's 2012

YORK CITY

tions   New York, Toronto, London, Sydney, Auckland

Eugene Fodor:
The Spy Who Loved Travel

As Fodor's celebrates our 75th anniversary, we are honoring the colorful and adventurous life of Eugene Fodor, who revolutionized guidebook publishing in 1936 with his first book, *On the Continent, The Entertaining Travel Annual.*

Eugene Fodor's life seemed to leap off the pages of a great spy novel. Born in Hungary, he spoke six languages and graduated from the Sorbonne and the London School of Economics. During World War II he joined the Office of Strategic Services, the budding spy agency for the United States. He commanded the team that went behind enemy lines to liberate Prague, and recommended to Generals Eisenhower, Bradley, and Patton that Allied troops move to the capital city. After the war, Fodor worked as a spy in Austria, posing as a U.S. diplomat.

In 1949 Eugene Fodor—with the help of the CIA—established Fodor's Modern Guides. He was passionate about travel and wanted to bring his insider's knowledge of Europe to a new generation of sophisticated Americans who wanted to explore and seek out experiences beyond their borders. Among his innovations were annual updates, consulting local experts, and including cultural and historical perspectives and an emphasis on people—not just sites. As Fodor described it, "The main interest and enjoyment of foreign travel lies not only in 'the sites,' . . . but in contact with people whose customs, habits, and general outlook are different from your own."

Eugene Fodor died in 1991, but his legacy, Fodor's Travel, continues. It is now one of the world's largest and most trusted brands in travel information, covering more than 600 destinations worldwide in guidebooks, on Fodors.com, and in ebooks and iPhone apps. Technology and the accessibility of travel may be changing, but Eugene Fodor's unique storytelling skills and reporting style are behind every word of today's Fodor's guides.

Our editors and writers continue to embrace Eugene Fodor's vision of building personal relationships through travel. We invite you to join the Fodor's community at fodors.com/community and share your experiences with like-minded travelers. Tell us when we're right. Tell us when we're wrong. And share fantastic travel secrets that aren't yet in Fodor's. Together, we will continue to deepen our understanding of our world.

Happy 75th Anniversary, Fodor's! Here's to many more.

Tim Jarrell, Publisher

FODOR'S NEW YORK CITY 2012

Editors: Rachel Klein (lead editor); Erica Duecy, Carolyn Galgano
Editorial Contributors: Maria Hart, Cate Starmer
Writers: Lynne Arany, Alexander Basek, Arthur Bovino, Robert Brenner, Samantha Chapnick, Jacinta O'Halloran, Anja Mutić, John Rambow, Adeena Sussman, Christina Valhouli

Production Editor: Carrie Parker
Maps & Illustrations: Mark Stroud, David Lindroth, *cartographers;* Bob Blake, Rebecca Baer, *map editors;* William Wu, *information graphics*
Design: Fabrizio La Rocca, *creative director;* Guido Caroti, Siobhan O'Hare, *art directors;* Tina Malaney, Nora Rosansky, Chie Ushio, *designers;* Melanie Marin, *senior picture editor*
Cover Photo: (Aerial view of Wall Street): Cameron Davidson/Corbis
Production Manager: Angela L. McLean

ISBN 978-0-679-00930-6

ISSN 0736-9395

SPECIAL SALES

This book is available at special discounts for bulk purchases for sales promotions or premiums. Special editions, including personalized covers, excerpts of existing books, and corporate imprints, can be created in large quantities for special needs. For more information, write to Special Markets/Premium Sales, 1745 Broadway, MD 6-2, New York, NY 10019, or e-mail specialmarkets@randomhouse.com.

AN IMPORTANT TIP & AN INVITATION

Although all prices, opening times, and other details in this book are based on information supplied to us at press time, changes occur all the time in the travel world, and Fodor's cannot accept responsibility for facts that become outdated or for inadvertent errors or omissions. So **always confirm information when it matters,** especially if you're making a detour to visit a specific place. Your experiences—positive and negative— matter to us. If we have missed or misstated something, **please write to us.** Share your opinion instantly through our online feedback center at fodors.com/contact-us.

PRINTED IN SINGAPORE

10 9 8 7 6 5 4 3 2 1

CONTENTS

1 **EXPERIENCE
NEW YORK CITY** 9

New York City Today 10

New York City Planner. 12

What's Where 14-17

New York City
Top Attractions. 18-20

New York City with Kids 21

New York City like a Local. 22

Sitting in a TV Audience 24

New York City for Free. 26

New York's Best Architecture . . 28-29

NYC's Waterfront Parks. 30

Sightseeing New York City 32

2 **LOWER MANHATTAN
with Ground Zero** 39

The Financial District and
South Street Seaport. 43

Chinatown and TriBeCa 61

3 **SOHO, NOLITA,
AND LITTLE ITALY** 65

SoHo. 69

Little Italy and NoLIta 73

4 **THE EAST VILLAGE
AND THE LOWER EAST SIDE** . . 77

East Village. 81

Lower East Side 85

5 **GREENWICH VILLAGE, THE WEST
VILLAGE, CHELSEA, AND THE
MEATPACKING DISTRICT**. 89

Greenwich Village and the West
Village. 93

Chelsea and the Meatpacking
District. 100

6 **UNION SQUARE, THE FLATIRON
DISTRICT, GRAMERCY PARK,
AND MURRAY HILL** 111

Fodor's Features

Gateway to the New World. 33

Ground Zero 48

The Metropolitan Museum of Art. 256

The American Museum of
Natural History. 268

New York Nights 304

7 **MIDTOWN
with Times Square
and Rockefeller Center** 127

8 **THE UPPER EAST SIDE** 147

9 **CENTRAL PARK** 155

10 **THE UPPER WEST SIDE** 171

11 **HARLEM** 181

12 **BROOKLYN** 191

13 **QUEENS, THE BRONX,
AND STATEN ISLAND**. 221

Queens 225

The Bronx. 234

Staten Island. 240

14 **MUSEUMS** 243

Muesums Planner. 244

15 **THE PERFORMING ARTS** 277

16 **NIGHTLIFE** 301

17 SHOPPING **333**
SoHo 340
NoLIta 352
Lower East Side 358
West Village 364
The Meatpacking District 368
Fifth Avenue and 57th Street 374
Madison Avenue 384

18 WHERE TO EAT **395**
New York City Dining Planner . . . 397
Best Bets for
New York City Dining 400
Lower Manhattan 402
SoHo, NoLIta, and Little Italy 404
East Village and Lower
East Side 406
Greenwich Village 408
Union Square 410
Midtown West and Chelsea 412
Midtown East/Upper East Side . . . 414
Upper West Side/Harlem 416
Restaurant Reviews 418

19 WHERE TO STAY **485**
New York City Lodging Planner . . . 488
Hotel Reviews 489
Best Bets for
New York City Lodging 490

**TRAVEL SMART
NEW YORK CITY** **527**

INDEX **545**

ABOUT OUR WRITERS **560**

MAPS

Lower Manhattan 40
East Village and the
Lower East Side 78
Greenwich Village, the West Village,
Chelsea, and the Meatpacking
District 90
Greenwich Village and the
West Village 94
Chelsea Galleries 106
Union Square, Gramercy, and
Murray Hill 112
The Upper East Side 148
The Upper West Side 172
Harlem 182
Brooklyn 192
Brooklyn Heights and DUMBO . . . 197
Williamsburg 205
Carroll Gardens, Cobble Hill,
Boerum Hill, and Fort Greene . . . 209
Park Slope and Prospect Park . . . 214
Queens, the Bronx and
Staten Island 222
Astoria and Long Island City 226
Jackson Heights 230
The New York Botanical Garden
and Bronx Zoo 236
Staten Island 241
Top Museums 247
Museums Worth Noting 248
Shopping in New York City 336
Dining in New York City 398

**NEW YORK CITY DINING AND
LODGING ATLAS** **471–484**

ABOUT THIS BOOK

Our Ratings

At Fodor's, we spend considerable time choosing the best places in a destination so you don't have to. By default, anything we recommend in this book is worth visiting. But some sights, properties, and experiences are so great that we've recognized them with additional accolades. Orange **Fodor's Choice** stars indicate our top recommendations; black stars highlight places we deem **Highly Recommended**; and **Best Bets** call attention to top properties in various categories. Disagree with any of our choices? Care to nominate a new place? Visit our feedback center at www.fodors.com/feedback.

TripAdvisor ⊙⊙

Fodor's partnership with TripAdvisor helps to ensure that our hotel selections are timely and relevant, taking into account the latest customer feedback about each property. Our team of expert writers selects what we believe will be the top choices for lodging in a destination. Then, those choices are reinforced by TripAdvisor reviews, so only the best properties make the cut.

> For expanded hotel reviews, visit **Fodors.com**

Hotels

Hotels have private bath, phone, TV, and air-conditioning, and do not offer meals unless we specify that in the review. We always list facilities but not whether you'll be charged an extra fee to use them.

Restaurants

Unless we state otherwise, restaurants are open for lunch and dinner daily. We mention dress only when there's a specific requirement and reservations only when they're essential or not accepted—it's always best to book ahead.

Credit Cards

We assume that restaurants and hotels accept credit cards. If not, we'll note it in the review.

Budget Well

Hotel and restaurant price categories from ¢ to $$$$ are defined in the opening pages of the respective chapters. For attractions, we always give standard adult admission fees; reductions are usually available for children, students, and senior citizens.

Listings		Hotels & Restaurants	Outdoors
★ Fodor's Choice	✉ E-mail	⊞ Hotel	🏌 Golf
★ Highly recommended	⌁ Admission fee	↙ Number of rooms	⛺ Camping
⊠ Physical address	⊙ Open/closed times	⚲ Facilities	**Other**
⊹ Directions or Map coordinates	Ⓜ Metro stations	⊗ Meal plans	⊙ Family-friendly
⌂ Mailing address	⊟ No credit cards	✕ Restaurant	⇨ See also
☎ Telephone		⊛ Reservations	⊠ Branch address
⊟ Fax		⌂ Dress code	☞ Take note
⊕ On the Web		⤵ Smoking	

Experience
New York City

NEW YORK CITY TODAY

Gotham doesn't stay on the mat for long, and that's most certainly the case in 2011. After a rough 2008 and 2009, the city has staggered back to its feet. Are things as peachy as they were pre-recession? Not quite. But real-estate prices are starting to climb again, restaurants big and small are opening apace, and new neighborhoods are gentrifying. This city, which thrives on work, is very eager to get back to business.

Indeed, things are businesslike thanks to our mayor, Mike Bloomberg, now in his third and final term. Any major gripes locals may have had with City Hall seem mostly to be in the rearview mirror. As for the mayor, most of the time you'll see bemusement at his gruff assessment of political problems in the city, from the Ground Zero mosque to MTA fare hikes.

As always, the state of the city's real estate is a top-of-mind for all New Yorkers. Despite hard times elsewhere in the country, prices continue to rise here. Rents in Manhattan are up, with vacancy a shade under 1 percent. Apartments in Manhattan, meanwhile, sell for an average of $1.33 million. So while Brooklyn continues to enjoy a steady influx, Manhattan is hot again among real-estate moguls in the know. The East Village keeps expanding east, SoHo keeps expanding west, and the Upper West Side gets more and more upper with each passing week.

On a more day-to-day level, a slice of pizza is usually $2.50, a glass of wine is rarely less than $10 (and can easily creep as high as $17), and a pack of cigarettes sets smokers back $11. Cab meters seem to hit $10 seconds after you get in, and even a bagel with a schmear is verging on $2 in some hoods.

What has really hit locals' wallets hard is increases for subway and bus fares the Metropolitan Transit Authority (MTA) has passed. A 12 to 2 vote at the end of 2010 bumped a single ride ticket to $2.50. Prices on 30-day unlimited cards made a 17 percent jump from $89 to $104. The only good news, if it can even be called that, is that a weekly unlimited pass—which tourists often rely upon heavily to sightsee—only went up $2 from $27 to $29.

So savvy New Yorkers are more attuned to bargains than ever before, signing up for restaurant discounts from Web sites like Groupon and Blackboard Eats, rummaging through the sales racks at the new airplane-hangar-size location of Century 21 in Queens, and taking advantage of

WHAT WE'RE TALKING ABOUT

What's on a New Yorker's plate these days? It's probably something from the mind of one of the city's two hottest restaurateurs, David Chang and Michael White. Chang is a media darling but continues to expand and evolve the Momofuku concept, while White has high-end

Italian covered, from the seafood delights of Marea to the fried lardo of Osteria Morini.

Also on the foodie front, the food-truck craze is in full swing, and it's hard to walk a couple of blocks in well-traversed neighborhoods without seeing at least one parked on the

corner. Office workers love 'em for fast, inexpensive, and often gourmet-quality lunches, as do tourists much for the same reason. Luckily, their addition hasn't pushed the hot-dog and pretzel stands off the streets, although now intersections seem even more crowded.

free concerts on Governors Island in summer.

The TKTS booth, overhauled in 2008, is popular with locals and visitors to Times Square alike, and on weekends, many a New Yorker finds his or her way to the Brooklyn Flea, with its cool knickknacks, inexpensive furniture, and a wide array of affordable street food, from pupusas to lobster rolls.

Despite the rising cost of living, New Yorkers eat out just as much as ever, and many restaurants have transitioned to small plates as a way to offer a variety of options, big or small, depending on one's appetite and checkbook.

As for Broadway, the lack of tourist dollars channeled to buy expensive tickets means that the Off Broadway scene is once again ascendant, with musicals such as *Bloody Bloody Andrew Jackson* making the transition to the Great White Way.

Concerts are rife, from arena rockers at Madison Square Garden to the hottest new act at the Bowery Ballroom; heck, there's even a distinct possibility that the Knicks will start winning again. (Don't count on it.) In other words, things are on the way up.

As history will attest, New York is always changing into something new in response to a fresh set of challenges. Given the tiny residences, high prices, and complexities of daily living here, locals are resourceful, and they're also capable of putting up with just about anything. Let us show you what we can do.

Escaping the city in summer is something locals think about way in advance of the season, making plans early in the year for housing shares in the Hamptons or Fire Island. But for those without the means, the summertime hotspot of late is Governors Island. The short ferry ride, free concerts, easy biking, and cool history make it popular with out-of-towners and locals alike.

An unfortunate continually discussed topic—and the number of subway ads reveal its presence—is bedbugs. Street furniture is shunned, offices are fumigated, and relationships are ended over these tiny critters that can infest mattresses and often cost of fortune to get rid of. Bring it up and you're sure to hear some strong opinions.

NEW YORK CITY PLANNER

When to Go

New York City weather, like its people, is a study in extremes. Much of winter brings bone-chilling winds and an occasional traffic-snarling snowfall, but you're just as likely to experience mild afternoons sandwiched by cool temperatures.

In late spring and early summer, streets fill with parades and street fairs, and Central Park has free performances. Late-August temperatures sometimes claw skyward, bringing subway station temperatures over 100°F (no wonder the Hamptons are so crowded). This is why September brings palpable excitement, with stunning yellow-and-bronze foliage complementing the dawn of a new cultural season. Between October and May, museums mount major exhibitions, most Broadway shows open, and formal opera, ballet, and concert seasons begin.

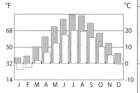

Getting Around

Without a doubt, the best way to explore New York is on foot. No matter what neighborhood you're headed to, you'll get a better sense of it by wandering around; you can check out the architecture, pop into cool-looking shops and cafés, and observe the walk-and-talk of the locals. And if you get lost, you'll find that New Yorkers are surprisingly helpful with directions.

Long gone are the days when New York's subways were dangerous. It's by far the city's most efficient and cost effective way to get around, and it runs 24 hours a day. But the subway is by no means flawless: good luck understanding loudspeaker announcements on all but the newest trains. The floors are sticky, stations are sweltering in summer, and platforms are grimy year-round. In other words, it's quite obvious that the subway is more than 100 years old. As you'd expect, it gets crowded during rush hours, when you'll likely find that all the subway car seats are taken—and have to join your fellow riders in the particular New York sport of "strap-hanging."

If you've got a long way to go and would rather be comfortable than thrifty, hail one of the ubiquitous yellow cabs that troll New York's streets around the clock. You'll be out $3 just for getting in, but you'll get to look at the scenery as you go and talk to the driver (who might be from as far away as Bangladesh or Ukraine). Avoid trying to hail a cab between 4 and 4:30 pm, unless you want to do a lot of futile street-side arm waving; it's when the drivers change shifts.

WHAT IT COSTS

	¢	$	$$	$$$	$$$$
Restaurants	under $10	$10–$17	$18–$24	$24–$35	over $35
Hotels		under $150	$150–$299	$300–$449	$450–$600	over $600

Restaurant prices are per person for a median main course or equivalent combination of smaller dishes. Note: if a restaurant offers only prix-fixe (set-price) meals, it has been given the price category that reflects the full prix-fixe price. Hotel prices are for a standard double room, excluding 14.75% city and state taxes.

A Guide to the Grid

The map of Manhattan is, for the most part, easy to follow: north of 14th Street, streets are laid out in a numbered grid pattern.

Numbered streets run east and west (crosstown), and broad avenues, most of them also numbered, run north (uptown) and south (downtown).

The main exception is Broadway, which runs the entire length of Manhattan on a diagonal. Below 14th Street, street patterns get chaotic.

In the West Village, West 4th Street intersects West 11th Street, Greenwich Street runs roughly parallel to Greenwich Avenue, and Leroy Street turns into St. Luke's Place for one block and then becomes Leroy again.

There's an East Broadway and a West Broadway, both of which run north–south, and neither of which is an extension of Broadway, leaving even locals scratching their heads.

Street Smarts

Avoid deserted blocks in unfamiliar neighborhoods. A brisk, purposeful pace helps deter trouble wherever you go. New York City is a safe city, but it's still a city, so keep jewelry out of sight on the street; better yet, leave valuables at home. Don't wear gold chains or large jewelry, even if it's fake.

When in bars or restaurants, never hang your purse or bag on the back of a chair or put it underneath the table.

Never leave any bags unattended, and expect to have yourself and your possessions inspected thoroughly in such places as airports, sports stadiums, museums, and city buildings. Police officers stationed by subway-token booths also reserve the right to check your bags before you pass through the turnstile to enter the platform.

Politely ignore panhandlers on the streets and subways, people who offer to hail you a cab (they often appear at Penn Station, the Port Authority, or the airport), and limousine and gypsy-cab drivers who (illegally) offer rides priced according to how desperate you look.

Knockoff wristwatches will keep excellent time until you're about an hour away from the vendor, so don't bother with them; ditto for pirated DVDs.

Opening Hours

Subways and buses run around the clock, and so do plenty of businesses—including restaurants, pharmacies, copy shops, and even fitness clubs (there's no wait for a treadmill at 4 am). Other shops and services have more extensive hours than you'll find elsewhere in the United States. For example, there are quite a few places where you can get groceries—or get your hair and nails done—at 11 pm. In general, though, you can safely assume that most shops are open seven days a week, from about 10 to 7 Monday–Saturday and from noon to 6 on Sunday. Bars generally close at 4 am, though some after-hours clubs are open later.

Money Saving Tips

Consider buying a CityPass, a group of tickets to six top-notch attractions in New York: the Empire State Building, the Guggenheim Museum, the American Museum of Natural History, the Museum of Modern Art, the Metropolitan Museum of Art (including the Cloisters), and Circle Line Cruises or admission to Liberty and Ellis islands. The $79 pass, which saves you half the cost of each individual ticket, is good for nine days from first use.

Discount coupons are available at the city's official tourism marketing bureau, **NYC & Company** (⊕ *www.nycvisit. com*), near Times Square.

WHAT'S WHERE

Numbers below correspond to chapter numbers.

2 Lower Manhattan. Heavy-duty landmarks anchor the southern tip: Wall Street and the Financial District; the breezy waterfront parks of Battery Park City and historic South Street Seaport; ferry terminals dispatching boats out to Ellis Island and the Statue of Liberty; and the gradually evolving construction site at Ground Zero, where thousands flock daily to pay their respects. To the north, Chinatown teems with street vendors selling knockoff handbags. Brave the crowds and explore some of the less-traveled side streets to find Chinese herb shops, exceptional noodle joints, and Hong Kong cakes. The tony streets of TriBeCa, to the west, are broader and also quieter, but it does have a busy restaurant scene.

3 SoHo, NoLIta, and Little Italy. The only struggling creative types in SoHo these days are sidewalk merchants hawking canvases, handmade jewelry, and T-shirts; the superluxe shops dominate here. To the east, NoLIta has more tiny boutiques and restaurants. And to the south, Little Italy is a shrinking zone of red-sauce eateries and gelaterias.

4 The East Village and the Lower East Side. Once an edgy neighborhood of artists and punks, now filled with a combination of artists, fashionable lawyers, and students, the East Village centers around the scruffy but beloved Tompkins Square Park. The neighborhood is one of the city's best for eating, both in terms of variety and quality. To the south, the once seedier, now trendier Lower East Side (bounded by the Bowery, Clinton, Houston, and Delancey streets) draws hipsters with live-music clubs, independent clothing shops, wine-and-tapas bars, and health-food joints.

5 Greenwich Village, the West Village, Chelsea, and the Meatpacking District. Happily, artists with rent-controlled apartments, out-and-proud gays, and university students are still in the Village today, but because those town houses have become so expensive, residents also include wealthy media moguls, celebrities, and socialites. From 14th Street south to Houston and from the Hudson River east to 5th Avenue, the blocks are a jumble of jazz clubs, posh restaurants, former speakeasies, and rainbow flags. Farther west, the once blue-collar Meatpacking District has evolved into a swanky clubbing and late-night restaurant scene for the young and scantily clad. Chelsea, like its namesake London district, has a small-town personality with big-city prices. Its leafy streets (which stretch from 14th to the upper 20s) are lined with renovated brownstones and spacious art galleries; its avenues (from 6th to the Hudson) brim with restaurants, bakeries, bodegas, and men's clothing stores. Chelsea has supplanted the Village as the center of gay life in the city.

6 Union Square, the Flatiron District, Gramercy Park, and Murray Hill. Bustling Union Square Park, bounded by 14th and 17th streets, Broadway, and Park Avenue, hosts the city's best greenmarket four times a week. On the 14th Street edge are broad stone steps where break-dancers and other performers busk for onlookers. North, up Broadway, is Madison Square Park, beloved for its outdoor summer jazz concerts. Nearby are the preening mansions and town houses of Gramercy in the East 20s, and of Murray Hill in the East 30s.

WHAT'S WHERE

7 Midtown. Chockablock with sightseeing blockbusters, this area holds Times Square and Rockefeller Center. Head to 42nd Street to see Times Square in all its neon, scrolling tickers, and massive-TV-screens glory. Towering office buildings continue to line Broadway going north, ending at Columbus Circle at the edge of Central Park. At Rockefeller Center you'll find the justly famous ice rink and tree (in season), and nearby are ultraswank Saks, Tiffany & Co., Henri Bendel, and Bergdorf Goodman, among others. St. Patrick's Cathedral, on 5th Avenue, is a key landmark. Heading south will bring you to the stately New York Public Library (and the adjacent Bryant Park), Grand Central Terminal, and the Chrysler Building.

8 The Upper East Side. North of 59th Street, between 5th and Park avenues, the Upper East Side is home to more millionaires than any other part of the city. Historic-district designation has kept the tony mansions and apartment buildings intact and largely uninterrupted by "plebeian" structures. Tucked into this stretch of 5th are the Museum Mile and, a block east, Madison Avenue's haute boutiques.

9 Central Park. Fredrick Law Olmstead's beautiful ode to the pastoral in the heart of New York, Central Park is where New Yorkers come to escape the bustle of the city. There's a small zoo, a boathouse, and activities as diverse as rock climbing, softball, and Frisbee. And don't forget getting a tan! The park starts at 59th Street and goes all the way to 110th at the north end; east to west, it runs from 5th to 8th avenues.

10 The Upper West Side. In the shadow of ornate prewar buildings, sidewalks burst with stroller-pushing caregivers, dog walkers, joggers, and students. By day the dominant draw is the American Museum of Natural History; by night, Lincoln Center. Way north sit the eminently walkable Columbia University campus and the grounds of the Cathedral Church of St. John the Divine, with catacombs and wandering peacocks.

11 Harlem. A hotbed of African-American and Hispanic-American culture for almost a century, Harlem still sizzles today. The brownstone-lined blocks between about 110th and 145th streets—many of which languished in the '70s and '80s—are being refurbished: Bill Clinton moved his post-presidency offices here in 2001. Chic boutiques and restaurants are popping up, and music venues from the 1920s and '30s are still in full swing.

12 Brooklyn. Our largest borough counts among its stars Coney Island, Prospect Park, and the Brooklyn Botanic Gardens. Its ultra-distinct neighborhoods include the hipster Neverland Williamsburg, the Italian-American Carroll Gardens, and family-friendly Park Slope.

13 Queens, the Bronx, and Staten Island. Queens has pocket communities of Greeks, Indians, and Dominicans (among others), as well as Flushing Meadows, Citi Field, and excellent museums. including the newly redone Museum of the Moving Image, MoMa PS1, and the Noguchi Museum. The Bronx was best known for the old Yankee Stadium—it's likely the new one will remain famous, too—but Arthur Avenue's Italian restaurants, the New York Botanical Garden, and the Bronx Zoo are no slouches. Staten Island harbors the famous Staten Island Ferry that residents use to commute and tourists hop on for the best—and free—view of the city's skyline and the Statue of Liberty.

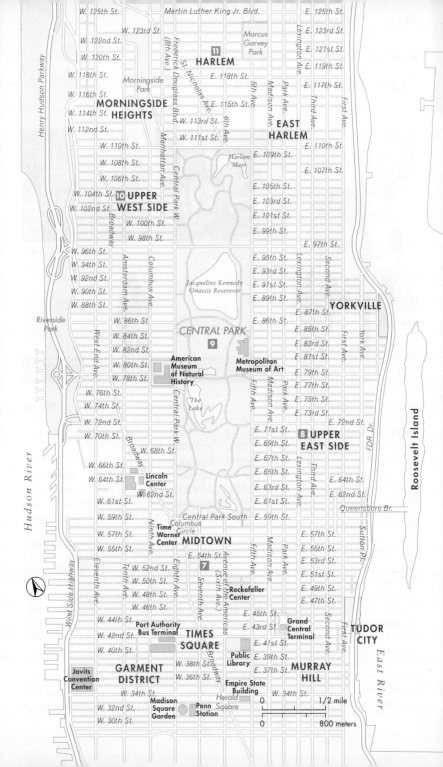

NEW YORK CITY TOP ATTRACTIONS

Metropolitan Museum of Art

(A) The largest art museum in the Western Hemisphere, the Met is—naturally—a mecca for art lovers of all stripes. Treasures from all over the world and every era of human creativity make up its expansive collection. It's easy to get dizzy circling all the Dutch master canvases, bronze Rodins, and ancient Greek artifacts—but if you need a breather, you can always retire to the Temple of Dendur or the rooftop café.

Times Square

(B) Times Square is the most frenetic part of New York City: a cacophony of flashing lights and shoulder-to-shoulder crowds that many New Yorkers studiously avoid. But if you like sensory overload, the chaotic mix of huge underwear billboards, flashing digital displays, on-location television broadcasts, and outré street performers will give you your fix. In an effort to make this headache-inducing mecca more traversable, Mayor Bloomberg banned cars on Broadway between 42nd and 49th streets in 2009, creating a pedestrian mall.

Empire State Building

(C) From the 86th-floor observatory, which towers 1,050 feet above the city, you can see up to 80 mi away on a clear day (and it's heated and air-conditioned, unlike the deck 16 stories farther up). The views at night are equally stunning, with the glittering city lights French architect Le Corbusier once called "a Milky Way come down to earth." If you're afraid of heights, gazing at the building from afar will still deliver a dose of dazzle—especially after dark, when it's illuminated by colored lights that correspond to different holidays and events.

Museum of Modern Art

(D) Described as a "modernist dream world" after its $425 million face-lift in 2004, MoMA has since become as famous

for its architecture as for its collections. Yoshio Taniguchi, the Japanese architect responsible for the redesign, created newly spacious, soaring-ceiling galleries suffused with natural light, where masterpieces like Monet's *Water Lilies,* Picasso's *Les Demoiselles d'Avignon,* and van Gogh's *Starry Night* can get the oohs and aahs they deserve. The museum's restaurant next door, the Modern, is nearly as breathtaking.

Brooklyn Bridge

(E) "A drive-through cathedral" is how critic James Wolcott described this, one of New York's noblest and most recognized landmarks. Spanning the East River, the Brooklyn Bridge connects the island of Manhattan to the borough of Brooklyn (once an independent city, and still worth a visit in its own right). A leisurely hour's stroll on the pedestrian walkway (which you'll share with bicyclists, in-line skaters, and entrepreneurs selling bottled water) is an essential New York experience. Traffic is beneath you, and the views along the East River and of Manhattan's Financial District are some of the best anywhere.

Statue of Liberty

(F) Presented to the United States in 1886 as a gift from France, Lady Liberty is a near-universal symbol of freedom and democracy, standing 152 feet high atop an 89-foot pedestal on Liberty Island. You can get a taste of the thrill millions of immigrants must have experienced as you approach Liberty Island on the ferry from Battery Park. The statue's crown was closed to visitors for almost eight years after the September 11 attacks, but reopened on July 4, 2009.

American Museum of Natural History

(G) The towering, spectacularly reassembled dinosaur skeletons that greet you when you enter this museum are practically worth the (suggested) price of admission. But there's tons more, including

exhibits of ancient civilizations, animals both stuffed and living (don't miss the live Butterfly Conservatory October–May), a hall of oceanic creatures overlooked by a 94-foot model of a blue whale, and space shows at the adjoining Rose Center for Earth and Space.

Central Park

(H) The literal and spiritual center of Manhattan, Central Park has 843 acres of meandering paths, tranquil lakes, ponds, and open meadows. For equestrians, softball and soccer players, strollers, ice- and roller-skaters, rock climbers, bird-watchers, boaters, picnickers, and outdoor performers, it's an oasis of fresh air and greenery that lets them forget—at least for a little while—the hustle and congestion of the city.

Bronx Zoo

(I) One urban jungle deserves another. Only at the world's largest urban zoo is there room for gorillas to lumber around a 6.5-acre simulated rain forest, or tigers and lions to roam nearly 40 acres of open meadows.

SoHo

(J) The elegant cast-iron buildings, cobblestone streets, art galleries, chic boutiques, and swanky hotels make this a wonderful area in which to shop, drink, and dream of a more glamorous life.

NEW YORK CITY WITH KIDS

Though much of New York revolves around the distinctly adult pursuits of making and spending money, it's also a great city for kids. Our top activities include the following:

American Museum of Natural History. The hands-down favorite for both visiting and local kids, this museum's many exhibits could entertain most children for a week. The dinosaurs alone are worth the trip, as is the live Butterfly Conservatory that runs each year from October through May. You'll also find an IMAX theater, ancient-culture displays, and wildlife dioramas with taxidermied creatures that hit the right mix of fascinating and creepy.

Bronx Zoo. The country's largest metropolitan wildlife park is home to more than 4,000 animals, including endangered and threatened species. Plan to spend a whole day here, so your kids don't have to choose between Congo Gorilla Forest and the Siberian cats at Tiger Mountain. Be sure to check out the World of Darkness, a black-lighted indoor exhibit of nocturnal creatures. Special tours with a docent for children can be arranged year-round.

Central Park Zoo. Three climatic regions—Rain Forest, Temperate Territory, and Polar Circle—are represented at this bite-size zoo. The rain-forest frogs, red pandas, and performing sea lions are all nifty—but the winner is the underwater viewing window into the polar bear pool.

Children's Museum of Manhattan. Interactive exhibits in this five-floor museum change frequently—but they're always fun. As well as visiting with TV friends like Dora the Explorer, your little ones can build castles in the sand laboratory, and—in warm weather—race boats on a zigzagging outdoor watercourse.

New York Aquarium. Alongside the creaky amusements of Coney Island, this aquarium is home to more than 10,000 marine species, including walrus, giant sea turtles, sand-tiger sharks, and sea otters.

New York Botanical Garden. Fifty gardens and plant collections fill this gorgeous 250-acre space; there are flowering rose and water-lily gardens in the warm months, and hothouses full of tropical flowers in winter. Don't miss the Children's Adventure Garden and its boulder maze.

Rose Center for Earth and Space. The appropriately space-age design of the new Hayden Planetarium (and its accompanying cosmos museum) has made waves among architects—but the thrilling daily space shows inside are a big bang with kids. The complex is part of the American Museum of Natural History, though planetarium tickets are sold separately.

Sony Wonder Technology Lab. The line to get into this futuristic fantasy world might be long (as well as having great interactive exhibits, the museum has free entry). But don't worry—a slightly freaky talking robot will keep your kids entertained while they wait. Inside, there are more robots and image and sound labs where kids can record their own digital music, movies, and games.

South Street Seaport Museum. The fleet of historic square-riggers with looming masts might be the first thing to catch your children's eyes—but there's much more going on here, including weekend concerts, performances by storytellers and chantey singers, and special guided tours for families.

NEW YORK CITY LIKE A LOCAL

The phrase "in a New York minute" is clichéd for a reason: in this wonderful, frenetic, and overwhelming city, things really do change in a flash. Even for those of us who live here, keeping up with the latest trends in fashion, art, music, food, and nightlife can be exhausting.

Thankfully, there are a few tricks to navigating this city—unspoken, hard-won bits of knowledge that help us locals get the most out of our hometown without driving ourselves crazy. And at the risk of compromising our New York credibility (after all, we consider ourselves members of an exclusive club and guard our secrets accordingly), we've decided to share those tricks here. Just don't tell anyone we told you.

Getting Around Like a Local

First, when distance is involved, take the subway. Skip the horse-drawn carriages, called hansom cabs, that wait for fares around Central Park. A jaunt in one will leave you exposed to the elements; stalled in exhaust-filled traffic; guilt-ridden about the poor, plodding horse; and broke. Pedicabs aren't of much use either, except for the novelty value.

When hailing a taxi, recognize which cabs to avoid flagging down. Don't wave at cars whose rooftop lights aren't illuminated; these already have passengers inside. Taxis whose roof lights are lighted only at the edges—not the center—are offduty, and will rarely pick you up unless your destination is on their way to the garage.

Think twice about getting into a cab whose driver has cut across three lanes of traffic to get to you; if he's willing to risk his life and the lives of others just to pick you up, he might not suddenly morph into a model of safe driving once you're inside.

Then again, he might be the only sure bet to get you to the airport when you're running late.

Once you're in a cab, know your passenger rights. Although your driver will likely careen at high speeds while simultaneously cursing, leaning on his horn, and chattering into his cell-phone headset, you're entitled to ask him to slow down. You're also allowed to ask him to turn off his phone or blaring car radio, and if he doesn't comply, refrain from tipping him. Cabbies make almost nothing aside from tips, so tack 15% to 20% onto your fare after any satisfactory ride; all cabs are now required to take credit cards, too.

Lastly, hailing a cab between the hours of 4 and 6 pm is near impossible. It's rush hour, when every workaday New Yorker is trying to get home, and available taxis are very scarce. They're all but nonexistent between 4 and 4:30, when the driver shifts change, so don't even waste your time trying to find one—head right for the subway or else hoof it.

Speaking of walking, it's crucial that you be aware of the implicit rules of the New York City sidewalk. Most important, when walking here, move quickly. Realize that New Yorkers are like sharks: if they stop moving forward, they die (and if you stop moving, one might bite your head off). Unless you're holding the hand of a small child, single file is the rule; walking two or three abreast will cause locals to jostle, sideswipe, and growl at you. Stopping on the sidewalk to take pictures of each other or consult your guidebook will also put you at risk for being hip-checked. If you need a moment to consult your map or text-message a friend, make like you're on the highway: pull over and get out of the way.

Dining Like a Local

The first rule of New York eating is, forget the heavy breakfast—at least on weekdays. Although weekend brunches are popular—as the lines in front of restaurants on Saturday and Sunday attest—when the rest of the city is on the clock, it's better to get up and go. Grab a cup of joe and a bagel from a café, a deli, or one of the ubiquitous sidewalk carts (they're passably good), and walk around while you eat. This will give you more valuable exploring time (trust us, there's too much to see to waste the whole morning lingering over omelets), and will also help you save money for the most important meal of the day: dinner.

While we're on the subject, you should plan to eat dinner later than you ordinarily would—if you want to experience the real New York dining scene, that is. Most New York restaurants are empty around 6 pm and don't fill up until at least 7:30 or 8, so if you eat early, you'll have your pick of tables. Prime-time dinner reservations—between 8 and 10 pm—are the hardest to score, but will ensure that you're surrounded by chic dining companions.

Of course, if you can't get a good reservation (and you don't have young kids in tow), you can always do what many savvy locals do: eat at the bar. You'll get the same great food and people-watching, plus you'll get to feel like an insider while other folks are still waiting for a table.

Going Out Like a Local

There's one major rule New Yorkers abide by when hitting the nightspots: avoid, avoid, avoid the big clubs on Friday and Saturday nights. The only people you're likely to see then are other visitors, the pickup artists trying to scam them, and kids too young to know better. Locals and A-listers go clubbing on Tuesday, Wednesday, and Thursday—on weekends you'll find them either at smaller, low-key bars and lounges or huddled in their apartments with Netflix and take-out Chinese.

When you do hit one of the superswanky spots in Chelsea or the Meatpacking District, don't over- or underdress. If you're female, don't confuse "dressy" with "formal"; leave the cocktail dress at home and go for something casually sexy: tight, dark jeans, a classy-yet-revealing top, a fabulous handbag, and heels are almost always a safe bet, as is the classic N.Y.C. black. If you're a guy, dress to impress—jeans are fine as long as they're dark—but leave the baseball cap at home.

SITTING IN A TV AUDIENCE

Tickets to tapings of TV shows are free, but can be very hard to come by on short notice. Most shows accept advance requests by email, phone, or online—but for the most popular shows, like *The Daily Show with Jon Stewart*, the request backlog is so deep, you might even have to wait a few months before they'll accept any new ones. Same-day standby tickets are often available—but be prepared to wait in line for several hours, sometimes starting at 5 or 6 am, depending on how hot the show is, or the wattage of that day's celebrity guests.

The Shows

The Colbert Report. More tongue-in-cheek than the Daily Show (with a more knowing audience, too), Stephen Colbert leads his "nation" through shows Monday through Thursday. Check the Web site for dates with open tickets. Sign-up for standby tickets happens in front of the studio at 4 pm the day of the show. ✉ *513 W. 54th St., between 10th and 11th Aves., Midtown West* ☎ 212/586–2477 ⊕ *www. colbertnation.com* Ⓜ *C, E to 50th St.*

The Daily Show with Jon Stewart. The smirking, amiable, and incisive Jon Stewart pokes fun at news headlines on this half-hour cable show. The program tapes from Monday through Thursday; you can request advance tickets by checking the calendar on the Web site. For standby tickets, show up well before the 5:45 pm doors-open time. Audience members must be 18 or older. ✉ *733 11th Ave., between W. 51st and W. 52nd Sts., Midtown West* ☎ 212/586–2477 ⊕ *www.thedailyshow. com* Ⓜ *C, E to 50th St.*

Good Morning America. Robin Roberts and George Stephanopoulos host this early-morning news and entertainment standby. *GMA* airs live, weekdays from 7 to 9 am, and ticket requests (online only) should be sent four to six months in advance. ✉ *7 Times Sq., at W. 44th St. and Broadway, Midtown West* ☎ 212/930– 7855 ⊕ *abcnews.go.com/GMA/tickets- good-morning-america-audience/story? id=144752* Ⓜ *1, 2, 3, 7, N, Q, R, S to 42nd St./Times Sq.*

Late Night with Jimmy Fallon. Jimmy Fallon is settling in nicely at 30 Rock—it helps when your house band is the Roots and when Justin Timberlake is a frequent visitor to your show. For tickets, call the Ticket Information Line for a maximum of four tickets, about one month in advance. Single standby tickets are available on taping days—Monday through Friday—at the West 49th Street side of 30 Rockefeller Plaza; arrive before 9 am. You must be 17 years or older. ✉ *30 Rocke- feller Plaza, Midtown West* ☎ 212/664– 3056 *ticket information line* ⊕ *www. latenightwithjimmyfallon.com* Ⓜ *B, D, F, M to 47th–50th Rockefeller Center.*

The Late Show with David Letterman. Letterman's famously offbeat humor and wacky top-10 lists have had fans giggling for more than two decades. Call 212/247– 6497 starting at 11 am on tape days— Monday through Thursday—for standby tickets. For advance tickets (two maximum), you can submit a request online or fill out an application in person at the theater. You must be 18 or older to sit in the audience. ✉ *Ed Sullivan Theater, 1697 Broadway, between W. 53rd and W. 54th Sts., Midtown West* ☎ 212/975–5853 ⊕ *www.cbs.com/late_night/late_show/ tickets* Ⓜ *1, C, E to 50th St.; B, D, E to 7th Ave.*

Live! with Regis and Kelly. The sparks fly on this morning program, which books an eclectic roster of guests. Standby tickets

become available weekdays at 7 am at the **ABC Studios** (✉ *7 Lincoln Sq., corner of W. 67th St. and Columbus Ave., Upper West Side*). Otherwise, write for tickets (four tickets maximum) a full year in advance or fill out a form online. Children under 10 aren't allowed in the audience. 🖱 *Live Tickets, Ansonia Station, Box 230-777, 10023* ☎ *212/456-3054* Ⓜ *1 to 66th St./Lincoln Center.*

The Martha Stewart Show. Master baker, crafts maker, and champion of all "good things," Martha Stewart hosts her show with a live studio audience and various celebrity guests. The program generally tapes weekdays at both 10 am and 2 pm. You can request tickets only through the Martha Stewart Web site. Often, show producers are recruiting for groups of people (like nurses, new moms, or brides-to-be), and if you fit that category, your chances of scoring tickets increase. Occasionally standby tickets are given out two hours before showtime. Audience members must be at least 10 years old. ✉ *221 W. 26th St., between 7th and 8th Aves., Chelsea* ☎ *212/727-1234* ⊕ *www.marthastewart.com/get-tickets* Ⓜ *C or 1 to 23rd St.*

Saturday Night Live. Influential from the start, *SNL* continues to captivate audiences. Standby tickets—only one per person—are distributed at 7 am on the day of the show at the West 49th Street entrance to 30 Rockefeller Plaza. You may ask for a ticket for either the dress rehearsal (8 pm) or the live show (11:30 pm). Requests for advance tickets (two per applicant) must be submitted by email only in August to snltickets@nbcuni.com; recipients are determined by lottery. You must be 16 or older to sit in the audience. ✉ *NBC Studios, Saturday Night Live, 30 Rockefeller*

Plaza, between W. 49th and W. 50th Sts., Midtown West ☎ *212/664-3056* Ⓜ *B, D, F, M to 47th–50th Sts./Rockefeller Center.*

Today. America's first morning talk–news show airs weekdays from 7 to 10 am in the glass-enclosed, ground-level NBC studio across from its original home at 30 Rockefeller Plaza. You may well be spotted on TV by friends back home while you're standing behind anchors Meredith Vieira, Al Roker, and Matt Lauer. (If you bring a funny sign, you're more likely to catch the cameraman's attention.) ✉ *Rockefeller Plaza at W. 49th St., Midtown West* Ⓜ *B, D, F, M to 47th–50th Sts./Rockefeller Center.*

NEW YORK CITY FOR FREE

If you think everything in New York costs too much, well, you're right—almost. In fact, the city has tons of free attractions and activities; you just need to know where to look for them.

Outdoor Fun

Walk across the Brooklyn Bridge for a spectacular view of the Financial District, Brooklyn, the seaport, and Manhattan.

Ride the Staten Island ferry to see the Statue of Liberty, Ellis Island, and the southern tip of Manhattan from the water. Check out the spiffy Whitehall terminal in Manhattan, completed in 2005 after a $200 million renovation. The ferry is popular as an inexpensive date spot—the cafeteria on board is a surprisingly inexpensive place to buy beer and snacks. Ⓜ *1 to South Ferry; 4, 5 to Bowling Green.*

Catch a free movie screening in Bryant Park in summertime. A tradition since 1992, watching films alfresco surrounded by tall Midtown buildings is a summertime rite of passage for New Yorkers. Bring a blanket and a picnic basket, and be prepared to stake out a good spot on the lawn well in advance. The park runs from 40th to 42nd streets between 5th and 6th avenues; movie schedules are posted on ⊕ *www. bryantpark.org* Ⓜ *B, D, F, M to 42nd St.*

Wander Battery Park City's waterfront promenade. The breeze and passing boats will make you forget you're in the gritty city, though the view of the Statue of Liberty will remind you that you couldn't be anywhere but New York. Ⓜ *4, 5 to Bowling Green; 1 to South Ferry.*

Kayak on the Hudson. The Downtown Boathouse gives free lessons and paddling tours, and there's even an indoor-swimming-pool program to hone kayaking skills in winter months. The boats are distributed on a first-come, first-served basis, so cloudy days and early mornings are the best times to avoid the crowds. ⊠ *Pier 40 at Houston St.* ⊕ *www.downtownboathouse.org* Ⓜ *B, D, F, M to 47th–50th Sts./Rockefeller Center.*

Watch wannabe trapeze artists swing and soar at the Trapeze School New York (as shown on *Sex and the City*). They've helped locals and visitors alike make leaps of faith since 2002. ⊠ *Pier 40 at Houston St.* ⊕ *www.trapezeschool.com* Ⓜ *A, C, E to Canal St.*

Taste the goods at the Union Square Greenmarket (on Monday, Wednesday, Friday, and Saturday), where farmers offer samples of their organically grown produce, artisanal cheeses, and fresh bread. The Greenmarket, a hip outing for all, is often filled with families shopping for dinner, famous chefs choosing ingredients, and foodies stalking Food Network hosts. Ⓜ *4, 5, 6 to Union Sq.*

Stroll the Coney Island boardwalk for some old-school kitsch (before it's redeveloped into swanky condos). There are also plenty of annual events for free here, including the outrageous Mermaid Parade and the Fourth of July hot-dog-eating contest. Ⓜ *B, F, N, Q to Stillwell Ave.*

Check out the street performers around New York's parks: break-dancing crews in Union Square, ragtime duets in Central Park, nutty unicyclists in Washington Square. Buskers in the subway are better than you'd expect—the MTA has a committee that vets official performers, with the top performers assigned to the busiest subway stops.

Smell the cherry blossoms in spring at the Central Park Conservatory; the pathways beneath the blossoming trees are gorgeous, and much closer than the botanical gardens in the outer boroughs. ⊠ *5th Ave. at 105th St.* Ⓜ *6 to 103rd.*

Music, Theater, and Dance

Watch tango dancers and jazz musicians *outside* Lincoln Center at the annual monthlong Out of Doors festival, held in August. It includes more than 100 performances of spoken word, beat boxing, and bigwigs like Dave Brubeck and Arlo Guthrie. Ⓜ *1 to 66th St./Lincoln Center.*

Hit Central Park Summerstage for big-name performers like Afrobeat bandleader Seun Kuti and Columbia's own Vampire Weekend. There's also a second series of concerts in Brooklyn.

Catch rising stars in classical music, drama, and dance at the Juilliard School's free student concerts (check ⊕ *www.juilliard. edu* for a calendar of events). Free tickets are available at the Juilliard box office for theater performances; there's also a line for standby an hour before the show. Smaller acts don't require tickets beforehand. ✉ *144 W. 65th St.* Ⓜ *1 to 66th St./ Lincoln Center.*

Entertain thyself at Shakespeare in the Park, one of New York City's most beloved events—80,000 watch each year. It's been going strong since 1962, and shows usually feature celebrities earning their olde English acting chops. Get in line early at the Public Theater for a shot at tickets, or head to the Delacorte Theater in Central Park. ✉ *425 Lafayette St.* Ⓜ *6 to Astor Pl.*

Get gratis giggles at the Upright Citizens Brigade Theatre's comedy shows. The theater has moved a few times since 1999, but the improv comedy, inspired by Chicago's Second City, remains sharp regardless of location. Professional comedians, including UCB cofounder and Saturday Night Live alumna Amy Poehler, are sprinkled in with amateurs during the shows. ✉ *307 W. 26th St.* ⊕ *www.ucbtheatre.com* Ⓜ *A, C, E to 23rd St.*

Art, Lit, and Architecture

Visit the Metropolitan Museum of Art. If you'll believe it, the $20 entry fee is really a suggested donation. You can pay as much, or as little, as you wish. Smaller donations may get some eye-rolling from the cashier, but it's a small price to pay for access to world-famous works. ✉ *1000 5th Ave. at 80th St.* ⊕ *www.metmuseum.org* Ⓜ *6 to 86th St.*

Browse through the galleries scattered throughout the city. Chelsea's full of expensive galleries with superstar artists, though things get edgier the closer you get to the West Side Highway; you'll also find a trendy art scene in Williamsburg, Brooklyn.

Marvel at Grand Central Terminal's spectacular main concourse. The ceiling painted with the constellations of the zodiac is one of the city's treasures. Ⓜ *4, 5, 6 to Grand Central/42nd St.*

Attend a reading at one of the city's hundreds of bookstores. Night owls shouldn't feel left out—they can attend readings of their own at bars like the Half King in Chelsea or Pete's Candy Store in Brooklyn.

Explore the new MoMA on Friday between 4 and 8 pm, when the $20 entry fee is waived during Target Free Friday Nights. Tickets are not available in advance, so plan to wait in line. ✉ *11 W. 53rd St., between 5th and 6th Aves.* ⊕ *www.moma. org* Ⓜ *E, M to 5th Ave./53rd St.; B, D, F to 47–50th St./Rockefeller Center.*

NEW YORK'S BEST ARCHITECTURE

Midtown is the heart of the city during the workday. From every direction, people pour into the city to give it a jolt of energy. That vibrancy is intense, but is also an unmissable aspect of city life worth exploring for the average visitor. Midtown is home to many beautiful architectural sights, so don't be embarrassed to look at them.

The East Side: from the United Nations to Grand Central

Start near the river, at New York City's first glass-curtain skyscraper, the UN Building (760 United Nations Plaza), completed in 1949 and designed by Le Corbusier. (Technically, it's not on New York's land, but we still count it.) The iconic structure is a monument to diplomacy, though being the city's first skyscraper isn't all glory: the air-conditioning is famously persnickety in the summer months. Continuing west, you'll pass the murals of the Daily News Building (220 E. 42nd) on the south side of the street. The lobby is home to a giant globe (from the era when the News had international correspondents) and murals are in the WPA-style, as the Art Deco building was finished in 1929. Also a can't-miss: the Chrysler Building (405 Lexington Ave.), which out–Art Decos any other structure in New York. (Dig the wheels with wings in place of gargoyles on the exterior.) Continue walking and you'll see Grand Central Terminal (1 E. 42nd St.), the largest train station in the world. This Beaux-Arts structure was saved from the wrecking ball by concerned citizens in the '70s, a fate that similarly styled Penn Station didn't escape. Peek inside for a look at the constellations painted on the soaring ceiling, for a nibble at the Grand Central Oyster Bar, or a cocktail at the swanky Campbell Apartment.

Midtown: Bryant Park and the New York Public Library

By the time you hit 5th Avenue, you'll be staring at the lions that guard the New York Public Library (455 5th Ave.). Built in 1911, the structure is a hub of learning and hosts many lecture series throughout the year. It's abutted by Bryant Park, which offers free Wi-Fi, ice skating in the winter, and films in the summer. It, too, was brought back from the dead during New York's darkest days. There's also the renovated Nat Sherman store (12 E. 42nd St.), which even has a room for smokers to sample their wares.

The West Side: The Heart of Times Square

Keep walking west and you'll hit the razzle and dazzle of Times Square. It's better than it's ever been. No, not from Guiliani's cleanup—those seedy days are long since past, and Disney predominates—but thanks to a series of pedestrian-friendly improvements, including the closure of some streets to traffic and the addition of lawn chairs, making it easy to navigate. Be sure to note the futuristic-looking 4 Times Square, where Anna Wintour of Vogue dictates the world of style from on high, and the kid-friendly confines of Madame Tussaud's (234 W. 42nd St.). Finish off by seeing the lights of Broadway from the many theaters on this stretch between 8th and 9th avenues.

NYC'S WATERFRONT PARKS

Does Central Park make you think, "been there, done that"? Then head to the waterfront. Even New Yorkers are just discovering some of these new green getaways. And with those helpful city bike lanes, doing a tour from one to the next is a great full-day outing, with one-way bike rentals available at key spots along the route. If biking isn't your thing, just hit the park to walk, kayak, watch stunning sunsets, or try to catch a free event from spring to fall.

The Hudson River Park

This 5-mi greenway park hugs the Hudson River from 59th Street to Battery Park. Although the park has a unified design, it's divided into seven distinct sections that reflect the different neighborhoods just across the West Side Highway. The star attraction here—especially for kids—is the freshly refurbished Intrepid Sea, Air, and Space Museum at Pier 86 across from 46th Street. A few blocks south, the Circle Line and World Yacht offer boat tours of the Hudson. At piers 96 and 40, the Downtown Boat House (⊕ *www.downtownboathouse.org*) offers free kayaking. A classic summer experience is the free outdoor movies with popcorn shown on Wednesday and Friday nights at Pier 54. Chelsea Piers, the mammoth sports center between piers 59 and 61, offers bowling, a driving range, ice skating, even trapeze classes. At Pier 66 Boathouse you can take a two-hour $80 introductory sailing course with Hudson River Community Sailing (⊕ *hudsonsailing.org*). The park also sponsors free tours and classes, including free fishing. (Yes, fishing in N.Y.C.) For a calendar of events and activities, go to ⊕ *www.hudsonriverpark.org*.

Getting Here With its location across the West Side Highway, the Hudson River Park isn't exactly easy to get to. Crosstown buses at 14th, 23rd, and 42nd will get you close, but you'll still have to hike across the highway. At Pier 84 across from 44th Street, you can rent a bike at Bike and Roll with an option of dropping it off at any of its locations in Central Park, Riverside Park, or Battery Park.

Governors Island

A new addition to the city's parks scene, this little island feels like a small New England town just 800 yards from N.Y.C.'s financial district. Tourists love the unparalleled views of the harbor and Lower Manhattan, and locals love the out-of-the-city experience. The 172-acre park, built in part from landfill from subway excavations, was a base for the U.S. Army and Coast Guard for almost two centuries. Until 2003 it was off-limits to the public, which could be why the 19th-century homes here are so well preserved. Anytime from May to October (when the park is open), you'll find numerous weekend programs, including art showings, concerts, and family programs. Bikers take a bike over on the ferry or rent one on the island. The biking conditions are ideal, with 5 mi of car-free lanes (although you will have to watch for people movers!). For more information, including updated ferry schedules and a calendar of activities, go to ⊕ *www.govisland.org*.

Getting Here Governors Island is accessible by a pleasant seven-minute ferry ride that leaves from a dock at 10 South St., next to the Staten Island Ferry. (Don't expect to get a seat for the trip!) By subway: 1 to South Ferry Station; 4, 5 to Bowling Green; or R, W to Whitehall St. Station. By bus: M1 (weekdays only), M6, M9, and M15.

The High Line

Another new attraction, the High Line was once an elevated railroad track that serviced the long-ago factories along the lower west side. Neglected and forgotten, it went through a dramatic conversion into a highly acclaimed park that integrates landscaping with witty rail-inspired design. Vegetation here includes 210 species of plants, trees, and shrubs intended to reflect the wild plants that flourished for decades after the tracks were abandoned in 1980. The park—30 feet above street level—is open between Gansevoort Street in the Meatpacking District to 20th Street, with another section extending up to 30th Street expected to open in 2010. The viaduct runs alongside and sometimes through buildings, including Chelsea Market. Wonderful sweeping views of the Hudson River and an extended sight line of the Meatpacking District are the highlights, but some visitors also report getting an eyeful of uninhibited couples at the nearby Standard Hotel. On Sunday at 2 pm during warm-weather months, the park offers guided tours. For more information and a calendar, go to ⊕ *www. thehighline.org* or call ☎ *212/500–6035.*

Getting Here The High Line is accessible at Gansevoort, 14th, 16th, 18th, and 20th streets with elevator access at 14th and 16th. Sorry, the elevated route is strictly for pedestrians, so park that bike and walk. The High Line is two blocks west of the subway station at 14th Street and 8th Avenue, which is served by the L/A/C/E. You can also take the C/E to 23rd Street and walk two blocks west. The 1/2/3 stops at 14th Street and 7th Avenue, three blocks away. By bus: M11 to Washington Street, M11 to 9th Avenue, M14 to 9th Avenue, M23 to 10th Avenue, M34 to 10th Avenue.

Battery Park City

Built over the past 30 years on landfill jutting out into the Hudson River, Battery Park City is a high-rise residential neighborhood split in two by the World Financial Center and its marina. Although the Hudson River Park promenade borders BPC alongside the West Side Highway, locals prefer the route that follows the river's edge through BPC—it's the more scenic path heading to the World Trade Center site from Battery Park. In South Battery Park City you'll pass by the Museum of Jewish Heritage, at 36 Battery Place. Nearby are several reasonably priced outdoor restaurants with stunning views of the Statue of Liberty. **Gigino at Wagner Park** (✉ *20 Battery Pl.* ☎ *212/528–2228*) offers Italian cuisine, and reservations for the outside patio are a must. Or skip the food in favor of high art; public exhibits are scattered throughout BPC. In Wagner Park, Louise Bourgeois has created *Eyes*, two large balls that represent oversize, ahem, body parts. At Vesey Street is the Irish Hunger Memorial by artist Brian Tolle, which includes an Irish cottage dismantled stone by stone and reassembled here. And in Rockefeller Park at Chambers Street, Tom Otterness has created *The Real World*, a popular collection of whimsical—and dark—bronze sculptures, including tiny workers rolling giant pennies.

Getting Here By subway: South Battery Park: 1, R to Rector Place; 4, 5 to Wall Street. North Battery Park: 1, 2, 3, A, C to Chambers Street; E to World Trade Center. By bus: M9, M20, M22.

SIGHTSEEING NEW YORK CITY

Taking a guided tour is a good idea, even if you prefer flying solo. It will help you get your bearings in this city, and it's a great way to investigate out-of-the-way areas, or learn about a particular facet of the city's history, inhabitants, or architecture.

Boat Tours

A **Circle Line Cruise** (✉ *Pier 83 at W. 42nd St., Midtown West* ☎ *212/563–3200* ⊕ *www.circleline42.com*) around Manhattan Island is one of the best ways to get oriented in the city. The three-hour, 35-mi circumnavigation gives a good sense of where things are. The cruises run at least once daily; the cost is $35 per person (there's also a shorter, two-hour "semi-Circle" option available for $31).

Manhattan By Sail (✉ *North Cove Marina, Lower Manhattan* ☎ *212/619–0885* ⊕ *www.shearwatersailing.com*) has an 82-foot yacht dating from the 1920s, sails from the North Cove Marina at the World Financial Center and makes daily 90-minute public sails and Sunday brunch sails from mid-April through mid-October. They also offer two-hour sunset sails in June, July, and August. Reservations are advised, but they can be made only a maximum of two weeks in advance for sunset sails. Fares start at $45.

Bus Tours

Gray Line New York (✉ *777 8th Ave., between 47th and 48th Sts., Midtown West* ☎ *800/669–0051* ⊕ *www.graylinenewyork.com*) runs a number of "hop-on, hop-off" double-decker bus tours in various languages, including a downtown Manhattan loop, upper Manhattan loop, Brooklyn loop, and evening tours of the city. Packages include entrance fees to attractions.

Walking Tours

Big Onion Walking Tours (☎ *212/439–1090* ⊕ *www.bigonion.com*) lead themed tours such as "Irish New York" and "Jewish Lower East Side," as well as famous multiethnic eating tours and guided walks through every neighborhood from Harlem to the Financial District and Brooklyn. Tours run daily and cost $15; add $5 for tours that include stops to eat.

Joyce Gold (☎ *212/242–5762* ⊕ *www.nyctours.com*) has been conducting neighborhood walking tours since 1976. Her theme walks, such as "Gangs of New York and the Bloody Five Points," and "Hell Ain't Hot: This Here's Hell's Kitchen," run on weekends and cost $15.

The **Municipal Art Society** (☎ *212/935–3960, 212/439–1049 recorded information* ⊕ *www.mas.org*) conducts walking tours that emphasize architecture and history. The cost is $15 per person. MAS also runs two weekly tours: downtown Manhattan on Tuesday, and Grand Central Station on Wednesday. Weekly tours begin at 12:30, and there's a $10 suggested donation.

New York City Cultural Walking Tours (☎ *212/979–2388* ⊕ *www.nycwalk.com*) have covered such topics as buildings' gargoyles and the Millionaire's Mile of 5th Avenue. Two-hour public tours run on some Sundays from March to December, and are $15 per person (no reservations needed); private tours can be scheduled throughout the week at $60 per hour (most tours run about three hours).

New York Food Tours (☎ *917/617–7158* ⊕ *www.foodtoursofny.com*) offers walking tours for the foodie on the go. Options include "The Freakiest and Funniest Food" and a "Chinatown Discovery" tour. Prices start at $43 for 2½ hours' worth of walking and noshing.

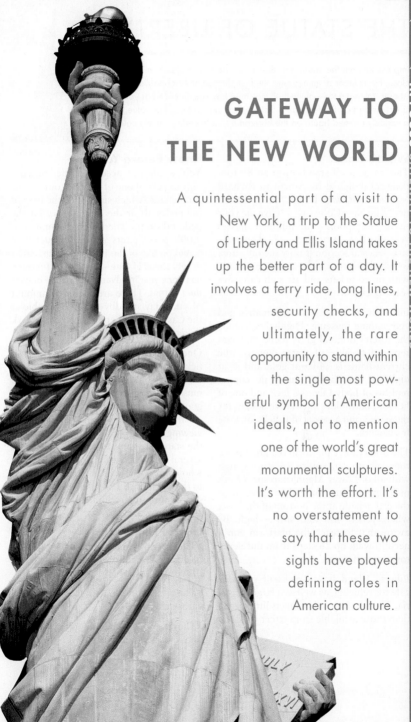

GATEWAY TO THE NEW WORLD

A quintessential part of a visit to New York, a trip to the Statue of Liberty and Ellis Island takes up the better part of a day. It involves a ferry ride, long lines, security checks, and ultimately, the rare opportunity to stand within the single most powerful symbol of American ideals, not to mention one of the world's great monumental sculptures. It's worth the effort. It's no overstatement to say that these two sights have played defining roles in American culture.

THE STATUE OF LIBERTY

Impressive from the shore, the Statue of Liberty is majestic in person and up close. For millions of immigrants, the first glimpse of America was the Statue of Liberty. You get a taste of the thrill they must have experienced as you approach Liberty Island on the ferry from Battery Park and witness the statue grow from a vaguely defined figure on the horizon into a towering, stately colossus.

What's Here
The statue itself stands atop an 89-foot pedestal designed by American Richard Morris Hunt, with Emma Lazarus's sonnet "The New Colossus" ("Give me your tired, your poor, your huddled masses yearning to breathe free . . ."). This massive pedestal section is now the only area to which visitors have access, and only with timed tickets and after an extensive security check.

Inside the pedestal is an informative and entertaining museum. Highlights include the torch's original glass flame that was replaced because of water damage (the current flame is 24-karat gold and lit at night by floodlights), full-scale copper replicas of Lady Liberty's face and one of her feet, Bartholdi's alternative designs for the statue, and a model of Eiffel's intricate framework.

The observatory platform is a great place for a photo op; you're 16 stories high with all of Lower Manhattan spread out in front of you. You'll then descend to the promenade at the bottom of the base, where you're still four stories high. Be aware that to reach the platform you'll need to walk up 26 steps from the elevator drop-off point.

Liberty Island has a pleasant outdoor café for refueling as well as a large cafeteria. The gift shop sells trinkets little better than those available from street vendors.

Know Before You Go
You're allowed access to the museum only as part of one of the free tours of the promenade (which surrounds the base of the pedestal) or the observatory (at the pedestal's top). The tours are limited to 3,000 participants a day. To guarantee a spot on one of the tours, you must order tickets ahead of time—they can be reserved up to one year in advance, by phone or over the Internet. There are a limited amount of same-day standby tickets available at the Castle Clinton and Liberty State Park ticket offices.

Once you reach the island, there are no tickets available. And without a ticket, there is absolutely no admittance into the museum or observatory. You can get a good look at the statue's inner structure on the observatory tour through glass viewing windows that look straight into the statue. Be sure to try the view from several different viewing spots to get the whole interior. There has been no access to the torch since 1916, however the park service now offers limited access to the statue's crown.

Liberty Highlights
■The surreal chance to stand next to, and be dwarfed by, the original glass torch and the copper cast of Lady Liberty's foot.

■The vistas of New York from the observatory platform.

■The rare opportunity to look up the skirt of a national monument.

Statue Basics

- 📠 212/363–3200; 877/523–9849 ticket reservations
- 🌐 www.statuecruises.com
- 🎫 Free; ferry $12.00 round-trip; crown tickets $3
- 🕙 Daily 9:30 AM–5:00; extended hours in summer.

Liberty helicopters

VIEWS OF THE CROWN
Some unique ways to see Lady Liberty:

Liberty Helicopter: Sightseeing tours that fly over the crown and torch (⇨ Chapter 1, Sightseeing Tours).
Kayak: Free kayak tours of the harbor depart from the NYC Downtown Boathouse (See Smart Travel Tips, Sports & the Outdoors).

FAST FACT: To move the Statue of Liberty from its initial home on a Paris rooftop to its final home in the New York Harbor, the statue was broken down into 350 individual pieces and packed in 214 crates. It took four months to reassemble it.

FAST FACT: The face of Lady Liberty is actually a likeness of sculptor Frederic-Auguste Bartholdi's mother—quite a tribute.

FAST FACT: *Liberty Enlightening the World*, as the statue is officially named, was presented to the United States in 1886 as a gift from France to celebrate the centennial of the United States, a symbol of unity and friendship between the two countries. The 152-foot-tall figure was sculpted by Frederic-Auguste Bartholdi and erected around an iron skeleton engineered by Gustav Eiffel (the same Eiffel who would later create the Eiffel Tower).

Foundation of the pedestal to torch: 305′6″

Heel to top head: 111′6″

ELLIS ISLAND

Chances are you'll be with a crowd of international tourists as you disembark at Ellis Island. Close your eyes for a moment and imagine the jostling crowd 100 times larger. Now picture that your journey has lasted weeks at sea and that your daypack contains all your worldly possessions, including all your money. You're hungry, tired, jobless, and homeless. This scenario just begins to set the stage for the story of the millions of poor immigrants who passed through Ellis Island at the turn of the 20th century. Between 1892 and 1924, approximately 12 million men, women, and children first set foot on U.S. soil at the Ellis Island federal immigration facility. By the time the facility closed in 1954, it had processed ancestors of more than 40% of Americans living today.

What's Here

The island's main building, now a national monument, reopened in 1990 as the Ellis Island Immigration Museum, containing more than 30 galleries of artifacts, photographs, and taped oral histories. The centerpiece of the museum is the white-tile Registry Room (also known as the Great Hall). It feels dignified and cavernous today, but photographs show that it took on a multitude of configurations through the years, always packed with humanity undergoing one form of screening or another. While you're there, take a look out the Registry Room's tall, arched windows and try to imagine what passed through immigrants' minds as they viewed lower Manhattan's skyline to one side and the Statue of Liberty to the other.

Along with the Registry Room, the museum's features include the ground-level Railroad Ticket Office, which has several interactive exhibits and a three-dimensional graphic representation of American immigration patterns; the American Family Immigration Center, where for a fee you can search Ellis Island's records for your own ancestors; and, outside, the American Immigrant Wall of Honor, where the names of more than 700,000 immigrant Americans are inscribed along a promenade facing the Manhattan skyline.

The gift shop has a selection of international dolls, candies, and crafts. You can also personalize a number of registry items here as well.

Making the Most of Your Visit

Because there's so much to take in, it's a good idea to make use of the museum's interpretive tools. Check at the visitor desk for free film tickets, ranger tour times, and special programs.

Consider starting your visit with a viewing of the free film *Island of Hope, Island of Tears*. A park ranger starts off with a short introduction, then the 25-minute film takes you through an immigrant's journey from the troubled conditions of European life (especially true for ethnic and religious minorities), to their nervous arrival at Ellis Island, and their introduction into American cities. The film is a primer into all the exhibits and will deeply enhance your experience.

The audio tour ($8) is also worthwhile: it takes you through the exhibits, providing thorough, engaging commentary interspersed with recordings of immigrants themselves recalling their experiences.

Ellis Island Highlights

- Surveying the Great Hall.

- The moving film *Island of Hope, Island of Tears*.

- Listening to the voices of actual immigrants who risked their lives to come to America.

- Reading the names on the American Immigrant Wall of Honor.

- Researching your own family's history.

Ellis Island Basics

☎ 212/363–3200 Ellis Island; 212/561–4500 Wall of Honor information

🌐 www.ellisisland.org

🎫 Free; ferry $12.00 round-trip

🕐 Daily 9:30–5:00; extended hours in summer.

IMMIGRANT HISTORY TIMELINE

Starting in the 1880s, troubled conditions throughout Europe persuaded both the poor and the persecuted to leave their family and homes to embark on what were often gruesome journeys to come to the golden shores of America.

1880s 5.7 million immigrants arrive in U.S.

1892 Federal immigration station opens on Ellis Island in January.

1901–1910 8.8 million immigrants arrive in U.S.; 6 million processed at Ellis Island.

1907 Highest number of immigrants (860,000) arrives in one year, including a record 11,747 on April 17.

1910 75% of the residents of New York, Chicago, Detroit, Cleveland, and Boston are now immigrants or children of immigrants.

1920s Federal laws set immigration quotas based on national origin.

1954 Ellis Island immigration station is closed.

Ellis Island: New arrivals line up to have their papers examined. ca. 1880 – 1910.

FAST FACT: Some immigrants who passed through Ellis Island later became household names. A few include Charles Atlas (1903, Italy); Irving Berlin (1893, Russia); Frank Capra (1903, Italy); Bob Hope (1908, England); Knute Rockne (1893, Norway); and Baron Von Trapp and his family (1938, Germany).

FAST FACT: In 1897, a fire destroyed the original pine immigration structure on Ellis Island, including all immigration records dating back to 1855.

FAST FACT: Only third-class, or "steerage," passengers were sent to Ellis Island. Affluent first- and second-class passengers, who were less likely to be ill or become wards of the state, were processed on board and allowed to disembark in Manhattan.

Four immigrants and their belongings, on a dock, look out over the water; view from behind.

PLANNING

Admission

There's no admission fee for either sight, but the ferry ride, run by Statue Cruises, costs $12.00 ($20.00 with an audio tour). Ferries leaving from **Battery Park** (See Chapter 2) every half hour take you to both islands. (Note that large packages and oversize bags and backpacks aren't permitted on board.) Reserve tickets in advance online—you'll still have to wait in line, both to pick up the tickets and to board the ferry, but you'll be able to pick up a Monument Pass allowing you access to the pedestal of the statue, the museum, and the statue's interior structure. There is no fee for the Monument Pass and you cannot enter inside the statue without it.

Where to Catch the Ferry

Broadway and Battery Pl., Lower Manhattan Ⓜ Subway: 4, 5 to Bowling Green.

When in New Jersey

Directly on the other side of the Hudson River from Battery Park, Liberty State Park is an impressive stretch of green with ample parking and quick ferries to the monuments. Lines are almost never an issue here, something that can't be said about the New York side.

Planning Tips

Buy tickets in advance. This is the only way to assure that you'll have tickets to actually enter the Statue of Liberty museum and observatory platform.

Be prepared for intense security. At the ferry security check, you will need to remove your coat; at the statue, you will need to remove your coat as well as your belt, watch, and any metal accessories. At this writing, no strollers, large umbrellas, or backpacks are allowed in the statue.

Check ferry schedules in advance. Before you go, check www.statuecruises.com.

Keep in mind that even though the last entry time for the monument is at 4:30 PM, **the last ferry to the Statue of Liberty and Ellis Island is at 3:30 PM.** You need to arrive by at least 3 PM (to allow for security checks and lines) if you want to make the last ferry of the day.

Lower Manhattan

WITH GROUND ZERO

WORD OF MOUTH

"A walk over the Brooklyn Bridge is great. If you don't want to walk over and back get the subway across to Brooklyn and walk back to downtown."

—baysidegirl

GETTING ORIENTED

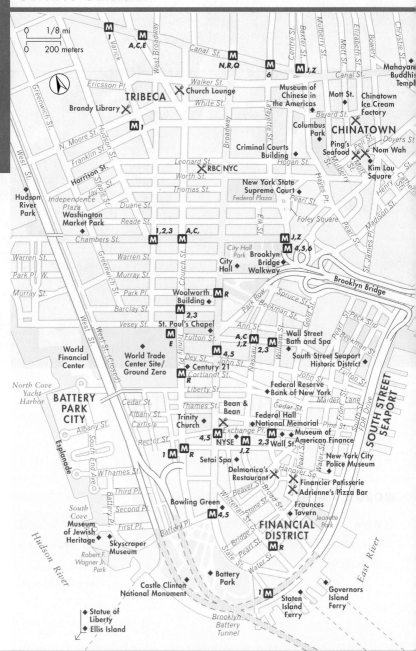

0   1/8 mi
0   200 meters

Varick

West Broadway

Greenwich St.

Ericsson Pl.

Canal St.

Walker St.

N,R,Q

6

J,Z

Canal St.

Mahayan
Buddhis
Templ

Church Lounge

White St.

TRIBECA

Brandy Library

Museum of
Chinese in
the Americas

Mott St.

Chinatown
Ice Cream
Factory

Bayard St.

Columbus
Park

CHINATOWN

Ping's
Seafood

Doyers St.

Nom Wah

Pell St.

N. Moore St.

Hudson St.

Franklin St.

Broadway

Lafayette St.

Criminal Courts
Building

Hogan St.

Kim Lau
Square

Henry St.

Catherine St.

West St.

Harrison St.

Staple St.

Leonard St.

Worth St.

Thomas St.

RBC NYC

New York State
Supreme Court
Federal Plaza

Pearl St.

Hester St.

Mulberry St.

St. James Pl.

Madison St.

Hudson
River
Park

Independence
Plaza

Washington
Market Park

Duane St.

Reade St.

Foley Square

Chambers St.

1,2,3

A,C,

Elk St.

J,Z

4,5,6

Warren St.

Park Pl. W.

Murray St.

Greenwich St.

Church St.

Warren St.

Murray St.

Park Pl.

City Hall
Park

City
Hall

Brooklyn
Bridge
Walkway

Park Row

Spruce St.

Beekman St.

Brooklyn Bridge

Peck Slip

Barclay St.

Vesey St.

Woolworth
Building

St. Paul's Chapel

2,3

E

Ann St.

Beekman St.

Pearl St.

World
Financial
Center

World Trade
Center Site/
Ground Zero

Fulton St.

Dey St.

John St.

Cortlandt St.

Liberty St.

A,C,
J,Z

4,5

Century 21

R

Nassau St.

William St.

2,3

Wall Street
Bath and Spa

South Street Seaport
Historic District

Fulton St.

**SOUTH STREET
SEAPORT**

Front St.

FDR Drive

John St.

Federal Reserve
Bank of New York

Maiden Lane

North Cove
Yacht
Harbor

West St. (Closed)

Cedar St.

Albany St.

Carlisle

Thames St.

Bean &
Bean

Trinity
Church

Federal Hall
National Memorial

Cedar St.

Pine St.

Water St.

**BATTERY
PARK
CITY**

Rector St.

4,5

NYSE

Exchange Pl.

2,3

J,Z

Wall St.

Museum of
American Finance

New York City
Police Museum

Esplanade

South End Ave.

1

R

Setai Spa

Delmonico's
Restaurant

Broad St.

Hanover Sq.

Financier Patisserie

Adrienne's Pizza Bar

W Thames St.

Third Pl.

Second Pl.

Battery Pl.

Bowling Green

4,5

Beaver St.

Stone St.

Whitehall St.

Bridge St.

**FINANCIAL
DISTRICT**

Fraunces
Tavern

Jeanette
Park

South
Cove

Museum
of Jewish
Heritage

First Pl.

Skyscraper
Museum

Battery Pl.

R

Hudson River

Robert F.
Wagner Jr.
Park

Castle Clinton
National Monument

State St.

Pearl St.

Battery
Park

Water St.

East River

Staten
Island
Ferry

Governors
Island
Ferry

1

Statue of
Liberty

Ellis Island

Brooklyn-
Battery
Tunnel

2

MAKING THE MOST OF YOUR TIME

Visit Lower Manhattan during business hours on a week-day to capture the district's true vitality—but expect to be jostled on the crowded sidewalks if you stand still too long or walk too slowly.

On weekends you could feel like a lone explorer in a canyon of buildings in the Financial District. If you look, you can find some spots for good food and nightlife, but the neighborhood largely shuts down at night. End your visit by watching the sunset over the Hudson River.

Chinatown is lively pretty much any time of day, but more so on weekends, when there's so much sidewalk shopping, you'll likely have to walk in the street.

GETTING HERE AND AROUND

Many subway lines service this area. The Fulton Street/Broadway-Nassau station, serviced by nine different subway lines, puts you within walking distance of City Hall, South Street Seaport, and the World Trade Center site.

If Chinatown is your downtown destination, don't even think of driving—its cramped streets and heavy congestion make it a tough place to navigate and an even more disastrous place to park. The subway is a better idea, with the J, N, R, Q, Z, and 6 (Canal Street) and the B and D (Grand Street) all serving the area. The 1 subway line stops in the heart of TriBeCa (Franklin Street).

FODOR'S CHOICE

Brooklyn Bridge

Ellis Island

Ground Zero

Statue of Liberty

TOP EXPERIENCES

Visiting Ground Zero

Riding the Staten Island Ferry

Eating dim sum in Chinatown

Touring Ellis Island and the Statue of Liberty

Snapping a photo in front of Wall Street's bull

Strolling down TriBeCa's Harrison Street

BEST FOR KIDS

Battery Park and Castle Clinton National Monument

South Street Seaport Historic District

Governors Island

WHAT'S NEARBY

Museum of American Finance (⇨ Ch. 14)

Museum of Jewish Heritage (⇨ Ch. 14)

Museum of Chinese in the Americas (⇨ Ch. 14)

New York City Police Museum (⇨ Ch. 14)

Skyscraper Museum (⇨ Ch. 14)

WFC Winter Garden (⇨ Ch. 15)

Century 21 (⇨ Ch. 17)

J&R Music World (⇨ Ch. 17)

Sightseeing
★★★★★
Nightlife
★★
Dining
★★★
Lodging
★★
Shopping
★★

Pirates, rogue politicians, upwardly mobile go-getters, robber barons, scrappy entrepreneurs, and roaming packs of pigs scouring the streets for garbage: what does this motley crew have in common? They're the citizenry that built and inhabited the southern tip of Manhattan in various eras, and in varying combinations.

Updated by
Arthur Bovino

Lower Manhattan, or in the parlance of New Yorkers emphatically giving directions to tourists, "all the way downtown," has long been where the action—or transaction—is. Back when the neighborhood was the village of New Amsterdam (1626–47), its director-general, Peter Minuit, made the quintessential deal on behalf of the Dutch, trading knives, tools, and cloth to an Algonquin tribe, the Canarsees, for all of Manhattan (that he bought it for $24 is more or less an urban myth).

In 1789, a year before New York City lost its title as America's capital, George Washington was sworn in as the nation's first president at Federal Hall, where, two years later, Congress ratified the Bill of Rights.

Little is left from Manhattan's colonial era, however: apart from a precious few structures built in the 1700s, the 19th-century brick facades of **South Street Seaport** are about as old as it gets here. As you'll notice immediately, the neighborhood has largely given way to the sometimes intimidating (and on weekends, seemingly deserted) skyscraper-lined canyons of the **Financial District** on Wall Street and lower Broadway. Bounded by the East and Hudson rivers to the east and west, respectively, and by Chambers Street and **Battery Park** to the north and south, this is an area you can fully and best appreciate by walking its streets.

You'll want to see what's here, but above all you'll want to see what's not, most notably in that empty but evolving gulf among skyscrapers: **the World Trade Center site**, known as **Ground Zero**.

The southern tip has often served as a microcosm for a city that offers as many first shots as it does second chances, so it's appropriate that it's the key point of departure for the **Statue of Liberty** and **Ellis Island**. This experience should never be dismissed as too touristy. Like nothing else, the excursion will remind you that this is a city of immigrants and survivors.

The city's downtown neighborhoods give you a close-up of the many cultures of Manhattan. Tucked to the west, south of Canal Street, residential **TriBeCa** (triangle below Canal Street) has a quieter vibe and owes some of its cred to Robert De Niro, whose investments in the area include the TriBeCa Grill and the nonprofit TriBeCa Film Center. Unlike nearby SoHo (south of Houston) and NoLIta's (north of Little Italy) in-your-face commercial presence, TriBeCa keeps more to itself. And although TriBeCa's money is hidden away behind grand industrial facades, you can get a taste of it at one of the posh neighborhood restaurants or when the stars turn out for the annual TriBeCa Film Festival in spring.

Chinatown, by contrast, is a living, breathing, anything-but-quiet ethnic enclave: a quarter of the city's 400,000 Chinese residents live here above storefronts crammed with souvenir shops and restaurants serving every imaginable regional Chinese cuisine, from modest dumplings to sumptuous Hong Kong feasts. What started as a 7-block area has morphed into more than 40 blocks above and below **Canal Street** with tea shops, restaurants, Buddhist temples, herbalists, acupuncturists, and pungent open-air markets.

THE FINANCIAL DISTRICT AND SOUTH STREET SEAPORT

TOP TOURING EXPERIENCES

THE BATTERY'S DOWN

The best piece of navigational advice about the city still resides in the tune "New York, New York" (the one from the musical *On the Town*): "The Bronx is up and the Battery's down." But once you head down (take the 4 or 5 train to the Bowling Green stop at Broadway and Battery Place, the 1 train to South Ferry, or the R train to Whitehall), you'll want a clue about what's actually down here.

Perhaps mercifully, after all your walking as well as standing on buses and trains with no available seats, **Battery Park** has plenty of places to sit, including tiers of wood benches that line the promenade facing New York Harbor. On a reasonably clear day you'll be able to see **Governors Island,** a former Coast Guard installation now managed by the National Park Service; a hilly Staten Island in the distance; the **Statue of Liberty**; **Ellis Island**; and the old railway terminal in Liberty State Park, on the mainland in Jersey City, New Jersey.

Your key point of interest within the park, as well as where to buy tickets for the Statue of Liberty and Ellis Island, is **Castle Clinton National Monument,** once a fort intended as a defense against the British, though the castle's cannons were never fired in war. The building saw far more action in later centuries as an opera house, an aquarium, and a processing center for immigrants. In 2005 the Bosque Gardens by landscape

Where can I find . . . ?

COFFEE	**Bean & Bean** (71 Broadway). The corner location of this local favorite makes it a convenient place to stop for a fantastic cup of organic, fair trade coffee. Standard sweets and sandwiches are served as well.	**RBC NYC** (71 Worth St.). Order the Vietnamese, a sweet, double-shot espresso drink made using the shop's handcrafted coffee machine, the Slayer, which allows for pre-infusion.
A QUICK BITE	**Adrienne's** (54 Stone St.). Come for a wide selection of artisanal pizza (many tout their square pies as the best in the city), small plates, and salads, along with a few well chosen choices of pasta and entrees.	**Financier Patisserie** (62 Stone St.). If you're done with Starbucks, the three Financier locations downtown offer decent coffee as well as offer a wide variety of pastries, soups, and salads.
COCKTAILS	**Church Lounge** (2 6th Ave., near White St.). Attracts a celeb crowd with 30+ signature cocktails.	**Brandy Library** (25 North Moore St.). Old-school, upscale chic across the street from Walker's, which serves a very underrated burger.

artist Piet Oudulf were opened, as was the Spiral Fountain, with 35 illuminated and interactive jets.

The northern tip of Battery Park skims **Bowling Green,** New York's first public park and a great place with fantastic views. On Bowling Green's south side a warren of blocks contain additional remnants of New York's colonial history, including **Fraunces Tavern,** established in 1762. It was the hostelry of Samuel Fraunces, George Washington's steward and one of the colonial era's most prominent black New Yorkers. George Washington was fond of the tavern, and the American Revolution was in part planned here. History buffs will want to view the American Revolution and other early New York City collections in the **Fraunces Tavern Museum,** which includes four 19th-century buildings in addition to the 18th-century Fraunces Tavern building.

SHOW ME THE MONEY

Late in the evening of December 15, 1989, sculptor Arturo Di Modica left a 7,000-pound surprise gift for N.Y.C. under the Christmas tree in front of the New York Stock Exchange—his bronze *Charging Bull* statue. The bull quickly became the icon of Wall Street. Ask New Yorkers who don't frequent the downtown area where the statue is and they'll usually tell you it's somewhere on Wall Street near the stock exchange. But the statue actually resides in Bowling Green, where it was moved after police complained that it was blocking traffic in its original location. Since the city never commissioned it, the bull is still officially dubbed a "temporary installation."

After you pose for snapshots with the bull, head northeast to **Wall Street,** one of the most famous thoroughfares in the world. The epicenter of Wall Street is—you guessed it—the **New York Stock Exchange**, at the intersection of Wall and Broad streets. The stock exchange traces its beginnings to a group of brokers who, in 1792, shortly after Alexander Hamilton issued the first bonds in an attempt to raise money to cover Revolution-caused debt, were in the habit of meeting under a button-wood tree that once grew on Wall Street. The exchange isn't open to visitors, but there is a related museum at the **Federal Hall National Memorial.** Look at the facade of 23 Wall Street, just across from the exchange. The deep pockmarks and craters were created on September 16, 1920, when, at noon, a horse-drawn wagon packed with explosives detonated in front of the building, killing 33 people and injuring 400. Those responsible were never apprehended, and no one ever claimed credit for what was the worst terrorist attack on American soil until the Oklahoma City bombing and later 9/11.

Marking Wall Street's far west end is **Trinity Church,** whose parish was founded by King William III of England in 1697. Trinity's burial ground serves as a resting place for a half-dozen notables, including Alexander Hamilton.

If you get tuckered out, do as the locals do and hit the spa. The **Wall Street Bath & Spa** (✉ *88 Fulton St.* ☎ *212/766–8600*) offers old-school saunas and plunging pools for $32.50 a day. Those with bigger bonuses should snag an appointment at **the Setai Spa** (✉ *40 Broad St., 3rd floor above SHO restaurant* ☎ *212/363–5418*). The luxurious massages and facials make for excellent top-tier pampering.

THE STREET OF SHIPS

It's hard to see history in Lower Manhattan's rebuilt and bustling streets. But at **South Street Seaport** history is right in your face. The seaport was created to time-warp visitors back to the days when N.Y.C. was a bustling nautical town, and it succeeds in part. Its spiffy little fleet does bring you back to the 19th century, when tall ships sailed from South Street, a time when pirates—Captain Kidd had a house near the wharves—and merchants walked the cobblestone streets and warehouses held treasures from exotic ports. What the seaport, in all its scrubbed tourist beauty, does not include among its careful restorations are the gambling houses, brothels, and saloons that were once so common in this area.

TOP ATTRACTIONS

Battery Park. Jutting out at the southernmost point of Manhattan, tree-filled Battery Park is a respite from the narrow, winding, and (on weekdays) jam-packed streets of the Financial District. Even if you don't plan to stay for long, carve out a couple of minutes from sightseeing time to sit on a bench and take in the view, which includes the Statue of Liberty and Ellis Island. On crystal-clear days you can see all the way to Port Elizabeth's cranes, which seem to mimic Lady Liberty's stance. Of course, looking away from the water and toward the buildings, there's a feeling that you're at the beginning of the city, and a sense of all the possibility it offers just a few blocks in.

The park's main structure is **Castle Clinton National Monument,** the ticket-office site and takeoff point for ferries to the Statue of Liberty and Ellis Island. This monument was once 200 feet off the southern tip of the island, located in what was called the Southwest Battery, and was erected during the War of 1812 to defend the city. (The East Battery sits across the harbor on Governors Island.) As dirt and debris from construction were dumped into the harbor, the island expanded, eventually engulfing the landmark. Later, from 1855 to 1890, it served as America's first official immigration center (Ellis Island opened in 1892).

The interior of the park is loaded with monuments and statues, including *The Sphere,* which for three decades stood on the plaza at the World Trade Center as a symbol of peace. Damaged but still intact after the collapse of the towers, it serves as a temporary memorial to those who lost their lives.

The southern link in a chain of parks connecting Battery Park north to Chambers Street, **Robert F. Wagner Jr. Park** has a flat, tidy lawn and wide benches from which to view the harbor or the stream of runners and in-line skaters on the promenade. A brick structure that holds public bathrooms and a restaurant provides additional views from its flat roof. ⊠ *Broadway and Battery Pl., Lower Manhattan* Ⓜ *4, 5 to Bowling Green.*

Fodor's Choice ★ **Brooklyn Bridge.** "A drive-through cathedral" is how the critic James Wolcott described one of New York's noblest and most recognized landmarks. "The best, most effective medicine my soul has yet partaken," said Walt Whitman upon seeing the nearly completed bridge. It spans the East River, connecting Manhattan and Brooklyn. A walk across its promenade—a boardwalk elevated above a roadway and shared by pedestrians, in-line skaters, and cyclists—takes about 40 minutes from the heart of Brooklyn Heights to Manhattan's civic center. It's worth traversing for the astounding views. ⊠ *Lower Manhattan* Ⓜ *4, 5, 6 to Brooklyn Bridge/City Hall; J, Z to Chambers St.; A, C to High St.–Brooklyn Bridge.*

Fodor's Choice ★ **Ellis Island.** *See highlighted feature at the end of Chapter 1.*

Federal Hall National Memorial. It's a museum now, but this site has a most notable claim: George Washington was sworn in here as the first president of the United States in 1789, when the building was Federal Hall of the new nation. When the city lost capital rights to Philadelphia in 1790, Federal Hall reverted to New York's City Hall, then was demolished in 1812 when the present City Hall was completed. The museum within covers 400 years of New York City's history, with a focus on the life and times of what is now the city's Financial District. You can spot this building easily—it was modeled on the Parthenon, and a statue of George Washington is planted quite obtrusively on the steps. ⊠ *26 Wall St., at Nassau St., Lower Manhattan* ☏ *212/825–6990* ⊕ *www.nps.gov/feha* ☒ *Free* ☉ *Weekdays 9–5* Ⓜ *1, 4, 5, N, R to Rector; 2, 3 to Wall St.; J, Z to Broad St.*

Ⓒ **Governors Island.** If visiting from May to October, take a quick ferry ride over to this charming park—which looks like a small New England town—popular with locals for its bike and running trails, festivals, art

A mix of old and new: Lower Manhattan's bright lights combine with the seaport's historic ships.

shows, concerts, and family programs. Wouter Van Twiller, a representative for Holland, supposedly purchased the island for his private use in 1637 from Native Americans for two ax heads, a string of beads, and a handful of nails. It was confiscated by the Dutch a year later, and for the next decade its ownership switched back and forth between the Dutch and British until the Brits gained firm control of it in the 1670s. The island was officially named in 1784 for "His Majesty's Governors", and was used by the American military until the 1960s, when the Coast Guard took it over. After their facilities were abandoned in 1995, the island was purchased by the public in 2002 and welcomed visitors in 2003. The free ferry to the island departs from the Battery Maritime Building. ⊠ *10 South St., Lower Manhattan* ✉ *Free* ⊙ *June–Oct., Fri. 10–5; weekends 10–7* Ⓜ *1 to South Ferry station; 4, 5 to Bowling Green; R to Whitehall Street.*

Fodor's Choice **Ground Zero.** *See highlighted feature in this chapter.*

★ **New York Stock Exchange (NYSE).** Unfortunately you can't tour it, but it's certainly worth ogling. At the intersection of Wall and Broad streets, the exchange is impossible to miss. The neoclassical building, designed by architect George B. Post, opened on April 22, 1903. It has six Corinthian columns supporting a pediment with a sculpture titled *Integrity Protecting the Works of Man*, featuring a tribute to what were then the sources of American prosperity: Agriculture and Mining to the left of Integrity; Science, Industry, and Invention to the right. The Exchange was one of the world's first air-conditioned buildings. ⊠ *11 Wall St., Lower Manhattan* Ⓜ *1, 4, 5, N, R to Rector; 2, 3 to Wall St.; J, Z to Broad St.*

Continued on page 56

A GLIMPSE OF THE FUTURE WORLD TRADE CENTER

An illuminated **antenna** will reach to 1,776 feet to commemorate America's founding.

Tower 2
Designed by Norman Foster. Ground was broken in 2010. Tentative finish: 2015.

Tower 1
Designed by David Childs. The roof will be 1,368 feet tall—identical to that of the tallest twin tower. Tentative finish: 2013.

Tower 3
Designed by Richard Rogers. Groundbreaking in 2010. Tentative finish: early 2015.

7 World Trade Center
Designed by David Childs. Opened in 2006.

Transportation Hub
Designed by Santiago Calatrava. Finish date 2014.

9/11 Museum
Tentative finish: 2012.

Tower 4
Designed by Fumihiko Maki. Finish date late 2013.

National September 11 Memorial
Entitled *Reflecting Absence*, this will feature 30-foot-tall waterfalls and will open by 9/11/11.

GROUND ZERO
THE WORLD TRADE CENTER SITE

A decade after September 11, 2001, Ground Zero still attracts thousands of visitors who come to connect with the events that unfolded here. At first, though, a visit here may feel like just gazing at a large construction site. (The space remains encircled by fencing.) But with a bit of knowledge you can appreciate places touched by that day. Many of the sites nearby, such as St. Paul's Chapel and the "10 House" firehouse on Liberty Street, are as essential to understanding the complete story as Ground Zero itself.

(above) Ground Zero view from the Winter Garden; (below) 9/11 memorial wall; (opposite) A rendition of the future World Trade Center site

LOOKING BACK AT THE TOWERS AND 9/11

THE TOWERS

The World Trade Towers, each 110 stories tall, were an impressive feat of engineering. Construction began in 1968, and the Twin Towers officially opened in 1973. Avoiding the typical construction used at the time, the architects gave each building an exterior skeleton made up of 244 slim steel columns and an inner "core" tube that supported the weight of the tower.

Approximately 50,000 people worked in the north tower (1 World Trade Center) and south tower (2 World Trade Center), and another 40,000 people visited the 16-acre complex every day. Beneath the towers was a multi-level mall with nearly 100 stores and restaurants.

The Twin Towers prior to 9/11

EVENTS OF THE DAY On September 11, 2001, terrorist hijackers steered two jets into the World Trade Center's Twin Towers, demolishing them and five outlying buildings.

- The first hijacked jet, American Airlines Flight 11, crashed into the north tower, 1 World Trade Center, at 8:46 AM, cutting through floors 93 to 99. The tower collapsed at 10:28 AM. Cantor Fitzgerald, a brokerage firm headquartered between the 101st and 105th floors, lost 658 of its 1,050 employees. At the Windows on the World restaurant (floors 106 and 107), 100 patrons and 72 staff members died.

- The second hijacked jet, United Airlines Flight 175, hit the south tower, 2 World Trade Center, at 9:03 AM, crashing through the 77th to 85th floors. The plane banked as it hit, so portions of the building remained undamaged on impact floors. Consequently, one stairwell initially remained passable from at least the 91st floor down. The tower collapsed at 9:58 AM.

- The attack killed 2,752 people. (Deaths are still being counted; the most recent casualty, Leon Heyward, died in fall 2008 from lymphoma caused by exposure to the toxic atmosphere that formed after the towers' collapse.) The fenced-in 16-acre work site that emerged from the rubble, almost immediately dubbed Ground Zero, has come to symbolize the personal and historical impact of September 11.

(above) Towers burning after attack; Pedestrians flee as the south tower falls

THE DAMAGE

Why *did* the towers fall? A three-year federal study revealed several reasons. The two airplanes used in the attack, both Boeing 767s, hit their respective towers at roughly 500 mph. They both damaged the exterior columns, destroying core supports for at least three of the north tower's floors and up to six of the south tower's floors. Ensuing fires, fed by tens of thousands of gallons of jet fuel, further weakened the buildings. The collapse of the most heavily damaged floors then triggered a domino effect, causing the towers to crumple at an estimated speed of about 125 mph.

Many other area buildings suffered collateral damage. The World Financial Center office complex, to the west of Ground Zero, has as its centerpiece the 10-story glass-domed Winter Garden. After having nearly all its glass blown out in the attacks, the atrium reopened in September 2002 after repairs that included the installation of 2,000 windows and 1.2 million pounds of stone.

The 47-story 7 World Trade Center, to the north of Ground Zero, was struck by large chunks of falling debris from the north and south towers. The building remained standing at first, but subsequent fires caused it to collapse later that afternoon. A new 52-story 7 World Trade Center opened in May 2006 with a much smaller footprint than its predecessor.

St. Paul's Chapel, across the street from Ground Zero, sustained no major damage; staff there credit a huge sycamore

that toppled over during the attack. Its gigantic root system, now above ground, helped to shield the building and the headstones in its attached cemetery from falling debris.

Although the New York Stock Exchange's building wasn't physically harmed during the attacks, the market remained closed for six days (including 9/11). When trading resumed on September 17, the Dow Jones industrial average dropped 684.81 points, or 7.13 percent. The American Stock Exchange (Amex), however, sustained some damage on 9/11, and for two weeks Amex stocks and exchange-traded funds were traded on the NYSE floor.

(above) Firefighters search the WTC rubble; A 9/11 memorial wreath; Protesters demonstrate against retaliation

A vision of the future Manhattan skyline

After years of delays, the process of filling the massive void at Ground Zero is well under way. The World Trade Center Memorial is on target to open on September 11, 2011. (The museum will not open to the public until a year later.) One World Trade Center, the tallest of the new office towers, is also moving along, and so, to varying degrees, are Santiago Calatrava's soaring, controversial new transportation hub and three other distinctive towers, each to be built by a notable architect. In addition, the portion of Greenwich Street that was paved over in 1966 in preparation for the building of the World Trade Center is likely to be reinstated, meaning that traffic will now cut through Ground Zero. The hope is that restoring the street grid will help revitalize nearby businesses and neighborhoods, which are now isolated by the site.

Future downtown skyline at dusk

NATIONAL SEPTEMBER 11 MEMORIAL AND MUSEUM AT THE WORLD TRADE CENTER

No building will occupy the space where the Twin Towers once stood. In their place, as part of the memorial titled "Reflecting Absence," will be recessed, thirty-foot-tall waterfalls. After the water cascades down into the two subterranean reflecting pools outlining the Twin Towers' original footprints, it will then tumble down into smaller square holes at the center of each pool. Surrounding each waterfall on the plaza level will be a low bronze wall with the names of the approximately 2,752 victims of 9/11 cut into it, so that the water and light can be seen through them. The work, designed by the architects Michael Arad and Peter Walker, will be set in a plaza filled with sugar gum and white oak trees.

The museum is to be built below the plaza surface, with just a small visitor center at plaza level. Visitors will walk down a long, twisting ramp that will take them down to the bedrock the towers were built on, 71 feet below. One exhibit here will be the "last column," the last piece of steel to be removed from the site, which was covered with slogans and memorials from rescue crews and others. The museum will also incorporate a 65-foot-high section of the original foundation, the so-called slurry wall that prevented the Hudson River from swamping the grounds after the attacks. The museum is on target to be finished by the tenth anniversary of 9/11, but nearby construction will keep it closed to the public until 2012. The memorial plaza will be open to the public by 9/11/11.

1 World Trade Center 1/1/2010

Fumihiko Maki, Larry Silverstein, and Norman Foster

ONE WORLD TRADE CENTER

Previously known as the Freedom Tower, One World Trade Center will occupy the northwest corner of Ground Zero. The largest building on the site will have a roof that's 1,368 feet tall—identical to that of the taller of the Twin Towers. An illuminated antenna will further increase the building's total height to 1,776 feet to commemorate America's founding. An observation deck is planned for the 100th and 101st floors, 1,265 feet from street level, and a restaurant will be on the floor above. Designed by David Childs of Skidmore, Owings & Merrill, the new 1 WTC is on schedule to reach its roof level by late 2011 and to be finished by the end of 2013. The three other office buildings on the site (all at various stages of construction) are each by a different prominent architect: Fumihiko Maki, Richard Rogers, and Norman Foster.

TRANSPORTATION HUB

About 1,000 feet of subway tunnels collapsed after the towers fell, closing the Cortlandt Street station across the street from Ground Zero. The Port Authority of New York and New Jersey's World Trade Center PATH train station was also damaged in the attacks, and its temporary train station is due to be replaced by a transportation hub designed by Spanish architect and engineer Santiago Calatrava. Inspired by the image of a child releasing a dove, the massive glass-roofed building will be larger than Grand Central Terminal, with many shops besides connections to the Hudson ferries and all nearby subway stations. It's currently on schedule for completion in 2014, although that date may change.

For more information on the new structures, visit ⊕ *www.lowermanhattan.info* and ⊕ *www.buildthememorial.org*.

A GROUND ZERO WALK

A woman watches the Ground Zero construction site

1 Begin your walk in front of the **Ground Zero construction site** (20 Vesey St.), where maps and a scale model help visitors picture both the original World Trade Center as well as what the site will look like once all the construction is over.

☞ Across the street is **St. Paul's**, the Episcopal chapel that became a dormitory, mess hall, and medical center in the months after 9/11. Even George Washington's pew was called back into service for the exhausted rescue workers.

Inspired by the giant sycamore that fell under the rubble and helped protect old headstones in St. Paul's graveyard, the *Trinity Root* sculpture, a 9/11 memorial pictured here, can be seen at Trinity Church

2 After exiting the chapel, head back to Vesey Street, keeping the chapel on your left. Continue west to reach the pedestrian bridge over the West Side Highway; the bridge takes you to the World Financial Center and its palm-tree-filled atrium, **the Winter Garden.**

☞ From its second floor you can see nearly all of Ground Zero.

The Winter Garden Atrium

3 Exit the World Financial Center and head to the Hudson River. From the ferry terminal here, many people fled on 9/11 on boats commanded by volunteer captains. The well-to-do neighborhood here, **Battery Park City**, is partially built on landfill excavated during the building of the first World Trade Center. After 9/11, many of the community's 9,000 residents were unable to return to their apartments for months.

Re-enter the World Financial Center complex and find your way to the southern pedestrian bridge, which leads to Liberty Street.

The firefighters' memorial

4 Once you reach street level, you'll be near the former **Deutsche Bank building**, at 130 Liberty. Severely damaged and filled with toxic dust from the south tower's collapse, the building is still being "deconstructed." Across Greenwich Street, at 124 Liberty, is **10 House**, a fire station nearly destroyed on 9/11. Now the station's restored exterior is covered with a 56-foot bronze bas-relief "dedicated to those who fell and to those who carry on." **The Tribute WTC Visitor Center,** a project of the September 11th Families' Association, is next-door. Its exhibits give a heartbreaking picture of the many lives lost on that day.

The Tribute WTC Visitor Center

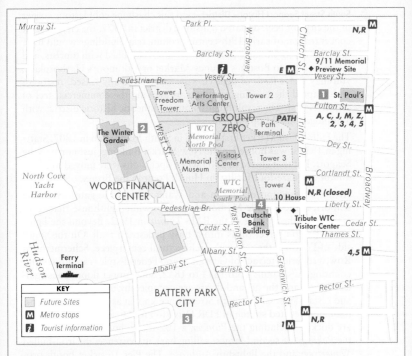

KEY
Future Sites
M Metro stops
i Tourist information

WHEN TO GO
There are no special viewing hours, and the site seldom feels crowded. Early weekday mornings, when many tourists and locals are still working on their first cups of coffee, are good times to go.

TIMING
Allow half a day to linger at all these sites.

INFORMATION AND VISITOR CENTERS
Stop at the information booth at Vesey Street, near the temporary PATH station, for maps of the area (as well as a free Wi-Fi hotspot). The **9/11 Memorial Preview Site** (20 Vesey St., 212/267–2047, ⊕ www. national911memorial.org, free) is open from 10–7 from Monday to Saturday, and 10–6 on Sunday. **The Tribute WTC Visitor Center** (120 Liberty St., 866/737–1184, ⊕ www. tributewtc.org, $10) is open from 10–6 on Monday and Wednesday through Saturday, noon–6 on Tuesday, and noon–5 on Sunday.

TOURS
The Tribute Center leads walking tours of Ground Zero several times daily. New York City Vacation Packages (877/692–8747, ⊕ www.nycvp.com, from $19) conducts guided tours of lower Manhattan and World Trade Center sites.

GETTING THERE

Subway:
1 , **N** , **R** to Rector St.;

2 , **3** , **4** , **5** , **A** , **C** , **J** , **Z** to Fulton St./Broadway-Nassau;

E to World Trade Center/Church St.

PATH:
Any line to World Trade Center stop.

IN FOCUS GROUND ZERO

2

☝ **South Street Seaport Historic District.** Had this charming cobblestone corner of the city not been declared a historic district in 1977, the city's largest concentration of early-19th-century commercial buildings would have been destroyed. But take note that this area is mobbed with tourists, and if you've been to Boston's Quincy Market or Baltimore's Harborplace, you may feel a flash of déjà vu—the same company leased, restored, and adapted the existing buildings, preserving the commercial feel of centuries past. The result blends a quasi-authentic historic district with a homogenous shopping mall.

The Fulton Fish Market first opened in South Manhattan in 1807. Starting in 1939 it was housed in the New Market Building, just north of the Seaport. But that closed in 2005 when operations were moved to a new 400,000-square-foot facility in Hunt's Point in the Bronx.

At the intersection of Fulton and Water streets, the gateway to the seaport, is the **Titanic Memorial,** a small white lighthouse that commemorates the sinking of the RMS *Titanic* in 1912. Beyond the lighthouse, Fulton Street turns into a busy pedestrian mall. On the south side of Fulton is the seaport's architectural centerpiece, **Schermerhorn Row,** a redbrick terrace of Georgian- and Federal-style warehouses and countinghouses built from 1811 to 1812. Some upper floors house gallery space, and the ground floors are occupied by upscale shops, bars, and restaurants. Cross South Street, once known as the Street of Ships, under an elevated stretch of FDR Drive to **Pier 16,** where historic ships are docked, including the *Pioneer,* a 102-foot schooner built in 1885; the *Peking,* the second-largest sailing bark in existence; the iron-hulled *Wavertree*; and the lightship *Ambrose.* The Pier 16 ticket booth provides information and sells tickets to the museum, ships, tours, and exhibits. Pier 16 is the departure point for various seasonal cruises.

To the north is **Pier 17,** a multilevel dockside shopping mall filled mostly with national chain retailers. The weathered-wood decks at the rear of the pier are a choice spot from which to catch sight of the river, with views as far north as Midtown Manhattan and as far south as the Verrazano-Narrows Bridge.

Also, at 12 Fulton Street, is the main lobby of the **South Street Seaport Museum** (☎ 212/748–8600 ⊕ *www.seany.org* ☉ *Apr.–Dec., Tues.–Sun. 10–6; Jan.–Mar., Fri.–Mon. 10–5 [all galleries open; ships open noon–4, weather permitting]*), which hosts walking tours, hands-on exhibits, and fantastic creative programs for children, all with a nautical theme. You can purchase tickets at either 12 Fulton Street or Pier 16 Visitors Center ($15). ✉ *South Street Seaport, Lower Manhattan* ☎ *212/732–7678 events and shopping information* ⊕ *www.southstreetseaport.com* 🎫 *Free; $8 to ships, galleries, walking tours, Maritime Crafts Center, films, and other seaport events* Ⓜ *2, 3, 4, 5, A, C, J, Z to Fulton St./ Broadway-Nassau.*

★ **Staten Island Ferry.** About 70,000 people ride the ferry every day, and you should be one of them. Without having to pay a cent, you get great views of the Statue of Liberty, Ellis Island, and the southern tip of Manhattan. You'll pass tugboats, freighters, and cruise ships—a reminder that this is still a working harbor. The boat embarks from the Whitehall

Terminal at Whitehall and South streets, near the east end of Battery Park. The ferry provides transport to Staten Island, one of the city's boroughs. But if you don't want to visit Staten Island, you can usually remain on board for the return trip. Occasionally a boat is taken out of service for a while; if you're told to disembark, walk down the main gangplank (the same one you used when you came aboard), enter the terminal, and catch the next boat back to the city. ⊠ *Lower Manhattan* ⊕ *www.siferry.com* Ⓜ *1 to South Ferry; R to Whitehall St.; 4, 5 to Bowling Green.*

Fodor's Choice **Statue of Liberty.** *See highlighted feature at the end of Chapter 1.*
★

WORTH NOTING

City Hall. You just might spot news crews jockeying on the front steps as they attempt to interview city officials, which is perhaps all you want to know about City Hall. But if the history of local politics is truly your thing, the hall is open for tours. Among the highlights within are the Victorian-style **City Council Chamber;** the Rotunda where President Lincoln lay in state in 1865 under a soaring dome supported by 10 Corinthian columns; and the **Governor's Room,** which includes a writing table that George Washington used in 1789 when New York was the U.S. capital. If nothing else, take a moment to snap a photo of the austere columned exterior.

Take a moment to enjoy the small but lovely **City Hall Park**, bounded by Broadway to the west and Chambers Street to the north. The layers of history buried under the city's compulsion to reinvent itself were interestingly revealed in portions of the northern part of the park in 1991, when an **African burial ground** was uncovered during construction of a federal office building nearby. It has since been declared a city landmark. Aside from historical interest, though, the park is also just a pleasant, underrated place to stop and take a breath. Enjoy the impressive fountain, and watch government workers and jury members taking a break from their day. ⊠ *City Hall Park, Lower Manhattan* ☎ *212/788–2656* ⊕ *www.nyc.gov/html/artcom/html/tours/city_hall.shtml for tours* ☑ *Free* ☉ *Tours weekdays; reservations required, call 311 or 212/639–9675 outside city* Ⓜ *2, 3 to Park Place; R to City Hall; 4, 5, 6 to Brooklyn Bridge/City Hall; J, Z, A, C to Chambers St.*

Federal Reserve Bank of New York. With its imposing mix of sandstone, limestone, and ironwork, the reserve looks the way a bank ought to: strong and impregnable. The gold ingots in the subterranean vaults here are worth roughly $140 billion—reputedly a third of the world's gold reserves. Hour-long tours (conducted six times a day and requiring reservations made at least five days in advance) include a visit to the gold vault, the trading desk, and "FedWorks," a multimedia exhibit center where you can track hypothetical trades. Visitors must show an officially issued photo ID, such as a driver's license or passport, and pass through scanning equipment to enter the building; the Fed advises showing up 20 minutes before your tour to accommodate security screening. Photography is not permitted. ⊠ *33 Liberty St., between*

William and Nassau Sts., Lower Manhattan ☎ *212/720–6130* ⊕ *www. newyorkfed.org* ☞ *Free* ☉ *1-hr tour by advance reservation, weekdays 9:30–3:30* Ⓜ *A, C to Broadway-Nassau; J, Z, 2, 3, 4, 5 to Fulton St.*

Fraunces Tavern. In his pre-presidential days as a general, George Washington celebrated the end of the Revolutionary War here in 1783, bidding a farewell to his officers upon the British evacuation of New York. Today the former tavern is a museum covering two floors above a restaurant and bar. It has two fully furnished period rooms—including the Long Room, site of Washington's address—and other modest displays of 18th- and 19th-century American history. The museum also hosts lectures. After both the bar and restaurant were closed for almost a year, 2011 has seen the reopening of the bar, the **Rum House**, with the restaurant supposedly following soon. ⊠ *54 Pearl St., at Broad St., Lower Manhattan* ☎ *212/425–1778* ⊕ *www.frauncestavernmuseum. org* ☞ *$10* ☉ *Mon.–Sat. noon–5* Ⓜ *R to Whitehall St.; 4, 5 to Bowling Green; 1 to South Ferry; J, Z to Broad St.*

St. Paul's Chapel. For more than a year after the World Trade Center attacks, the chapel's fence served as a shrine for visitors seeking solace. People from around the world left tokens of grief and support, or signed one of the large drop cloths that hung from the fence. After having served as a 24-hour refuge where rescue and recovery workers could eat, pray, rest, and receive counseling, the chapel, which amazingly suffered no damage, reopened to the public in fall 2002. The powerful ongoing exhibit, titled Unwavering Spirit: Hope & Healing at Ground Zero, honors the efforts of rescue workers in the months after September 11 with photos, drawings, banners, and other items sent to them or as memorials. Open since 1766, St. Paul's is the oldest public building in continuous use in Manhattan. ⊠ *209 Broadway, at Fulton St., Lower Manhattan* ☎ *212/233–4164* ⊕ *www.saintpaulschapel. org* ☉ *Weekdays 10–6, Sat. 10–4, Sun. 7–3* Ⓜ *2, 3, 4, 5, A, C, J, Z to Broadway-Nassau; 4, 5 to Broadway-Nassau; E to Chambers; 6 to Brooklyn Bridge/City Hall.*

Trinity Church. Alexander Hamilton is buried under a white-stone pyramid in the church's graveyard, not far from a monument commemorating steamboat inventor Robert Fulton (buried in the Livingston family vault with his wife). The church (the third on this site) was designed in 1846 by Richard Upjohn. Its most notable feature is the set of enormous bronze doors designed by Richard Morris Hunt to recall Lorenzo Ghiberti's doors for the Baptistery in Florence, Italy. *Trinity Root,* a 12½-foot-high, 3-ton sculpture by Steven Tobin cast from the sycamore tree struck by debris on 9/11 behind St. Paul's Chapel, was installed in front of the church in 2005. A museum outlines the church's history; a daily tour is given at 2. Trinity Church was the city's tallest building until 1890, when the New York World Building took the title (currently held by the Empire State Building). Don't look too hard for the former New York World Building, however: it bit the dust in 1955 to make way for automobile access to the Brooklyn Bridge. ⊠ *74 Trinity Pl., entrance at Broadway and the head of Wall St., Lower Manhattan* ☎ *212/602–0800* ⊕ *www.trinitywallstreet.org* ☉ *Weekdays 7–6, Sat. 8–4, Sun. 7–4; churchyard Nov.–Apr., daily 7–4; May–Oct., weekdays*

7–5, Sat. 8–4, Sun. 7–3; museum weekdays 9–5:30 Ⓜ *2, 3, 4, 5 to Wall St.; 1, R to Rector St.; J, Z to Broad St.*

Woolworth Building. Until 40 Wall Street stole the title in 1930, the 792-foot Woolworth Building, opened in 1913, was the world's tallest building. Make a quick stop in the lobby to check out the stained-glass skylight and sculptures set into the portals to the left and right: one represents an elderly F. W. Woolworth counting his nickels and dimes, another depicts the architect, Cass Gilbert, cradling in his arms a model of his creation. ✉ *233 Broadway, between Park Pl. and Barclay St., Lower Manhattan* Ⓜ *2, 3 to Park Pl.; R to City Hall.*

CHINATOWN AND TRIBECA

TOP TOURING EXPERIENCES

A STREET THAT DEFINES THE COMMUNITY

For a quick taste of Chinatown, head to **Mott Street**, Chinatown's main thoroughfare. This is where the first Chinese immigrants (mostly men) settled in tenements in the late 1880s. Today the street is dense with restaurants, hair salons and barbershops, bakeries, tea parlors, and souvenir shops, most of them lying below Canal Street.

If you plan it right, you can create a movable feast, starting with soup dumplings, a specialty from Shanghai, and continuing with Peking duck, a yellow custard cake, and a jasmine bubble tea, each at a different place. Or, you can have it all come to you at **Ping's Seafood** (✉ *22 Mott St.* ☎ *212/602–9988*) with dim sum for lunch. The few blocks above Canal overflow with food markets selling vegetables and fish (some still alive and squirming). Walk carefully, as the sidewalks can be slick from the ice underneath the eels, blue crabs, snapper, and shrimp that seem to look back at you as you pass by. A good place to get oriented or arrange a walking tour is the **Museum of Chinese in the Americas.**

MOVIE-PERFECT BUT WITH A SHADY PAST

To the right off restaurant-lined Pell Street is alley-size **Doyers Street,** the site of early-20th-century gang wars and today a favorite location for film shoots. Tobey McGuire and Kirsten Dunst had a heart-to-heart talk in *Spider-Man 2,* and Woody Allen used it in two of his films, *Alice* and *Small Time Crooks.*

Quirky, angled, and authentic, this curving roadway is where you can find Chinatown's oldest teahouse, dating from 1920, **Nom Wah Tea Parlor** (✉ *13 Doyers St.* ☎ *212/962–6047*). There's also a relatively hidden and grungy underground passage, formerly a storage place for liquor and now lined with Chinese travel agencies and other very low-tech businesses (don't expect to see signs in English). The street makes a sharp angle (according to legend, it was built this way by Chinatown merchants to thwart straight-flying ghosts who brought bad luck; history says it's because the street was once the entryway to brewer Heinreich Doyers's elegant home) before it reaches the **Bowery,** a point known as

Getting decked out for the carnival of colors and sounds that is the Chinese New Year's parade in Chinatown.

"Bloody Angle" because of the visibility-challenged victims' inability to anticipate a gang's attacks from the corner.

The Bowery itself was once lined with theaters and taverns, but earned a reputation well into the late 20th century as the city's skid row. The Bowery Mission is still there, but today the street is a busy commercial thoroughfare with several restaurant-equipment and lighting stores, and is also the home of the New Museum, in the Lower East Side, which houses contemporary art exhibitions. The oldest row building in New York City, the **Edward Mooney House,** is at 18 Bowery on the corner of Pell Street. Erected in 1785 by Edward Mooney, the house was a residence until the 1820s, and was at one time or another a hotel, tavern, pool hall, restaurant, and bank. Today, it's a historic landmark and opened to the public.

STAR POWER AND STELLAR LOOKS

Walking the photogenic streets of TriBeCa, full of cast-iron factories as well as a time-defying stretch of Federal row houses on **Harrison Street,** you can understand why everyone from Robert De Niro to J.F.K. Jr. has bought apartments here.

The two-block-long Staple Street, with its connecting overhead walkway, is a favorite of urban cinematographers. At 60 Hudson Street is the Art Deco Western Union Building—try to sneak a peek at its magnificent lobby.

The Gangs of Five Points

In the mid-19th century the Five Points area was perhaps the city's most notorious and dangerous neighborhood. The confluence of five streets—Mulberry, Anthony (now Worth), Cross (now Park), Orange (now Baxter), and Little Water (no longer in existence)—had been built over a drainage pond that had been filled in the 1820s. When the buildings began to sink into the mosquito-filled muck, middle-class residents abandoned their homes. Buildings were chopped into tiny apartments that were rented to the poorest of the poor, who at this point were newly emancipated slaves and Irish immigrants fleeing famine.

Newspaper accounts at the time tell of robberies and other violent crimes on a daily basis. And with corrupt political leaders like William M. "Boss" Tweed more concerned with lining their pockets than patrolling the streets, keeping order was left to the club-wielding hooligans portrayed in *Gangs of New York*.

But the neighborhood, finally razed in the 1880s to make way for Columbus Park, has left a lasting legacy. In the music halls where different ethnic groups grudgingly came together, the Irish jig and the African-American shuffle combined to form a new type of fancy footwork called tap dancing.

TOP ATTRACTIONS

Harrison Street. One of TriBeCa's most compelling attractions isn't a collection of monuments or destinations as much as its having a different feel from the rest of the city. With cobblestone streets like Greenwich and Washington and a more subdued pace, it's a chance to get a fleeting glimpse of age in a city determined to constantly reinvent itself. Take a deep breath, take it all in, and make sure not to miss the Federal-style houses on Harrison Street that were relocated here in the 1970s. ⊠ *TriBeCa* Ⓜ *1 to Franklin St.*

Hudson River Park. If the chaos of New York City starts to get to you and you need a new perspective, take a walk along the Hudson River. Parts of the five-mile area from Battery Place to 59th Street are still being renovated to create a park with a unifying style, but you have the opportunity to rent bicycles and explore the bike paths, take boat excursions, and use the basketball courts and batting cages. The TriBeCa portion consists of Piers 25 and 26. ⊠ *TriBeCa* Ⓜ *1 to Franklin St.*

WORTH NOTING

Columbus Park. People-watching is the thing in this park. If you swing by in the morning, you'll see men and women practicing tai chi; the afternoons bring intense games of mah-jongg. In the mid-19th century the park was known as Five Points—the point where Mulberry Street, Anthony (now Worth) Street, Cross (now Park) Street, Orange (now Baxter) Street, and Little Water Street (no longer in existence) intersected—and was notoriously ruled by dangerous Irish gangs. In the 1880s a neighborhood-improvement campaign brought about the park's creation. ⊠ *Chinatown* Ⓜ *4, 6 J, N, Q, Z to Canal St.*

Kim Lau Square. Ten streets converge at this labyrinthine intersection crisscrossed at odd angles by pedestrian walkways. Standing on an island in this busy area is the **Kim Lau Arch,** honoring Chinese casualties in American wars. A statue on the square's eastern edge pays tribute to a Qing Dynasty official named Lin Ze Xu, the Fujianese minister who sparked the Opium War by banning the drug. ⊠ *Chinatown* Ⓜ *4, 5, 6 to Brooklyn Bridge/City Hall; J, Z to Chambers St.*

Mahayana Buddhist Temple. You'll be able to say you saw New York's largest Buddha here at the largest Buddhist temple in Chinatown; it's at the foot of the Manhattan Bridge Arch on the Bowery. A donation of $2 is requested. There's a great gift shop on the second floor. Before its incarnation as a place of worship in 1997, this was the Rosemary, an adult-movie theater. ⊠ *133 Canal St., at the Bowery, Chinatown* ☎ *212/343–9592* ⊙ *Daily 8–7* Ⓜ *B, D to Grand St.*

Washington Market Park. This landscaped recreation space with a gazebo and playground—ideal for permitting the kids to blow off steam—was named after the great food market that once sprawled over the area. Across the street at the elementary school are a stout red tower resembling a lighthouse and a fence with iron ship figures—reminders of the neighborhood's dockside past. There's a small greenmarket here on Wednesday and Saturday. ⊠ *Greenwich St. between Chambers and Duane Sts., TriBeCa* Ⓜ *1, 2, 3 to Chambers St.*

SoHo, NoLIta, and Little Italy

WORD OF MOUTH

"I took the subway to SoHo and had a great breakfast at Balthazar. It was just eggs, sausage, and toast, but just the atmosphere alone made it just seem better. The waitress was very nice and sent the maitre'd over to give me directions. He had it all—he was handsome and French!"

—MichelleY

GETTING ORIENTED

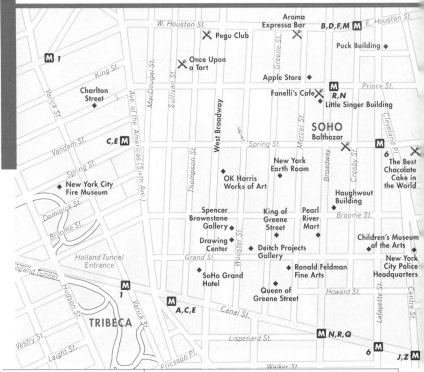

FODOR'S CHOICE	MAKING THE MOST OF YOUR TIME

FODOR'S CHOICE

King of Greene Street

St. Patrick's Old Cathedral

TOP EXPERIENCES

Browsing boutiques in SoHo and NoLIta

Architecture-ogling along Greene Street

Engage in some gallery hopping

Grazing at Little Italy's Grand Street grocers

Doing brunch at Balthazar

MAKING THE MOST OF YOUR TIME

If you're coming to shop in SoHo (south of Houston) and NoLIta (north of Little Italy), plan to arrive after 11 am, as most shops open late and stay open until early evening. If art is your thing, avoid Sunday, because most galleries are closed. SoHo, with national chains lining its section of Broadway, is almost always a madhouse (unless it's raining), but weekdays are somewhat less frenetic. NoLIta is calmer and less crowded, with fewer chains and more boutiques. Little Italy represents a very small area nowadays—just four blocks—having lost ground to a growing Chinatown. You can see it all in a half hour, or spend an afternoon exploring the grocers and the stores hawking touristy Italian-theme T-shirts, bumper stickers, and assorted tchotchkes, capped off with a meal at one of Mulberry Street's kitschy Italian-American restaurants or its touted newcomer, Torrisi Italian Specialties. If you come in mid-September during the San Gennaro festival (a huge street fair in honor of the patron saint of Naples) you—along with thousands of others—can easily spend an entire day and night exploring the many food and souvenir booths and playing games of chance.

WHAT'S NEARBY

Children's Museum of the Arts (⇨ Ch. 14)

New York City Fire Museum (⇨ Ch. 14)

Museum of Comic and Cartoon Art (⇨ Ch. 14)

Angelika Film Center (⇨ Ch. 15)

Housing Works Used Books Cafe (⇨ Ch. 15)

Tribeca Performing Arts Center (⇨ Ch. 15)

Broome Street Bar (⇨ Ch. 16)

Pegu Club (⇨ Ch. 16)

S.O.B.'s (⇨ Ch. 16)

Apple Store (⇨ Ch. 17)

Fragments (⇨ Ch. 17)

Jacques Torres Chocolate (⇨ Ch. 17)

Kirna Zabête (⇨ Ch. 17)

MarieBelle (⇨ Ch. 17)

McNally Jackson (⇨ Ch. 17)

Pearl River Mart (⇨ Ch. 17)

Resurrection (⇨ Ch. 17)

Lafco NY Santa Maria Novella (⇨ Ch. 17)

UNIQLO (⇨ Ch. 17)

GETTING HERE AND AROUND

SoHo is roughly bounded by Houston Street, Canal Street, 6th Avenue, and Lafayette Street.

To the east, NoLIta grows daily but lies pretty much between Houston, the Bowery, Kenmare, and Lafayette.

Plenty of subways service the area; take the 6 or A, C, E to Spring Street; the R to Prince Street; or the B, D, F, to Broadway-Lafayette.

WORD OF MOUTH

"Sunday. Our SoHo day. Based largely on Fodorite advice, we [had] brunch at Balthazar. The decor is perfect—it really did feel as if we were in a classic French brasserie. Much cheaper than going to Paris, and no jet lag. Well fortified, we head out to Spring Street for a spot of shopping/browsing through Kate's Paperie, Sur la Table, down to Pearl River, and then (more walking) past enticing windows." —SB_Travlr

Sightseeing
★★

Nightlife
★★★

Dining
★★★

Lodging
★★★★

Shopping
★★★★★

SoHo (south of Houston) and NoLlta (north of Little Italy) are shopper's paradises, super-trendy, painfully overcrowded on weekends, often overpriced, and undeniably glamorous. A few decades ago, though, these neighborhoods were quiet warrens of artists' lofts and galleries, and the only reason to visit was to go gallery hopping.

Updated by
Arthur Bovino

SoHo was the epicenter of New York's art scene in the late 1970s, and has since evolved into a Mecca of mostly chain retailers. On the side streets, however, a handful of galleries still exist, tucked away between higher-end stores such as Chanel and Louis Vuitton and a few local boutiques. That said, SoHo hasn't lost its charm. In between whipping out your credit card or feverishly searching for a café with empty seats, take a few seconds to savor the Belgian brick cobblestones and turn-of-the-20th-century lampposts, adorned with cast-iron curlicues from their bases to their curved tops.

Compared to SoHo, **NoLlta** is the place to hit for unique boutiques and quieter cafés. The area feels significantly more like a neighborhood where locals eat, shop, and live. A great place to stop for break or picnic is DeSalvio Playground at the corner of Spring and Mulberry streets, where kids play on red, white, and green equipment (colors in honor of the Italian flag) and people play chess on stone game tables.

Just east of Broadway, find the remains of what once was a thriving, lively community of Italian Americans: the tangle of streets that make up **Little Italy**. The few nostalgic blocks surrounding Mulberry Street between NoLlta and ultrabusy Canal Street are still a cheerful salute to all things Italian, with red-green-and-white street decorations on permanent display and specialty grocers and cannelloni makers dishing up delights. And every September, Mulberry Street becomes the giant Feast of San Gennaro, a crowded 11-day festival that sizzles with the smell of sausages and onions (don't miss John Fasullo's braciole, an iconic sandwich filled with fillet of pork roasted over a coal pit and topped with peppers and onions). This is by far the city's most extensive annual street fair.

SOHO

TOP TOURING EXPERIENCES

SHOP 'TIL YOU DROP

The stretch of Broadway between Houston and Broome streets is a flurry of pedestrian traffic with retail giants like H&M, Banana Republic, and Victoria's Secret, as well as local city favorites such as **Scoop NYC** (⊠ *532 Broadway* ☎ *212/925–2266*) and **Pearl River Mart** (⊠ *477 Broadway* ☎ *212/431–4770*).

To the west or east in SoHo are boutiques from established contemporary designers such as **Catherine Malandrino, Kate Spade, 3.1 Phillip Lim, Marc Jacobs, Alexander Wang, Anja Hindmarch, and Vivienne Tam,** just to name a few. If the crowds of fashionistas and tourists start to become too much, head a few blocks over to West Broadway—also lined with mostly chain stores—where the action is less interesting but the sidewalk is also less trafficked.

In NoLIta, on Elizabeth, Mulberry, and Mott streets, mix with models and magazine editors at one-off shops by young designers just starting to make their marks. There, amid lingering remnants of the neighborhood's Italian immigrant past, custom-designed jewelry, hand-sewn dresses, trendy home furnishings, and high-concept lighting fill the storefronts.

When you're shopped out and ready to drop, hit **Bliss SoHo** (⊠ *568 Broadway, 2nd Fl., between Prince and Houston Sts.*) for a muscle-soothing Ginger Rub massage. Just be warned, this type of pampering isn't the "walk-in" variety, so book at least a month ahead on ⊕ *www. blissworld.com* or just enjoy the spa store with its lotions and potions to cart back to your hotel.

MODERN ART AND DESIGN

Even if you're not in the market for a $1,000 skirt, the 23,000-square-foot **Prada** design store (⊠ *575 Broadway* ☎ *212/334–8888*) is worth a stop to check out the Rem Koolhaas design. ■ **TIP→** Try something on just to experience the drama of the dressing room, just as hyperdesigned as the rest of the space. A showcase of everything wired, the **Apple Store** (⊠ *103 Prince St.* ☎ *212/226–3126*) is a tech-head's Nirvana.

Edgy in the '70s and '80s, SoHo still retains some of the artists' galleries that brought the neighborhood to the forefront of the city's art scene at the time. Several of SoHo's better exhibition spaces, including **Deitch Projects** and the **Drawing Center,** are clustered in the vicinity of Greene and Wooster streets near Grand and Canal. Many a rainy day can be spent enjoying the often outré collections inside, no purchase necessary.

19TH CENTURY ARCHITECTURE

SoHo has the world's greatest concentration of cast-iron buildings, built in response to fires that wiped out much of Lower Manhattan in the mid-18th century. It's hard to single out any one block, as almost all have gorgeous examples of the various cast-iron styles (Italianate, Victorian Gothic, Greek Revival), but Greene Street has two buildings

DID YOU KNOW?

Despite the attention-grabbing store windows, many feel the real eye candy of SoHo is the cast-iron buildings and cobblestone streets, preserving a 19th-century elegance in the face of 21st-century consumerism.

that are architectural standouts: the **Queen of Greene Street** and the **King of Greene Street.**

Other notable buildings are the Beaux-Arts **Little Singer Building** and the **Haughwout Building** on Broadway, and the 1885 Romanesque Revival **Puck Building** (⊠ *295 Lafayette St.*), a former magazine headquarters and now a busy event space. Lastly, the "Look down, look around" admonishment need not apply only to commuters in Penn Station. In SoHo you'll notice lights in the sidewalk along Broadway and neighboring streets. Starting in the 1850s, these vault lights were set into sidewalks to permit daylight to reach basements.

TOP ATTRACTIONS

Fodor'sChoice
★
King of Greene Street. This five-story Renaissance-style 1873 building has a magnificent projecting porch of Corinthian columns and pilasters. Today the King is painted in high-gloss ivory and houses a boutique on the ground floor with an array of fashion-forward international labels and an espresso bar that among other things, serves mochas, affogatos and green tea lattes. ⊠ *72–76 Greene St., between Spring and Broome Sts., SoHo* Ⓜ *R to Prince St.*

Queen of Greene Street. The regal grace of this 1873 cast-iron beauty is exemplified by its dormers, columns, window arches, projecting central bays, and Second Empire–style roof. ⊠ *28–30 Greene St., between Grand and Canal Sts., SoHo* Ⓜ *J, N, Q, R, Z, 6 to Canal St.*

WORTH NOTING

OFF THE
BEATEN
PATH
Charlton Street. The city's longest stretch of Federal-style redbrick row houses from the 1820s and '30s runs along the north side of this street, which is west of 6th Avenue and south of West Houston Street. The high stoops, paneled front doors, leaded-glass windows, and narrow dormer windows are all intact. Nearby King and Vandam streets have more historic houses. Much of this area was once the site of a mansion called Richmond Hill. In the late 18th century Richmond Hill was set in what is described as a beautiful wild meadow with glimpses of the nearby city and the "hamlet" of Greenwich Village, which served variously as George Washington's headquarters and the home of Abigail Adams and Aaron Burr. ⊠ *SoHo* Ⓜ *1 to Houston St.; C, E to Spring St.*

Haughwout Building. Perhaps best known for what's no longer inside—the world's first commercial passenger elevator, invented by Elisha Graves Otis—the building's exterior is still well worth a long look. Nicknamed the Parthenon of Cast Iron, this five-story, Venetian palazzo–style structure was built in 1857 to house department-store merchant E. V. Haughwout's china, silver, and glassware store. Each window is framed by Corinthian columns and rounded arches. ⊠ *488–492 Broadway, at Broome St., SoHo* Ⓜ *6 to Spring St.; R to Prince St.*

Little Singer Building. Ernest Flagg's 1904 masterpiece reveals the final flower of the cast-iron style with a delicate facade covered with curlicues of wrought iron. The central bay windows are recessed, allowing the top floor to arch over like a proscenium. The L-shape building's second facade is around the corner on Prince Street. ⊠ *561 Broadway, SoHo* Ⓜ *R to Prince St.*

LITTLE ITALY AND NOLITA

TOP TOURING EXPERIENCES

THE BEST ITALIAN AMERICAN EATS

Around Grand Street near Mulberry and Mott are a number of fine family-run Italian grocers, including the fifth-generation **DiPalo's Fine Foods** (⊠ *200 Grand St.* ☎ *212/226–1033*), known for its amazing cheese and cured meats (ask for a sample!), and fourth-generation **Alleva** (⊠ *188 Grand St.* ☎ *212/226–7990*), where the mozzarella and fried rice balls are among the best in the city. Although it's technically NoLIta, newcomer **Torrisi Italian Specialties** (⊠ *250 Mulberry St.* ☎ *212/965–0955*), with former cooks from Babbo (a Mario Batali enoteca in Greenwich Village), has brought high-quality Italian-American food back to the area. Try to avoid visiting before dinner, when locals hit them after work, and have a much less frenzied experience and more of a chance to taste the goods. (DiPalo's in particular has long lines most days.)

It's practically a crime to visit Little Italy without a stop into **Ferrara** (⊠ *195 Grand St.* ☎ *212/226–6150*), a fifth-generation business that was started in 1892. Grab a Baba Rum, an espresso, some gelato, and, of course, a cannoli. Because of the restaurant's popularity, waits for tables—especially on summer weekends—can top out at an hour or more. An alternative is to hop on the to-go line (it's usually significantly shorter), and have your sweets boxed to go to savor in your hotel room.

Speaking of crime, there's a bit of food-related mob history at the corner of Hester and Mulberry streets, at what was once **Umberto's Clam House** (*now Da Gennaro Restaurant* ⊠ *129 Mulberry St.* ☎ *212/431–3934*), where in 1972 mobster Joey Gallo was gunned down by mob hit men during dinner. Although this was Little Italy's most notorious whack job, there are less-well-known mob spots here, like John "The Dapper Don" Gotti's former Manhattan headquarters at 247 Mulberry Street in NoLIta.

THE HEART OF LITTLE ITALY

St. Patrick's Old Cathedral (⊠ *263 Mulberry St.*) was established in 1809, and described by the *New York Gazette* as "a grand and beautiful church, which may justly be considered one of the greatest ornaments of our city." Step inside this Gothic Revival church, once the scene of race riots, vehement anti-Catholic protests, and other less savory bits of N.Y.C. history, to see a peaceful space with a grandeur that far exceeds what you might expect to find in this neighborhood (once Little Italy but is now technically in NoLIta).

Where can I find . . . ?

COFFEE	Aroma Espresso Bar (145 Greene St.) Locals skip Starbucks to come here for quick service, soups, sandwiches, and pastries.	Once Upon a Tart (135 Sullivan St.) Great name with the goods to back it up.
A QUICK BITE	Lombardi's (32 Spring St.) It kicked off New York's (and America's) love of pizza.	The Best Chocolate Cake in the World (55a Spring St.) Locations in Lisbon, São Paulo, and now New York. Try it for yourself.
COCKTAILS	Fanelli's (94 Prince St.) It's a scene, but it's worth stopping in this neighborhood bar at least once.	Pegu Club (77 West Houston St.) The fine art of drinking, elevated with great martinis.

TOP ATTRACTIONS

Most Precious Blood Church. A replica of the grotto at Lourdes is the high point of the Most Precious Blood Church's richly painted interior. The church becomes a focal point during the annual San Gennaro festival. ⊠ *109 Mulberry St., Little Italy* ☎ *212/226–6427* ☺ *Mass Sat. noon, 5:30; Sun. 9, noon, 2 (Vietnamese)* Ⓜ *N, Q, R, 6 to Canal St.; J, Z to Canal St.*

Fodor'sChoice
★
St. Patrick's Old Cathedral. If you've watched *The Godfather*, you've peeked inside St. Patrick's Old Cathedral—the interior shots of the infamous baptism scene were filmed here.

The unadorned exterior of the cathedral gives no hint to the splendors within, including an 1868 Henry Erben pipe organ. The enormous marble altar surrounded by hand-carved niches (reredos) house an extraordinary collection of sacred statuary and other Gothic exuberance.

There's a maze of mortuary vaults underneath the cathedral (older residents of Little Italy recall playing hide-and-seek in the vaults), and the outdoor cemetery is the final resting place for notable New Yorkers, such as the Venerable Pierre Toussaint, an African-American who was born a slave in Haiti and made his fortune as a New York hairdresser, and whose many charitable works have resulted in his consideration for sainthood. Also interred here is Bishop Hughes—better known during his time as "Dagger John," a nickname he earned for his fiery temperament and the distinctive pointed cross he always scrawled after signing his name. ⊠ *263 Mulberry St., corner of Mott and Prince Sts., NoLIta* ☎ *212/226–8075* ☺ *Hrs. may vary, usually open 8–5. Mass weekdays 8:30 am (Spanish) and 12:10 (English); Sat. 8:30 am (Spanish), 12:10 (English), and 5:30 (English); Sun. 9:15 (English), 10:15 (Chinese), 11:30 (Spanish), 12:45 (English), and 7 pm (English)* Ⓜ *R to Prince St.; 6 to Bleecker St.*

The stark, simple interior of OK Harris Works of Art illustrates the typical gallery space in SoHo.

WORTH NOTING

New York City Police Headquarters. Seen in Martin Scorsese's *Gangs of New York*, this magnificent 1909 Edwardian baroque structure with a striking copper dome served as the headquarters of the New York City Police Department until 1973. Designed to "impress both the officer and the prisoner with the majesty of the law," it was converted into luxury condos in 1988 and is known today as the Police Building Apartments. Big-name residents have included Cindy Crawford, Winona Ryder, and Steffi Graf. ⊠ *240 Centre St., between Broome and Grand Sts., Little Italy* Ⓜ *6 to Spring St.; J, Z to Bowery.*

GALLERIES

Deitch Projects. This energetic enterprise composed of two gallery spaces shows works from the global art scene, as well as performance groups such as the Citizens Band. Artists on view have included Swoon, Ryan McGinness, and Kihinde Wiley. ⊠ *76 Grand St., between Greene and Wooster Sts., SoHo* ☎ *212/343–7300* ☽ *Tues.–Sat., noon–6* ⊕ *www. deitch.com* Ⓜ *C, E to Spring St.* ⊠ *18 Wooster St., between Grand and Canal Sts., SoHo* ☎ *212/343–7300* Ⓜ *N, Q, R, J, Z, 6, A, C, E to Canal St.*

Drawing Center. At this nonprofit organization the focus is on contemporary and historical drawings seen nowhere else. Works often push the envelope on what's considered drawing; many projects are commissioned especially by the center. A second gallery is across the street at 40 Wooster Street. ⊠ *35 Wooster St., between Broome and Grand*

Sts., SoHo ☎ *212/219–2166* ⊕ *www.drawingcenter.org* Ⓜ *N, Q, R, J, Z, 6, A, C, E to Canal St.*

New York Earth Room. Walter De Maria's 1977 avant-garde work consists of 140 tons of gently sculpted soil (22 inches deep) filling 3,600 square feet of a second-floor gallery maintained by the Dia Art Foundation. You cannot touch or tread on the dirt, nor can you take its photo, but it has been valued at $1 million. If you like the work, check out de Maria's *Broken Kilometer* a few blocks away at 393 West Broadway. ⊠ *141 Wooster St., between W. Houston and Prince Sts., SoHo* ☎ *212/989–5566* ⊕ *www.earthroom.org* ⊠ *Free* ☉ *Wed.–Sun. noon–6 (closed 3–3:30 and during the summer)* Ⓜ *R to Prince St.; B, D, F, M to Broadway-Lafayette.*

OK Harris Works of Art. This SoHo stalwart hosts a wide range of visual arts: paintings, digitally enhanced photographs, trompe-l'oeil reliefs, and sculptures. The gallery closes from mid-July to early September. ⊠ *383 West Broadway, between Spring and Broome Sts., SoHo* ☎ *212/431–3600* ⊕ *www.okharris.com* Ⓜ *C, E to Spring St.*

Ronald Feldman Fine Arts. Founded in 1971, this gallery represents more than 30 international contemporary artists. It has a large selection of Andy Warhol prints, paintings, and drawings. ⊠ *31 Mercer St., between Grand and Canal Sts., SoHo* ☎ *212/226–3232* ⊕ *www.feldmangallery. com* Ⓜ *N, Q, R, J, A, C, E, 6 to Canal St.*

The East Village and the Lower East Side

WORD OF MOUTH

"We thought the Tenement Museum was one of the best 'museums' we've been to in a long time. The Tenement Museum, a walk around the Lower East Side, and lunch at Katz's Deli—a perfect morning/afternoon!"

—sf3707

GETTING ORIENTED

M 4,5,6, L,
N,Q,R

M L

Third Ave.

Second Ave.

First Ave.

E. 13th St.

◆ The Strand

Fourth Ave.

E. 12th St.

Broadway

E. 11th St.

St. Mark's
Church-in-the-Bowery

E. 10th St.

Stuyvesant Fish House

Russian &
◆ Turkish Baths

Stuyvesant St. ◆   ◆ Renwick Triangle

◆ P.S. 122

Astor Place
Subway
Station

E. 9th St.

Sculpture for
Living ◆

PDT
✗

Astor Pl.

Cooper Union
Foundation
Building

St. Mark's Place

Tompkins
Square Park
◆

M
R

Fourth Ave.

Cooper Union
Science & Art
Building

✗ McSorley's Old Ale House

Astor Pl.

M 6

Taras Shevchenko Pl.

E. 7th St.

Colonnade
Row ◆

Third Ave.

◆ St. George's Ukranian
Catholic Church

✗ Abraço

Ave. A

Ave. B

Joseph Papp
Public Theater

E. 6th St.

EAST VILLAGE

Merchant's
House Museum

E. 5th St.

◆

Cooper
Square

E. 4th St.

**ALPHABET
CITY**

Lafayette St.

Gt. Jones St.

E. 3rd St.

E. 2nd St.

Nuyorican
Poets Café →

E. 1st St.

Angel Orensanz
Center for the Arts
◆

6 **M**

Bleecker St.

F

Katz's Delicatessen

M Russ & Daughters ✗

Essex St.

Norfolk St.

Suffolk St.

B,D,F,M **M**

E. Houston St.

Allen St.

Orchard St.

Ludlow St.

Forsyth St.

✗ D'Espresso

Mulberry St.

Mott St.

Elizabeth St.

Chrystie St.

Eldridge St.

Stanton St.

Economy
Candy

Prince St.

Bowery

New
Museum
◆

**LOWER
EAST SIDE**

← **SOHO**

NOLITA

Rivington St.

Gallery
Onetwentyeight

Essex Street
Market

Bialystoker
Synagogue

Spring St.

6 **M**

Delancey St.

J,M,Z,F **M**

J,Z **M**

Lower East Side
Tenement Museum

◆ Il Laboratorio
✗ del Gelato

0 ———— 1/8 mile

Kehila Kedosha Janina ◆

Broome St.

0 ———— 200 meters

Eldridge St.
Synagogue

MAKING THE MOST OF YOUR TIME

Houston Street, which runs the entire width of this part of Manhattan, somewhat neatly divides the area south of 14th Street and east of 4th Avenue and the Bowery into the East Village (above) and the Lower East Side (below). So many communities converge in these neighborhoods that each block seems like a new neighborhood unto itself.

The East Village lets loose on weekend nights, when reservations fill up and bar-hoppers converge. Visiting on weekdays makes for a less frenetic experience, when establishments attract mostly locals shuffling on errands and visitors enjoying the mellow shopping and café vibe. (It should be noted that "locals" always includes a large number of students from New York University.) Weekend days see the street life at its most vibrant, with brunch spots like Prune and Back Forty filled with lingering patrons, and boutique shoppers trying on vintage dresses.

The Lower East Side is not an early riser any day of the week. Although there's plenty to see during the day, nightfall offers a different vision: blocks that were previously empty rows of pulled-down gratings transform into clusters of throbbing bars. When shopping, be aware that a number of traditional food and clothing establishments close on Saturday to observe the Jewish Sabbath, and on Sunday Orchard Street below Houston becomes a pedestrian-only strip where street vendors set up their stands outside the many "bargain district" clothing and specialty shops. On the increasingly trendy streets around Rivington and Stanton, stores, bars, and cafés buzz all week but are less crowded by day.

GETTING HERE AND AROUND

Take the R subway line to 8th Street or the 6 to Astor Place. To reach Alphabet City, take the L to 1st Avenue or the F to 2nd Avenue. Head southeast from the same stop on the F, or take the F to Delancey or the J, M, Z to Essex Street. Driving is not recommended, as parking here is very difficult.

FODOR'S CHOICE

Essex Street Market

TOP EXPERIENCES

People-watching on St. Marks Place

Stopping for a beer at McSorley's

Strolling through the Strand Bookstore

Visiting the Lower East Side Tenement Museum

Wandering around the Lower East Side's funky boutiques

Having a classic New York deli at Katz's or Russ & Daughters

WHAT'S NEARBY

Lower East Side Tenement Museum (⇨ Ch. 14)

Merchant's House Museum (⇨ Ch. 14)

New Museum (⇨ Ch. 14)

The Public Theater (⇨ Ch. 15)

The Strand Bookstore

The Bowery Ballroom (⇨ Ch. 16)

4

Sightseeing
★★

Nightlife
★★★★★

Dining
★★★★★

Lodging
★★

Shopping
★★★★

The high concept of "La Bohème meets hipsters in vintage clothing," better known as the musical *Rent*, accurately pegs the East Village as a community of artists, activists, and other social dissenters. Spend some time wandering these bohemian side streets, and you'll be struck by the funky pastiche of ethnicities whose imprints are visible in the neighborhood's restaurants, shops, and, of course, people.

Updated by
Arthur Bovino

Another defining point in the neighborhood's history, American punk was born here at the now-defunct CBGB; the punk rock and indie scene is kept alive at the many small music venues both here and on the Lower East Side.

These days a walk along the lively but somewhat homogenized **St. Marks Place** barely evokes this once-gritty and counterculture scene. The arrival of Whole Foods, a Trader Joe's, and the new glass-and-chrome condos signal that a tamer neighborhood has taken hold.

Enter the Lower East Side. Often referred to as simply as LES, the historic "Gateway to America" for many seeking a better life has seen waves of Irish, German, Jewish, Hispanic, and Chinese immigrants. Now it's their great-grandchildren who pay top dollar for tiny apartments here, coming in droves to revel in the very place their forebears fought to leave for the greener "suburbs" of Brooklyn and Queens. On Saturday nights the scene can be as raucous as a college town, especially on Rivington and Orchard streets.

But during the day the Lower East Side is a wonderful place to catch of glimpse of the past, especially if it includes a visit to the **Lower East Side Tenement Museum** *(⇨ Chapter 14)*. And then, of course, there's noshing the neighborhood is famous for, from pastrami on rye at the age-old **Katz's Delicatessen** or **Russ & Daughters** to the wide selection of top gourmet eats at the fantastic **Essex Street Market**.

EAST VILLAGE

TOP TOURING EXPERIENCES

ASTOR PLACE: ANCHORED IN TIME

Stop for a moment at Astor Place, the triangle formed by the intersections of East 8th Street, Lafayette Street, Astor Place, and 4th Avenue. The area seems frozen in time, in a way, with both a university and an arts community holding on to the idealism of the neighborhood's past. On any given day there are students from NYU or Cooper Union shooting a film or sketching a scene, political groups soliciting signatures, and punks and rockers boldly evincing the city's bohemian subculture.

Distinctive architecture and design are also part of this area's legacy. On East 4th Street off Lafayette is the **Merchant's House Museum**, an example of upscale residential Manhattan life in the 19th century and open for a self-guided tour. **Colonnade Row**, around the corner along Lafayette Street, is marked by marble Corinthian columns in front of a sweep of Greek Revival mansions once home to millionaires John Jacob Astor and Cornelius Vanderbilt. It's easy to miss, as they're above the mix of theaters, restaurants, and other retail establishments that now fill their lower levels.

New design-forward buildings are also popping up in the area, including **Cooper Union's Science and Art Building**, built in 2009. The **Sculpture for Living** building, a much-maligned glass-and-steel tower of million-dollar apartments, sits smack in the middle of numerous low-rises in jarring contrast. Its name and shape seem to ironically refer to what had previously been Astor Place's focal point, **the Alamo**, a giant spinning cube on the central traffic island. At the entrance to the **Astor Place Subway Station** is a cast-iron replica of the Beaux-Arts kiosks that covered most subway entrances in the early 20th century.

TAKING IN LOCAL FLAVOR

Those living in the East Village come from a wide range of ethnicities and sub-cultures. East 6th Street between 2nd and 3rd avenues is known as Little India, and spilling around the corners to each of the avenues there are Bangladeshi and Indian grocery stores, boutiques, and restaurants that offer inexpensive dining choices. Two blocks east, the strip between Avenues A and B is a South American enclave, with an eclectic mix of generally affordable eateries as well.

East 7th Street between 2nd and 3rd avenues is dominated by **St. George's Ukrainian Catholic Church**, the meeting place for the local Ukrainian community and the site of an annual Ukrainian folk festival in spring. Incongruously, the block also has an odd assortment of brewpubs, including the grizzly **McSorley's Old Ale House**, made famous by the writer Joseph Mitchell in his 1945 essay, which has remained unchanged in both menu and decor over its 100-plus-year history (but now allows women to partake in the revelry).

One block north is **St. Marks Place**, aka 8th Street between 3rd Avenue and Avenue A. Over the years, beatniks, artists, and musicians have congregated at this hub of the East Village scene.

Today the block between 2nd and 3rd avenues feels like a shopping arcade for the vinyl-pants set. It's crammed with body-piercing and tattoo salons; shops selling cheap jewelry, sunglasses, incense, and caustic T-shirts; and restaurants and bars. And if you're craving Asian food, there seems to be a new restaurant opening here every day. ■ TIP→ Many attest that the egg cream was hatched at Gem Spa (⊠ 131 2nd Ave. ☎ 212/995–1866), a 24-hour newsstand at the corner of St. Marks and 2nd Avenue. Cold milk, seltzer, and chocolate or vanilla syrup combine to make this peculiarly New York drink, $2.50.

One block north in what feels like a world away is Stuyvesant Street, a strip of historic redbrick row houses—and the oldest street in Manhattan—laid out along a precise east–west axis (other streets in the city follow the island's geographic orientation). Fitting in perfectly is **St. Mark's Church in-the-Bowery**, a charming 1799 fieldstone country church that occupies the former site of Dutch governor Peter Stuyvesant's family chapel.

THE CITY'S BOHEMIA

East of 1st Avenue is **Alphabet City**. The streets of Avenues A, B, and C were once burned-out slums and drug haunts, but the neighborhood started to turn around in the 90s and has managed to hold onto the same young, artistic rawness it established more than two decades ago.

At the center of the crowded tenements is **Tompkins Square Park**, a popular hangout with playgrounds, green expanses, and active dog runs. The Avenue A side has one of the city's most interesting arrays of inexpensive ethnic restaurants, Internet cafés, collectibles shops, and low-rent bars.

Contributing to the artistic bent is the popular Friday-night poetry slam at the **Nuyorican Poets Cafe** on East 3rd Street between Avenues B and C. At 151 Avenue B, on the east side of the park, stands a brownstone where jazz saxophonist Charlie Parker lived in the '50s.

TOP ATTRACTIONS

Alphabet City. The north–south avenues east of 1st Avenue, from Houston Street to 14th Street, are all labeled with letters, not numbers, which gives this area its nickname. While Avenues A, B, and C are mostly gentrified, Avenue D is still a bit rough around the edges.

Avenues A and B along the park have a wide variety of cafés, bars, and a steadily growing restaurant scene. A close-knit Puerto Rican community makes its home around Avenue C, also called Loisaida Avenue (a Spanglish creation meaning "Lower East Side"), with predominantly Latino shops and bodegas. Avenue C also has plenty of fun spots for booze and food, ranging from a Bavarian indoor beer garden to local joints serving up tacos to eclectic Australian and Brazilian eateries. ⊠ *East Village* Ⓜ *6 to Astor Pl.; L to 1st Ave.; F to 2nd Ave.*

McSorley's Old Ale House. Joseph Mitchell immortalized this spot, which claims to be one of the city's oldest, in *The New Yorker*. Opened in 1854, it didn't admit women until 1970. Fortunately, it now offers separate restrooms. The mahogany bar, gas lamps, potbellied stove, and yellowing newspaper clips are originals.

Vibrant vintage clothing boutiques and pop culture shops display the funky, freewheeling vibe of the East Village.

Try to visit on a weekday before 7 pm to enjoy one of the two McSorley's ales and a cheese plate with onions in relative peace. Be warned: on weekends this place is a zoo, and there can be a line to get in day or night. ⊠ *15 E. 7th St., between 2nd and 3rd Aves., East Village* ☎ *212/473–9148* Ⓜ *6 to Astor Pl.*

St. Marks Place. The longtime hub of the edgy East Village, St. Marks Place is the name given to idiosyncratic East 8th Street between 3rd Avenue and Avenue A. During the 1950s beatniks Allen Ginsberg and Jack Kerouac lived and wrote in the area; the 1960s brought Bill Graham's Fillmore East, Andy Warhol's the Dom, the Electric Circus nightclub, and hallucinogenic drugs.

The studded, pink-haired, and shaved-head punk scene followed, continuing today, although a little more diluted, with pierced rockers and teenage Goths. The blocks between 2nd and 3rd avenues have time-tested alternative-clothing boutiques and Asian restaurants galore. The cafés between 2nd Avenue and Avenue A attract customers late into the night. Ⓜ *6 to Astor Pl.*

Tompkins Square Park. This leafy spot amid the East Village's crowded tenements is a release valve. The park fills up with locals year-round, partaking in picnics, drum circles, the playground, and two dog runs. The Charlie Parker Jazz Festival, honoring the former park-side resident and noted jazz saxophonist, packs the park in late August, and since 2003 it has been the site of the annual Howl! Festival, which commemorates Allen Ginsberg's famous poem.

But it wasn't always so rosy. In 1988 police followed then-mayor David Dinkins's orders to clear the many homeless who had set up makeshift homes here, and homeless rights and anti-gentrification activists fought back with sticks and bottles. The park was reclaimed and reopened in 1992 with a midnight curfew, still in effect today. ⊠ *Bordered by Aves. A and B and E. 7th and E. 10th Sts., East Village* Ⓜ *6 to Astor Pl.; L to 1st Ave.*

WORTH NOTING

Colonnade Row. Marble Corinthian columns on the second level front this shabby-but-grand sweep of four Greek Revival mansions (originally nine) constructed in 1833, with stonework by Sing Sing penitentiary prisoners. These once-elegant homes served as residences to millionaires John Jacob Astor and Cornelius Vanderbilt until they moved uptown. Today they house apartments, a lounge, and a restaurant. The north-ernmost building is the home of the Astor Place Theatre and *Blue Man Group.* ⊠ *428–434 Lafayette St., between Astor Pl. and E. 4th St., East Village* Ⓜ *6 to Astor Pl.*

Astor Place Subway Station. At the beginning of the 20th century almost every Interborough Rapid Transit (IRT) subway entrance resembled the ornate cast-iron replica of a Beaux-Arts kiosk that covers the stairway leading to the uptown No. 6 train here.

Inside, plaques of beaver emblems line the tiled station walls, a reference to the fur trade that contributed to John Jacob Astor's fortune. Milton Glaser, a Cooper Union graduate, designed the station's murals. ⊠ *On traffic island at E. 8th St. and 4th Ave., East Village* Ⓜ *6 to Astor Pl.*

Russian and Turkish Baths. It's clear from the older Soviet types devouring blintzes and Baltika beer served in the lobby that this is no cushy, uptown spa. But the three-story public bathhouse, which dates to 1892, isn't about pampering as much as hearty, Slavic-style cleansing.

The baths have five saunas and steam rooms, an aromatherapy steam room, a Finnish sauna, a Turkish room with a pull chain shower, and a Russian room for dousing yourself with cold water. You're encouraged to alternate cooking in the hot rooms with plunges in the cold pool to stimulate circulation, a bathing cultures staple.

Traditional massages and scrubs are offered without appointment. Except for a few single-sex hours per week on Wednesday, Thursday, and Sunday, the baths are coed, with bathing suits or shorts worn, and felt hats (alleged to decrease lightheadedness) for the seriously old-school. ⊠ *268 E. 10th St., between 1st Ave. and Ave. A, East Village* ☎ *212/674–9250* ⊕ *www.russianturkishbaths.com* 🖃 *$30* ☯ *Mon., Tues., Thurs., and Fri. noon–10, Wed. 10–10, Sat. 9 am–10 pm, Sun. 8 am–10 pm* Ⓜ *L to 1st Ave.*

St. Mark's Church in-the-Bowery. This charming 1799 fieldstone country church stands on what was once Governor Peter Stuyvesant's *bouwerie,* or farm. St. Mark's is Manhattan's oldest continually used Christian site, and both Stuyvesant and Commodore Perry are buried here in vaults.

Be sure to check out the gorgeous modern stained-glass windows on the balcony, which replaced the more traditional windows like those on the ground level after a fire in the late '70s.

Over the years St. Mark's has hosted many progressive arts events, including readings by poet Carl Sandburg and dance performances by Martha Graham and Merce Cunningham. The tradition has continued with Danspace, the Poetry Project, and the Incubator Arts Project, which give performances throughout the year. ⊠ *131 E. 10th St., at 2nd Ave., East Village* ☎ *212/674–6377* Ⓜ *6 to Astor Pl.; L to 3rd Ave.*

Sculpture for Living. A few steps down from the Public Theater near Cooper Union sits this residential skyscraper, an anomaly among the predominantly low-rise, traditional architecture of this neighborhood. The curving-glass building was designed by postmodern architect Charles Gwathmey (known for his addition to the Guggenheim Museum), who passed away in 2009. ⊠ *445 Lafayette St., at Astor Pl., East Village* Ⓜ *6 to Astor Pl.; R to 8th St./Broadway.*

Stuyvesant Street. This diagonal slicing through the block bounded by 2nd and 3rd avenues and East 9th and 10th streets is unique in Manhattan: it's the oldest street laid out precisely along an east–west axis. Among the handsome 19th-century redbrick row houses are the Federal-style **Stuyvesant-Fish House** (⊠ *21 Stuyvesant St., East Village*), built as a wedding gift for a great-great-granddaughter of the Dutch governor Peter Stuyvesant, and **Renwick Triangle,** an attractive group of Anglo-Italianate brick and brownstone residences that face Stuyvesant and East 10th streets. Ⓜ *6 to Astor Pl.*

LOWER EAST SIDE

TOP TOURING EXPERIENCES

GATEWAY TO AMERICA

Directly south of the East Village, on the other side of Houston Street, is the traditional Lower East Side, a juxtaposition of old and new worlds, where a hot nightlife scene is growing amid aged businesses that hark back to the area's immigrant heritage. The historic heart of the Lower East Side is **Orchard Street,** the center of New York's fabric and garment district at the turn of the 20th century.

At the **Lower East Side Tenement Museum** *(⇨ Chapter 14)* different tours draw you into Irish, German, Polish, Jewish, and Sicilian family life of the period. Some of the old building fronts remain, as do discount shops (the so-called Bargain District), but younger fashion-furious boutiques and other cool shops have moved in as well.

THE LIVES OF JEWISH IMMIGRANTS

Several historic synagogues, their gorgeous facades squeezed among the tenements, are still in use. The **Eldridge Street Synagogue** was the first Orthodox synagogue erected by the large number of Eastern European Jews who settled on the Lower East Side in the late 1880s. A glorious restoration of its main sanctuary has just been completed, allowing the

Where can I find . . . ?

COFFEE	Abraço 86 E. 7th St. Coffee, custard, frittatas, house-made sandwiches, and sweets.	D'espresso 100 Stanton St. Italian-style coffee, plus the pastries to match.
A QUICK BITE	Katz's Delicatessen 205 E. Houston St. Sample pastrami at the counter while waiting. Just don't lose your ticket.	Il Laboratorio del Gelato 95 Orchard St. Seasonal flavors make this gelato la crème de la crème.
COCKTAILS	PDT 113 St. Marks Pl. Back-room bar serving some of the city's best cocktails. Enter through the telephone booth in the hot-dog shop.	McSorley's Old Ale House 15 E. 7th St. Sawdust, crowds, and rounds of multiple glasses of beer at a time per person, old New York alive all around you.

synagogue to become a permanent museum and home to its practicing Orthodox congregation.

The only Romaniote (Greek Jewish) synagogue in the Western Hemisphere, **Kehila Kedosha Janina** also functions as a museum to this obscure branch of Judaism. The city's oldest synagogue, dating to 1850, is now the funky **Angel Orensanz Center for the Arts,** named for the sculptor who purchased the synagogue when it fell into disrepair. This originally German synagogue was modeled after the Cathedral of Cologne, and now hosts exhibits and dramatically lighted events such as the wedding of Sarah Jessica Parker and Matthew Broderick.

The busiest of the Lower East Side synagogues today is the Orthodox **Bialystoker Synagogue,** with its dramatic blue-sky-clouds-and-stars ceiling; scenes from the zodiac; and "hidden" balcony door (you can open it), which was once used by the Underground Railroad to hide slaves during the synagogue's former days as a Methodist church.

Starting on Houston Street and heading south along Essex, Allen, and Orchard streets, munch on traditional pickles, bialys, knishes, and strudel as you walk by buildings with Hebrew letters and antique Jewish books in the windows.

EAT AND SHOP WITH THE HIPSTERS

The epicenter of the trendy, gentrified Lower East Side falls along parallel Rivington and Stanton streets, between Orchard and Essex streets, and the section of Ludlow Street that crosses them. Among the restaurants, boutiques, and bars are stores that fluctuate from hip to historic, like **Babeland,** a women-oriented sex shop, and **Economy Candy,** every kid's fantasy and a pseudo-general store literally crammed to the rafters with barrels of nuts and shelves of old-time and current candy favorites. The area also has a handful of quirky shops, most of which sell vintage-y clothing and knickknacks.

A stretch of Second Avenue on the Lower East Side.

The indoor **Essex Street Market** took the place of the pushcarts that once dominated Hester Street, and has a colorful assortment of fish markets, butchers, cheesemongers, and more, where sellers are more than happy to pass out samples.

TOP ATTRACTIONS

Eldridge Street Synagogue. This was the first Orthodox synagogue erected by the large number of Eastern European Jews who settled in the Lower East Side in the late 19th century. The exterior is a striking mix of Romanesque, Gothic, and Moorish motifs. Inside is an exceptional hand-carved ark of mahogany and walnut, a sculptured wooden balcony, jewel-tone stained-glass windows, stenciled walls, and an enormous brass chandelier.

The synagogue can be viewed as part of a tour, which begins at the small museum downstairs where interactive "touch tables" teach all ages about Eldridge Street and the Lower East Side. The crowning piece of the museum's restoration of the synagogue is a new stained-glass window by artist Kiki Smith and architect Deborah Gans, weighing 6,000 pounds and with more than 1,200 pieces of glass. ⊠ *12 Eldridge St., between Canal and Division Sts., Lower East Side* ☎ *212/219–0302* ⊕ *www.eldridgestreet.org* ✉ *$10* ☺ *Sun.–Thurs. 10–5; tours on the hr* Ⓜ *F to E. Broadway; B, D to Grand St.; N, R to Canal St.*

Fodor'sChoice ★ **Essex Street Market.** Started in 1940 as an attempt by Mayor Fiorello LaGuardia to establish a place for street pushcarts and vendors, the Essex Street Market's character was defined early on by the Jewish and Italian immigrants of the Lower East Side. After being run cooperatively by the merchants for years, the market was taken over by a private developer in 1992 until the New York City Economic Development Corporation assumed control of it. They started their $1.5 million renovation and consolidation of the space in 1995.

These days the market has been reinvigorated, and is filled with terrific stands of produce, meat, fish, and gourmet cheeses. Standouts include Jeffrey's Meats, Saxelby Cheesemongers, and local favorite Shopsins General Store, which moved there in 2007 after decades in the West Village. The store's extensive and creative menu is an all-around feast (you need a microscope to read the menu, and it's filled with delicious and creatively named items such as Blisters on My Sisters sliders). ⊠ *120 Essex St., between Rivington and Delancey Sts., Lower East Side* ☎ *212/388–0449* ⊕ *www.essexstreetmarket.com* ⊗ *Tues.–Sat. 8–7* Ⓜ *F, V to Delancey St.; J, M, Z to Essex St.*

WORTH NOTING

Gallery Onetwentyeight. Inside the jewel-box space, artist Kazuko Miyamoto directs crisp and provocative group shows. ⊠ *128 Rivington St., between Essex and Norfolk Sts., Lower East Side* ☎ *212/674–0244* ⊕ *www.galleryonetwentyeight.org* Ⓜ *F to Delancey St.; J, M, Z to Essex St.*

Greenwich Village, the West Village, Chelsea, and the Meatpacking District

WORD OF MOUTH

"We enjoyed the Chelsea Market tour very much. It's a fun place to shop but the tour adds history plus the yummy tastings. Also, don't miss walking on the High Line."

—dfrostnh

GETTING ORIENTED

0 | 1/4 mile
0 | 400 meters

See Chelsea Galleries map

W. 34th St.

M A,C,E
M 1,2,3
M B,D,F,M N,Q,R

W. 31st St.
W. 32nd St.
Madison Square Garden /Penn Station
W. 30th St.

Seventh Ave.
Broadway
Fifth Ave.

W. 29th St.
W. 28th St.
Robert Miller ◆
M N,R
Avenue of the Americas

Gagosian ◆
CHELSEA
W. 27th St.
W. 26th St.
W. 25th St.
Madison Square Park

London Terrace
W. 24th St.
F,M

Chelsea Art Museum ◆
◆ Matthew Marks
C,E
M W. 23rd St.
1
M
◆ Chelsea Hotel
W. 22nd St.
N,R
FLATIRON DISTRICT

Cushman ◆ Row
W. 21st St.
W. 20th St.
GRAMERCY →

David Zwirner Gallery ◆
Joyce Theater ◆
W. 19th St.
W. 18th St.
1
M

Chelsea Piers ◆
W. 17th St.
◆ Rubin Museum
W. 16th St.
W. 15th St.
UNION SQUARE →

Chelsea Market ◆
Ninth St. Espresso
MEATPACKING DISTRICT
A,C,E,L
M
M W. 14th St.
1,2,3
F,M,L
M

Hotel Gansevoort ◆
W. 13th St.
W. 12th St.
W. 11th St.
Patchin Pl. ◆
GREENWICH VILLAGE

The High Line
West Side Hwy.
Eleventh Ave.
Little W. 12th St.
Gansevoort St.
Horatio St.
Jane St.
W. 12th St.
Bethune St.
Greenwich St.
Greenwich Ave.
Abingdon Square
Bank St.
W. 11th St.
W. 4th St.
Waverly
Gay St.
W. 10th St.
W. 9th St.
Fifth Ave.

W. 8th St.
Washington Memorial Arch
Waverly Pl.
Wash. Pl.
Washington Square Park
Washington Sq. S.

Perry St.
Charles St.
Hudson St.
W. 10th St.
Christopher St.
Christopher Park ◆
W. 4th
Cornelia
A,B,C,D,E,F,M
M
W. 3rd

Hudson River Park ◆
WEST VILLAGE
75 1/2 Bedford ◆
Grove St.
Bedford St.
Seventh Ave. South
Leroy St.
Carmine St.
Father Demo Sq.
Bleecker St.
Downing St.
Sixth Ave.

Barrow
Morton St.
Commerce St.
Leroy St.
Washington St.
West St.
Promenade
Clark St.
W. Houston St.
M
MacDougal St.
Sullivan St.
Thompson St.
La Guardia Pl.

See Greenwich Village and West Village map

Ⓝ

MAKING THE MOST OF YOUR TIME

Weekday afternoons the streets of the West Village are nearly empty. Because of the many artists, students, and writers who live here, you'll have just enough company at the cafés and shops to make you feel like an insider instead of a tourist. To truly appreciate the Meatpacking District, make a 9 pm or later dinner reservation at a hot restaurant, then hit the bars to see where the glitterati are this week. If shopping is your pleasure, weekdays are great; come after noon, though, or you'll find most spots shuttered.

Chelsea has a dual life: typical gallery hours are Tuesday–Saturday 10–6, but at night the neighborhood changes into a party town, with gay bars and difficult-to-enter clubs that don't rev up until after 11.

GETTING HERE AND AROUND

The West 4th Street subway stop—serviced by the A, B, C, D, E, F, and M—puts you in the center of Greenwich Village. Farther west, the 1 train has stops on West Houston Street and Christopher Street/Sheridan Square. The A, C, E, 1, 2, 3, and L trains stop at 14th Street for both the Meatpacking District and Chelsea. The latter is further served by the C, E, 1, F, and M lines at the 23rd Street stop and the 1 stop at 28th Street. The L train connects Union Square on 14th Street to the Meatpacking District at 8th Avenue and 14th Street. 14th Street and 23rd Street are both also served by the PATH trains.

WORD OF MOUTH (WWW.FODORS.COM/FORUMS)

"Weave your way through the West Village and definitely go down Bleecker Street (all the way down) for amazing bakeries and cheese shops, and grab a slice of cake at Amy's or a dessert and coffee/hot chocolate with homemade whipped cream at Rocco's." —amanda Amanda

FODOR'S CHOICE

Chelsea Market

The High Line

Washington Square Park

TOP EXPERIENCES

Gallery hopping in Chelsea

Walking on the High Line

Checking out nightlife in the Meatpacking District

Catching live music at the Village Vanguard or a movie at the Film Forum

People-watching in Washington Square Park

Eating your way through Chelsea Market

WHAT'S NEARBY

The Film Forum (⇨ Ch. 15)

Le Poisson Rouge (⇨ Ch. 15)

The Joyce Theater (⇨ Ch. 15)

The Village Vanguard (⇨ Ch. 16)

Plunge (⇨ Ch. 16)

Books of Wonder (⇨ Ch. 17)

5

Sightseeing
★★★
Nightlife
★★★★★
Dining
★★★★★
Lodging
★★★
Shopping
★★★★

Long the home of writers, artists, bohemians, and bons vivants, Greenwich Village is a singular section of the city. High-rises and office towers have no business among the small curving streets, peculiar alleys, and historic town houses here, although a new boom in distinctive apartment living by designer architects has emerged around the west edges of the West Village north to Chelsea.

Updated by
Arthur Bovino

Primarily residential, **Greenwich Village** and the **West Village** have many specialty restaurants, cafés, and boutiques with a warm and charming neighborhood vibe. Tiny as they might be, hot spots such as Little Owl and 'ino invite you to linger, as do larger restaurants with outside dining areas.

Of course, the Village has a long history of people lingering on sidewalks and in cafés. In the late 1940s and early 1950s abstract expressionist painters Franz Kline, Jackson Pollock, Mark Rothko, and Willem de Kooning congregated here, as did Beat writers Jack Kerouac, Allen Ginsberg, and Lawrence Ferlinghetti. The '60s brought folk musicians and poets, notably Bob Dylan. **New York University** students keep the idealistic spirit of the neighborhood alive, but polished professionals have also moved into the high-rent town houses.

The Meatpacking District, in the far northwest part of the Village, has cobblestone streets whose original meatpacking tenants are being replaced by a different kind of meat-market life: velvet-rope clubs, trendy restaurants, and trendy-chic shops. Now, with the opening of the **High Line** in the Meatpacking District and its continued plans for expansion northward, there's a new artery of life happening in this part of the city, bringing new foot traffic and gentrification.

Overlapping the Meatpacking District to the north, the **Chelsea** has usurped SoHo as the world's contemporary-art-gallery headquarters. *(An extensive gallery list and map at the end of this chapter will help you find your way.)* **Chelsea's galleries** along the west edge of the neighborhood are housed in cavernous converted warehouses that are easily identified by their ultracool, glass-and-stainless-steel doors. Other former warehouses, unremarkable by day, pulsate through the night as the city's hottest nightclubs. Chelsea has also replaced the West Village as the heart of the city's gay community. One-of-a-kind boutiques and gay-friendly shops are scattered among unassuming grocery stores and other remnants of Chelsea's immigrant past.

GREENWICH VILLAGE AND THE WEST VILLAGE

TOP TOURING EXPERIENCES

GORGEOUS PARKS AND ARCHITECTURE

At **Washington Square Park** the city's central business artery, 5th Avenue, officially ends, and the student-bohemian feel of the West Village begins. Circle the recently spruced-up open square, but don't expect to find a bench or fountain-side seat not occupied by New York University students, professors, pigeon-feeders, or idlers of all sorts. On the park's north side is the grand **Washington Memorial Arch**, which looks upon the **Row**, two blocks of lovingly preserved Greek Revival and Federal-style town houses.

Make sure to stop to take a peek down a few residential streets tucked away in little enclaves in the Village. **Washington Mews** and **MacDougal Alley** are two cobblestone private streets just above the park. **Grove Court**, a cluster of brick-front homes, seems like a precursor to today's gated communities. West of 6th Avenue on 10th Street is the wrought-iron gateway to a tiny courtyard called **Patchin Place**. Around the corner is another alley filled with homes, **Milligan Place**.

The beautiful blocks of 19th-century redbrick town houses that predominate in the Village are occasionally marked by attempts at nonconformity. At **18 West 11th Street** sits a home with a modern, angled bay window, a building erected to replace the town house inadvertently blown up by the antiwar group the Weathermen in 1970. The triangle formed by West 10th Street, 6th Avenue, and Greenwich Avenue originally held a market, a jail, and the magnificent towered courthouse that is now the **Jefferson Market Library.** Where Christopher Street crosses Waverly Place is the triangular 1831 brick **Northern Dispensary building.**

THE VILLAGE'S GAY COMMUNITY

Christopher Street has long been the symbolic heart of New York's gay and lesbian community. On this street, among cafés, lifestyle boutiques, and clothing shops, is one of the city's most acclaimed off-Broadway theaters, the **Lucille Lortel**, where major off-Broadway playwrights like David Mamet, Eugene Ionesco, and Edward Albee have their own markers in the sidewalk. There's also an active nightlife scene, anchored by the **Duplex** piano bar and cabaret at the corner of 7th Avenue. Nearby, at **51–53 Christopher Street**, is the site of the Stonewall Inn and the historic Stonewall riots, which marked the beginning of the gay rights movement. Across the street is a green triangle named **Christopher Park**, where there are commemorative statues of gay and lesbian companions. Far west, where Christopher Street continues to the river, a fountain

5

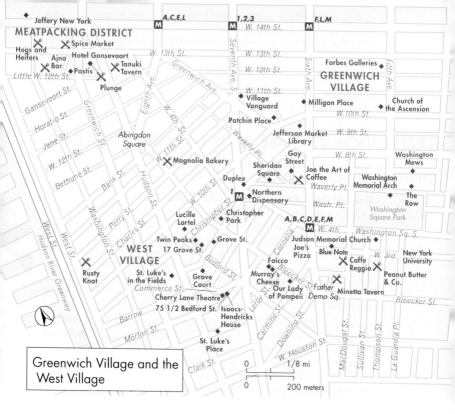

Greenwich Village and the West Village

and a landscaped pier with benches are a green and peaceful part of **Hudson River Park**.

GETTING LOST ON THE VILLAGE'S STREETS

On purpose, that is. Even long-time residents will reluctantly admit to not knowing their way around this area, as the city's grid gives way to a maze of streets that date back to the 19th century.

Walk from one end of Bleecker Street to another and you'll pass through a smattering of everything Village: NYU buildings, used-record stores, Italian cafés and food shops, charming restaurants and bakeries, and funky boutiques, plus a park with a playground and tables and benches. Grab an espresso, check out century-old butcher shops, and sample some of the city's best pizza. At 119 MacDougal Street is **Caffe Reggio**, one of the Village's first coffeehouses, pretty much unchanged since it opened in 1927.

Afterward, make a quick stop at **Our Lady of Pompeii Church** at Bleecker and Carmine, where Mother Cabrini, a naturalized Italian immigrant who became the first American saint, often prayed.

Partly because of the proximity of NYU, the streets attract a young crowd to its theaters, cabarets, and jazz clubs. Two of the best for getting a jazz fix are the **Blue Note**, at West 3rd near 6th Avenue, and the **Village Vanguard** on 7th Avenue South just below West 11th Street,

Where can I find . . . ?

COFFEE	Ninth Street Espresso (75 Ninth Ave. inside Chelsea Market) No matter what time of day, the line for this local favorite is always long. But the wait is worth it.	Joe the Art of Coffee (141 Waverly Pl.) Java with swirled milk almost too beautiful to gulp down.
A QUICK BITE	Three Tarts (164 9th Ave.) Artisanal sweets in pocket-size portions.	Peanut Butter & Co. (240 Sullivan St.) From smooth to crunchy to superfunky.
COCKTAILS	Rusty Knot (425 West St.) Dive bar extraordinaire. Have a pickle back shot and a pretzel dog.	Plunge (18 Ninth Ave.) If you want to set your eyes on fantastic views and beautiful people, hit the Gansvoort Hotel's rooftop bar.

5

considered by many to be "the Carnegie Hall of jazz." A more recent but much-loved jazz club is Smalls, a small subterranean club started in 1993 by jazz impresario Mitch Borden. Forced to close after 9/11, **Smalls** reopened with a full bar in 2007.

West of 7th Avenue South the Village turns into a picture-book town of twisting tree-lined streets, quaint houses, and tiny restaurants. Greenwich Street and Greenwich Avenue bear no relation to each other, West 4th inexplicably crosses West 10th and West 11th streets, and names of streets become confusing in a seemingly random way.

The area where Grove and Bedford streets intersect is among the most beautiful in the Village. These streets still feel like 19th-century New York, with simple redbrick homes from the early part of the century as well as a clapboard home and even a home built to resemble a Swiss chalet. Commerce Street, the location of the historic **Cherry Lane Theatre,** is undoubtedly one of the city's most romantic lanes. Minetta Lane, a "hidden" alley dating from the city's speakeasy history, lies between Washington Square Park and 6th Avenue, and is now home to the innovative **Minetta Lane Theatre** and **Minetta Tavern.**

TOP ATTRACTIONS

75½ Bedford Street. Rising real-estate rates inspired the construction of New York City's narrowest house—just 9½ feet wide and 32 feet deep—in 1873. Built on a lot that was originally a carriage entrance for the Isaacs-Hendricks House next door, this sliver of a building was home to actor John Barrymore and poet Edna St. Vincent Millay. ⊠ 75½ Bedford St., between Commerce and Morton Sts., Greenwich Village Ⓜ A, B, C, D, E, F, M to W. 4th St.

Gay Street. A curved, one-block lane lined with small row houses, Gay Street is named after Sydney Howard Gay, managing editor of the long-defunct New York Tribune, who lived here during the Civil War with

Bleecker Street's Little Italy

Little Italy can be besieged by slow-moving crowds, touristy shops, and restaurant hosts hollering invites as you pass to dine inside. With its crowded cafés, bakeries, pizza parlors, and old-world merchants, Bleecker Street between 6th and 7th avenues seems more vital as a true Italian neighborhood.

For an authentic Italian bakery experience, step into **Pasticerria Rocco** (No. 243) for wonderful cannoli, cream puffs, and cookies packed up, or order an espresso to linger over the treats.

Step into the past at the old-style butcher shops, such as **Ottomanelli & Sons** (No. 285) and **Faicco's Sausage Store** (No. 260), where Italian locals have gotten their pork custom cut since 1900.

The sweet (or stinky) smell of success seems nowhere more evident than at **Murray's Cheese** (No. 254), at Cornelia Street. The original shop, opened in 1940 by Murray Greenberg

(not Italian), was not much larger than the display case that stocked the stuff. Now it's a fromage fiend's emporium, with everything from imported crackers and bamboo cutting boards to a full-service sandwich counter. Samples of cheese, gelato, salami, and other goodies are frequently offered.

In a town that's fierce about its pizza, some New Yorkers swear by **John's Pizzeria** (No. 278). But be forewarned: they do whole thin-crust pies only—no individual slices. Luckily, one of the city's best slice joints is right around the corner, Joe's Pizza (7 Carmine St.). To complicate the Bleecker Street pizza situation further, newcomer **Kesté Pizza & Vino** (271 Bleecker St.) is serving up Neapolitan pies that some would argue give even Da Michele in Naples a run for its money. It is also the official location in the United States for the Associazione Pizzaiuoli Napoletani, whose mission is to protect and promote the Neapolitan pizza tradition.

his wife and fellow abolitionist Lucretia Mott. In the 1930s this darling thoroughfare and nearby Christopher Street became famous nation-wide when, from No. 14, Ruth McKenney wrote her somewhat zany autobiographical stories published in *The New Yorker* and later in *My Sister Eileen*, based on what happened when she and her sister moved to Greenwich Village from Ohio. ⊠ *Between Christopher St. and Waverly Pl., Greenwich Village* Ⓜ *1 to Christopher St./Sheridan Sq.; A, B, C, D, E, F, M to W. 4th St.*

Patchin Place. This little cul-de-sac off West 10th Street between Greenwich and 6th avenues has 10 diminutive 1848 row houses. Around the corner on 6th Avenue is a similar dead-end street, **Milligan Place,** with five small homes completed in 1852. The houses in both quiet enclaves were originally built for waiters who worked at 5th Avenue's high-society Brevoort Hotel, long since demolished. Later Patchin Place residents included writers Theodore Dreiser, e. e. cummings, Jane Bowles, and Djuna Barnes. Milligan Place became popular among playwrights, including Eugene O'Neill. ⊠ *Greenwich Village* Ⓜ *A, B, C, D, E, F, M to W. 4th St.*

DID YOU KNOW?

Greenwich Village has a long bohemian history: for years it was an enclave of counter-culture, from beatniks to the antiwar movement to gay rights. Today this neighborhood is better known for its celebrity residents and sky-high housing costs.

Washington Square Park. NYU students, street musicians, skateboarders, jugglers, chess players, and those just watching the grand opera of it all generate a maelstrom of activity in this physical and spiritual heart of the Village. The partially restored 9½-acre park had inauspicious beginnings as a cemetery, principally for yellow fever victims—an estimated 10,000–22,000 bodies lie below. (A headstone was actually unearthed in 2009.) At one time, plans to renovate the park called for the removal of the bodies; however, local resistance prevented this from happening. In the early 1800s the park was a parade ground and the site of public executions; bodies dangled from a conspicuous Hanging Elm that still stands at the northwest corner of the square. Today that gruesome past is all but forgotten, as playgrounds attract parents with tots in tow, dogs go leash-free inside the popular dog runs, and everyone else seems drawn toward the large central fountain.

The triumphal European-style **Washington Memorial Arch** stands at the square's north end, marking the start of 5th Avenue. In 1889 Stanford White designed a wood-and-papier-mâché arch, originally situated a half block north, to commemorate the 100th anniversary of George Washington's presidential inauguration. The arch was reproduced in Tuckahoe marble in 1892, and the statues—*Washington as General Accompanied by Fame and Valor* on the left, and *Washington as Statesman Accompanied by Wisdom and Justice* on the right—were added in 1916 and 1918, respectively. Completion of the renovation, which includes upgrading the northeast, southeast, and southwest quadrants and the perimeter sidewalks, and reorienting the Giuseppe Garibaldi monument, was scheduled for the winter of 2011. ⊠ *5th Ave. between Waverly Pl. and 4th St., Greenwich Village* Ⓜ *A, B, C, D, E, F, M to W. 4th St.*

WORTH NOTING

Christopher Park. You might have to share a bench in this tiny park with George Segal's life-size sculptures of a lesbian couple. A gay male couple is also captured in mid-chat nearby. The park was a punch line in the '90s gay comedy *Jeffrey.* ⊠ *Bordered by W. 4th, Grove, and Christopher Sts., Greenwich Village* Ⓜ *1 to Christopher St./Sheridan Sq.*

The Row. Built from 1833 through 1837, this series of beautifully preserved Greek Revival row houses along Washington Square North, between University Place and MacDougal Street, once belonged to merchants and bankers, then writers and artists such as John Dos Passos and Edward Hopper. ⊠ *1–13 and 19–26 Washington Sq. N, between University Pl. and MacDougal St., Greenwich Village* Ⓜ *A, B, C, D, E, F, M to W. 4th St./Washington Sq.*

St. Luke's Place. Steeped in New York City history and shaded by graceful gingko trees, this street officially called Leroy Street has 15 classic Italianate brownstone and brick town houses (1851–54). Novelist Theodore Dreiser wrote *An American Tragedy* at No. 16, and poet Marianne Moore resided at No. 14. Mayor Jimmy Walker (first elected in 1926) lived at No. 6; the lampposts in front are "mayor's lamps," which were sometimes placed in front of the residences of New York

Halloween in the Village

All things weird and wonderful, all creatures great and squall, all things witty and fantastical, New York City has them all—and on All Hallows' Eve they freak through the streets in New York's Halloween parade. White-sheeted ghouls feel dull compared with fishnets and leathers, sequins and feathers posing and prancing along 6th Avenue in this vibrant display of vanity and insanity.

In 1973 mask maker and puppeteer Ralph Lee paraded his puppets from house to house visiting friends and family along the winding streets of his Greenwich Village neighborhood. His merry march quickly outgrew its original, intimate route and now, decades later, it parades up 6th Avenue, from Spring Street to 21st Street, attracting 90,000 creatively costumed exhibitionists, artists, dancers, and musicians, hundreds of enormous puppets, scores of bands, and more than 2 million spectators. Anyone with a costume can join in, no advance registration required, although the enthusiastic

interaction between participants and spectators makes it just as much fun to watch. It's a safe "street event" for families and singles alike, and a joyful night unlike any other.

The parade lines up on 6th Avenue between Canal and Spring streets from 6:30 pm to 8:30 pm. The walk actually starts at 7 pm, but it takes about two hours to leave the staging area. It's best to arrive from the south to avoid the crush of strollers and participants. Get there a few hours early if possible. Costumes are usually handmade, clever, and outrageous, and revelers are happy to strike a pose. The streets are crowded along the route, with the most congestion below 14th Street. Of course the best way to truly experience the parade is to march, but if you're not feeling the face paint, it's possible to volunteer to help carry the puppets. For information, contact ⊕ *www.halloween-nyc. com.*

—Jacinta O'Halloran

5

mayors. This block is often used as a film location: No. 12 was shown as the Huxtables' home on *The Cosby Show* (although on the show it was in Brooklyn), and No. 4 was the setting of the Audrey Hepburn movie *Wait Until Dark.* Before 1890 the playground on the south side of the street near Hudson was a graveyard where, according to legend, the dauphin of France—the lost son of Louis XVI and Marie Antoinette—is buried. ⊠ *Between Hudson St. and 7th Ave. S, Greenwich Village* Ⓜ *1 to Houston St.*

Washington Mews. A rarity in Manhattan, this private, gated street is lined on one side with the former stables of the houses on "The Row," as it's know, on Washington Square North. ⊠ *Between 8th St. and Washington Sq. N, between 5th Ave. and University Pl., Greenwich Village* Ⓜ *A, B, C, D, E, F, M to W. 4th St.*

Out and On Display: George Segal's sculptures of two gay couples in Christopher Park illustrate gay pride in Greenwich Village.

CHELSEA AND THE MEATPACKING DISTRICT

TOP TOURING EXPERIENCES

THE CONTEMPORARY ARTS

North of the Meatpacking District, Chelsea is the nexus of the American art scene, with a thriving gallery culture that spans from 20th to 27th streets, primarily between 10th and 11th avenues. The range of contemporary art on display includes almost every imaginable medium and style; if it's going on in the art world, it'll be in one of the 300 or so galleries here. Standouts include the enormous **David Zwirner Gallery** on West 19th Street, across from the amazing Frank Gehry–designed IAC office building; the **Robert Miller Gallery** on West 26th Street, whose proprietor is a titan in the New York art world and represents the estate of Diane Arbus, among others; and the galleries of **Gagosian** and **Matthew Marks**, both showing the latest in painting, photography, and sculpture. For a taste of the artistic past, there's the **Chelsea Art Museum** on West 22nd Street, housed in a former Christmas ornament factory. If it's performing arts that you're more interested in, the **Joyce Theater** on 8th Avenue and 19th Street showcases modern dance troupes like Pilobolus, Elisa Monte Dance, and Momix.

ARCHITECTURAL ICONS

The neighborhood's history is on display a few blocks east on West 23rd Street at the legendary **Chelsea Hotel**, one of the best-known reminders of the street's heyday as a gathering point for the literati and creatures of counterculture. Equally distinguished long-term digs can be found on West 20th Street in the **Cushman Row** town houses, dating from the 1820s, and at **London Terrace** on West 23rd Street, home to such notables as Isaac Mizrahi and Annie Leibovitz. Regardless of whether they rent or own, nearly all neighborhood residents make frequent pilgrimages to block-long **Chelsea Market** at 15th Street between 9th and 10th avenues, the former National Biscuit Company Building, now filled with gourmet and specialty stores, restaurants, bakeries, a florist, and the headquarters of the Food Network.

GLAM, NIGHTLIFE, AND THE CITY THAT NEVER SLEEPS

The **Meatpacking District** is concentrated in a few blocks of the West Village, between the Hudson River and 9th Avenue, from Little West 12th Street to West 14th Street, with some fringe activity heading toward West 16th Street. Besides beloved meat purveyor Pat LaFrieda, there are few meat markets left in this burgeoning cobblestoned area, but it's certainly a metaphorical one at night, when the city's trendiest frequent the equally trendy restaurants and bars here. Attracting a late-day shopping crowd, affluent-angled retailers and services line West 14th Street and include boutiques of fashion designers **Alexander McQueen** and **Stella McCartney**. For one of the city's most extensive and expensive shoe departments, visit **Jeffrey,** the district's pioneer retailer. The ever-popular **High Line**, a formerly abandoned railroad track recently turned promenade and park is becoming a runway of sorts for fashionistas as they strut past the gleaming windows of the new über-chic hotel **The Standard.**

The city's recent crop of slick mega-restaurants seem to have found their homes in the streets between Little West 12th and West 16th, with huge Asian-food and Asian-style "temples" like **Buddakan** (⊠ *16th Street and 9th Avenue*), **Morimoto** (⊠ *16th Street and 10th Avenue*), **Matsuri** (⊠ *16th Street and 9th Avenue*), and **Ajna Bar,** formerly Buddha Bar (⊠ *Little West 12th between 9th Avenue and Washington Street*). Equally sexy but somewhat smaller, Jean-Georges's **Spice Market** has a rich Southeast Asian design, **Tanuki Tavern** dishes up Japanese tapas, and late-night hot spot **Pastis** is a wall-to-wall French bistro scene. Mario Batali and Joe Bastianich's huge Italian restaurant, **Del Posto**, one of the city's newest four-star restaurants, can also be found nearby (⊠ *85 10th Avenue*). The scene-y **Hotel Gansevoort** is brilliant purple at night and has a rooftop bar. From the top, look down at the pool at the private SoHo House, used in *Sex and the City*. A notable exception among all the glitz is the rough-and-tumble **Hogs and Heifers,** a neighborhood drinking hole infamous for its bra-covered bar and the movie *Coyote Ugly,* based on it.

TOP ATTRACTIONS

Chelsea Hotel. The shabby aura of the hotel is part of its bohemian allure. This 12-story Queen Anne–style neighborhood landmark (1884) became a hotel in 1905, although it has always catered to long-term tenants with a tradition of broad-mindedness and creativity. Its literary roll call of live-ins is legendary: Mark Twain, Eugene O'Neill, O. Henry, Thomas Wolfe, Tennessee Williams, Vladimir Nabokov, Mary

McCarthy, Brendan Behan, Arthur Miller, Dylan Thomas, and William S. Burroughs. In 1966 Andy Warhol filmed a group of fellow artists in eight rooms; the footage was included in *The Chelsea Girls* (1967). The hotel was also seen on-screen in *I Shot Andy Warhol* (1996) and in *Sid and Nancy* (1986), a dramatization of the real-life murder of Nancy Spungen, stabbed to death here by her Sex Pistols bassist boyfriend Sid Vicious. Read the commemorative plaques outside, then check out the eclectic collection of art in the lobby, some rumored to have been donated in lieu of rent. ⊠ *222 W. 23rd St., between 7th and 8th Aves., Chelsea* ☎ *212/243–3700* ⊕ *www.hotelchelsea.com* Ⓜ *1, 2, C, E to 23rd St.*

↻ **Chelsea Market.** In the former Nabisco plant, where the first Oreos were
Fodor's Choice baked in 1912, nearly two-dozen food wholesalers flank what is pos-
★ sibly the city's longest interior walkway in a single building—from 9th to 10th avenues. Snack your way from one end to the other, nibbling Fat Witch brownies, Ronnybrook farmer's cheese, and Amy's Bread sourdough, or just watch the bread being made as it perfumes the halls. If it's a meal you're after, Friedman's Lunch is a standout for its excellent, well-priced food. The market's funky industrial design— a tangle of glass and metal creates the awning and art, artifacts, and a factory pipe converted into an indoor waterfall—complements the eclectic assortment of bakers, butchers, grocers, and cafés inside. ⊠ *75 9th Ave., between W. 15th and W. 16th Sts., Chelsea* ☎ *212/243–6005* ⊕ *www.chelseamarket.com* ⊙ *Mon.–Sat. 7–10, Sun. 8–8* Ⓜ *A, C, E, L to 14th St.*

↻ **Chelsea Piers.** This sports-and-entertainment complex along the Hudson River between 17th and 23rd streets (entrance on 23rd), a phenomenal example of adaptive reuse, is the size of four 80-story buildings lying flat. There's pretty much every kind of sports activity going on inside and out, from golf to ice-skating, rock climbing, soccer, bowling, gymnastics, and basketball. Plus there's a spa, elite sport-specific training, film studios, and a brewery. It's the jumping-off point for some of the city's varied water tours and dinner cruises. Trips on the river via private yacht can be arranged by **Surfside 3 Marinemax Marina** (☎ *212/336–7873*). Lunch cruises, dinner cruises, and cabaret sails can be reserved on *Bateaux New York* or *Spirit of New York*, which both leave from **Pier 62** (☎ *866/211–3805*). Sophisticated themed cruises on the retro-designed *schooner Adirondack*, and the *yacht Manhattan* leave from Pier 62 through **Classic Harbor Line** (☎ *646/336–5270*). ⊠ *Piers 59–62 on Hudson River from 17th to 23rd Sts.; entrance at 23rd St., Chelsea* ☎ *212/336–6666* ⊕ *www.chelseapiers.com* Ⓜ *C, E to 23rd St.*

▰▰ DID YOU
KNOW?
The *Titanic* was scheduled to arrive at Chelsea Piers on April 16, 1912. Fate intervened and the "unsinkable" ship struck an iceberg on April 14 and went down. Of the 2,200 passengers aboard, 675 were rescued by the Cunard liner *Carpathia*, which arrived at Chelsea Piers eight days later. Check out Chelsea Piers' historical photos on the wall between piers 60 and 61.

Cushman Row. Built in 1840, this string of homes between 9th and 10th avenues represents some of the country's most perfect examples of Greek Revival row houses. Original details include small wreath-encircled attic windows, deeply recessed doorways with brownstone frames, and striking iron balustrades and fences. Note the pineapples, a traditional symbol of welcome, on top of the black iron newels in front of No. 416. ⊠ *406–418 W. 20th St., between 9th and 10th Aves., Chelsea* Ⓜ *C, E to 23rd St.*

Fodor'sChoice
★
The High Line. Once a 1.5-mi elevated railroad track carrying freight trains, this space is now being transformed into Manhattan's newest green retreat in the spirit of Paris's Promenade Plantée. A long "walking park" with benches, public art installations, and views of the Hudson River and the Manhattan skyline, the High Line is set above the streets in West Chelsea and the West Village. Reclining chaise longues that roll along the track give it a playful air. The first section between Gansevoort and West 20th streets opened in 2009, and at this writing the second section was slated for a spring 2011 opening; doubling the length of the park by extending it up to West 30th Street, with scattered access points. The final section of the High Line, between West 30th and West 34th streets at the West Side Rail Yards, is privately owned and has not yet been secured for park use. Future plans include water features, children's attractions, viewing platforms, sundecks, and performance areas. Check the Web site for announcements and openings. ⊠ *10th Ave. from Gansevoort St. to 30th St., Meatpacking District* ⊕ *www.thehighline.org* Ⓜ *L to 8th Ave.; 1, 2, 3 to 14th St. and 7th Ave.; A, C, E to 14th St. and 8th Ave.*

GALLERIES

Alan Klotz Gallery. Fine 19th- and 20th-century and contemporary photography is the focus of the exhibitions here. Shows range from the modern photo-realistic domestic scenes by Melissa Ann Pinney to the more playful portraits of photojournalist Jonathan Torgovnik. Also here are extensive collections from some of history's most important photographers, including Josef Sudek, Berenice Abbott, and Eugene de Salignac. ⊠ *511 W. 25th St., Suite 701, between 10th and 11th Aves., Chelsea* ☎ *212/741–4764* ⊕ *www.klotzgallery.com* Ⓜ *C, E to 23rd St.*

Andrea Rosen. The gallery showcases artists on the cutting edge, such as sculptor Andrea Zittel, Felix Gonzalez-Torres, and painter and installation artist Matthew Ritchie. ⊠ *525 W. 24th St., between 10th and 11th Aves., Chelsea* ☎ *212/627–6000* ⊕ *www.andrearosengallery.com* Ⓜ *C, E to 23rd St.*

ATM Gallery. On an industrial cobblestone block just off the West Side Highway, this gallery is now in a larger space. Eleven artists, six from Japan, are represented here in a gallery that began in the East Village in 2002. ⊠ *621 W. 27th St., between 11th and 12th Aves., Chelsea* ☎ *212/375–0349* ⊕ *www.atmgallery.com* Ⓜ *C, E to 23rd St.*

Casey Kaplan. Founded in 1995, this gallery represents 17 contemporary artists from Europe and the Americas. Casey Kaplan showcases sophisticated and ambitious exhibitions of works by such artists as

Chelsea Galleries

Henning Bohl, Matthew Brannon, Johannes Wohnseifer, and Julia Schmidt. ✉ *525 W. 21st St., between 10th and 11th Aves., Chelsea* ☎ *212/645–7335* ⊕ *www.caseykaplangallery.com* Ⓜ *C, E to 23rd St.*

Cheim & Read. This prestigious gallery represents artists such as Louise Bourgeois, William Eggleston, Joan Mitchell, Jenny Holzer, Donald Baechler, and Jack Pierson. ✉ *547 W. 25th St., between 10th and 11th Aves., Chelsea* ☎ *212/242–7727* ⊕ *www.cheimread.com* Ⓜ *C, E to 23rd St.*

David Zwirner. Proving his finger is on the pulse of contemporary art, Zwirner shows works in all mediums by such emerging artists as Luc Tuymans, Stan Douglas, Thomas Ruff, Diana Thater, and Yutaka Sone. ✉ *525 W. 19th St., between 10th and 11th Aves., Chelsea* ☎ *212/727–2070* ⊕ *www.davidzwirner.com* Ⓜ *C, E to 23rd St.*

Gagosian. This enterprising modern gallery has two large Chelsea branches and a third on the Upper East Side, one in Beverly Hills, plus one in London. All present works by heavy hitters, such as sculptor Richard Serra, the late pop-art icon Roy Lichtenstein, and Willem de Kooning. ✉ *555 W. 24th St., at 11th Ave., Chelsea* ☎ *212/741–1111* ✉ *522 W. 21st St., between 10th and 11th Aves., Chelsea* ☎ *212/741–1717* ⊕ *www.gagosian.com* Ⓜ *C, E to 23rd St.*

Galerie Lelong. This large gallery presents challenging installations and art, as well as many Latin American artists. Look for Alfredo Jaar, Andy Goldsworthy, Cildo Meireles, Ana Mendieta, Hélio Oiticica, Sean Scully, and Petah Coyne. ⊠ *528 W. 26th St., between 10th and 11th Aves., Chelsea* ☎ *212/315–0470* ⊕ *www.galerielelong.com* Ⓜ *C, E to 23rd St.*

Gladstone Gallery. The international roster of artists in this gallery's two locations includes sculptor Anish Kapoor, photographer Sharon Lockhart, and multimedia artists Matthew Barney and Richard Prince. ⊠ *515 W. 24th St., between 10th and 11th Aves., Chelsea* ☎ *212/206–9300* ⊠ *530 W. 21st St., between 10th and 11th Aves., Chelsea* ☎ *212/206–7606* ⊕ *www.gladstonegallery.com* Ⓜ *C, E to 23rd St.*

Jack Shainman. Both emerging and established artists are shown here, such as Subodh Gupta, a young sculptor from India, and Kerry James Marshall, who deals with African-American issues. You might find works by Phil Frost, whose imagery is derived from graffiti, or Zwelethu Mthethwa, a South African photographer. ⊠ *513 W. 20th St., between 10th and 11th Aves., Chelsea* ☎ *212/645–1701* ⊕ *www.jackshainman. com* Ⓜ *C, E to 23rd St.*

Luhring Augustine. Since 1985 owners Lawrence Luhring and Roland Augustine have worked with established and emerging artists from Europe, Japan, and America. ⊠ *531 W. 24th St., between 10th and 11th Aves., Chelsea* ☎ *212/206–9100* ⊕ *www.luhringaugustine.com* Ⓜ *C, E to 23rd St.*

Marlborough. With galleries in London, Monaco, and Madrid, the Marlborough empire also operates two of the largest and most influential galleries in New York City. The Chelsea location (the other's in Midtown) shows the latest work of modern artists, with a special interest in sculptural forms, such as the large-scale work of Michele Oka Doner. Red Grooms, Richard Estes, and Fernando Botero are just a few of the 20th-century luminaries represented. ⊠ *545 W. 25th St., between 10th and 11th Aves., Chelsea* ☎ *212/463–8634* ⊕ *www.marlboroughgallery. com* Ⓜ *C, E to 23rd St.*

Mary Boone. It was once a hot gallery in SoHo during the 1980s, but this venue now resides both in Midtown and in the newer flash point of Chelsea. Boone continues to show established artists such as Barbara Kruger and Eric Fischl, as well as newcomers. ⊠ *541 W. 24th St., between 10th and 11th Aves., Chelsea* ☎ *212/752–2929* ⊕ *www. maryboonegallery.com* Ⓜ *C, E to 23rd St.*

Matthew Marks. A white-hot venue for both the New York and international art crowd, openings at any of the three Matthew Marks galleries are always an interesting scene. Swiss artist Ugo Rondinone made his U.S. debut here, as did Andreas Gursky. Nan Goldin, Ellsworth Kelly, Brice Marden, Katharina Fritsch, and a cast of illustrious others also show here. ⊠ *523 W. 24th St., between 10th and 11th Aves., Chelsea* ☎ *212/243–0200* Ⓜ *C, E to 23rd St.* ⊠ *522 W. 22nd St., between 10th and 11th Aves., Chelsea* ☎ *212/243–0200* Ⓜ *C, E to 23rd St.* ⊠ *526 W. 22nd St., between 10th and 11th Aves., Chelsea* ☎ *212/243–0200* ⊕ *www.matthewmarks.com* Ⓜ *C, E to 23rd St..*

5

Chelsea Galleries 101

Good art, bad art, edgy art, downright disturbing art—it's all here waiting to please and provoke in the contemporary art capital of the world. For the uninitiated, the concentration of nearly 300 galleries within a seven-block radius can be overwhelming, and the sometimes cool receptions upon entering and deafening silence, intimidating. Art galleries are not exactly famous for their customer-service skills, but they're free, and you don't need a degree in art appreciation to stare at a canvas or any installation.

There's no required code of conduct, although most galleries are library-quiet and cell phones are seriously frowned upon. Don't worry, you won't be pressured to buy anything; staff will probably be doing their best to ignore you.

Galleries are generally open Tuesday through Saturday from 10 am to 6 pm. Gallery-hop on a Saturday afternoon—the highest-traffic day—if you want company. You can usually find a binder with the artist's résumé, examples of previous work, and exhibit details (usually including prices) at the front desk. If not, ask. Also ask whether there's information you can take with you.

You can't see everything in one afternoon, so if you have specific interests, plan ahead. Find gallery information and current exhibit details by checking the listings in the weekend section of *The New York Times*. Learn more about the galleries and the genres and artists they represent at ⊕ *www.artincontext.org.*

—Jacinta O'Halloran

Nancy Hoffman. Contemporary painting, sculpture, drawing, photography, and video works by an impressive array of international artists are on display here. Gallery artists range from Viola Frey, known for her heroic-scale ceramic male and female figures, to other well-established artists such as Don Eddy and Joseph Raffael, to a strong group of young artists embarking on their first solo shows. ⊠ *520 W. 27th St., between 10th and 11th Aves., Chelsea* ☎ *212/966–6676* ⊕ *www.nancyhoffmangallery.com* Ⓜ *C, E to 23rd St.*

Metro Pictures. The hottest talents in contemporary art shown here include Cindy Sherman, whose provocative photographs have brought her international prominence. ⊠ *519 W. 24th St., between 10th and 11th Aves., Chelsea* ☎ *212/206–7100* ⊕ *www.metropicturesgallery.com* Ⓜ *C, E to 23rd St.*

Pace Wildenstein. The Midtown specialist in 20th- and 21st-century art now has two spaces in Chelsea. The West 25th Street location can fit the largest sculpture and installations. Their roster concentrates on upper-echelon artists, sculptors, and photographers, including Elizabeth Murray, Chuck Close, Sol LeWitt, and Robert Rauschenberg. ⊠ *534 W. 25th St., between 10th and 11th Aves., Chelsea* ☎ *212/929–7000* Ⓜ *C, E to 23rd St.* ⊠ *545 W. 22nd St., between 10th and 11th Aves., Chelsea* ☎ *212/989–4258* ⊕ *www.pacewildenstein.com* Ⓜ *C, E to 23rd St..*

Contemporary art finds a home in the Pace Wildenstein Gallery, one of many such spaces in Chelsea.

Paula Cooper. SoHo pioneer Paula Cooper moved to Chelsea in 1996, and enlisted architect Richard Gluckman to transform a warehouse into a dramatic space with tall ceilings and handsome skylights. Now she has three galleries that showcase the minimalist sculptures of Carl André, among other works. ⊠ *534 W. 21st St., between 10th and 11th Aves., Chelsea* ☎ *212/255–1105 C, E to 23rd St.* ⊠ *521 W. 21st St., 2nd fl., between 10th and 11th Aves., Chelsea* ☎ *212/255–5247* ⊕ *www. paulacoopergallery.com* Ⓜ Ⓜ *C, E to 23rd St.* ⊠ *465 W. 23rd St., at 10th Ave., Chelsea* ☎ *212/255–4499* Ⓜ *C, E to 23rd St..*

Postmasters. Postmasters shows new and established conceptual artists, with one room devoted to multimedia shows. Recent exhibits have included Claude Wampler's *Pomerania*—a series of photographs, sculptures, video, and drawings examining the artist's relationship with her pet Pomeranian. ⊠ *459 W. 19th St., between 9th and 10th Aves., Chelsea* ☎ *212/727–3323* ⊕ *www.postmastersart.com* Ⓜ *C, E to 23rd St.*

Robert Miller. Miller, a titan of the New York art world, represents some of the biggest names in modern painting and photography, including Diane Arbus and the estates of Lee Krasner and Alice Neel. ⊠ *524 W. 26th St., between 10th and 11th Aves., Chelsea* ☎ *212/366–4774* ⊕ *www.robertmillergallery.com* Ⓜ *C, E to 23rd St.*

Sean Kelly. Drop in at this large space for works by top contemporary American and European artists, including Marina Abramovic, Robert Mapplethorpe, Antony Gormley, Joseph Kosuth, and James Casebere. ⊠ *528 W. 29th St., between 10th and 11th Aves., Chelsea* ☎ *212/239–1181* ⊕ *www.skny.com* Ⓜ *1 to 28th St.; C, E to 23rd St.*

Sonnabend. This pioneer of the SoHo art scene continues to show important contemporary artists in its Chelsea space, including Jeff Koons, Ashley Bickerton, and British art duo Gilbert & George. ⊠ *536 W. 22nd St., between 10th and 11th Aves., Chelsea* ☎ *212/627–1018* Ⓜ *C, E to 23rd St.*

Tanya Bonakdar. This gallery presents such contemporary artists as Uta Barth, whose blurry photos challenge ideas about perception, and Ernesto Neto, a Brazilian artist who has made stunning room-size installations of large nylon sacks filled with spices. ⊠ *521 W. 21st St., between 10th and 11th Aves., Chelsea* ☎ *212/414–4144* ⊕ *www. tanyabonakdargallery.com* Ⓜ *C, E to 23rd St.*

303. International cutting-edge artists shown here include photographer Doug Aitken and installation artists Karen Kilimnik, and Jane and Louise Wilson. 303 is closed in August and weekends between July 5 and Labor Day. ⊠ *547 W. 21st St., between 10th and 11th Aves., Chelsea* ☎ *212/255–1121* ⊕ *www.303gallery.com* Ⓜ *C, E to 23rd St.*

Union Square, the Flatiron District, Gramercy Park, and Murray Hill

WORD OF MOUTH

"Union Square is very lively and very busy . . . on any given day there is a protest or a commercial filming or a news crew grabbing 'man on the street' interviews . . . and 2 blocks south is one of the best bookstores in the US—the Strand."

—mp

GETTING ORIENTED

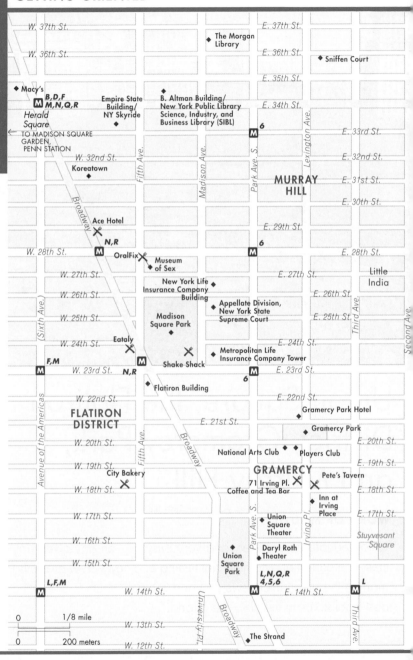

The Morgan Library

Sniffen Court

Macy's

**B,D,F
M,N,Q,R**

*Herald
Square*

← TO MADISON SQUARE
GARDEN,
PENN STATION

Empire State
Building/
NY Skyride

B. Altman Building/
New York Public Library
Science, Industry, and
Business Library (SIBL)

6

W. 37th St.
W. 36th St.

E. 37th St.
E. 36th St.
E. 35th St.
E. 34th St.
E. 33rd St.
E. 32nd St.

W. 32nd St.
Koreatown

Fifth Ave.
Madison Ave.
Park Ave. S.
Lexington Ave.

**MURRAY
HILL**

E. 31st St.
E. 30th St.

Broadway

Ace Hotel

N,R

W. 28th St.

OralFix

Museum
of Sex

New York Life
Insurance Company
Building

Madison
Square Park

Eataly

F,M

W. 23rd St.

N,R

Shake Shack

Flatiron Building

E. 29th St.

6

E. 28th St.

W. 27th St.
W. 26th St.
W. 25th St.
W. 24th St.

Little
India

E. 27th St.
E. 26th St.
E. 25th St.
E. 24th St.

Appellate Division,
New York State
Supreme Court

Metropolitan Life
Insurance Company Tower

6

E. 23rd St.

(Sixth Ave.)

Third Ave.
Second Ave.

**FLATIRON
DISTRICT**

W. 22nd St.

E. 22nd St.

Gramercy Park Hotel

Gramercy Park

W. 20th St.

E. 21st St.

Fifth Ave.

Broadway

National Arts Club

Players Club

E. 20th St.
E. 19th St.

W. 19th St.
City Bakery

W. 18th St.

GRAMERCY

Pete's Tavern

71 Irving Pl.
Coffee and Tea Bar

Inn at
Irving
Place

E. 18th St.

W. 17th St.

Union
Square
Theater

E. 17th St.

Avenue of the Americas

W. 16th St.
W. 15th St.

Daryl Roth
Theater

Park Ave. S.
Irving Pl.

Stuyvesant
Square

Union
Square
Park

**L,N,Q,R
4,5,6**

L,F,M

W. 14th St.

E. 14th St.

L

0   1/8 mile

0   200 meters

W. 13th St.

University Pl.
Broadway

The Strand

W. 12th St.

FODOR'S CHOICE

Empire State Building

Gramercy Park

Union Square Park and Greenmarket

TOP EXPERIENCES

Taking in Union Square Park and the Greenmarket

Browsing the piles of books in The Strand

Viewing the rare manuscripts at the Morgan Library and Museum

Soaking in the history and elegance of Gramercy Park

Picnicking in Madison Square Park with goodies from Shake Shack or Eataly

Dining with locals in Koreatown

Shopping on lower 5th Avenue

WHAT'S NEARBY

Morgan Library and Museum (⇨ Ch. 14)

The Ace Hotel (⇨ Ch. 16)

Pete's Tavern (⇨ Ch. 16)

ABC Carpet & Home (⇨ Ch. 17)

6

MAKING THE MOST OF YOUR TIME

If you're planning to visit the Empire State Building, try to do so either early or late in the day—morning is the least crowded time, and late at night the city lights are dazzling. Allow at least two hours for your visit if you plan to visit the observation deck. Then, you can stroll at your ease from the Empire State Building to Union Square (about 20 blocks), taking in Madison Square Park, the Flatiron Building, and Gramercy Park along the way. Note: Union Square is at its liveliest on market days—Monday, Wednesday, Friday, and Saturday.

GETTING HERE AND AROUND

Both Union Square/14th Street and Herald Square/34th Street are major subway hubs, connected by the N, Q, and R lines. Any of these trains can bring you right to the center of the action. For Madison Square Park, take the local R to 23rd Street. You can reach the Empire State Building via the B, D, F, N, Q, R, or M line to 34th Street or the 6 to 33rd Street. The 6 also stops at 23rd, 28th, and 33rd streets.

WORD OF MOUTH (WWW.FODORS.COM/FORUMS)

"I've been to New York many times for business and pleasure, but somehow in these trips I've overlooked Madison Square Park. What an omission!... What caught our eyes was staring up at the amazing architecture surrounding the park on its east and south sides. Sure we've seen the Flatiron Building before while zipping down to Lower Manhattan or up to Midtown, but we've never paid attention to its spectacular surroundings... the New York Life Building (topped off with its immediately-recognizable dazzling gold pyramid I'd seen from other vantage points in the city), the squattier Metropolitan Life North Building... the Metropolitan Life Tower, and the new dizzyingly pencil-thin 50-story One Madison Park high rise..." —MRand

Sightseeing
★★★★
Nightlife
★★
Dining
★★★★★
Lodging
★★★
Shopping
★★★★

The neighborhood defined as Union Square refers to the few blocks that surround Union Square Park, which lies between 14th and 17th streets and Broadway and Park Avenue South. If visiting on Monday, Wednesday, Friday, or Saturday, don't miss one of the best things this hood has to offer—the Union Square Greenmarket.

Updated
by Jacinta
O'Halloran

But don't despair if it's a nonmarket day. **Union Square** regularly has vendors of all kinds, selling everything from art to jewelry to T-shirts. New York University students, nannies with their charges, visitors, and locals alike all gather in this open space that can at times feel more like an outdoor version of Grand Central Station than a park.

The Flatiron District—anchored by **Madison Square Park** on the north and Union Square to the south—is one of the city's busiest neighborhoods, particularly along 5th Avenue and Park Avenue South. In some ways it should still be called Ladies' Mile: the area is a favorite for spotting models because of the number of agencies and photography studios here. Fine chain stores are mixed with local boutiques, and some of the city's coolest hotels and trendiest restaurants. To top it off, the elegant turn-of-the-20th-century skyline that hovers above is magical and brilliantly lighted at night.

The haste and hullabaloo of the city calms considerably once you reach the more residential neighborhoods of **Gramercy Park** and **Murray Hill** to the east.

Dignified Gramercy Park, named for its 1831 gated garden square ringed by historic buildings and private clubs, is an early example of the city's best creative urban planning. Even though you can't unpack your picnic in the exclusive residents-only park, pick a spot on the sidewalk in front of the cast-iron gate and gaze upward to take in the beautiful Greek Revival, Italianate, Gothic Revival, and Victorian Gothic buildings that flank its sides. Off its southern edge is **Irving Place**, a short street honoring Washington Irving, where there's one of the city's most charming inns, the **Inn at Irving Place**, and a number of casual restaurants.

Just north of the park is Ian Schrager's cooler-than-cool reincarnation of the **Gramercy Park Hotel** on Lexington Avenue.

Murray Hill stretches from 30th to 40th streets between 5th and 3rd avenues and is a mix of high rises, restaurants and bars filled mostly with a post-college crowd, and the small but solid enclave of **Little India**, where you can sample authentic cuisine and shop for traditional clothing and other goods in a handful of boutiques. Farther north a few side streets are tree-lined and town-house-filled with some high-profile haunts, including the **Morgan Library and Museum** with its vast book stacks and rare manuscripts. But perhaps the biggest reason to visit this neighborhood is to see New York's biggest skyscraper, the **Empire State Building**.

TOP TOURING EXPERIENCES

A WELL-ROUNDED NEIGHBORHOOD WALK

The energy of **Union Square** reaches its peak during its Greenmarket days, when more than 25 farms and food purveyors set up shop on the square's north and west sides to peddle everything from produce to meat, fresh fish to baked goods. The market is a great place to rub elbows with—and get elbowed by—local shoppers and chefs and a great source for tasty souvenirs (locally produced honeys, jams, and cheeses) as well as lunch.

Take your loot to a bench in the park and take in the scene. It was here, on September 5, 1882, that Labor Day was born, when more than 10,000 New York City union workers took an unpaid day off to march from City Hall to Union Square.

Head northeast to Irving Place (the stretch between East 14th and East 20th streets) for a trip back in time. It feels calm, green, and exclusive, and has a combination of old and new eateries, stores, and architecture. **Pete's Tavern**, residing on Irving Place since 1864, maintains its claim as the oldest original bar in the city and its reputation as a neighborhood hangout. Two famous writers, O. Henry (*Gift of the Magi*) and Ludwig Bemelmans (*Madeline*), were "inspired" here, probably from the amazing eggnog or Pete's House Ale.

At the top of Irving Place sits serene, look-but-don't touch **Gramercy Park**. The park oozes urbane theatrical and artistic ambience, surrounded by the tony likes of the **Players Club** (technically just called "The Players") and the **National Arts Club**, both established to indulge and encourage a passion for the arts. Only residents living in buildings immediately surrounding the park have keys to get in, as do guests of the **Gramercy Park Hotel**.

Heading north, walk along less touristy Park Avenue South, looking west all the while for glimpses of Madison Square Park, and, if its time for a break, get on line to sample what many call the city's best burger and shakes at the ever-popular **Shake Shack** inside the park. Afterward, stroll over to Lexington Avenue and away from the magnetic pull of the **Empire State Building** to Sniffen Court, a gated cul-de-sac two blocks away from the Morgan Library. These 10 brick Romanesque Revival

6

carriage houses were built in 1863–64 on a small court perpendicular to East 36th Street, and are a peaceful spot to end before tackling frenetic Midtown.

ARCHITECTURE AT ITS MOST ELABORATE

Rimming **Madison Square Park** is a slice of Manhattan's most impressive skyline. In the northeast corner, the gold-top **New York Life Insurance** building was the tallest in the city when it opened in 1903. The elaborately carved Beaux-Arts structure one block down at East 25th Street is the **Appellate Division, New York State Supreme Court,** with its main entrance tucked onto the side street.

Towering over the park between East 23rd and 24th streets is another classically inspired spire, the **Metropolitan Life Insurance Tower,** which has a stunning clock face keeping time of all four sides.

One of the buildings most emblematic of New York City, the **Flatiron Building,** is a limestone-and-terra-cotta vessel sailing its prowlike shape uptown from its berth on 23rd Street.

At the edge of Murray Hill, at between 33rd and 34th streets and 5th and 6th avenues, looms the inimitable **Empire State Building.** Canonized in postcards, books, and on film, the building majestically reaches toward the sky, which colorfully illuminates the night sky according to an elaborate calendar. For an excellent view of it, head one block north on 5th Avenue to the steps of the Italian-Renaissance-style **B. Altman Building,** worth a look in its own right.

TOP ATTRACTIONS

Ⓒ **Empire State Building.** Bittersweet though it is, this landmark is once again the city's tallest building. Its pencil-slim silhouette, recognizable virtually worldwide, is an Art Deco monument to progress, a symbol for New York City, and a star in some great romantic scenes, on- and off-screen. Its cinematic résumé—the building has appeared in more than 200 movies—means that it remains a fixture of popular imagination, and many visitors come to relive favorite movie scenes. You might just find yourself at the top of the building with *Sleepless in Seattle* look-alikes or even the building's own *King Kong* impersonator.

Fodor's Choice
★

Built in 1931 at the peak of the skyscraper craze, this 103-story limestone giant opened after a mere 13 months of construction. The framework rose at an astonishing rate of 4½ stories per week, making the Empire State Building the fastest-rising skyscraper ever built. Unfortunately, your rise to the observation deck might not be quite so record-breaking.

But before hopping on the elevator, take a moment to stare up at the ceiling in the lobby, which was beautifully restored in 2009. The gilded gears and sweeping Art Deco lines, long hidden under a drop ceiling and decades of paint, are a romantic tribute to the machine age and part of the original vision for the building.

The Empire State Building

At night the Empire State Building lights up the Manhattan skyline with a colorful view as awe-inspiring from a distance as the view from the top. The colors at the top of the building are changed regularly to reflect seasons, events, and holidays, so New Yorkers and visitors from around the world always have a reason to look at this icon in a new light.

The building's first light show was in November 1932, when a simple searchlight was used to spread the news that New York–born Franklin Delano Roosevelt had been elected president of the United States. Douglas Leigh, sign designer and mastermind of Times Square's kinetic billboard ads, tried to brighten up prospects at the "Empty State Building" after the Depression by negotiating with the Coca-Cola Company to occupy the top floors. He proposed that Coca-Cola could change the lights of the building to serve as a weather forecast and then publish a small guide on its bottles to decipher the colors. Coca-Cola loved this idea, but the deal fell through because of the bombing at Pearl Harbor, when the U.S. government needed office space in the building.

In 1956 the revolving "freedom lights" were installed to welcome people

to America; then in 1964 the top 30 floors of the building were illuminated to mark the New York World's Fair. Douglas Leigh revisited the lights of the ESB in 1976, when he was made chairman of City Decor to welcome the Democratic Convention. He introduced the idea of color lighting, and so the building's tower was ablaze in red, white, and blue to welcome the convention and to mark the celebration of the American Bicentennial. The color lights were a huge success, and they remained red, white, and blue for the rest of the year.

Leigh's next suggestion of tying the lights to different holidays, a variation on his weather theme for Coca-Cola, is the basic scheme still used today. In 1977 the lighting system was updated to comply with energy conservation programs and to allow for a wider range of colors. Leigh further improved this new system in 1984 by designing an automated color-changing system so vertical fluorescents in the mast could be changed with the flick of a switch, the only automated portion of the building's lighting system to date.

For a full lighting schedule, visit ⊕ www.esbnyc.com.

—Jacinta O'Halloran

There are three lines to get to the top of the Empire State Building; a line for tickets, a line for security, and a line for the elevators. ■ TIP➔ Save time and skip a line by purchasing your tickets in advance online (esbnyc. com). You can't skip the security line, but you can skip to the front of both this line and the line for elevators by purchasing an Express Pass for an extra $45—if time is tight, it guarantees you'll get to the observation deck in twenty minutes. If you don't want to pony up for express service, do yourself a favor and skip that last elevator line at the 80th floor by taking the stairs.

If this is your first visit, keep yourself entertained during your ascent by renting a headset with an audio tour from Tony, a fictional but "authentic" native New Yorker, available in eight languages.

The 86th-floor observatory (1,050 feet high) has both a glass-enclosed area (heated in winter and cooled in summer) and an outdoor deck spanning the building's circumference. Don't be shy about going outside into the wind (even in winter) or you'll miss half the experience. Also, don't be deterred by crowds; there's an unspoken etiquette when it comes to sharing the views and backdrop, and there's plenty of city to go around. Bring quarters for the high-powered binoculars—on clear days you can see up to 80 mi—or bring binoculars of your own so you can get a good look at some of the city's rooftop gardens. If it rains, the deck will be less crowded and you can view the city between the clouds or watch the rain travel sideways around the building from the shelter of the enclosed walkway.

While the views of the city from the 86th-floor deck are spectacular, what can be seen 16 stories up on the 102nd-floor observatory is even more astounding—and yet, fewer visitors make it this far. Instead of rushing back to elevator lines, ask yourself when you'll be back again and then head up to the enclosed 102nd floor. It will cost you an extra $15 (at the 86th-floor kiosk), but you will be rewarded with peaceful, bird's-eye views of the entire city. Also, there are fewer visitors angling for photo ops, so you can linger a while and really soak in the city and experience.

Although some parents blanch when they discover both how much it costs and how it lurches, the second-floor **NY SKYRIDE,** New York's only aerial virtual tour simulator, is a favorite of the 7- and 8-year-old set and a fun and fast way to get a sense of the city's highlights.

Narrated by actor Kevin Bacon, the ride takes the viewer on a virtual tour of New York, swinging by the Brooklyn Bridge, the Statue of Liberty, Central Park, Times Square, Yankee Stadium, and other top attractions along the way. There's also a brief but poignant trip back in time to visit the World Trade Center's Twin Towers—a sight sure to drive you straight into the arms of the first I Heart NY T-shirt vendor you see when you leave the building. ■TIP➜ When you purchase a Skyride–Empire State Building combo ticket, you will visit the Skyride first and then join the line for the observation deck at the elevators, skipping up to half the wait. ☎ 212/279–9777 or 888/759–7433 ⊕ www.nyskyride.com ☞ $41; $52 combo Skyride and observatory (discounts are available on their Web site) ⊙ Daily 8 am–10 pm. ⊠ 350 5th Ave., at E. 34th St., Murray Hill ☎ 212/736–3100 or 877/692–8439 ⊕ www.esbnyc.com ☞ $20 ⊙ Daily 8 am–2 am; last elevator up leaves at 1:15 am Ⓜ B, D, F, N, Q, R, M to 34th St./Herald Sq.; 6 to 33rd St.

Flatiron Building. When completed in 1902, the Fuller Building, as it was originally known, caused a sensation. Architect Daniel Burnham made ingenious use of the triangular wedge of land at 23rd Street, 5th Avenue, and Broadway, employing a revolutionary steel frame that allowed for the building's 22-story, 286-foot height.

The Flatiron Building

Covered with a limestone and white terra-cotta skin in the Italian Renaissance style, the building's shape resembled a clothing iron, hence its nickname. When it became apparent that the building generated strong winds, gawkers would loiter at 23rd Street hoping to catch sight of ladies' billowing skirts. Local traffic cops had to shoo away the male peepers—one purported origin of the phrase "23 skidoo."

There is a small display of historic building and area photos in the lobby, but otherwise you will have to settle for appreciating this building from the outside . . . at least for now; the building may be converted to a luxury hotel when current occupant leases expire in 2013. ⊠ *175 5th Ave., bordered by E. 22nd and E. 23rd Sts., 5th Ave., and Broadway, Flatiron District* Ⓜ *R, W to 23rd St.*

Fodor's Choice **Gramercy Park.** You may not be able to enter this private park, but a look
★ through the bars in the wrought-iron fence that encloses it is well worth your time, as is a stroll around its perimeter. The beautifully planted 2-acre park, designed by developer Samuel B. Ruggles, dates from 1831, and is flanked by grand examples of early-19th-century architecture and permeated with the character of its many celebrated occupants.

When Ruggles bought the property, it was known as Krom Moerasje ("little crooked swamp"), named by the Dutch settlers. He drained the swamp and set aside 42 lots for a park to be accessible exclusively to those who bought the surrounding lots in his planned London-style residential square.

The park is still owned by residents of buildings in the surrounding square, although neighbors from the area can now buy visiting privileges. ■TIP➜ Guests of the Gramercy Park Hotel (⇨ Chapter 19) can enjoy coveted access to this private park.

In 1966 the New York City Landmarks Preservation Commission designated Gramercy Park a historic district. Notable buildings: **No. 15** was once home to Samuel Tilden, governor of New York. It was designed by Calvert Vaux in Gothic Revival brownstone with black granite trim and included a secret passageway to 19th Street so Tilden could escape his political enemies. It is now home to the 100-year-old National Arts Club. Next door at **No. 16** Gramercy Park South lived the actor Edwin Booth, perhaps most famous for being the brother of Lincoln's assassin. In 1888 he turned his Gothic-trim home into the Players, a clubhouse for actors and theatrical types who were not welcome in regular society. A bronze statue of Edwin Booth as Hamlet has pride of place inside the park.

Other notables include the School of Visual Arts' women's residence at **No. 17**, which contains the former home of Joseph Pulitzer, and the mock-Tudor at **No. 38**, home to John Steinbeck from 1925 to 1926 when he struggled as a reporter for a New York newspaper.

Before leaving this elegant oasis and returning to the city's hustle and bustle a few blocks away, be sure to stroll along **Irving Place**, named by Samuel Ruggles for Washington Irving, and running from 14th Street to Gramercy Park South between 3rd Avenue and Park Avenue South. A few places not to be missed are The Inn at Irving Place, Pete's Tavern, and Lady Mendl's Tea Salon. While you're walking, wander down "The Block Beautiful"—a charming tree-lined stretch on East 19th Street between 3rd Avenue and Irving Place. ⊠ *175 5th Ave., bordered by E. 20th and E. 21st Sts., and Gramercy Park West and Gramercy Park East, Gramercy Park* Ⓜ *L, N, Q, R, 4, 5, 6 to Union Sq./14th St.*

Macy's. Sure, you can shop in Macy's in other cities, but there's a say-you-did-it appeal to walking that indoor city block between 6th Avenue (where it meets Broadway) to 7th Avenue, from 34th to 35th streets, verifying that yes, it is indeed the world's largest store (11 floors, 2 million square feet of selling space).

In that spirit, be sure to ride on one of the narrow wooden escalators you can find tucked among its metallic brethren: installed in 1902, they were the first escalators ever used in an American store. ⊠ *W. 34th St. between Broadway at 6th and 7th Aves., Murray Hill* ☎ *212/695–4400* ⊕ *www.macys.com* ☽ *Hrs vary seasonally; Mon.–Sat. 10–9:30, Sun. 11–8* Ⓜ *B, D, F, N, Q, R, M to 34th St./Herald Sq.; 1, 2, 3 to 33rd St.*

★ **Madison Square Park.** The benches of this elegant tree-filled park afford great views of some of the city's oldest and most charming skyscrapers (the Flatiron Building, the Metropolitan Life Insurance Tower, the New York Life Insurance Building, and the Empire State Building) and serve as a perfect vantage point for people-, pigeon-, dog-, or squirrel-watching. Add free Wi-Fi, the Shake Shack, temporary art exhibits, and a summer music series, and you'll realize that a bench here is definitely the place to be.

Where can I find . . . ?

COFFEE	Coffee & Tea Bar 71 Irving Pl. Owners roast their own beans—always a good sign.	OralFix Aphrodisiac Cafe 233 5th Ave. Bored with that latte? Experiment with 3,000-year-old aphrodisiacs and elixirs instead!
A QUICK BITE	City Bakery 3 W. 18th St. Signature "pretzel croissants" and super-thick hot chocolate.	Shake Shack in Madison Square Park A true contender for New York's best burger.
DRINKS	Ace Hotel 20 W. 29th St. Cool and inviting hot spot for visiting and local hipsters.	Pete's Tavern 129 E. 18th St. Iconic bar, neighborhood feel, and good beer selection.

New York City's first baseball games were played in this 7-acre park in 1845 (though New Jerseyans are quick to point out that the game was actually invented across the Hudson in Hoboken, New Jersey).

On the north end of the park, an imposing 1881 statue by Augustus Saint-Gaudens memorializes Civil War naval hero Admiral David Farragut. An 1876 statue of Secretary of State William Henry Seward (the Seward of the term "Seward's Folly," coined when the United States purchased Alaska from the Russian Empire in 1867) sits in the park's southwest corner, though it's rumored that the sculptor placed a reproduction of the statesman's head on a statue of Abraham Lincoln's body. ⊠ *E. 23rd to E. 26th Sts., between 5th and Madison Aves., Flatiron District* Ⓜ *R to 23rd St.*

★ **The Strand Bookstore.** Opened in 1927, and still run by the same family, this monstrous book emporium—home to 2 million volumes and "18 Miles of Books"—is a symbol of a bygone era, a mecca for serious bibliophiles, and a local institution.

The store has survived the Great Depression, World War II, the competition of a giant Barnes & Noble bookstore a few blocks away, and the tremendous shift in how readers are consuming literature. The Strand has also survived the challenges of being an intellectual oasis as well as a profit-making machine.

Stock includes both new and secondhand books, plus thousands of collector's items. A separate rare-book room is on the third floor and closes at 6:20 daily. Check out the basement, with discounted, barely touched reviewers' copies of new books, organized by author. ■**TIP**➔ If you're looking for souvenirs, visit the New York tables at The Strand; you'll find New York–centric literature, poetry, history, photography, and cookbooks, as well as T-shirts, gadgets, and totes. ⊠ *828 Broadway, at E. 12th St., Union Square* ☎ *212/473–1452* ☉ *Mon.–Sat. 9:30 am– 10:30 pm, Sun. 11–10:30* Ⓜ *L, N, Q, R, 4, 5, 6 to Union Sq./14th St.*

Fodor's Choice **Union Square Park and Greenmarket.** A park, farmers' market, meeting
★ place, and site of rallies and demonstrations, this pocket of green space
sits in the center of a bustling residential and commercial neighborhood.
The name Union originally signified that two main roads—Broadway
and 4th Avenue—crossed here, but it took on a different meaning in the
late 19th and early 20th centuries, when the square became a rallying
spot for labor protests; many unions, as well as fringe political parties,
moved their headquarters nearby.

Union Square is at its best on Monday, Wednesday, Friday, and Saturday (8–6), when the largest of the city's **greenmarkets** brings farmers
and food purveyors from the tri-state area. Browse the stands of fruit
and vegetables, flowers, plants, fresh-baked pies and breads, cheeses,
cider, New York State wines, fish, and meat. Between Thanksgiving
and Christmas, artisans sell gift items in candy-cane-stripe booths at
the square's southwest end.

New York University dormitories, theaters, and cavernous commercial spaces occupy the handsomely restored 19th-century commercial
buildings that surround the park, along with chain coffee shops and
restaurants. The run of diverse architectural styles on the building at 33
Union Square West, the **Decker Building,** is as imaginative as its former
contents: this was once home to Andy Warhol's studio. The redbrick-
and-white-stone **Century Building** (⊠ *33 E. 17th St., Flatiron District*),
built in 1881, on the square's north side, is now a Barnes & Noble
bookstore, with original cast-iron columns. The building at 17th Street
and Union Square East, now housing the New York Film Academy
and the Union Square Theater, was the final home of **Tammany Hall,**
an organization famous in its day as a corrupt and powerful political
machine. Two blocks south at Union Square East and 15th Street is the
former U.S. Savings Bank, now the Daryl Roth Theatre.

Statues in the park include those of George Washington, Abraham Lincoln, Mahatma Gandhi (often wreathed in flowers), and the Marquis de
Lafayette sculpted by Frederic Auguste Bartholdi, creator of the Statue
of Liberty. Plaques in the sidewalk on the southeast and southwest sides
chronicle the park's history from the 1600s to 1800s. ⊠ *E. 14th to E.
17th Sts., between Broadway and Park Ave. S, Flatiron District* Ⓜ *L,
N, Q, R, 4, 5, 6 to Union Sq./14th St.*

WORTH NOTING

Appellate Division Courthouse. Sculpted by Frederick Ruckstuhl, figures
representing Wisdom and Force flank the main portal of this imposing
Beaux-Arts courthouse, built in 1899. Melding the structure's purpose
with artistic symbolism, statues of great lawmakers line the roof bal-
ustrade, including Moses, Justinian, and Confucius. In total, sculptures
by 16 artists adorn the ornate building, a showcase of themes relating
to the law.

This is one of the most important appellate courts in the country: it
hears more than 3,000 appeals and 6,000 motions a year, and also
admits approximately 3,000 new attorneys to the bar each year. Inside
the courtroom is a stunning stained-glass dome set into a gilt ceiling.

All sessions, which are generally held Tuesday to Friday afternoons, are open to the public. (Visitors can call the main number ahead of time to be sure court is in session.) ⊠ *27 Madison Ave., entrance on E. 25th St., Flatiron District* ☎ *212/340–0400* ⊕ *www.nycourts.gov* ☉ *Weekdays 9–5* Ⓜ *R, 6 to 23rd St.*

B. Altman Building/New York Public Library–Science, Industry, and Business Library (SIBL). In 1906 department-store magnate Benjamin Altman gambled that his fashionable patrons would follow him uptown from his popular store in the area now known as the Ladies' Mile Historic District. His new store, one of the first of the grand department stores on 5th Avenue, was designed to blend with the mansions nearby. Note in particular the beautiful entrance on 5th Avenue.

In 1996 the New York Public Library set up a high-tech library here. A 33-foot-high atrium unites the building's two floors, the lending library off the lobby and the research collections below. Downstairs a wall of electronic ticker tapes and TVs tuned to business-news stations beams information and instructions to patrons. Tours are offered Thursday at 2. ⊠ *188 Madison Ave., between E. 34th and E. 35th Sts., Murray Hill* ☎ *212/592–7000* ⊕ *www.nypl.org* ☉ *Mon. 11–6, Tues.–Thurs. 10–8, Fri. and Sat. 11–6* Ⓜ *6 to 33rd St.*

Koreatown. Despite sitting in the shade of the Empire State Building, and within steps of Herald Square, Koreatown, or K-Town as it is locally referred to, is not a tourist destination. In fact, it feels decidedly off-the-beaten track and insulated, as though New Yorkers wryly planted their own place to eat, drink, and be merry, and then detoxed right on the beaten track and under the noses of millions of tourists.

Technically, Koreatown runs from 31st to 36th streets and between Fifth and Sixth avenues, though the main drag, and the only street you really need to know, is 32nd Street between Fifth and Broadway. Known as Korea Way, this strip is home to 24-7 Korean barbecue joints, kara-oke bars, and spas. Fill up on kimchi (spicy pickled cabbage), kimbap (seaweed rice), and red bean doughnuts (delicious), then afterward try some authentic Asian karaoke. Expect bang for your buck and brag-ging rights over other visitors who missed the experience. ⊠ *Bordered by 31st and 36th Sts., 5th and 6th Aves., Murray Hill* Ⓜ *B, D, F, N, Q, R, M to 34th St./Herald Sq.; 6 to 33rd St.*

Metropolitan Life Insurance Company Tower. When it was added in 1909, the 700-foot tower resembling the campanile of St. Mark's in Venice made this 1893 building the world's tallest; it was surpassed in height a few years later (by the Woolworth Building).

It was stripped of much of its classical details during renovations in the early 1960s, but it remains a prominent feature of the Midtown skyline today. The clock's four faces are each three stories high, and their minute hands weigh half a ton each. A bench across the street in Madison Square Park is the perfect place to appreciate this National Historic building with its lighted tower and quarter-hourly chimes.

✉ *1 Madison Ave., between E. 23rd and E. 24th Sts., Flatiron District* Ⓜ *R, 6 to 23rd St.*

New York Life Insurance Company Building. Cass Gilbert, better known for the Woolworth Building, capped this 1928 building with a gilded octagonal spire that is stunning when illuminated. Its soaring lobby's coffered ceilings and ornate bronze gates are equally grand. The building sits on the site of the former P. T. Barnum Hippodrome and the original Madison Square Garden designed by Stanford White. ✉ *51 Madison Ave., between E. 26th and E. 27th Sts., Flatiron District* Ⓜ *R, 6 to 28th St.*

Sniffen Court. In a gated cul-de-sac two blocks from the Morgan Library, these 10 brick Romanesque Revival carriage houses were built in 1863–64 on a small court perpendicular to East 36th Street. The cover of the Doors album *Strange Days* was shot here. ✉ *150–158 E. 36th St., between Lexington and 3rd Aves., Murray Hill.*

7

Midtown

WITH TIMES SQUARE AND ROCKEFELLER CENTER

WORD OF MOUTH

"We allowed ourselves a quick look into St Patrick's Cathedral . . . and continued walking heading toward Times Square. Despite the reputation, I loved it. There's nothing like it anywhere—it really is like the throbbing heart of New York. I know, I know only a tourist would see it like that. So full of people, color, and movement."

—mazj

GETTING ORIENTED

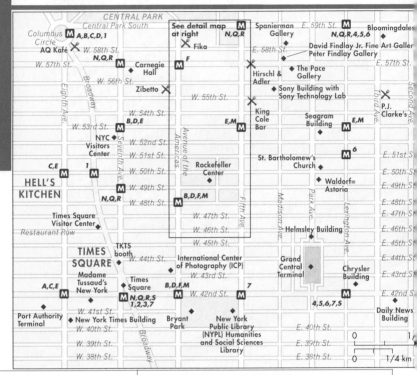

FODOR'S CHOICE	MAKING THE MOST OF YOUR TIME
Bryant Park	If you're staying in Midtown, take advantage of your prime location: rise early and be first in line at landmarks and museums. To avoid crowds while shopping or sightseeing, hit the streets at midday on weekdays or early on weekends. (Alternatively, to experience the thrill of thousands of racing workaday suits, visit Grand Central Terminal or Rockefeller Center at rush hour.)
Grand Central Terminal	

TOP EXPERIENCES

Elbowing through Times Square

Lounging in the grass at Bryant Park

Seeing the tree at Rockefeller Center at Christmas

Standing in the center of Grand Central Station's main concourse

Strolling down Fifth Avenue

At night, stroll through Rockefeller Plaza or gaze up at the Chrysler Building shimmering in the dark. You'll see Midtown at its quieter moments, when the romance of the city washes over you.

WHAT'S NEARBY

International Center of Photography (⇨ Ch. 14)

Intrepid Sea, Air, and Space Museum (⇨ Ch. 14)

Japan Society

Museum of Modern Art

The Paley Center for Media

Carnegie Hall (⇨ Ch. 15)

American Girl Place (⇨ Ch. 17)

Apple Store (⇨ Ch. 17)

B&H Photo (⇨ Ch. 17)

Bergdorf Goodman (⇨ Ch. 17)

Bloomingdale's (⇨ Ch. 17)

Chanel (⇨ Ch. 17)

F.A.O. Schwarz, Fifth Avenue (⇨ Ch. 17)

Louis Vuitton (⇨ Ch. 17)

Saks Fifth Avenue (⇨ Ch. 17)

Toys "R" Us (⇨ Ch. 17)

WORD OF MOUTH (WWW.FODORS.COM/FORUMS)

"You've got to admit that Times Square is halfway between most of the destinations. They don't call it Midtown for nuthin'…If I only have a few days in the city, I want to 'spend' my time as economically as possible. The time spent going up and down via subway is cut in half if you are staying in Midtown." —starrs

"Make sure you stop in at the map exhibit in the public library behind the Bryant Park Grill and go to their gift shop as well."— SueNYC

GETTING HERE AND AROUND

You can get to Midtown via (almost) all the subways; many make numerous stops throughout the area. The B, D, F, and M trains serve Rockefeller Center and 42nd Street at 6th Avenue. The 1, 2, 3, 7, A, C, E, N, Q, and R serve Times Square and West 42nd Street. The 4, 5, 6, and 7 take you to Grand Central. The S or Shuttle travels back and forth between Grand Central and Times Square.

Sightseeing
★★★★★

Nightlife
★★

Dining
★★★

Lodging
★★★★★

Shopping
★★★★

Just as Washington, D.C., has its Mall, New York City has Midtown, mobbed with more massive urban monuments— Rockefeller Center, Grand Central Terminal, the Chrysler Building, and the Empire State Building among them—than any other part of the city. This is the New York City of opening-credit aerial views, the heart of the world's most recognizable skyline.

Updated by
Robert Brenner

When movies need a big-city backdrop, they come to Midtown. Even the small screen is drawn to New York, as *Today* show early risers and Saturday Night Live night owls know. But even though Midtown's attractions seem obvious, there are gems less familiar to visitors, such as **Rockefeller Center's Top of the Rock** or **St. Bartholomew's Church**, that are every bit as showstopping.

And who could forget the origin of that phrase "bright lights, big city": **Times Square**. The shopping here may be ordinary and the restaurants average, but the amazing theaters of the Great White Way still have a gravitational pull. Seeing a show can be pricey, but join the line at the **TKTS booth** (⇨ *Chapter 15*) and suddenly orchestra seats don't seem out of the question.

The funny thing is that most locals come to think of Midtown as simply the end point for their workaday commute: they often forget the wonder its skyscrapers elicit, the magic of the department-store windows decked out in razzle-dazzle display.

It's true that Midtown is mostly nonstop hustle-bustle, but don't dismiss this part of town as a place without pockets of local flavor and finds. They can be hard to spot, tucked away on random side streets traversed by relatively few pedestrians, where workers load boxes onto trucks, mounds of garbage bags are piled high at curbs, and parking garages are a dime a dozen. So as you try to keep pace with the mass of crowds and fight your way across intersections—even when you have the light—take a moment to tune out the frenzy and open your eyes to what you're passing by.

TOP TOURING EXPERIENCES

THE MANY FACES OF MIDTOWN

Midtown Manhattan is a study in contrasts, most visibly in its architecture, a mind-boggling patchwork of styles spanning two centuries. Walk west from residential **Tudor City** on 42nd Street and, in the span of a few blocks, you'll pass the stately **Chrysler Building** (considered an Art Deco triumph), the bustling Beaux-Arts masterpiece **Grand Central Terminal,** and the tranquil Beaux-Arts masterpiece **New York Public Library.** Savor a book in neighboring **Bryant Park,** but travel only an avenue farther west and lose your page in that hurricane of people and lights, **Times Square.**

Continue to 8th Avenue, where you're just as likely to stand amid the moss and birch trees of the **New York Times Building** lobby as to dodge intrepid coach buses in the Port Authority melee outside.

Midtown Manhattan's juxtapositions aren't only in stone and glass. Here buttoned-down, world-class musical theater performances elicit encores at street level while unbuttoned, top-notch crooners, musicians, and break-dancers entertain in the subway stations below. Restaurants fit for power lunches and marriage proposals meet street-corner stands bearing some of the city's freshest fruit.

The digital screen LEDs of Times Square neighbor the gas lamps and wrought-iron railings of Restaurant Row (✉ *46th Street between 8th and 9th avenues*). And the excuse-me-coming-through briskness of 100,000 commuting suits gives way to the heartwarming narrative holiday window displays of **Saks Fifth Avenue** (✉ *611 5th Avenue*), **Bloomingdale's** (✉ *1000 Third Avenue at 59th Street*), **Lord and Taylor** (✉ *39th Street at 5th Avenue*), and other department stores each year. All this—plus very late hours—combines to create an energy that is uniquely, quintessentially "New York."

THE WHOLE SONG AND DANCE

Whether you want to see a Broadway show, visit a museum, or tour a television studio, Midtown is the place to be. Score good seats to some of the hottest Broadway and Off Broadway shows for half the going rate at the TKTS booth in Duffy Square at 47th Street and Broadway.

Although people think of Broadway as the heart of the theater scene, few theaters actually line the thoroughfare. For some of the grandes dames, head west on 45th Street. There are several Broadway beauties here, including the **Booth,** the **Schoenfeld,** the **Jacobs,** the **Music Box,** and the **Imperial.** On the southern side of 45th Street there's the pedestrians-only **Shubert Alley,** distinguished by colorful posters advertising the latest hit plays and musicals, and the **Shubert Theatre,** one of Broadway's most lustrous gems.

Head west along 44th Street to see its neighbors, the **Helen Hayes,** the **Broadhurst,** the **Majestic,** and the **St. James.** Tucked among them, at No. 243, is **Sardi's,** the legendary Broadway watering hole, and nearby is the former speakeasy **'21' Club,** with its row of jockeys out front, once the ultimate retreat for New York high society.

Music lovers can get their fix. In the West 40s–50s area are the jazz venues **Birdland** and **Iridium.** Continue north to 57th Street to **Carnegie Hall,** the world-famous performance venue for classical music and other showstoppers.

Where can I find . . . ?

COFFEE	Fika (41 W. 58th St.) Coffee break with a Swedish twist.	Zibetto (1385 6th Ave.) No seats, but arguably the best espresso drinks in New York.
A QUICK BITE	AQ Kafé (1800 Broadway) Classic and Scandinavian-influenced sandwiches and fresh breads.	John's Pizzeria (260 W. 44th St.) Best pizza in the nabe. Try the "essence of garlic" on your pie.
COCKTAILS	King Cole Bar (2 E. 55th St.) A swank and storied watering hole at the St. Regis Hotel.	P. J. Clarke's (915 3rd Ave.) New York's most famous Irish bar, and for good reason.

TOP ATTRACTIONS

Fodor's Choice ★

Bryant Park. This is one of Manhattan's most popular parks—and for good reason, as it's a lovely green space nestled among landmarks and skyscrapers. Lining the perimeter of the sunny central lawn, tall London plane trees cast welcome shade over stone terraces, formal flower beds, gravel pathways, and a smattering of kiosks selling everything from sandwiches to egg creams (in season).

In the afternoon the garden tables scattered about fill with lunching office workers and folk enjoying the park's free Wi-Fi (signs show you how to log on). In good weather, arrive before happy hour for a chance at snagging a couch swing at the Southwest Porch, with its cozy seating and bar serving seasonal brews.

In summer you can check out free live jazz and "Broadway in Bryant Park" musical theater performances, and author readings. Most popular of all is the Summer Film Festival: locals leave work early to snag a spot on the lawn for its outdoor screenings each Monday at dusk.

At the east side of the park, near a squatting bronze cast of Gertrude Stein, is the stylish Bryant Park Grill, which has a rooftop garden, and the adjacent open-air Bryant Park Café, open seasonally. On the south side of the park is an old-fashioned **carousel** (🎠 $2) where kids can ride fanciful rabbits and frogs instead of horses, and attend storytellings and magic shows.

Come late October the park rolls out the artificial frozen **"pond"** (⊙ *Nov.–Feb., Sun–Thurs. 8 am–10 pm, Fri. and Sat. 8 am–midnight*) for ice skating. Rental for skates will run you $13 for skates and $9 for a lock to use with a "free" locker. Surrounding the ice rink are the Christmas market–like stalls of the **Holiday Shops** (⊙ *Nov.–Jan. 2*), selling handcrafted and designer goods from around the world. ✉ *6th Ave. between W. 40th and W. 42nd Sts., Midtown West* ☎ *212/768–4242*

⊕ *www.bryantpark.org* ⊙ *Hrs vary by month. See Web site for exact times.* Ⓜ *B, D, F, M to 42nd St.; 7 to 5th Ave.*

Chrysler Building. A monument to modern times and the mighty automotive industry, the former Chrysler headquarters wins many a New Yorker's vote for the city's most iconic and beloved skyscraper (the world's tallest for 40 days until the Empire State Building stole the honor).

Architect William Van Alen, who designed this 1930 Art Deco masterpiece, incorporated car details into its form: American eagle gargoyles made of chromium nickel sprout from the 61st floor, resembling car-hood ornaments used on 1920s Chryslers; winged urns festooning the 31st floor reference the car's radiator caps. Most breathtaking is the pinnacle, with tiered crescents and spiked windows that radiate out like a magnificent steel sunburst.

View it at sunset to catch the light gleaming off the tip. Even better, observe it at night, when its peak illuminates the sky like the backdrop to a Busby Berkeley musical. The inside is off-limits apart from the amazing time-capsule lobby replete with chrome "grillwork," intricately patterned wood elevator doors, marble walls and floors, and an enormous ceiling mural saluting transportation and the human endeavor. ⊠ *405 Lexington Ave., at E. 42nd St., Midtown East* Ⓜ *4, 5, 6, 7, S to 42nd St./Grand Central.*

Fodor's Choice
★

Grand Central Terminal. Grand Central is not only the world's largest (76 acres) and the nation's busiest (nearly 700,000 commuters and subway riders use it daily) railway station, but also one of the world's most magnificent, majestic public spaces. Past the glimmering chandeliers of the waiting room is the jaw-dropping **main concourse,** 200 feet long, 120 feet wide, and 120 feet (roughly 12 stories) high, modeled after an ancient Roman public bath.

In spite of its being completely cavernous, it manages to evoke a certain sense of warmth rarely found in buildings its size. Overhead, a twinkling fiber-optic map of the constellations covers the robin's egg–blue ceiling. To admire it all in relative solitude, definitely avoid visiting at rush hour; those willing to brave it will be swept into the tides and eddies of human traffic swirling around the central information kiosk, the room's crown jewel with its polished marble counter and backlit, multifaced clock beaming the time in four directions.

After enjoying the thrill of the main concourse, escape up the sweeping staircases at either end, where three upscale restaurants occupy the balcony space. Any would make an enjoyable perch from which to survey the concourse, but for a real taste of the station's early years, head beyond the western staircase to the **Campbell Apartment,** a clubby cocktail lounge housed in the restored private offices and salon of 1920s tycoon John W. Campbell. Located around and below the main concourse are fantastic shops and eateries, making this one of the best—if somewhat labyrinthine—"malls" in the city.

To best admire Grand Central's exquisite Beaux-Arts architecture, start from its ornate south face on East 42nd Street, modeled after a Roman triumphal arch. Crowning the facade's Corinthian columns and 75-foot-high arched windows, a graceful clock keeps time for

Eat and Shop at Grand Central

For a great meal around Grand Central, dine at one of these go-to restaurants.

Amid the hustle and bustle of Grand Central Station is the elegant **Grand Central Oyster Bar & Restaurant** (✉ *89 E. 42nd St., at Vanderbilt Ave.* ☎ *212/490–6650* ⊗ *Closed Sun.*). This sprawling space, with a tiled-vaulted ceiling, brings a sense of grandeur to a chaotic transportation hub. Famous for its architecture and décor, the Oyster Bar's impressive raw bar (29 varieties of oysters on a typical day) and fresh seafood are the real reason customers have been returning for the past 90 years.

If you want to indulge yourself, stop at the stylish **Michael Jordan's The Steak House N.Y.C.** (✉ *Grand Central Terminal, 23 Vanderbilt Ave.* ☎ *212/655–2300*) on the balcony of Grand Central Station. The prime dry-aged rib eye or the succulent 2½-pound lobster are reason enough to dine here. But if you don't have time to sit for a meal, pull up a stool at the restaurant's bustling bar and have a drink off the impressive wine list.212-406-7900 ext 120,

For lighter fare and top-notch picnic provisions, visit these eateries:

The French-style pastries at **Financier Patisserie** (✉ *87 E. 42nd St., in the 42nd Street Passage* ☎ *212/973–1010*) have won it citywide acclaim; it also serves quiches, tarts, sandwiches, and light breakfast fare.

A huge international selection of cheeses as well as cooked and cured meats awaits at **Murray's Cheese** (✉ *43rd Street at Lexington Ave., center of the Grand Central Market* ☎ *212/922–5410*).

For a thoughtful gift on the go, try one of these shops:

With two locations in the terminal, **Dahlia** (✉ *Biltmore Passage and Lower Level dining concourse Grand Central Terminal* ☎ *212/697–5090*) sells flowers imported directly from overseas producers (so that they last longer), as well as vases of ceramic, glass, and other materials, at reasonable prices.

The independent **Posman Books** (✉ *9 Grand Central Terminal, at Vanderbilt Ave. and 42nd St.* ☎ *212/983–1111*) has an outstanding selection of cheeky and serious high-quality greeting cards, as well as a great range of contemporary and classic books across genres.

---

hurried commuters. In the central window stands an 1869 bronze statue of Cornelius Vanderbilt, who built the station to house his railroad empire. Also noteworthy is the 1½-ton, cast-iron bald eagle displaying its 13-foot wingspan atop a ball near the corner of 42nd Street and Vanderbilt Avenue.

Grand Central still functions primarily as a railroad station, and might resemble its artless cross-town counterpart, Penn Station, were it not for Jackie Kennedy Onassis's public information campaign to save it as a landmark. Underground, more than 60 ingeniously integrated railroad tracks carry trains upstate and to Connecticut via Metro-North Commuter Rail. The subway connects here as well. A massive four-year

The high-steppin' Rockettes show off their signature moves at Radio City Music Hall.

renovation completed in October 1998 restored the 1913 landmark to its original splendor—and then some.

The **Municipal Art Society** (☎ *212/935–3960* ⊕ *www.mas.org*) leads architectural tours of the terminal that begin here on Wednesday at 12:30. Reservations are not required, and a $10 donation is suggested. Meet at the information booth, Main Concourse. ✉ *Main entrance, E. 42nd St. at Park Ave., Midtown East* ☎ *212/935–3960* ⊕ *www. grandcentralterminal.com* Ⓜ *4, 5, 6, 7, S to 42nd St./Grand Central.*

Radio City Music Hall. This icon of New York City was built to enchant everyone who stepped inside its doors. Shortly after the stock market crash of 1929, John D. Rockefeller wanted to create a symbol of hope in what was a sad, broke city. He selected a piece of real estate in an area of Manhattan then known as "the speakeasy belt," and partnered with the Radio Corporation of America to build a grand theater, a place where everyday people could see the finest entertainment at sensible prices.

Every inch of the interior was designed to be extraordinary. RCA head David Sarnoff named their creation Radio City Music Hall. When it opened, some said it was so grand that there was no need for performances, because people would get more than their money's worth simply by sitting there and enjoying the space. Early shows included vaudeville acts and film premieres.

Despite being the largest indoor theater in the world with its city-block-long marquee, it feels warm and intimate. One-hour walking tours run year-round, but avoid taking the tour during show times, as access is limited. Day-of tickets are sold at the Radio City Avenue Store on a first-come, first-served basis; advanced tickets are available by phone.

Ice skating under the sculpture of Prometheus is a winter ritual for many local and visiting families.

📧 *Radio City Music Hall "Stage Door Tour" $17* ☎ *212/247–4777* 🕑 *Tours Mon.–Sat. 11:30–6.*

Although there are concert performances and media events here year-round, most people (more than a million visitors every year, in fact) want to see the **Radio City Christmas Spectacular**, starring the iconic Rockettes. Make reservations as early as possible, especially if you want to attend near the Christmas holidays or on weekends. The shows tend to sell out, but you can usually find tickets until mid-October. Happily, there are no bad seats at Radio City Music Hall, so if you are booking late, grab what you can get. Tickets—$45–$105 per person for the 90-minute show—can be purchased at the Radio City Music Hall; on the Web (⊕ *www.radiocitychristmas.com*); by phone on the Christmas Spectacular hot line (☎ *866/858–0007*); or at Ticketmaster. ✉ *1260 6th Ave., at W. 51st St., Midtown West* ☎ *800/745–3000* ⊕ *www.radiocity. com* Ⓜ *B, D, F, M to 47th–50th St./Rockefeller Center; N, R to 49th St.*

★ **Rockefeller Center.** If Times Square is New York's crossroads, Rockefeller Center is its communal gathering place, where the entire world converges to snap pictures, skate on the ice rink, peek in on a taping of the *Today* show (or—with luck—NBC's *30 Rock*), shop, eat, and take in the monumental Art Deco structures and public sculptures from the past century.

Totaling more than 75 shops and 40 eateries (1.4 million square feet in all), the complex runs from 47th to 52nd streets between 5th and 7th avenues. Special events and huge pieces of art dominate the central plazas in summer.

In December an enormous twinkling tree towers above the ice-skating rink, causing huge crowds of visitors from across the country and the globe to shuffle through with necks craned and cameras flashing. This holiday tradition began in 1931, when workers clearing away the rubble for Rockefeller Center erected a 20-foot-tall balsam. It was two years into the Great Depression, and the 4,000 men employed at the site were grateful to finally be away from the unemployment lines. The first official tree-lighting ceremony was held in 1933. Visit ⊕ *www. rockefellercenter.com* for more information.

At the complex's center is the sunken **Lower Plaza**, site of the world's most famous ice-skating rink October through April (it's a café in summer). Skaters swoop or stumble across the ice while crowds gather above on the Esplanade to watch the spins and spills.

Hovering above, the gold-leaf statue of the fire-stealing Greek hero **Prometheus**—Rockefeller Center's most famous sculpture—forms the backdrop to zillions of photos. Carved into the wall behind it, a quotation from Aeschylus reads "Prometheus, teacher in every art, brought the fire that hath proved to mortals a means to mighty ends."

The Lower Plaza provides access to the marble-lined corridors underneath Rockefeller Center, which house restaurants (everything from the high-end Sea Grill to pizza parlors), a post office, and clean public restrooms—a rarity in Midtown. ⊠ *Between 5th and 6th Aves. and W. 49th and W. 50th Sts., Midtown West* ☎ *212/332–7654 for the rink* Ⓜ *B, D, F, M to 47th–50th Sts./Rockefeller Center.*

Rising up on the Lower Plaza's west side is the 70-story (850-foot-tall) Art Deco **GE Building** (☎ *212/332–6868*), a testament to modern urban development. Here Rockefeller commissioned and then destroyed a mural by Diego Rivera upon learning that it featured Vladimir Lenin. He replaced it with the monumental *American Progress* by José María Sert, still on view in the lobby, flanked by additional murals by Sert and English artist Frank Brangwyn.

While in the lobby, pick up a free "Rockefeller Center Visitor's Guide" at the **information desk.** Up on the 65th floor sits the now shuttered **Rainbow Room,** a glittering big-band ballroom from 1934 through 2009.

The GE Building also houses **NBC Studios,** whose news tapings, visible at street level, attract gawking crowds. For ticket information for NBC shows or the 70-minute studio tour, visit the NBC Experience Store at the building's southeast corner. ⊠ *30 Rockefeller Plaza, between 5th and 6th Aves. at 49th St., Midtown West* ☎ *212/664–7174* ⊕ *www. nbcstudiotour.com* 🖻 *NBC Studio Tour $18.50* ☞ *Children under 6 not permitted* ☉ *Tours depart every 30 mins Mon.–Sat. 8:30–5:30, Sun. 9:30–4:30* Ⓜ *B, D, F, M to 47th–50th Sts./Rockefeller Center.*

★ **St. Patrick's Cathedral.** This Gothic edifice—the largest Catholic cathedral in the United States, seating approximately 2,400 people—is among the city's most striking churches, with its double spires topping out at 330 feet. St. Pat's, as locals call it, holds a special place in the hearts of many New Yorkers and Catholics around the country and indeed the world, receiving more than 3 million visitors annually. Its widely broadcast midnight Mass at Christmas has become somewhat of a social event for politicians and celebrities, yet tickets are always made available to the general public months in advance.

The church dates back to 1858–79. Among the statues in the alcoves around the nave is a modern depiction of the first American-born saint, Mother Elizabeth Ann Seton, and its pietà is three times larger than the pietà in St. Peter's in Rome. Its rose window by Charles Connick is considered to be the stained-glass artist's greatest work. The 5th Avenue steps are a convenient, scenic rendezvous spot. Sunday Masses can overflow with tourists; off-hours are significantly more peaceful. Many of the funerals for fallen New York City police and firefighters after 9/11 were held here. ⊠ *5th Ave. between E. 50th and E. 51st Sts., Midtown East* ☎ *212/753–2261 rectory* ⊕ *www.ny-archdiocese.org* ☉ *Daily 6:30 am–8 pm* Ⓜ *E, M to 5th Ave./53rd St.*

Fodor's Choice
★

Times Square. Manhattan's entertainment capital began its history when the Olympia Theatre opened in 1895, the first of many entertainment venues—from theaters to movie palaces to porn cinemas to strip clubs—for which the thoroughfare is famous. Speakeasies alive with jazz in the 1920s became cheaper burlesques and peep shows during the Depression, and it wasn't until the early 90s that a massive cleanup began. Today, it's theme park–like, with the ESPN Zone, the M&M store, the world's largest McDonald's, and a newly redone TKTS booth. After its $1.8 million renovation, the **Visitor Center** has a New Year's Eve "Wishing Wall," where you can write on confetti that will become one of the actual pieces to flutter down at midnight on January 1. You can also take a free walking tour and watch a video on Times Square's unsavory past in a mock-peep booth. Stop by for multilingual kiosks, MetroCards, a peek in the gift shop, sightseeing and theater tickets, and (most important!) free restrooms. ⊠ *1560 Broadway, between 46th and 47th Sts., Midtown West* ☎ *212/869–1890* ⊕ *www.timessquarenyc.org* 🎫 *Times Square Exposé tour, free* ☉ *Tours leave Fri. at noon from the Visitor Center* ☉ *Weekdays 9–7, weekends 8–8* Ⓜ *1, 2, 3, 7, N, Q, R, S to 42nd St./Times Sq.*

Top of the Rock. Rockefeller Center's multifloor observation deck, first opened in 1933 and closed in the early 1980s, reopened in 2005 to be embraced by visitors and locals alike. Arriving just before sunset affords a view of the city that morphs before your eyes into a dazzling wash of colors, with a bird's-eye view of the tops of the Empire State Building, the Citicorp Building, and the Chrysler Building, and sweeping views northward to Central Park and south to the Statue of Liberty.

Transparent elevators lift you to the 67th-floor interior viewing area, and then an escalator leads to the outdoor deck on the 69th floor for sightseeing through nonreflective glass safety panels. Then, take another elevator or stairs to the 70th floor for a 360-degree outdoor panorama of New York City on a deck that is only 20 feet wide and nearly 200 feet long.

Reserved-time ticketing eliminates long lines. Indoor exhibits include films of Rockefeller Center's history and a model of the building. Especially interesting is a Plexiglas screen on the floor with footage showing Rock Center construction workers dangling on beams high above the streets; the brave can even "walk" across a beam to get a sense of what it might have been like to erect this skyscraper. ■ TIP➔ The local consensus is that the views from the Top of the Rock are better than those from the Empire State Building, in part because the Empire State is part of the skyline here. ✉ *Entrance on 50th St., between 5th and 6th Aves., Midtown West* ☎ *877/692–7625 or 212/698–2000* ⊕ *www.topoftherocknyc.com* 🎫 *$21 adult* ☞ *children under 6 not admitted* ☉ *Daily 8–midnight; last elevator at 11 pm* Ⓜ *B, D, F, M to 47th–50th Sts./Rockefeller Center.*

WORTH NOTING

Daily News Building. One of the city's most unusual lobbies resides in Raymond Hood's Art Deco and modernist tower. An illuminated 12-foot globe revolves beneath a black glass dome. Around it, spreading across the floor like a giant compass and literally positioning New York at the center of the world, bronze lines indicate mileage to various international destinations. The *Daily News,* however, hasn't called this building home since the mid-1990s, 15 years after it played the offices of the fictional newspaper the *Daily Planet* in the original Superman movie. ✉ *220 E. 42nd St., between 2nd and 3rd Aves., Midtown East* Ⓜ *4, 5, 6, 7, S to 42nd St./Grand Central.*

Helmsley Building. "With its outline and decoration, it was able to indicate clearly its relationship to the height of a man," wrote Nathan Silver in his 1967 book *Lost in New York*, "and so was like an enormous measuring-rod, and from miles off along Park Avenue the dimensions of half a city could be perceived." This Warren & Wetmore–designed 1929 landmark was intended to match neighboring Grand Central Station in bearing, and it succeeded, with a gold-and-copper-roof topped with an enormous lantern (originally housing a 6,000-watt light) and distinctive dual archways for traffic on Park Avenue.

But its history turns quirky: When the millionaire real estate investor Harry Helmsley purchased the building in 1977, he changed its name from the New York Central Building to the New York General Building in order to save money by replacing only two letters in the facade. Only later did he rename it after himself. During a renovation the following year, however, he went so far as to gild the building, applying gold paint even to limestone and bronze (it was later removed by a succeeding owner).

However, in September 2010, after a $100 million renovation, the Helmsley Building became the first prewar office tower to receive LEED Gold certification for energy efficiency. Despite being blocked from view from the south by the MetLife Building (originally, the Pan Am Building), the Helmsley Building remains a defining—and now "green," as opposed to gold—feature of one of the world's most lavish avenues. ✉ *230 Park Ave., between 45th and 46th Sts., Midtown East* Ⓜ *4, 5, 6, 7, S to 42nd St./Grand Central.*

Madame Tussaud's New York. Sit in the Oval Office with President Obama, sing along with an American Idol, party in the V.I.P. room with the Jonas Brothers and Paris Hilton, or forecast tomorrow's weather with Al Roker. Much of the fun here comes from the photo opportunities—you're encouraged to pose with and touch the nearly 200 realistic replicas of the famous and infamous (disposable cameras are for sale).

But there's more to do here than just pal around with the waxworks. Interactive options include a karaoke café, a celebrity walk down the red carpet, and a haunted town, the latter populated with both wax figures and real people. ⊠ *234 W. 42nd St., between 7th and 8th Aves., Midtown West* ☎ *212/512–9600* ⊕ *www.madame-tussauds.com* 🖅 *35.50* ⊗ *Sun.–Thurs. 10–8, weekends 10–10* Ⓜ *1, 2, 3, 7, A, C, E, N, Q, R, S to 42nd St.*

New York Public Library (NYPL) Humanities and Social Sciences Library. The "Library with the Lions" in 2011 celebrated its centennial as a masterpiece of Beaux-Arts design and one of the great research institutions in the world, with more than 6 million books, 12 million manuscripts, and 3 million pictures.

But you don't have to crack a book to make it worth visiting: an hour or so at this National Historic Landmark is a peaceful (and free!) alternative to Midtown's bustle, along with some pretty incredible architecture, especially when combined with a stroll through adjacent **Bryant Park.** Buy a drink at a park kiosk, and then head to the library's grand 5th Avenue entrance to people-watch from the block-long marble staircase and check out the opulent interior.

The library's bronze front doors open into **Astor Hall,** which leads to several special exhibit galleries and, to the left, a stunning periodicals room with wall paintings of New York publishing houses. Walk up the sweeping double staircase to a second-floor balconied corridor overlooking the hall, with panels highlighting the library's development.

Make sure to continue up to the magisterial **Rose Main Reading Room**—297 feet long (almost two full north–south city blocks), 78 feet wide, and just over 51 feet high; walk through to best appreciate the rows of oak tables and the extraordinary ceiling of this space.

Several additional third-floor galleries show rotating exhibits on print and photography (past exhibits have included old New York restaurant menus and a 1455 Gutenberg Bible). Free one-hour tours leave Monday–Saturday at 11 and 2, and Sunday at 2 from Astor Hall. Women's bathrooms are on the ground floor and third floor, and there's a men's bathroom on the third floor. ⊠ *5th Ave. between E. 40th and E. 42nd Sts., Midtown West* ☎ *212/930–0800 for exhibit information* ⊕ *www. nypl.org* ⊗ *Mon. and Thurs.–Sat. 10–6, Sun. 1–5, Tues. and Wed. 10–8; exhibitions until 6* Ⓜ *B, D, F, M to 42nd St.; 7 to 5th Ave.*

⟳ **New York Times Building.** This Renzo Piano–designed testament to clean-lined modernism is perhaps most famous for two visitors it received on June 5, 2008, both of whom climbed straight to the top but didn't take the stairs—or even set foot inside—to do so.

The first to grab the 52-story building's distinctive, ladder-like ceramic rods without using ropes or harnesses was Alain Robert, a then-46-year-old stuntman who had previously climbed the Sydney Opera House and Eiffel Tower, among other architectural icons. Upon reaching the top, he unfurled a banner warning against global warming. Hours later, a Brooklyn man made the same climb, later claiming his intention was to raise awareness of the dangers of malaria, and replying "no" to the question of whether he was a copycat. Both men were arrested.

The architect extended the ceramic rods beyond the top of the building so that it would give the impression of dissolving into the sky. Escape congested streets in the building's lobby atrium, which includes an open-air moss garden with 50-foot paper birch trees and a wooden footbridge, a 560-screen media art installation titled *Moveable Type* streaming a mix of the newspaper's near-real time and archival content, and a flagship store by minimalist home goods designer MUJI. Plus, you never know which famous journalists you'll spy. Unfortunately, tours are not offered. ⊠ *620 8th Ave., between 40th and 41st Sts., Midtown West* ☎ *212/556–1234* Ⓜ *A, C, E to 42nd St.; 1, 2, 3, 7, N, Q, R, S to 42nd St./Times Sq.*

The Plaza Hotel. With two sides of Central Park *and* 5th Avenue at its doorstep, this world-famous 19-story 1907 building claims one of Manhattan's prize real-estate corners. Henry Hardenbergh, who built the Dakota on Central Park West, here concocted a birthday-cake effect of highly ornamented white-glazed brick topped with a copper-and-slate French mansard roof.

The original hotel was home to Eloise, the fictional star of Kay Thompson's children's books, and has appeared in many movies, including Alfred Hitchcock's *North by Northwest, Plaza Suite,* and *Home Alone 2.*

After a $400 million renovation, the Plaza reopened in early 2008. The legendary Oak Room, Oak Bar, and Grand Ballroom are all back, as are new high-end shops (including an Eloise-themed mecca), an upscale dining court by celebrity chef Todd English, luxury hotel rooms, and condo hotel units. ⊠ *5th Ave. at W. 59th St., Midtown West* ☎ *212/759–3000* Ⓜ *N, R to 5th Ave./59th St.*

St. Bartholomew's Church. Known to locals as St. Bart's, this handsome 1919 limestone-and-salmon-color brick church represents a generation of Midtown Park Avenue buildings long since replaced by modernist behemoths and contemporary glass-and-steel towers.

It's a pleasant surprise to stumble upon its triple-arched Romanesque portal and see the intricately tiled Byzantine dome set against the skyscrapers, and then have a bite at its popular outdoor café open in good weather.

St. Bart's also sponsors major music events throughout the year, including the summer's Festival of Sacred Music, with full-length masses and other choral works; an annual Christmas concert; and an occasional organ recital series that showcases the church's 12,422-pipe organ, the city's largest. The church has been associated with VIPs in many capacities, including weddings. ⊠ *325 Park Ave., at 51st St., Midtown East* ☎ *212/378–0222, 212/378–0248 for concert information* ⊕ *www.stbarts.org* ✑ *Free* ۞ *Tours leave Sun. after services (around 12:15)* ۞ *Mon., Tues., Thurs., Fri., and Sat. 9–6, Sun. 7:45–6, Wed. 9–8:30* Ⓜ *6 to 51st St./Lexington Ave.; E, M to Lexington–3rd Aves./53rd St.*

Seagram Building. Ludwig Mies van der Rohe, a pioneer of modern architecture, built this boxlike bronze-and-glass tower in 1958. The austere facade belies its wit: I-beams, used to hold buildings up, here are merely attached to the surface, representing the *idea* of support. The Seagram Building's innovative ground-level plaza, extending out to the sidewalk,

Art in Rockefeller Center

The mosaics, murals, and sculptures that grace Rockefeller Center—many of them considered Art Deco masterpieces—were all part of the plan of John D. Rockefeller Jr. In 1932, as the steel girders on the first of the buildings were heading heavenward, Rockefeller put together a team of advisers to find artists who could make the project "as beautiful as possible." More than 50 artists were commissioned for 200 individual works.

Some artists scoffed at the idea of decorating an office building: Picasso declined to meet with Rockefeller to discuss the project, and Matisse replied that busy business executives would not be in the "quiet and reflective state of mind" necessary to appreciate his art. Those who agreed to contribute, including muralists Diego Rivera and José María Sert, were relatively unknown at the time and not popular with the public. A group of American artists protested Rockefeller's decision to hire these "alien" artists.

As Rockefeller Center neared completion in 1932, Rockefeller still needed a mural to grace the lobby of the main building. The industrialist's taste dictated that the subject of the 63-by-17-foot mural was to be grandiose: "human intelligence in control of the forces of nature." He hired Rivera for the job.

With its depiction of massive machinery moving mankind forward, Rivera's *Man at the Crossroads* seemed exactly what Rockefeller wanted—until it was realized that a portrait of Soviet Premier Vladimir Lenin surrounded by red-kerchiefed workers occupied a space in the center. Rockefeller, who was building what was essentially a monument to capitalism, was less than thrilled. When Rivera was accused of willful propagandizing, the artist famously replied, "All art is propaganda."

Rivera refused to remove the portrait. Despite negotiations to move it to the Museum of Modern Art, Rockefeller was determined to get rid of it. Not content to have it painted over, he ordered ax-wielding workers to chip away the entire wall.

Rockefeller ordered the mural replaced by a less offensive one by Sert. But Rivera had the last word. He re-created the mural in the Palacio de Bellas Artes in Mexico City, adding a portrait of Rockefeller among the champagne-swilling swells ignoring the plight of the workers.

The largest of the original artworks that remained is Lee Lawrie's 2-ton sculpture, *Atlas. Its building also stirred* controversy, as it was said to resemble Italy's fascist dictator, Benito Mussolini. The sculpture, depicting a muscle-bound man holding up the world, drew protests in 1936. Some even derided Paul Manship's golden *Prometheus,* which soars over the ice-skating rink, when it was unveiled the same year.

Lawrie's sculpture *Wisdom,* perched over the main entrance of 20 Rockefeller Plaza, is another gem. Also look for Isamu Noguchi's stainless-steel plaque *News* over the entrance of the Bank of America Building at 50 Rockefeller Plaza and Attilio Piccirilli's 2-ton glass-block panel called *Youth Leading Industry* over the entrance of the International Building. René Chambellan's bronze dolphins in the fountains of the Channel Gardens are also crowd-pleasers.

The view of Midtown from across the Hudson River shows the skyline punctuated by the Empire State Building.

has since become a common element in urban skyscraper design. ✉ *375 Park Ave., between E. 52nd and E. 53rd Sts., Midtown East* Ⓜ *6 to 51st St./Lexington Ave.; E, M to Lexington–3rd Aves./53rd St.*

Sony Building. Designed by Philip Johnson in 1984, the Sony Building's rose-granite columns and its giant-size Chippendale-style pediment made the skyscraper an instant landmark. The first-floor public arcade includes electronics stores, an upscale kosher restaurant, a café, and an atrium filled with people playing chess.

Have kids in tow? The free **Sony Wonder Technology Lab** (☎ *212/833–8100, 212/833–7875 for week-of screening reservations* ⊕ *www. sonywondertechlab.com* ☾ *Tues.–Sat. 10–5, Sun. noon–5; last entrance 30 mins before closing*) in the Sony Building lets them program robots, create movie trailers, perform virtual heart surgery, and work as a team to produce a high-definition news broadcast. The lab also shows classic and contemporary films for both young and adult audiences in its 73-seat HD theater. Admission is free, but call at least seven days ahead for reservations, as it's very popular. ✉ *550 Madison Ave., between E. 55th and E. 56th Sts., Midtown East* ☾ *Daily 7 am–11 pm* Ⓜ *E, M to 5th Ave./53rd St.*

Trump Tower. The tallest all-glass building in Manhattan when it was completed in 1983, this skyscraper's ostentatious atrium flaunts that decade's unbridled luxury, with expensive boutiques and gaudy brass everywhere. One half expects the pleasant-sounding waterfall streaming down to the lower-level food court to flow with champagne. Half-price specialty cocktails 5–7 pm weeknights at the cozy, burgundy-tented Trump Bar are a consolation.

If you can see past the glitz, you'll find the building connects not only to Niketown but also to 590 Atrium, a pleasant, glass-enclosed space with tables, chairs, and an Italian café counter selling coffee, panini, and the like. ⊠ *725 5th Ave. at E. 56th St., Midtown West* ☎ *212/832–2000* ⊕ *www.trump.com* Ⓜ *N, R to 5th Ave./59th St.*

Tudor City. Before Donald Trump, there was Fred F. French. In 1925 the prominent real-estate developer became one of the first to buy up a large number of separate buildings—more than 100, in fact, most of them tenements—and join their properties into a single new development.

He designed a collection of nine apartment buildings and two parks in the "garden city" mode, which placed a building's green space not in an enclosed courtyard but in the foreground. French also elevated the entire development 70 feet (40 stone steps) above the river and built a 39-by-50-foot "Tudor City" sign atop one of the 22-story buildings. The development's residential towers opened between 1927 and 1930, borrowing a marketable air of sophistication from Tudor-style stonework, stained-glass windows, and lobby design flourishes.

An official city landmark, Tudor City has featured in numerous films, including all three *Spider-Man* movies, and its gardens remain a popular lunch spot among office workers. The street overpass on Tudor Place (its main drag) offers a unique view straight down 42nd Street, made even better when the sun sets directly over the street on May 28 and July 12 or 13 each year. Brian K. Thompson, a local real-estate agent and historian, leads private 45-minute architecture, finance, and real-estate history tours of the development; email him for details (☏ *Tudor City tour $10* ✍ *briankthompson@yahoo.com*). ⊠ *Between 41st and 43rd Sts and 1st and 2nd Aves., Midtown East* Ⓜ *4, 5, 6, 7, S to 42nd St./Grand Central.*

United Nations Headquarters. Officially an "international zone" and not part of the United States, the U.N. Headquarters is a working symbol of global cooperation. Built between 1947 and 1961, the headquarters sit on a lushly landscaped, 18-acre tract on the East River, fronted by flags of member nations.

The main reason to visit is the 45-minute guided tour (given in 20 languages), which includes the **General Assembly** and major council chambers, though some rooms may be closed on any given day. The tour includes displays on war, peacekeeping, nuclear nonproliferation, human rights, and refugees, and passes corridors overflowing with imaginatively diverse artwork.

Free tickets to assemblies are sometimes available on a first-come, first-served basis before sessions begin; pick them up in the General Assembly lobby. If you just want to wander around, the grounds include a beautiful riverside promenade, a rose garden with 1,400 specimens, and sculptures donated by member nations.

The complex's buildings (the slim, 505-foot-tall green-glass **Secretariat Building**; the much smaller, domed **General Assembly Building**; and the **Dag Hammarskjöld Library**) evoke the influential French modernist Le Corbusier (who was on the team of architects that designed the complex), and the surrounding park and plaza remain visionary.

A statue of Atlas stands across the street from the looming Gothic St. Patrick's Cathedral.

The public concourse, beneath the visitor entrance, has a coffee shop, gift shops, a bookstore, and a post office where you can mail letters with U.N. stamps. ⊠ *Visitor entrance, 1st Ave. at E. 46th St., Midtown East* ☎ *212/963–8687* ⊕ *www.un.org* 🖼 *Tour $12.50* ☞ *Children under 5 not admitted* ⊗ *Tours weekdays 9:30–4:45; tours in English leave General Assembly lobby every 30 mins; for other languages, call* ☎ *212/963–7539 on the day of your visit* Ⓜ *4, 5, 6, 7, S to 42nd St./ Grand Central.*

University Club. Among the best surviving works of McKim, Mead & White, New York's leading turn-of-the-20th-century architects, this 1899 pink Milford granite palace was built for an exclusive club of degree-holding men. (The crests of various prestigious universities are engraved into the facade above its windows.)

The club's popularity declined as individual universities built their own clubs and as gentlemen's clubs became less important to the New York social scene. Still, the nine-story Italian High Renaissance Revival building (the facade looks as though it's three stories) stands out, grand as ever, among the shiny 5th Avenue shops. ⊠ *1 W. 54th St., at 5th Ave., Midtown West* Ⓜ *E, M to 5th Ave./53rd St.*

GALLERIES

David Findlay Jr. Fine Art. This gallery concentrates on contemporary and 20th-century American artists from Whistler to Herman Cherry, Byron Brown, and David Aronson, and specializes in the New York

School. ✉ *41 E. 57th St., 11th fl., at Madison Ave., Midtown East* ☎ *212/486–7660* ⊕ *www.davidfindlayjr.com* Ⓜ *N, R to 5th Ave.*

Hirschl & Adler. Although this gallery has a selection of European works, it's best known for its American paintings, prints, and decorative arts. The celebrated 19th- and 20th-century artists whose works are featured include Stuart Davis, Childe Hassam, Camille Pissarro, and John Singleton Copley. ✉ *730 5th Ave at W. 57th St., 4th fl., Midtown East* ☎ *212/535–8810* ⊕ *www.hirschlandadler.com* Ⓜ *N, R to 5th Ave. St./ Hunter College.*

Marlborough. With its latest branch in Chelsea, Marlborough has raised its global visibility yet another notch. The gallery represents modern artists such as Claudio Bravo, Magdalena Abakanowicz, and photorealist Richard Estes. Look for sculptures by Tom Otterness—his whimsical bronzes are found in several subway stations. ✉ *40 W. 57th St., between 5th and 6th Aves., Midtown West* ☎ *212/541–4900* ⊕ *www. marlboroughgallery.com* Ⓜ *F to 57th St.*

Pace Wildenstein. The giant gallery—now in Chelsea as well—focuses on such modern and contemporary painters as Julian Schnabel, Mark Rothko, and New York School painter Ad Reinhardt. ✉ *32 E. 57th St., between Park and Madison Aves., 2nd fl., Midtown East* ☎ *212/421– 3292* ⊕ *www.thepacegallery.com* Ⓜ *N, R to 5th Ave.*

Spanierman. This venerable gallery deals in 19th- and early-20th-century American painting and sculpture. Their inventory list and scholarship is amazing, and they frequently sell to museums looking to broaden their own collections. Next-door, Spanierman Modern (⊕ *www. spaniermanmodern.com*) represents contemporary artists such as Dan Christensen and Frank Bowling. ✉ *45 E. 58th St., between Park and Madison Aves., Midtown East* ☎ *212/832–0208* ⊕ *www.spanierman. com* Ⓜ *N, R to 5th Ave.*

Tibor de Nagy. Founded in 1950, this gallery shows work by 20th-century artists such as Biala, Nell Blaine, Jane Freilicher, and Shirley Jaffee. Instrumental in bringing many of America's finest abstract expressionist artists to public attention in the mid-20th century, the gallery now shows abstract and realistic work. It's open Tuesday–Saturday, closed weekends June through mid-August, and closes up completely from mid-August to Labor Day. ✉ *724 5th Ave., between W. 56th and W. 57th Sts., Midtown West* ☎ *212/262–5050* ⊕ *www.tibordenagy.com* Ⓜ *N, R to 5th Ave.*

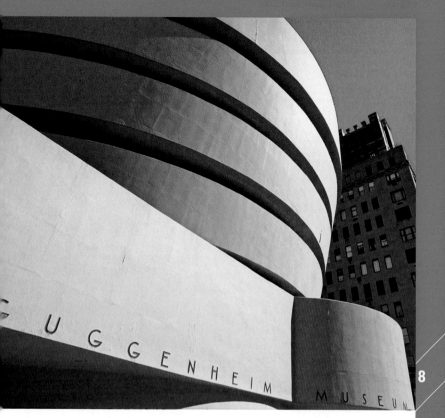

The Upper East Side

WORD OF MOUTH

"If you are an art buff, the Frick is a magnificent home and gallery.
Mr. Frick had an eye for art, and the fortune to make the best of it!"
—Johnnyman7

GETTING ORIENTED

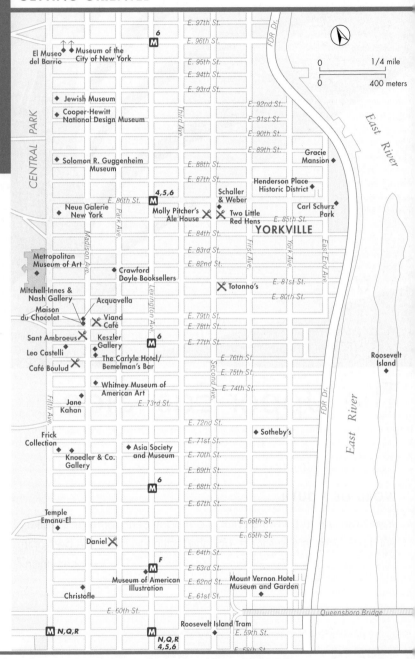

El Museo del Barrio

Museum of the City of New York

6

Jewish Museum

Cooper-Hewitt National Design Museum

Solomon R. Guggenheim Museum

CENTRAL PARK

Neue Galerie New York

4,5,6

Molly Pitcher's Ale House

Schaller & Weber

Henderson Place Historic District

Gracie Mansion

Carl Schurz Park

Two Little Red Hens

YORKVILLE

Metropolitan Museum of Art

Crawford Doyle Booksellers

Mitchell-Innes & Nash Gallery

Acquavella

Totonno's

Maison du Chocolat

Viand Café

Sant Ambroeus

Keszler Gallery

6

Leo Castelli

Café Boulud

The Carlyle Hotel/ Bemelman's Bar

Whitney Museum of American Art

Jane Kahan

Frick Collection

Knoedler & Co. Gallery

Asia Society and Museum

Sotheby's

6

Temple Emanu-El

Daniel

F

Museum of American Illustration

Mount Vernon Hotel Museum and Garden

Christofle

Queensboro Bridge

N,Q,R

N,Q,R 4,5,6

Roosevelt Island Tram

Roosevelt Island

East River

FDR Dr.

0   1/4 mile
0   400 meters

MAKING THE MOST OF YOUR TIME

The Upper East Side lends itself to a surprising variety of simple but distinct itineraries: regimented hopping up and down Museum Mile; languorous gallery-grazing; window-shopping on Madison Avenue; or bar-hopping for just-out-of-college kids on 2nd Avenue. The Upper East Side's town houses, boutiques, consignment stores, and hidden gardens are easy to miss unless you take some time to wander. If all that walking wears you out, you can always hit one of the nail salons and indulge in a neighborhood stereotype of the pampered Upper East Sider. A well-deserved post–Museum Mile foot rub and mani/pedi are surprisingly reasonably priced.

GETTING HERE

Take the Lexington Avenue 4 or 5 express trains to 59th or 86th Street. The 6 local train also stops at 59th, 68th, 77th, 86th, and 96th streets. If you're coming from Midtown, the F train will let you out at Lexington Avenue at 63rd Street, where you can transfer to the 4, 5, and 6 after a short walk (and without paying subway fare again). From the Upper West Side, take one of the crosstown buses, the M66, M72, M79, M86, and M96. You can also take the N or R train to 59th Street and Lexington Avenue.

WORD OF MOUTH (WWW.FODORS.COM/FORUMS)

"For the East Side, window-shopping on Madison is always enjoyable. Just about every high-end store you can think of has a shop there. One huge plus to the [Upper East Side] is that there are far fewer tourists around. I know that everyone likes to come here and see Times Square, and it is certainly something to see, but having to navigate through the ridiculous crowds becomes exhausting. I think you might enjoy coming uptown and just being able to walk leisurely without people bumping into you." —elysag

FODOR'S CHOICE

Central Park

Gracie Mansion

TOP EXPERIENCES

Enjoying a spin through the Neue Galerie and eating at Café Sabarksy

Spending an afternoon at locals' favorite, the Frick Collection

Seeing permanent collections at the Guggenheim or the Whitney

Window-shopping on Madison Avenue

WHAT'S NEARBY

Central Park (⇨ Ch. 9)

Asia Society and Museum (⇨ Ch. 14)

Cooper-Hewitt National Design Museum (⇨ Ch. 14)

El Museo del Barrio (⇨ Ch. 14)

Frick Collection (⇨ Ch. 14)

Jewish Museum (⇨ Ch. 14)

Museum of American Illustration (⇨ Ch. 14)

Museum of the City of New York (⇨ Ch. 14)

Neue Galerie New York (⇨ Ch. 14)

Solomon R. Guggenheim Museum (⇨ Ch. 14)

Whitney Museum (⇨ Ch. 14)

8

Sightseeing
★★★

Nightlife
★★

Dining
★★★

Lodging
★★

Shopping
★★★★

To many New Yorkers the Upper East Side connotes old money and high society. Alongside Central Park, between 5th and Lexington avenues, up to East 96th Street, the trappings of wealth are everywhere apparent: posh buildings, Madison Avenue's flagship boutiques, and doormen in braided livery.

Updated by
John Rambow

Although a glance up and down the manicured grass meridian of Park Avenue may conjure scenes from *Bonfire of the Vanities* or *Gossip Girl*, there are more than palatial apartments, elite private schools, and highfalutin clubs up here—starting with fantastic museums. **The Metropolitan Museum of Art**, the **Solomon R. Guggenheim Museum**, the **Whitney Museum**, and many others lie on and around "Museum Mile" (⇨ *Chapter 14)*, as do a number of worthy art galleries. For a local taste of the luxe life, hit up the platinum-card corridor that is Madison Avenue for its lavish boutiques, marble-counter cafés, and the epitome of class, the **Carlyle Hotel**.

Venture east of Lexington Avenue and you encounter a less wealthy—and more diverse—Upper East Side, one inhabited by couples seeking some of the last (relatively) affordable places to raise a family south of 100th Street, and recent college grads getting a foothold in the city (on weekend nights 2nd Avenue resembles a miles-long fraternity and sorority reunion).

One neighborhood particularly worth exploring is northeast-lying **Yorkville**, especially between 78th and 86th streets east of 2nd Avenue. Once a remote hamlet with a large German population, its several remaining ethnic food shops, 19th-century row houses, and, one of the city's best-kept secrets, **Carl Schurz Park**, make for a good half-day's exploration, as does touring most striking residence there, **Gracie Mansion.**

TOP TOURING EXPERIENCES

NEW YORK'S LAP OF LUXURY

Walking up Madison Avenue between East 60th and East 82nd Street is like stepping into the pages of a glossy magazine. Many fashion houses have their flagships here and showcase their lush threads in equally exquisite settings.

Compared with the megastores of Midtown, Madison Avenue feels quieter; it's significantly less crowded and more conducive to leisurely shopping (window or otherwise). Beyond clothing, the boutiques here carry baubles to satisfy anyone's champagne wishes, whether it's a box of truffles at **La Maison du Chocolat,** an intriguing read at **Crawford Doyle Booksellers,** or a piece of contemporary silver tableware at **Christofle** (⊠ *680 Madison Ave.* ☎ *212/308–9390*).

For a break, grab a seat at a café, such as **Sant Ambroeus,** and take in the fashion show on the sidewalk. End the day in style with dinner at **Café Boulud** or a drink at one of the neighborhood's sleek lounges or bars.

A NEIGHBORHOOD IN EVERY BLOCK

The Upper East Side is more than just an enclave for the wealthy. In fact, a great way to experience Manhattan's hodgepodge of communities is to walk east from 5th Avenue to the East River—zigzagging to include both avenues and side streets—and watch the neighborhoods change.

One good place to start is along lavish East 65th Street, passing the Romanesque **Temple Emanu-El;** the double town house at No. 47 built for Sara Delano Roosevelt and her son, Franklin; and the acclaimed French restaurant **Daniel** across the street. End several blocks and a world away at the 18th-century **Mount Vernon Hotel Museum and Garden** on 61st Street between 1st and York avenues.

Another good route starts at the cooperative apartments at 1040 5th Avenue, at East 85th Street, the former home of Jacqueline Kennedy Onassis. It overlooks the reservoir that now bears her name.

Heading east beyond Park Avenue, the town houses and boutiques give way to the residential high-rises of **Yorkville** (the one at 185 E. 85th appeared in the opening credits of the TV show *The Jeffersons*). Few remaining shops recall the neighborhood's German and Hungarian immigrant past (which earned 2nd Avenue the nickname "Goulash Avenue"). One delicious reminder is the 1937 food shop **Schaller & Weber** (⊠ *1654 2nd Ave., at East 86th St.*), where you can pick up homemade bratwurst or imported stollen, cookies, and other goodies. From here, continue east to see the official mayoral residence, **Gracie Mansion,** and the serene riverside **Carl Schurz Park.**

TOP ATTRACTIONS

Fodor'sChoice
★

Central Park. (⇨ *Chapter 9*).

Fodor'sChoice
★

Gracie Mansion. The official mayor's residence, Gracie Mansion was built in 1799 by shipping merchant Archibald Gracie, with an enlargement in 1966. Tours of the highly impressive interior—which must be scheduled in advance and take place under limited hours—take you through its history and colorful rooms furnished over centuries and packed with American objets d'art.

Nine mayors have lived here since it became the official residence in 1942, but New York City's current mayor, Michael Bloomberg, broke with tradition; he chose to stay in his own 79th Street town house. He does use it, however, for meetings and functions. ⊠ *Carl Schurz Park, East End Ave. opposite 88th St., Upper East Side* ☏ *212/570–4751* ✉ *$7* ⊘ *45-min guided tours by advance reservation only; Wed. 10–2* Ⓜ *4, 5, 6 to 86th St.*

WORTH NOTING

☙ **Carl Schurz Park.** Facing the East River, this park, named for a German immigrant who was a prominent newspaper editor in the 19th century, is so tranquil you'd never guess you're directly above FDR Drive. Walk along the promenade, where you can take in views of the river and the Roosevelt Island Lighthouse across the way. To the north are Randall's and Wards islands and newly renamed RFK Bridge (aka the Triborough Bridge)—as well as the more immediate sight of locals pushing strollers, riding bikes, or exercising their dogs.

If you're visiting with kids, there's a very worthwhile playground at the 84th Street end with climbing equipment, swings, and other diversions for toddlers and older children. If you enter the park at its 86th Street entrance or you're exiting there, you'll find yourself approaching the grounds of a Federal-style wood-frame house that belies the grandeur of its name—Gracie Mansion. ■**TIP→** If you exit the park at 86th Street, cross East End Avenue for a stroll through Henderson Place, a miniature historic district of 24 connected Queen Anne–style houses in a dead end. The small redbrick houses, built in 1881 "for persons of moderate means," have turrets marking the corner of each block and symmetrical roof gables, pediments, parapets, chimneys, and dormer windows. ⊠ *Carl Schurz Park spans East End Ave. to the East River, E. 84th to E. 90th Sts., Upper East Side* ⊕ *www.carlschurzparknyc.org* Ⓜ *4, 5, 6 to 86th St.*

Mount Vernon Hotel Museum and Garden. Built in 1799, this former carriage house (i.e., stable) became a day hotel (a sort of country club) in 1826. Now restored and owned by the Colonial Dames of America, it provides a glimpse of the days when the city ended at 14th Street and this area was a country escape for New Yorkers. The 45-minute tour passes through the eight rooms that display furniture and artifacts of the Federal and Empire periods. Many rooms have real artifacts such as clothes, hats, and fans that children can handle. There is a lovely adjoining garden, designed in an 18th-century style. ⊠ *421 E. 61st St., between York and 1st Aves., Upper East Side* ☏ *212/838–6878* ⊕ *www.mvhm.org* ✉ *$8* ⊘ *Tues.–Sun. 11–4* Ⓜ *4, 5, 6, F, N, R to 59th St./Lexington Ave.*

Roosevelt Island. The 2-mi-long East River slice of land that parallels Manhattan from East 48th to East 85th streets is now a quasi-suburb of 10,000 people, and the vestiges of its infamous asylums, hospitals, and prisons make this an offbeat trip for the historically curious.

Where can I find . . . ?

COFFEE	Sant Ambroeus (1000 Madison Ave., by 77th St.) A bustling café with great cappuccino and even better people-watching.	Two Little Red Hens (1652 2nd Ave., by 86th St.) First-rate joe and the cupcakes to match.
A QUICK BITE	Viand Cafe (1011Madison Ave., by 78th St. Classic New York diner.	Totonno's (1544 2nd Ave., by 80th St.) No slices, but the best white pizza you'll ever eat.
COCKTAILS	Bemelmans Bar (35 E. 76th St., by Madison Ave.) Classy (and pricey) but unpretentious.	Molly Pitcher's Ale House (1641 2nd Ave., by 85th St.) A sports bar with 16 beers on tap.

At the south tip are the eerie ruins of a **Smallpox Hospital,** built in 1854 in a Gothic Revival style by the prominent architect James Renwick Jr. (Among many other works, Renwick also designed St. Patrick's and the Smithsonian's Castle.) On a small park at the island's north tip is a lighthouse built in 1872 by island convicts. Most of what's in between (new as well as 1970s-era condominiums and a modern-day hospital) is fairly banal, but riverside esplanades provide nice panoramas of Manhattan.

You can get here by subway, but more fun is the five-minute ride on the **Roosevelt Island Tramway,** the only commuter cable car in North America, which lifts you 250 feet in the air, with impressive views of Queens and Manhattan. A visitor center, made from an old trolley kiosk, stands to your left as you exit the tram. Red buses service the island, 25¢ a ride. ⊠ *Tramway entrance at 2nd Ave. and either 59th St. or 60th St., Upper East Side* 🕿 *212/832–4555* ⊕ *www.rioc.com* 🖃 *$2.25 (subway Metrocard accepted)* ⊙ *Tram Sun.–Thurs. 6 am–2 am, Fri. and Sat. 6 am–3:30 am; leaves approximately every 15 min* Ⓜ *F to Roosevelt Island.*

Temple Emanu-El. The world's largest Reform Jewish synagogue seats 2,500 worshippers. Built in 1928–29 of limestone and designed in the Romanesque style with Byzantine influences, the building has Moorish and Art Deco ornamentation, and its sanctuary is covered with mosaics. A free museum displays artifacts detailing the congregation's history and Jewish life. The synagogue stands on the site of what was once the house of the ultimate society maven, Mrs. William Astor. ⊠ *1 E. 65th St., at 5th Ave., Upper East Side* 🕿 *212/744–1400* ⊕ *www. emanuelnyc.org* ⊙ *Sabbath services Fri. 5:15 pm, Sat. 10:30 am; regular services Sun.–Thurs. 5:30 pm. Temple daily 10–4:30, museum Sun.– Thurs. 10–4:30 (call to confirm); tours Sun.–Thurs., Fri., and Sat. after services* Ⓜ *6 to 68th St./Hunter College.*

GALLERIES

Chelsea, Midtown's West 57th Street, the Lower East Side, and other parts of town all have their own art galleries, but those on the Upper East Side are in a class of their own. In keeping with the tony surroundings, the emphasis here is on works by established masters rather than up-and-coming (or even still-living) artists. Their locations are eminent as well: large town houses and upper stories in and around Madison and Fifth avenues. Note that galleries often have limited hours, so make sure to check times in advance.

Acquavella. The 19th- and 20th-century art shown inside this five-story marble-floored mansion tends to be by the big names, from Impressionists through Pop artists, including Picasso, Lucian Freud, and James Rosenquist. ⊠ *18 E. 79th St., between 5th and Madison Aves., Upper East Side* ☎ *212/734–6300* ⊕ *www.acquavellagalleries.com* Ⓜ *6 to 77th St..*

Jane Kahan. This welcoming gallery represents very lofty works. Besides ceramics by Picasso and modern master tapestries, one of this gallery's specialties, you'll see works by late-19th- and early-20th-century modern artists such as Fernand Léger, Joan Miró, and Marc Chagall. ⊠ *922 Madison Ave., 2nd fl., between E. 73rd and E. 74th Sts., Upper East Side* ☎ *212/744–1490* ⊕ *www.janekahan.com* Ⓜ *6 to 77th St.*

Keszler Gallery. Inside a warren of rooms on the ground floor of the same building that holds the Gagosian you'll find contemporary works by celebrity painter Russell Young and the street artist Banksy. ⊠ *984 Madison Ave., at E. 77th St., Upper East Side* ☎ *212/744–1906* ⊕ *www. keszlergallery.com.* Ⓜ *6 to 77th St.*

Knoedler & Company. Knoedler helped many major American collectors, including industrialist Henry Clay Frick, start their collections. Now this blue-chip gallery represents 20th-century painters such as Helen Frankenthaler, Frank Stella, and John Walker. ⊠ *19 E. 70th St., between 5th and Madison Aves., Upper East Side* ☎ *212/794–0550* ⊕ *www. knoedlergallery.com* Ⓜ *6 to 68th St./Hunter College.*

★ **Leo Castelli.** Castelli was one of the most influential dealers of the 20th century. He helped foster the careers of many important artists, including one of his first discoveries, Jasper Johns. The gallery continues to show works by Roy Lichtenstein, Ed Ruscha, Jackson Pollock, Robert Morris, and other heavies. ⊠ *18 E. 77th St., between 5th and Madison Aves., Upper East Side* ☎ *212/249–4470* ⊕ *www.castelligallery. com* Ⓜ *6 to 77th St.*

Mitchell-Innes & Nas. This sleek spot represents the estates of Roy Lichtenstein and Jack Tworkov as well as other Impressionist, modern, and contemporary masters. ⊠ *1018 Madison Ave., between 78th and 79th Sts., Upper East Side* ☎ *212/744–7400* ⊕ *www.miandn.com* Ⓜ *6 to 77th St.*

★ **Sotheby's.** Occupying its own 10-story building, this branch of the storied U.K. auction house puts on display many of the items it will be auctioning. A sizeable portion of these are extremely high-profile: a copy of the Magna Carta, Fabergé eggs, rare Tiffany lamps, and Norman Rockwell's 1943 painting *Rosie the Riveter* have all been sold through this Sotheby's. ⊠ *1334 York Ave., at E. 72nd St., Upper East Side* ☎ *212/606–7000* ⊕ *www.sothebys.com* Ⓜ *6 to 77th St.*

Central Park

WORD OF MOUTH

"For anybody reading this who has never been to NYC before, listen carefully: get up early, and walk in Central Park on the weekend. Do it. As soon as you take two steps inside, you realize that you are going to LOVE New York with all your heart and soul, and that you want to have her babies."

— MacSporran

OUR BACKYARD

HOW A SWAMP BECAME AN OASIS

1855 Using eminent domain, New York City acquires 843 acres of undeveloped swamp for the then-obscene sum of $5 million, displacing 1,600 people living there.

1857 Frederick Law Olmsted becomes superintendent of a park that does not yet exist. He spends days clearing dirt and evicting squatters and evenings working with architect friend Calvert Vaux on what will become the Greensward plan. The plan is the winning entry in the city's competition to develop a design for the park.

The Panic of 1857 creates widespread unemployment. Thousands of workers begin the task of moving five million cubic yards of dirt and planting more than five million trees, plants, and shrubs. Beleaguered by bureaucrats, Olmsted and Vaux unsuccessfully submit their resignations several times.

1873 The Greensward plan is completed. It has been the basic blueprint for Central Park ever since.

Thirty-five million people use Central Park each year; on an average summer weekend day, a quarter-million children and adults flood these precincts from all over the city and the world, frolicking in the 21 playgrounds, bellying up the 150 drinking fountains (water not guaranteed), and collapsing on more than 9,000 benches, which would span seven miles if you lined them up. There are more than 50 monuments and sculptures in the park, but many more ways to make your own fun.

⟨30⟩ THINGS WE LOVE TO DO IN CENTRAL PARK

1 Take a rowboat out on the Lake

2 Watch the sea lions play at feeding time

3 Walk around the Reservoir

4 Ice-skate at Wollman Rink

5 Watch rollerbladers show off

6 Go bird watching at the Ramble

7 Lie in the grass at Sheep Meadow

8 Rent a bike at the Boathouse

9 Sit on the hill behind the Met Museum

10 See a free concert or play

11 Catch a softball game

12 Clap for the jugglers

13 Remember John Lennon at Strawberry Fields

14 Run through an icy playground sprinkler

15 Rent a gondola and a gondolier

16 Cross the park on the bridle path

17 Stand under the gnarly 72nd Street pergola

18 Hear the Delacorte Clock's musical chimes

19 Crunch the snow before anyone else

20 Pilot a tiny boat at Conservatory Water

21 Stroll through Shakespeare Garden

22 Fish at Harlem Meer

23 Watch dogs play

24 Smell the Conservatory Garden tulips

25 Shoot photos from Bow Bridge

26 Ride the Carousel; wave at everyone

27 People-watch at Bethesda Fountain

28 Picnic on the Great Lawn

29 Pet the bronze Balto statue

30 Climb to the top of Belvedere Castle

(top left) Monarch butterfly pollinates at Conservatory Garden (top center) Hansom driver between fares (top right) Chrysanthemums near Sheep Meadow (center) The skyline with some of the park's 26,000 trees (bottom) Park skaters in the 1860s.

PARK BASICS

Several entrances lead into the park. You can enter from the east, west, south, and north by paved pedestrian walkways, just off Fifth Avenue, Central Park North (110th St.), Central Park West, and Central Park South (59th St.).

Four roads, or transverses, cut through the park from east to west—66th, 79th, 86th, and 96th streets. The East and West drives are both along the north–south axis; Center Drive enters the south edge of the park at Sixth Avenue and connects with East Drive around 66th Street.

Five Visitor Centers—the Dairy (just south of the 66th St. transverse), Belvedere Castle (just north of the 79th Street transverse), the Chess & Checkers house (mid-park at 64th St.), and the Charles A. Dana Discovery Center (at the top of the park at Central Park North)—have directions, park maps, event calendars, and volunteers who can guide you. Until a new restaurant opens in its place, the former Tavern on the Green (west side near 66th St.) is also serving as a visitor center, with food vendors as well.

TOURS

The **Central Park Conservancy** gives several different free walking tours of the park based on the season. Most tours are 60 to 90 minutes, and custom tours are also available. If you'd rather go it alone, the Conservancy also offers an audio guide you can follow on your cell phone. Each description is read by a different celebrity or NYC VIP. Dial 646/862-0997 then the extension that corresponds to each landmark and hit pound. For more information, see centralparknyc.org.

WHERE AM I?

Along the main loop and some smaller paths, lampposts are marked with location codes. Posts bear a letter—always "E" (for east) or "W" (for west)—followed by four numbers. The first two numbers tell you the nearest cross street. The second two tell you how far you are from either 5th Avenue or Central Park West (depending on whether it's an "E" or "W" post). So E7803 means you're near 78th Street, three posts in from 5th Avenue. For street numbers above 99, the initial "1" is omitted, for example, E0401 (near 104th Street, one post in from 5th Avenue).

PERFORMERS AND THE PARK: SOULMATES

It was inevitable that Central Park, conceived to give so much and ask little in return, would attract artists and arts lovers who feel the same way.

Be they superstars like Paul Simon, Diana Ross, or Barbra Streisand or one of the amateur musicians, animal handlers, or jugglers who delight passersby, they all share the urge to entertain and give back to the city, the park, and its visitors.

Information on scheduled events is provided, but if you can't catch one, don't fret: you'll be rewarded by the serendipitous, particularly on summer and autumn days. Just keep your ears peeled for the music, applause, and laughter. The Central Park Conservancy, in cooperation with other arts patrons, drives a series of free events, including the Harlem Meer Performance Festival and the Great Lawn performances by the Metropolitan Opera and New York Philharmonic. One standout is Summer-Stage, which yields a cornucopia of international performers.

Perhaps the brass ring of park performances is the more than four-decade-old Shakespeare in the Park, which wows about 80,000 New Yorkers and visitors during any given summer. Free tickets (two per person) are given out starting at 1 PM for the performance that evening, but you need to line up by midmorning or earlier depending on the show. The wait is worth it, though, as casts are often studded with the likes of Meryl Streep, Philip Seymour Hoffman, Natalie Portman, Morgan Freeman, Denzel Washington, and Kevin Kline.

GOINGS ON

Central Park Film Festival: Five nights at end of summer; Rumsey Playfield, near E. 72nd St. entrance.

Harlem Meer Performance Festival: Late June–early Sept., Sun.; at Dana Discovery Center, near Lenox Ave. entrance.

New York Grand Opera: Performances July.–Sept.; Naumburg Bandshell; mid-park near 72nd St.

New York Philharmonic: Two performances in June or July; Great Lawn.

Shakespeare in the Park: June–early Aug., Tues.–Sun. evenings.

Storytelling: June–Sept., Sat. 11 AM; Hans Christian Andersen Statue at 72nd St. and 5th Ave.

SummerStage: Late May or June–early Sept.; Rumsey Playfield. Big-name, up-and-coming, and international musicians perform here, sometimes for free.

Swedish Cottage Marionette Theatre: Since 1947, puppeteers have entertained in this 1876 Swedish schoolhouse. $8 adults/$5 kids. Daily hours vary; reservations required.

(center) N.Y. Philharmonic associate conductor Xian Zhang (right) Shakespeare's *Much Ado About Nothing*

FROM 59TH TO 72ND ST.

 The busy southern section of Central Park is where most visitors get their first impression. Artists line the entrances off Central Park South, and drivers of horse carriages await passengers. But no matter how many people congregate in this area, you can always find a spot to picnic, ponder, or just take in the beauty, especially on a sunny day.

At the southeast corner of the park, you will come upon one of its prettiest areas, the **Pond**. Swans and ducks cruise on its calm waters, and if you follow the shore line to Gapstow Bridge and look southward, you'll see much of New York City's skyline: to the left (east) are the peak-roofed Sherry-Netherland Hotel, the black-and-white GM Building, the Chippendale-style top of the Sony Building, and the black-glass Trump Tower. In front of you is the château-style Plaza Hotel.

Opening in late October, **Wollman Memorial Rink** sits inside the park against a backdrop of Central Park South skyscrapers. You can rent skates there, buy snacks, and have a perfect city-type outing. There's a lively feeling here with lots of great music playing and

a terrace so you can watch if you're not into skating.

The **Friedsam Memorial Carousel**, also known as the Central Park Carousel, was built in 1908. It has 58 nearly life-size hand-carved horses and remains a favorite among young and old. Its original Wurlitzer organ plays calliope waltzes, polkas, and standards. Even if you don't need visitor infomation, the **Dairy** is worth a stop for its Swiss-chalet exterior.

If you saw the film *Madagascar*, you may recognize the Central Park Zoo, officially known as the **Central Park Wildlife Center**. Here, the polar bears play at the Polar Circle, monkeys frolic in the open-air Temperate Territory, and the Rain Forest showcases flora and fauna that you wouldn't expect to see in Manhattan. An unusual exhibit is the ant colony—even New York City's zoo has a sense of humor. Stick around to see the sea lion feedings (call for times) and to watch the animal statues dance to a variety of nursery rhymes at the **Delacorte Musical Clock** just outside, on the hour and half-hour from 8 AM to 5 PM.

Wedged between the zoo and the clock is **The Arsenal**, the second-oldest building in the park. Inside are rotating

QUICK BITES

Zabar's, on 80th and Broadway, is a perennial pit stop for picnic fare, but you can avail yourself of many grab-and-go eateries and supermarkets on either side of the park. Your best bet for rations: west of Columbus Ave. and east of Park Ave.

If you prefer a more formal (and pricier) bite, **The Boathouse Restaurant** (Midpark at 74th St.) is an open-air restaurant and bar. An adjacent café dishes up good, cheap meals. The Moorish-style Mineral Springs Pavilion (Midpark at W. 69th St.) houses the **Sheep Meadow Café**, which serves sandwiches, salads, and grilled steak and fish.

The site of the Tavern on the Green, east of Central Park West and 67th Street, has food trucks on hand for speedy noshing.

exhibits that often cover park history and landscape art.

North of the clock is **Tisch Children's Zoo**, where kids can pet and feed sheep, goats, rabbits, cows, and pigs. Enter through the trunk of a make-believe tree and arrive at The Enchanted Forest, filled with huge "acorns,"

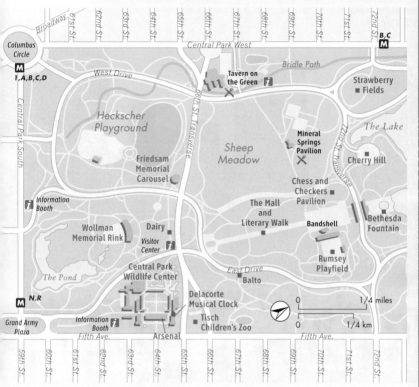

a climbable "spider web," and hoppable "lily pads."

Perhaps more pettable than any of the zoo's occupants is a decidely more inert creature, perched on a rockpile at East Drive and 67th Street: **Balto.** Shiny in places from constant touching, this bronze statue commemorates a real-life sled dog who led a team of huskies that carried medicine for 674 mi across perilous ice to Nome, Alaska, during a 1925 diphtheria epidemic.

The Mall, at the intersection of Central Drive and East Drive, is arguably the most elegant area of Central Park. In the beginning of the 20th century, it was the place to see and be seen. Today, these formal walkways are still a wonderful place to stroll, meander, or sit and take in the "parade" under a canopy of the largest collection of American elms in North America. The mall's southern end, known as **Literary Walk,** is lined with statues of authors and artists such as Robert Burns and William Shakespeare.

(from left to right) Riding on the outside track (recommended) of the Carousel; Getting in a workout on a park drive loop; The Mall, where Dustin Hoffman's character famously teaches his son to ride a bike in *Kramer vs. Kramer.*

The large expanse to the west of the Mall is known as **Sheep Meadow**, the only "beach" that some native New Yorkers have ever known. Join in on a Frisbee or football game, admire the tenacity of kite flyers, or indulge simultaneously in the three simplest meadow pleasures of them all—picnicking, sunbathing, and languorously reading a book.

There's a reason why the ornate **Bethesda Fountain**, off the 72nd Street transverse, shows up in so many movies set in New York City: the view from the staircase above is one of the most romantic in the city. The statue in the center of the fountain, **The Angel of the Waters**, designed by Emma Stebbins, is surrounded by four figures symbolizing Temperance, Purity,

Health, and Peace. There's a good amount of New York–style street entertainment here, too, with break dancers, acrobats, and singers all vying for your spare change. It's also a great place to meet, sit, and admire the beautiful lake with its swans. For a glimpse of the West Side skyline, walk slightly west to **Cherry Hill**. Originally a watering area for horses, this circular plaza has a small

wrought-iron-and-gilt fountain. It's particularly beautiful in the spring when the cherry trees are in full pink-and-white bloom. Farther west are the Oak Bridge and the lovely Ladies Pavilion, emblematic of the park's past.

Across from the Dakota apartment building on Central Park West is **Strawberry Fields**, named for the Beatles' 1967 classic, "Strawberry Fields Forever." Sometimes called the "international garden of peace," this spot draws fans in pilgrimages who reflect among its shrubs, trees, and flower beds, and lay flowers on the black-and-white "Imagine" mosaic. On December 8, hundreds of Beatles fans mark the anniversary of Lennon's death by gathering here.

(top from left to right) Seals cavorting at the zoo; Artist painting the oft-rendered Gapstow bridge, which spans the northeast end of the Pond; Cutting through the park is a classic midday timesaver and post-work respite; Meeting up and chilling out at world-famous Bethesda Fountain (center left); Nighttime at Wollman Rink serves up twinkling skyscrapers and skaters of all abilities (center right); The late John Lennon and his widow, Yoko Ono, often visited the site of what would become Strawberry Fields.

FROM 72ND ST. TO THE RESERVOIR

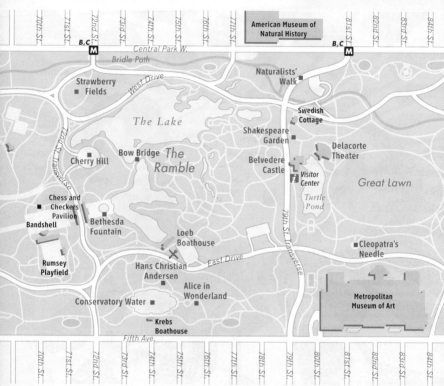

Playgrounds, lawns, jogging and biking paths, and striking buildings populate the midsection of the park. You can soak up the sun, have a picnic, or even play in a pick-up basketball or baseball game by the Great Lawn; get your cultural fix at the Metropolitan Museum of Art; or train for the next New York City Marathon along the Reservoir.

A block from Fifth Avenue, just north of the 72nd Street entrance, is a peaceful section of the park where you'll find the **Conservatory Water**, named for a conservatory that was never built. Generations of New Yorkers have grown up racing radio-controlled model sailboats here. It's a tradition that happens each Saturday at 10 AM from April through Oct. Smaller boats are available for rent. At the north end is

the **Alice in Wonderland** statue; on the west side of the pond, a bronze statue of **Hans Christian Andersen**, the Ugly Duckling at his feet, is the site of Saturday story-telling hours during summer.

At the brick neo-Victorian **Loeb Boathouse** on the park's 18-acre Lake, you can rent a rowboat, kayak, or a bicycle as well as ride in an authentic Venetian gondola. The attached café is a worthy pit stop.

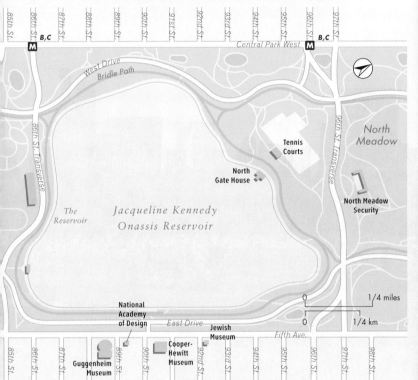

IN FOCUS CENTRAL PARK

9

Designed to resemble upstate New York's Adirondack Mountain region, the **Ramble** covers 38 acres and is laced with twisting, climbing paths. This is prime bird-watching territory, since it's a rest stop along a major migratory route and a shelter for many of the more than 230 species of birds that have been sighted in the park; bring your binoculars. Because the Ramble is so dense and isolated,

however, don't wander here alone, or after dark. Head south through the Ramble and you'll come to the beautiful cast-iron **Bow Bridge**, spanning part of the Lake between the Ramble and Bethesda Fountain. From the center of the bridge, you can get a sweeping view of the park as well as of the apartment buildings on both the East Side and the West Side.

North of the Ramble atop Vista Rock, **Belvedere Castle** is the second-highest natural point in the park. If you can't get tickets for Delacorte Theater, you can climb to one of the castle's

(from left to right) Belvedere means "beautiful view" in Italian, a clue to why we climb to the top of Belvedere Castle; Birders, photographers, and couples of all ages are drawn to Bow Bridge; Red-eared slider turtles frolic in Turtle Pond, at the base of Belvedere Castle.

three terraces and look down on the stage. You'll also get a fantastic view of the Great Lawn—it's particularly beautiful during the fall foliage months—and of the park's myriad bird visitors. Since 1919 the castle has served as a U.S. Weather Bureau station, and meteorological instruments are set on top of the tower. If you enter the Castle from the lower level, you can visit the Henry Luce Nature Observa-tory, which has nature exhibits, children's workshops, and educational programs.

Somewhat hidden behind Belvedere Castle, **Shakespeare Garden** is an informal jumble of flowers, trees, and pathways, inspired by the flora mentioned in Shakespeare's plays and poetry. Bronze plaques throughout the garden bear the bard's lines mentioning the plants.

The Great Lawn hums with action on weekends, on warm days, and on most summer evenings, when its baseball fields and picnic grounds fill with city folks and visitors alike. Its 13 acres have endured millions of footsteps, thousands of ball games, hundreds of downpours, dozens of concerts, fireworks displays, and even a papal mass. On a beautiful day, everyone seems to be here.

Chancing upon the 70-ft-tall **Cleopatra's Needle** always feels a bit serendipitous and delightfully jarring, even to the most cynical New Yorkers. This weathered hieroglyphic-covered obelisk began life in Heliopolis, Egypt, around 1500 BC, but has only a little to do with Cleopatra—it's just New York's nickname for the work. It was eventually carted off to Alexandria by the Romans in 12 BC, and

it landed here on January 22, 1881, when the khedive of Egypt made it a gift to the city.

At the southwest corner of the Great Lawn is the fan-shaped **Delacorte Theater**, home to the summer Shakespeare in the Park festival.

If you want to take in several sites in a single brisk jaunt, consider walking the **Naturalists' Walk**. On this path you can wind your way

toward the Swedish Cottage, the Shakespeare Garden, and Belvedere Castle on a landscaped nature

(top, from left to right) A female Canada goose and goslings on Turtle Pond; Cyclists make good use of the bike paths; Bikers as well as joggers boost their egos by outpacing the hansom carriages; Racing boats at Conservatory Water (center) In the 1930s, a flock of mutant sheep was evicted from what would later be known as Sheep Meadow.

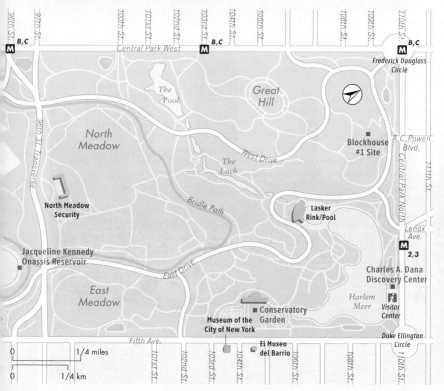

walk with spectacular rock outcrops, a stream that attracts bird life, a woodland area with various native trees, stepping-stone trails, and, thankfully, benches.

North of the Great Lawn and the 86th Street transverse is a popular gathering place for New Yorkers and visitors alike, the **Jacqueline Kennedy Onassis Reservoir**. Rain or shine, you'll see runners of all ages and paces heading counterclockwise around the 1.58-mi cinder path that encircles the water. The path in turn is surrounded by hundreds of trees that burst into color in the spring and fall. The 106-acre reservoir, finished in 1862, was a source of fresh water for Manhattanites. It holds more than a billion gallons, but it's no longer used for drinking water; the city's main reservoirs are upstate. From the top of the stairs at 90th Street just off 5th Avenue you have a 360-degree panorama of the city's exciting skyscrapers and often-brilliant sunsets. On the south side, there are benches so you can rest and recharge.

FROM THE RESERVOIR TO 110TH ST.

 More locals than tourists know about the wilder-looking, less-crowded northern part of Central Park, and there are hidden gems lurking here that enable even the most tightly wound among us to decompress, at least for a short while.

Walking along Fifth Avenue to 105th Street, you'll see a magnificent wrought-iron gate—once part of the 5th Avenue mansion of Cornelius Vanderbilt II—that marks the entrance to the **Conservatory Garden**. As you walk through it, you enter a different world, a quiet place that's positively idyllic for reading and slowing down. The Italian-style Central Garden is a beauty, with an expansive lawn, a strikingly simple fountain, and a wisteria-draped pergola that just oozes romance.

The French-inspired **North Garden** is a colorful place with plants placed into elaborate patterns. Springtime is magical—thousands of tulips come to life in a circle around the garden's striking Untermyer Fountain and its three bronze dancers; in the fall, chrysanthemums take their place. The English-style **South Garden** conjures up images from the classic children's book *The Secret Garden*. The garden is a beautiful hodgepodge of trees, bushes, and flowers that bloom year-round. A free tour is conducted on Saturday at 11 AM, from April through October.

At **Harlem Meer**, the third-largest body of water in Central Park, you can borrow fishing poles (identification required) from mid-April through October and try your hand at catching (and releasing) the largemouth bass, catfish, golden shiners, and bluegills that are stocked in the water's 11 acres. You can also learn about the upper park's geography, ecology, and history at the Victorian-style Charles A. Dana Discovery Center.

Although only a shell of this stone building remains, **Blockhouse #1** serves as a historical marker: the structure was built in 1814 as a cliffside fortification against the British. The area is deserted and dense with trees, so go as a group here, and avoid it at night.

(left) A pensive raccoon in the park's northern reaches (center); Indulging in a park favorite, soccer, near East Meadow (right); A jogger makes her counterclockwise progress along the Reservoir.

CONTACT INFORMATION

Central Park Conservancy
☎ 212/310–6600
🌐 www.centralparknyc.org

Central Park SummerStage
☎ 212/360–2756
🌐 www.summerstage.org

Central Park Wildlife Center (Central Park Zoo)
☎ 212/439–6500
🌐 www.centralparkzoo.org

Central Park Visitor Centers
☎ 212/794–6564
🌐 www.nycgovparks.org

Charles A. Dana Discovery Center
☎ 212/860–1370

Delacorte Theater
☎ 212/539–8500
🌐 www.publictheater.org

Loeb Boathouse, Boathouse Restaurant
☎ 212/517–2233
🌐 www.thecentral parkboathouse.com

Swedish Cottage Marionette Theatre
☎ 212/988–9093

Wollman Memorial Rink
☎ 212/439–6900
🌐 www.wollmanskating rink.com

PALE MALE: IF YOU CAN MAKE IT HERE . . .

Telescoping the nest from within the park; Pale Male returns home; watching the brood like a hawk; Pale Male's progeny.

From 1993 to 2004, the red-tailed hawk Pale Male sired and raised 23 offspring in a nest on the 12th floor of 927 Fifth Avenue. Despite his upscale digs, life wasn't always easy. He's lost mates (current partner Lola is his fourth), eggs, chicks, and even his home. In 2004, the co-op trashed Pale Male and Lola's nest and blocked their return. Under pressure from the news media and protesters (some holding signs that urged passing drivers to "Honk-4-Hawks"), the board relented less than a month later. A platform was installed to hold the nest, and Pale Male and Lola returned and began to rebuild, although their eggs had trouble hatching. The privileged bird's fame continues to grow: the film *The Legend of Pale Male*, which premiered in 2010, revealed that New Yorkers were big softies at heart while telling his tale.

The Upper West Side

WORD OF MOUTH

". . . we stopped in at Zabar's Cafe, which was fun. It's a tiny place, and the one long table that everyone shares made it easy to eavesdrop on the other people there. I felt like I got a peek (and listen) at how the locals live, which was fun for me. The food was good, too."

—Traveler_A

GETTING ORIENTED

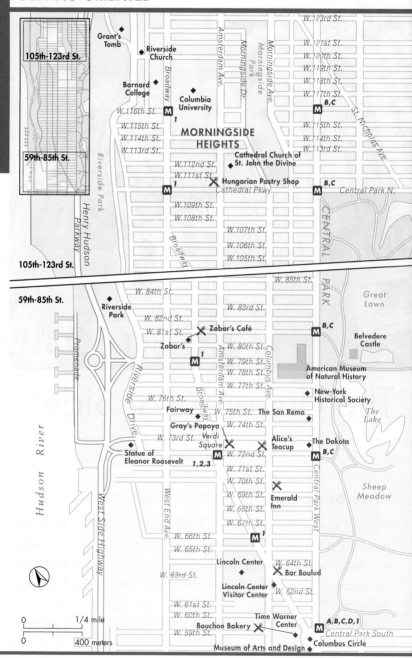

105th–123rd St.

59th–85th St.

Grant's Tomb
Riverside Church
Barnard College
Columbia University
Broadway
Amsterdam Ave.
Morningside Park
Morningside Dr.
Morningside Ave.
W. 123rd St.
W. 121st St.
W. 120th St.
W. 119th St.
W. 118th St.
W. 117th St.
W. 116th St.
W. 115th St.
W. 114th St.
W. 113rd St.
B,C
St. Nicholas Ave.
W. 115th St.
W. 114th St.
W. 113rd St.

MORNINGSIDE HEIGHTS

Cathedral Church of St. John the Divine
W. 112nd St.
W. 111st St.
Hungarian Pastry Shop
Cathedral Pkwy.
W. 109th St.
W. 108th St.
W. 107th St.
W. 106th St.
W. 105th St.
B,C
Central Park N.
Broadway
CENTRAL PARK

Riverside Park
Henry Hudson Parkway

105th–123rd St.

59th–85th St.

Riverside Park
W. 84th St.
W. 85th St.
W. 83rd St.
W. 82nd St.
W. 81st St.
Zabar's Café
Zabar's
W. 80th St.
W. 79th St.
W. 78th St.
W. 77th St.
B,C
Great Lawn
Belvedere Castle
American Museum of Natural History
New-York Historical Society
The Lake
Amsterdam Ave.
Columbus Ave.

Promenade
Riverside Drive
W. 76th St.
Fairway
W. 75th St. The San Remo
Gray's Papaya
Verdi Square
W. 73rd St.
Statue of Eleanor Roosevelt
W. 74th St.
Alice's Teacup
W. 72nd St.
1,2,3
The Dakota
B,C
Central Park West
Broadway
West End Ave.
Hudson River
West Side Highway

W. 71st St.
W. 70th St.
W. 69th St.
Emerald Inn
W. 68th St.
W. 67th St.
W. 66th St.
W. 65th St.
Sheep Meadow

Lincoln Center
W. 64th St.
Bar Boulud
W. 63rd St.
Lincoln Center Visitor Center
W. 62nd St.
W. 61st St.
W. 60th St.
Time Warner Center
Bouchon Bakery
W. 59th St.
Museum of Arts and Design
A,B,C,D,1
Central Park South
Columbus Circle

0   1/4 mile
0   400 meters

MAKING THE MOST OF YOUR TIME

Broadway is hands down the most walkable and interesting thoroughfare on the Upper West Side, largely because of its broad sidewalks and aggressive mix of retail stores, restaurants, and apartment buildings. If you head north from the Lincoln Center area (around 65th Street) to about 81st Street (about 1 mi), you'll get a feel for the neighborhood's local color, particularly above 72nd Street. Up here you'll encounter residents of every conceivable age and ethnicity either shambling or sprinting (New Yorkers wouldn't know a medium pace if they tripped over it, quite literally), street vendors hawking used and newish books, and such beloved landmarks as the 72nd Street subway station, the Beacon Theater, the produce mecca Fairway (the cause of perhaps the most perpetually congested block), and Zabar's, a food spot that launches a memorable assault on all five of your senses—and your wallet.

Should you venture farther uptown, you'll encounter a high concentration of apartments and the families that complain about outgrowing them, along with a smattering of decent and enduring restaurants. If you're intrigued by having the city's only Ivy League school close at hand, hop the 1 train to 116th Street and emerge on the east side of the street, which puts you smack in front of Columbia University and its Graduate School of Journalism. Pass through the gates and up the walk for a look at a cluster of buildings so elegant you'll understand why it's an iconic N.Y.C. setting.

GETTING HERE

The A, B, C, D, and 1 subway lines will take you to Columbus Circle. From there, the B and C lines run along Central Park, stopping at 72nd, 81st, 86th, 96th, 103rd, and 110th streets. The 1 train runs up Broadway, making local stops at 66th, 72nd, 79th, 86th, 96th, 103rd, 110th, 116th, and 125th streets. The 2 and 3 trains, which also go along Broadway, stop at 72nd and 96th.

FODOR'S CHOICE

Cathedral Church of St. John the Divine

Central Park (⇨ *Chapter 9*)

Lincoln Center

TOP EXPERIENCES

Walking along Broadway—and stopping to sit on a bench in its median or a chair in the pedestrian-only sections that run along it

Grabbing lox and cream cheese and a cup of coffee at Zabar's

Strolling through Riverside Park past the boat basin

Standing below the gigantic blue whale at the Museum of Natural History

Watching performers and students rushing to rehearsals and classes at Lincoln Center

Taking in the Gothic mood of the Cathedral of St. John the Divine

Standing in awe at Grant's Tomb

WHAT'S NEARBY (⇨ *Ch. 9*)

Central Park (⇨ *Chapter 14*)

American Museum of Natural History

Museum of Art and Design

New-York Historical Society

10

Updated by
John Rambow

Residents of the Upper West Side will proudly tell you that they live in one of the last real neighborhoods in the city. That's highly debatable, but people actually do know their neighbors in this primarily residential section of Manhattan, and away from the high-rent stretches of Broadway, some small owner-operated businesses still flourish.

The Upper West Side is one of the city's quieter hoods, with a much slower pace than most other areas of the city. And it's for that reason—along with a large and somewhat more affordable housing stock—that families choose to live here.

On weekends, stroller-pushing parents cram sidewalks along the wide avenues, shuttling their kids to soccer practice and birthday parties. Shoppers jam gourmet food emporiums such as **Zabar's** and **Fairway**, and other specialty stores along **Broadway** and **Columbus Avenue**.

Side streets are tree-lined, with high stoops leading up to stately brownstones straight out of Woody Allen films. The area has traditionally had a sizeable Jewish community, and so on the Sabbath large families can be seen walking to and from one of the Upper West Side's many synagogues. And everyone, no matter the season or time of day, enjoys **Central Park** and **Riverside Park**, two of the neighborhood's communal backyards.

The Upper West Side also has its share of cultural institutions, from the stunning buildings that sit on the 16-acre **Lincoln Center** complex, to the impressive collection at the **New-York Historical Society** to Columbus Circle's **Museum of Art and Design** to the much-loved **American Museum of Natural History**.

Most people think the area north of 106th Street and south of 125th Street on the West Side is just an extension of the Upper West Side. But technically it's called **Morningside Heights**, and it's largely dominated by **Columbia University**, along with a cluster of academic, religious, and medical institutions—Barnard College, St. Luke's Hospital, and the **Cathedral of St. John the Divine**, to name a few.

Within the gates of the Columbia or Barnard campuses or inside the hushed St. John the Divine, New York City takes on a different character. This is an *uptown* student neighborhood—less hip than the Village, but friendly, fun, and intellectual.

TOP TOURING EXPERIENCES

LIVE LIKE A NEW YORKER

The upper 70s and lower 80s of the Upper West Side present a very livable, bourgeois New York. Families and young couples settled here, attracted to the peaceful side streets and broad avenues combined with the best accessories of urban living: museums and performance centers, plentiful stores, restaurants, gourmet markets, and parks.

You could shop and eat your way up and down this stretch of Broadway and Columbus Avenue for hours, turning along tree-lined side streets of gorgeous brownstones. Museum lovers should stroll right up Central Park West—passing the **Dakota** and other elegant residences—to reach the **New-York Historical Society** and the **American Museum of Natural History.** Need a rest? Go for a spot of tea at **Alice's Teacup** (⊠ *102 W. 73rd St.* ☎ *212/799–3006*) or assemble a picnic from what some say is the city's best gourmet market and place to get a bagel and lox, **Zabar's** (⊠ *80th St. at Broadway*), and take it to **Central Park** or farther west to **Riverside Park.**

TAKE A TRIP UPTOWN

Feeling a world away (actually, only 50 blocks) from the hustle of Midtown, much of Morningside Heights moves at the scholarly pace of its many schools, including **Columbia University** and **Barnard College.**

Both campuses have beautiful buildings, but the area's architectural winner is the **Cathedral Church of St. John the Divine,** the world's largest Gothic-style cathedral. And when you get hungry, well . . . with students come great cheap eats: peruse a local newspaper at an old-school diner, or sample the authentic Mexican and South American cooking on Amsterdam Avenue.

ENJOY A LITTLE NIGHT MUSIC

Have a night on the town without heading south of Central Park. The Upper West Side is New York's epicenter of the performing arts, especially classical music. The acoustic star is **Lincoln Center** (⇨ *Chapter 15*), a 16-acre collective of concert halls and other institutions (including Juilliard) that draws the world's greatest musicians, dancers, and other performers. In 2009 the center finished major renovations, making the complex much more a part of the neighborhood. Its sparkling main plaza (⊠ *W. 63rd St. at Columbus Ave., Upper West Side*), with its gorgeous and dramatic fountain, is a thrilling place to wander through.

Sharing the neighborhood's energetic vibe are the busy Columbus Circle destinations, **the Museum of Art and Design** (⇨ *Chapter 14*), and the 55-story **Time Warner Center.** The skyscraper complex, essentially a supercharged mall, includes a great collection of shops, Jazz at Lincoln Center, and a blue-chip lineup of restaurants, including **Per Se, Masa,** and **Porter House New York.**

10

And the area around Lincoln Center isn't the only place to find star turns on the Upper West Side. **Symphony Space**, at Broadway and 95th Street, is famed for its "Selected Shorts" reading series as well as other events, and the jazz club **Cleopatra's Needle**, a few blocks away, is an institution.

TOP ATTRACTIONS

Fodor's Choice
★

Cathedral Church of St. John the Divine. The largest Gothic-style cathedral in the world, even with its towers and transepts still unfinished, this divine behemoth comfortably asserts its bulk in the country's most vertical city.

The seat of the Episcopal diocese in New York, it acts as a sanctuary for all, giving special services that include a celebration of New York's gay and lesbian community as well as the annual Blessing of the Bikes, when cyclists of all faiths bring their wheels for a holy-water benediction. The cathedral hosts **musical performances** (⊕ *www.stjohndivine. org*) and has held funerals and memorial services for such artists as Duke Ellington, Jim Henson, George Balanchine, James Baldwin, and Alvin Ailey. Reopened at the end of 2008 after a 2001 fire left it damaged, the church now looks newly scrubbed and magnificent.

Built in two long spurts starting in 1892, the cathedral remains only two-thirds complete. What began as a Romanesque-Byzantine structure under the original architects George Heins and Christopher Grant Lafarge shifted (upon Heins's death in 1911) to French Gothic under the direction of Gothic Revival purist Ralph Adams Cram. You can spot the juxtaposition of the two medieval styles by comparing the finished Gothic arches, which are pointed, with the still-uncovered arches, which are rounded in the Byzantine style.

To get the full effect of the cathedral's size, approach it from Broadway on West 112th Street. Above the 3-ton central bronze doors is the intricately carved **Portal of Paradise,** which depicts St. John witnessing the Transfiguration of Jesus, and 32 biblical characters. Then step inside to the cavernous nave. More than 600 feet long, it holds some 5,000 worshippers, and the 162-foot-tall dome crossing could comfortably contain the Statue of Liberty (minus its pedestal). Turn around to see the **Great Rose Window,** made from more than 10,000 pieces of colored glass, the largest stained-glass window in the United States.

At the end of the nave, surrounding the altar, are seven chapels expressing the cathedral's interfaith tradition and international mission—with menorahs, Shinto vases, and dedications to various ethnic groups. The **Saint Saviour Chapel** contains a three-panel bronze altar in white-gold leaf with religious scenes by artist Keith Haring (his last work before he died in 1990).

Outside, in the cathedral's south grounds, don't miss the eye-catching **Peace Fountain.** It depicts the struggle of good and evil in the form of the archangel Michael decapitating Satan, whose head hangs from one side. Encircling it are whimsical animals cast in bronze from pieces sculpted by children.

On the first Sunday of October the Cathedral Church of St. John the Divine is truly a zoo. In honor of St. Francis of Assisi, the patron saint of animals, the church holds its usual Sunday service with a twist: the service is attended by men, women, children, dogs, cats, rabbits, hamsters, and the occasional horse, sheep, or ant farm. In past years upward of 3,500 New Yorkers have shown up to have their pets blessed. A procession is led by such guest animals as elephants, camels, llamas, and golden eagles. Seats are first-come, first-served for this popular event, so come at least an hour ahead of time. ⊠ *1047 Amsterdam Ave., at W. 112th St., Morningside Heights* ☏ *212/316–7540* ⊕ *www.stjohndivine. org* ⊠ *Tours $6* ☾ *Mon.–Sat. 7–6, Sun. 7–7; tours Tues.–Sat. at 11 and 1, Sun. at 2. A vertical tour with a climb of 124 feet to the top is given on Sat. at noon and 2 (reservations required; $15). Sun. services at 8, 9, 11, 1, and 4* Ⓜ *1 to 110th St./Cathedral Pkwy.*

Fodor's Choice **Central Park.** (⇨ *Chapter 9*)

★ **Columbus Circle.** This busy traffic circle at Central Park's southwest corner anchors the Upper West Side and makes a good starting place for exploring the neighborhood if you're coming from south of 59th Street. The central 700-ton granite monument (capped by a marble statue of Christopher Columbus) serves as a popular meeting place.

To the west looms the **Time Warner Center** (☏ *212/823–6300* ⊕ *www. shopsatcolumbuscircle.com*), its 80-story twin glass towers designed by skyscraper architect David M. Childs. The concave front of its lower floors envelops Columbus Circle's curve, and the upper towers mirror the angle of Broadway and the lines of the city's street grid.

Its first three floors and basement house stores that include Whole Foods (good for a quick bite), Sephora, Williams-Sonoma, Borders, and Coach. The third and fourth floors have restaurants, including Masa, an outrageously priced and acclaimed sushi restaurant (a meal for two starts at $900); plus A Voce; and Thomas Keller's famed (and also costly) Per Se as well as his takeout-friendly Bouchon Bakery.

Above are luxury condos, offices, and the Mandarin Oriental Hotel, whose restaurant and beautiful lobby bar (on the 35th floor) make a bird's-eye perch for surveying the city below. The performing arts center **Jazz at Lincoln Center** (⊕ *www.jalc.org*) is also in the complex.

10

Just north of Columbus Circle, the **Trump International Hotel and Tower** fills the wedge of land between Central Park West and Broadway; it's home to the self-named Jean Georges restaurant, where the celebrity chef works his culinary magic.

On the circle's south side, at 2 Columbus Circle, is the former Huntington Hartford building, built in 1964 from the owner's A&P fortune. In 2008 it reopened as the new home of the **Museum of Arts and Design** (⇨ *Chapter 14*) after extensive renovation that clad its exterior in lots of zigzags and narrow slits of glass. Ⓜ *A, B, C, D, 1 to 59 St./ Columbus Circle.*

Fodor's Choice **Lincoln Center.** This massive travertine-clad complex contains Avery ★ Fisher Hall, the Juilliard School, the New York City Ballet, and the Film Center of Lincoln Center, making it one of the most concentrated

Where can I find . . . ?

COFFEE	Hungarian Pastry Shop (1030 Amsterdam Ave.) Encourages lingering over a Danish with the Columbia kids. If there's room.	Zabar's Café (2245 Broadway, at 80th St.) Brewed with the beans from their store next door.
A QUICK BITE	Bouchon Bakery (10 Columbus Circle, Time Warner Center, 3rd fl.) Boulangerie sandwiches and macaroons.	Gray's Papaya (2090 Broadway, at 72nd St.) Hot-dog gods. Go to the counter and say, "Two with everything, medium papaya."
COCKTAILS	Emerald Inn (205 Columbus Ave., at 69th St.) Longtime neighborhood Irish bar near Lincoln Center.	Bar Boulud (1900 Broadway, bet. 63rd and 64th Sts.) Elegant wine bar/bistro.

places for the performing arts in the nation. Its 16-acre campus was built over the course of several years, from 1962 to 1969.

Renovations that were done to celebrate its recent 50th anniversary season included remodeling centerpiece of the plaza, the Revson Fountain, as well as the completely transformed Alice Tully Hall, which has won accolades from critics for its design. Its largest hall, the Metropolitan Opera House, is notable for its dramatic arched entrance as well as its lobby's immense chandeliers and Marc Chagall paintings, both of which can be seen from outside.

To get oriented, head to the David Rubenstein Atrium on Broadway between 62nd and 63rd streets. There you can get schedules and buy tickets (there's a special TKTS-like booth for same-day tickets at 25%–50% off full price). In addition to having free Wi-Fi, a sandwich shop, and lots of seating, the Atrium is the site for free performances every Thursday at 8:30 pm. ⊠ W. 62nd to W. 66th Sts., Broadway to Amsterdam Ave., Upper West Side Ⓜ 1 to 66th St. ☎ 212/546–2656 ⊕ www. lincolncenter.org.

WORTH NOTING

Columbia University. Wealthy, private, and Ivy League, New York's first college has a pedigree that has always attracted students. But for a visitor, the why-go resides within its campus, bucolic and quietly energetic at once.

The main entrance is at 116th Street and Broadway, site of the Columbia Graduate School of Journalism. To your left is the Miller Theater (⊕ www.millertheater.com), which brings an impressive roster of classical and early-music performers to the school. After walking past the "J-School" on your right, follow the herringbone-pattern brick pathway of College Walk to the main quadrangle, the focal point for campus life. (When you eventually leave, exit through the quad's south gate to

West 114th Street's Frat Row, where brownstones housing Columbia's frats display quirky signs of collegiate pride.)

Dominating the quad's south side is **Butler Library** (1934), modeled after the Roman Pantheon, which holds the bulk of the university's 8 million books. Looking north, you'll see **Low Memorial Library**, its steps presided over by Daniel Chester French's statue *Alma Mater*. Low is one of the few buildings you can enter (on weekdays), to check out the former Reading Room and marble rotunda, to pick up a map, or to take a campus tour at the **visitor center**. (Alternatively, you can visit Columbia's Web site ahead of time for a podcast and map covering architectural highlights.)

North of the quad (near a cast bronze of August Rodin's *Thinker*) is the interdenominational **St. Paul's Chapel,** an exquisite little Byzantine-style dome church with salmon-color Guastavino tile vaulting inside. This same design can be seen in Grand Central Terminal and many other buildings throughout the city. Right across Broadway from Columbia's main gate lies the brick-and-limestone campus of women-only **Barnard College** (☎ *212/854–2014*), which also gives tours. ⊠ *Morningside Heights* ☎ *212/854–4900* ⊕ *www.columbia.edu* ☻ *Visitor center weekdays 9–5. Tours begin at 1 weekdays from Room 213, Low Library* Ⓜ *1 to 116th St./Columbia University.*

The Dakota. One of the first residences built on the Upper West Side, the château-style Dakota (1884) remains an architectural fixture with its lovely gables, gaslights, copper turrets, and a central courtyard. Celebrity residents have included Boris Karloff, Rudolf Nureyev, José Ferrer, Rosemary Clooney, Lauren Bacall, Leonard Bernstein, Gilda Radner, and Connie Chung, but none more famous than John Lennon, who in 1980 was shot and killed at the Dakota's gate by a deranged fan. Yoko Ono and their son, Sean, still live there. ⊠ *1 W. 72nd St., at Central Park W, Upper West Side* Ⓜ *B, C to 72nd St.*

Grant's Tomb (*General Grant National Memorial*). Walk through upper Riverside Park and you're sure to notice this towering granite mausoleum (1897), the final resting place of Civil War general and two-term president Ulysses S. Grant and his wife, Julia Dent Grant. But who's buried here, as the old joke goes? Nobody—they're *entombed* in a crypt beneath a domed rotunda, surrounded by photographs and Grant memorabilia.

Once a more popular sight than the Statue of Liberty, this pillared Classical Revival edifice feels more like a relic of yesteryear, but it remains a moving tribute. The words engraved on the tomb, "Let Us Have Peace," recall Grant's speech to the Republican convention upon his presidential nomination.

Surrounding the memorial are the so-called "rolling benches," which are swoopy and covered with colorful mosaic tiles that bring to mind the works of architect Antonio Gaudí's Parque Güell, in Barcelona. Made in the 1970s as a public art project, they are now as beloved as they are incongruous with the grand memorial they surround. ⊠ *Riverside Dr. at W. 122nd St., Morningside Heights* ☎ *212/666–1640*

10

⊕ *www.nps.gov/gegr* ⬚ *Free* ⊘ *Daily 9–5; 20-min tours at 10, noon, 2, and 4* Ⓜ *1 to 116th St. St.*

Riverside Church. This enormous, 21-story church, built by John D. Rockefeller Jr. in 1930, has stained-glass windows and other Gothic touches that were modeled on those on the cathedral at Chartres, France. Its nearly 400-foot tower, which is primarily given over to office space, is a local landmark. ⊠ *Main entrance at 91 Claremont Ave., 490 Riverside Dr., between W. 120th and W. 122nd Sts., Morningside Heights* ☎ *212/870–6700* ⊕ *www.theriversidechurchny.org* ⬚ *Free* ⊘ *Daily 7 am to 10 pm* Ⓜ *1 to 116th St.*

☺ **Riverside Park.** Walking around concrete and skyscrapers all day, you can easily miss the expansive waterfront park just blocks away. Riverside Park—which along with the Riverside Park South extension runs along the Hudson from 58th to 156th streets—dishes out a dose of tranquillity.

Its original sections, designed by Frederick Law Olmsted and Calvert Vaux of Central Park fame and laid out between 1873 and 1888, are outshone by Olmsted's "other" park. But with its waterfront bike and walking paths and lighter crowds, Riverside Park holds its own.

One of the park's loveliest attributes is a half-mile path along the waterfront, a rare spot in Manhattan where you can walk right along the river's edge. Reach it entering the park at West 72nd Street and Riverside Drive (look for the **statue of Eleanor Roosevelt**) and then heading through an underpass beneath the West Side Highway.

Head north along the Hudson River, past the **79th Street Boat Basin,** where you can watch a flotilla of houseboats bobbing in the water. Above it, a ramp leads to the **Rotunda,** home in summer to the Boat Basin Café, an open-air, dog-friendly spot for a burger, a beer, and river views.

Leave the riverside path near 92nd Street by taking another underpass and then heading up the path on the right. The **91st Street Garden,** planted by community gardeners, explodes with flowers in most seasons. To the south, cresting a hill along Riverside Drive at West 89th Street, stands the Civil War **Soldiers' and Sailors' Monument** (1902), an imposing 96-foot-high circle of white-marble columns designed by Paul M. Duboy, who also designed the Ansonia Hotel. ⊠ *W. 72nd to W. 156th Sts. between Riverside Dr. and Hudson River, Upper West Side* ⊕ Ⓜ *1, 2, 3 to 72nd St.*

The San Remo. You're likely to notice its twin towers rising above the trees in Central Park, looking like the fairy-tale spires of some urban palace, which it more or less is. Rita Hayworth, Paul Simon, Tiger Woods, and Steven Spielberg are among the celebrities who've resided in the 1930 building's giant apartments.

At their peaks, the towers recede into circular columned Greek temples (modeled after the cathedral in Seville, Spain). They make a useful "compass" if you get disoriented in Central Park and want to know which way is west. ⊠ *145 Central Park W, between W. 74th and W. 75th Sts., Upper West Side* Ⓜ *B, C to 72nd St.*

Harlem

WORD OF MOUTH

"Memorial [Baptist] Church is very small and had a wonderfully intimate feeling even if it was 'wired for sound'! The gospel music service was excellent—audience participation [was] encouraged in the form of standing and clapping. A really good choir made it all the better. We were ushered out after an hour and this would have emptied the church by about half. We were certainly made to feel very welcome and not intrusive. We're glad we went."

—mazj

GETTING ORIENTED

Morris-Jumel Mansion
W. 155th St.

Hispanic Society of America

409 Edgecombe Avenue
W. 153rd St.

Sugar Hill
W. 152nd St.

Highbridge Park

B,D

W. 151st St.

W. 150th St.

W. 149th St.

W. 148th St.

W. 147th St.

W. 146th St.

W. 145th St.

HAMILTON HEIGHTS
W. 144th St.

Hamilton Terrace

W. 140th St.

Hamilton Grange

City College
W. 138th St.

Strivers' Row
W. 139th St.

Abyssinian Baptist Church
W. 137th St.

ST. NICHOLAS HISTORIC DISTRICT
W. 136th St.

B,C

E. 135th St.

W. 135th St.

W. 133rd St.

W. 129th St.

W. 128th St.

W. 127th St.

Apollo Theatre
W. 126th St.

A,B,C,D

African Sq.

Hue-Man Bookstore & Cafe

Studio Museum in Harlem
W. 124th St.

Dr. Martin Luther King Jr. Blvd. (125th St.)

2,3

125th St. Metro North Station

Uptown Juice Bar

Lenox Lounge
W. 123rd St.

Grant's Tomb
W. 121st St.

HARLEM

Marcus Garvey Park

Patisserie des Ambassades

Barnard College

Columbia University
W. 116th St.

Make My Cake

Canaan Baptist Church of Christ

B,C

Native

Amy Ruth's

2,3

Minton's Playhouse

Malcolm Shabazz Harlem Market

First Corinthian Baptist Church

Masjid Malcolm Shabazz

Cathedral Church of St. John the Divine
W. 113th St. **67 Orange St.**

B,C
W. 111th St.

2,3

Miss Mamie's Spoonbread Too

Central Park North

E. 110th St.

CENTRAL PARK

Harlem Meer

THE BRONX

145 St. Bridge

Harlem River

Madison Ave. Bridge

0   1/4 mile

0   400 meters

MAKING THE MOST OF YOUR TIME

One enduring simple pleasure in Harlem is its terrific architecture: take a little time to walk the areas around Strivers' Row, Hamilton Heights, and 116th Street for some impressive and often fanciful brownstone. While you're at it, visit the Studio Museum in Harlem, which showcases contemporary works of Harlem's artist community, or the Morris-Jumel Mansion, for a trip back to colonial New York.

GETTING HERE AND AROUND

The 2 and 3 subway lines stop on Lenox Avenue; the 1 goes along Broadway, to the west; and the A, B, C, and D trains travel along St. Nicholas and 8th avenues. And yes, as the song goes, the A train is still usually "the quickest way to Harlem."

The city's north–south avenues take on different names in Harlem: 6th Avenue is called both Malcolm X Boulevard *and* Lenox Avenue ; 7th Avenue is Adam Clayton Powell Jr. Boulevard (it's named for the influential minister and congressman); and 8th Avenue is Frederick Douglass Boulevard. West 125th Street, the major east–west street and Harlem's commercial center, is sometimes called Dr. Martin Luther King Jr. Boulevard.

SAFETY

In the past two decades Harlem's crime rate has decreased far below the heights it reached in the 1980s. Like everywhere else in New York, however, you should still use common sense. Stay close to main commercial areas like 125th Street and Lenox Avenue if you visit at night.

WORD OF MOUTH (WWW.FODORS.COM/FORUMS)

"You can go by yourself to a gospel service, or BB King's in Times Square has a gospel brunch with the Harlem Gospel choir on Sundays." —mclaurie

TOP EXPERIENCES

Attending a gospel service at one of the many Baptist churches

Grooving to a jazz session at Lenox Lounge

Indulging in a soul-food lunch or dinner

Seeing the historic Apollo Theater

Taking a stroll along 125th Street

Walking around Hamilton Heights, Strivers' Row, or Sugar Hill to see elegant brownstones

WHAT'S NEARBY

Hispanic Society of America (⇨ Ch. 14)

Studio Museum in Harlem (⇨ Ch. 14)

Apollo Theater (⇨ Ch. 15)

Amy Ruth's (⇨ Ch. 15)

Miss Mamie's Spoonbread Too (⇨ Ch. 18)

Native (⇨ Ch. 18)

Sightseeing
★★★

Nightlife
★★

Dining
★★★

Lodging
★

Shopping
★

Harlem is known throughout the world as a center of African-American culture, music, and life. Today many renovated and new buildings join such historic jewels as the Apollo Theatre, architecturally splendid churches, and cultural magnets like the Studio Museum in Harlem and the Schomburg Center for Research in Black Culture.

Updated by
John Rambow

As overcrowded apartments and expensive rents downtown make Harlem a more and more attractive area, black and white professionals and young families are restoring many of Harlem's classic brownstone and limestone buildings. This new growth has brought much new life and commerce to the community, but it has also priced out some longtime residents.

Back in 2001, former president Bill Clinton's selection of 55 West 125th Street as the site of his New York office was an inspiration to businesses considering a move to Harlem; now the busy thoroughfare sprouts outposts of Starbucks, Old Navy, MAC Cosmetics, and H&M side by side with local restaurants and clothing stores, including a smattering of boutiques.

Outside, the sidewalk is a continuous traffic jam of people, offering a concentrated glimpse of neighborhood life. Pedestrians compete with street-side hawkers selling bootleg DVDs, books, and homemade essential oils in nondescript bottles.

TOP TOURING EXPERIENCES

FIND RELIGION IN HARLEM

Some of Harlem's most interesting religious buildings—especially its Baptist churches—stand on 116th Street, particularly between St. Nicholas Avenue and Lenox (Malcolm X) Boulevard. Admire the ornate theatrical facade of the giant **First Corinthian Baptist Church** or fill your soul with the mellifluous gospel music of the **Canaan Baptist Church of Christ's** choir during a Sunday service. Take a hint from the parishioners and follow up with the smothered chicken and waffles at **Amy Ruth's**, at 113 W.

11

116th. After lunch, walk by the green-domed **Masjid Malcolm Shabazz**—a mosque attended primarily by West Africans and African-Americans. Finish at **Malcolm Shabazz Harlem Market** to stock up on African jewelry, masks, crafts, and caftans at good prices. On Saturday, the jazz players jam at the market from 1:30 to 3.

RELIVE THE JAZZ AGE

Many of Harlem's historic jazz venues (found mostly on 125th Street) are still active, so pay respect to the legends like Duke Ellington and Louis Armstrong, then listen to one of their musical heirs. A giant digital marquee announces the **Apollo Theatre**, where jazz and funk godfather James Brown debuted in 1956 and was laid out in splendor after his death in 2006. (Following this tradition, king of pop Michael Jackson was also given a final farewell here in 2009.)

Around the corner, the **Lenox Lounge** (⊠ *288 Lenox Ave., at W. 125th St.*) is a trip back in time. Continue the pilgrimage at **Minton's Playhouse** (⊠ *206 W. 118th St.*), the birthplace of bebop, where Thelonious Monk was house pianist in the 1940s. It reopened in 2006 after being closed since 1974. If you're here on Thursday or Friday, when exhibits are open until 9 pm, check out the contemporary African-American–oriented artworks at the **Studio Museum in Harlem**.

HUNT THE GHOSTS OF THE HARLEM RENAISSANCE

Take the subway up to the 140s and lower 150s (between Edgecombe and Convent avenues) and find yourself on a rocky bluff above lower Harlem. Here, in the enclaves of **Sugar Hill** and **Hamilton Heights**, the Harlem elite in the early 1900s could literally "look down " on their neighbors. Some blocks will require more imagination than others to re-create their former glory (especially Edgecombe Avenue, where many leaders of the Harlem Renaissance once resided), but the brownstones of Convent Avenue and adjacent streets remain in mint condition.

Finish your walk at **Strivers' Row**, a pair of posh blocks that have attracted well-to-do African-Americans since 1919, or head a bit farther north to the Morris-Jumel Mansion, where George Washington slept and three other future presidents once dined.

TOP ATTRACTIONS

Abyssinian Baptist Church. This 1923 Gothic-style church holds one of Harlem's richest legacies, dating to 1808 when a group of parishioners defected from the segregated First Baptist Church of New York City and established the first African-American Baptist church in New York State. Among its legendary pastors was Adam Clayton Powell Jr., a powerful orator and civil rights leader and the first black U.S. congressman.

Today sermons by pastor Calvin Butts III are fiery, and the seven choirs are excellent. Because of its services' popularity, the church maintains separate lines for parishioners and tourists at its 11 am service. Dress your best, remember to not take pictures or videos, and get there early—at least two hours ahead of time. ⊠ *132 Odell Clark Pl., W. 138th St., between Adam Clayton Powell Jr. Blvd., 7th Ave., and Malcolm*

Where can I find . . . ?

COFFEE	**Hue-Man Bookstore & Cafe** (2319 Frederick Douglass Blvd., near 125th St.) Good joe and fun bookstore.	**Patisserie des Ambassades** (2200 Frederick Douglass Blvd.) Classic combo of pastries and java.
A QUICK BITE	**Uptown Juice Bar** (54 W. 125th St.) Tasty veggie fare; snacks; "detoxifying" juices.	**Make My Cake** (121 St. Nicholas Ave., at 116th St.) Especially made for red velvet cake lovers.
COCKTAILS	**67 Orange Street** (2082 Frederick Douglas Blvd., near 113th St.) Speakeasy setting with expertly mixed drinks.	**Lenox Lounge** (288 Lenox Ave., near 125th St.) Quintessential Harlem jazz spot.

X Blvd., Lenox Ave./6th Ave., Harlem ☎ *212/862–7474* ⊕ *www. abyssinian.org* ⊘ *Sun. services for visitors at 11*; no such services on major holidays Ⓜ *2, 3 to 135th St.*

Canaan Baptist Church of Christ. The heavenly gospel music during Sunday-morning services makes up for this church's unassuming, concrete-box-like exterior (visitors may enter once parishioners are seated). Pastor emeritus Wyatt Tee Walker worked with Dr. Martin Luther King Jr. (who delivered his famous "A Knock at Midnight" sermon here). To attend, arrive at least an hour before services, and dress up. ⊠ *132 W. 116th St., between Malcolm X Blvd., Lenox Ave./6th Ave., and Adam Clayton Powell Jr. Blvd., 7th Ave., Harlem* ☎ *212/866–0301* ⊕ *www. cbccnyc.org* ⊘ *Services Sun. at 8 and 11 am* Ⓜ *2, 3 to 116th St.*

Hamilton Heights. To taste this neighborhood's Harlem Renaissance days, walk down tree-lined Convent Avenue, detouring onto adjacent **Hamilton Terrace,** and see a time capsule of elegant stone row houses in mint condition. (Until 2008 Hamilton Grange, founding father Alexander Hamilton's Federal-style mansion, stood at 287 Convent Avenue. The clapboard structure, owned by the National Park Service, has been moved around the corner to Saint Nicholas Park.

At this writing it's closed for refurbishment and scheduled to reopen for tours in summer 2011: visit ⊕ *www.nps.gov/hagr* for updates). Continue down Convent Avenue and see the looming Gothic spires (1905) of **City College.** The stately Oxford-inspired buildings here are New York to the core: they are clad with the schist rock unearthed when the city was building what is now the 1 subway line. When you're ready to move on, head east through Saint Nicholas Park, which will bring you to Strivers' Row. ⊠ *Convent Ave. between 138th and 150th Sts., Harlem* Ⓜ *A, B, C, D to 145th St.*

Morris-Jumel Mansion. During the Revolutionary War, General George Washington used this wooden, pillared 8,500-square-foot house (built

11

Harlem's Jazz Age

It was in Harlem that Billie Holiday got her first singing job, Duke Ellington made his first recording, and Louis Armstrong was propelled to stardom. Jazz was king during the Harlem Renaissance in the 1920s and '30s, and though Chicago and New Orleans may duke it out for the "birthplace of jazz" title, New York was where jazz musicians came to be heard.

In the 1920s socialites made the trek uptown to Harlem's Cotton Club and Connie's Inn (131st Street and 7th Avenue) to hear "black" music. Both clubs were white-owned and barred blacks from entering, except as performers. (The rules changed years later.) Connie's introduced New Yorkers to Louis Armstrong. The Cotton Club—Harlem's most popular nightspot by far—booked such big names as Fletcher Henderson, Coleman

Hawkins, Duke Ellington, Cab Calloway, and Ethel Waters. After shows ended at the paying clubs, musicians would head to after-hours establishments with black patrons, such as Small's Paradise, Minton's Playhouse, and Basement Brownies, where they'd hammer out new riffs into the wee hours.

Today several parts of Manhattan are known for their jazz venues, but old-time clubs like the Lenox Lounge still hash it out unlike anywhere else. Why? Partly because of history and sense of place, and partly because of—as musicians claim—the more easygoing nature of uptown clubs, which tend to have more flexible sets and open jam sessions. You can't go back in time to Harlem's jazz heyday, but you might catch a modern-day jazz great in the making.

in1765) as his headquarters, Later, as president, he visited again for dinner, bringing along with him John and John Quincy Adams, Thomas Jefferson, and Alexander Hamilton.

Inside are rooms furnished with period decorations—upstairs, keep an eye out for the hand-painted wallpaper (original to the house) and a "commode chair," stuck in a corner. Outside, behind the house, is a Colonial-era marker that says it's 11 miles to New York: it's a reminder of what a small sliver of Manhattan the city was at that time.

West of the house is the block-long Sylvan Terrace, a row of crisp two-story clapboard houses built in the 1880s. ⊠ *65 Jumel Terrace, north of W. 160th St.; between St. Nicholas Ave. and Edgecombe Ave., Harlem* ☎ *212/923–8008* ⊕ *www.morrisjumel.org* ⊡ *$5; guided tours $6* ⊙ *Wed. to Sun., 10–4; guided tours Sat. noon.*

Strivers' Row. This block of gorgeous 1890s Georgian and neo-Italian homes earned its nickname in the 1920s from less affluent Harlemites who felt its residents were "striving" to become well-to-do. Some of the few remaining private service alleys, used when deliveries arrived via horse and cart, lie behind these houses and are visible through iron gates. Note the gatepost between No. 251 and 253 on West 138th Street that says, "Private Road. Walk Your Horses."

The houses were built by the contractor David H. King Jr., whose works also include the base for the Statue of Liberty and the oldest parts of

Taking a Gospel Tour

For the past decade or so, the popularity of gospel tours, conducted by bus, has greatly increased, especially among Europeans. Some of the tours include only a 20-minute stop at a church to hear some of the sermon and the gospel music. Then you're off to another Harlem sight or to a soul-food brunch. Prices may be as high as $99. The tours are a speedy, if not authentic, way to experience a bit of Harlem.

Tours garner mixed reactions from church officials and parishioners. Some see it as an opportunity to broaden horizons and encourage diversity. But others find tours disruptive and complain that tourists take seats away from regular parishioners (churches regularly fill to capacity). If you decide to go on one of these tours or to visit a church on your own, plan ahead. Most churches have services at 11, but you may need to arrive as much as two hours ahead of time to actually get in. Most important, remember that parishioners do not consider the service, or themselves, to be tourist attractions or entertainment. Dress nicely—no shorts, sneakers, or jeans. Harlem churchgoers take the term "Sunday best" to heart. Be as quiet as possible, and do not take photos or videos or use

your cell phone. One tour company based in the neighborhood that does get high marks for its gospel tours is **Harlem Heritage Tours** (⊠ 104 Malcolm X Blvd., Lenox Ave./6th Ave., Harlem ☎ 212/280–7888 ⊕ www. harlemheritage.com).

The following are some of the uptown churches with gospel choirs:

Abyssinian Baptist Church is one of the few churches that does not allow tour groups. Services for visitors are at 11. Arrive at least two hours ahead of time for this service. **Canaan Baptist Church of Christ** has services at 8 and 11. **Convent Avenue Baptist Church** (⊠ 420 W. 145th St., between Convent and St. Nicholas Aves., Harlem ☎ 212/234–6767 ⊕ www. conventchurch.org) has services at 8, 11, and 5. **First Corinthian Baptist Church** has services at 8 and 11.

Greater Refuge Temple (⊠ 2081 Adam Clayton Powell Jr. Blvd., at 124th St., Harlem ☎ 212/866–1700 ⊕ www.greaterrefugetemple.org) has services at 11, 4, and 7:30. **Memorial Baptist Church** (⊠ 141 W. 115th St., between Adam Clayton Powell Jr. and Malcolm X Blvds., Harlem ☎ 212/663–8830 ⊕ www.mbcvisionharlem.org) has services at 8 and 11.

the Cathedral Church of St. John the Divine. When the houses failed to sell to whites, the properties on these blocks were sold to African-American doctors, lawyers, and other professionals; the composers and musicians W. C. Handy and Eubie Blake were also among the residents.

If you have the time, detour a block north to see the palazzo-style group of houses designed by Stanford White, on the north side of West 139th Street. ⊠ W. 138th and W. 139th Sts. between Adam Clayton Powell Jr. and Frederick Douglass Blvds., Harlem Ⓜ B, C to 135th St.

Gospel at St. Luke's church

WORTH NOTING

First Corinthian Baptist Church. One of the most ornate structures in Harlem, this church kicked off its life in 1913 as the Regent Theatre, one of the country's early movie palaces that replaced the nickelodeons. Its elaborately columned and arched facade loosely resembles the Doges' Palace in Venice. The Regent was sold to the church in 1964. To attend services, arrive at least an hour ahead of time. ⊠ *1912 Adam Clayton Powell Jr. Blvd., at 7th Ave., Harlem* ☎ *212/864–5976* ⊘ *Services Sun. at 8 and 11* Ⓜ *2, 3 to 116th St.*

🐾 **Marcus Garvey Park.** At the center of this historic, tree-filled public square, atop a 70-foot-high outcrop of Manhattan schist (the same bedrock that anchors our skyscrapers) stands a 47-foot cast-iron **watchtower** (Julius Kroel, 1865), the last remnant of a citywide network used to spot and report fires in pre-telephone days. Around it, an **Acropolis** provides great views of Manhattan and the handsome neoclassical row houses of **Mount Morris Park Historic District,** which extends west from the park. ⊠ *Interrupts 5th Ave. between W. 120th and W. 124th Sts., Madison Ave. to Mt. Morris Park W, Harlem* ⊕ *www.nycgovparks. org* Ⓜ *2, 3 to 125th St.*

Masjid Malcolm Shabazz *(Mosque).* Talk about religious conversions. In the mid-'60s the Lenox Casino was transformed into this house of worship and cultural center, and given bright yellow arches and a huge green onion dome that loudly proclaims its presence in a neighborhood of churches.

Once functioning as Temple No. 7 under the Nation of Islam with a message of pro-black racism, the mosque was bombed after the assassination of Malcolm X, who had preached here. It was then rebuilt and renamed for the name Malcolm took at the end of his life, El-Hajj Malik Shabazz; its philosophy now is one of inclusion.

These days the Sunni congregation has a large proportion of immigrants from Senegal, many of whom live in and around 116th Street. Next door is Graceline Court, a 16-story luxury condominium building that opened in 2008. ⊠ *102 W. 116th St., at Malcolm X Blvd., Lenox Ave./6th Ave., Harlem* ☎ *212/662–2200* Ⓜ *2, 3 to 116th St.*

Sugar Hill. Standing on the bluff of Sugar Hill overlooking Jackie Robinson Park, outside the slightly run-down **409 Edgecombe Avenue,** you'd never guess that here resided such influential African-Americans as NAACP founder W.E.B. DuBois and Supreme Court Justice Thurgood Marshall, or that farther north at **555 Edgecombe,** known as the "Triple Nickel," writers Langston Hughes and Zora Neale Hurston and jazz musicians Duke Ellington, Count Basie, and others lived and played. ■TIP➔ For over a decade, musician Marjorie Eliot (☎ 212/781–6595) has been hosting Sunday jazz concerts with prominent local musicians in her apartment (3F) at 555 Edgecombe. The shows run from 4 to 6:30 pm. If you're in Sugar Hill after 9:30 pm, drop by St. Nick's Jazz Pub (⊠ 773 St. Nicholas Ave., near 149th St. ☎ 212/283–9728 ⊕ www.stnicksjazzpub.net), a laid-back, tiny basement club that has been a local fixture for ages. Bring some bills to stuff into the tip jar that circulates, grab a drink, and enjoy the late-night jam sessions. ⊠ *Bounded by 145th and 155th Sts. and Edgecombe and St. Nicholas Aves., Harlem* Ⓜ *A, B, C, D to 145th St.*

Brooklyn

WORD OF MOUTH

"Walking over the Brooklyn Bridge was a really neat experience; I liked being elevated above the bridge deck, with the traffic below us on both sides . . . A word of caution . . . be sure to stay out of the bike lane, as the cyclists come whipping past you like they're being chased by the law."

—artstuff

GETTING ORIENTED

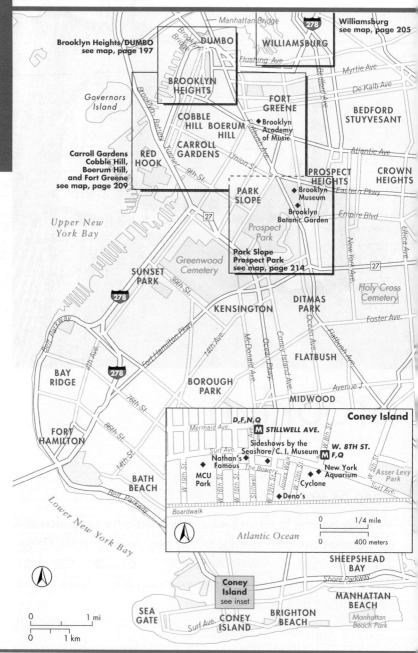

MAKING THE MOST OF YOUR TIME

The best way to enter this borough is by its most majestic bridge. Walking across the wooden pedestrian path of the Brooklyn Bridge—a classic New York experience—takes about 30 minutes, all worth it for the panoramic views of the skylines and the harbor. It's also a great way to transition from the bustle of Manhattan into Brooklyn's slower pace. After you exit onto Cadman Plaza, walk southwest to poke around Brooklyn Heights, a charming neighborhood of posh 19th-century brownstone homes, or walk north into the hip neighborhood of DUMBO to check out its adorable shops and stunning waterfront parks. To get to Brooklyn's sights more quickly, take the 2 or 3 train to the Eastern Parkway/ Brooklyn Museum stop. The museum, the Botanic Garden, the Children's Museum, and Prospect Park are all close.

GETTING HERE

To get to Williamsburg, take the L train from any 14th Street station in Manhattan to Bedford Avenue, the first stop in Brooklyn. You can reach Brooklyn Heights by the 2 or 3 train to Clark Street, the R to Court Street, or the 4 or 5 to Borough Hall. To get to DUMBO, take the F train to York Street or walk from Brooklyn Heights. The F to 7th Avenue will take you to the center of Park Slope. From there, walk uphill to reach Prospect Park or walk north on 7th Avenue to sample the shops. The hipper boutiques and eateries are two long blocks west, on 5th Avenue, best accessed on the R train to Union Street. To reach the Brooklyn Museum, Brooklyn Botanic Garden, and Prospect Park take the 2 or 3 train to Eastern Parkway/Brooklyn Museum. Coney Island is the last stop on the D, F, N, and Q trains, and the Q or B will take you to Brighton Beach. Allow a good part of the day for these trips, since it takes about an hour to reach the ocean from Manhattan.

FODOR'S CHOICE

The Brooklyn Bridge
Brooklyn Heights Promenade
Coney Island
Prospect Park

TOP EXPERIENCES

Hitting restaurants and bars in Williamsburg, or on Smith Street in Cobble Hill and Carroll Gardens

Screaming on the Cyclone in Coney Island

Spending an afternoon at the Brooklyn Botanic Garden or Prospect Park

Taking in the Manhattan skyline at night from the Brooklyn Heights Promenade

Catching a show at The Brooklyn Academy of Music (BAM)

BEST FOR KIDS

Brooklyn Children's Museum
Brooklyn Ice Cream Factory
Brooklyn Superhero Supply Co.
MCU Park
Lefferts Historic House
New York Aquarium
Transit Museum

NEARBY MUSEUMS

Brooklyn Children's Museum
Brooklyn Historical Society
Brooklyn Museum
Coney Island Museum
C. V. Starr Bonsai Museum at the Brooklyn Botanic Garden
Transit Museum

Sightseeing
★★

Nightlife
★★★

Dining
★★★★★

Lodging
★

Shopping
★★★

Updated by
Anja Mutić

To put it mildly, Brooklyn is exploding. Hardly Manhattan's wimpy sidekick, this is the largest and most populous of all the boroughs, with more than 2.5 million residents. If it were an independent city, it would be the fourth largest in the country.

Brooklyn was in fact its own city until the end of the 19th century, with its own widely circulated newspaper, the *Brooklyn Eagle,* its own expansive park, Prospect Park, and its own baseball team that would eventually be called the Brooklyn Dodgers.

And in 1883 it got its own bridge. The Brooklyn Bridge, which drew the attention of the entire country, essentially became the final push that would rob the borough of its city status and fuel its merge with Manhattan. The marriage of the two cities took effect in 1898, much to the objection of Brooklynites, as it was widely dubbed, "the great mistake of 1898."

Today, for many who've chosen to leave the island of Manhattan behind for Brooklyn in search of more living space (although not necessarily lower rent) living here is about celebrating the borough's diverse neighborhoods that share a down-to-earth character. Neighborly chats take place on the stoops of brownstones, family-owned businesses preserve their heritages, and people are happy to eat and drink without the see-or-be-seen scene.

That's not to say that restaurateurs and bar owners don't mind drawing the attention of those across the river. The dining scene here is huge—so much so that Manhattanites are more than willing to hop on the subway to come—with new eateries opening seemingly on a weekly basis.

Aside from Brooklyn's mellow family-friendly vibe in areas such as **Brooklyn Heights, Cobble Hill, Carroll Gardens,** and **Boerum Hill,** added to the mix is a group described with an overly-used moniker for which there's no other appropriate word: hipster. Hipsters here are most strongly associated with **Williamsburg,** where the young artists flocked more than a decade ago, and soon after the area became known for its galleries, along with its pricy real estate to match.

It's largely Brooklyn that has lent New York its streetwise and sincere personality, famously captured in films such as *Do the Right Thing, Moonstruck,* and *Brighton Beach Memoirs.* As it's continually been dubbed "the new Manhattan," this borough now attracts visitors not only from the city's other boroughs but tourists from far and wide as well.

12

TOP TOURING EXPERIENCES

LOCAL LANDMARKS AND PERFECT PARKS

In the midst of urban bustle, Brooklyn is full of green getaways and natural attractions. Relax like a real Brooklynite by packing a picnic lunch and heading to **Prospect Park**'s lush Long Meadow. Or find its hidden nooks and surprises, like the Zoo, the Ravine, and great summer concerts in the Bandshell.

Next door is the **Brooklyn Botanic Garden,** the borough's beloved 52-acre retreat with more than 10,000 plant species from around the world. Take an unexpected detour to **Green-Wood Cemetery,** which dates back to 1838, where you can walk along its hills and lakes or hunt for the headstones of V.I.P.s among the R.I.P.s.

No tour of Brooklyn would be complete without a pilgrimage to **Coney Island,** where the boardwalk, Nathan's hot dogs, and the Cyclone have thrilled generations of New Yorkers.

BOUTIQUE BONANZA

Manhattan is slowly being taken over by chain stores, but Brooklyn's boutique scene is thriving. It's easy to spend an afternoon looking at ladylike knits or punchy, bright-color sundresses, chuckling at hipster-esque home items (resin deer antlers, anyone?), or simply discovering new designers.

Start off in Williamsburg at **Future Perfect,** a modern-home-decor lover's dream, then hop over to other Brooklyn spots like **Catbird** or **Love Brigade Co-op** (✉ *230 Grand St.* ☎ *718/715–0430* ⊕ *www.lovebrigade.com*). In Park Slope, stroll down 5th and 7th avenues for a more sophisticated range at **Bird** or **Serene Rose** (✉ *329 5th Ave.* ☎ *718/832–0717* ⊕ *www. serenerose.com),* among others.

Over in Carroll Gardens, Cobble Hill, and Boerum Hill, hit the antiques and home-design stores as well as the handful of galleries on Atlantic Avenue, then head over to Court Street and **Smith Street** to combine boutique hopping with a meal at one of the area's many celebrated restaurants.

EPICURE'S PARADISE

Eating your way through Brooklyn is one of the best ways to experience the mix of old, new, and immigrant cultures that make the borough so vibrant. Carroll Gardens perhaps best epitomizes this mix; here 50 years of Italian heritage meet a more recent and highly acclaimed restaurant scene on and near Smith Street.

Take the F train to the Bergen or Carroll Street stop to try standout eateries like **Char No. 4** or **Saul,** then walk off your meal along leafy Court Street, stopping at one of its bakeries for dessert. (Try **Sweet**

Melissa [✉ *276 Court St.* ☎ *718/855–3410*] for sour-cherry clafoutis; or anything from **The Chocolate Room** [✉ *269 Court St.* ☎ *718/246–2600*] just across the street.)

For more international adventures, head to **Brighton Beach** for smoked fish at elaborate Russian palaces beneath the train tracks—**Primorski** (✉ *282 Brighton Beach Ave.* ☎ *718/891–3111*) is a classic—or browse the Central Asian eateries on Brighton Beach Avenue. Local fave **Café Kashkar** (✉ *1141 Brighton Beach Ave.* ☎ *718/743–3832*) serves Uyghur food. In Sunset Park, wallet-friendly fare from Latin America (clustered on 5th Avenue) and East Asia (on 8th Avenue) compete for your taste buds' time. **Ba Xuyen** (✉ *4222 8th Ave.* ☎ *718/633–6601*) vies for the title of New York's best *Banh Mi* (Vietnamese hero sandwiches), and **Tacos Matamoros** (✉ *4508 5th Ave.* ☎ *718/871–7627*) packs in locals for its authentic tacos and tortas.

WHAT IT COSTS					
	¢	$	$$	$$$	$$$$
AT DINNER	under $10	$10–$17	$18–$24	$25–$35	over $35

Price per person for a median main course or equivalent combination of smaller dishes. Note: if a restaurant offers only prix-fixe (set-price) meals, it has been given the price category that reflects the full prix-fixe price.

BROOKLYN HEIGHTS

Brooklyn's toniest neighborhood offers residents something wealthy Manhattanites will never have: a stunning view of the Manhattan skyline from the **Brooklyn Heights Promenade.** First developed in the mid-1800s as the business center of the then-independent city of Brooklyn, it showcases historic cobblestone streets of pristine brownstones.

In the early to mid-20th century the Heights was a bohemian haven, home to writers like Arthur Miller, Truman Capote, Alfred Kazin, Marianne Moore, Norman Mailer, and W. E. B. DuBois. In the '80s a new generation of gentrifiers moved in, and—even with a softening real estate market—homes here are still as pricey as their Manhattan counterparts.

Much of its early architecture has been preserved, thanks to its designation in the 1960s as New York's first historic district. Some 600 buildings built in the 19th century represent a wide range of American building styles. Many of the best line **Columbia Heights,** a residential street that runs parallel to the promenade, but any of its adjoining streets are also worth strolling.

On **Willow Street** be sure to note No. 22, Henry Ward Beecher's prim Greek Revival brownstone, and Nos. 155–159. These three brick Federal row houses are said to have been stops on the Underground Railroad. The skylight in the pavement by the gate to No. 157 provided the light for an underground tunnel leading to an 1880 carriage house.

Don't miss a stroll around the leafy Pier 1, the newly expanded section of the Brooklyn Bridge Park, accessible from Old Fulton Street. And if

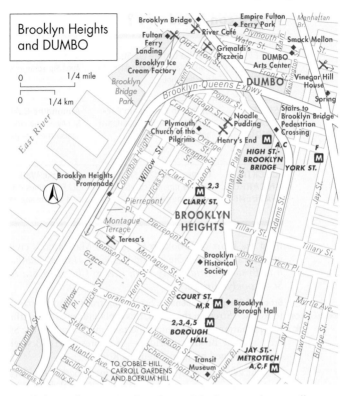

Brooklyn Heights and DUMBO

0 ____ 1/4 mile

0 ____ 1/4 km

Brooklyn Bridge
Empire Fulton Ferry Park
Manhattan Br.
Fulton Ferry Landing
River Café
Plymouth St.
Old Fulton St.
Water St.
Front St.
Smack Mellon St.
Grimaldi's Pizzeria
DUMBO Arts Center
Brooklyn Ice Cream Factory
Washington St.
DUMBO
Vinegar Hill House
12
Brooklyn Bridge Park
Brooklyn-Queens Expwy.
Poplar St.
Middagh St.
Cranberry St.
Spring
East River
Plymouth Church of the Pilgrims
Noodle Pudding
Stairs to Brooklyn Bridge Pedestrian Crossing
Orange St.
Henry's End **M** A,C
Columbia Heights
Willow St.
Pineapple St.
Cadman Plaza West
HIGH ST.-BROOKLYN BRIDGE
YORK ST. **M** F
Brooklyn Heights Promenade
Clark St.
Henry St.
M 2,3
CLARK ST.
Pierrepont Pl.
Montague Terrace
Pierrepont St.
BROOKLYN HEIGHTS
Tillary St.
Teresa's
Remsen St.
Montague St.
Brooklyn Historical Society
Johnson St.
Tech Pl.
Tillary St.
Grace Ct.
Hicks St.
Joralemon St.
Henry St.
Clinton St.
COURT ST. **M,R** **M** Brooklyn Borough Hall
Myrtle Ave.
Willow Pl.
State St.
2,3,4,5 **M** **BOROUGH HALL**
Livingston St.
Jay St.
Bridge St.
Lawrence St.
Columbia St.
Atlantic Ave.
Pacific St.
Amity St.
Congress St.
TO COBBLE HILL CARROLL GARDENS AND BOERUM HILL
Schermerhorn St.
Transit Museum
JAY ST.-METROTECH A,C,F **M**
Boerum Pl.
Adams St.
Cadman Plaza West

you didn't walk it coming from Lower Manhattan, take a stroll across the majestic **Brooklyn Bridge.**

Brooklyn Borough Hall. Built in 1848 as Brooklyn's City Hall, this Greek Revival landmark is one of Brooklyn's handsomest buildings. Adorned with Tuckahoe marble, it features a hammered square rotunda and a two-story Beaux-Arts courtroom.

Today the building serves as the office of Brooklyn's borough president and the home of the **Brooklyn Tourism & Visitors Center** (☎ 718/802–3846 ⊕ *www.visitbrooklyn.org*), which has historical exhibits, a gift shop, and helpful information. It's open weekdays 10–6. Each Tuesday and Saturday as well as Thursday from April through December a greenmarket sets up on the flagstone plaza in front. ⊠ *209 Joralemon St., between Court and Adams Sts., Brooklyn Heights* ☎ 718/802–3700 *Free* **M** *2, 3, 4, 5 to Borough Hall; M, R to Court St; A, C, F to Jay St.*

Fodor'sChoice ★ **Brooklyn Bridge.** "A drive-through cathedral" is how the critic James Wolcott described one of New York's noblest and most recognized landmarks. "The best, most effective medicine my soul has yet partaken," said Walt Whitman upon seeing the nearly completed bridge. It spans the East River, connecting Manhattan and Brooklyn. A walk across its promenade—a boardwalk elevated above a roadway, shared by pedestrians, in-line skaters, and cyclists—takes about 40 minutes

Where can I find . . . ?

COFFEE IN PARK SLOPE	**Gorilla Coffee** (97 5th Ave.) Grab a fair-trade Brooklyn-roasted shot.	**Red Horse Café** (497 6th Ave.) Sip some micro-roast.
SWEETS NEAR THE BRIDGE	**Brooklyn Ice Cream Factory** (1 Water St.) Superlative hot fudge.	**Almondine Bakery** (85 Water St.) Awesome croissants and sandwiches are picnic-perfect.
COCKTAILS IN CARROLL GARDENS	**Clover Club** (210 Smith St.) Swanky modern cocktails in a cozy atmosphere.	**The Jake Walk** (282 Smith St.) Fifty wines, 130 whiskies, and 40 artisanal cheeses.

from the heart of Brooklyn Heights to Manhattan's civic center. It's worth traversing for the astounding views. *Lower Manhattan* Ⓜ *4, 5, 6 to Brooklyn Bridge/City Hall; J, Z to Chambers St.; A, C to High St.–Brooklyn Bridge.*

Ⓢ
Fodor'sChoice
★
Brooklyn Heights Promenade. Stretching from Orange Street in the north to Remsen Street in the south, this esplanade provides enthralling views of Manhattan. Find a bench and take in the skyline, the Statue of Liberty, and the Brooklyn Bridge—an impressive 1883 steel suspension bridge designed by John Augustus Roebling.

To your left is Governors Island, a former Coast Guard base that's now become a prime picnic and summertime festival destination for locals. Below you are the Brooklyn–Queens Expressway and Brooklyn's industrial waterfront of warehouses, piers, and parking lots.

A greenway initiative is moving forward in a bid to build a 14-mi waterfront park for pedestrians and bikers. The first 6 acres of the park opened in March 2010 at Pier 1, including the park's first waterfront promenade and a playground. Pier 6 opened in June 2010, and Pier 1 got another 3.5 acres of parkland in August 2010. The plan is to complete the entire park by 2013. For updates, check the Brooklyn Bridge Park Conservancy Web site at ⊕ *www.brooklynbridgepark.org.* Ⓜ *2, 3 to Clark St.; A, C to High St.*

Brooklyn Historical Society. Housed in an 1881 Queen Anne–style National Landmark building (one of the gems of the neighborhood), the Brooklyn Historical Society displays memorabilia, artifacts, art, and interactive exhibitions. Upstairs, an impressive library—which contains an original copy of the Emancipation Proclamation—is invaluable to researchers. ⊠ *128 Pierrepont St., at Clinton St., Brooklyn Heights* ☎ *718/222–4111* ⊕ *www.brooklynhistory.org* 🎫 *$6* 🕙 *Wed.–Fri. and Sun. noon–5, Sat. 10–5* Ⓜ *2, 3, 4, 5 to Borough Hall; A, C, F to Jay St.; M, R to Court St.*

Plymouth Church of the Pilgrims. Built in 1849, this Protestant Congregational church was a center of abolitionist sentiment, thanks to the stirring oratory of Brooklyn's most eminent theologian and the church's first minister, Henry Ward Beecher (brother of Harriet Beecher Stowe, who wrote *Uncle Tom's Cabin*). Because it provided refuge to slaves, the church was known to some as the Grand Central Depot of the Underground Railroad.

Though the architecture of this brick building may seem simple, it was enormously influential on subsequent American Protestant churches. Three Louis C. Tiffany stained-glass windows were added in the 1930s. In the gated garden beside the church a statue of Beecher by Gutzon Borglum (who later sculpted Mount Rushmore) depicts one of the slave "auctions"—publicity stunts wherein church members purchased the slaves' freedom. A fragment of Plymouth Rock is in an adjoining arcade. ⊠ *75 Hicks St., at Orange St., Brooklyn Heights* ☎ *718/624–4743* ⊕ *www.plymouthchurch.org* ☉ *Services Sun. at 11; tours by appointment* Ⓜ *2, 3 to Clark St.; A, C to High St.*

🕐 **Transit Museum.** Step down into a 1930s subway station, where you'll find more than 60,000 square feet devoted to the history of public transportation. Interact with the collection of vintage trains and turnstiles, sit behind the wheel of city buses, and laugh over old subway advertisements and signs. The gift store is a great place for N.Y.C.-theme souvenirs. ⊠ *Boerum Pl. at Schermerhorn St., Brooklyn Heights* ☎ *718/694–1600* ⊕ *www.mta.info/museum/* 🎫 *$6* ☉ *Tues.–Fri. 10–4, weekends noon–5* Ⓜ *2, 3, 4, 5 to Borough Hall; A, C, F to Jay St.; M, R to Court St.*

WHERE TO EAT

$$
AMERICAN
✕ **Henry's End.** At this nearly 40-year-old neighborhood favorite, the casual decor belies the quality of the food and wines. Wild game such as elk, kangaroo, and ostrich take center stage during the Wild Game Festival in the late fall and winter months; seasonal seafood and foraged vegetables star in the springtime. ⊠ *44 Henry St., near Cranberry St., Brooklyn Heights* ☎ *718/834–1776* ⊕ *www.henrysend.com* ▭ *AE, D, DC, MC, V* ☉ *No lunch* Ⓜ *2, 3 to Clark St.; A, C to High St.*

$$
ITALIAN
✕ **Noodle Pudding.** The name is bad, but the food is great at this cozy restaurant serving the best regional Italian fare in Brooklyn Heights. Locals especially rave about the osso buco served with goat-cheese polenta. It does get crowded, but that means it's noisy enough that you can bring the kids. Note that reservations are accepted only for parties of six or more. ⊠ *38 Henry St., near Cranberry St., Brooklyn Heights* ☎ *718/625–3737* ▭ *No credit cards* ☉ *No lunch* Ⓜ *A, C to High St.; 2, 3 to Clark St.*

$
POLISH
✕ **Teresa's.** At the end of Montague Street, right before the entrance to the Promenade, this busy mom-and-pop coffee shop serves Polish and American comfort food, including breakfast all day. Fill up on delicate cheese blintzes, pierogi, and juicy kielbasa. ⊠ *80 Montague St., near Hicks St., Brooklyn Heights* ☎ *718/797–3996* ▭ *MC, V* Ⓜ *2, 3 to Clark St.; R to Court St.*

DUMBO

A downhill walk from Brooklyn Heights is the area called DUMBO (*Down Under the Manhattan Bridge Overpass*). It was once known as Fulton Landing, after the inventor and engineer Robert Fulton, who introduced steamboat ferry service from Brooklyn to Manhattan in 1814.

Factories and dry-goods warehouses thrived here until the Manhattan Bridge was completed in 1909. DUMBO then fell on hard times, but since the 1970s artists have been drawn by the historic warehouses for use as spacious studios. Today the area is full of luxury condos, art galleries, and small businesses.

The **Fulton Ferry Landing**'s view of Manhattan and the Brooklyn Bridge makes it a favorite site for wedding photos; the New York Water Taxi stops here as well. When all that sightseeing makes you hungry, walk uphill to the always excellent, always crowded, **Grimaldi's Pizzeria** and the **Brooklyn Ice Cream Factory**. Wander the empty, old cobblestone streets for photo ops (try to frame the Empire State Building within the anchorage of the Manhattan Bridge), and visit the art galleries and boutiques.

☺ **Empire Fulton Ferry Park.** This charming 9-acre park is a great place for a riverside picnic or to just enjoy the view. The large playground includes a replica of a boat for make-believe voyages across the East River. From April to October the park is home to a wide range of arts performances, and on Thursday nights in July and August, Movies with a View projects New York classic films on an outdoor screen with no cover charge. ⊠ *New Dock St. at Water St., DUMBO* ☎ *718/858–4708* ⊕ *nysparks. state.ny.us* ✆ *Free* ☉ *Daily dawn–dusk* Ⓜ *A, C to High St.; F to York St.*

WHERE TO EAT

$ ✕ **Grimaldi's Pizzeria.** This classic New York–style parlor serves excellent
PIZZA   pizza pies from its coal ovens. Although sometimes inconsistent, when they're good, the thin crisp crust is slightly blackened, and the fresh mozzarella oozes satisfyingly. Grimaldi's popularity allows them to be picky: no slices, no reservations, no credit cards, and no empty tables (expect a wait). Impatient foodies have been known to phone in a to-go order, swoop past the lines, and then enjoy their pizza in the nearby Brooklyn Bridge Park. ⊠ *19 Old Fulton St., between Front and Water Sts., DUMBO* ☎ *718/858–4300* ⊕ *www.grimaldis.com* ✆ *Reservations not accepted* ▭ *No credit cards* Ⓜ *A, C to High St.; 2, 3 to Clark St.; F to York St.*

$$$$ ✕ **River Café.** The River Café's incredible views of the Manhattan skyline
NEW AMERICAN   across the way, lush flowers, and live piano music make it a waterfront favorite for romantic meals, marriage proposals, fancy birthdays, and special celebrations. The menu offers a contemporary take on local and exotic ingredients. For the ultimate experience, snag a window seat and try the chef's six-course tasting menu ($125 per person). Gentlemen: jackets are required after 5 pm. ⊠ *1 Water St., near Old Fulton St., DUMBO* ☎ *718/522–5200* ⊕ *www.rivercafe.com* ▭ *AE, D, DC, MC, V* Ⓜ *F to York St.; A, C to High St.; 2, 3 to Clark St.*

$$ ✕ **Vinegar Hill House.** In an offbeat enclave on the edge of DUMBO
NEW AMERICAN   called Vinegar Hill, this relative newcomer to Brooklyn's dining scene

has formed a fiercely loyal following. Foodies trek out to its rustic-chic dining room for well-prepared seasonal food and cozy ambience. Favorites include the moist and crispy cast-iron chicken and oven-roasted octopus. ✉ *72 Hudson Ave., between Front and Water Sts., DUMBO*☎ *718/522–1018* ⊕ *www.vinegarhillhouse.com* ⌂ *Reservations not accepted* ☰ *AE, MC, V* ☉ *No lunch weekdays* Ⓜ *F to York St.*

GALLERIES

No trip to DUMBO would be complete without some gallery hopping—most are open afternoons Wednesday or Thursday through Sunday. The **DUMBO Arts Center** (*DAC* ✉ *30 Washington St., between Water and Plymouth Sts.* ☎ *718/694–0831* ⊕ *www.dumboartscenter.org*) exhibits contemporary art in a 3,000-square-foot gallery.

Inside a 6,000-square-foot restored boiler building, **Smack Mellon Studios** (✉ *92 Plymouth St., at Washington St.* ☎ *718/834–8761* ⊕ *www.smackmellon.org*) exhibits up-and-coming artists, and nurtures them with studio space and other support. At exhibition space and design shop **Spring** (✉ *126a Front St.* ☎ *718/222–1054* ⊕ *www.spring3d.net*) you can view contemporary art, then satisfy your shopping urges with quirky home goods.

Don't miss the annual **DUMBO Arts Festival** (⊕ dumboartsfestival.com) in September, with three art- and music-packed days in the area's galleries, open studios, warehouses, parks, and streets.

NIGHTLIFE

Galapagos Art Space. Performances here could almost take a backseat to the unique architecture of supper-club red banquettes floating above a huge lagoon of water. (Hold on to your purse!) Thankfully, the theater, music, and performance art is dynamic enough to grab your attention. ✉ *16 Main St., DUMBO* ☎ *718/222–8500* ⊕ *www.galapagosartspace.com* ▭ *Ticket prices vary* ☉ *Opening times vary* Ⓜ *F to York St.; A, C to High St.*

reBar. Occupying several rooms inside a former factory, this cavernous industrial space does multiple duty as bar, lounge, indie movie theater, gastropub, and supper club. Sample one of its 15 brews and vivacious vibe under terra-cotta ceilings and antique chandeliers. ✉ *147 Front St., DUMBO* ☎ *718/766–9110* ⊕ *www.rebarnyc.com* Ⓜ *F to York St.; A, C to High St.*

Superfine. The huge orange pool table takes center stage for the young crowd at this sprawling restaurant and bar at the base of the Manhattan Bridge. Rotating artwork, exposed-brick walls lined with tall windows, sunken secondhand chairs, and mellow music (including a bluegrass brunch on Sunday) make for a distinctive scene. ✉ *126 Front St., between Jay and Pearl Sts., DUMBO* ☎ *718/243–9005* ☉ *Closed Mon.* Ⓜ *F to York St.*

SHOPPING

At **Jacques Torres Chocolate** (✉ *66 Water St.* ☎ *718/875–9772* ⊕ *www.mrchocolate.com*) you'll feel like Charlie getting a peek at the Oompa Loompas as you peer into the small factory while munching on a few unusually flavored chocolate bonbons and sipping a thick, rich cup of hot chocolate. (For the latter, try the "wicked" flavor, spiked with chipotle peppers and cinnamon.)

Don't skip the adjacent ice-cream shop, for a treat of mango sorbet or a scoop of caramel-rum vanilla served sandwich-style between two chocolate-chip cookies.

Forget the touristy "I Heart NY" shirts. Pick up souvenirs they'll actually wear at **Neighborhoodies** (⊠ *26 Jay St.* ☎ *718/243–2265* ⊕ *www. neighborhoodies.com* ⊙ *Weekdays 10–6*), where locals swear allegiance by emblazoning sweatshirts and other clothing with their favorite nabe. The Brooklyn branch allows you to instantly create custom pieces.

Blueberi (⊠ *143 Front St., DUMBO* ☎ *718/422–7724* ⊕ *www.blueberi. net*) is a sleek boutique with vintage and contemporary designer wear, shoes, and accessories hailing from the five boroughs as well as the faraway corners of the world. Striking window displays make it near impossible not to pop in for at least a browse.

powerHouse Arena (⊠ *37 Main St., DUMBO* ☎ *718/666–3049* ⊕ *www. powerhousearena.com*) is a definite must-stop in the neighborhood for culture hawks and bookworms. This stunning 5,000-square-foot space with soaring 24-foot ceilings, glass frontage, and amphitheater-style seating does multiple duty as gallery, boutique, bookstore, and performance space.

WILLIAMSBURG

For much of the 20th century this industrial area on the East River was home to a mix of Latin Americans, Poles, Hasidic Jews, and factories. Then, as Manhattan rents rose in the 1990s, artists, misfits, and indie rockers migrated across on the L train to transform the neighborhood into a creative bohemian center.

Today Williamsburg's main drag of Bedford Avenue is a veritable catwalk of fabulously dressed starving artists and wealthy hipsters on their way from the L train to a range of stylish bars and clubs, artists' studios, vintage stores, and costly boutiques. Meanwhile, the area's young families and migrating Manhattanites head to one of the many posh restaurants near the Williamsburg Bridge.

Note that the shops and attractions listed here are spread out, so be prepared to walk a few blocks on generally safe (though sometimes graffitied and abandoned) blocks filled with former factories.

WHERE TO EAT

$$

NEW AMERICAN

✕ **The Bedford.** With its farm-to-table philosophy, this newly opened restaurant offers superb market-fresh interpretations of American mainstays such as pasture-raised burgers with Gorgonzola cheese, charred lamb ribs, and cornmeal-crusted catfish. The seemingly slapdash aesthetics of the two rooms features planked floors, reclaimed wood benches, repurposed U.S. Army field desks, and vintage school chairs. There's a good selection of craft beer and organic wines, poured out to a rock-and-roll soundtrack. ⊠ *110 Bedford Ave., at N. 11th St., Williamsburg* ☎ *718/302–1002* ⊕ *www.thebedfordonbedford.com* ▭ *AE, MC, V* Ⓜ *L to Bedford Ave.*

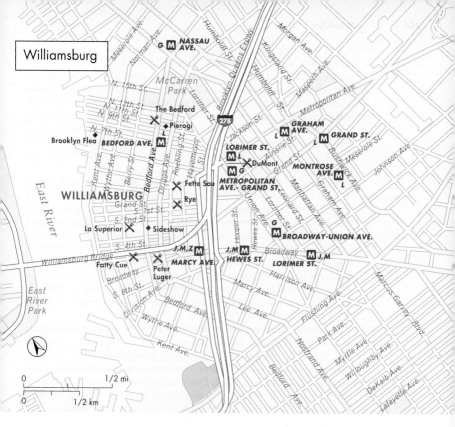

Williamsburg

$$ ✕ **Diner.** Tucked inside a 1927 dining car, this restaurant serves simple
AMERICAN seasonal fare and so many specials that your waiter scrawls their names
on the paper tablecloth to help you remember them all. Save room for
the intense flourless chocolate cake. ✉ *85 Broadway, at Berry St., Wil-
liamsburg* ☎ *718/486–3077* ⊕ *www.dinernyc.com* ⊜ *Reservations not
accepted* ═ *AE, MC, V* Ⓜ *J, M, Z to Marcy Ave.; L to Bedford Ave.*

$$$ ✕ **Dressler.** The critically acclaimed Dressler has a modern menu full of
AMERICAN meaty foods and an impressive wine list, served in a refined setting—
a classic example of the "New Brooklyn Cuisine." One standout is
the braised lamb shank, served with pearled barley, roasted tomato,
and Swiss chard. ✉ *149 Broadway, between Bedford and Driggs Aves.,
Williamsburg* ☎ *718/384–6343* ⊕ *www.dresslernyc.com* ═ *AE, MC,
V* ⊘ *No lunch weekdays* Ⓜ *J, M, Z to Marcy Ave.; L to Bedford Ave.*

$$ ✕ **DuMont.** Slide into a candlelit leather booth and order what is perhaps
AMERICAN the best mac 'n cheese in the city, served bubbling hot and punctuated
with (optional) smoky bacon. The juicy burgers, which also have a large
fan club, are best enjoyed at a table in the charming back garden. ✉ *432
Union Ave., between Metropolitan Ave. and Devoe St., Williamsburg*
☎ *718/486–7717* ⊕ *www.dumontrestaurant.com* ═ *AE, MC, V* Ⓜ *L
to Lorimer St.*

$$ ✕ **Fatty Cue.** This offshoot of Fatty Crab in the West Village features
SOUTHEAST the similarly quirky aesthetics in its series of low-lighted, low-ceilinged
ASIAN

rooms where the decibel level is as high as the enjoyment of chowing on deliciously juicy smoked fare with a Southeast Asian twist. Locally sourced meats and fish are thrown into two Ole Hickory smokers and rubbed with unique flavors, resulting in a delicious medley of snacks and more substantial dishes. Favorites include pork ribs with smoked-fish palm syrup and Indonesian long pepper, and the beef brisket with chili jam, aioli, bao (a Vietnamese steamed bun filled with meat or vegetables), pickled red onion, and bone broth. ✉ *91 S. 6th St., at Berry St., Williamsburg* ☎ *718/599–3090* ⊕ *www.fattycue.com* ▤ *AE, MC, V* Ⓜ *L to Bedford Ave.*

$
SOUTHERN

✕**Fette Sau.** It may surprise you to come to a former auto-body repair shop to eat meat, but the funky building and outside courtyard seem just right for some serious 'cue. Here a huge wood-and-gas smoker delivers well-smoked brisket, sausages, ribs, and even duck, ordered by the pound. Avoid the disappointing salads and sides, and instead order some of the more than 40 American whiskeys and 10 microbrews. Come early, as tables fill up quick, and even with 700 pounds of meat a night, the good stuff sometimes runs out by 9 pm. ✉ *354 Metropolitan Ave., between Havemeyer and Roebling Sts., Williamsburg* ☎ *718/963–3404* ⊕ *fettesaubbq.com* ⌕ *Reservations not accepted* ▤ *MC, V* ⊘ *No lunch weekdays* Ⓜ *L to Lorimer St.*

$$$
MEXICAN

✕**La Superior.** Serving some of Brooklyn's best Mexican grub this side of the Red Hook ball fields, La Superior melds Mexican street food with the Williamsburg ethic. The service is slapdash and the decor is unremarkable, but the food—from beef-tongue tacos to pescadillas (fish quesadillas)—always delivers. Don't be surprised if your waiter has a seat at your table while discussing the menu. ✉ *295 Berry St., Williamsburg* ☎ *718/388–5988* ⊕ *lasuperiornyc.com* ⌕ *Reservations not accepted* ▤ *No credit cards* Ⓜ *L to Bedford Ave.; J, M, Z to Marcy Ave.*

$$$$
STEAK

✕**Peter Luger Steak House.** Long before Brooklyn was chic, even the snobbiest Manhattanites flocked to Luger's. Other steak houses have more elegant ambience, bigger wine lists, and less brusque service, but the steak makes the trip to this 122-year-old temple of red meat worth it. Three tips: bring a buddy (individual steaks are available, but porterhouse is served only for two, three, or four), make a reservation (prime slots fill up more than a month in advance), and bring lots of cash—Luger's doesn't take plastic. The lunch-only burger is beloved among locals. ✉ *178 Broadway, at Driggs Ave., Williamsburg* ☎ *718/387–7400* ⊕ *www.peterluger.com* ⌕ *Reservations essential* ▤ *No credit cards* Ⓜ *J, M, Z to Marcy Ave.*

$$$
AMERICAN
Fodor's Choice
★

✕**Rye.** Chow down on delicious bistro classics and more creative American fare at this dark and moody speakeasy-style hideaway on a little-trodden block. Enter through the unmarked door and find yourself in a world of leather cushions, pressed-tin ceilings, dark woods, mosaic floors, and a 100-year-old oak bar. The signature meat-loaf sandwich is a must-have, served with crispy buttermilk onions and horseradish sauce. Wash it down with one of the great cocktails; try the Havemayer with overproof rye whiskey. Note that reservations are accepted for parties of six or more. ✉ *247 S. 1st St., at Havemeyer St., Williamsburg*

☎ *718/218–8047* ⊕ *www.ryerestaurant.com* ▪ *AE, DC, MC, V* ⊗ *No lunch weekdays* Ⓜ *L to Lorimer St.; J, M, Z to Marcy Ave.*

GALLERIES

Williamsburg's 70-plus galleries are distributed randomly, with no single main drag. Plan your trip ahead of time using the online **Brooklyn Art Guide** at ⊕ *www.wagmag.org.* (You can also pick up a copy at neighborhood galleries and some cafés.) Hours vary widely, but almost all are open weekends. Call ahead.

Although serendipitous poking is the best way to sample the art, two longtime galleries are must-sees. **Pierogi** (✉ *177 N. 9th St., between Bedford and Driggs Aves., Williamsburg* ☎ *718/599–2144* ⊕ *www. pierogi2000.com*) remains hip yet cheerfully accessible. Be sure to check out the famous "Flat Files," an online collection of the portfolios of more than 700 young contemporary artists.

At **Sideshow Gallery** (✉ *319 Bedford Ave., between S. 2nd and S. 3rd Sts., Williamsburg* ☎ *718/486–8180* ⊕ *www.sideshowgallery.com*) enjoy the diverse exhibitions as well as readings and concerts.

NIGHTLIFE

Barcade. Like Chuck E. Cheese for grown-ups, Barcade invites you to reminisce about your arcade-loving youth by playing one of more than 30 vintage arcade games for only a quarter. Casual players will love familiar favorites like Ms. Pacman, and serious video gamers will gravitate toward rarities like Rampage. But it's not just about the games; enjoy a full menu of small-label beers while you check out the hipster crowd. ✉ *388 Union Ave., near Ainslie, Williamsburg* ☎ *718/302–6464* ⊕ *www.barcadebrooklyn.com* Ⓜ *L to Lorimer St.*

Brooklyn Brewery. Brooklyn was once known as America's brewing capital; at the turn of the 20th century Williamsburg alone was home to nearly 60 breweries. The originals are mostly gone, but this relative newcomer has been bringing back the hops since opening here in 1996.

The Friday-evening happy hour means $4 beers—try the popular Brooklyn Lager, the Belgian-inspired Local 1, or one of the seasonal brews. Beer buffs can join a free guided tour on Saturday or Sunday afternoon. ✉ *79 N. 11th St., between Berry St. and Wythe Ave., Williamsburg* ☎ *718/486–7422* ⊕ *www.brooklynbrewery.com* ⊗ *Fri. 6–11 pm, Sat. and Sun. noon–6 pm* Ⓜ *L to Bedford Ave.*

Pete's Candy Store. Off Williamsburg's beaten path, this bar has a retro feel, a friendly crowd, and cheerful bartenders. The back room, smaller than a subway car, hosts intimate music performances nightly. Brainy hipsters come here for spelling bees and bingo, and the infamous quiz-off contest every Wednesday night. There's no actual candy here, so try a sandwich or craft beer instead. ✉ *709 Lorimer St., between Frost and Richardson Sts., Williamsburg* ☎ *718/302–3770* ⊕ *www. petescandystore.com* Ⓜ *L to Lorimer St.*

Radegast Hall & Biergarten. The perfect alternative if you don't want to schlep all the way out to Queens for alfresco Slavic beers, Radegast Hall & Biergarten serves Central European suds and hearty eats under a retractable roof. Schnitzel, goulash, and pretzels make for some authentic complements to the beers here, together with live music on some nights. ✉ *113 N. 3rd St., Williamsburg* 🕿 *718/963–3973* ⊕ *radegasthall.com* Ⓜ *L to Bedford Ave.*

SHOPPING

Though the boutiques on Bedford Avenue are best for people-watching, you'll also find stores along Grand Street, and on many side streets, especially North 6th.

At the **Realform Girdle Building** (✉ *218 Bedford Ave., Williamsburg*)—the closest thing Williamsburg has to a mall—pick up free newspapers and magazines that will help you get a read on the local scene. Attractions include a small café, a new/used record store, achingly hip boutiques, and an art bookstore.

The small size of the **Bedford Cheese Shop** (✉ *229 Bedford Ave., at N. 4th St., Williamsburg* 🕿 *718/599–7588* ⊕ *www.bedfordcheeseshop.com*) belies the fact that this is one of the city's best cheese stores, packed with an encyclopedic assortment of artisan cheeses as well as small-producer cured meats, gourmet imported oils, chocolates, and other dry goods. Don't miss the quirky and occasionally salacious descriptions of the cheeses ("looks like dirty scrimshaw but tastes like a peat-covered goat teat").

One of the standout boutiques on Bedford, **Catbird** (✉ *219 Bedford Ave., near N. 5th St., Williamsburg* 🕿 *718/599–3457* ⊕ *www.catbirdnyc. com*), is a dollhouse-size shop whose shelves are filled with handmade jewelry, home accessories, and whimsical hats.

Brooklyn's thriving home-design scene is often credited to **Future Perfect** (✉ *115 N. 6th St., at Berry St., Williamsburg* 🕿 *718/599–6278* ⊕ *www. thefutureperfect.com*), which has since opened a Manhattan branch.

Even if you're not planning on shipping home a Bone Chair made entirely of cow ribs, you'll have a great time browsing the playful and often ironic furnishings from better-known local Brooklyn designers and international exclusives. **A&G Merch** (✉ *111 N. 6th St., Williamsburg* 🕿 *718/388–1779* ⊕ *www.aandgmerch.com*) sells affordable home accessories that are both contemporary and stylish.

Local fashionistas and out-of-towners alike flock to **Beacon's Closet** (✉ *88 N. 11th St., Williamsburg* 🕿 *718/486–0816* ⊕ *www.beaconscloset.com*) for its huge selection of used and vintage clothing and accessories where real deals can be scored if you devote some time to browsing.

Mandate of Heaven (✉ *158 Cook St., Williamsburg* 🕿 *718/366–2565* ⊕ *mandateofheavenclothing.com*) sells quirky, delicately reimagined pieces sourced from the ample vintage clothing stores of Williamsburg. You'll find one-of-a-kind and handmade clothes, from jeans to capes.

CARROLL GARDENS, COBBLE HILL, AND BOERUM HILL

On Atlantic Avenue's south side, the three adjacent neighborhoods of Carroll Gardens, Cobble Hill, and Boerum Hill form a quiet residential area of leafy streets lined with 19th-century town houses.

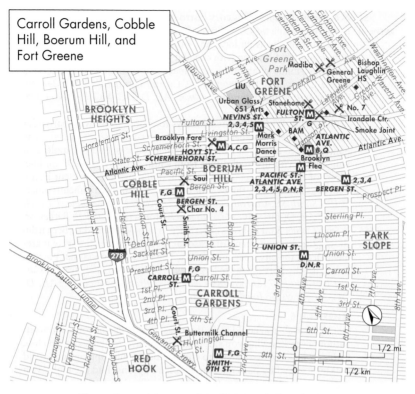

Carroll Gardens, Cobble Hill, Boerum Hill, and Fort Greene

The action swirls around **Smith Street**, a famed restaurant row augmented by fresh, fashionable boutiques, as well as **Court Street's** restaurants, bookstores, and old-fashioned bakeries.

Nearby on **Atlantic Avenue** between Court and Clinton is a rapidly gentrifying Middle Eastern enclave, which includes the emporium **Sahadi's** (⊠ *187 Atlantic Ave.* ☎ *718/624–4550*) great for purchasing a veritable bazaar of olives, baklava, and other treats. Get to this neighborhood by taking the F train to Bergen Street or Carroll Street.

WHERE TO EAT

$$$$ ✕ **Brooklyn Fare.** At Brooklyn's only restaurant with two coveted
GLOBAL Michelin stars, local star chef César Ramirez and his sous-chefs offer an inimitable culinary performance during three nightly seatings. Out of the multitude of copper pots and pans and on to dainty dishes come 20 seafood-focused concoctions presented to 18 diners seated at a semicircular steel counter. Examples include king salmon parfait with basil gelee, avocado, maple syrup, and mustard, and fresh tofu and king crab blended with matsutake mushrooms and dashi sauce. It's BYOB. ⊠ *200 Schermerhorn St., near Hoyt St., Downtown* ☎ *718/243–0050* ⊕ *www.brooklynfare.com* ⌔ *Reservations essential.* ▭ *AE, D, DC, MC, V* ☉ *Closed Sun. and Mon. No lunch* Ⓜ *A, C to Hoyt–Schermerhorn; 2, 3 to Hoyt St.; 4, 5 to Nevins St.; B, M, Q, R to Dekalb Ave.*

$$ ✕ **Buttermilk Channel.** This cozy bistro serves up a spirited slice of down-
AMERICAN   home Americana on Court Street. Locals swear by comfort-food main-
stays with emphasis on local and organic, especially the all-time fave:
buttermilk-fried chicken with cheddar waffles. Other standouts include
the house-made charcuterie and snacks like handmade mozzarella.
✉ *524 Court St.at Huntington St., Carroll Gardens* ☎ *718/852–8490*
⊕ *www.buttermilkchannelnyc.com* ▭ *AE, D, DC, MC, V* ☺ *No lunch
weekdays.* Ⓜ *F to Carroll St.*

$ ✕ **Char No. 4.** With 300-plus whiskeys to choose from, with particular
AMERICAN   accent on American labels, Char No. 4 is a connoisseur's dream. (The
name refers to barrels in which the golden liquor is aged.) Complement
your tipple with updated dishes from south of the Mason-Dixon line.
Many of the appetizers involve bacon; don't miss the thick-cut bacon
with peas and carrots, the BLT, or the cheese curds with pimento sauce.
✉ *196 Smith St., Carroll Gardens* ☎ *718/643–2106* ⊕ *www.charno4.
com* ▭ *AE, D, DC, MC, V* ☺ *No lunch Mon.–Thurs.* Ⓜ *F to Bergen St.*

$$$ ✕ **Saul.** Owner Saul Bolton's experience as a cook at famed Le Bernardin
AMERICAN   shows; the dynamic menu of seasonal specials features first-rate ingre-
dients from the city's best purveyors. The food is so good that patrons
only wish the portions were larger. ✉ *140 Smith St., near Bergen, Carroll Gardens* ☎ *718/935–9844* ⊕ *www.saulrestaurant.com* ▭ *AE, D,
DC, MC, V* ☺ *No lunch* Ⓜ *F to Bergen St.*

NIGHTLIFE

Brooklyn Social. You could walk right past this inconspicuous storefront
without even knowing you skipped past a converted men's social club.
Inside, a local crowd listens to the jukebox while sipping old-world
cocktails served by bartenders in butcher's aprons. End the night with
a game of pool. ✉ *335 Smith St., between President and Carroll Sts.,
Carroll Gardens* ☎ *718/858–7758* ⊕ *www.brooklynsocialbar.com* Ⓜ *F
to Carroll St.*

FORT GREENE

One of Brooklyn's most diverse neighborhoods, Fort Greene has long
been a home to writers like Richard Wright, Marianne Moore, and
John Steinbeck, and many musicians such as Betty Carter, Branford
Marsalis, and even rapper Ol' Dirty Bastard. Architecture buffs will see
many great examples of Eastlake and Italianate styles, especially in the
facade of BAM, Brooklyn's performing arts powerhouse.

Today the city has built on the success of BAM by creating a cultural
district around it. Here, you can take a modern dance class at the **Mark
Morris Dance Center** (✉ *3 Lafayette Ave.* ⊕ *www.markmorrisdancegroup.
org*), see African diaspora performances by **651Arts** (⊕ *www.651arts.
org*) in various venues around the neighborhood, catch avant-garde
theater at the **Irondale Center** (✉ *85 S. Oxford St.* ⊕ *www.irondale.org*),
or spend a weekend learning to blow glass at **UrbanGlass** (✉ *647 Fulton
St.* ⊕ *www.urbanglass.org*).

Fodor'sChoice   **The Brooklyn Academy of Music.** BAM is a comprehensive arts anchor for
★   the borough, with diverse and cutting-edge offerings in opera, theater,
dance, music, film, and more shown in a 1908 neo-Italianate showpiece.

The Brooklyn Flea Market

Quirky, inclusive, and full of unclaimed treasures—that's Brooklyn in a nutshell, and it also aptly describes the Brooklyn Flea. This little market that could is now one of Brooklyn's most popular shopping attractions, luring locals and bargain hunters from afar with vintage finds, hip crafts, and crazy-delicious eats.

The Flea is a hybrid of traditional flea market, garage sale, and crafts fair. It's a tumble of the expensive, the cheap, and the strange. Some vendors hawk high-end items like antique doors refashioned into tables, rescued fixtures from prewar houses, or midcentury lamps identical to those in *Mad Men*.

The most "Brooklyn-y" component is the local artisans, and buying their one-of-a-kind handmade wares gives shoppers the altruistic feeling of supporting arts and crafts, whether that's silk-screen T-shirts of giant squid, tongue-and-cheek charm bracelets with little daggers, or hand-stitched stuffed elephants. You'll also find not a small number of oddly specialized booths. Exhibit A: the vendor who sells nothing beyond oil paintings of bicycles. Why not? Finally, there is plenty of bric-a-brac to sift through: great stuff that may not be practical (mink stoles, nonfunctional alarm clocks, *Star Wars* collectibles), but it makes for fun browsing.

When you've exhausted the shopping side of things, the Flea boasts some fantastic food options. You'll find fat pretzels from Sigmund Pretzel Shop, funny franks from Asia Dogs, cold cuts and sandwiches from Mile End delicatessen, organic ice cream from Blue Marble, even the popular McClure's pickles, all with plenty of Crop to Cup family-farmed coffee to get a second wind.

The Flea takes place in two locations every weekend from mid-March to late November. The market splits time between the parking lot of a local school on Saturday and the stunning interior of the landmark Williamsburgh Savings Bank (now an event space known as Skylight One Hanson) on Sunday. During the colder months the Flea happens at its indoor location on both Saturday and Sunday. ✉ *Mid-Mar.–late Nov., Sat.: Bishop Laughlin Memorial High School, 176 Lafayette Ave., between Clermont and Vanderbilt Ave., Fort Greene; Sun.: One Hanson Pl., Fort Greene* ✉ *Winter: One Hanson Pl., Fort Greene* ⊕ *www.brooklynflea.com* 💲 *Free* ☾ *Sat. and Sun. 10–5* Ⓜ *A, C to Lafayette Ave. for outdoor location; 2, 3, 4, 5, B, Q to Atlantic Ave.; D, N, R to Atlantic Ave.–Pacific St. for indoor location.*

Late choreographer Pina Bausch, director Milos Forman, and composer Philip Glass have all recently presented work here. The BAM Rose Cinemas shows both art-house and mainstream films. The season's biggest annual event is the Next Wave Festival each fall, which showcases work by emerging and established artists.

BAM holds performances in the Beaux-Arts–style Howard Gilman Opera House and at the nearby **Harvey Theater** (✉ *651 Fulton St.*), a 1904 vaudeville house whose renovation purposefully retained some of its crumbling beauty. ✉ *Peter Jay Sharp Bldg., 30 Lafayette Ave.,* *between Ashland Pl. and St. Felix St., Fort Greene* ☎ 718/636–4100 ⊕ *www.bam.org* Ⓜ *C to Lafayette Ave.; 2, 3, 4, 5, B, Q to Atlantic Ave.; D, N, R to Atlantic Ave.–Pacific St.*

WHERE TO EAT

$$

NEW AMERICAN

✕ **BAMcafé.** Starting two hours before opera-house performances, enjoy nouveau American fare in the dramatic Lepercq Space on the mezzanine level. On Friday and Saturday, when free concerts take place as part of BAMcafé Live (June–September), BAMcafé opens at 8 pm with a limited menu. ✉ *30 Lafayette Ave., at Ashland Pl., Fort Greene* ☎ 718/623–7811 ⊕ *www.bam.org* ▭ *D, DC, MC, V* Ⓜ *D, M, N, R to Pacific St.; 2, 3, 4, 5, B, Q to Atlantic Ave.; C to Lafayette Ave.*

$

AMERICAN

✕ **The General Greene.** A good example of the hearty, stick-to-your-ribs fare that Brooklyn serves up these days, the General Greene is a neighborhood darling. Waiting for a table is part of the experience, especially at brunch time on weekends, as are the cocktails and the famous salted-caramel sundae. ✉ *229 DeKalb Ave., Fort Greene* ☎ 718/222–1510 ⊕ *www.thegeneralgreene.com* ▭ *MC, V* Ⓜ *C to Lafayette Ave.; B, M, Q, R to DeKalb Ave.*

$$$

SOUTH AFRICAN

✕ **Madiba.** The borough's only South African restaurant (and the city's first), is styled after a traditional shebeen, a local bar known for its convivial atmosphere and lively conversation. This eatery—with its wooden benches, colorful African-theme paintings, and quirky folk art—has staple curries and stews, as well as offbeat options such as ostrich carpaccio and spicy peri-peri prawns. ✉ *195 Dekalb Ave., Fort Greene* ☎ 718/855–9190 ⊕ *www.madibarestaurant.com* ▭ *AE, D, DC, MC, V* Ⓜ *C to Lafayette Ave.; 2, 3, 4, 5, B, Q to Atlantic Ave*

$$

NEW AMERICAN

✕ **No. 7.** Sit at the marble-top bar or on the banquettes in the back at this buzzy neighborhood bistro lighted up by Edison bulbs. The frequently changing menu takes American classics and throws them for a global spin. The result is a nouveau fusion that pulls in local diners in droves. Recent dishes have included cashew-crusted tofu with noodles, poached egg, and pickled coconut as well as bouchot mussels with quince, Chinese sausage, and spaghetti squash. ✉ *7 Greene Ave., Fort Greene* ☎ 718/522–6370 ⊕ *www.no7restaurant.com* ▭ *MC, V* ⊘ *No lunch weekdays; bar only Mon.* Ⓜ *C to Lafayette Ave; 2, 3, 4, 5, B, Q to Atlantic Ave.*

$

BARBECUE

✕ **Smoke Joint.** Up the street from BAM, find in-house-smoked "real New York barbecue," which translates to a mix of regional specialties like incredibly moist chicken, spicy dry-rubbed beef short ribs, collard greens, and meaty barbecued beans. Several kinds of sauces are served on the side, and the counter service couldn't be friendlier at this truly local joint. ✉ *87 S. Elliot Pl., Fort Greene* ☎ 718/797–1011 ⊕ *www.thesmokejoint.com* ⌲ *Reservations not accepted* ▭ *AE, DC, MC, V* Ⓜ *C to Lafayette Ave.; 2, 3, 4, 5, B, Q to Atlantic Ave.; D, M, N, R to Pacific St.*

$$

NEW AMERICAN

✕ **Stonehome Wine Bar & Restaurant.** The place to go before or after BAM if you want your food to match your wine, this dimly lighted basement hideaway serves great tasting flights—three samples for $18—and 35 wines by the glass. The cheese and charcuterie are stellar, as are the in-house-made pâtés and sausages. The small and uncomplicated menu features market-fresh new American fare, such as the all-time fave: organic air-dried chicken served with seasonal sides. On a recent fall night, those included cheddar grits, kale, and dark chicken jus. ✉ *87 Lafayette Ave., at S. Portland Ave., Fort Greene* ☎ *718/624–9443* ⊕ *www.stonehomewinebar.com* ▭ *AE, MC, V* ⊘ *No lunch* Ⓜ *C to Lafayette Ave.*

12

PROSPECT PARK/PROSPECT HEIGHTS/PARK SLOPE

Follow dog walkers and bicyclists to idyllic 585-acre **Prospect Park**, designed by Olmsted and Vaux of Central Park fame. Along with rolling meadows, shady forests, and a series of lakes, there are concerts and kids' programs.

Adjacent to the park are two of Brooklyn's main attractions: the **Brooklyn Botanic Garden**, a must-see during its springtime Cherry Blossom Festival, and the **Brooklyn Museum**, known for its Egyptian and feminist art collections.

The neighborhood that literally slopes down from the park, **Park Slope** is known affectionately as "Stroller Land." This family-friendly neighborhood is full of academics, writers, and late-blooming couples pushing Bugaboo strollers to its cafés and designer boutiques.

One of Brooklyn's most comfortable places to live, Park Slope contains row after row of immaculate brownstones that date from its turn-of-the-20th-century heyday, when it had the nation's highest per-capita income. To see some of the neighborhood's most beautiful houses, walk between 7th Avenue and Prospect Park along any of the streets between Sterling Place and 4th Street.

☾ ★ **Brooklyn Botanic Garden.** The 52 acres of this beloved Brooklyn retreat, one of the finest botanic gardens in the country, are a must-see, especially in spring and summer. A major attraction is the beguiling Japanese Hill-and-Pond Garden—complete with a pond, blazing red *torii* gate, and Shinto shrine. Nearby, the Japanese cherry arbor turns into a breathtaking cloud of pink every spring; the Sakura Matsuri, a two-day cherry blossom festival, is a hugely popular event.

Also be sure to wander through the Cranford Rose Garden (5,000 plants, 1,200 varieties); the Fragrance Garden, designed especially for the blind; and the Shakespeare Garden, featuring more than 80 plants immortalized by the Bard. At the Steinhardt Conservatory, desert, tropical, temperate, and aquatic vegetation thrives. Don't miss the extraordinary C. V. Starr Bonsai Museum for close to 100 miniature Japanese specimens, some more than a century old. Near the conservatory are a café and a gift shop, with bulbs, plants, and gardening books as well as jewelry.

Entrances to the garden are on Eastern Parkway, next to the subway station; on Washington Avenue, behind the Brooklyn Museum; and on Flatbush Avenue at Empire Boulevard. Free garden tours meet at the front gate every weekend at 1 pm. ✉ *900 Washington Ave., between Crown and Carroll Sts., Prospect Heights* ☎ *718/623–7200* ⊕ *www. bbg.org* ⊠ *$8; free all day Tues., Sat. before noon, and weekdays from*

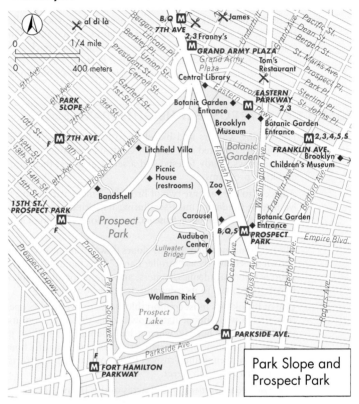

Park Slope and Prospect Park

mid-Nov. to mid-Mar. Combo ticket with Brooklyn Museum $16 ⊙ *Mid-Mar.–late Oct.: grounds Tues.–Fri. 8–6, weekends 10–6; conservatory daily 10–5:30. Nov.–mid-Mar.: grounds Tues.–Fri. 8–4:30, weekends 10–4:30; conservatory daily 10–4. Closed Mon. except holidays* Ⓜ *2, 3 to Eastern Pkwy.; B, Q to Prospect Park.*

★ **Brooklyn Museum.** The Brooklyn Museum has long stood in the shadow of Manhattan's Metropolitan. With more than 1 million pieces in its permanent collection, from Rodin sculptures to Andean textiles and Assyrian wall reliefs, the city's second-largest art museum now has a welcoming new design, more populist shows, and neighborhood events. The city is finally starting to appreciate this hidden gem.

Along with changing exhibitions, highlights include Egyptian art, one of the best collections of its kind in the world; African and pre-Columbian art; and Native American art. Seek out the museum's works by Georgia O'Keeffe, Winslow Homer, John Singer Sargent, George Bellows, Thomas Eakins, and Milton Avery—all stunners. Also check out the Elizabeth A. Sackler Center for Feminist Art, which hosts traveling exhibits in addition to serving as the permanent home to Judy Chicago's installation *The Dinner Party* (1974–79).

12

On the first Saturday of each month the museum throws an extremely popular free evening of art, music, dancing, film screenings, and readings, starting at 5 pm. ⊠ *200 Eastern Pkwy., at Washington Ave., Prospect Heights* ☎ *718/638–5000* ⊕ *www.brooklynmuseum.org* ⊠ *$10 suggested donation. Combo ticket with Brooklyn Botanic Garden $16* ⊘ *Wed. and weekends 11–6, Thurs. and Fri. 11–10; 1st Sat. of month 11–11; call for program schedule* Ⓜ *2, 3 to Eastern Pkwy./Brooklyn Museum.*

Central Library. Across Grand Army Plaza from the park entrance is this sleek, modern temple of learning—the central location of the Brooklyn Public Library. The building resembles an open book, with the entrance at the book's spine; on the facade, gold-leaf figures celebrate art and science.

Bright limestone walls and perfect proportions make this an impressive 20th-century New York building. Inside, more than 1.5 million books, public programs, and exhibitions in the lobby will keep you busy for at least a few hours. ⊠ *10 Grand Army Plaza, Prospect Heights* ☎ *718/230–2100* ⊕ *www.brooklynpubliclibrary.org* ⊘ *Mon.–Thurs. 9–9, Fri. and Sat. 10–6, Sun. 1–5* Ⓜ *2, 3 to Grand Army Plaza; Q to 7th Ave.*

☾
Fodor's Choice
★

Prospect Park. Brooklyn residents are fiercely passionate about Prospect Park. Designed by Frederick Law Olmsted and Calvert Vaux, the park was completed in the late 1880s. Olmsted once said that he was prouder of it than of any of his other works—including Manhattan's Central Park.

A good way to experience the park is to walk along its 3.5-mi circular drive and make detours off it as you wish. The drive is closed to cars at all times except weekday rush hours. Families with children should head straight for the eastern side, where most kids' attractions are clustered.

The park's north entrance is at **Grand Army Plaza,** where the Soldiers' and Sailors' Memorial Arch honors Civil War veterans. (Look familiar? It's patterned after the Arc de Triomphe in Paris.) Three heroic sculptural groupings adorn the arch: atop, a dynamic four-horse chariot; to either side, the victorious Union Army and Navy of the Civil War. The inner arch has bas-reliefs of presidents Abraham Lincoln and Ulysses S. Grant, sculpted by Thomas Eakins and William O'Donovan, respectively.

To the northwest of the arch, Neptune and a passel of debauched Tritons leer over the edges of the **Bailey Fountain.** On Saturdays year-round a greenmarket at the plaza sells produce, flowers and plants, cheese, and baked goods to throngs of locals. Other days, you can find a few vendors selling snacks here and at the 9th Street entrance.

If you walk down the park's west drive from Grand Army Plaza, you'll first encounter **Litchfield Villa** (☎ *718/965–8951* ⊠ *Free* ⊘ *Weekdays 9–5*), an Italianate hilltop mansion built in 1857 for a prominent railroad magnate. It has housed the park's headquarters since 1883; visitors are welcome to step inside and view the domed octagonal rotunda.

The **Prospect Park Band Shell** (☎ *718/855–7882 Celebrate Brooklyn Festival* ⊕ *www.bricartsmedia.org*) is the home of the annual Celebrate Brooklyn Festival, which from early June through mid-August sponsors free films and concerts that have included Afro-Caribbean jazz, flamenco dance troupes from Spain, David Byrne, and the Brooklyn Philharmonic.

Styled after Sansovino's 16th-century Library at St. Mark's in Venice, the **Prospect Park Audubon Center and Visitor Center at the Boathouse**, built in 1904, sits opposite the Lullwater Bridge, creating an idyllic spot for watching pedal boats and wildlife, or just taking a break at the café. Here, learn about nature through interactive exhibits, park tours, and educational programs especially for kids. On a nice day, take a ride on the electric boat to tour the Lullwater and Prospect Lake. You can also sign up for a bird-watching tour to see some of the 200 species spotted here. ⊠ *Prospect Park* ☎ *718/287–3400* ⊕ *www.prospectpark. org/audubon* 🖆 *Audubon Center free; electric-boat tours $8* ⊙ *Audubon Center: Apr.–Sept., Thurs.–Sun. noon–5; Oct.–Mar., weekends noon–4; closed in Jan.; call for program and tour times. Electric-boat tours: May–Aug., Thurs.–Sun. noon–4:30; Sept.–mid-Oct., weekends noon–3:30, every 30 mins.*

Lefferts Historic House (☎ *718/789–2822* 🖆 *Free* ⊙ *Apr. and May, Sat. and Sun. noon–5; June and Sept., Thurs.–Sun. noon–5; July and Aug., Thurs.–Sun. noon–6; Oct., Thurs.–Sun. noon–4; Nov. and Dec., and Feb. and Mar., Sat. and Sun. noon–4*) is a Dutch Colonial farmhouse built in 1783 and moved to Prospect Park in 1918. Rooms of the historic house-museum are furnished with antiques and reproductions from the 1820s, when the house was last redecorated. The museum hosts all kinds of activities for kids; call for information.

Climb aboard a giraffe or sit inside a dragon-pulled chariot at the immaculately restored **Prospect Park Carousel**, handcrafted in 1912 by master carver Charles Carmel. ☎ *718/282–7789* 🖆 *$2 per ride* ⊙ *Apr.–June, Sept., and Oct., Thurs.–Sun. noon–5; July–Labor Day, Thurs.–Sun. noon–6.*

Small and friendly, **Prospect Park Zoo** is perfect for those children who may be overwhelmed by the city's larger animal sanctuaries. Of the 400 inhabitants and 125 species, kids seem to be especially fond of the sea lions and the red pandas. An outdoor discovery trail has a simulated prairie-dog burrow, a duck pond, and kangaroos and wallabies in habitat. Be aware that there are no cafés, only vending machines. ⊠ *450 Flatbush Ave., Prospect Heights* ☎ *718/399–7339* ⊕ *www. prospectparkzoo.com* 🖆 *$8* ⊙ *Apr.–Oct., weekdays 10–5, weekends 10–5:30; Nov.–Mar., daily 10–4:30; last ticket 30 mins before closing* Ⓜ *2, 3 to Eastern Pkwy.; B, Q to Prospect Park.*

OFF THE BEATEN PATH

☾ **Brooklyn Children's Museum.** A mile east of Grand Army Plaza is the oldest children's museum in the world, now housed in a sparkling Rafael Viñoly–designed "green" building. Here kids can trek through natural habitats found in the city, run a bakery, create African-patterned fabric, and even become DJs, mixing the rhythms of the outdoors to make music. ⊠ *145 Brooklyn Ave., at St. Marks Ave., Crown Heights* ☎ *718/735–4400* ⊕ *www.brooklynkids.org* ⊠ *$7.50* ⊘ *Tues.–Sun. 10–5* Ⓜ *C to Kingston–Throop Aves.; 3 to Kingston Ave., A, C to Nostrand Ave.*

WHERE TO EAT

$$ ✕ **al di là.** This northern Italian hot spot has been consistently packed
ITALIAN since it first opened in 1998, and it's easy to understand why: affordable
★ prices, a relaxed and charming environment, and simple yet soulfully comforting cuisine such as the red beet ravioli swimming in butter and poppy seeds. The no-reservations policy ensures that the place always has a buzz around it from waiting patrons. ⊠ *248 5th Ave., at Carroll St., Park Slope* ☎ *718/783–4565* ⊕ *www.aldilatrattoria.com* ⊠ *Reservations not accepted* ⊟ *MC, V* ⊘ *No lunch Tues.* Ⓜ *F to 15th St.–Prospect Park; R to Union St.*

$$ ✕ **applewood.** Do the math: lavish devotion to seasonal ingredients +
NEW AMERICAN supporting local farmers + relaxed service in a pretty pale-yellow dining room + simple flavors layered in interesting ways = one thing—an amazing restaurant. The menu changes constantly; recent highlights have included a sautéed North Carolina wreckfish with tomato-okra stew, parsnips, and mixed greens. ⊠ *501 11th St., at 7th Ave. Park Slope* ☎ *718/788–1810* ⊕ *www.applewoodny.com* ⊟ *D, MC, V* ⊘ *Closed Mon. No lunch Tues.–Fri.* Ⓜ *F to 7th Ave.*

$ ✕ **Franny's.** Though many swear by Grimaldi's for the borough's best pie
PIZZA (or the two Brooklyn newcomers: Roberta's in Bushwick and Lucali in Carroll Gardens), this Park Slope pizza upstart has developed quite a following of its own. The crisp, thin-crust pizzas run the gamut, from a "naked" pie with olive oil and salt to their justly famous clam-and-garlic iteration. Many of the toppings are seasonal and locally sourced. ⊠ *295 Flatbush Ave., Park Slope* ☎ *718/230–0221* ⊕ *www.frannysbrooklyn. com* ⊠ *Reservations not accepted* ⊟ *MC, V* ⊘ *No lunch weekdays* Ⓜ *B, Q to 7th Ave.; 2, 3 to Bergen St., 4, 5, N, R to Pacific St.*

$$ ✕ **James.** Occupying the ground floor of a brownstone on a leafy corner
NEW AMERICAN of historic residential blocks, this neighborhood find is serious about its seasonal food and dedicated service. Pressed-tin ceilings, an antique bar, leather banquettes, and a dazzling light fixture on the ceiling grace the softly lighted dining room. The food reflects old-world European techniques, with fresh herbs picked from the restaurant's adjacent garden. ⊠ *605 Carlton Ave., Prospect Heights* ☎ *718/942–4255* ⊕ *www. jamesrestaurantny.com*

¢ ✕ **Tom's Restaurant.** For friendly service and great diner fare, like fluffy
AMERICAN pumpkin-walnut pancakes served with homemade flavored butters, head three blocks north of the Brooklyn Museum to this family-owned restaurant, which opened in 1936. On weekends lines are long, but your wait is eased by free coffee and orange slices. ⊠ *782 Washington Ave., at Sterling Pl., Prospect Heights* ☎ *718/636–9738* ⊠ *Reservations not accepted* ⊟ *No credit cards* ⊘ *No dinner* Ⓜ *2, 3 to Grand Army Plaza.*

12

NIGHTLIFE

Barbès. It's not *quite* like stepping into the funky Parisian neighborhood of the same name, but this cozy bar does have French-accented bartenders, pressed-tin ceilings, and a red-tinted back room. Diverse events range from the energetic Slavic Soul Party performance on Tuesday to classical music concerts. ⊠ *376 9th St., at 6th Ave., Park Slope* ☏ *347/422–0248* ⊕ *www.barbesbrooklyn.com* Ⓜ *F to 7th Ave.*

Southpaw. Folk, rock, and pop for refined tastes are on the bill at this Park Slope hangout, recognized as one of South Brooklyn's most popular music venues. The sprawling space is packed with glam twentysomethings on any given night, but country music showcases and the occasional kid-friendly family show on weekends keep everyone in the neighborhood happy. ⊠ *125 5th Ave., between St. Johns Pl. and Sterling Pl., Park Slope* ☏ *718/230–0236* ⊕ *www.spsounds.com* Ⓜ *R to Union St., F to 7th Ave.*

Union Hall. You'll feel immediately comfortable at this large, airy hangout. Grab a beer up front in the classy library, or, if you're up for a little sport, join friendly locals in a game of bocce ball. In the basement, check out some rising indie rock stars on stage. ⊠ *702 Union St., at 5th Ave., Park Slope* ☏ *718/638–4400* ⊕ *www.unionhallny.com* Ⓜ *R to Union St.*

SHOPPING

Seventh Avenue is Park Slope's main shopping street, with long-established restaurants, bookstores, shops, cafés, bakeries, churches, and real-estate agents (one favorite neighborhood pastime is window-shopping for new apartments). More fun, however, are the newer restaurants and cute boutiques along 5th Avenue.

Start out with a snack from gourmet food store **Bierkraft** (⊠ *191 5th Ave., near Union St., Park Slope* ☏ *718/230–7600* ⊕ *www.bierkraft. com*). In addition to nearly 1,000 craft beers (available by the bottle), they also sell artisan cheeses, boutique chocolates, olives, and other edible goodies.

Just one of the many excellent women's clothing stores dotting the area, **Bird** (⊠ *316 5th Ave., between 2nd and 3rd Sts., Park Slope* ☏ *718/768–4940* ⊕ *www.shopbird.com*) is one of the oldest and best. In addition to their many well-curated brands of women's clothing, like Martin Margiela and 3.1 Phillip Lim, Bird also stocks both men's apparel and baby clothes, and has two other Brooklyn locations (in Cobble Hill, at 220 Smith St., ☏ *718/797–3775*, and in Williamsburg, at 203 Grand St. ☏ *718/388–1656*).

At **Brooklyn Superhero Supply Co.** (⊠ *372 5th Ave. at 7th St., Park Slope* ☏ *718/499–9884* ⊕ *www.superherosupplies.com*) young superheroes can purchase capes, grappling hooks, secret identity kits, and more from staff who never drop the game of pretend. Proceeds benefit the free drop-in tutoring center (run by nonprofit organization 826NYC) in a "secret lair" behind a swinging bookcase.

CONEY ISLAND AND BRIGHTON BEACH

Fodor's Choice
★

Experience the sounds, smells, and sights of a New York City summer: hot dogs and ice cream, suntan lotion, excited crowds, and weathered old men fishing.

Named Konijn Eiland (Rabbit Island) by the Dutch for its wild rabbit population, the Coney Island peninsula has a boardwalk, a 2.5-mi-long beach, amusement parks, and the **New York Aquarium**. Eating a Nathan's Famous hot dog (✉ *1310 Surf Ave., Coney Island*) and strolling seaside has been a classic New York experience since 1916.

12

And then there are the freakish attractions at **Sideshows by the Seashore** and the **Coney Island Museum**, the heart-stopping plunge of the grand-daddy of all roller coasters—the **Cyclone**—and the thwack of bats swung by the minor-league team the Cyclones at **MCU Park**. The area's banner day is the raucous Mermaid Parade, held in June. A fireworks display lights up the sky Friday nights from late June through Labor Day.

A pleasant stroll down the boardwalk is Brighton Beach, named after Britain's longstanding beach resort. In the early 1900s Brighton Beach was a resort in its own right, with seaside hotels that catered to rich Manhattan families visiting for the summer. Since the 1970s and '80s Brighton Beach has been known for its 100,000 Soviet émigrés.

To get to the heart of "Little Odessa" from Coney Island, walk about a mile east along the boardwalk to Brighton 1st Place, then head up to Brighton Beach Avenue. To get here from Manhattan directly, take the B or Q train to the Brighton Beach stop; the trip takes about an hour.

Cyclone. One of the oldest roller coasters still operating, this world-famous, wood-and-steel colossus first roared around the tracks in 1927. Unfortunately, the adjacent, carnivalesque Astroland recently shut down, after pressure from developers. But fear not, thrill seekers: the landmark Cyclone will keep running, ensuring future generations of New Yorkers and visitors their most satisfying case of whiplash ever. ✉ *834 Surf Ave., at W. 10th St., Coney Island* ☎ *718/265–2100* 💲 *$8 for first ride, $5 for additional rides* ⊙ *Memorial Day–Labor Day, daily; call for seasonal hrs* Ⓜ *B, F, N, Q to Coney Island–Stillwell Ave.*

Deno's Wonder Wheel Amusement Park. You get a new perspective atop the 150-foot-tall Wonder Wheel, built in 1920. Though it appears tame, its swinging cars will quicken your heart rate. Fortunately, Deno's lease runs until 2020, so Coney-lovers still have time for the Spook-A-Rama, the Thunderbolt, and bumper cars. ✉ *3059 Denos Vourderis Pl., at W. 12th St., Coney Island* ☎ *718/372–2592* ⊕ *www.wonderwheel.com* 💲 *$6 per ride, 5 rides for $25* ⊙ *Memorial Day–Labor Day, daily 11 am–midnight; Apr., May, Sept., and Oct., weekends noon–9* Ⓜ *D, F, N, Q to Coney Island–Stillwell Ave.*

MCU Park. Rekindle your Brooklyn baseball memories (or make some new ones) at a Brooklyn Cyclones game. When this Mets-owned single-A farm team moved to Brooklyn, it brought professional baseball to the borough for the first time since 1957. Now the intimate, bright park is especially great for introducing kids to the game. The park often holds special promotions to get the little ones on the field. ✉ *1904 Surf Ave.,* *between 17th and 19th Sts., Coney Island* ☎ *718/449–8497* ⊕ *www. brooklyncyclones.com* ✉ *$8–$17* ◷ *Games June–Sept.; call for schedule* Ⓜ *D, F, N, Q to Coney Island–Stillwell Ave.*

New York Aquarium. Home to more than 8,000 creatures of the ocean, New York City's only aquarium is also the nation's oldest. Tropical fish, sea horses, and jellyfish luxuriate in large tanks; otters, walruses, penguins, and seals lounge on a replicated Pacific coast; and a 90,000-gallon tank is home to several different types of sharks. ✉ *502 Surf Ave., at W. 8th St., Coney Island* ☎ *718/265–3474* ⊕ *www.nyaquarium.com* ✉ *$17* ◷ *Early Apr.–Memorial Day and Labor Day–Oct., weekdays 10–5, weekends 10–5:30; Memorial Day–Labor Day, weekdays 10–6, weekends 10–7; Nov.–early Apr., daily 10–4:30; last ticket sold 45 mins before closing* Ⓜ *F, Q to W. 8th St.; N, D to Coney Island–Stillwell Ave.*

Sideshows by the Seashore and the Coney Island Museum. Step right up for a lively circus sideshow, complete with a fire-eater, sword swallower, snake charmer, and contortionist. Upstairs, the small museum has Coney Island memorabilia and a great deal of tourist information. ✉ *1208 Surf Ave., at W. 12th St., Coney Island* ☎ *718/372–5159* ⊕ *www.coneyisland.com* ✉ *Sideshow $7.50, museum 99¢* ◷ *Sideshows: Memorial Day–Labor Day, daily shows; Sept.–May, some weekends. Museum: weekends noon–5. Hrs vary, so call ahead.* Ⓜ *D, F, N, Q to Coney Island–Stillwell Ave.*

WHERE TO EAT

¢ **Nathan's Famous.** No visit to Coney Island would be complete without a

AMERICAN hot dog from this stand that first opened in 1916. On the Fourth of July

★ thousands come to see their world-famous hot dog–eating contest; the record stands at 68 in 10 minutes. ✉ *1310 Surf Ave., at Stillwell Ave., Coney Island* ☎ *718/946–2202* ☰ *AE, D, DC, MC, V* Ⓜ *D, F, N, Q to Coney Island–Stillwell Ave.*

Queens, The Bronx, and Staten Island

WORD OF MOUTH

"[Combine] a visit to Arthur Avenue with a visit to the New York Botanical Garden which is located just north of the Belmont section. Take a MetroNorth train from Grand Central to the Botanical Garden stop. Walk across the street and enter the gardens. There are many acres of outdoor exhibits."

—ellenem

GETTING ORIENTED

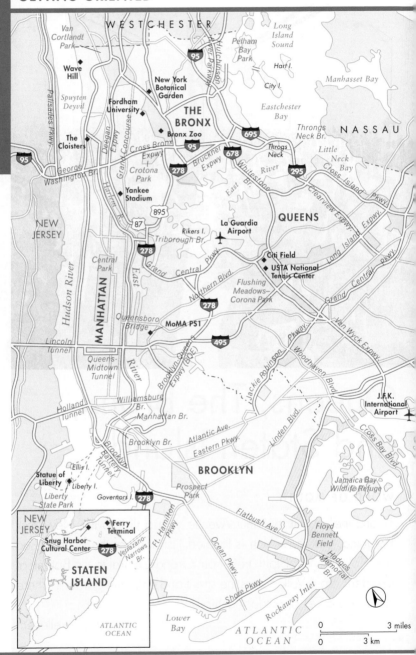

MAKING THE MOST OF YOUR TIME

Queens is rich with superb museums. An afternoon in Long Island City and Astoria will enable you to take in the PS1 Contemporary Art Center, the Museum of the Moving Image, and the Noguchi Museum. After that, jump on the 7 train and have dinner in Jackson Heights or Flushing at one of the borough's excellent restaurants.

It is easy to spend a full day at either of the Bronx's treasures: the New York Botanical Garden or the Bronx Zoo. To visit both, start early and plan on a late lunch or early dinner in the Arthur Avenue area. The garden and the zoo are less crowded on weekdays during the school year.

Many tourists' only sight of Staten Island is during a round-trip ride on the ferry, but the borough also holds unexpected offerings in its small museums and historic villages. Set aside the better part of a day for Historic Richmond Town, and add on a couple of hours for the Museum of Tibetan Art.

GETTING HERE

Queens is served by many subway lines. To get to Astoria, take the N train. For Long Island City, take the E, M, or 7 train. To get to Jackson Heights, take the 7 subway train to the 74th Street–Broadway stop. You can also take the E, F, R, or M train to Roosevelt Avenue.

The Bronx is serviced by the 2, 4, 5, 6, B, and D subway trains. The attractions in the Bronx are spread out across the borough, so you'll need to take different lines to get where you want to go, and it's not necessarily convenient to make connections across town. The B, D, and 4 trains all go to Yankee Stadium, and the B and D continue uptown to take you to Arthur Avenue from the west. The 2 and 5 trains take you to the Bronx Zoo and to Arthur Avenue.

From the scenic and free Staten Island Ferry you can catch a local bus to attractions. Tell the driver where you're going, and ask about the return schedule.

FODOR'S CHOICE

Bronx Zoo

New York Botanical Garden

MoMA PS1

Staten Island Ferry

13

TOP EXPERIENCES

Traveling around the world through the restaurants of Queens

Standing in the shadow of the World's Fair Unisphere

Catching a game at the new Yankee Stadium or Citi Field

Taking a free ride on the Staten Island Ferry

BEST FOR KIDS

Bronx Zoo

The Museum of the Moving Image

Queens Zoo

NEARBY MUSEUMS

Jacques Marchais Museum of Tibetan Art

Museum of the Moving Image

New York Hall of Science

The Noguchi Museum

Queens Museum of Art

AREA SHOPS

Arthur Avenue Retail Market

Sightseeing
★★★

Nightlife
★

Dining
★★★

Lodging
★

Shopping
★

Many tourists miss out on seeing these three boroughs, and that's a shame. They contain some of the city's best restaurants, museums, and attractions, and the subway's handful of express trains means that they're closer than you might think.

Updated by
Alexander
Basek

A patchwork of diverse neighborhoods best describes **Queens**, each a small world with a distinct culture, all fascinating to explore. Thanks especially to the borough's strong immigrant population (almost 50%), you'll also find some of the city's most interesting cuisine here. Art lovers will definitely want to make the short trip for museums such as PS1 Contemporary Art Center and the Noguchi Museum.

The **Bronx** is the city's most maligned and misunderstood borough. Its reputation as a gritty, down-and-out place is a little outdated, and more than a little incorrect.

There's lots of beauty in the Bronx, including more parkland than any other borough, one of the world's finest botanical collections, and the largest metropolitan zoo in the country.

Be aware that the borough covers a large area and its attractions are spread out. Whether you're relaxing at a ball game or scoping out exotic species at the zoo, there's plenty of fun to be had here.

Staten Island is legally a part of New York City, but in many ways it's a world apart. The "Forgotten Borough," as some locals refer to it, is geographically more separate, less populous, politically more conservative, and ethnically more homogeneous than the rest of the city.

Along with suburban sprawl, there are wonderful small museums, walkable woodlands, and a historic village replicating New York's rural past. And for a view of the skyline and the Statue of Liberty, nothing beats the 25-minute free ferry trip to Staten Island.

WHAT IT COSTS					
	¢	$	$$	$$$	$$$$
AT DINNER	under $10	$10–$17	$18–$24	$25–$35	over $35

Price per person for a median main course or equivalent combination of smaller dishes. Note: if a restaurant offers only prix-fixe (set-price) meals, it has been given the price category that reflects the full prix-fixe price.

13

QUEENS

Just for the museums and restaurants alone, a short 15-minute trip on the 7 train from Grand Central or Times Square to **Long Island City** and **Astoria** is truly worth it. In Long Island City, major must-sees are **MoMA PS1** and the **Noguchi Museum**. No trip to Astoria, nicknamed "Little Athens" would be complete without sampling Greek cuisine and stopping at newly-renovated **Museum of the Moving Image**.

Jackson Heights is home to the city's largest Indian population. It's a wonderful place to spend an afternoon browsing its shops and dining in one of the many authentic restaurants.

Top reasons to trek out to **Flushing** and **Corona** include seeing the New York Mets new stadium, **Citi Field**, spending time at the expansive **Flushing Meadows—Corona Park**—especially if traveling with kids—and enjoying Italian ices from the **Lemon Ice King of Corona**, a neighborhood institution.

LONG ISLAND CITY AND ASTORIA

Long Island City (L.I.C. for short) is the outer-borough art capital, with **MoMA PS1**, which presents experimental and formally innovative work; the **Noguchi Museum**, showcasing the work of Japanese-American sculptor Isamu Noguchi in a large, peaceful garden and galleries; and **Socrates Sculpture Park**.

Nearby Astoria, nicknamed Little Athens, was the center of Greek immigrant life in New York City for more than 60 years. An increase in Greek affluence has meant that many have left the borough, but they still return for authentic restaurants, grocery stores, and churches. Here you can buy kalamata olives and salty sheep's-milk feta from storeowners who can tell you where to go for the best spinach pie.

Today substantial numbers of Asian, Eastern European, Irish, and Latino immigrants also live in Astoria. The heart of what remains of the Greek community is on Broadway, between 31st and Steinway streets. Thirtieth Avenue is another busy thoroughfare, with almost every kind of food store imaginable.

Astoria is also home to the nation's only museum devoted to the art, technology, and history of film, TV, and digital media. The newly-redone **Museum of the Moving Image** has countless hands-on exhibits that allow visitors to edit, direct, and step into favorite movies and television shows.

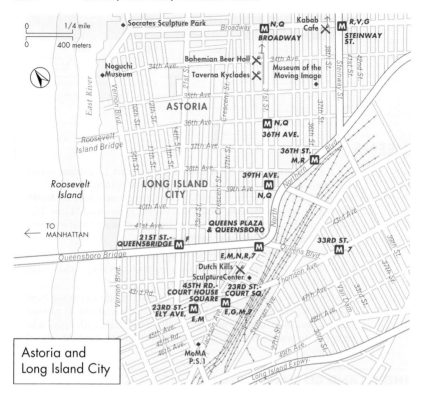

0 ——— 1/4 mile
0 ——— 400 meters

Socrates Sculpture Park • Broadway N,Q Kabab Cafe ✕ R,V,G
BROADWAY STEINWAY ST.

Bohemian Beer Hall ✕ 34th Ave. Museum of the Moving Image
Noguchi ♦Museum 34th Ave.
Taverna Kyclades ✕
East River
Vernon Blvd.
ASTORIA
35th Ave.
36th Ave. N,Q 36TH AVE.
Roosevelt Island Bridge
37th Ave. 36TH ST. M,R
38th Ave. 39TH AVE.
Roosevelt Island
LONG ISLAND CITY
39th Ave. N,Q
40th Ave.
TO ← MANHATTAN
41st Ave. QUEENS PLAZA & QUEENSBORO
21ST ST.- QUEENSBRIDGE F
33RD ST. 7
Queensboro Bridge
E,M,N,R,7
Dutch Kills ✕
SculptureCenter ♦
45TH RD.- COURT HOUSE SQUARE 23RD ST.- COURT SQ.
23RD ST.- ELY AVE. E,G,M,7
E,M
MoMA P.S.1
Long Island Expwy.

Astoria and Long Island City

TOP ATTRACTIONS

Fodor'sChoice ★ **MoMA PS1.** A pioneer in the "alternative-space" movement, PS1 rose from the ruins of an abandoned school in 1976 as a sort of community arts center for the future. MoMA PS1 focuses on the work of currently active experimental and innovative artists. Long-term installations include work by Sol LeWitt and Pipilotti Rist. Every available corner of the enormous 100-room building is used; discover art not only in galleries but also on the rooftop, in the boiler room, and even in some bathrooms. On summer Saturdays from 3 to 9 pm outdoor dance parties attract a hip art-school crowd. ✉ *22–25 Jackson Ave., at 46th Ave., Long Island City* ☎ *718/784–2084* ⊕ *www.ps1.org* 💲 *$10 suggested donation, free with MoMA entrance ticket* ☼ *Thurs.–Mon. noon–6* Ⓜ *7 to 45th Rd.–Courthouse Sq.; E, M to 23rd St.–Ely Ave.; G to 21st St.*

★ **Museum of the Moving Image.** Like switching to a widescreen television, the newly renovated Museum of the Moving Image is twice as nice as before. The new Thomas Lesser design includes a three-story addition and a panoramic entrance to this museum full of Hollywood and television memorabilia. Exhibitions range from "Behind the Screen" which demonstrates how movies are produced and shot to watching the live editing of Mets baseball games as they happen on SNY. Classic family films are shown as matinees on Saturdays and Sundays, while the

Where can I find . . . ?

DRINKS IN QUEENS	**Dutch Kills** 27–24 Jackson Ave. Swank cocktails at Queens prices.	**Bohemian Hall & Beer Garden** 29-19 24th Ave. Perfect on a summer night.
SNACKS IN THE BRONX	**Zero Otto Nove** 2357 Arthur Ave. Serious Neapolitan pizza without the hassle.	**Mike's Deli** 2344 Arthur Ave. Sandwiches as big as your head, friendly service, and a convenient location.
GOOD EATS IN STATEN ISLAND	**Adobe Blues** 63 Lafayette Ave. Southwestern food and more than 200 beers.	**Café Botanica** Snug Harbor Cultural Center, Cottage Row American classics, like fresh biscuits with whipped butter.

13

museum also has a section devoted to video artists for visitors looking for some culture. Film buffs will love the film retrospectives, lectures, and other special programs. ⊠ *35th Ave. at 37th St., Astoria* ☎ *718/784–0077* ⊕ *www.movingimage.us* ⛁ *$10; free after 4 on Fri.* ☉ *Wed. and Thurs. 10:30–5, Fri. 11–8, weekends 10:30–7:00* Ⓜ *R, M to Steinway St.; N to 36th Ave.*

Noguchi Museum. In 1985 the Japanese-American sculptor Isamu Noguchi (1904–88) transformed this former photo-engraving plant into a place to display his modernist and earlier works. A peaceful central garden is surrounded by gallery buildings, providing room to show more than 250 pieces done in stone, metal, clay, and other materials. Temporary exhibits have featured his collaborations with others, such as industrial designer Isamu Kenmochi. The museum is about a mile from subway stops; check the Web site for complete directions. On Sunday a shuttle bus leaves from the northeast corner of Park Avenue and 70th Street in Manhattan (in front of the Asia Society) hourly, beginning at 12:30; the round-trip costs $10. ⊠ *9–01 33rd Rd., at Vernon Blvd., Long Island City* ☎ *718/204–7088* ⊕ *www.noguchi.org* ⛁ *$10; 1st Fri. of month, pay what you wish* ☉ *Wed.–Fri. 10–5, weekends 11–6* Ⓜ *N or Q to Broadway.*

WORTH NOTING

SculptureCenter. Founded by artists in 1928 to exhibit innovative contemporary work, SculptureCenter now occupies a former trolley repair shop renovated by artist Maya Lin and architect David Hotson, not far from MoMA PS1. Their indoor and outdoor exhibition spaces sometimes close between shows; call ahead before visiting. ⊠ *44–19 Purves St., at Jackson Ave., Long Island City* ☎ *718/361–1750* ⊕ *www. sculpture-center.org* ⛁ *$5 suggested donation* ☉ *Thurs.–Mon. 11–6* Ⓜ *7 to 45th Rd.—Courthouse Sq.; E, M to 23rd St.–Ely Ave.; G to Court Sq.*

Socrates Sculpture Park. In 1986 local artist Mark di Suvero and other residents rallied to transform what had been an abandoned landfill

TIPS FOR QUEENS ADDRESSES

Addresses in Queens can seem confusing at first. Not only are there 30th Street and 30th Avenue, but there are also 30th Place and 30th Road, all next to one another. Then there are those hyphenated building numbers.

But the system is actually much more logical than you might think. Sequentially numbered avenues run east-to-west, and sequentially numbered streets run north-to-south. If there are any smaller roads between avenues, they have the same number as the nearest avenue, and are called roads or drives.

Similarly, smaller side roads between streets are called places or lanes. Thus, 30th Place is one block east of 30th Street. Most buildings have two pairs of numbers, separated by a hyphen. The first pair indicates the cross street nearby, and the second gives the location on the block. So 47-10 30th Place is between 47th and 48th avenues. Logical, right? If this all still seems confusing to you, there's good news: locals are used to giving directions to visitors.

and illegal dump site into this 4.5-acre waterfront park devoted to public art. Today a superb view of the river and Manhattan frames changing exhibitions of contemporary sculptures and multimedia installations. Free public programs include art workshops and an annual outdoor film series (July and August, Wednesday evenings). ⊠ *32–01 Vernon Blvd., at Broadway, Long Island City* ☎ *718/956–1819* ⊕ *www. socratessculpturepark.org* ⊡ *Free* ☉ *Daily 10–sunset* Ⓜ *N to Broadway, then walk 8 blocks west or take Q104 bus along Broadway to Vernon Blvd.*

WHERE TO EAT

After you're finished with the sights, why head back to Manhattan? End your day with dinner at one of Astoria's legendary Greek restaurants (on or near Broadway), or venture to the Middle Eastern restaurants farther out on Steinway Street.

$
EASTERN
EUROPEAN
✕ **Bohemian Hall & Beer Garden.** If your favorite outdoor activities include drinking beer and eating kielbasa, you'll love this place. The last survivor of the more than 800 beer gardens that once graced New York, this popular spot offers imported Czech beers and Central-European eats like pierogi and schnitzel. Get there early to avoid long lines. Just drinking? Bring cash, as credit cards are reserved for orders from the kitchen. Bad weather? Don't worry: indoor seating is available. ⊠ *29–19 24th Ave., between 29th and 31st Sts., Astoria* ☎ *718/728–9278* ⊟ *MC, V* Ⓜ *N to Astoria Blvd.*

$
MIDDLE EASTERN
✕ **Kabab Café.** Middle-Eastern restaurants are a dime a dozen in N.Y.C., but Egyptian-Mediterranean spots are a rarer find, attracting foodies like celebrity chef Anthony Bourdain. This charming yet eccentric 16-seat café, which excels at interesting home-style dishes, is a true hidden treasure. The menu changes nightly, but exceedingly tender lamb stuffed with pomegranate is always great. ⊠ *25–12 Steinway St., Asto-*

CLOSE UP

Filmmaking in Astoria

Hollywood may be the king of movie-making now, but in the early days of sound Queens was where it was at. In the 1920s such stars as Gloria Swanson, Rudolph Valentino, and Claudette Colbert all acted in one of the more than 100 films made at Astoria Studios. Opened in 1920 by the film company that would become Paramount, "the Big House" was the largest and most important filmmaking studio in the country.

Though Astoria's ideal location provided easy access to Broadway and vaudeville stars, Hollywood's weather soon lured away most studios. Astoria was able to hold its own for a while longer, creating such films as the Marx Brothers classics *The Cocoanuts* and *Animal Crackers.* But in 1942 the studio was sold to the U.S. Army.

It became the Signal Corps Photographic Center, producing training films and documentaries, including Frank's Capra's classic seven-film series *Why We Fight.* The army retained the studio until 1970.

In 1980 the city leased the studio to real-estate developer George S. Kaufman, in partnership with Alan King and Johnny Carson. Kaufman-Astoria Studios, with six stages, is a thriving operation once again, used for television series (*Sesame Street, Law & Order*) as well as movies (*The Wiz, Hair,* and *The Pink Panther*). Although the studio is not open to the public, movie buffs can hope to spot stars at the Studio Café and learn more about the craft next door at the fantastic Museum of the Moving Image.

---

ria ☎ *718/728–9858* ⌧ *Reservations not accepted* 🚫 *No credit cards* 🕐 *Closed Mon.* Ⓜ *N to Astoria–Ditmars Blvd.*

$ ✕ **Taverna Kyclades.** The current powerhouse of Hellenic eats in the
GREEK neighborhood, Taverna Kyclades offers Greek classics at a higher level than you'd expect, given the simple decor and unassuming location. Fried calamari and grilled octopus make appearances at rock-bottom prices, despite their obvious quality, as do more out-of-the-ordinary dishes like "caviar dip" and swordfish kebabs. Be prepared to wait for a table at peak times, as they don't take reservations. ⌧ *33–07 Ditmars Blvd., Astoria* ☎ *718/545–8666* ⊕ *tavernakyclades.com* ⌧ *Reservations not accepted* 🚫 *AE, MC, V* Ⓜ *N to Astoria–Ditmars Blvd.*

JACKSON HEIGHTS

Even in the diverse borough of Queens, Jackson Heights stands out for being a true polycultural neighborhood. In just a few blocks surrounding the three-way intersection of Roosevelt Avenue, 74th Street, and Broadway, you can find shops and restaurants catering to the area's strong Indian, Bangladeshi, Colombian, Mexican, and Ecuadorian communities.

Built as a planned "garden community" in the late 1910s, the area boasts many prewar apartments with elaborate block-long interior gardens as well as English-style homes. Celebs who grew up in the area

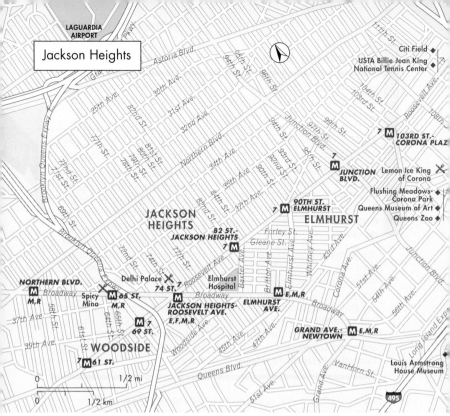

include Lucy Liu and Gene Simmons. It's also the birthplace of the board game Scrabble.

WHERE TO EAT

$ ✕ **Delhi Palace**. Jackson Heights is full of Indian restaurants, but Delhi
INDIAN   Palace, specializing in north Indian cuisine, stands out from the competition. Fans cite their varied daily $10 buffet, friendly service, and fewer crowds than the popular Jackson Diner down the street. Try the thin and crispy potato-filled crepes called masala *dosa*, made to order. ⊠ *37–33 74th St., between Roosevelt and 37th Aves., Jackson Heights* ☎ *718/507–0666* ═ *AE, D, MC, V* Ⓜ *E, F, R, M to Jackson Heights–Roosevelt Ave.; 7 to 74th St.–Broadway.*

$ ✕ **Spicy Mina**. Since 2003, fans of Mina Azad's Bangladeshi food have
ASIAN   eagerly followed her career. They mourned when her Sunnyside restaurant closed, and cheered when she briefly popped up again, cooking in Manhattan. Now they trek to the border of Jackson Heights and Woodside to wait patiently through spotty service while she prepares elaborately spiced feasts from scratch, an anomaly in a sea of steam-table buffet restaurants. It's also BYOB. ⊠ *64–23 Broadway, Woodside* ☎ *718/205–2340* ═ *MC, V* Ⓜ *G, R, M to 65th St.*

CLOSE UP

The 7 Train: A Food Lover's Favorite Subway Line

13

Manhattan may be known for its fine four-star restaurants, but food lovers know there's one train line to take to some of the best eats in the city. The 7 train snakes its way through the middle of Queens, and conveniently also through some of the best eating neighborhoods in New York. Because the tracks are elevated, it's easy to get a handle on your surroundings—and to know where to find the train once your explorations are through.

Irish expats have long settled in the adjoining neighborhoods of Woodside and Sunnyside (near the 61st Street stop), the site of many great Gaelic bars and a few restaurants. Get a proper Irish breakfast, including black and white pudding, at the casual **Stop Inn** (✉ 6022 Roosevelt Ave., Woodside ☎ 718/779–0290). At **Donovan's** (✉ Roosevelt Ave. and 58th St., Woodside ☎ 718/429–9339) ask for extra napkins and get one of the best burgers in New York City, nicely charred and served with home-cut steak fries.

But the main reason foodies flock to Woodside is for the Thai restaurant **Sripraphai** (✉ 64–13 39th Ave., Woodside ☎ 718/899–9599), pronounced See-PRA-pie, widely considered the best Thai restaurant in New York. Don't miss the crispy watercress salad and the larb (ground pork with mint, lime juice, and onions). It's closed on Wednesday.

At either the 74th Street or 82nd Street stop, diverse Jackson Heights offers not only outstanding Indian restaurants but also many other Southeast Asian spots and fantastic eats from all over Latin America. Named after a town in Puebla, Mexico, **Taqueria Coatzingo** (✉ 76–05 Roosevelt Ave., Jackson Heights ☎ 718/424–1977) has deeply flavorful mole poblano. Those in the know stick to daily handwritten specials like Pipian en Puerco Rojo—pork cooked in red pumpkin-seed sauce. El **Chivito D'Oro III** (✉ 84–02 37th Ave., Jackson Heights ☎ 718/424–0600), a Uruguayan diner, serves up parades of grilled meats called parrilladas—easily enough for two. Since many Uraguayans are of Italian heritage, Chivito also serves delicate pastas.

The 7 train may save the best for last: at the end of the line is Flushing, home to the second-largest Chinatown in the United States. (First is San Francisco's.) Wide streets have few tourists and many interesting stores and restaurants, making the long trip worth it. The standout is **Spicy and Tasty** (✉ 39–07 Prince St., at 39th Ave., Flushing ☎ 718/359–1601), which lives up to its name with numbing Szechuan peppercorns and slicks of red chili oil. Tea-smoked duck has crispy skin and smoky, salty meat. Eggplant with garlic sauce tastes of ginger, tomatoes, and red chilies. Cool it all down with a Tsingtao beer.

A few tips: Bring cash, because not many of these restaurants accept credit cards. Be prepared to encounter language difficulties, as English speakers are in the minority. In Manhattan, catch the 7 train at Times Square or Grand Central Terminal.

—Nina Callaway

SHOPPING

At **Patel Brothers** (✉ *37–27 74th St., near 37th Ave.* ☎ *718/898–3445*) let your nose lead your way through the aisles of this Indian grocery store minichain, inhaling the heady scents of rich spices, rare Kesar mangoes, and other exotic produce. Then follow your curiosity through dozens of varieties of lentils and an entire aisle devoted to rice before stocking up on spicy fried snacks and cheap souvenirs for the folks back home.

For special keepsakes, head to **Sahil Sari Palace** (✉ *37–39 74th St., between Roosevelt and 37th Aves.* ☎ *718/426–9526*), filled with bolts of colorful silks and ready-to-wear sequined saris.

FLUSHING AND CORONA

Before it became a part of New York City, Queens was once many small independent townships. So it makes sense that the historic town of Flushing is today a microcosm of a larger city, including a bustling downtown area, fantastic restaurants, and bucolic suburbanlike streets nearby.

Flushing may seem like a strange name for a town, but it's an English adaptation of the original (and hard-to-pronounce) Dutch name Vlissingen. The Dutch named it for a favorite port city in the Netherlands.

Next door, quiet Corona could easily be overlooked, but that would be a mistake. Here are two huge legacies: the music of Satchmo and the cooling simplicity of an Italian ice.

TOP ATTRACTIONS

Citi Field. The Mets are justly proud of their brand-new stadium, designed to hark back to Ebbets Field (where the Dodgers played in Brooklyn) with a brick exterior and plenty of bells and whistles, from a batting cage and wiffle-ball field to the original giant apple taken from the team's old residence, Shea Stadium.

The Mets unfortunately christened the stadium in 2009 with a terrible season, but even those who aren't Mets fans and simply love baseball should come to see the Jackie Robinson Rotunda, a soaring multistory entrance and history exhibit dedicated to the Dodgers player who shattered baseball's color barrier.

While here, don't miss making a stop at the more-than-fabulous food court behind center field, Shake Shack burgers, surprisingly inexpensive beers such as Czechvar and Leffe, and even lobster rolls and tacos.

Though it seats fewer people than Shea by about 10,000, tickets are not hard to come by, especially later in the season. Still feeling nostalgic for the old Shea? Pay your respects at the plaque in the parking lot. ✉ *Roosevelt Ave. off Grand Central Pkwy.* ☎ *718/507–8499* ⊕ *www. mets.com* Ⓜ *7 to Mets/Willets Point.*

☺ **Flushing Meadows–Corona Park**. Standing in the lush grass of this park, you'd never imagine that it was once a swamp and a dumping ground. But the gleaming Unisphere (an enormous 140-foot-high steel globe) might tip you off that this 1,255-acre park was also the site of two World's Fairs.

Unisphere globe in Flushing Meadows, Corona Park.

Take advantage of the park's barbecue pits and sports fields, but also don't forget that there's an art museum, a petting zoo, golf and minigolf, and even a model-plane field.

There's way too much to see here to pack into a day, so aim to hit a few primary spots, noting that while several are clustered together on the northwest side of the park, visitors should be prepared for long peaceful walks in between. The flat grounds are ideal for family biking; rent bikes near the park entrance or Meadow Lake from March to October.
■TIP➔ Although the park is great in daytime, avoid visiting once it gets dark; there has been some crime in this area.

At the northwestern edge of the park, the **New York Hall of Science** (☎ *718/699–0005* ⊕ *www.nysci.org* ✉ *$11; free Fri. 2–5 and Sun. 10–11 Sept.–June* ☉ *Sept.–June, Mon.–Thurs. 9:30–2, Fri. 9:30–5, weekends 10–6; July and Aug., weekdays 9:30–5, weekends 10–6*) has more than 400 hands-on exhibits that make science a playground for inquisitive minds of all ages. Climb aboard a replica of John Glenn's space capsule, throw a fastball and investigate its speed, or explore Charles and Ray Eames's classic Mathematica exhibition.

Behind the Hall of Science lies the intimate **Queens Zoo** (☎ *718/271–1500* ⊕ *www.queenszoo.com* ✉ *$8* ☉ *Early Apr.–late Oct., weekdays 10–5, weekends 10–5:30; late Oct.–early Apr., daily 10–4:30; last ticket sold 30 mins before closing*), whose small scale is especially well suited to easily tired young visitors. In only 11 acres you'll find North American animals such as bears, mountain lions, bald eagles, and pudu—the world's smallest deer. Buckminster Fuller's geodesic dome from the 1964 World's Fair is now the aviary. Across the street is a petting zoo.

Between the zoo and the Unisphere, you'll find the **Queens Museum of Art** (☎ 718/592–9700 ⊕ *www.queensmuseum.org* ⊠ *$5 suggested donation* ☉ *Sept.–June, Wed.–Sun. noon–6; call for extended hrs in July and Aug.*). Don't miss the astonishing Panorama, a nearly 900,000-building model of N.Y.C. made for the 1964 World's Fair. Many unsuspecting park visitors looking for a bathroom instead find themselves spending hours checking out the intricate structures that replicate every block in the city. There are also rotating exhibitions of contemporary art and a permanent collection of Louis Comfort Tiffany stained glass. ⊠ *Between 111th St./Grand Central Pkwy. and Van Wyck Expressway at 44th Ave., Flushing* Ⓜ *7 to 111th St. or Willets Point.*

USTA Billie Jean King National Tennis Center. Each August, 700,000 fans come here for the U.S. Open, which claims the title of highest-attended annual sporting event in the world. The rest of the year the 45 courts (33 outdoor and 12 indoor, all Deco Turf II) are open to the public for $20–$60 hourly. Make reservations up to two days in advance. ⊠ *Flushing Meadows–Corona Park* ☎ *718/760–6200* ⊕ *www.usta.com* Ⓜ *7 to Willets Point.*

WORTH NOTING

Louis Armstrong House Museum. For the last 28 years of his life the famed jazz musician lived in this modest three-story house in Corona with his wife Lucille. Take a guided 40-minute tour and note the difference between the rooms vividly decorated by Lucille in charming midcentury style and Louis's dark den, cluttered with phonographs and reel-to-reel tape recorders. Although photographs and family mementos throughout the house impart knowledge about Satchmo's life, it's in his den that you'll really understand his spirit. ⊠ *34–56 107th St., at 37th Ave., Corona* ☎ *718/478–8274* ⊕ *www.louisarmstronghouse.org* ⊠ *$8* ☉ *Tours hourly Tues.–Fri. 10–5, weekends noon–5* Ⓜ *7 to 103rd St.–Corona Plaza.*

NEED A BREAK? If you're looking for authentic Queens experiences, there are few as true as eating an Italian ice from the **Lemon Ice King of Corona** (⊠ *52–02 108th St., at 52nd St., Corona* ☎ *718/699–5133*) while strolling by a nearby bocce court on a hot summer day. There are no seats and the service can often be gruff at this neighborhood institution of more than 60 years, but none of that will matter after your first taste.

THE BRONX

Many tourists feel as if getting up to the city's northernmost borough is a schlep because it looks so far away from midtown Manhattan on the map. But in actuality, travel time from Grand Central is no longer than taking the subway from the Upper West Side to the Financial District.

That said, if you're looking to spend the better part of a day outside at the **Bronx Zoo** or **New York Botanical Gardens**—considered top sites in all of New York, not just in the Bronx—and want to sample what some call the city's most authentic Italian food on **Arthur Avenue**, it's well worth a visit.

The Jungle habitat at the Bronx Zoo will make you forget the surrounding urban jungle.

TOP ATTRACTIONS

Fodor's Choice ★

The Bronx Zoo. When it opened its gates in 1899, the Bronx Zoo had only 843 animals. But today, with 265 acres and more than 4,000 animals (of more than 600 species), it's the largest metropolitan zoo in the United States. Get up close and personal with exotic creatures in outdoor settings that re-create natural habitats; you're often separated from them by no more than a moat or wall of glass.

Don't miss the **Congo Gorilla Forest** ($5) a 6.5-acre re-creation of a lush African rain forest with two troops of lowland gorillas, as well as white-bearded DeBrazza's monkeys, okapis, and red river hogs. At **Tiger Mountain** an open viewing shelter lets you get incredibly close to Siberian tigers, who frolic in a pool, lounge outside (even in cold weather), and enjoy daily "enrichment sessions" with keepers. As the big cats are often napping at midday, aim to visit in the morning or evening. In the new $62 million exhibit **Madagascar!**, the formality of the old Lion House has been replaced with a verdant re-creation of one of the most threatened natural habitats in the world. Here you'll see adorable lemurs and far-from-adorable hissing cockroaches.

Go on a minisafari via the **Wild Asia Monorail** ($4), open May–October, weather permitting. As you wend your way through the forest, see Asian elephants, Indo-Chinese tigers, Indian rhinoceroses, gaur (the world's largest cattle), Mongolian wild horses, and several deer and antelope species. ■TIP→ Try to visit the most popular exhibits, such as Congo Gorilla Forest, early to avoid lines later in the day. In winter the outdoor exhibitions have fewer animals on view, but there are also fewer crowds, and plenty of indoor exhibits to savor. From mid-November to

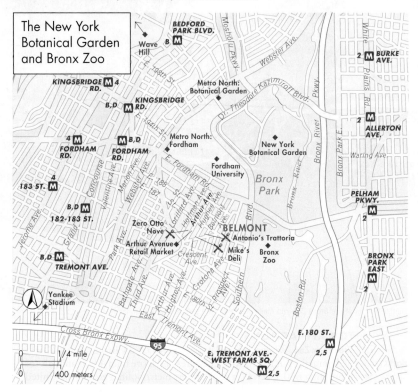

January 1 the zoo is decorated with holiday lights and open until 9 pm.
✉ *Bronx River Pkwy. and Fordham Rd., Fordham* ☎ *718/367–1010*
⊕ *www.bronxzoo.com* ⊑ *$16; extra charge for some exhibits; free
Wed., donation suggested; parking $13* ☉ *Apr.–Oct., weekdays 10–5,
weekends 10–5:30; Nov.–Mar., daily 10–4:30; last ticket sold 30 mins
before closing* Ⓜ *2, 5 to E. Tremont/West Farms, then walk 2 blocks
up Boston Rd. to zoo's Asia entrance; Bx11 express bus to Bronx River
entrance.*

Fodor's Choice **New York Botanical Garden.** Considered one of the leading botany centers
★ of the world, this 250-acre garden is one of the best reasons to make a
trip to the Bronx. Built around the dramatic gorge of the Bronx River,
the Garden offers lush indoor and outdoor gardens, and acres of natural
forest, as well as classes, concerts, and special exhibits. Be astounded by
the captivating fragrance of the Peggy Rockefeller Rose Garden's 2,700
plants of more than 250 varieties; see intricate orchids that look like the
stuff of science fiction; relax in the quiet of the forest or the calm of the
Conservatory; or take a jaunt through the Everett Children's Adventure
Garden: a 12-acre, indoor-outdoor museum with a boulder maze, giant
animal topiaries, and a plant discovery center.

The Garden's roses bloom in June and September, but there's plenty
to see year-round. The Victorian-style **Enid A. Haupt Conservatory**

(✉ *$20, part of the Combination Ticket*) houses re-creations of misty tropical rain forests and arid African and North American deserts as well as exhibitions, such as the annual Holiday Train Show and the Orchid Show. The **Combination Ticket** (✉ *$20*) gives you access to the Conservatory, Rock Garden, Native Plant Garden, Tram Tour, Everett Children's Adventure Garden, and exhibits in the library.

The most direct way to the Garden is via **Metro-North Railroad** (⊕ *www.mta.info/mnr*) from Grand Central Terminal (Harlem Local Line, Botanical Garden stop). Round-trip tickets are $10.50 to $14, depending on time of day. A cheaper alternative is to take the D or 4 train to Bedford Park Boulevard, then walk east. ⊠ *200th St. at Kazimiroff Blvd., Bedford Park* ☎ *718/817–8700* ⊕ *www.nybg.org* ✉ *Grounds only $6, free Sat. 10–noon and all day Wed.; All-Garden Pass $20; parking $12* ◷ *Tues.–Sun. 10–6* Ⓜ *B, D, 4 to Bedford Park Blvd., then walk 8 blocks downhill to the garden; Metro-North to Botanical Garden.*

Yankee Stadium. Fans are still mourning the original, legendary Yankee Stadium, which saw its last season in 2008. Though the team is still breaking it in, the new Yankee Stadium—right next to the House that Ruth Built—has gotten off to a good start, with the Yankees winning the World Series in its inaugural year.

Tickets can be ridiculously expensive, but the experience is like watching baseball in Las Vegas's Bellagio hotel. It's incredibly opulent and over-the-top: traditional white frieze adorns the stadium's top; inside, limestone-and-marble hallways are lined with photos of past Yankee greats; lower-level seats have cushions, cup holders, and a boffo meatery, NYY Steak.

Like the team, all the amenities here don't come cheap. But the spirit of the original stadium still remains. History buffs and hard-core fans should be sure to visit Monument Park, with plaques of past team members, by Center Field—it survived from the old stadium. Aside from the subway, you can also get here by Metro-North, to the Yankees–153rd Street Station. ⊠ *River Ave. at 161st St., South Bronx* ☎ *718/293–6000* ⊕ *www.yankees.com* Ⓜ *B (weekdays only), D, or 4 to 161st St.–Yankee Stadium.*

★ **Arthur Avenue (Belmont).** Manhattan's Little Italy is sadly overrun with mediocre restaurants aimed at tourists, but Belmont, the Little Italy of the Bronx, is a real, thriving Italian-American community. Unless you have family in the area, the main reason to come here is for the food: eating it, buying it, looking at it fondly through windows. A secondary, but just as important, reason is chatting with shopkeepers so you can steal their recipes.

Nearly a century after pushcarts on Arthur Avenue catered to Italian-American workers constructing the zoo and Botanical Garden, the area teems with meat markets, bakeries, and cheese makers. There are long debates about which store or restaurant is the "best," but thanks to generations of Italian grandmothers, vendors here wouldn't dare offer anything less than superfresh, handmade foods.

Although the area is no longer solely Italian—many Latinos and Albanians share this neighborhood now—Italians dominate the food scene. Regulars mostly shop on Saturday afternoon; you'll find many stores shuttered on Sunday and after 6 pm. ⊠ *Arthur Ave. between Crescent Ave./E. 184th St. and E. 188th Sts., and 187th St. from Lorillard Pl. to Hughes Ave. Belmont* Ⓜ *B, D, 4 to Fordham Rd., then Bx12 east; 2, 5 to Pelham Pkwy., then Bx12 west.*

WORTH NOTING

OFF THE BEATEN PATH

Wave Hill. Drawn by stunning views of the Hudson River and New Jersey's dramatic cliffs, 19th-century Manhattan millionaires built summer homes in the Bronx suburb of Riverdale. One of the most magnificent, Wave Hill, is now a 28-acre public garden and cultural center that attracts green thumbs from all over the world.

Along with exquisite gardens, grand beech and oak trees adorn wide lawns, an elegant pergola overlooks the majestic river view, and benches on curving pathways provide quiet respite. Wave Hill House (1843) and Glyndor House (1927) now house art exhibitions, Sunday concerts, and gardening workshops. Even England's queen stayed here during a visit. It's worth the schlep. ⊠ *Independence Ave. at W. 249th St., Riverdale* ☎ *718/549–3200* ⊕ *www.wavehill.org* 🎫 *$6; free Tues. and Sat. mornings* ⊙ *Mid-Apr.–mid-Oct., Tues.–Sun. 9–5:30; mid-Oct.– mid-Apr., Tues.–Sun. 9–4:30; closed Mon. except holidays. Free garden tours Sun. at 2* Ⓜ *1 to 231st St., then Bx7 or Bx10 bus to 252nd St. and Riverdale Ave. or free van service hourly from W. 242nd St. station between 9:10 am and 4:10 pm.*

WHERE TO EAT

$

ITALIAN

✕ **Antonio's Trattoria.** Antonio's bills itself as "an Italian restaurant serving simple food," but that's underselling it by far. Fantastic classic Italian fare is dished out here; do not miss the baked clams, the house-made ravioli, and the excellent pizzas. It's a bit off the main Arthur Avenue strip, but worth the trek. ⊠ *2370 Belmont Ave., Belmont* ☎ *718/733– 6630* ⊕ *antoniostrattoria.com* ⊙ *Closed Mon.* ⊟ *MC, V* Ⓜ *B, D to 182nd.*

$

ITALIAN

✕ **Zero Otto Nove.** Though insiders who can get a table swear by Rao's on 114th in Manhattan, Zero Otto Nove chugs along as one of the best Italian restaurants north of 96th Street. The draw? Wood-ovenfired pizza, perfectly chewy and larded with buffalo mozzarella. The San Matteo, which adds broccoli rabe to the mix, is just as addictive as the plain Jane margherita. ⊠ *2357 Arthur Ave., Belmont* ☎ *718/220– 1027* 🍴 *Reservations not accepted* ⊟ *MC, V* ⊙ *Closed Mon.* Ⓜ *B, D to 182nd.*

SHOPPING

★ The covered **Arthur Avenue Retail Market** (⊠ *2344 Arthur Ave., at E. 187th St., Belmont* ☎ *718/367–5686* Ⓜ *B, D, 4 to Fordham Rd., then 15-min walk or Bx12 east*), which houses more than a dozen vendors, was opened by Mayor Fiorello LaGuardia in an effort to get the pushcarts off the crowded streets. Inside, you'll find great sandwiches and pizza, barrels of olives, a butcher specializing in offal, and lots of fresh pastas. Cigars are rolled by hand right at the building's entrance,

LIFE RING BUOY WITH LINE

alongside Italian gifts and kitchenware. It's open Monday through Saturday 6–6.

Let an Italian nonna (grandmother) sell you homemade fresh pastas of every kind, shape, and flavor at **Borgatti's Ravioli & Egg Noodles** (⊠ 632 *E. 187th St., between Belmont and Hughes Aves., Belmont* ☎ 718/367–3799). It's closed all day Monday and Sunday afternoon, and frequently has shorter hours in summer.

Don't miss the porcine spectacle of **Calabria Pork Store** (⊠ 2338 *Arthur Ave., between 186th St. and Crescent Ave., Belmont* ☎ 718/367–5145), where a forest of house-aged salamis dangles thickly from the rafters.

At **Calandra Cheese** (⊠ 2314 *Arthur Ave., between 186th St. and Crescent Ave., Belmont* ☎ 718/365–7572) bulbous spheres of freshly made cheese hang from the ceiling. Go for the cacciocavallo—a dry, salty mozzarella—or the clean-tasting ricotta.

The brick ovens at **Madonia Brothers Bakery** (⊠ 2348 *Arthur Ave., at 187th St., Belmont* ☎ 718/295–5573) have been turning out golden-brown loaves since 1918, but the true stars are fresh, crispy cannoli, filled only when you order, with not-too-sweet ricotta cream.

At **Teitel Bros** (⊠ 2372 *Arthur Ave., at E. 186th St., Belmont* ☎ 718/733–9400), grab a number and stand elbow-to-elbow with locals buying pungent olives, hulking hunks of hard cheeses, pounds of dried beans, and gallons of olive oil.

STATEN ISLAND

Staten Island is full of surprises, from a premier collection of Tibetan art to a multifaceted historic village. To explore the borough, take the **Staten Island Ferry** from the southern tip of Manhattan. After you disembark, grab an S40 bus to the **Snug Harbor Cultural Center (about 10 minutes)** or take the S74 and combine visits to the **Tibetan Museum** and **Historic Richmond Town.**

TOP ATTRACTIONS

Ⓒ **Historic Richmond Town.** Think of Virginia's Colonial Williamsburg (the polar opposite of Brooklyn's scene-y Williamsburg), and you'll understand the appeal of Richmond Town. This 100-acre village, constructed from 1695 to the 19th century, was the site of Staten Island's original county seat.

Fifteen of the site's 27 historic buildings are open to the public. Highlights include the Gothic Revival **Courthouse,** the one-room **General Store,** and the **Voorlezer's House,** one of the oldest buildings on the site. It served as a residence, a place of worship, and an elementary school.

Also on-site is the **Staten Island Historical Society Museum,** built in 1848 as the second county clerk's and surrogate's office, which now houses Staten Island artifacts plus changing exhibits about the island. Audio tours are free with admission. You may see staff in period dress demonstrate Early American crafts and trades such as tinsmithing or basket making, though the general era meant to be re-created is 1820–1860. December brings a monthlong Christmas celebration.

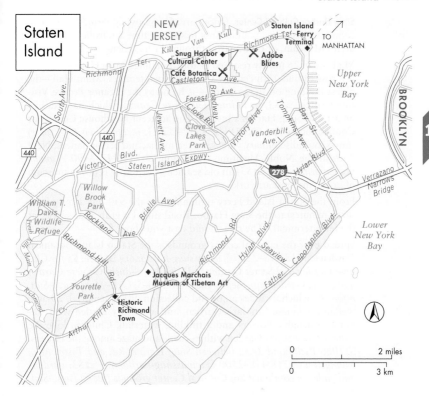

Staten Island

Take the S74–Richmond Road bus (30 minutes) or a car service (about $15) from the ferry terminal. ✉ *441 Clarke Ave., Richmondtown* ☎ *718/351–1611* ⊕ *www.historicrichmondtown.org* 🎫 *$5* ☉ *July and Aug., Wed.–Sun. 11–5; Sept.–June, Wed.–Sun. 1–5* Ⓜ *S74 bus to St. Patrick's Pl.*

Fodor's Choice **Staten Island Ferry.** One of Staten Island's biggest attractions is free—the
★ phenomenal view of Manhattan and the Statue of Liberty afforded by the 25-minute ferry ride across New York Harbor. From Whitehall Terminal at the southern tip of Manhattan, catch the ferry, which leaves every 15 minutes to half hour. ✛ *Runs between Manhattan's Whitehall Terminal, Whitehall and South Sts., and Staten Island's St. George Terminal* ⊕ *www.siferry.com* Ⓜ *4, 5 to Bowling Green; R to Whitehall St.; 1 to South Ferry.*

WORTH NOTING

Jacques Marchais Museum of Tibetan Art. At the top of a hill sits this replica of a Tibetan monastery containing one of the largest collections of Tibetan and Himalayan sculpture, paintings, and artifacts outside Tibet. Meditate with visiting Buddhist monks, or just enjoy the peaceful views from the terraced garden. ✉ *338 Lighthouse Ave., Richmondtown* ☎ *718/987–3500* ⊕ *www.tibetanmuseum.org* 🎫 *$5* ☉ *Thurs.–Sun. 1–5* Ⓜ *S74 bus to Lighthouse Ave. and walk uphill 15 mins.*

Snug Harbor Cultural Center. Once part of a sprawling farm, this 83-acre community is now a popular spot to see maritime art, frolic in the **Children's Museum,** or take a stroll through lush gardens.

Made up of 26 mostly restored historic buildings, Snug Harbor's center is a row of mid-19th-century Greek Revival temples. Main Hall—the oldest building on the property—is home to the **Eleanor Proske Visitors Center** (⌨ *$3, including Newhouse Center*), which has exhibits on art and Snug Harbor's history. The adjacent **Newhouse Center for Contemporary Art** (☎ 718/425–3524 ⌨ *$3, including visitor center*) shows multidisciplinary videos, mixed media, and performances. Next door at the **Noble Maritime Collection** (☎ 718/447–6490 ⊕ *www. noblemaritime.org* ⌨ *$5*) an old seamen's dormitory is now a museum of ocean-inspired artwork.

From the Staten Island Ferry terminal, take the S40 bus 2 mi (about seven minutes) to the Snug Harbor Road stop. Or grab a car service at the ferry terminal. (The ride should cost you about $5.)

Spread over the cultural center grounds is the **Staten Island Botanical Garden** (☎ 718/448–2500 ⊕ *www.snug-harbor.org* ⌨ *Free; $5 for Chinese Garden and Secret Garden* ☉ *Daily dawn–dusk; Chinese Garden and Secret Garden Apr.–Sept., Tues.–Sun. 10–5; Oct.–Mar., Tues.–Sun. noon–4*), which includes an orchid collection, 9/11 memorial, 20-acre wetland, Chinese Scholar's Garden, and a sensory garden with fragrant, touchable flowers and a tinkling waterfall. Children love the Connie Gretz Secret Garden with its castle and maze among the flowers. ⊠ *1000 Richmond Terr., between Snug Harbor Rd. and Tyson Ave., Livingston* ☎ 718/448–2500 ⊕ *www.snug-harbor.org* ⌨ *$3; gardens and galleries combined $6; Cultural Center grounds free* ☉ *Tues.–Sun. 10–5; Noble Maritime Thurs.–Sun. 10–5; grounds dawn–dusk every day except major holidays.*

Museums

WORD OF MOUTH

"If you go to the Neue [Galerie] museum, definitely stop into Café Sabarsky for a fabulous dessert and Viennese coffee. The coffee here is some of the best I have ever tasted."

—Cries_Van_Notebook

MUSEUMS PLANNER

Fodor's Choice	Making the Most of Your Time
Metropolitan Museum of Art American Museum of Natural History Solomon R. Guggenheim Museum Museum of Modern Art Whitney Museum of American Art Lower East Side Tenement Museum Frick Collection ## Highly Recommended Morgan Library and Museum Museum of the City of New York Neue Galerie New York New-York Historical Society	Manhattan could be called Museumpalooza—within just one 30-block area (the main stage, aka Museum Mile, 5th Avenue from 82nd Street to 105th Street) there are nine heavy hitters, and within that general vicinity there are a dozen or so merely excellent ones. Trying to see all of this wonderfulness in a week or two is, unfortunately, impossible. Attempting to see all of even one or two of the big museums is equally futile; your feet will go on strike shortly before your brain shuts down with sensory overload. So consider this your permission slip to think small. Pick one—at most, two—of the bigger museums—the Metropolitan Museum of Art and/or the American Museum of Natural History are the obvious choices, though the Museum of Modern Art is a definite contender—check out their Web sites, and choose just two exhibit halls to tour in depth. For a first visit to the Met, perhaps choose the Egyptian gallery and some of the period rooms off the majorly renovated American Wing; in Natural History, the Dinosaur and Ocean Life halls. See them, and then turn your attention to the city's smaller museums, where there are hidden treasures; elsewhere, many of them could be a city's cultural centerpiece. Among our favorites are the Rubin Museum of Art on West 17th Street, the first museum in the Western world dedicated to the art of the Himalayas; the Museum of the City of New York on 5th Avenue at 103rd Street, which provides an outstanding overview of the city's origins; the American Folk Art Museum on West 53rd Street; the International Center of Photography on 6th Avenue and 43rd Street; and El Museo del Barrio at 104th Street and 5th Avenue, dedicated to Latino art and culture. (Bonus: all our picks also have outstanding gift shops.) But choose the museums that suit your interests, however niche they may be—there are institutions dedicated to water, toys, money, film, television, transportation, assorted cultural heritages, fashion, gardening, and many more.

Updated by
Samantha
Chapnick

Artists have long since called New York home, and for centuries they've drawn inspiration from the bustling mash-up of cultures found here. But the city's museums do more than just display the works of its native sons and daughters—they provide the best the world has to offer at a depth and volume arguably unfound in any other city in the world.

Visitors can easily fill their first half-dozen trips to New York visiting the Metropolitan Museum of Art, the American Museum of Natural History, and the Museum of Modern Art, and still be intimidated by what's left for their next N.Y.C. weekend. A trip down Museum Mile, spanning 23 blocks along 5th Avenue, has nine museums, including the Jewish Museum; El Museo Del Barrio; the Museum of the City of New York; and the Cooper-Hewitt, National Design Museum. And the less-hyped but much-loved museums locals would recommend—the Frick Collection, the Whitney, the Cloisters, the Morgan Library, and the Tenement Museum—are virtually unrivaled for the perspectives on old masters, 20th- and 21st-century art, medieval Europe, manuscripts, and the international immigrant experience, respectively.

But enough highbrow. On a different level, New York's specialty boutique museums offer new perspectives on everyday objects and life. With names like the Museum of Sex, the Museum of Comic and Cartoon Art (MoCCA), the Skyscraper Museum, and Schomburg Center for Research in Black Culture, their collections speak for themselves.

Choose museums to visit before you arrive and check Web sites if it's necessary to purchase advance tickets for special exhibitions. If traveling with kids, ask about family or educator programs for interesting activities—scavenger hunts, puzzles, doodling—that can make the trip more fun.

(⇨ For museums in Brooklyn, see Chapter 12; for venues in Queens, the Bronx, and Staten Island, see Chapter 13.)

LOWER MANHATTAN AND CHINATOWN

Museum of American Finance. Visiting the New York Stock Exchange was the ultimate high for many. The energy of the floor and the proximity to so much power couldn't be beat. But since 9/11 security has tightened and tours are no longer allowed. However, you can get a glimpse of what makes the financial world go 'round by stopping by this museum.

This Smithsonian Institution affiliate moved from a room in the Standard Oil Building on Broadway to the grandiose former banking hall of the Bank of New York in 2008. On view are artifacts of the financial market's history; interactive exhibits on the financial markets, banking, entrepreneurship, and Alexander Hamilton; and well-executed temporary exhibits. ⊠ *48 Wall St., at William St., Lower Manhattan* ☎ *212/908–4110* ⊕ *www.financialhistory.org* ☐ *$8* ⊙ *Tues.–Sat. 10–4* Ⓜ *2, 3 to Wall St.*

The Museum of Chinese in America (MOCA). Founded in 1980, this museum is dedicated to preserving and presenting the history of the Chinese people and their descendants in the United States. MOCA moved in early 2009 to its new home on Centre Street, where the 14,000-square-foot gallery space increased the size of the museum by more than five times.

Designed by Maya Lin, architect of the Vietnam Veterans Memorial in Washington, D.C., MOCA features a permanent exhibit on Chinese-American history, *With a Single Step: Stories in the Making of America*, which includes artworks, personal and domestic artifacts, historical documentation, and films. Chinese laundry tools, a traditional general store, and antique business signs are some of the unique objects on display.

Rotating shows such as *Here & Now*, a contemporary art exhibit, are on display in the second gallery. MOCA sponsors workshops, walking tours, lectures, and family events. ⊠ *215 Centre St., between Grand and Howard Sts., Chinatown* ☎ *212/619–4785* ⊕ *www.mocanyc.org* ☐ *$7* ⊙ *Thurs. 11–9, Mon. and Fri. 11–5, weekends 10–5* Ⓜ *6, J, M, N, Q, R, Z to Canal St.*

Museum of Jewish Heritage—A Living Memorial to the Holocaust. In a granite 85-foot hexagon at the southern end of Battery Park City, this museum pays tribute to the 6 million Jews who perished in the Holocaust. Architects Kevin Roche and John Dinkeloo built the museum in the shape of a Star of David, with three floors of exhibits demonstrating the dynamism of 20th-century Jewish culture.

Visitors enter through a gallery that provides a context for the early-20th-century artifacts on the first floor: an elaborate screen hand-painted for the fall harvest festival of Sukkoth, wedding invitations, and tools used by Jewish tradesmen. Original documentary films play throughout the museum.

The second floor details the rise of Nazism and anti-Semitism, and the ravages of the Holocaust. A gallery covers the doomed voyage of the SS *St. Louis*, a ship of German Jewish refugees that crossed the Atlantic twice in 1939 in search of a safe haven. Signs of hope are also on display, including a trumpet that Louis Bannet (the "Dutch Louis

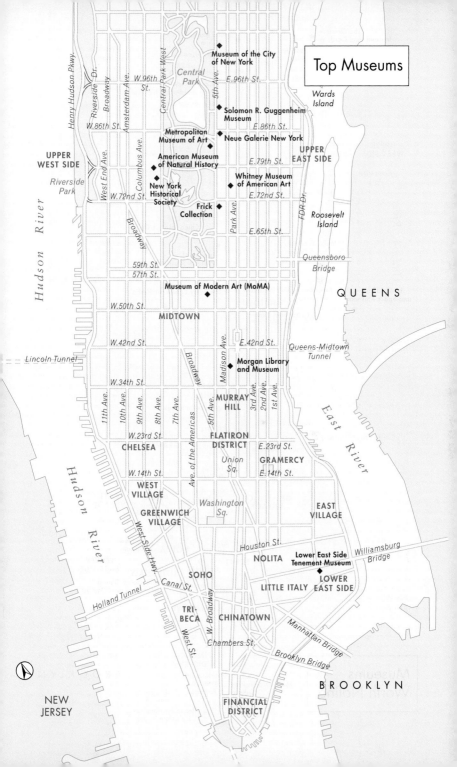

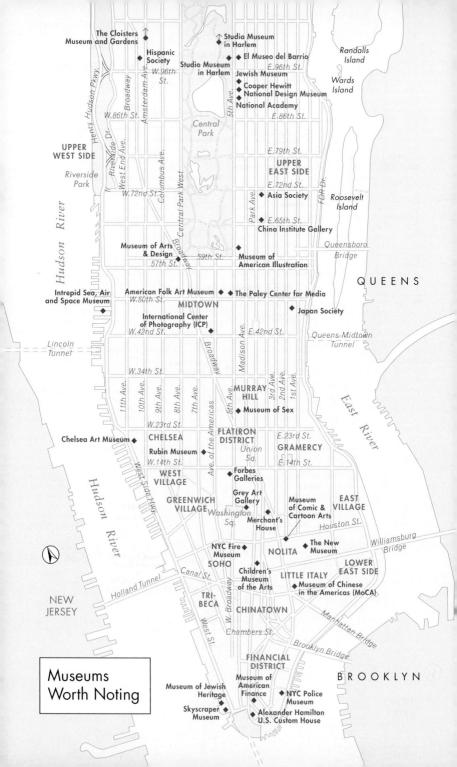

Museums
Worth Noting

The Cloisters
Museum and Gardens

Hispanic
Society
W.96th
St.

Studio Museum
in Harlem

Studio Museum
in Harlem

El Museo del Barrio
E.96th St.

Jewish Museum

Cooper Hewitt
National Design Museum

National Academy
E.86th St.

UPPER
WEST SIDE

Central
Park

E.79th St.

UPPER
EAST SIDE

E.72nd St.

Riverside
Park

W.86th St.

W.72nd St.

Asia Society

E.65th St.

China Institute Gallery

Roosevelt
Island

Randalls
Island

Wards
Island

Queensboro
Bridge

QUEENS

Museum of Arts
& Design
57th St.

59th St.

Museum of
American Illustration

Intrepid Sea, Air
and Space Museum

American Folk Art Museum

The Paley Center for Media

W.50th St.

MIDTOWN

International Center
of Photography (ICP)
W.42nd St.

E.42nd St.

Japan Society

Queens-Midtown
Tunnel

Lincoln
Tunnel

W.34th St.

MURRAY
HILL

Museum of Sex

Hudson River

W.23rd St.

Chelsea Art Museum

CHELSEA

Rubin Museum

W.14th St.

WEST
VILLAGE

FLATIRON
DISTRICT

Union
Sq.

GRAMERCY

E.23rd St.

E.14th St.

Forbes
Galleries

Grey Art
Gallery

GREENWICH
VILLAGE

Washington
Sq.

Merchant's
House

Museum
of Comic &
Cartoon Arts

EAST
VILLAGE

Houston St.

Williamsburg
Bridge

NYC Fire
Museum

SOHO

Children's
Museum
of the Arts

NOLITA

The New
Museum

LITTLE ITALY

LOWER
EAST SIDE

Museum of Chinese
in the Americas (MoCA)

Canal St.

TRI-
BECA

CHINATOWN

Manhattan Bridge

Holland Tunnel

NEW
JERSEY

Chambers St.

Brooklyn Bridge

FINANCIAL
DISTRICT

BROOKLYN

Museum of Jewish
Heritage

Museum of
American
Finance

NYC Police
Museum

Skyscraper
Museum

Alexander Hamilton
U.S. Custom House

Henry Hudson Pkwy.

Broadway

Amsterdam Ave.

Riverside Dr.

West End Ave.

Columbus Ave.

Central Park West

5th Ave.

Park Ave.

FDR Dr.

East River

11th Ave.

10th Ave.

9th Ave.

8th Ave.

7th Ave.

Ave. of the Americas

5th Ave.

Madison Ave.

3rd Ave.

2nd Ave.

1st Ave.

Broadway

West St.

West Side Hwy.

W. Broadway

Armstrong") played for three years in the Auschwitz-Birkenau inmate orchestra.

The third floor covers postwar Jewish life. The east wing contains a theater, memorial garden by artist Andy Goldsworthy, resource center, library, more galleries, classrooms, and a café. ✉ *36 Battery Pl., Battery Park City, Lower Manhattan* ☎ *646/437–4200* ⊕ *www.mjhnyc. org* 🎟 *$12, free Wed. 4–10* ☉ *Thurs. and Sun.–Tues. 10–5:45, Wed. 10–8, Fri. and eve of Jewish holidays 10–3* Ⓜ *4, 5 to Bowling Green.*

National Museum of the American Indian (Smithsonian Institution). This museum is housed in the Beaux-Arts Alexander Hamilton U.S. Custom House (1907), one of Lower Manhattan's finest buildings. Massive granite columns rise to a pediment topped by a double row of statues. Inside, the egg-shape stairwell and rotunda embellished with shipping-theme murals (completed in the 1930s) are incredibly impressive.

Changing presentations drawn from the National Museum of the American Indian in New York, a branch of the Smithsonian, are exhibited here with modern stylishness. The museum recently opened a new public gallery called *Infinity of Nations*, which presents an encyclopedic survey of Native cultures from throughout the Americas, including 700 objects from ancient times to present day.

The Diker Pavilion provides a venue for dance, music, and storytelling programs. Videos and films made by indigenous people from around the world are shown here regularly. ✉ *1 Bowling Green, between State and Whitehall Sts., Lower Manhattan* ☎ *212/514–3700* ⊕ *www. americanindian.si.edu* 🎟 *Free* ☉ *Mon.–Wed. and Fri.–Sun. 10–5, Thurs. 10–8* Ⓜ *4, 5 to Bowling Green.*

🄲 **New York City Police Museum.** Why are police called cops? Why does a police badge have eight points? When was fingerprinting first used to solve a crime? Find the answers at this museum dedicated to New York's finest.

The force's history from colonial times through the present is covered through permanent and rotating exhibits. A permanent exhibit, *9/11 Remembered*, includes a video with interviews with those who were first responders to the attack. The Hall of Heroes honors police officers who have fallen in the line of duty. Special events include a vintage police-car show the first weekend in June. ✉ *100 Old Slip, near South St., Lower Manhattan* ☎ *212/480–3100* ⊕ *www.nycpolicemuseum.org* 🎟 *$5 suggested donation* ☉ *Mon.–Sat. 10–5* Ⓜ *2, 3 to Wall St.*

Skyscraper Museum. This small museum will either delight or disappoint skyscraper fans. To evoke space, the stainless-steel floor and ceiling are polished to mirror quality, but the open room with column partitions does not include a comprehensive overview of the rise of the skyscraper.

Focused exhibits change every few months; the newly expanded permanent display features highlights of New York and Chicago skyscraper history, including the daily photo journal a contractor kept during the Empire State Building's construction. Models of current or future buildings; short videos; and exhibits that reveal the influence of history, real estate, and individuals on architecture are regular features. ✉ *39 Battery*

Pl., Battery Park City, Lower Manhattan ☎ *212/968–1961* ⊕ *www. skyscraper.org* ◷ *$5* ⊗ *Wed.–Sun. noon–6* Ⓜ *4, 5 to Bowling Green.*

SOHO

◐ **Children's Museum of the Arts.** In this bi-level space a few blocks from Broadway, children ages 1 to 14 can amuse and educate themselves with various activities, including diving into a pool of colorful balls; playacting in costume; music making with real instruments; and art making, from computer art to old-fashioned painting, sculpting, and collage. ✉ *182 Lafayette St., between Grand and Broome Sts., SoHo* ☎ *212/274–0986* ⊕ *www.cmany.org* ◷ *$10* ⊗ *Wed. and Fri.–Sun. noon–5, Thurs. noon–6* Ⓜ *6 to Spring St.*

Museum of Comic and Cartoon Art. The Museum of Comic and Cartoon Art features smartly curated artist spotlights (such as Will Eisner, Todd McFarlane, and Kim Deitch) and genre exhibits. Recent shows included a retrospective of Saturday morning cartoons, which included a Smurf village along with the more predictable (but still swell) sketches, animation cells, videos, a horror-theme *Things That Go Bump* review, modern fairy tales, and a comprehensive look at the history and future of independent comics.

New shows are mounted frequently, but MoCCA's Web site tends to list only coming-very-soon shows, so don't worry if nothing seems to be happening while you're planning your trip; check the site a week or so before you arrive in the city to see what's scheduled. And stay on the lookout for MoCCA's annual Art Festival, a comic and cartoon bonanza typically in June. ✉ *594 Broadway, Suite 401, between W. Houston and Broome Sts., SoHo* ☎ *212/254–3511* ⊕ *www.moccany.org* ◷ *$5* ⊗ *Tues., Wed., Fri., and Sat. noon–5; Thurs. noon–6* Ⓜ *B, D, F, G to Broadway–Lafayette St.; N, R to Prince St.*

New York City Fire Museum. In the former headquarters of Engine 30, a handsome Beaux-Arts building dating from 1904, retired firefighters volunteer their time to answer visitors' questions. The collection of firefighting tools from the 18th century to the present includes hand-pulled and horse-drawn engines, pumps, and uniforms.

A memorial exhibit with photos, paintings, children's artwork, and found objects relating to the September 11 attacks is also on view. On 9/11 the city's fire department lost 343 members at the World Trade Center. The museum is two subway stops (via the E train) north of the Ground Zero site. ✉ *278 Spring St., near Varick St., SoHo* ☎ *212/691–1303* ⊕ *www.nycfiremuseum.org* ◷ *$7 suggested donation* ⊗ *Tues.–Sat. 10–5, Sun. 10–4* Ⓜ *C, E to Spring St.*

EAST VILLAGE AND LOWER EAST SIDE

◐ **Lower East Side Tenement Museum.** Step back in time and into the partially
Fodor'sChoice restored 1863 tenement building at 97 Orchard St., where you can
★ squeeze through the preserved apartments of immigrants on one of four one-hour tours. This is America's first urban living-history museum ded-

icated to the life of immigrants—and one of the city's most underrated and overlooked.

Getting By visits the homes of Natalie Gumpertz, a German-Jewish dressmaker (dating from 1878) and Adolph and Rosaria Baldizzi, Catholic immigrants from Sicily (1935). *Piecing It Together* visits the Levines' garment shop/apartment and the Rogarshevsky family from Eastern Europe (1918). The tour through the Confino family apartment is designed for children, who are greeted by a costumed interpreter playing Victoria Confino. Her family of Sephardic Jews came from Kastoria, Turkey, which is now part of Greece (1916). Another tour explores the life of the Moores, an Irish American family living in the building in 1869, and shows a re-created tenement rear yard.

14

Building tours are limited to 15 people, so consider buying tickets in advance. A two-hour extended experience tour with a chance for in-depth discussion is offered every day. Walking tours of the neighborhood are also held daily. The visitor information center and excellent gift shop displays a video with interviews of Lower East Side residents past and present. ⊠ *108 Orchard St., between Delancey and Broome Sts., Lower East Side* ☎ *212/982–8420* ⊕ *www.tenement.org* ✉ *Tenement and walking tours $35; Confino apartment tour $20* ☉ *Tours July and Aug., Fri.–Wed., 10–5, Thurs. 10–7:15; Sept.–June, daily 11:15–5; check Web site for full details. Visitor center and gift shop daily 10–6* Ⓜ *B, D to Grand St.; F to Delancey St.; J, M, Z to Essex St.*

Merchant's House Museum. Built in 1832, this redbrick house, combining Federal and Greek Revival styles, provides a glimpse into domestic life for the three decades before the Civil War. Retired merchant Seabury Tredwell and his descendants lived here from 1835 until 1933. The home became a museum in 1936 with the original furnishings and architectural features preserved; family memorabilia are also on display. Self-guided tours are available without reservations. Kids under 12 get in free. ⊠ *29 E. 4th St., between Bowery and Lafayette St., East Village* ☎ *212/777–1089* ⊕ *www.merchantshouse.org* ✉ *$8* ☉ *Thurs.–Mon. noon–5* Ⓜ *6 to Astor Pl. or Bleecker St.; B, D, F, M to Broadway–Lafayette St.; R to 8th St.*

The New Museum. Focused on contemporary art, the New Museum moved to 235 Bowery in late 2007, marking the first time in its 30 years of existence that the institution has had its very own building. It's also the first building in downtown Manhattan constructed from the ground up with the purpose of being a museum.

The seven-story, 60,000-square-foot structure—a glimmering metal mesh-clad assemblage of off-centered squares—was designed by avant-garde architects Kazuyo Sejima and Ryue Nishizawa. Previous exhibits include *Live Forever: Elizabeth Peyton,* the painter's first survey in an American institution, and shows on computer hacking and life inside "the grid" of modern society.

Be sure to run up to the seventh-floor "sky room" for a twirl around the panoramic balcony above Lower Manhattan. ⊠ *235 Bowery, at Prince St., Lower East Side* ☎ *212/219–1222* ⊕ *www.newmuseum.org*

⌨ *$12* ⊙ *Wed. and Fri.–Sun. 11–6, Thurs. 11–9* Ⓜ *6 to Spring St.; F, M to 2nd Ave.*

CHELSEA

Chelsea Art Museum. In a former Christmas-ornament factory, this contemporary art museum was created to display a collection of postwar European art and to host traveling exhibitions from European museums. Exhibits examine relatively unexplored dimensions of 20th- and 21st-century art, as well as display the work of French abstract painter Jean Miotte. ⊠ *556 W. 22nd St., at 11th Ave., Chelsea* ☎ *212/255–0719* ⊕ *www.chelseaartmuseum.org* ⌨ *$8* ⊙ *Tues., Wed., Fri., and Sat. 11–6, Thurs. 11–8* Ⓜ *C, E to 23rd St.*

Rubin Museum of Art. Opened in 2004, this sleek and serene museum is the largest in the Western Hemisphere dedicated to art of the Himalayas. It provides a great deal of explanation for the colorful works, which are religious and rich with symbols.

Six floors contain paintings on cloth, metal sculptures, and textiles dating from the 2nd century onward. Many of the works from areas such as Tibet, Nepal, southwest China, and India are related to Buddhism, Hinduism, Bon, and other eastern religions. A pleasant café and gift shop are on the ground floor. ⊠ *150 W. 17th St., near 7th Ave., Chelsea* ☎ *212/620–5000* ⊕ *www.rmanyc.org* ⌨ *$10* ⊙ *Mon. and Thurs. 11–5, Wed. 11–7, Fri. 11–10, weekends 11–6* Ⓜ *1 to 18th St.*

MURRAY HILL AND THE FLATIRON DISTRICT

★ **Morgan Library and Museum.** The treasures inside this museum, gathered by John Pierpont Morgan (1837–1913), one of New York's wealthiest financiers, are exceptional: medieval and Renaissance illuminated manuscripts, old master drawings and prints, rare books, and autographed literary and musical manuscripts.

Architect Renzo Piano's redesign of the museum was unveiled in April 2006. The original Renaissance-style building (1906) by Charles McKim of McKim, Mead & White has been preserved, but now there's twice the gallery space, an enlarged auditorium, a dining room, and a café.

Crowning achievements produced on paper, from the Middle Ages to the 20th century, are on view here: letters penned by John Keats and Thomas Jefferson; a summary of the theory of relativity in Einstein's own elegant handwriting; three Gutenberg Bibles; drawings by Dürer, Leonardo da Vinci, Rubens, Blake, and Rembrandt; the only known manuscript fragment of Milton's *Paradise Lost;* Thoreau's journals; and original manuscripts and letters by Charlotte Brontë, Jane Austen, Thomas Pynchon, and many others.

The library shop is within an 1852 Italianate brownstone, once the home of Morgan's son, J. P. Morgan Jr. Outside on East 36th Street, the sphinx in the right-hand sculptured panel of the original library's facade was rumored to wear the face of architect Charles McKim. ⊠ *225 Madison Ave., at 36th St., Murray Hill* ☎ *212/685–0008* ⊕ *www.themorgan.*

org ✉ *$12* ⊙ *Tues.–Thurs. 10:30–5, Fri. 10:30–9, Sat. 10–6, Sun. 11–6*
Ⓜ *B, D, F, N, Q, R, V to 34th St./Herald Sq.; 6 to 33rd St.*

Museum of Sex. Ponder the profound history and cultural significance
of sex while staring at vintage pornographic photos, S&M parapher-
nalia, anti-masturbation devices from the 1800s, vintage condom tins,
and silent movies. The subject matter is given serious curatorial treatment, though an alternative museum like this has to credit sex-product
companies rather than foundations for sponsorship, and the gift shop
preceding the galleries is full of fun sexual kitsch.

On two floors, special exhibits and the permanent collection probe
topics such as Japanese pornographic art from the 1700s or classic
American pinup art. Evenings bring readings by cutting-edge authors
and performance artists. No one under 18 is admitted. ✉ *233 5th
Ave., entrance on 27th St., Flatiron District* ☎ *212/689–6337* ⊕ *www.
museumofsex.com* ✉ *$16.75* ⊙ *Sun.–Thurs. 10–8, weekends 10–9* Ⓜ *R
to 28th St.*

MIDTOWN

American Folk Art Museum. Weather vanes, quilts, pottery, scrimshaw,
sculpture, and paintings give an excellent overview of the freewheeling
folk-art genre, but the exterior is a work of art as well: the eight-story
building was designed in 2001 by husband-and-wife-team Tod Williams
and Billie Tsein, and the facade, consisting of 63 hand-cast panels of
alloyed bronze, reveals individual textures, sizes, and plays of light.

You'll also find a large collection of contemporary self-taught artists
of the 20th and 21st centuries, including the single largest collection of
reclusive Chicago artist Henry Darger, known for his mythic, mural-
size painting. The museum's gift shop has an outstanding collection
of handcrafted items. ✉ *45 W. 53rd St., between 5th and 6th Aves.,
Midtown West* ☎ *212/265–1040* ⊕ *www.folkartmuseum.org* ✉ *$12;
Fri. 5:30 pm–7:30 pm, free* ⊙ *Tues.–Sun. 10:30–5:30, Fri. 10:30–7:30*
Ⓜ *E, M to 5th Ave./53rd St.; B, D, E to 7th Ave.; B, D, F, M to 47th–
50th Sts./Rockefeller Center.*

International Center of Photography. Founded in 1974 by photojournalist Cornell Capa (photographer Robert Capa's brother), this leading
photography museum and school has a permanent collection focused
on American and European documentary photography of the 1930s
to the 1990s.

Changing exhibits display work by famous and should-be-famous photographers and theme group shows on topics such as ecology, health,
religion, science, war, and candid street shots. The gift shop offers
amazing imagery on postcards, posters, and prints, and outstanding
photography books. ✉ *1133 6th Ave., at W. 43rd St., Midtown West*
☎ *212/857–0000* ⊕ *www.icp.org* ✉ *$12* ⊙ *Tues.–Thurs. and weekends
10–6, Fri. 10–8* Ⓜ *B, D, F, M to 42nd St.*

Intrepid Sea, Air & Space Museum. The centerpiece of the newly renovated
Intrepid Sea, Air & Space Museum complex is the 900-foot *Intrepid* aircraft carrier, making it Manhattan's only floating museum. The carrier's

14

MUSEUM OF MODERN ART (MOMA)

✉ 11 W. 53rd St., between 5th and 6th Aves., Midtown East ☎ 212/708–9400 ⊕ www. moma.org 🎟 $20 ☉ Sat.– Mon., Wed., and Thurs. 10:30– 5:30, Fri. 10:30–8. Closed Tues. Ⓜ E, M to 5th Ave./53rd St.; B, D, F, M to 47th–50th Sts./ Rockefeller Center.

TIPS

■ Consider the free audio guide, especially if the scribbled and rather ambiguous nature of modern art occasionally confounds you.

■ Entrance between 4 and 8 pm on Friday is free, but expect to wait in line.

■ Check out the free Wi-Fi in the museum to listen to audio tours as you wander through MoMA (log on to www.moma. org/wifi with your HTML browser-enabled device).

■ With so much art on display, it's hard to remember that the MoMA has three movie theaters. Film passes to the day's screenings are included with the price of admission.

■ Tickets to MoMA also include free admission to its affiliated MoMA PS1 in Queens. Don't worry; you won't need to trek out to Queens on the same day. Save your ticket and you can go in for free any time within 30 days of your original purchase.

Art enthusiasts and novices alike are often awestruck by the masterpieces before them here, including Monet's *Water Lilies*, Picasso's *Les Demoiselles d'Avignon*, and van Gogh's *Starry Night*. In 2004 the museum's $425 million face-lift by Yoshio Taniguchi increased exhibition space by nearly 50%, including space to accommodate large-scale contemporary installations. Its current building gave the museum an opportunity for an increased focus on contemporary art, evident in the recent creation of a Media and Performance Art department. The museum continues to collect: most recently it obtained important works by Martin Kippenberger, David Wojnarowicz, Jasper Johns, Kara Walker, and Neo Rauch. One of the top research facilities in modern and contemporary art is housed inside the museum's eight-story Education and Research building.

HIGHLIGHTS

In addition to the artwork, one of the main draws of MoMA is the building itself. A maze of glass walkways permits art viewing from many angles.

The 110-foot atrium entrance (accessed from the museum's lobby on either 53rd or 54th Street) leads to the movie theaters and the main-floor restaurant, Modern, with Alsatian-inspired cuisine.

A favorite resting spot is the Abby Aldrich Rockefeller Sculpture Garden. Designed by Philip Johnson, it features Barnett Newman's *Broken Obelisk* (1962–69). The glass wall lets visitors look directly into the surrounding galleries from the garden, where there's also a reflecting pool and trees.

Contemporary art (1970 to the present) from the museum's seven curatorial departments shares the second floor of the six-story building, and the skylighted top floor showcases an impressive lineup of changing exhibits.

most trying moment of service, the day it was attacked in World War II by kamikaze pilots, is recounted in a multimedia presentation.

Aircraft on deck include an A-12 Blackbird spy plane, a Concorde, helicopters, and 30 other aircraft. Docked alongside, and also part of the museum, is the *Growler,* a strategic-missile submarine. The interactive Exploreum contains 18 hands-on exhibits.

You can experience a flight simulator, transmit messages in Morse code, and see what it was like to live aboard the massive carrier. ⊠ *Hudson River, Pier 86, 12th Ave. at W. 46th St., Midtown West* ☎ *212/245–0072 or 877/957–7447* ⊕ *www.intrepidmuseum.org* ✑ *$20; free for children under 3* ☉ *Apr.–Oct., weekdays 10–5, weekends 10–6; Nov.–Mar., Tues.–Sun. 10–5; last admission 1 hr before closing* Ⓜ *A, C, E to 42nd St.; M42 bus to pier.*

14

Japan Society. The stylish and serene lobby of the Japan Society has interior bamboo gardens linked by a second-floor waterfall. Works by well-known Japanese artists are exhibited in the second-floor gallery—past shows have included the first-ever retrospective of Yoko Ono's works and *Hiroshi Sugimoto: History of History.* ⊠ *333 E. 47th St., between 1st and 2nd Aves., Midtown East* ☎ *212/832–1155* ⊕ *www. japansociety.org* ✑ *$10* ☉ *Building weekdays 9:30–5:30; gallery Tues.–Thurs. 11–6, Fri. 11–9, weekends 11–5* Ⓜ *6 to 51st St./Lexington Ave.; E, M to Lexington–3rd Aves./53rd St.*

The Paley Center for Media. Three galleries of photographs and artifacts document the history of broadcasting in this 1989 limestone building by Philip Johnson and John Burgee. But the main draw here is the computerized catalog of more than 100,000 television and radio programs. If you want to see a performance of "Turkey Lurkey Time" from the 1969 Tony Awards, for example, type the name of the song, show, or performer into a computer terminal.

You can then proceed to a semiprivate screening area to watch your selection. People nearby might be watching classic comedies from the '50s, miniseries from the '70s, or news broadcasts from the '90s. Adding to the delight of screening TV shows from yesteryear is that the original commercials are still embedded in many of the programs; if ads are your thing you can also skip the programming altogether and watch different compilations of classic commercials. ⊠ *25 W. 52nd St., between 5th and 6th Aves., Midtown West* ☎ *212/621–6800* ⊕ *www. paleycenter.org* ✑ *$10* ☉ *Tues. and Wed.–Sun. noon–6* Ⓜ *E, M to 5th Ave./53rd St.; B, D, F, V to 47th–50th Sts./Rockefeller Center.*

UPPER EAST SIDE

Asia Society and Museum. The Asian art collection of Mr. and Mrs. John D. Rockefeller III forms the core of the museum's holdings, which include South Asian stone and bronze sculptures; art from India, Nepal, Pakistan, and Afghanistan; bronze vessels, ceramics, sculpture, and paintings from China; Korean ceramics; and paintings, wooden sculptures, and ceramics from Japan.

Continued on page 263

THE METROPOLITAN MUSEUM OF ART

Mesmerizing carvings in the ancient Egyptian Temple of Dendur.

If the city held no other museum than the colossal Metropolitan Museum of Art, you could still occupy yourself for days roaming its labyrinthine corridors. Because the Metropolitan Museum has more than 2 million works of art representing 5,000 years of history, you're going to have to make tough choices. Looking at everything here could take a week.

Before you begin exploring the museum, check the museum's floor plan, available at all entrances, for location of the major wings and collections. Pick up the "Today's Events" flier at the desk where you buy your ticket. The museum offers gallery talks on a range of subjects; taking a tour with a staff curator can show you some of the collection's hidden secrets.

The posted adult admission, though only a suggestion, is one that's strongly encouraged. Whatever you choose to pay, admission includes all special exhibits and same-day entrance to the Cloisters (see page 231). The Met's audio guide costs an additional $7, and if you intend to stay more than an hour or so, it's worth it. The generally perceptive commentary covers museum highlights and directors' picks, with separate commentary tracks directed at kids.

If you want to avoid the crowds, visit weekday mornings. Also good are Friday and Saturday evenings, when live classical music plays from the Great Hall balcony. If the Great Hall (the main entrance) is mobbed, avoid the chaos by heading to the street-level entrance to the left of the main stairs, near 81st Street. Ticket lines and coat checks are much less ferocious here.

What to see? Check out the museum highlights on the following pages.

> ✉ 5th Ave. at 82nd St., Upper East Side
> Ⓜ Subway: 4, 5, 6 to 86th St.
> ☎ 212/535-7710
> ⊕ www.metmuseum.org
> 💲 $20 suggested donation
> 🕐 Tues.–Thurs. and Sun. 9:30–5:30, Fri. and Sat. 9:30–9

Left, Great Hall

MUSEUM HIGHLIGHTS

Egyptian Art

A major star is the **Temple of Dendur** (circa 15 BC), in a huge atrium to itself and with a moatlike pool of water to represent its original location near the Nile. The temple was commissioned by the Roman emperor Augustus to honor the goddess Isis and the sons of a Nubian chieftain. Look for the scratched-in graffiti from 19th-century Western explorers on the inside. Egypt gave the temple as a gift to the U.S. in 1965; it would have been submerged after the construction of the Aswan High Dam.

Temple of Dendur

The Egyptian collection as a whole covers 4,000 years of history, with papyrus pages from the Egyptian Book of the Dead, stone sarcophagi inscribed with hieroglyphics, and tombs. The galleries should be walked through counterclockwise from the Ancient Kingdom (2650–2150 BC), to the period under Roman rule (30 BC–400 AD). In the latter, keep an eye out for the enormous, bulbous **Sarcophagus of Horkhebil**, sculpted from basalt.

ART TO TAKE HOME

You don't have to pay admission to get to the mammoth gift shop on the first floor. One of the better souvenirs here is also one of the more reasonable: the Met's own **illustrated guide** to 858 of the best items in its collection ($19.95).

Greek and Roman Art

Today's tabloids have nothing on ancient Greece and Rome. They had it all—sex, cults, drugs, unrelenting violence, and, of course, stunning art. The recently redone Greek and Roman galleries encompass 6,000 works of art that reveal fascinating aspects of everyday life in these influential cultures.

The urnlike terracotta kraters were used by the Greeks for mixing wine and water at parties and other events. Given that, it's not surprising that most depict slightly racy scenes. Some of the most impressive can be found in the gallery covering 5th century BC.

Engelhard Court

On the mezzanine of the Roman galleries, the Etruscan bronze chariot from 650 BC depicts scenes from the life of Achilles. Notice how the simplistic Etruscan style in combination with the Greek influence evolved into the naturalistic Roman statues below.

The frescoes from a bedroom in the Villa of P. Fannius Synistor preserved by the explosion of Mt. Vesuvius in 79 AD give us a glimpse into the stylistic achievement of perspective in Roman painting.

Greek and Roman Galleries

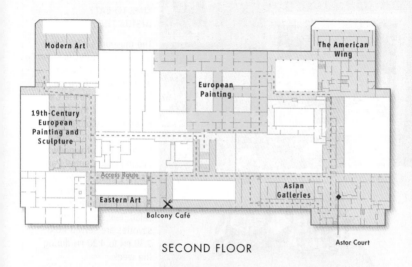

SECOND FLOOR

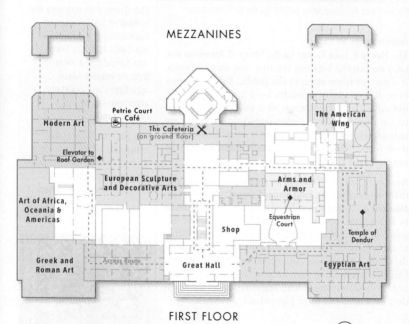

MEZZANINES

FIRST FLOOR

5th Avenue

Visitors ponder European paintings on the 2nd floor.

American Wing

The **Henry R. Luce Center for the Study of American Art,** on a mezzanine between the first and second floors, is a storage room open to the public. Row after row of multilevel glass enclosures hold furniture, decorative objects, and paintings that couldn't otherwise be on display due to space constraints. There are enough works here to make up a small museum of their own—the **Pennsylvania Dutch chests** in row 25 are especially cool.

Also part of the collection is a group of five larger-than-life portraits by **John Singer Sargent.** One of them, *Madame X,* caused a scandal when it was first exhibited in Paris. The woman's pose, with one strap of her gown falling off her shoulder, seemed very suggestive to the onlookers of the time. Sargent later repainted the strap back up in its current, more proper position. Unfortunately these Sargent paintings are currently not on view, but check with information to see when they expect to put these pieces back on display.

TIME TO EAT?
INSIDE THE MUSEUM

The museum's restaurants are almost always full, and going to lunch at 2 PM doesn't mean there won't be a line. The **Petrie Café,** at the back of the 1st-floor European Sculpture Court, has waiter service, but aside from its wall of windows looking onto Central Park, it's very plain. Prices range from $12 for a sandwich to $21 for organic chicken salad. Tea, sweets, and savories are served from 2:30 PM to 4:30 PM during the week.

The **Great Hall Balcony Bar** is located on the second floor belcony overlooking the Great Hall. On Fridays and Saturdays, 4 PM TO 8:30 PM waiters serve appetizers and cocktails accompanied by live classical music.

The basement **cafeteria,** which has white tiles and a vaulted ceiling, has stations for pasta, main courses, antipasti, and sandwiches.

Tiffany

Arms and Armor

The **Equestrian Court,** where the knights are mounted on armored models of horses, is one of the most dramatic rooms in the museum. For a bird's-eye view, check it out again from the balconies in the Musical Instruments collection on the second floor.

European Sculpture and Decorative Arts

Among the many sculptures in the sun-filled Petrie Court, *Ugolino and His Sons* still stands out for the despairing poses of its subjects. Ugolino, a nobleman whose family's tragic story is told in Dante's *Inferno,* was punished for treason by being left to starve to death with his grandsons and sons in a locked tower. (It's not clear if putting such a sculpture so near the Petrie Court's café is some curator's idea of a joke or not.) By the way, the redbrick and granite wall on the court's north side is the museum's original entrance.

The newly renovated Wrightsman Galleries for French Decorative Arts on the first floor displays the opulence that caused Louis the XVI to lose his head. The blindingly golden Boiserie from the Hotel de Cabris, a remnant of French 18th century Neo-classical interiors, represents the finest collection of French decorative arts in the country.

Modern Art

The museum's most famous Picasso is probably his 1906 portrait *Gertrude Stein* in which the writer's face is stern and masklike. The portrait was bequeathed to the museum by Stein herself.

Of the Georgia O'Keeffes on view, 1931's *Red, White, and Blue* painting of a cow skull is a standout. The color, composition, and natural motif work together to create a work with religious as well as nationalist overtones.

European Paintings

On the second floor, the 13th- to 18th-century paintings are in one block, at the top of the Great Hall's stairs. To get to the 19th-century paintings and sculptures, walk through the the narrow corridor of Drawings, Prints, and Photographs. Both sections can be hard to navigate quickly, with a masterpiece around every corner.

Recently, the Met spent about $45 million to buy Duccio di Buoninsegna's *Madonna and Child,* painted circa 1300. The last remaining Duccio in private hands,

TIME TO EAT?
OUTSIDE THE MUSEUM

Because museum admission is good all day, you can always leave for lunch and come back later. The deli-style **City Market Café** (1100 Madison Ave., between. 82nd and 83rd Sts., 212/535–2070) with 10 small tables, serves pizzas, sandwiches, and make-your-own salad. At the fairly inexpensive sit-down eatery **Le Pain Quotidien** (1131 Madison Ave., at 84th St., 212/327–4900), the hungry dine at long communal tables for sandwiches (around $9), salads, and pastries high in both calories and quality. If you'd rather try for a typical New York diner, head for the **Amity Restaurant** (1134 Madison Ave, between 84th and 85th Sts.). A burger with fries costs under $10.

14

IN FOCUS THE METROPOLITAN MUSEUM OF ART

Equestrian Court (1930)

this painting, the size of a piece of typewriter paper, is unimpressive at first glance. The work, though rigid, represents a revolution in Byzantine art. The humanity reflected in the baby Jesus grabbing his mother's veil changed European painting.

The Triumph of Fame, a round, double-sided "commemorative birth tray" by Scheggia, shows a crowd of mounted knights saluting winged Fame, who holds both a cupid and a sword (they symbolize two timeless ways to get famous). The tray heralds the arrival of Lorenzo de' Medici (1449–92), who did indeed become a famed figure of the Italian Renaissance.

Vincent van Gogh,
Wheatfield with Cypresses

Rembrandt's masterful *Aristotle with a Bust of Homer* (1653) shows a philosopher contemplating worldly gains versus values through its play of light and use of symbols. Around Aristotle is a gold medal of Alexander the Great, one of the philosopher's students.

In the room dedicated to **Monet** you can get to all his greatest hits—poplar trees, haystacks, water lilies, and the Rouen Cathedral. The muted tones of Pissaro are followed by a room full of bright and garish colors announcing works by Gauguin, Matisse, and Van Gogh.

Asian Galleries

The serene **Astor Court,** which has its own skylight and pond of real-life koi (goldfish), is a model of a scholar's court garden in Soochow, China.

The Han dynasty (206 BC–220 AD) introduced the practice of sending the dead on to the afterlife with small objects to help them there. Keep an eye out for these **small clay figures,** which include farm animals (enclosed in barnyards) and dancing entertainers.

On display in a glass case in the center of an early-Chinese gallery is a complete set of 14 **bronze altar vessels.** Dating 1100 BC—800 AD, these green and slightly crusty pieces were used for worshipping ancestors. The Met displays some of its finest **Asian stoneware and porcelain** along the balcony overlooking the Great Hall.

The teak dome and minature balconies from a **Jain meeting hall** in western India were carved in the 16th century. Just about the entire surface is covered with musicians, animals, gods, and servants.

GREAT VIEWS

Looking for one of the best views in town? The Roof Garden (open May–October) exhibits contemporary sculptures, but most people take the elevator here to have a drink or snack while checking out Central Park and the skyline.

Founded in 1956, the society has a regular program of lectures, films, and performances, in addition to changing exhibitions of traditional and contemporary art. Trees grow in the Garden Court Café, which serves an eclectically Asian menu for lunch and dinner. ⊠ *725 Park Ave., at 70th St., Upper East Side* ☎ *212/288–6400* ⊕ *asiasociety.org* ⊠ *$10, Fri. 6–9 free* ☉ *Tues.–Sun. 11–6, open until 9 on Fri. from the day after Labor Day to July 1* Ⓜ *6 to 68th St./Hunter College.*

Cooper-Hewitt, National Design Museum. More than 2,000 years of international design are on display inside the 64-room mansion, formerly home to industrialist Andrew Carnegie. The 200,000-plus objects here include drawings, textiles, furniture, metalwork, ceramics, glass, and woodwork.

Changing exhibitions are drawn from the permanent collection, highlighting everything from antique cutlery and Japanese sword fittings to robotics and animation. The museum's shows are invariably enlightening and often amusing. In summer some exhibits are displayed in the museum's lush garden. ⊠ *2 E. 91st St., at 5th Ave., Upper East Side* ☎ *212/849–8400* ⊕ *www.cooperhewitt.org* ⊠ *$15* ☉ *Weekdays 10–5, Sat. 10–6, Sun. 11–6* Ⓜ *4, 5, 6 to 86th St.*

El Museo del Barrio. *El barrio* is Spanish for "the neighborhood" and the nickname for East Harlem, a largely Spanish-speaking Puerto Rican and Dominican community. The museum, on the edge of this neighborhood, focuses on Latin American and Caribbean art.

The more than 6,500-object permanent collection includes numerous pre-Columbian artifacts, sculpture, photography, film and video, and traditional art from all over Latin America. The collection of 360 *santos,* carved wooden folk-art figures from Puerto Rico, is a popular attraction. Thanks to a renovation in 2009, the museum now sports a glass facade and a redesigned courtyard. ⊠ *1230 5th Ave., between E. 104th and E. 105th Sts., Upper East Side* ☎ *212/831–7272* ⊕ *www. elmuseo.org* ⊠ *$9* ☉ *Wed.–Sun. 11–5* Ⓜ *6 to 103rd St.*

Fodor's Choice
★

Frick Collection. Henry Clay Frick made his fortune amid the soot and smoke of Pittsburgh, where he was a coke (a coal fuel derivative) and steel baron. Decidedly removed from soot is this facility, once Frick's private New York residence.

Édouard Manet's *The Bullfight* (1864) hangs in the East Gallery, which also exhibits a Chinard portrait bust (1809; bought in 2004). Two of the Frick's three Vermeers—*Officer and Laughing Girl* (circa 1658) and *Girl Interrupted at Her Music* (1660–61)—hang by the front staircase.

Nearly 50 additional paintings, as well as sculpture, decorative arts, and furniture, are in the West and East galleries. Three Rembrandts, including *The Polish Rider* (circa 1655) and *Self-Portrait* (1658), as well as a third Vermeer, *Mistress and Maid* (circa 1665–70), hang in the former; paintings by El Greco, Goya, Millet, Greuze, and Hogarth in the latter.

An audio guide, available in several languages, is included with admission, as are the year-round temporary exhibits. The tranquil indoor garden court is a great spot for a rest. Children under 10 are not admitted, 10–16 with adult only. ⊠ *1 E. 70th St., at 5th Ave., Upper East*

14

Side ☎ *212/288–0700* ⊕ *www.frick.org* ✉ *$18* ⊙ *Tues.–Sat. 10–6, Sun. 11–5* Ⓜ *6 to 68th St./Hunter College.*

Jewish Museum. Within a Gothic-style 1908 mansion, the museum draws on a large collection of art and ceremonial objects to explore Jewish identity and culture spanning more than 4,000 years.

The two-floor permanent exhibition *Culture and Continuity: The Jewish Journey* displays nearly 800 objects complemented by interactive media. The wide-ranging collection includes a 3rd-century Roman burial plaque, 20th-century sculpture by Elie Nadelman, and contemporary art from artists such as Marc Chagall and Man Ray. ✉ *1109 5th Ave., at E. 92nd St., Upper East Side* ☎ *212/423–3200* ⊕ *www.jewishmuseum.org* ✉ *$12, Sat. free* ⊙ *Sat.–Tues. 11–5:45, Thurs. 11–8, Fri. 11–4* Ⓜ *6 to 96th St.*

Museum of American Illustration. Founded in 1901, the museum of the Society of Illustrators presents its annual "Oscars," a juried, international competition, from January to March. The best in children's book illustrations is featured October through November. In between are eclectic exhibitions on science fiction, fashion, political, and historical illustration. ✉ *128 E. 63rd St., between Lexington and Park Aves., Upper East Side* ☎ *212/838–2560* ⊕ *www.societyillustrators.org* ✉ *Free* ⊙ *Tues. 10–8, Wed.–Fri. 10–5, Sat. noon–4* Ⓜ *F to 63rd St.; 4, 5, 6, N, R to 59th St./Lexington Ave.*

★ **Museum of the City of New York.** Within a Colonial Revival building designed for the museum in the 1930s, the city's history and many quirks are revealed through engaging exhibits. Beginning in early 2010 and through 2012, the museum's permanent galleries will undergo a major renovation.

The museum will still have a series of rotating exhibitions on subjects such as architecture, fashion, history, and politics. Don't miss *Timescapes*, a 25-minute media projection that innovatively illustrates New York's physical expansion and population changes. The museum hosts New York–centric lectures, films, and walking tours. ■**TIP→** When you're finished touring the museum, cross the street and stroll through the Vanderbilt Gates to enter the Conservatory Garden, one of Central Park's hidden gems. ✉ *1220 5th Ave., at E. 103rd St., Upper East Side* ☎ *212/534–1672* ⊕ *www.mcny.org* ✉ *$10 suggested donation* ⊙ *Tues.–Sun. 10–5* Ⓜ *6 to 103rd St.*

★ **Neue Galerie New York.** Early-20th-century German and Austrian art and design are the focus here, with Gustav Klimt, Wassily Kandinsky, Paul Klee, Egon Schiele, Josef Hoffman, and other designers from the Wiener Werkstätte. The Neue Galerie was founded by the late art dealer Serge Sabarsky and cosmetics heir and art collector Ronald S. Lauder.

The two-floor gallery, Viennese-style café, and design shop are in a 1914 wood- and marble-floor mansion designed by Carrère and Hastings, which was home to Mrs. Cornelius Vanderbilt III. An audio guide is included with admission. Note that children under 12 are not admitted, and teens 12–16 must be accompanied by an adult.

SOLOMON R. GUGGENHEIM MUSEUM

✉ *1071 5th Ave., between E. 88th and E. 89th Sts., Upper East Side* ☎ *212/423–3500* ⊕ *www.guggenheim.org* 🎟 *$18* ⊙ *Sun.–Wed. 10–5:45, Fri. 10–5:45, Sat. 10–7:45. Closed Thurs.* Ⓜ *4, 5, 6 to 86th St.*

14

TIPS

■ Gallery talks provide richer understanding of the masterpieces in front of you. The museum offers tours at a terrific price: free!

■ Eat before trekking over to 5th Avenue; restaurants on Lexington offer more varied fare than the museum's cafeteria.

■ The museum is pay-what-you-wish on Saturday from 5:45 to 7:45. Lines can be long, so go early. The last tickets are handed out at 7:15.

Frank Lloyd Wright's landmark museum building is visited as much for its famous architecture as for its superlative art. Opened in 1959, shortly after Wright's death, the Guggenheim is acclaimed as one of the greatest buildings of the 20th century. After a three-year restoration project completed at the end of October 2008, the Guggenheim building is once again a glorious vision. Eleven coats of paint were removed, exterior cracks were fixed, and supporting structures were reinforced. Inside, under a 92-foot-high glass dome, a seemingly endless ramp spirals down past changing exhibits. The museum has strong holdings of Wassily Kandinsky, Paul Klee, Marc Chagall, Pablo Picasso, and Robert Mapplethorpe.

HIGHLIGHTS

Wright's design was criticized by some who believed that the distinctive building detracted from the art within, but the interior nautilus design allows artworks to be viewed from several different angles and distances. Be sure to notice not only what's in front of you but also what's across the spiral from you.

Even if you aren't planning to eat, stop at the museum's modern American restaurant, the Wright, for its stunning design created by Andre Kikosk.

On permanent display, the museum's Thannhauser Collection is made up primarily of works by French impressionists and postimpressionists van Gogh, Toulouse-Lautrec, Cézanne, and Matisse. Perhaps more than any other 20th-century painter, Wassily Kandinsky, one of the first "pure" abstract artists, has been closely linked to the museum's history. Beginning with the acquisition of his masterpiece *Composition 8* (1923) in 1930, the collection has grown to encompass more than 150 works.

WHITNEY MUSEUM OF AMERICAN ART

✉ *945 Madison Ave., at E. 75th St., Upper East Side* ☎ *800/944-8639* ⊕ *www. whitney.org* 🎟 *$18* ⊙ *Wed., Thurs., and weekends 11–6; Fri. 1–9* Ⓜ *6 to 77th St.*

TIPS

■ After 6 pm on Friday the price of admission is pay-what-you-wish. On some of those nights the Whitney Live series presents new artists and reinterpretations of American classics. Be forewarned that this combination may result in long lines.

With its bold collection of 20th- and 21st-century and contemporary American art, this museum presents an eclectic mix drawn from more than 18,000 works in its permanent collection. The museum was originally a gallery in the studio of sculptor and collector Gertrude Vanderbilt Whitney, whose talent and taste were accompanied by the money of two wealthy families. In 1930, after the Met turned down Whitney's offer to donate her collection of 20th-century American art, she established an independent museum in Greenwich Village. Now uptown, the minimalist gray-granite building opened in 1966 and was designed by Marcel Breuer and Hamilton Smith.

HIGHLIGHTS

Start your visit on the fifth floor, where the galleries house rotating exhibitions of postwar and contemporary works from the permanent collection by artists such as Jackson Pollock, Jim Dine, Jasper Johns, Mark Rothko, Chuck Close, Cindy Sherman, and Roy Lichtenstein.

Although the collection on display constantly changes, notable pieces often on view include Hopper's *Early Sunday Morning* (1930), Bellows's *Dempsey and Firpo* (1924), Alexander Calder's beloved *Circus,* and several of Georgia O'Keeffe's dazzling flower paintings.

The lower floors feature exhibitions of contemporary artists such as Kara Walker and Gordon Matta-Clark as well as retrospective exhibitions that focus on movements and themes in American art.

The often-controversial Whitney Biennial, which showcases the most important developments in American art over the previous two years, takes place in the spring of even-numbered years.

In an elegant, high-ceiling space below the Neue Galerie, **Café Sabarsky** serves Viennese coffee, cakes, strudels, and Sacher tortes (Monday and Wednesday 9–6, Thursday–Sunday 9–9). If you seek something more than a sugar fix, the savory menu includes trout crepes and Hungarian goulash. ⊠ *1048 5th Ave., at E. 86th St., Upper East Side* ☎ *212/628–6200* ⊕ *www.neuegalerie.org* ⊠ *$15* ☞ *Children under 12 not admitted* ☼ *Thurs.–Mon. 11–6* Ⓜ *4, 5, 6 to 86th St.*

UPPER WEST SIDE

Museum of Arts and Design. In a whimsical building right next door to the Time-Warner Center, the Museum of Arts and Design celebrates joyful quirkiness and personal, sometimes even obsessive, artistic visions. The art is human-scale here, much of it neatly housed in display cases rather than on the walls, with a strong focus on contemporary jewelry, glass, ceramic, fiber, wood, and mixed-media works.

Recent exhibits included *Slash: Paper Under the Knife,* which show-cased contemporary artworks entirely made from cut paper, and *Read My Pins,* which displayed the brooch collection of former secretary of state Madeline Albright. Thursday is a good time to drop by; the admission is pay-what-you-wish. ⊠ *2 Columbus Circle, 59th St. at 8th Ave., Upper West Side* ☎ *212/299–7777* ⊕ *www.madmuseum.org* ⊠ *$15* ☼ *Tues.–Sun. 11–6, Thurs. 11–9* Ⓜ *A, B, C, D, 1 to Columbus Circle/59th St.; N, Q, R to 57th St./7th Ave.; F to 57th St./6th Ave.*

★ **New-York Historical Society.** Manhattan's oldest museum, founded in 1804, has one of the city's finest research libraries and a collection of 6 million pieces of art, literature, and memorabilia. Special exhibitions shed light on New York's—and America's—history, art, and architecture. Major exhibits have included Hudson River School landscapes and an examination of New York City's role in the slavery debate and the Civil War.

Unlike other museums that keep much of their collections in storage, virtually all of the museum's huge and eclectic permanent collection—ranging from 19th-century cockroach traps to the armchair that George Washington sat in during his inaugural ceremony—are displayed in glass shelves in the museum's Henry Luce III Center for the Study of American Culture. It's a bit of a jumble, but you're bound to stumble across many wonderful things.

The recently completed $65-million renovation has snatched this museum from the purview of history buffs and placed it center stage for all New York visitors. The already spectacular block-long neoclassical building has been enhanced with long overdue features offering a more contemporary experience on a par with its large cousins across Central Park.

History and grandeur have now been made personal and tangible. Visitors enter through the Great Hall where they use kiosks and view original objects tied to key themes of American history such as commerce and immigration. Every year one major history exhibit demonstrates how the past is anything but dead. Currently, *Revolution* uses

Continued on page 276

INSECTS AND MYRIAPODS

INSECTS AND MYRIAPODS

SEGMENTED WOR

AMERICAN MUSEUM ᴼᶠ NATURAL HISTORY

Theodore Roosevelt
Memorial Hall

The largest natural history museum in the world is also one of the most impressive sights in New York. Four city blocks make up its 46 exhibition halls, which hold more than 30 million artifacts and wonders from the land, the sea, and outer space. With all those wonders, you won't be able to see everything on a single visit, but you can easily hit the highlights in half a day.

Before you begin, plan a route before setting out. Be sure to pick up a map when you pay your admission. The museum's four floors (and lower level) are mazelike.

To get the most from the museum's stunning riches, try to allow enough time to slow down and take advantage of the computer stations and the volunteer "Explainers," who are knowledgeable and able to point out their own favorite exhibits.

Getting into the museum can be time consuming. For the shortest lines, use the below-street-level entrance connected to the 81st Street subway station (look for the subway entrance to the left of the museum's steps). This entrance gives you quick access to bathrooms and the food court. The entrance on Central Park West, where the vast steps lead up into the impressive, barrel-ceilinged Theodore Roosevelt Rotunda, is the most impressive and memorable entrance at

the museum. Its central location makes a good starting place for exploring.

The Rose Center for Earth and Space, a must-visit, is attached to the museum. Enter from West 81st Street, where a path slopes down to the entrance, after which elevators and stairs descend to the ticket line on the lower level.

What to see? Check out the museum highlights on the following pages.

✉ Central Park West at W. 79th St., Upper West Side

Ⓜ Subway: B, C to 81st St.

☎ 212/769-5200

🌐 www.amnh.org

🎫 $16 suggested donation, includes admission to Rose Center for Earth and Space

🕙 Daily 10–5:45. Rose Center until 8:45 on Fri.

MUSEUM HIGHLIGHTS

Left, Tyrannosaurus rex
Above, Hadrosaurus

Dinosaurs and Mammals

An amazing assembly of dinosaur and mammal fossils covers the entire floor. The organization can be hard to grasp at first, so head to the **Wallace Orientation Center,** where a short film explains how each of the Fossil Halls lead into each other. You'll want to spend at least an hour here—the highlights include a *T. rex,* an *Apatosaurus* (formerly called a Brontosaurus), and the *Buettneria,* which resembles a modern-day crocodile.

The specimens are not in chronological order; they're put together based on their shared characteristics. Key branching-off points—a watertight egg, a grasping hand—are highlighted in the center of rooms and surrounded by related fossil groups. Check out the touch screens here; they make a complex topic more comprehensible.

Reptiles and Amphibians

Head for the Reptiles and Amphibians Hall to check out the Komodo dragon lizards and a 23-foot-long python skeleton. The weirdest display is the enlarged model of the Suriname toad *Pipa pipa,* whose young hatch from the female's back. The Primates Hall carries brief but interesting comparisons between apes, monkeys, and humans. Also on the third floor is the upper gallery of the famed Akeley Hall of African Mammals.

SPECIAL SHOWS AND NEW EXHIBITS

Special exhibits, the IMAX theater, and the Space Show cost extra. The timed tickets are available in advance at the museum's Web site and are sold same day at the door. Between October and May, don't miss the warm, plant-filled Butterfly Conservatory, where blue morphos, monarchs, and other butterflies flit and feed. Ten minutes is probably enough time to enjoy it.

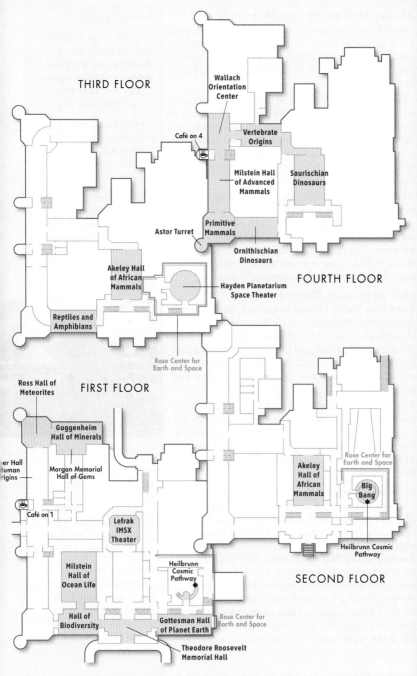

THIRD FLOOR

Wallach
Orientation
Center

Café on 4

Vertebrate
Origins

Milstein Hall
of Advanced
Mammals

Saurischian
Dinosaurs

Astor Turret

Primitive
Mammals

Ornithischian
Dinosaurs

FOURTH FLOOR

Akeley Hall
of African
Mammals

Hayden Planetarium
Space Theater

Reptiles and
Amphibians

Rose Center for
Earth and Space

Ross Hall of
Meteorites

FIRST FLOOR

Guggenheim
Hall of Minerals

er Hall
uman
rigins

Morgan Memorial
Hall of Gems

Rose Center for
Earth and Space

Akeley
Hall of
African
Mammals

Big
Bang

Café on 1

Lefrak
IMSX
Theater

Heilbrunn Cosmic
Pathway

Milstein
Hall of
Ocean Life

Heilbrunn
Cosmic
Pathway

SECOND FLOOR

Hall of
Biodiversity

Gottesman Hall
of Planet Earth

Rose Center for
Earth and Space

Theodore Roosevelt
Memorial Hall

Akeley Hall of African Mammals

Opened in 1936, this hall is one of the most beloved parts of the museum. Its 28 dramatically lighted dioramas may seem merely kitschy at first glance, but take a little time to let their beauty and technical brilliance shine through.

The hall was the life's work of the explorer Carl Akeley, who came up with the idea for the hall, raised the funds for the expeditions, gathered specimens, and sketched landscape studies for what would become the stunning backgrounds. (The backgrounds themselves were painted by James Perry Wilson, whose works can be found throughout the museum.)

Akeley died a decade before the hall opened on an expedition in what's now Rwanda. His grave site is near the landscape portrayed in the gorilla diorama, completed after his death as a memorial to him and his work. The dioramas make irresistible photo ops. If you want to snap one yourself, it's best to turn off your flash to prevent reflections off the glass.

Hall of Human Origins

The Spitzer Hall of Human Origins is a comprehensive exhibit that allows visitors to draw their own conclusions about human evolution by presenting both the scientific methods and the material evidence that goes into evolutionary theory. Visitors gain insight into the techniques and thinking of scientists and anthropologists.

The exhibit then traces the evolution of our species over six million years of fossil record and spells out our ancestors' physical and intellectual advancements. Highlights include casts of our famous hairy relative "Lucy," who walked the plains of Africa over 1.8 million years ago.

Hall of Biodiversity

The small **Hall of Biodiversity** includes a shady replica of a Central African Republic rain forest. Within a few yards are 160 species of flora and fauna—and also evidence of the forest's destruction. Nearby, the **Spectrum of Life Wall** showcases 1,500 specimens and models, helping show just how weird life can get. The wall opens into the gaping Milstein Hall of Ocean Life, designed to give it an underwater glow and to show off the 94-foot model of a **blue whale** that's suspended from the ceiling. The hall focuses on the vast array of life in the ocean that covers our planet.

AMNH ON FILM

Does the inside of AMNH look familiar? It should. The museum is a popular location for movies filming in New York. Here are a few of its recent close ups:

Spider-Man 2: Peter Parker (Toby Maguire) has yet another bad day wrestling with his secret identity while in the Rose Center.

Night at the Museum: Larry (Ben Stiller) is chased through the halls by a t. Rex and outsmarts a monkey in the Hall of African Mammals while working as a night security guard.

Blue Whale

The Squid & the Whale: Walt Berkman (Jesse Eisenberg) comes to a revelation that he is the squid and his father is the whale in front of the Hall of Ocean Life's famous diorama.

The Devil Wears Prada: Andrea (Anne Hathaway) wins over Miranda (Meryl Streep) by remembering the names of high society guests while attending a benefit here.

FREDERICK PHINEAS & SANDRA PRIEST ROSE CENTER FOR EARTH AND SPACE

ROSE CENTER
FOR EARTH AND SPACE

The vast expanses of space and time involved in the creation of the universe can be hard to grasp even with the guiding hand of a museum, so visit the center when you're at your sharpest. The stunning glass building's centerpiece is the aluminum-clad Hayden Sphere, 87 feet in diameter. Enclosed within are the planetarium, called the Space Theater, and an audiovisual Big Bang presentation consisting of four minutes of narration by Maya Angelou, indistinct washes of color, and frightening bursts of sound. The rock-filled **Hall of Planet Earth** is particularly timely given the earthquakes and other natural disasters of recent years: one section uses a working earthquake monitor to help explain just what causes such seismic violence.

The Space Theater

At the Space Theater, the stage is the dome above you and the actors, heavenly projections. One of the world's largest virtual reality simulators, the theater uses surround sound and slight vibrations in the seats, to immerse you in scenes of planets, star clusters, and galaxies. The music of U2, Audioslave, and David Byrne among others inspire Sonic Vision, a digitally animated performance given every Friday and Saturday night.

TIME TO EAT?

Inside the Museum: The main food court on the lower level serves sandwiches for about $7.95; hamburgers cost $5.50. The animal- and planet-shaped cookies are draws for kids; adults should check out the barbecue station.

The small Café on 4, in a turret next to the fossil halls, sells pre-made sandwiches and salads, and yogurt and desserts, but nothing warm.

The über-white Café on 1, tucked away beside the Hall of Human Origins, sells warm sandwiches, soup, salads, beer and wine at New York prices.

Outside the Museum: The nearest restaurants are expensive; to keep to a budget, head to a popular chain: Uno Chicago Grill (✉ Columbus Ave. and W. 81st St. ☎ 212/595–4700), where lunch specials run until 3 PM and kids' meals are $3.99 and up. For something special, try Nice Matin (Amsterdam Ave. and W. 79th St.), a French restaurant that specializes in food from the Nice region of France. They offer a brunch on the weekend from $7.50. Another option is a three course prix fixe dinner from 5:00–6:30 Monday–Friday that offers an array of selections from the menu for $32.50.

14

IN FOCUS AMERICAN MUSEUM OF NATURAL HISTORY

AMNH TALKS TO FODOR'S

Rose Center for Earth and Space

Interview with Ellen V. Futter, President of the American Museum of Natural History, conducted by Michelle Delio.

If You Only Have an Hour: The American Museum of Natural History has the world's finest collection of dinosaur fossils, so a visit to the fourth-floor's Fossil Halls, where more than 600 specimens are on display, is a must. An extraordinarily high percentage of the specimens on view—85%—are real fossilized bones as opposed to casts. At most museums those percentages are reversed, so here visitors have the chance to see the real thing including T. rex, velociraptor, and triceratops.

What to Hit Next? The museum also is renowned for its habitat dioramas, which are considered among the finest examples in the world. Visits to the Akeley Hall of African Mammals, the Hall of North American Mammals, and the Sanford Hall of North American Birds provide an overview of the diorama arts—pioneered and advanced at the museum—while allowing visitors to come face-to-face with some glorious and beautiful animals depicted in their natural habitats—habitats which in many cases no longer exist in such pristine conditions.

If You're Looking to Be Starstruck: Even if you don't have time to take in a space show in the Hayden Planetarium, the Rose Center for Earth and Space has lots of fascinating exhibits describing the vast range of sizes in the cosmos; the 13-billion-year history of the universe; the nature of galaxies, stars, and planets; and the dynamic features of our own unique planet Earth—all enclosed in a facility with spectacular award-winning architecture.

Hidden gems

The museum consists of 45 exhibition halls in 25 interconnected buildings so there are gems around every corner. Some lesser-known treasures include:

Star of India: The 563-carat Star of India, the largest and most famous star sapphire in the world, is displayed in the Morgan Memorial Hall of Gems.

WHERE'S PLUTO?

With all the controversy about what constitutes a planet, some visitors enjoy hunting for Pluto in the Cullman Hall of the Universe in the Rose Center for Earth and Space. We'll give you a hint: it's not with the other planets.

Black Smokers: These sulfide chimneys—collected during groundbreaking museum expeditions to the Pacific Ocean—are the only such specimens exhibited anywhere. Black smokers form around hot springs on the deep ocean floor and support a microbial community that does not live off sunlight but instead on the chemical energy of the Earth. Some of these microbes are considered the most ancient forms of life on Earth and may offer clues to the development of life here and the possibility of life elsewhere. See them in the Gottesman Hall of Planet Earth.

14

Spectrum of Life: The Hall of Biodiversity aims to showcase the glorious diversity of life on Earth resulting from 3.5 billion years of evolution. The impressive "Spectrum of Life" display is a 100-foot-long installation of more than 1,500 specimens and models—microorganisms and mammals, bacteria and beetles, fungi and fish. Use the computer workstations to learn more about the species depicted in each area.

Star of India

Dodo: One of the museum's rarest treasures is the skeleton of a dodo bird, displayed along with other endangered or extinct species in the "Endangered Case" in the Hall of Biodiversity.

Small Dioramas: Tucked along the sides of the Hall of North American Mammals are two easy-to-miss corridors displaying a number of exquisitely rendered dioramas. In these jewel-box-like displays, some a mere 3 feet deep, you will see the smaller animals such as wolves galloping through a snowy night, a Canada lynx stalking a snowshoe hare, and a spotted skunk standing on its hands, preparing to spray a cacomistle, to name just a few of the evocative scenes.

Dinosaur Eggs: In 1993 museum scientists working in the Gobi Desert of Mongolia were the first to unearth fossilized embryos in dinosaur eggs, as well as the fossil of an adult oviraptor in a brooding posture over its nest. This discovery provided invaluable information about dinosaur gestation and revolutionized thinking about dinosaur behavior. Look for the display in the museum's Fossil Halls on the fourth floor.

Ross Terrace: In warmer months the Ross Terrace, with its fountains and cosmic theme, offers a wonderful outdoor spot for resting and reflecting, while providing a spectacular view of the Rose Center for Earth and Space.

IN FOCUS AMERICAN MUSEUM OF NATURAL HISTORY

MOST INTERESTING OBJECT?

What's most interesting about the American Museum of Natural History is not any single object on exhibit, but the sheer range and scope of what you can experience here. Think of it is a field guide to the natural world, the universe, and the cultures of humanity—all under one roof. The experience of visiting the museum is ultimately about awakening a sense of discovery, wonder, awe, and stewardship of this Earth we call home.

the common winds of liberty and freedom to connect the American, French, and Haitian Revolutions.

Foodies are encouraged to explore small plates at the latest Starr (of Buddakan and Morimoto) restaurant on the first floor. Families rejoice in what might just be one of the few museums showing historical figures as they were when they were young themselves in the relatively huge 2,300 square foot DiMenna Children's History Museum and Barbara K. Lipman Children's History Library. ✉ *2 W. 77th St., at Central Park W, Upper West Side* ☎ *212/873–3400* ⊕ *www.nyhistory.org* ✐ *$12* ⊙ *Tues.–Thurs. and weekends 10–6, Fri. 10–8* Ⓜ *B, C to 81st St.*

OFF THE BEATEN PATH

The Cloisters Museum and Gardens. Perched on a wooded hill in Fort Tryon Park, near Manhattan's northwestern tip, the Cloisters Museum and Gardens, which shelters the medieval collection of the Metropolitan Museum of Art, is a scenic destination on its own.

Colonnaded walks connect authentic French and Spanish monastic cloisters, a French Romanesque chapel, a 12th-century chapter house, and a Romanesque apse. One room is devoted to the 15th- and 16th-century Unicorn Tapestries from around 1500—a must-see masterpiece of medieval mythology.

The tomb effigies are another highlight. Two of the three enclosed gardens shelter more than 250 species of plants similar to those grown during the Middle Ages, including flowers, herbs, and medicinals; the third is an ornamental garden planted with both modern and medieval plants, providing color and fragrance from early spring until late fall.

Concerts of medieval music are held here regularly (concert tickets include same-day admission to the museum), and an outdoor café decorated with 15th-century carvings serves biscotti and espresso from May through October. ✉ *99 Margaret Corbin Dr., Upper West Side* ☎ *212/923–3700* ⊕ *www.metmuseum.org* ✐ *$20 suggested donation* ⊙ *Mar.–Oct., Tues.–Sun. 9:30–5:15; Nov.–Feb., Tues.–Sun. 9:30–4:45* Ⓜ *A to 190th St.*

HARLEM

Hispanic Society of America. This is the best collection of Spanish art outside the Prado in Madrid, with (primarily 15th- and 16th-century) paintings, sculptures, textiles, and decorative arts from Spain, Portugal, Italy, and South America. There are notable pieces by Goya, El Greco, and Velázquez. An entire room is filled with a collection of antique brass knockers. ✉ *Audubon Terr., Broadway, between W. 155th and W. 156th Sts., entrance up steps to left, Harlem* ☎ *212/926–2234* ⊕ *www.hispanicsociety. org* ✐ *Free* ⊙ *Sept.–July, Tues.–Sat. 10–4:30, Sun. 1–4* Ⓜ *1 to 157th St.*

Studio Museum in Harlem. Contemporary art by African-American, Caribbean, and African artists is the focus of this small museum with a light-filled sculpture garden. Its changing exhibits have included *Black Artists and Abstraction* and *Africa Comics*. Three artists in residence present their works each year. ✉ *144 W. 125th St., between Lenox Ave. and Adam Clayton Powell Jr. Blvd., Harlem* ☎ *212/864–4500* ⊕ *www. studiomuseum.org* ✐ *$7 suggested donation* ⊙ *Thurs. and Fri. noon–9, Sat. 10–6, Sun. noon–6* Ⓜ *2, 3 to 125th St.*

The Performing Arts

WORD OF MOUTH

"Seating is personal preference and does depend on the theater. I like aisle seats best and will always opt for one if it's available. For a musical, often first few rows of the mezzanine is better than back of the orchestra but try to get as close to the center of the theater as possible (not on extreme sides)."

—mclaurie

Updated by
Lynne Arany

"Where do you wait tables?" is the not-so-ironic question New York performers get when they say they're in the arts. But even more telling is that most of these toughened artists won't miss a beat when they respond with the restaurant's name. Fact is, if you're an aspiring performer here, you'd better be tough and competitive. There is a constant influx of artists from around the globe, and all these actors, singers, dancers, and musicians striving for their big break infuse the city with a crackling creative energy.

Just as tough are the audiences, many out-of-towners, many discerning local patrons, who help drive the arts scene as they thrive on keeping up with the latest—flocking to a concert hall to hear a world-class soprano deliver a flawless performance, then crowding into a cramped café to support young writers floundering through their own prose.

New York has somewhere between 200 and 250 legitimate theaters (meaning those with theatrical performances, not movies or strip shows), and many more ad hoc venues—parks, churches, lofts, galleries, rooftops, even parking lots.

The city is also a revolving door of special events: summer jazz, one-act-play marathons, film festivals, and music and dance celebrations from the classical to the avant-garde, to name just a few. It's this unrivaled wealth of culture and art that many New Yorkers cite as the reason why they're here, and the reason why many millions more say they're visiting here.

BUYING TICKETS AT FULL PRICE

What do tickets sell for, anyway? Not counting the limited "premium seat" category (or discount deals), the top ticket price for Broadway musicals is now hovering at $136; the low end for musicals is in the $50 range. Nonmusical comedies and dramas start at about $70 and top out at about $120. Off Broadway show tickets average $50–$90, and Off Off Broadway shows can run as low as $15–$25.

Tickets to an opera start at about $25 for nosebleed seats and can soar close to $400 for prime locations. Classical music concerts go for $25 to $100 or more, depending on the venue. Dance performances are usually in the $15 to $60 range, but expect seats for the ballet in choice spots to cost more.

Scoring tickets is fairly easy, especially if you have some flexibility. But if timing or cost is critical, the only way to ensure you'll get the seats you want is to make your purchase in advance—and that might be months ahead for a hit show. In general, tickets for Saturday evening and for weekend matinees are the toughest to secure.

For opera, classical music, and dance performances, go to the box office or order tickets through the venue's Web site.

For smaller performing-arts companies, and especially for Off Broadway shows, try **Ticket Central** (⊠ *416 W. 42nd St., between 9th and 10th Aves., Midtown West* ☎ *212/279–4200* ⊕ *www.ticketcentral.com* ☉ *Daily noon–8* Ⓜ *A, C, E to 42nd St.*), which is right in the center of Theater Row; service charges are nominal here. **SmartTix** (☎ *212/868– 4444* ⊕ *www.smarttix.com*) is a reliable resource for (usually) smaller performing-arts companies, including dance and music; their service charges are nominal as well.

Inside the Times Square Information Center is the **Broadway Concierge and Ticket Center** (⊠ *1560 Broadway, between W. 46th and W. 47th Sts., Midtown West* ☎ *888/BROADWAY* ⊕ *www.broadwayleague.com* ☉ *Tickets: Mon.–Sat. 9–7, Sun. 10–6* Ⓜ *1, 2, 3, 7, N, Q, R, S to 42nd St./Times Sq.; N, R to 49th St.*), where you can purchase full- and premium-price tickets for most Broadway (and some Off Broadway) shows.

Sure bets for Broadway (and some other big-hall events) are the box office or either **Telecharge** (☎ *212/239–6200, 800/432–7250 outside N.Y.C.* ⊕ *www.telecharge.com*) or **Ticketmaster** (☎ *212/307–4100, 866/448–7849 automated service, 212/220–0500 premium tickets* ⊕ *www.ticketmaster.com*). Virtually all larger shows are listed with one service or the other, but never both; specifying "premium" will help you get elusive—and expensive (upward of $200–$350)—seats. A broker or your hotel concierge should be able to procure last-minute tickets, but prices may even exceed "premium" rates. Be prepared to pay steep add-on fees (per ticket *and* per order) for all ticketing services.

■ TIP➔ Although most online ticket services provide seating maps to help you choose, the advantage of going to the box office is twofold: there are no add-on service fees, and a ticket seller can personally advise you about sight lines—and knee room—for the seat location you are considering. Broadway box offices do not usually have direct phone lines; their walk-in hours are generally 10 am until curtain.

BUYING DISCOUNT TICKETS

The cheapest—though chanciest—ticket opportunities are found at participating theater box offices on the day of the performance. These rush tickets, usually about $25, may be distributed by lottery and are usually for front-row (possibly neck-craning) seats. Check the comprehensive planner on ⊕ *www.nytix.com* or go to the box office of the show you are interested in to find out whether they have such an offer and how to pursue it. Obstructed-view seats or those in the very rear balcony are sometimes available for advance purchase; the price point on these is usually in the $35–$40 range.

But for advanced discount purchases, the best seating is likely available by using a discount "code"—procure these codes, good for 20% to 50% off, online. (You will need to register on each Web site.) The excellent no-subscription-required ⊕ *www.broadwaybox.com* site is comprehensive and posts all discount codes currently available for Broadway shows. As with all discount codes offered through online subscriber services—**TheaterMania** (⊕ *www.theatermania.com*), **Playbill** (⊕ *www.playbill.com*), and **Best of Off Broadway** (⊕ *bestofoffbroadway. com*) among them—to avoid service charges, you must bring a printout of the offer to the box office, and make your purchase there.

For seats at 25%–50% off the usual price, go to one of the **TKTS booths** (⊠ *Father Duffy Sq., W. 47th St. and Broadway, Midtown West* Ⓜ *1, 2, 3, 7, N, Q, R, S, W to 42nd St./Times Sq.; N, R, W to 49th St.; 1 to 50th St.* ⊠ *South St. Seaport, Front and John Sts., Lower Manhattan* Ⓜ *2, 3, 4, 5, A, C, E, J, M, Z to Fulton St./Broadway–Nassau* ⊠ *Downtown Brooklyn, at the Myrtle St. Promenade and Jay St., Brooklyn* Ⓜ *A, C, F to Jay St.–Borough Hall; R, 2, 3, 4, 5 to Court St.–Borough Hall* ⊕ *www.tdf.org*). Although they do tack on a $4 per ticket service charge, and not all shows are predictably available, the broad choices and ease of selection—and of course, the solid discount—make TKTS the go-to source for the flexible theatergoer.

Check the electronic listings board near the ticket windows to mull over your options while you're in line. At the spiffed-up Duffy Square location (look for the red glass staircase), there is a separate *"Play Express"* window (for nonmusical events) to further simplify—and speed—things.

Duffy hours are Monday and Wednesday–Saturday 3–8, and Tuesday 2–8 (for evening performances); for Wednesday and Saturday matinees 10–2; for Sunday matinees 11–3; Sunday evening shows, from 3 until a half hour before curtain. Seaport hours are Monday–Saturday 11–6, Sunday 11–4.

Brooklyn hours are Tuesday–Saturday 11–6. With the exception of matinee tickets at the Seaport and Brooklyn locations, which sell these for next-day performances only, all shows offered are for that same day. Credit cards, cash, or traveler's checks are accepted *at all locations.*
■**TIP**➜ Planning ahead? The TKTS Web site lists what was available at the booths in the previous week to give you an idea of what shows you'll find. Note: Ticket booth hours may vary over holiday periods.

LOWER MANHATTAN

MUSIC

Count on the **WFC Winter Garden** (⊠ *World Financial Center, West St., between Vesey and Liberty Sts., Lower Manhattan* ☎ *212/945–0505* ⊕ *www.artsworldfinancialcenter.com* Ⓜ *E to World Trade Center; 1*

Best Tips for Broadway

Whether you're handing over a hundred bucks for a top ticket or shoestringing it in a nosebleed seat, seeing one show or seven, you'll have better Broadway experiences to brag about if you take our advice.

Do your homework. Remember— your friends' "must-see" may not be yours. If you're new to theater, or not a regular, try to discover Broadway for yourself. Subscribe to online services ahead of your trip; you'll get access to show synopses, special ticket offers, and more. If it's a classic play, try to read it before you go; for a musical, listen to the score.

Reserve ahead. The TKTS booth is great when you're up for what the fates make available, but for must-sees, we recommend booking early. While you're at it, don't forget to ask whether the regular cast is expected. (An in-person stop at the box office is the most reliable way to score this information ahead of time, but don't hold them to it unless it's the day of performance. If there is a change then—and the replacement cast is not acceptable to you—you may get a refund.) For musicals, live music will always add a special zing; confirm when ticketing to avoid surprises on the rare occasion when recorded music is used.

Check theater seating charts. Front mezzanine is a great option; with seats that overhang the stage, they can be better (though not always less expensive) than many orchestra locations. Always book with a seating chart at hand (available online and at the box office); although even the priciest seats might be tight, it is always worth splurging for the best sight lines. Check accessibility, especially at older theaters with multiple flights of stairs and scarce elevators.

Know when to go. Surprisingly, Friday evening is a good option; Saturday night and weekday matinees are the most difficult. Do as the locals do and go on weeknights. Tuesday is especially promising, and typically an earlier curtain—7 or 7:30 instead of the usual 8 pm—helps ensure that you'll get a good night's sleep for your next day of touring.

Dress right. You can easily throw on jeans to go to the theater these days, but personally we feel Bermuda shorts have no place on Broadway. Bring binoculars if your seats are up high, leave behind the heavy coat (coat checks are *not* the norm), and drop packages off at your hotel room in advance.

Travel smart. Trying to get to the show in time? Unless you don't mind watching the meter run up while you're stuck in traffic, avoid cabs into or out of Times Square. The pre- and post-theater crush will render Broadway virtually unwalkable, but that said, walk, especially if you're within 10 blocks of the theater. Otherwise, take the subway.

Dine off Broadway. Dining well on a budget and doing Broadway right are not mutually exclusive notions. Key is avoiding the temptation to eat in Times Square proper—even the national chains are overpriced. Consider instead supping in whatever neighborhood you're touring that day. Or, if you're already in Midtown, head west of the district to 9th Avenue. That's where many actors and other theater folk actually live, and you never know who you'll see on the street or at the next table. Prix-fixe deals and ethnic eateries are plentiful.

to Rector St.) for an inspired array of musical events from gospel to site-specific sonic installations—and a little theater, dance, and film as well—all presented within its spectacular crystal-encased atrium or on its outdoor plaza. It's all free, and all befitting the incomparable setting overlooking the Hudson.

READINGS AND LECTURES

Having settled into a new home hard by the Hudson in 2009, **Poets House** (✉ *10 River Terr., at Murray St., Battery Park City* ☎ *212/431–7920* ⊕ *www.poetshouse.org* Ⓜ *E to World Trade Center; 1, 2, 3 to Chambers St.*) finally has a setting that rises to its theme: it is an open resource for all ages, one that offers a huge library and readings and events that exalt the art of poetry.

TRIBECA AND SOHO

TRIBECA

FILM

The film programs at **92YTribeca** (✉ *200 Hudson St., at Canal St., TriBeCa* ☎ *212/601–1000* ⊕ *www.92y.org/92yTribeca* Ⓜ *1, E to Canal St.*), a branch of the 92nd Street Y, emphasize participation, with directors often on hand, and a Q&A afterward is the norm. View a fresh and eclectic take on series concepts, with the likes of Closely Watched Films (classics revisited) and a late-night sing-along series.

MUSIC

☕ The **Tribeca Performing Arts Center** (✉ *199 Chambers St., at Greenwich St., TriBeCa* ☎ *212/220–1460* ⊕ *www.tribecapac.org* Ⓜ *1, 2, 3 to Chambers St.*) celebrates theater (with a clever children's series) and dance, but more so, jazz in all its forms. Highlights in Jazz and Lost Jazz Shrines are two of its special series.

READINGS AND LECTURES

Local favorite WNYC Radio invites the public into its intimate (125 seats), technologically forward-thinking digs, **the Jerome L. Greene Performance Space (the Greene Space)** (✉ *44 Charlton St., at Varick St. Tribeca* ☎ *646/829–4400* ⊕ *www.thegreenespace.org* Ⓜ *C, E to Spring St.; 1 to Houston St. or Canal St.*). Live shows—music, audio theater, interviews—match its renowned, and equally forward-thinking, on-air programming.

The intent at **92YTribeca** (✉ *200 Hudson St., at Canal St., Tribeca* ☎ *212/601–1000* ⊕ *www.92y.org* Ⓜ *1, E to Canal St.*) is to appeal to a twenty- to thirty-ish set, but just about anyone should find something to his or her liking in their extensive daytime and evening lineups. Try talks on American Media & the Green Movement to JewBu: Exploring Jewish Dharma, and themes from the arts, food, and technology.

SOHO

FILM

★ Foreign, independent, and, some mainstream films are screened at the **Angelika Film Center** (✉ *18 W. Houston St., at Mercer St., Greenwich Village* ☎ *212/995–2570* ⊕ *www.angelikafilmcenter.com* Ⓜ *B, D, F, M to Broadway–Lafayette St.; 6 to Bleecker St.*). Despite its (six) tunnel-like theaters, small screens, and the occasionally audible subway rumble below, it's usually packed; get a snack at their café while you wait for your movie to be called.

READINGS AND LECTURES

★ Amid its collection of 45,000 titles for sale, the **Housing Works Used Book Café** (✉ *126 Crosby St., between E. Houston and Prince Sts., SoHo* ☎ *212/334–3324* ⊕ *www.housingworksbookstore.com* Ⓜ *R, W to Prince St.; B, D, F, M to Broadway–Lafayette St.; 6 to Bleecker St.*) sponsors readings—often by breakout local authors or from books on social issues—and a monthly acoustic music series. Events at this cozy nonprofit benefit homeless people with HIV/AIDS.

THEATER

HERE Arts Center (✉ *145 6th Ave., between Spring and Broome Sts., SoHo* ☎ *212/352–3101 tickets* ⊕ *www.here.org* Ⓜ *C, E to Spring St.*), the original home of Eve Ensler's 1997 Obie winner *The Vagina Monologues*, 2007's lauded *Removable Parts,* and all manner of genre-bending productions, also has an art gallery and café.

EAST VILLAGE AND LOWER EAST SIDE

THE EAST VILLAGE

FILM

Dedicated to preserving and exhibiting independent and avant-garde film, **Anthology Film Archives** (✉ *32 2nd Ave., at E. 2nd St., East Village* ☎ *212/505–5181* ⊕ *anthologyfilmarchives.org* Ⓜ *F, V to 2nd Ave.*) comprises a film repository and two gemlike screening rooms in a renovated redbrick courthouse. Committed cinephiles make their way here for hard-to-find films and videos. The Essential Cinema series delves into the works of filmmakers from Stan Brakhage and Charles Ludlam to Robert Bresson and Jean Cocteau.

The **Village East Cinema** (✉ *181–189 2nd Ave., at E. 12th St., East Village* ☎ *212/529–6799* ⊕ *www.villageeastcinema.com* Ⓜ *6 to Astor Pl.; L to 1st Ave.*), with programming more on the indie side than that of its SoHo sister the Angelika, is housed in a former Yiddish theater that was restored and converted to a six-screen multiplex. Catch a film that's screening in the original theater space upstairs (you can call ahead to find out); its Moorish Revival–style decor, domed ceiling, and grand chandelier are best appreciated from the balcony.

THEATER

At the cozy 178-seat theater belonging to the **Classic Stage Company** (✉ *136 E. 13th St., between 3rd and 4th Aves., East Village* ☎ *212/677–4210; 212/352–3101 or 866/811–4111 tickets* ⊕ *www.classicstage.org* Ⓜ *4, 5, 6, L, N, Q, R to Union Sq.*) you can see excellent literary revivals—such as Chekhov's *Three Sisters* or Shakespeare's *The Tempest*—perhaps with a modern spin, and often with reigning theatrical stars.

Ellen Stewart, also known as La Mama, founded **La MaMa E.T.C.** (✉ *74A E. 4th St., between Bowery and 2nd Ave., East Village* ☎ *212/475–7710* ⊕ *lamama.org* Ⓜ *F to 2nd Ave.; B, D, F, M to Broadway–Lafayette St.; 6 to Bleecker St.*) in a small basement space in 1961. It's grown now, and her influential Experimental Theater Club continues to support new works that cross cultures and performance disciplines.

The **New York Theater Workshop (NYTW)** (✉ *79 E. 4th St., between Bowery and 2nd Ave., East Village* ☎ *212/460–5475, 212/279–4200 tickets* ⊕ *www.nytw.org* Ⓜ *F, M to 2nd Ave.; B, D, F, M to Broadway–Lafayette St.; 6 to Bleecker St.*) produces work by new and established playwrights. Jonathan Larson's *Rent* got its pre-Broadway start here, and current works by Tony Kushner (*Homebody/Kabul*), Caryl Churchill, and Paul Rudnick are staged. Hit the box office for Sunday night Cheap-Tix; those seats are $20—in cash, in advance only—as available.

Performance Space 122 (P.S. 122) (✉ *150 1st Ave., at E. 9th St., East Village* ☎ *212/352–3101 tickets* ⊕ *www.ps122.org* Ⓜ *6 to Astor Pl.*) became a launching pad for now well-recognized talent like Karen Finley, Spalding Gray, Ann Magnuson, and Eric Bogosian back in the day, and continues to offer a dazzling repertoire of performance from the fringe. Their Avant-Garde-Arama! festival has drawn crowds since the nonprofit's founding in 1980.

★ **The Public Theater** (✉ *425 Lafayette St., south of Astor Pl., East Village* ☎ *212/539–8500, 212/967–7555 tickets* ⊕ *www.publictheater.org* Ⓜ *6 to Astor Pl.; R to 8th St.*) presents fresh theater such as the 2010 six-hour F. Scott Fitzgerald marathon, *Gatz*, a 2008 Stephen Sondheim debut, *and* the latest work of Suzan-Lori Parks. Many noted productions that began here (*Hair, A Chorus Line*) went on to Broadway.

Go to the Public's box office one hour before curtain to snag limited-availability $20 rush standby tickets (two tickets max; cash only). In summer you won't want to miss their incomparable—and free—Shakespeare in the Park performances, which are held at the Delacorte Theatre in Central Park.

■TIP→ Because you can stand in line for hours—and still not get a ticket voucher—the easiest way to score these scarce tickets is to register online with their "virtual line" after midnight on the night before the performance you would like to attend; an email response confirms (or denies) success.

A four-theater cultural complex, **Theater for the New City** (✉ *155 1st Ave., between E. 9th and E. 10th Sts., East Village* ☎ *212/254–1109* ⊕ *www.theaterforthenewcity.net* Ⓜ *6 to Astor Pl.*) stages short runs of shows by new and emerging American playwrights. Favorite longtime troupers and presenters of seriously giant puppets (upward of 12 feet is typical), the 1960s N.Y.C.-rooted, and still seriously political, Bread & Puppet Theater put in an annual appearance as well.

READINGS AND LECTURES

The reigning arbiter of poetry slams, the **Nuyorican Poets Café** (✉ *236 E. 3rd St., between Aves. B and C, East Village* ☎ *212/505–8183* ⊕ *www.nuyorican.org* Ⓜ *F, M to 2nd Ave.*) schedules open-mike events, most often on Wednesday night, and hosts the influential granddaddy (b. 1989) of the current spoken-word scene, the Friday Night Poetry Slam.

The Poetry Project (✉ *St. Mark's Church in-the-Bowery, 131 E. 10th St., at 2nd Ave., East Village* ☎ *212/674–0910* ⊕ *poetryproject.org* Ⓜ *6 to Astor Pl.*) had its start in 1966, and has been a source of sustenance

15

for poets (and their audiences) ever since. This is where Allen Ginsberg, Amiri Baraka, and Sam Shepard first found their voices, and where you're likely to find folks of the same caliber today. Prime times: Monday, Wednesday, and Friday.

Fodor's Choice ★ The famed **Strand Bookstore** (⊠ *828 Broadway, at E. 12th St., East Village* ☎ *212/473–1452* ⊕ *www.strandbooks.com* Ⓜ *L, N, Q, R, 4, 5, 6 to 14th St./Union Sq.*) hosts nonfiction panels, special Family Hour events, and current fiction readings with authors like Marisha Pessl, Thomas McGuane, Calvin Trillin, and Mark Kurlansky.

LOWER EAST SIDE

FILM

With vestiges of its life as a vaudeville theater all but gone, the **Sunshine Cinema** (⊠ *143 E. Houston St., between 1st and 2nd Aves., Lower East Side* ☎ *212/330–8182* ⊕ *www.landmarktheatres.com* Ⓜ *F, M to 2nd Ave.*), with its five decent-size screens, is the neighborhood go-to for a mix of art-house and smaller-release mainstream films.

OPERA

The **Gotham Chamber Opera** (⊠ *410 W. 42nd St., between 9th and 10th Aves., Midtown West* ☎ *212/868–4460* ⊕ *www.gothamchamberopera. org* Ⓜ *A, C, E to 42nd St./Port Authority*) presents less-known chamber works from the baroque era to the present in inspired productions.

Catching a broader audience's attention, shows include Moisés Kaufman's acclaimed rendition of the 1947 *El Gato Con Botas* by Xavier Montsalvatge (staged at the New Victory Theater); Handel's *Arianna in Creta;* a collaboration with choreographer Karole Armitage, *Ariadne Unhinged;* and a joint venture with the Hayden Planetarium of Haydn's *Il Mondo della Luna,* or *The World on the Moon.*

READINGS AND LECTURES

"Poetry Czar" Bob Holman's **Bowery Poetry Club** (⊠ *308 Bowery, at Bleecker St., East Village* ☎ *212/614–0505* ⊕ *www.bowerypoetry.com* Ⓜ *B, D, F, M to Broadway–Lafayette St.; 6 to Bleecker St.*) serves up coffee and comestibles along with its ingenious poetry events. Expect slams and every other permutation of the spoken word—as well as art and music.

GREENWICH VILLAGE, WEST VILLAGE, AND CHELSEA

GREENWICH VILLAGE

FILM

Cinema Village (⊠ *22 E. 12th St., between University Pl. and 5th Ave., Greenwich Village* ☎ *212/924–3363* ⊕ *www.cinemavillage.com* Ⓜ *4, 5, 6, L, N, Q, R to 14th St./Union Sq.*) has three tiny screening rooms (with surprisingly good sight lines) that show a smart selection of hard-to-find (some might say obscure) first-run domestic and foreign films.

★ In addition to premiering new releases, **Film Forum** (⊠ *209 W. Houston St., between 6th Ave. and Varick St., Greenwich Village* ☎ *212/727–8110* ⊕ *www.filmforum.org* Ⓜ *1 to Houston St.*), a very special non-profit theater with three small screening rooms, hosts movies by directors from Hitchcock to Bertolucci, genre series with themes from pre-Code to Fritz Lang's Hollywood, and newly restored prints of classic works. The café in their sleek little Euro-style lobby serves tasty cakes and fresh-popped popcorn.

Movie lovers are quite attached to the **Quad Cinema** (✉ *34 W. 13th St., between 5th and 6th Aves., Greenwich Village* ☎ *212/255–2243* ⊕ *www.quadcinema.com* Ⓜ *1, 2, 3, F, M to 14th St.; L to 6th Ave.*) despite the patina of its early 1970s vintage—probably because the four teacup-size theaters feel so much like their own private screening rooms. A finely balanced selection of first-run art documentaries and foreign films is the fare here.

MUSIC

★ Bleecker Street holds onto its musical history a bit longer with the timely conversion of the venerable Village Gate location to the 2008 upstart **(Le) Poisson Rouge** (✉ *158 Bleecker St., between Sullivan and Thompson Sts., Greenwich Village* ☎ *212/503–3474* ⊕ *lepoissonrouge.com* Ⓜ *A, B, C, D, E, F, M to W. 4th St./Washington Sq.*). The sound system is quite good, and the layout rewards those who like to get up close to the artists—which is especially nice if you're there for one of their classical chamber shows or a fine guitarist.

Other times the music mix runs from Afropop to electronic, indie, jazz, and DJ. As at most clubs, you're not assured a seat, so get here early and be prepared for a minimum drink charge as well.

READINGS AND LECTURES

The **Center for Architecture** (✉ *536 LaGuardia Pl., between W. 3rd and Bleecker Sts., Greenwich Village* ☎ *212/683–0023* ⊕ *www.aiany.org* Ⓜ *A, B, C, D, E, F, M to W. 4th St./Washington Sq.*), a contemporary glass-faced gallery, hosts lively discussions (which may be accompanied by films or other visuals) on topics like radical architecture in Mexico City or visionary American architects of the 1930s.

The **Cornelia Street Café** (✉ *29 Cornelia St., between W. 4th and Bleecker Sts., Greenwich Village* ☎ *212/989–9319* ⊕ *www.corneliastreetcafe. com* Ⓜ *A, B, C, D, E, F, M to W. 4th St./Washington Sq.*) is a good bet for original poetry—the Pink Pony West open-mike series takes place here—and fiction and nonfiction readings, live jazz, and a good meal serving up dishes such as steak frites and black sesame–crusted salmon as well.

At **The New School** (✉ *66 W. 12th St., between 5th and 6th Aves., Greenwich Village* ☎ *212/229–5488* ⊕ *www.newschool.edu/events* Ⓜ *1, 2, 3, F, M to 14th St.*) topical panels predominate (Women Writers of the Diaspora), but are complemented with poetry (An Evening with John Ashbery) and film; expect incisive and thought-provoking results, whether the subject is philosophy, economics, or design. Jazz and chamber music performances are also part of New School's low-priced lineup ($5 is typical for panel events; free–$20 for music).

The venerable **New York Studio School** (✉ *8 W. 8th St., between 5th and 6th Aves., Greenwich Village* ☎ *212/673–6466* ⊕ *www.nyss.org* Ⓜ *A, B, C, D, E, F, M to W. 4th St./Washington Sq.*) hosts two—usually free, almost always on Tuesday and Wednesday—evening lecture series on

15

contemporary issues in art. Hear from both emerging and established artists, and from some of the biggest names in art history and criticism.

THEATER

A pristine wood-lined theater, the 866-seat **Skirball Center for the Performing Arts** (✉ *566 LaGuardia Pl., at Washington Sq. S, Greenwich Village* ☎ *212/352–3101 tickets* ⊕ *www.skirballcenter.nyu.edu* Ⓜ *A, B, C, D, E, F, M to W. 4th St./Washington Sq.*), supports emerging artists, with a growing repertoire of interesting dance, music, and theater events, often in collaboration with other esteemed companies—including its Village neighbor, the Public.

The Skirball was built in 2003 and designed by Kevin Roche. This contemporary venue on the New York University campus provides a rare larger-scale anchor for the arts in this part of town.

WEST VILLAGE

READINGS AND LECTURES

The **Lesbian, Gay, Bisexual & Transgender Community Center** (✉ *208 W. 13th St., between 7th and 8th Aves., West Village* ☎ *212/620–7310* ⊕ *www. gaycenter.org* Ⓜ *1, 2, 3, A, C, E, F, M to 14th St.; L to 8th Ave.*) sponsors Second Tuesdays, Center Voices, and other series of engaging and topical talks (and occasional films, dance, or theatrical events), with themes ranging from out lawyers to Elaine Stritch.

THEATER

A venerable neighborhood survivor, the **Lucille Lortel Theatre** (✉ *121 Christopher St., between Hudson and Bleecker Sts., West Village* ☎ *212/279–4200 tickets* ⊕ *www.lucillelorteltheatre.com* Ⓜ *1 to Christopher St.*) became known in the 1950s for its influential interpretations of works by Brecht and Dos Passos. Previously known as the Theatre De Lys, this 299-seater has forged on to become the home to 21st-century productions of the MCC Theater company (known for Neil LaBute's challenging plays in the century's first decade), the Atlantic Theater company, and free summer shows that appeal to both children and adults by Theatreworks/USA.

CHELSEA

DANCE

☺ **Dance Theater Workshop** (✉ *219 W. 19th St., between 7th and 8th Aves., Chelsea* ☎ *212/691–6500* ⊕ *www.dancetheaterworkshop.org* Ⓜ *1 to 18th St.; A, C, E, L to 14th St.–8th Ave.*), an important venue for the dance world since its founding in 1965, serves as a laboratory for new choreographers; performances are often accompanied by enlightening post-show talks with the dance makers themselves. DTW is also known for its multimedia and kid-friendly Family Matters series.

★ In a former Art Deco movie house in Chelsea, the 472-seat **Joyce Theater** (✉ *175 8th Ave., at W. 19th St., Chelsea* ☎ *212/691–9740, 212/242–0800 tickets* ⊕ *www.joyce.org* Ⓜ *A, C, E to 14th St.; L to 8th Ave.*) has superb sight lines and presents a full spectrum of contemporary dance. **Garth Fagan Dance** (⊕ *garthfagandance.org*), **Ballet Hispanico** (⊕ *www.ballethispanico.org*), and taut and athletic **Parsons Dance** (⊕ *www.parsonsdance.org*) are regulars on the Joyce's always rewarding lineup.

New York's Film Festivals

New York's extreme diversity is also what makes it a cinephile's heaven: dozens of festivals for both niche interests and for those just wanting to be at the front end of what's out there. New releases and premieres dominate the festival scene, but the city has its share of retrospective events, especially in summer.

The city's preeminent film event is the annual **New York Film Festival** (⊕ www.filmlinc.com); sponsored by the **Film Society of Lincoln Center**, it runs annually from late September into October. Its screenings feature many U.S. premieres and are announced more than a month in advance to often-rapid sell-out. Film venues are usually Lincoln Center's Alice Tully Hall and Walter Reade Theater. In January, the Film Society joins forces with the Jewish Museum to produce the **New York Jewish Film Festival**, in March it joins with MoMA to present **New Directors/New Films**, and June brings its collaboration with the **Human Rights Watch Film Festival**.

Another popular festival, the **TriBeCa Film Festival** (⊕ www. tribecafilmfestival.org)—was an immediate success when it launched in 2002 as a Robert De Niro–spearheaded community response to the events of 9/11. It takes place in mostly downtown venues for about two weeks starting in late April, and features mainstream premieres along with indie treasures, as well as a **Family Festival,** which attracts big crowds for its street fair and movies for ages eight and up.

Summer in New York sees a bonanza of alfresco film. Even better, it's usu-

ally free (but arrive early to secure a space; screenings begin at dusk).

You'll want to check out lovely **Bryant Park** (☎ 212/512–5700 ⊕ www. bryantpark.org) for the classic films—and the scene—at its Monday night HBO Bryant Park Summer Film Festival, June–August.

Hudson River Park (⊕ www. hudsonriverpark.org) runs its RiverFlicks series in July and August. Movies for "grown-ups" screen on Wednesday evening on Pier 54; RiverFlicks for kids are shown on Pier 46, on Friday.

Riverside Park South's Summer on the Hudson (⊕ www.nycgovparks.org) offers Wednesday-night screenings on Pier 1, in this park along the Hudson on the Upper West Side.

Rooftop Films' (⊕ www.rooftopfilms. com) Underground Movies Outdoors is N.Y.C.'s most eclectic film series, with shows outdoors in summer on rooftops in all five boroughs. Check their schedule for off-season screenings as well.

On Thursday night in summer, make your way over the Brooklyn Bridge to Movies with a View in **Brooklyn Bridge Park** (⊕ www. brooklynbridgepark.org). There's a bike valet, and of course that competing waterfront view; this one has a lineup that alternates kid-pleasing shows with more strictly adult fare.

15

The **Joyce SoHo** (✉ *155 Mercer St., between Houston and Prince Sts., SoHo* ☎ *212/431–9233, 212/242–0800 tickets* ⊕ *www.joyce.org* Ⓜ *R to Prince St.; B, D, F, M to Broadway–Lafayette St.*), their satellite location, is a 74-seat theater that shows smaller-scale, experimental work. Both offer $10 tickets for some performances.

THEATER

The Kitchen (✉ *512 W. 19th St., between 10th and 11th Aves., Chelsea* ☎ *212/255–5793* ⊕ *www.thekitchen.org* Ⓜ *C, E to 23rd St.*) is *the* place for multimedia performance art, and has been a crucible for artists on the experimental edge—think Charles Atlas, Kiki Smith, Elizabeth Streb—since 1971. Literary events are often free; most others can be seen for as little as $10–$15.

MIDTOWN

DANCE

The 299-seat Jerome Robbins Theater opened in 2010, and with it the first full season of the **Baryshnikov Arts Center (BAC)** (✉ *37 Arts, 450 W. 37 St., between 9th and 10th Aves., Midtown* ☎ *646/731–3200* ⊕ *www. bacnyc.org* Ⓜ *A, C, E, to 34th St./Penn Station*). Mikhail Baryshnikov's longtime vision has come to fruition in this modern venue for contemporary performance dedicated to movement, which can be as much about theater as it is about dance.

The seminal Wooster Group (⊕ *www.thewoostergroup.org*) is now in residence, and their productions along with those of a roster of boundary-breaking international choreographers (George Stamos, Donna Uchizono, and Emmanuèle Phuon), co-productions with The Kitchen, and BAC Flicks (*Mondays with Merce* and more) are all part of the vibrant—and very well-priced—programming here.

FILM

Fodor's Choice
★

The **Museum of Modern Art (MoMA)** (✉ *11 W. 53rd St., between 5th and 6th Aves., Midtown West* ☎ *212/708–9400* ⊕ *www.moma.org* Ⓜ *E, M to 5th Ave./53rd St.; B, D, F, M to 47th–50th Sts./Rockefeller Center*) has some of the most engaging international repertory you'll find anywhere; it's shown in the state-of-the-art Roy and Niuta Titus Theaters 1 and 2.

Movie tickets are available at the museum for same-day screenings (a limited number are released up to one week in advance for an extra fee); they're free if you have purchased museum admission.

★ Adjacent to the Plaza Hotel sits the **Paris** (✉ *4 W. 58th St., between 5th and 6th Aves., Midtown West* ☎ *212/688–3800* ⊕ *www.theparistheatre. com* Ⓜ *N, R to 5th Ave./59th St.; F to 57th St.*)—a rare stately remnant of the single-screen era. Opened in 1948, it retains its wide screen (and its balcony) and is a fine showcase for new movies, often foreign and with a limited release.

☾ **SonyWonder Technology Lab** (✉ *550 Madison Ave., between E. 55th and E. 56th Sts., Midtown East* ☎ *212/833–8100, 212/833–7858 tickets* ⊕ *www.sonywondertechlab.com* Ⓜ *E, M to 5th Ave.–53rd St.*), the kid-oriented hands-on extravaganza of high-tech how-to for moviemaking and more, shows films as well on Thursday and Saturday.

Though mostly of the *Dora the Explorer* and *Sesame Street* genre, it's worth checking their schedule for teen and adult options. Children under 18 must be accompanied by an adult. You can reserve tickets—all free—by phone in the week of a screening.

★ Its vintage is late 1960s, but the **Ziegfeld** (⊠ *141 W. 54th St., between 6th and 7th Aves., Midtown West* ☎ *212/307–1862* ⊕ *www. clearviewcinemas.com* Ⓜ *F to 57th St./6th Ave.; N, Q, R to 57th St./ 7th Ave.*) is as close as you'll come to a movie-palace experience in New York today. Its chandeliers and crimson decor, raised balcony, wide screen, some 1,200 seats, good sight lines, and solid sound system make the Ziegfeld a special place to view anything it serves up. Grand-opening red-carpet galas often take place here as well.

MUSIC

Historic **Town Hall** (⊠ *123 W. 43rd St., between 6th and 7th Aves., Midtown West* ☎ *212/840–2824* ⊕ *www.the-townhall-nyc.org* Ⓜ *1, 2, 3, 7, N, Q, R, S to 42nd St./Times Sq.*) is where Garrison Keillor's *A Prairie Home Companion* radio show broadcasts from in December. It also hosts programs of jazz, cabaret, and rock, the Peoples Symphony Concert series, and a variety of international music, theater, and dance events.

☾ **Carnegie Hall** (⊠ *881 7th Ave., at W. 57th St., Midtown West* ☎ *212/247–*
Fodor'sChoice *7800* ⊕ *www.carnegiehall.org* Ⓜ *N, Q, R to 57th St.; B, D, E to 7th*
★ *Ave.*) is, of course, one of the world's most famous concert halls. Its incomparable acoustics make it one of the best venues—anywhere—to hear classical music, but its presentations of jazz, pop, cabaret, and folk music are superlative as well.

Since Tchaikovsky conducted the opening-night concert on May 5, 1891, virtually every important musician the world has known has performed in this Italian Renaissance–style building, often at the peak of his or her creative powers. Leonard Bernstein had his debut here; Vladimir Horowitz made his historic return to the concert stage here.

The world's top orchestras perform in the grand and fabulously steep 2,804-seat **Isaac Stern Auditorium,** the 268-seat **Weill Recital Hall** often features young talents making their New York debuts, and the subterranean 644-seat **Judy and Arthur Zankel Hall** attracts big-name artists such as the Kronos Quartet, Milton Nascimento, and Ravi Shankar to its modern and stylish space. A noted roster of family concerts is also part of Carnegie's programming.

■TIP→ The Carnegie box office offers $10 rush tickets on the day of performance, or you may buy partial-view seating in advance at 50% off the full ticket price.

PERFORMANCE CENTERS

★ **City Center** (⊠ *131 W. 55th St., between 6th and 7th Aves., Midtown West* ☎ *212/581–1212 CityTix* ⊕ *www.nycitycenter.org* Ⓜ *N, Q, R to 57th St./7th Ave.; F to 57th St./6th Ave.*) has a neo-Moorish look, built in 1923 for the Ancient and Accepted Order of the Mystic Shrine. Pause as you enter to admire the beautifully ornate tile work that plasters the lobby; a painstaking 2011 renovation makes the freshly refurbished detail hard to miss.

The 2,200-seat main stage is perfectly suited for its role as a show-place for dance and special theatrical events. **Alvin Ailey American Dance Theater** (⊕ *www.alvinailey.org*) and **Paul Taylor Dance Company** (⊕ *www.ptdc.org*) present their primary New York seasons here.

City Center's annual Fall for Dance festival is a must; all tickets are $10, the performances sell out very quickly. Another seasonal highlight—usually throughout January—is the lively productions of the **New York Gilbert & Sullivan Players** (☎ *212/769–1000* ⊕ *www.nygasp. org*), which feature such G&S favorites as *The Pirates of Penzance* and *The Mikado,* plus rarities like Sullivan's last completed work, *The Rose of Persia.*

The popular Encores! musicals-in-concert series is staged here, as are—on the smaller **City Center Stages I** and **II**—a number of productions and programs of the Manhattan Theatre Club and the Pearl Theatre Company.

★ **Radio City Music Hall** (✉ *1260 6th Ave., between W. 50th and W. 51st Sts., Midtown West* ☎ *212/247–4777* ⊕ *www.radiocity.com* Ⓜ *B, D, F to 47th–50th/Rockefeller Center*) is the famed home of the scissor-kicking Rockettes and the Radio City Christmas Spectacular, but this stunning Art Deco showplace also packs its some 6,000 seats for spectacles like Cirque du Soleil, musical events, and the occasional film, set, perhaps, to a live orchestra.

READINGS AND LECTURES

The nonprofit **Municipal Art Society (MAS)** (✉ *111 W. 57th St., between 6th and 7th Aves., Midtown West* ☎ *212/935–3960, 212/453–0050 Tour Hotline* ⊕ *www.mas.org* Ⓜ *F to 57th St.; D, E to 7th Ave./53rd St.*) is a committed advocate for smart urban planning and the architectural treasures that define this metropolis.

Count on their walking tours—on weekends mostly, plus a downtown series that sets out at midday on Tuesday—to offer a fresh perspective and feature the rarely seen, from Dawn Powell's Greenwich Village to a rolling tour of Grand Central Station to a visit to Little Syria in Manhattan's lower west side. Their resource library has the corner on NYC arcana.

The **New York Public Library** (✉ *Celeste Bartos Forum, W. 42nd St. at 5th Ave., Midtown West* ☎ *212/930–0855, or 888/718-4253* ⊕ *www.nypl. org/* Ⓜ *B, D, F, M to 42nd St.*) presents LIVE from the NYPL, a rich program of lectures and reading events at the famous main library and its branches elsewhere in the city.

THEATER

The onetime Selwyn—the venerable home to the works of Coward, Kaufman, and Porter in their heyday—is now known as the **American Airlines Theatre** (✉ *227 W. 42nd St., between 7th and 8th Aves., Midtown West* ☎ *212/719–1300* tickets ⊕ *www.roundabouttheatre.org* Ⓜ *1, 2, 3, 7, N, Q, R, S to 42nd St./Times Sq.; A, C, E to 42nd St./Port Authority*).

After incarnations as a burlesque hall and pornographic movie house, this splendidly restored 1918 Venetian-style playhouse is now home to the not-for-profit Roundabout Theatre Company, which is acclaimed for its revivals of classic musicals and plays, such as a Doug Hughes–directed production of *A Man for All Seasons*.

The **Barrymore Theatre** (✉ *243 W. 47th St., between Broadway and 8th Ave., Midtown West* ☎ *212/239–6200* tickets ⊕ *www.shubertorganization.com* Ⓜ *1, 2, 3, 7, N, Q, R, S to 42nd St./Times Sq.; C, E to 50th St.*) was that rare Broadway house that stayed legit throughout the Depression and still honors its original namesake, Ethel Barrymore. The 1928 Elizabethan wonder greets theatergoers with two stone archways. Shows within have included David Rabe's original *Hurly Burly* in 1984 and the innovative revival of Sondheim's *Company* in 2006.

In 1997 Disney refurbished the elaborate 1903 Art Nouveau **New Amsterdam Theater** (✉ *214 W. 42nd St., between 7th and 8th Aves., Midtown West* ☎ *212/282–2907* ⊕ *www.newamsterdamtheatre.org* Ⓜ *1, 2, 3, 7, N, Q, R, S to 42nd St./Times Sq.; A, C, E to 42nd St./Port Authority*), where Eddie Cantor, Will Rogers, Fanny Brice, and the Ziegfeld Follies once drew crowds. *The Lion King* ruled here for the first nine years of its run; *Mary Poppins* has prevailed ever since.

☺ In a magnificently restored century-old performance space, **the New Victory Theater** (✉ *209 W. 42nd St., between 7th and 8th Aves., Midtown West* ☎ *646/223–3010* ⊕ *www.newvictory.org* Ⓜ *1, 2, 3, 7, A, C, E, N, Q, R, S to 42nd St./Times Sq.*) presents an international roster of supremely kid-pleasing plays, music, and dance performances. Be dazzled by the likes of Canada's Circus INcognitus; Mabou Mines's Peter & Wendy—featuring Bunraku puppets and Celtic music; Mischief, a brilliant U.K.-based introduction to dance—with the inspired help of giant foam noodles; and Australian puppet madness, in The Tragical Life of Cheeseboy.

Count on reasonable ticket prices ($17 is the average), high-energy and high-class productions, and the opportunity for kids to chat with the artists after many performances.

Playwrights Horizons (✉ *416 W. 42nd St., between 9th and 10th Aves., Midtown West* ☎ *212/564–1235, 212/279–4200* tickets ⊕ *www.playwrightshorizons.org* Ⓜ *A, C, E to 42nd St./Port Authority*) is known for its support of new work by American playwrights. The first home for eventual Broadway hits such as *Grey Gardens* and Wendy Wasserstein's *Heidi Chronicles*, this is where you will find the latest work from Craig Lucas, Doug Wright, and Edward Albee.

Signature Theatre Company (✉ *Peter Norton Space, 555 W. 42nd St., between 10th and 11th Aves., Midtown West* ☎ *212/244–7529* info and tickets ⊕ *www.signaturetheatre.org* Ⓜ *A, C, E to 42nd St./Port Authority*) devotes each season to works by a single playwright (August Wilson, Horton Foote, Sam Shepard, and Tony Kushner among them), or an entire tradition, such as the seminal works of the Negro Ensemble Company.

15

All tickets are $20 for a show's first run. Come 2012, when, at this writing, the theater's new Frank Gehry–designed digs one block east are expected to be complete, the same ticket policy will be in place.

Moorish Revival in style, the **St. James** (✉ *246 W. 44th St., between Broadway and 8th Ave., Midtown West* ☎ *212/239–6200 tickets* ⊕ *www.jujamcyn.com* Ⓜ *1, 2, 3, 7, N, Q, R, S to 42nd St./Times Sq.; A, C, E to 42nd St./Port Authority*) went up in 1927, and has been running legit at least since the late 1930s. Home of Mel Brooks's juggernaut *The Producers* in its heyday, and where a Tony-laden revival of *Gypsy* held sway late in the first decade of the 21st century, the St. James is where Lauren Bacall was an usherette in the '40s, and where a little show called *Oklahoma!* premiered, with a rousing score and choreography to match, and changed the musical forever.

UPPER EAST SIDE

MUSIC

In its Grace Rainey Rogers Auditorium (and occasionally in the Medieval Sculpture Hall and the Temple of Dendur) the **Metropolitan Museum of Art** (✉ *1000 5th Ave., at E. 82nd St., Upper East Side* ☎ *212/570–3949* ⊕ *www.metmuseum.org* Ⓜ *4, 5, 6 to 86th St.*) offers a rich year-round music program with concerts by leading classical and jazz musicians.

Also part of the Met, and well worth the trip farther uptown, is **The Cloisters** (✉ *Fort Tryon Park, Washington Heights* ☎ *212/650–2290* Ⓜ *A to 190th St.*), which has matinee performances of sacred and secular music from the Middle Ages. It all takes place within a 12th-century chapel that was brought here from Spain.

OPERA

Ⓒ **Dicapo Opera Theatre** (✉ *184 E. 76th St., between Lexington and 3rd Aves. Upper East Side* ☎ *212/288–9438, 212/868–4444 tickets* ⊕ *www. dicapo.com* Ⓜ *6 to 77th St.*) may be in a church basement (albeit that of the distinctively French Provincial St. Jean Baptiste), but the 204-seater's boffo reputation—and its thoroughly modern facility—belie its humble-sounding setting. Productions range from Puccini to Tobias Picker's *Emmeline*. Their complementary children's programming, Opera for Kids, offers—at nominal seat prices—one-hour renditions of the classics on weekends.

PERFORMANCE CENTER

★ Well-known soloists, jazz musicians, show-tune stylists, and chamber
Ⓒ music groups perform in the **92nd Street Y's** 905-seat **Kaufmann Concert Hall**. But the Y's programming is hardly limited to music—purchase tickets early for their popular lectures-and-readings series featuring big-name authors, poets, playwrights, political pundits, and media bigwigs. Also worth the Upper East Side trek here are the Harkness Dance Festival, film programs, and all manner of family-friendly events. (✉ *1395 Lexington Ave., at E. 92nd St., Upper East Side* ☎ *212/415–5440, 212/415–5500 tickets* ⊕ *www.92y.org* Ⓜ *6 to 96th St.*).

Film Series and Revivals

Although many of the screens listed here also show first-run releases, old favorites and rarities are the heart of their programming. These gems—which include every genre from noir to the most au courant experimental work—frequently screen at museums, cultural societies, and other public spaces, such as the **French Institute** (☎ 212/355–6100 ⊕ www.fiaf.org) and even branches of the **New York Public Library** (⊕ www.nypl.org). Silent films (⊕ www.silentclowns.com) are the fare at Lincoln Center's **Library for the Performing Arts**.

And a reliably creative range of repertory screenings can always be found at **Anthology Film Archives** (☎ 212/505–5181 ⊕ www.anthologyfilmarchives.org), **Film Forum** (☎ 212/727–8110 ⊕ www.filmforum.org), the **Museum of Modern Art (MoMA)** (☎ 212/708–9400 ⊕ www.moma.org), the **Museum of the Moving Image** (☎ 718/784–0077 ⊕ www.movingimage.us), **BAM Rose Cinemas/BAMcinématek** (☎ 718/636–4100 ⊕ www.bam.org), and **Walter Reade Theater** (☎ 212/875–5600 ⊕ www.filmlinc.com).

15

READINGS AND LECTURES

Insight into the creative process is what the superb **Works & Process** (✉ *Guggenheim Museum, 1071 5th Ave., at E. 89th St., Upper East Side* ☎ *212/423–3587* ⊕ *www.worksandprocess.org* Ⓜ *4, 5, 6 to 86th St.*) program is all about. Often drawing on dance and theater works-in-progress, live performances are complemented with illuminating discussions with their (always top-notch) choreographers, playwrights, and directors.

CENTRAL PARK

THEATER

The **Swedish Cottage Marionette Theatre** (✉ *Swedish Cottage, West Dr. at W. 79th St., Central Park* ☎ *212/988–9093 [reservations required]* ⊕ *www.cityparksfoundation.org* Ⓜ *B, C to 81st St.*) was originally part of Sweden's exhibit at the 1876 Centennial Exposition in Philadelphia (park designer Frederick Law Olmsted had it moved here the following year). The charming wooden 100-seat (and technically modern) playhouse presents classics like *Hansel and Gretel* and *Cinderella*.

UPPER WEST SIDE

MUSIC

Anything you come to hear at the **Cathedral Church of St. John the Divine** (✉ *1047 Amsterdam Ave., at W. 112th St., Upper West Side* ☎ *212/316–7540 performance line* ⊕ *www.stjohndivine.org* Ⓜ *1, B, C to 110th St./Cathedral Pkwy.*) will likely be an unforgettable experience, but the seasonal programming of the **Early Music New York** (☎ *212/749–6600, 212/280–0330 tickets* ⊕ *www.earlymusicny.org*) ensemble is essential.

An outpost a few blocks south of the Lincoln Center main campus was dedicated to **Jazz at Lincoln Center** (✉ *Time Warner Center, Broadway* *at W. 60th St., Columbus CircleUpper West Side* ☎ *212/258–9800* ⊕ *www.jalc.org* Ⓜ *1, A, B, C, D to 59th St./Columbus Circle*) in 2004. Stages in Rafael Viñoly's crisply modern **Frederick P. Rose Hall** feature the 1,100-seat **Rose Theater** (where a worthy Jazz for Young People series joins the buoyant adult programming a few times each year).

Also here is the **Allen Room,** an elegant and intimate 310–460-seater, and the even more intimate 140-seat Dizzy's Club Coca-Cola.

Adventurous programming of jazz, classical, early and modern music, and dance continues at the **Miller Theatre** (⊠ *Columbia University, 2960 Broadway, at W. 116th St., Morningside Heights* ☎ *212/854–1633, 212/854–7799 box office* ⊕ *www.millertheatre.com* Ⓜ *1 to 116th St.*). A well-designed 688-seater, this is a hall that rewards serious listeners.

PERFORMANCE CENTERS

Fodor's Choice
★
Lincoln Center for the Performing Arts (⊠ *W. 62nd to W. 66th Sts., Broadway/Columbus Ave. to Amsterdam Ave., Upper West Side* ☎ *212/875–5456 Customer Service daily 9–9, 212/721–6500 CenterCharge, 212/875–5375 for accessibility information* ⊕ *www.lincolncenter.org* Ⓜ *1 to 66th St./Lincoln Center*) is the uncontested star of New York City's performance universe. Just in time for its 50th anniversary—which coincided with the 2009–2010 season—the wraps came off most of the construction geared to improving and enhancing its timeless, elegant buildings. And from the moment you approach the main plaza and its exuberant centerpiece, the Revson Fountain, it's clear the revitalization effort has more than succeeded.

Rising in stages from 1962 to 1969, the sprawling 16-acre campus was aptly built on the once gritty urban grounds that set the scene for the deeply energized music and dance in *West Side Story.* The predominantly white, travertine-clad buildings were originally designed by a host of "who"s in 20th-century architecture, all of whom applied a classical aesthetic to their cleanly modern structures.

Formal and U-shaped, the massive **Avery Fisher Hall** (⊠ *Columbus Ave., at W. 65th St.* ☎ *212/875–5030*) opened in 1962. Then known as Philharmonic Hall, the 2,738-seater's original design, by Max Abramovitz, was given an overhaul in 1976 by Philip Johnson and John Burgee, resulting in the much-improved acoustics that draw the world's greatest musicians today.

Avery Fisher is home to the stellar **New York Philharmonic** (☎ *212/875–5656* ⊕ *nyphil.org*), which Alan Gilbert conducts to great acclaim from late September to early June. Orchestra rehearsals at 9:45 am are open to the public on selected weekday mornings (usually Wednesday or Thursday) for $18. A popular Young People's Concert series is offered on Saturday afternoon, four times throughout the season. In August, Lincoln Center's longest-running classical series, the **Mostly Mozart Festival** (☎ *212/875–5399*), captures the crowds.

A handful of Mozart festival events are held at **Alice Tully Hall,** (⊠ *1941 Broadway, at W. 65th St.* ☎ *212/671–4050*), but its primary resident is the **Chamber Music Society of Lincoln Center** (☎ *212/875–5788* ⊕ *www.chambermusicsociety.org*). The hall is considered to be as acoustically perfect as a concert hall can get. It was designed in 1969 by Pietro Belluschi for a music and film audience of 1,100, and was an instant success.

When it reopened for the spring 2009 season, after a hiatus for an aesthetic (and acoustic) transformation by Diller Scofidio + Renfro, it's fair to say event goers were utterly transfixed with its new transparency. The once rather subdued facade has become an angular glass beacon, with an illuminated indoor rehearsal space and lobby.

Just down the street is the lovely 250-seat **Stanley H. Kaplan Penthouse,** (⌧ *165 W. 65th St., between Broadway and Amsterdam Ave.*), a high-rise space for intimate chamber ensembles.

The 3,800-seat **Metropolitan Opera House,** (⌧ *30 Lincoln Center Plaza, Columbus Ave., between W. 62nd and W. 65th Sts.* ☎ *212/362–6000*) with its suitably luxe Austrian-crystal chandeliers and immense, multi-story Marc Chagall paintings, premiered in 1966.

The titan of American opera companies and an institution since its founding in 1883, the **Metropolitan Opera** (☎ *212/362–6000* ⊕ *www.metfamilyopera.org*) brings the world's leading singers to the vast stage here from October to April. The company's music director and principal conductor, James Levine, despite ongoing health challenges, ensures that the Met's orchestra rivals the world's finest symphonies; its programming eagerly embraces the 21st century. From a controversial new *Tosca* in 2009 to a senses-defying staging for *Das Rheingold* in 2010, all performances, including those sung in English, are unobtrusively subtitled on small screens on the back of the seat in front of you.

Also resident at the Met is **American Ballet Theatre (ABT)** (☎ *212/477–3030* ⊕ *www.abt.org*), which is renowned for its gorgeous full-program renditions of the 19th-century classics (*Swan Lake, Giselle, The Sleeping Beauty*) with choreography reenvisioned by 20th-century masters. Since its founding in 1940, the company has nurtured the likes of Baryshnikov, Makarova, and Gregory, and 21st-century principal dancers Gillian Murphy, David Hallberg, and Herman Cornejo. ABT has two New York seasons: eight weeks of performances begin in May here at the Met, and starting with the 2010 holiday season, their Nutcracker is staged at the **Brooklyn Academy of Music (BAM)**.

Now known as the **David H. Koch Theater** (⌧ *Columbus Ave., at W. 62nd St.* ☎ *212/870–5570*), the Philip Johnson–designed former New York State Theater opened its doors here in 1964. Although perhaps not as famous as the Met next door, here at the spruced-up Koch the **New York City Opera** (☎ *212/870–5570* ⊕ *www.nycopera.com*) is distinguished by its own vibrant personality. Founded in 1943, the company is known for its diverse repertory and its soft spot for American composers—a theme that has only been strengthened with the 2009 appointment of George Steel as artistic director.

Ever more innovative, and often rarely staged, productions (Leonard Bernstein's *A Quiet Place*, Richard Strauss's *Intermezzo*) provide fine vehicles for this company's great voices, which follow in the footsteps of Placido Domingo and Beverly Sills, who began their careers here. City Opera performs October to November and March to April. Super-titles—the opera's libretto, line-by-line—are displayed above the stage.

15

Sharing the Koch is the equally formidable **New York City Ballet** (NYCB) (☎ *212/870–5570* ⊕ *www.nycballet.com*), with its unmatched repertoire of 20th-century works, predominantly by George Balanchine, Jerome Robbins, and Peter Martins. The NYCB's 90 dancers—Jock Soto, Kyra Nichols, and Wendy Whelan have all graced this stage—are superb in the short-form programs this company has excelled in since its first performances, in 1948.

Its fall season starts in September and early October, then returns in late November through December for their beloved annual production of Balanchine's *The Nutcracker*. Its winter repertory program runs in January and February, and a spring season runs from May into June.

Housed in Eero Saarinen's finely scaled 1965 Lincoln Center Theater complex, and home to a rich tradition of plays and musicals, the 1,047-seat **Vivian Beaumont** and the 334-seat **Mitzi E. Newhouse** theaters are being joined in 2012 by the rooftop **Claire Tow Theater**. With 131 seats and a small grassy terrace for attendees, this Hugh Hardy–designed add-on has been created to offer full stagings of works by the newest directors, playwrights, and designers.

The comfy 268-seat auditorium of the **Walter Reade Theater** (✉ *165 W. 65th St., between Broadway and Amsterdam Ave.* ☎ *212/875–5600* ⊕ *www.filmlinc.com*) has what may be the best sight lines in town. It presents series devoted to "the best in world cinema" that run the gamut from silents (with occasional live organ accompaniment) and documentaries to retrospectives and recent releases, often on the same theme or from the same country. And here's where to come on certain Saturdays to catch The Met: Live in HD screenings.

Tucked under the Illuminated Lawn on the main campus, across the street, the **Elinor Bunin-Monroe Film Center,** which opened in 2011, offers two small screening rooms (a 150-seater and a 90-seater), a café, and an archive that encourages further immersion into NYC's film arts. (✉ *165 W. 65th St., between Broadway and Amsterdam Ave.* ☎ *212/875–5610* ⊕ *www.filmlinc.com*)

■ **TIP→** Discounted day-of-show tickets for most Lincoln Center venues may be purchased in person at the David Rubenstein Atrium (Broadway between W. 62nd and W. 63rd; www.lincolncenter.org/live/index.php/atrium), which also functions as a lounge with a cafe and free Wi-Fi. For programs Monday–Thursday, a limited number of same-day $20 rush orchestra-seat tickets are available at the Met box office two hours before curtain.

Symphony Space (✉ *2537 Broadway, at W. 95th St., Upper West Side* ☎ *212/864–5400* ⊕ *www.symphonyspace.org* Ⓜ *1, 2, 3 to 96th St.*) presents an energetic roster of music (including its famed Wall to Wall composer programs), from world to classical. On the literary front, its two halls—the **Peter Jay Sharpe Theatre** and the **Leonard Nimoy Thalia** host a celebrated roster of literary events, including Bloomsday and the famed Selected Shorts series of stories read by prominent actors and broadcast live on National Public Radio. Opera on film and Thalia Film Sundays (usually a true-to-its-roots art-house screening) round out the adult programming.

For the family, turn to their hugely popular **Just Kidding** lineup for a nonstop parade of zany plays, sing-alongs, midday Saturday (and sometimes Sunday) movies, and animations, like the Gustafer Yellowgold Show.

HARLEM

MUSIC

★ **Apollo Theater.** If the Apollo's famed Amateur Night doesn't get you off the couch, keep in mind its more intimate Apollo Music Cafe events on Friday, Saturday, and Monday nights, featuring some of the finest artists in jazz and other music traditions—and some right on the edge of fame.

The Apollo's notable weeklong Harlem Jazz Shrines festival in May is held in venerable nearby venues Lenox Lounge, Minton's Playhouse, and Showman's Cafe. ⊠ *253 W. 125th St., at 8th Ave./Frederick Douglass Blvd., Harlem* ☎ *212/531–5300, 800/745–3000 tickets (Ticketmaster)* ⊕ *www.apollotheater.org* Ⓜ *A, B, C, 2, 3, 4, 5, 6 to 125th St.*

BROOKLYN

MUSIC

In Brooklyn, **Bargemusic** (⊠ *Fulton Ferry Landing, Old Fulton and Furman Sts., Brooklyn Heights* ☎ *718/624–2083* ⊕ *www.bargemusic.org* Ⓜ *A, C to High St.; 2, 3 to Clark St.*) keeps chamber music groups busy year-round on a re-outfitted harbor barge with a fabulous view of the Manhattan skyline.

PERFORMANCE CENTERS

Fodor'sChoice America's oldest performing arts center, the **Brooklyn Academy of Music**
★ **(BAM)** (⊠ *Peter Jay Sharp Bldg., 30 Lafayette Ave., between Ashland Pl. and St. Felix St., Fort Greene* ☎ *718/636–4100* ⊕ *www.bam.org* Ⓜ *C to Lafayette Ave.; 2, 3, 4, 5, B, Q to Atlantic Ave.; D, N, R to Atlantic Ave.–Pacific St.*), presented its first show in 1861. Today BAM has a much-deserved reputation for the unusual and the unexpected, presented in grand-scale stagings. The most contemporary dance, music, opera, and cross-media productions mingle here with an array of classics. A restored Renaissance Revival palace built in 1908—the 2,100-seat **Howard Gilman Opera House**—and the 874-seat **Harvey Theater,** an updated 1904 theater a block away at 651 Fulton Street, are BAM's primary performance spaces. Every fall their Next Wave Festival fills the house with crackling energy and events that highlight a global mix of remarkable artists. The holidays bring a run of American Ballet Theatre's 2010-debuted Nutcracker, and with springtime comes a top-notch roster of international theater companies (such as Ireland's renowned Abbey) in repertory. Year-round you can catch a movie at the four-screen **BAM Rose Cinemas,** which offers BAMcinématek, an eclectic repertory series (from Kurosawa's Samurai to Hungarians in Hollywood), as well as first-run indies, documentaries, and foreign-language films. Or, hit the industrial-glam **BAMcafé** (☎ *718/623–7811 reservations*) for Between the Lines, a synapse-sparking lecture series on Thursday night; it becomes a cabaret venue on Friday and Saturday

15

nights. ■TIP→ BAM gets kudos for its down-to-earth range of ticket prices; $25 to $60 is typical.

THEATER

Finely detailed wooden marionettes and hand puppets are on the bill at **Puppetworks** (⊠ *338 6th Ave., at 4th St., Park Slope* ☎ *718/965–3391 Reservations essential* ⊕ *www.puppetworks.org* Ⓜ *F to 7th Ave.*). Familiar childhood tales like *Little Red Riding Hood* and *Peter and the Wolf* come to life most weekends in this 75-seat neighborhood theater.

St. Ann's Warehouse (⊠ *38 Water St., between Main and Dock Sts., DUMBO* ☎ *718/254–8779, 866/911–4111 tickets* ⊕ *stannswarehouse. org* Ⓜ *A, C to High St.; F to York St.*) has hosted everything from the boundary-stretching 2009 opera *La Didone* to award-winning performances from the famous Edinburgh Fringe Festival, all in a onetime spice-milling factory.

QUEENS

FILM

The **Museum of the Moving Image** (⊠ *35th Ave. at 36th St., Astoria* ☎ *718/784–0077* ⊕ *www.movingimage.us* Ⓜ *R, M to Steinway St.; N to 36th Ave.*) presents special film programming to go along with the museum's radical, well-received face-lift and re-launch in 2011.

Video art, digital screenings, live musical collaborations, and in-person appearances by moviemaker luminaries are regular features, as are the sort of retrospectives and themed repertory they programmed previously, like an Alain Resnais series, Recovered Treasures (from world archives), or Avant-Garde Masters.

It's also a great choice for kids: weekend Family Film matinees take place in Tut's Fever Movie Palace, the fab Red Grooms and Lysiane Luong–designed installation that's a holdover from this 1920 Astoria Studio building's first incarnation as a museum in the late 1980s.

Nightlife

WORD OF MOUTH

"The Iridium is an intimate and funky room where we spent a delightful evening on a recent visit to New York. The late, great Les Paul played there on Monday nights until shortly before his death."

—happytrailstoyou

Updated by
Alexander
Basek

New York is fond of the "work hard, play hard" maxim, but the truth is that Gothamites don't need much of an excuse to gather together when the sun goes down (or before it goes down, sometimes). Monday is the new Thursday, which replaced Friday and Saturday, but it doesn't matter. The bottom line is that there's always plenty to do at night in this 24-hour city, and visitors will quickly see that whether it's going to a divey 1930s saloon, a gay sports bar, or a swanky rooftop hotel lounge, it isn't hard to get a piece of the action.

The nightlife scene still resides largely downtown—in dives in the East Village and Lower East Side, classic jazz joints in the West Village, and the Meatpacking District's and Chelsea's see-and-be-seen clubs. Midtown, especially around Hell's Kitchen, has developed quite the vibrant scene, too, and plenty of preppy hangouts dot the Upper East and Upper West sides.

Keep in mind that *when* you go is just as important as *where* you go. A spot sizzles only when it's hopping—a club that is packed at 11 might empty out by midnight, and a bar that raged last night may be completely empty tonight. These days, night prowlers are more loyal to floating parties, DJs, and club promoters than to any specific addresses.

For those of you trying to give N.Y.C. its "Fun City" rep back, *Paper* magazine has a good list of the roving parties. You can check their online nightlife guide, *PM* (N.Y.C.), via their Web site ⊕ *www.papermag.com*. Another streetwise mag, *The L Magazine* (⊕ *www.thelmagazine.com*), lists what's happening day by day at many of the city's lounges and clubs, as well as dance and comedy performances. Be sure to scour industry-centric Web sites, too, like Eater and Grub Street, which catalog the comings and goings of many a nightlife impresario.

The *New York Times* has listings of cabaret and jazz shows, most comprehensively in their Friday and Sunday Arts section. Bear in mind that a venue's life span is often measured in months, not years. Phone ahead to make sure your target hasn't closed or turned into a polka hall (although you never know—that could be fun, too).

(⇨ *For venues in Brooklyn, see Chapter 12; for venues in Queens, the Bronx, and Staten Island, see Chapter 13)*

LOWER MANHATTAN

TRIBECA

BARS

B-flat. The decor is red-on-red here, and the Asian-style cocktails are particularly groovy (literally—one, with citrusy Japanese yuzu juice and vodka, is dubbed the Groovy) at this Japan-meets-'50s America lounge. Get some fine Japanese food treats and check out the upstairs area with amazing wall and ceiling murals of the Tokyo Bar. ⊠ *277 Church St., between Franklin and White Sts., TriBeCa* ☎ *212/219–2970* ⊕ *www. bflat.info* Ⓜ *1 to Franklin St.*

★ **Brandy Library.** Alas, the only book in this exquisite, wood-paneled room is the leather-bound menu listing hundreds of brandies and single-malt scotches. The bottles are on gorgeous backlighted "bookshelves," though, and you can learn what makes each of them special by chatting with the spirit sommelier—or by attending the twice-weekly Spirit School tastings. ⊠ *25 N. Moore St., between Varick and Hudson Sts., TriBeCa* ☎ *212/226–5545* ⊕ *www.brandylibrary.com* Ⓜ *1 to Franklin St.*

Canal Room. Polished wood floors, potted palms, and stylish chairs give this intimate club an air of glamour. Musicians perform here several times a month, but they also come just to enjoy themselves. The owners' record-business connections, a spectacular sound system, celeb sightings, and DJs with reputations as big as their turntables (size does matter) keep the crowds moving. ⊠ *285 West Broadway, at Canal St., TriBeCa* ☎ *212/941–8100* ⊕ *www.canalroom.com* Ⓜ *A, C, E to Canal St.*

M1-5. For the more bohemian of TriBeCa pub goers, this lipstick-red, high-ceiling spot is a vast playground (as in pool and darts). A reggae jukebox helps keep it real, as do discounts for local artists on the diverse cocktail menu. Extra points, too, for the bar's name, which cites TriBeCa's warehouse zoning law. ⊠ *52 Walker St., between Broadway and Church St., TriBeCa* ☎ *212/965–1701* ⊕ *www.m1-5.com* Ⓜ *J, M, Z, N, Q, R, 6 to Canal St.*

Smith and Mills. Attractive scenesters frolic giddily at this tiny gem of a gin mill, where mixologists who resemble Daniel Day-Lewis dispense elixirs (and caviar) from a bar hung with pots and pans. There are cozy table-nooks for couples, and an elevator-toilet (yes, you read that correctly) for anyone who feels "nature's call" while heeding "the call of the wild." ⊠ *71 N. Moore St., between Hudson and Greenwich Sts., TriBeCa* ☎ *212/219–8568* ⊕ *www.smithandmills.com* Ⓜ *1 to Franklin St.*

16

Continued on page 312

NEW YORK NIGHTS

New York is the city that never sleeps—and when you come to visit, you might not, either. It doesn't matter if you're a disco queen, a lounge lizard, a class act, or a prisoner of rock n' roll; the nightlife options here will give you your fix. So pop some No-Doz, drink that third cup of coffee, do whatever it takes for you to rev up. You can catch up on sleep when you're dead . . . or in Cleveland.

A NIGHT OF JAZZ
GREENWICH VILLAGE

It's no surprise that the Village, a legendary haunt for Beat poets, avant-garde performance artists, and countercultural politicos, is also a hotbed of jazz. This neighborhood's vibe is all about experimentation and free expression . . . so put on your dark glasses and your artfully distressed leather jacket, grab your Gauloises (for the sidewalk, anyhow), and get ready to groove.

Making advance reservations may not entirely jibe with jazz's spontaneous sensibility, but it's necessary if you want to get into some of the Village's best-known venues. Booking weeks ahead for a table at the **Blue Note** will only ensure that you have a memorable night; you'll be able to see jazz greats like Herbie Hancock,

McCoy Tyner, Cassandra Wilson, Eddie Palmer, Nellie McKay, and Chris Botti right up close from one of the cramped 40-or-so tables. This is also a great place to have dinner; the Note serves up some bodacious barbecue, especially at Sunday brunch.

Another spot that's worth pre-booking for is the nearby "Carnegie Hall of Cool," the **Village Vanguard**. John Coltrane and Sonny Rollins used to jam here regularly, and modern-day jazz giants like Wynton Marsalis make rare appearances. When the headline act's not huge, though, you can sometimes wander in at 8 (when the doors open) and still snag a seat.

OUTSIDE THE BOX

Although the Village has the highest concentration of jazz clubs in the city, a few fabulous venues that are worth the cab fare uptown. Smoke, way up near Columbia University, is a true jazz-lover's haven. The 16-piece "Smoke Big Band" blasts your brain-pan off on Thursdays. A less arduous trip to Midtown will bring you to Iridium, where late guitar great Les Paul once played on Monday nights. A bit farther south near Times Square is the famous 60-year-old Birdland, named for the late great Charlie Parker; the cover charge here includes a drink.

Above, jazz bassist Ron Carter.

Jazz legends, Charles Lloyd at the Blue Note (above)
and Joe Wilder at the Village Vanguard (right).

With smaller, less famous Village venues,
you can extemporize a bit; these places are
almost always packed with jazzers, but
you can show up without a reservation
(often without paying a cover charge) and
still catch some top-quality music. The
Garage Restaurant & Café is one such spot;
you can have a steak dinner in front of
the giant fireplace while listening to great
local trios and quartets (or, on Monday,
big-band swing). The **Knickerbocker Bar &
Grill** is another place where you can satisfy
both your gastronomic and musical appetites; on Friday and Saturday nights live
ensembles play while diners dig in to St.
Louis ribs or slow baked salmon.

Arthur's Tavern is another no-cover venue,
with a coolly grotty dark-wood (or, more
accurately, dark wood–veneer) ambi-

ence; you can chill out in the piano bar
or catch a jazz trio from one of the dining room tables. **Sweet Rhythm**, also a
great choice, is even greater if you're
a starving student; on Monday nights, a
jazz ensemble from the nearby New School
University's music program takes the stage,
and anyone with student ID gets in free.

For addresses and phone numbers of these venues, see the main Nightlife listings in this chapter.

A NIGHT OF CLUBBING
THE MEATPACKING DISTRICT AND CHELSEA

Ever since Studio 54 hung its first mirrored ball and ignited a citywide disco inferno, New York has been a playground for the young late-night club set. The '70s may be over; the multilevel megaclubs of the '80s and pulsing raves of the '90s are now largely in the past. But if DJ-spun grooves and packed dance floors are what you love, there's still plenty of New York spots where you can party like it's 1999 (or 1989, or 1979).

It's best to start your long evening with some sustenance, so your first stop—no earlier than 9 PM—should be one of the Meatpacking District's super-hip eater-

ies. **Spice Market** and **Pastis** serve excellent food (Southeast Asian and French bistro, respectively), and will also ease you into the clubland vibe; they both have killer cocktails, a see-and-be-seen crowd, and sometimes even lines of people waiting to get inside (hence advance reservations are highly recommended).

Once you've lingered until a more respectable hour (midnight so), meander over to one of the neighborhood's more civilized clubs. **APT's** basement room, where funk and soul are in heavy rotation, has just a narrow slice of dance floor between the bar and a seating area; it's a safe place to do some preliminary

OUTSIDE THE BOX

Although the Meatpacking and Chelsea neighborhoods are Clubland Central, a couple of New York's best clubs are a bit off the beaten path and worth seeking out.

If you've had your fill of velvet-rope snootiness, direct your dancing feet to the Santos Party House, where a democratic entry policy rules. What it lacks in frills, Santos more than makes up for in fun.

HOW TO GET IN

Unless you're a model, movie star, or recording artist, there's no surefire way to make sure you'll get past the velvet ropes at top New York clubs. But there are some things you can do to increase your chances.

■ **Arranging for bottle service** is an expensive proposition, but it's one of the only ways to reserve a table for you and your friends inside a club. Bottle service means you agree to purchase an entire bottle (or several) of, say, vodka or champagne, which is then used to serve your group. You won't be paying liquor-store prices, though; a bottle of Grey Goose with mixers can easily set you back a couple hundred dollars.

■ **Surrounding yourself with good-looking, sexily dressed females** is always a good bet when you're trying to catch the doorman's eye. Club owners and managers want to keep their venues packed with eye candy—so if you're a girl, pour yourself into tight jeans, stiletto heels, and some sort of dressy top, and grab your friends. If you're a guy, do your best to cobble together an entourage, and steer clear of sports jerseys, baseball hats, sneakers.

■ **Showing up early** may make you feel like a loser—nothing's more dismal than a cavernous, empty dance floor—but it's easier to get in when the door staff is simply trying to get bodies inside.

■ **Cash** has been known to part even the most stubborn velvet ropes like the Red Sea. So if you're not famous, good-looking, or rich enough for bottle service, you can always try slipping the doorman a $20 (just do it discreetly, and don't consider it a guarantee).

head-bobbing. **Cielo,** where deep-house DJs reign, is another relatively chill and intimate place to dance. A glorious new Meatpacking marvel is **Kiss and Fly,** where plenty of groovy dancing gets done along with all the kissing and flying. An incandescent interior based on a butterfly motif is eye-popping, but the crowd and how they move grabs the most attention.

When the wee hours arrive, it's time to get serious; New York's biggest and wildest clubs only really come alive around 1 AM. Many of these are in Chelsea, the next neighborhood over and just a short cab ride away from the Meatpacking District. **Marquee** (289 10th Ave., 646/473–0202) is similarly fabulous, but with with a high quotient of beautiful people. It, like the other ultra-glamorous dance clubs in town (Oak, the Gates, Avenue, M2), can be a tough door to get past.

No matter where your night of clubbing takes you, have at least $150 on you. Many places don't take plastic, and if they do, you'll only exasperate the people behind you if you whip it out. Most clubs charge a cover ranging from $5 to $25, depending on the night and venue. Have another $40–$50 socked away for round-trip cab fare: it's a relatively small price to pay for the convenience and the designated driver.

For addresses and phone numbers of these venues, see the main Nightlife listings in this chapter.

A NIGHT OF ELEGANCE
MIDTOWN, THE UPPER EAST AND UPPER WEST SIDES

I like the city air
I like to drink of it
The more I know New York
The more I think of it

It hardly matters that these Cole Porter lyrics (from "I Happen to Like New York") are decades old. The nighttime Manhattan that Porter knew—of moonlit walks in Central Park, swanky piano bars, chandeliered dining rooms, and dancing cheek to cheek—is still alive and kicking. Some of the city's classiest nightspots have been around since Porter himself was a regular, and some are more newly minted—but all of them share a sense of old-world, uniquely New York style.

If you prefer a clubbier, less formal but still elegant meal, try the **'21' Club**, where you can enjoy one of the city's best, and most expensive, hamburgers ($30) in front of a roaring fire. (Jackets are required for men at dinnertime.)

For post-dinner drinks, head east to the gorgeously wood-paneled **Campbell Apartment**—a small warren of rooms inside Grand Central that was once the private residence of a New York tycoon.

Cocktails with Fitzgerald-esque names will literally help get you in the spirit. Or, head north to the posh Carlyle Hotel, where you can slip into one of the leather banquettes and listen to live piano music at **Bemelmans Bar.** The Carlyle is also home to the famed **Café Carlyle**, where big-name entertainers like Judy Collins dazzle in an intimate setting (you'll need to buy tickets well in advance for these shows). Another nearby spot for live music (except in the summertime, when it's closed) is **Feinstein's** at the Regency Hotel (540 Park Ave., 212/759–4100).

CLASSIC CHAMPAGNE COCKTAILS

If sipping bubbly while gazing at the New York skyline sounds like the epitome of class, you're in luck; many of the elegant nightspots listed here serve up signature Champagne cocktails. Here are a few you can try:

The Flapper's Delight, at the Campbell Apartment: Champagne with papaya juice and amaretto

The ChamPino, at Bemelmans Bar: A concoction made with Champagne, Campari, and sweet vermouth

The Kir Royale, once served at the now-closed, Rainbow Room: An oldie but goodie, made with Champagne and crème de cassis

A cheeky row of lawn jockeys mark the entrance to the '21' Club

Featured performers here have included Florence Henderson.

Another sort of elegance is the urban intellectual sort, and this too can be found. At the venerable **Lexington Bar and Books**, the shelves are filled with those pre-Kindle curios, otherwise known as books, giving it a clubby feel. Even if these book-lined walls don't draw you in, the waitresses in pearl, the cozy furnishings, and the elite cocktails, cognacs, and malts will.

As mentioned, some of the swankiest bars and cocktail lounges are located in Manhattan's fabled hotels, the grand dames of lodging, such as the St. Regis, home to the tiny but essential **King Cole Bar** where artist Maxfield Parrish's bar-long mural looks as luminous as ever. The Plaza, the Pierre, and the Sherry-Netherland, also offer supremely elegant nightcap settings.

BACK IN THE DAY

The '21' Club, founded during Prohibition, began its life as a speakeasy. The club was raided several times, but it never closed, largely because of the ingenious preventive measures set up by its owners, Jack Kreindler and Charlie Berns. One of these was a mechanical system of pulleys that, when activated, immediately swept all the alcohol bottles off the bar shelves and down a chute, away from the prying eyes of police.

A glorious newcomer to this group is the dark-wood paneled **Lobby Lounge** of the Mandarin Oriental hotel. The Lounge's views are flat-out sensational and their signature cocktails, like the Blood and Seoul (made of vodka, lemon juice, tomato juice, and spicy Korean kimchee), are good enough to become a conversation piece.

For addresses and phone numbers of these venues, see the main Nightlife listings in this chapter.

A NIGHT OF ROCK N' ROLL
THE LOWER EAST SIDE

The Ramones, Patti Smith, the New York Dolls, the Velvet Underground, Television, Blondie . . . easily half the bands that are today considered American punk rock legends cut their teeth in the gritty grottoes of the Lower East Side. Now that the neighborhood's undergone a revival—it's become home base for a new generation of jaded, creative young things—new live-music venues have been popping up around the old dives like weeds in a junkyard. Some of these are full-blown performance spaces, others just bars with a guitarist, an amp, and a drummer crammed into a corner; but the good news is, if you don't like the band playing in one place, you'll have to walk only a block or two to get to the next one. And hey—now that smoking's been banned, you can actually see what's happening on stage.

The venerable **Bowery Ballroom**, a staple of the downtown music scene, is the perfect place to start your a rock n' roll pilgrimage. You'll need advance tickets to see the bands that play here, especially ultra-hip headliners like Arctic Monkeys, Dr. Dog, and the Yeah Yeah Yeahs. But the relatively small size of the auditorium, the great acoustics, and the beer-sloshing enthusiasm of the crowd make it worth the Ticketmaster prices. On your way out, you may find yourself passing 315 Bowery, the address of the legendary and now defunct **CBGB**. A battle-scarred, stinking pit even in its 1970s heyday—when bands like Suicides, Talking Heads, and Blondie launched their careers here—the club finally closed its doors in October of 2006 and is now a rock-themed clothing store.

The nearby intersection of Ludlow and Stanton streets is a mecca of sorts; small but rocking clubs seem to radiate in every direction for several blocks. This is the part of the LES that can get as crowded as a suburban mall late at night; between around 11 and 3 or 4 AM., the sidewalks are awash in young hipsters smoking Luckies and parading their thrift-store best. (If you want to blend in here, think scruffy retro-chic; no logos, no Manolos, no bling.) A favorite of this crowd is **Pianos,** once a piano shop (the new owners didn't bother to change the sign) and now an intimate performance space for acoustic and rock bands. **Arlene's Grocery,** just a block away, has been pulling in alternative music acts for more than a decade; The Strokes played here before anyone else had heard of them. If you need to channel your own inner Julian Casablancas, come on Monday night and join in the super-popular Rock n' Roll Karaoke party.

Heading less than a block east on Stanton will bring you to the deceptively un-rocklike **Cake Shop,** which looks like a record store crossed with a bakery. It is—at least on the first floor—but downstairs is a whole other story. Here, up-and-coming punk and garage bands play for a crowd of too-cool twenty-somethings (who also like to tank up on Fridays with the two-for-one happy hour, 5–8). Following Ludlow up to Houston, though, will take you right to **Mercury Lounge,** whose back room is famous for hosting big names before they were big. The White Stripes played here in their early days—the late, great Jeff Buckley would try out new material here; more recent performers, like Cold War Kids and Voxtrot are already starting to hit the mainstream.

Hopping from one LES music bar to another is a blast—until the killer headache sets in. If you need a place to chill out between venues and wait for the Tylenol to take effect, try one of these lower-key neighborhood lounges:

■ **Local 138.** This unpretentious pub, with neon signs and sports on the television, has a back room with low lighting and couches—perfect for nursing a $3 draft.

■ **The Pink Pony.** A book-lined eatery with good café au lait and a sort-of-French menu, the Pony is one of the more relaxing places on the sceney Ludlow strip.

■ **Teany.** This café is no longer owned by Moby, but it still keeps musician hours: open until 11 during the week (1 AM during the weekend). You'll find lots of teas, juices, and vegetarian fare the perfect antidote for a bender.

For addresses and phone numbers of these venues, see the main Nightlife listings in this chapter.

The Best Karaoke Bars

If you're looking for a venue other than the shower to bust out your rendition of Queen's "Somebody to Love," you're in good company. Otherwise jaded New Yorkers have become hooked on the goofy, addictive pleasure of karaoke. The K-word means "empty orchestra" in Japanese, and seems to tickle both downtown hipsters (who dig the irony of kitsch) and uptown financiers (who need a good rebel yell after the end of a workday), and everybody in between who loves to flex the golden pipes after a few drinks.

There are three ways of getting your lead-vocalist groove on: doing it in public, at a barwide Karaoke Night; reserving a private space at a bar ("karaoke boxes," they're called), where only your friends can hear you scream—er, sing; and bounding up onstage in front of a live band like Rock Star Karaoke, which plays all your favorites every Thursday night at Brother Jimmy's (✉ 1644 3rd Ave. ☎ 212/426-2020).

The hard-core karaoke places tend to be either grungy or glitzy, with as many as 15 available boxes for rent by the hour or full night (each box including music machine, microphones, and bar service), as well as up to 80,000 songs on tap for you to warble. (Don't worry, that figure includes stuff by Journey, REO Speedwagon, Britney Spears, and other grotesquely catchy Top 20 music.)

The most popular of this lot include Chinatown's scruffy Winnie's (✉ 104 Bayard St., at Baxter St. ☎ 212/732-2384), the East Village's Sing-Sing (✉ 9 St. Marks Place ☎ 212/387-7800), the triple-serving-of-cheesiness at Midtown's Pulse (✉ 135 W. 41st St., between Broadway and 6th Ave. ☎ 646/461-7717), and just about anywhere else in the unofficial Koreatown that sprawls around Herald Square. Try Karaoke Duet 35 (✉ 53 W. 35th St., 2nd fl., between 5th and 6th Aves. ☎ 646/233-2685).

For those who crave a cooler, and more public, karaoke experience, head to the Lower East Side's hottest karaoke night: Monday at Arlene's Grocery (✉ 95 Stanton St. ☎ 212/995-1652) as well as Piano's (✉ 158 Ludlow St. ☎ 212/505-3733).

DANCE CLUBS AND DJ VENUES

Santos Party House. "Now *this* is what I call a dance club," says Arthur Baker, the legendary DJ (and legendary record producer), about this glorious downtown dance club, where the velvet ropes part for everyone. Co-owned by the rocker Andrew W. K., the bi-level Santos ain't fancy, but that's the point, and the customers are as eclectic (everybody from punks to Upper East Siders) as the DJs, including Mr. Baker, who flies in regularly from London. Hence the musical vibe—underground dance, mostly—is simply kaleidoscopic. ✉ 96 Lafayette St., between White and Walker Sts., TriBeCa ☎ 212/584-5892 ⊕ www.santospartyhouse.com Ⓜ J, M, Z, N, Q, R, 6 to Canal St.

SOHO

BARS

Broome Street Bar. A local hangout since 1972, the casual yet essential Broome still feels like the old SoHo, before trendy boutiques replaced artists' lofts. There's an impressive selection of draft beers and a full menu of hefty burgers and other sturdy pub fare. ⊠ *363 West Broadway, at Broome St., SoHo* ☎ *212/925–2086* ⊕ *broomestreetbar.ypguides.net* Ⓜ *C, E to Spring St.*

Ear Inn. Since the early 1800s this sturdy old New York classic (at one time also a bordello) has been packing in, and amiably spooking, customers. According to legend, the place is haunted by a randy ghost, so beware—that hand you feel in your lap might not be your lover's. That hardly scares away patrons. In fact, it may be a selling point, as the staff encourages you to report all sightings. (No doubt "sightings" increase after a few drinks.) ⊠ *326 Spring St., between Greenwich and Washington Sts., SoHo* ☎ *212/226–9060* ⊕ *www.earinn.com* Ⓜ *1 to Houston St., C, E to Spring St.*

★ **Fanelli's.** Linger over the *New York Times* at this terrific neighborhood bar and restaurant, which is pretty down-to-earth for a SoHo landmark that's been serving drinks (and amazing cuisine—dig those burgers!) since 1847. Check out the hilarious old-timey photos on the walls, too. ⊠ *94 Prince St., at Mercer St., SoHo* ☎ *212/226–9412* Ⓜ *R to Prince St.*

Jimmy. Way up on the top floor of the new James Hotel, Jimmy is the second project from the team behind the West Village's Hotel Griffou. Here their take on the rooftop hotel bar is better than it has to be, given the stellar views; sit in a corner nook to gaze at the Empire State Building, or head toward the outdoor pool area to survey the bridges over the East River. Cocktails are a highlight, featuring seasonal ingredients and innovations like ice cubes made from cinnamon water. ⊠ *15 Thompson St., at Grand St., SoHo* ☎ *212/465–2000* ⊕ *www.jameshotels.com* Ⓜ *C, E to Spring St.*

★ **Lani Kai.** Julie Reiner, the brains behind the beloved Flatiron Lounge and Clover Club, has expanded her portfolio with a tiki bar. It sounds out of place in SoHo, but it works—and it's authentic, or as authentic as a tiki bar gets, thanks to Reiner's upbringing in Hawaii. Tropical plants, shells, and even a "fire pit" make it feel like a luau. Many of the cocktails are rum based, and the punches seem to include everything but the kitchen sink. Pupu, it's not. ⊠ *525 Broome St., between Sullivan and Thompson Sts., SoHo* ☎ *646/596–8778* ⊕ *www.lanikainy.com* Ⓜ *1, 2 to Canal St.*

16

MercBar. This neighborhood staple keeps packing in the crowds. Eleven different martinis, 9 bourbons, and 13 single-malt scotches are just the beginning of the extensive drink menu. ⊠ *151 Mercer St., between Prince and W. Houston Sts., SoHo* 🕾 *212/966–2727.*

Pegu Club. Modeled after an officers' club in what's now Myanmar, the Pegu manages to feel expansive and calm even when packed. The well dressed and flirtatious come here partly for the exotically lovely surroundings, but primarily for the cocktails, which are innovative, prepared with superlative ingredients, and predictably pricey. ⊠ *77 W. Houston St., 2nd fl., between West Broadway and Wooster St., SoHo* 🕾 *212/473–7348* ⊕ *www.peguclub.com* Ⓜ *B, D, F, M to Broadway– Lafayette St.; 6 to Bleecker St.*

Pravda. This Russian retreat has more than 70 brands of vodka, including 10 house-infused flavored vodkas, which means your choice of martinis is nearly endless. And teetotalers need not feel left out, because just about anywhere will serve New York's favorite nonalcoholic cocktail, the Lippy, which is simply a mix of every fruit juice that the bartender has on hand. Trust us—it's every bit as delicious as the harder stuff. ⊠ *281 Lafayette St., between Prince and W. Houston Sts., SoHo* 🕾 *212/226–4944*

WORLD MUSIC VENUES

★ **S.O.B.'s.** The initials stand for "Sounds Of Brazil" (no, not what you— and everybody else—might think), and this is *the* place for reggae, African, and Latin music, with some jazz gigs like Marcus Miller sprinkled in. The late, great Cuban sensation Cachao used to hold court here, as does calypso's Mighty Sparrow when he's up north. Don't miss the monthly Southeast Asian party Basement Bhangra, the Haitian dance parties, or the bossa nova brunches. Dinner is served as well. ⊠ *204 Varick St., at W. Houston St., SoHo* 🕾 *212/243–4940* ⊕ *www.sobs. com* Ⓜ *1 to Houston St.*

EAST VILLAGE AND LOWER EAST SIDE

EAST VILLAGE
BARS

Beauty Bar. Grab a seat in a barber chair or under a dryer at this made-over hair salon where, during happy hour, the manicurist will do your nails for a fee that includes a drink. (How's that for multitasking?) The DJ spins everything from Britpop to rock—a great soundtrack for primping. ⊠ *231 E. 14th St., between 2nd and 3rd Aves., East Village* 🕾 *212/539–1389* ⊕ *www.thebeautybar.com* Ⓜ *4, 5, 6, L, N, Q, R to 14th St./Union Sq.*

The Bourgeois Pig. What do you get when you serve all kinds of different fondue concoctions as well as all kinds of inventively delicious cocktails in a velvety yet chilled-out French bordello setting that's smack dab in the middle of the East Village? This keeper of a lounge, that's what. ⊠ *111 E. 7th St., between 1st Ave. and Ave. A, East Village* 🕾 *212/475–2246* ⊕ *www.thebourgeoispigny.com* Ⓜ *F to Lower East Side/2nd Ave.; 6 to Astor Pl.*

The Bowery Hotel Lobby Bar and Patio. Combining old-world hunting-lodge elegance with the height of comfort, the Bowery sets a standard for what all hotel lobbies should feature: sofas you can get lost in, a grand fireplace, a beautiful garden, an unusually friendly staff, and enough good vibes to compensate for the loss of CBGB down the block. ⊠ *333 The Bowery, between 2nd and 3rd Aves. East Village* ☎ *212/505–9100* ⊕ *www.theboweryhotel.com* Ⓜ *F to Lower East Side/2nd Ave.; 6 to Astor Pl.*

Death + Company. It's all about "speakeasy chic" at this sister lounge to the equally imaginative and classy nearby bars Mayahuel and Bourgeois Pig. A hilarious wall mural toward the rear sets the tone for the tongue-and-cheek satanic vibe here, but in the end, it's all about the outlandishly delicious cocktails. ⊠ *433 E. 6th St., between 1st Ave. and Ave. A, East Village* ☎ *212/388–0882* ⊕ *www.deathandcompany.com* Ⓜ *F to Lower East Side/2nd Ave.; 6 to Astor Pl.*

★ **Mayahuel.** This is the newest kid on the downtown, designer-bar block, and what a kid: all manner of Aztec spirits (raspberry tea–infused tequilas! pineapple-infused mescal!) make for the fiendishly rococo cocktails here, courtesy of master mixologist Philip Ward. Equally good are snacks such as popcorn with lime, cheese, and chili. The bi-level setting conjures a sort of demonic south-of-the-border bordello. As for the name, it derives from an Aztec legend (the fun menu fills you in). ⊠ *304 E. 6th St., between 1st and 2nd Aves., East Village* ☎ *212/253–5888* ⊕ *www.mayahuelny.com* Ⓜ *F to Lower East Side/2nd Ave.; 6 to Astor Pl., R, W to 8th St.–Broadway.*

McSorley's Old Ale House. One of New York's oldest saloons (it claims to have opened in 1854) and immortalized by *New Yorker* writer Joseph Mitchell, McSorley's is a must-visit for beer lovers, even if only two kinds of brew are served: McSorley's Light and McSorley's Dark. It's also essential for blarney lovers, and much friendlier to women than it was before the '80s. (The motto here once was "Good ale, raw onions, and no ladies.") Go early to avoid the down-the-block lines on Friday and Saturday night. ⊠ *15 E. 7th St., between 2nd and 3rd Aves., East Village* ☎ *212/473–9148* ⊕ *www.mcsorleysnewyork.com* Ⓜ *6 to Astor Pl.*

Otto's Shrunken Head. Who says N.Y.C. doesn't appeal to all tastes? Should you get a sudden urge to visit a tiki bar while in the East Village—and who doesn't sometimes?—the ultra-popular Otto's is your ticket. You'll find more than just a bamboo bar here: namely fish lamps, a tattooed, punk rock crowd, cute little banquettes, drinking mugs in the form of shrunken heads, beef jerky for sale, and DJs prone to spinning anything from '50s rock to "Soul Gidget." surf music. ⊠ *538 E. 14th St., between Aves. A and B, East Village* ☎ *212/228–2240* ⊕ *www.ottosshrunkenhead.com* Ⓜ *L to 1st Ave.*

PDT. Those who crave their cocktails with a little cloak-and-dagger will flip over PDT (which stands for "Please Don't Tell"). Housed below the unassuming hot-dog joint Crif Dogs, this pseudo-speakeasy can be reached only through a phone booth on the main floor. Patrons with phoned-in reservations are escorted through the phone booth's false back into the building's underbelly, which is decorated with warm

16

wooden beams and tongue-in-cheek taxidermy. ⊠ *113 St. Marks Pl., between 1st Ave. and Ave. A, East Village* ☎ *212/614–0386* ⊕ *www. pdtnyc.com* Ⓜ *6 to Astor Pl.*

Summit Bar. Manhattan's easternmost cocktail bar, Summit Bar serves up high-end sips in a low-key environment. Still, much thought and care is put into the drinks, right down to the herbs that come from the Summit's rooftop garden. The menu aims to please, and splits between "classic" and more ambitious "alchemist" sections, the latter boasting drinks with caraway-infused agave and shiso leaf. There's a snug outdoor patio as well, ideal for sampling the Summit's surprising take on a margarita come summer. ⊠ *133 Ave. C, between 8th and 9th Sts., East Village* ☎ *No phone* ⊕ *www.thesummitbar.net* Ⓜ *L to 1st Ave.*

CABARET AND PIANO BARS

Joe's Pub. Wood paneling, red-velvet walls, and comfy sofas make a lush setting for top-notch performers and the A-list celebrities who love them, or pretend to. Named for the Public Theater's near-mythic impresario Joe Papp, and located inside the Public, Joe's doesn't have a bad seat—but if you want to occupy one, buy tickets beforehand and/or arrive at least half an hour early for the Italian-inspired dinner menu. ⊠ *425 Lafayette St., between E. 4th St. and Astor Pl., East Village* ☎ *212/539–8770* ⊕ *www.joespub.com* Ⓜ *6 to Astor Pl.*

GAY NIGHTLIFE

Beige. Gay men in fashion and advertising predominate at this long-running Tuesday get-together at the B-Bar. An occasional celebrity or two keeps it lively, and with the right weather, the garden doubles or even triples the populace. Dress up, or look so freaking hot that you don't have to. ⊠ *B Bar, 40 E. 4th St., at the Bowery, East Village* ☎ *212/475–2220* Ⓜ *6 to Astor Pl.*

Urge. A bi-level bastion of East Village boy action, Urge has two levels of muscly hipsters, go-go boys, drag acts on Sunday, Bingo Monday, and a contest on Wednesday whose name we can't print here. Best of all, it's cheek by jowl with several other fun East Village gay bars like the new **DTOX**. ⊠ *33 2nd Ave. at 2nd St., East Village* ☎ *212/645–8613* Ⓜ *F to Lower East Side/2nd Ave.*

ROCK CLUBS

Fodor'sChoice ★ **Lit Lounge.** With a rock roster that's included musical forces as diverse as Devendra Banhart and the Hold Steady, Lit is a wonderfully grungy East Village classic. The raucous arty crowd hits not only shows but its charming art gallery Fuse and its theme parties, which cater to fans of specific bands (the White Stripes, Devo, and the Buzzcocks, to name just three). ⊠ *93 2nd Ave., East Village* ☎ *212/777–7987* ⊕ *www. litloungenyc.com* Ⓜ *F to Lower East Side/2nd Ave., 6 to Astor Pl.*

LOWER EAST SIDE

ACOUSTIC AND BLUES VENUES

Living Room. Terre Roche, Connie Acher, and other ace singer-songwriters—some solo, some with their bands—are found at this unpretentiously delightful club. Craving a more intimate experience? Head upstairs to Googie's Lounge, their humbler acoustic space with just a piano. (Or else sashay next door to **Cakeshop,** which has music and boozin' in a shabby-chic setting.) ⊠ *154 Ludlow St., between Stanton and Rivington Sts., Lower East Side* ☎ *212/533–7235* ⊕ *www. livingroomny.com* Ⓜ *F to 2nd Ave.*

BARS

Back Room. The Prohibition-era atmospheric touches here include tin ceilings, chandeliers, velvet wallpaper, mirrored bars, an amply sized fireplace, and a "hidden" outdoor entrance (which you'll find easily enough, though the back-alley walk to the second, indoor entrance puts you in the speakeasy spirit). The music consists of rock CDs rather than a live spinmeister, and the drinks come in old-fashioned teacups or wrapped in paper bags. These, and other prize quirks, attract a slightly older clientele than many of its rowdy "boho" (aka bohemian) neighbors do. ⊠ *102 Norfolk St., between Delancey and Rivington Sts., Lower East Side* ☎ *212/228–5098* Ⓜ *F to Delancey St.; J, M, Z to Essex St.*

The Pink Pony. Maintaining a defiantly boho feel on trendy Ludlow Street, this shabby-chic bar-café draws young writers, filmmakers, and designers who come to escape the cacophony from nearby music venues and make conversation over bottles of cheap wine and cup after cup (after cup) of coffee. ⊠ *176 Ludlow St., between E. Houston and Stanton Sts., Lower East Side* ☎ *212/253–1922* ⊕ *www.pinkponynyc. com* Ⓜ *F to 2nd Ave.*

Sweet and Vicious. The name of this unpretentious butterfly-logo'ed lounge doesn't signify the looks (sweet) and attitude (vicious) of certain downtown pretty things that frequent the bars on this LES stretch. So what makes this bar in particular so sweet? A lovely back garden perfect for rendezvous more private than the sceney bars they might otherwise hit in Soho and NoLITa. ⊠ *5 Spring St., between the Bowery and Elizabeth St., Lower East Side* ☎ *212/224–7915* Ⓜ *6 to Spring St.; J, M to Bowery.*

White Star. Master mixologist Sasha Petraske won kudos for his innovative cocktails at Milk and Honey, but the hassles associated with that bar (reservations, membership, and so on) mean that White Star, its elegantly less-is-more sister bar, is a better choice. Named for the Moroccan lamps that hang above the bar (and front door), the Star features nattily dressed barkeeps, a scintillating drinks menu, and a tiny sunken back room that is one of N.Y.C.'s best sites for a double date. ⊠ *21 Essex St., between Canal and Hester Sts., Lower East Side* ☎ *212/995–5464* Ⓜ *F to East Broadway.*

ROCK CLUBS

Arlene's Grocery. On Monday nights crowds pack into this converted convenience store for Rock and Roll Karaoke, where they live out their rock-star dreams by singing favorite punk anthems onstage with a live band. The other six nights of the week are for local bands, and are accordingly hit-or-miss. ⊠ *95 Stanton St., between Ludlow and Orchard Sts., Lower East Side* ☎ *212/995–1652* ⊕ *www.arlenesgrocery. net* Ⓜ *F to 2nd Ave.*

Fodor's Choice ★ **Bowery Ballroom.** This theater with Art Deco accents is probably the city's top midsize concert venue. Packing in the crowds here is a rite of

16

Indie band Beirut blows away the Bowery Ballroom

passage for musicians on the cusp of stardom, including the Gossip, Manic Street Preachers, and the exuberant Go! Team. Grab one of the tables on the balcony (if you can), stand (and thus get sandwiched) on the main floor, or retreat to the comfortable bar in the basement, which really fills up after each show. ⊠ *6 Delancey St., between the Bowery and Chrystie St., Lower East Side* ☎ *212/533–2111* ⊕ *www.boweryballroom.com* Ⓜ *J, M, Z to Bowery St.*

The Delancey. From the palm-studded rooftop deck (heated in wintertime, hosting barbecues in summertime) down to the basement, where noisy rock and punk bands hold court, the multifaceted Delancey at the foot of the Williamsburg Bridge strikes an invigorating balance between classy and trashy. ⊠ *168 Delancey St., between Clinton and Attorney Sts., Lower East Side* ☎ *212/254–9920* ⊕ *www.thedelancey.com* Ⓜ *F, J, M, Z to Delancey St.–Essex St.*

★ **Mercury Lounge.** You'll have to squeeze past all the sardine-packed hipsters in the front bar to reach the stage, but it's worth it. Not only does this top-quality venue, a "little sister to the Bowery Bar," specialize in cool bands on the indie scene (Holly Golightly, Echo and the Bunnymen, and the Apostle of Hustle, anyone?), but it was where the late great Jeff Buckley used to stop by to do spontaneous solo shows. ⊠ *217 E. Houston St., at Ave. A, Lower East Side* ☎ *212/260–4700* ⊕ *www.mercuryloungenyc.com* Ⓜ *F to 2nd Ave.*

GREENWICH VILLAGE, WEST VILLAGE, THE MEATPACKING DISTRICT, AND CHELSEA

GREENWICH VILLAGE

BARS

Cornelia Street Café. Share a bottle of merlot at a street-side table on this quiet West Village lane. Downstairs you can catch live jazz or a poetry reading, or take in the superb monthly Entertaining Science evenings hosted by the Nobel laureate chemist Roald Hoffmann. ⊠ *29 Cornelia St., between W. 4th and Bleecker Sts., Greenwich Village* ☎ *212/989– 9319* ⊕ *www.corneliastreetcafe.com* Ⓜ *A, B, C, D, E, F, M to W. 4th St./Washington Sq.*

Corner Bistro. Opened in 1961, this neighborhood saloon serves what many think are the best hamburgers in town. Once you actually get a seat, the space feels nice and cozy, but until then, be prepared to drink a beer amid loud and hungry patrons. ⊠ *331 W. 4th St., at 8th Ave., Greenwich Village* ☎ *212/242–9502* Ⓜ *A, C, E to 14th St.; L to 8th Ave.*

Little Branch. The owners of the secretive, hard-to-access lounge Milk & Honey (now closed) created this open-to-everyone cousin, the site of N.Y.'s legendary '80s Milk Bar, with the same simple yet high-quality cocktails. The dim lighting and snug booths make it the ideal spot for you to hide from creditors or share a romantic first kiss in equal measure. ⊠ *20 7th Ave., at Leroy St., Greenwich Village* ☎ *212/929–4360* Ⓜ *1 to Houston St.*

Vol de Nuit. Tucked away from the street, the "Belgian Beer Bar" (as everybody calls it) features a European-style, enclosed outdoor courtyard and a cozy interior, all red light and shadows. NYU grad-student types come for the mammoth selection of beers on tap as well as for the fries, which are served with a Belgian flair, in a paper cone with an array of sauces on the side. ⊠ *148 W. 4th St., at 6th Ave., Greenwich Village* ☎ *212/982–3388* ⊕ *www.voldenuitbar.com* Ⓜ *A, B, C, D, E, F, M to W. 4th St./Washington Sq.*

★ **White Horse Tavern.** According to New York legend, Dylan Thomas drank himself to death in this historic and quintessential West Village tavern founded in 1880. The Horse remains perpetually popular with literary types, but thankfully it's lacking more death-by-alcohol-poisoning cases of late. When the weather's nice, try to snag a seat at one of the sidewalk tables for prime—and, given the neighborhood, we do mean prime—people-watching. ⊠ *567 Hudson St., at W. 11th St., Greenwich Village* ☎ *212/989–3956* Ⓜ *1 to Christopher St./Sheridan Sq.*

CABARET AND PIANO BARS

The Duplex. No matter who's performing, the largely gay audience hoots and hollers in support of the often kitschy performers at this music-scene staple on busy Sheridan Square since 1951. Singers and comedians hold court in the cabaret theater, while those itching to take a shot at open mike head downstairs to the lively piano bar. ⊠ *61 Christopher St., at 7th Ave. S, Greenwich Village* ☎ *212/255–5438* ⊕ *www.theduplex. com* Ⓜ *1 to Christopher St.*

16

GAY NIGHTLIFE

The Cubby Hole. Early in the evening the crowd is mixed at this neighborhood institution, where the DJs, the unpretentious decor, and the inexpensive margaritas are popular. Later on, the women take charge—and how. ⊠ *281 W. 12th St., at W. 4th St., Greenwich Village* ☎ *212/243–9041* ⊕ *www.cubbyholebar.com* Ⓜ *A, C, E to 14th St.; L to 8th Ave.*

Henrietta Hudson. The nightly parties at this laid-back West Village HQ for the Sapphic set attract young professional women, out-of-towners, and longtime regulars. Because the DJ and the pool table quickly create a crowd, though, stake your claim to a spot early, especially on—yup, you guessed it—weekends. ⊠ *438 Hudson St., at Morton St., Greenwich Village* ☎ *212/924–3347* ⊕ *www.henriettahudson.com* Ⓜ *1 to Christopher St./Sheridan Sq.*

JAZZ VENUES

Bitter End. On a fabled street of West Village bohemia, this Greenwich Village standby has served up its share of talent since 1961, with Billy Joel, David Crosby, and Dr. John among the stars who've played here. These days you're more likely to find (much) lesser-known musicians playing blues, rock, funk, and jazz. If you don't like what you hear, there's always the similar **Kenny's Castaways** just down the block—and **(Le) Poisson Rouge** nearby. ⊠ *147 Bleecker St., between Thompson St. and LaGuardia Pl., Greenwich Village* ☎ *212/673–7030* ⊕ *www.bitterend.com* Ⓜ *A, B, C, D, E, F, M to W. 4th St.*

Blue Note. Considered by many (not least its current owners) to be "the jazz capital of the world," the Blue Note was once the stomping ground for such legends as Dizzy Gillespie, and still hosts a varied repertoire from Chris Botti to the Count Basie Orchestra to Boz Scaggs. Expect a steep cover charge except for late shows on weekends, when the music goes from less jazzy to more funky. ⊠ *131 W. 3rd St., near 6th Ave., Greenwich Village* ☎ *212/475–8592* ⊕ *www.bluenotejazz.com* Ⓜ *A, B, C, D, E, F, M to W. 4th St.*

Garage Restaurant & Café. Good news for you budget-minded jazzers: there's no cover *and* no minimum at this Village hot spot, where two jazz groups jam seven nights a week and a fireplace sets the mood upstairs. ⊠ *99 7th Ave. S, between Bleecker and Christopher Sts., Greenwich Village* ☎ *212/645–0600* ⊕ *www.garagerest.com* Ⓜ *1 to Christopher St./Sheridan Sq.*

Knickerbocker Bar and Grill. Jazz acts are on the menu on Friday and Saturday nights at this old-fashioned steak house, a longtime staple of the city's more intimate music scene. ⊠ *33 University Pl., at E. 9th St., Greenwich Village* ☎ *212/228–8490* ⊕ *www.knickerbockerbarandgrill.com* Ⓜ *R to 8th St.*

Terra Blues. A true charmer, this second-story haven for blues lovers is a cozy Greenwich Village club surprisingly short on NYU students (unlike other places in this neighborhood). Everyone from great national acts like Buddy Guy to local R&B'ers graces the stage year-round. ⊠ *149 Bleecker St., between Thompson St. and LaGuardia Pl., Greenwich Village* ☎ *212/777–7776* ⊕ *www.terrablues.com* Ⓜ *A, C, E, B, D, F, M to W. 4th St.; 4, 6 to Bleecker St.*

Village Vanguard. This prototypical jazz club, tucked into a cellar in Greenwich Village since the 1940s, has been the haunt of legends like Thelonious Monk and Barbra Streisand (who recently came back for a one-night-only gig). Today you can hear jams from the jazz-star likes of Bill Charlap and Ravi Coltrane, and on Monday night the sizable resident Vanguard Jazz Orchestra blows its collective heart out. ⊠ *178 7th Ave. S, between W. 11th and Perry Sts., Greenwich Village* ☎ *212/255–4037* ⊕ *www.villagevanguard.com* Ⓜ *1, 2, 3 to 14th St.*

WEST VILLAGE

BARS

The Dove. On a colorful block that evokes the Greenwich Village of yore—cigar store, vegetarian cafés, a bootleg music shop, and not one but two stores specializing in chess—is this wonderful bar whose elegant atmosphere (red-velvet wallpaper, white-wood paneling) is belied by the revelry of the very sexy young customers. ⊠ *228 Thompson St., between W. 3rd and Bleecker Sts., West Village* ☎ *212/254–1435* ⊕ *www.thedoveparlour.com* Ⓜ *E to Spring St.*

Employees Only. The dapper, white coated bartenders—many of them impressively mustachioed—at this Prohibition era–style bar mix delicious, well-thought out cocktails with debonair and aplomb. Sip one in the dimly lit, unpretentious bar area and you'll feel as if you've stepped back in time—if it weren't for the crush of trendy West Village locals and visitors in the know at your back. Look for the green awning that says EO and the neon "Psychic" sign out front. Dinner is served in the restaurant at the back: it's quality, but pricey. ⊠ *510 Hudson St. West Village* ☎ *212/242–3021* ⊕ *www.employeesonlynyc.com* Ⓜ *1 to Christopher St, A, B, C, D, E, F, M to West 4th St.*

Hudson Bar and Books. Along with its sister branches—Beekman Bar and Books on Beekman Place and Lexington Bar and Books on, yep, Lexington—the Hudson reflects a literary bent on its cocktails with names like the Dewey Decimal, the Cervantes Spritzer, and Alphabet Absinthe (topped off with floating letter-shape sugar cubes). Despite that, it's hardly a hushed library where well-read butlers serve you; no—the atmosphere here is more about book decor than serious literature. (It's usually too dim to read or write anyway.) Still, it is seriously gorgeous in a clubby way with wood paneling and leather banquettes. And the cigars and swell cocktail menu stimulate all kinds of conversation, literary or otherwise. ⊠ *636 Hudson St., at Horatio St., West Village* ☎ *212/229–2642* ⊕ *www.barandbooks.cz* Ⓜ *A, C, E to 14th St.; L to 8th Ave.*

ROCK CLUBS

★ **(Le) Poisson Rouge.** Underneath the site of the late, lamented Village Gate jazz emporium is this cutting-edge jewel of a place, whose name means "the Red Fish" and whose parentheses around Le remain a sacred mystery. Blending just the right mix of posh notes (the lush decor, the fine dining) and brave music programming (jazz, classical, electronic, cabaret, rock, folk—even, with the splendiferous Ralph's World, children's

16

music), the Poisson is quite simply an essential N.Y.C. fixture. ✉ *158 Bleecker St., at Thompson St., West Village* ☎ *212/796–0741* ⊕ *www. lepoissonrouge.com* Ⓜ *A, B, C, D, E, F, M to W. 4th St.*

THE MEATPACKING DISTRICT

BARS

675 Bar. How can you not love a spot where the bouncer greets you with a grin instead of a scowl, board games abound, a giant black-lacquered horse stands guard next to the pool table, the drinks get amply poured, and each small room along the subterranean stone corridor is decorated in a different creative way? As an ideal spot for both dates (plenty of dark corners) and raucous merriment (bright, big central space), the 675 scores highest for having less attitude than the rest of this supremely haughty nightlife neighborhood. ✉ *675 Hudson St., between Hudson St. and 9th Ave. (enter on 13th St.), Meatpacking District* ☎ *212/699–2410* ⊕ *www.675bar.com* Ⓜ *A, C, E to 14th St.; L to 8th Ave.*

Hogs & Heifers. This raucous place is all about the saucy barkeeps using megaphones to berate male customers and bait the females to get up on the bar and dance (and add their bras to the collection on the wall). Celebrities of the *Us Weekly* variety still drop in from time to time to get their names in the gossip columns. ✉ *859 Washington St., at W. 13th St., Meatpacking District* ☎ *212/929–0655* ⊕ *www.hogsandheifers.com* Ⓜ *A, C, E to 14th St.; L to 8th Ave.*

Plunge. The Gansvoort Hotel's slick rooftop bar would be worth visiting even without its mouthwatering views, though that helps. The adjectives sleek and glossy could easily be illustrated by Plunge, where the lighting is soft, the furnishings are cool and comfy (at least to a degree), the music isn't too loud, servers of both sexes are sexy, and the ample space—indoor as well as outdoor—make it practically iconic. ✉ *18 9th Ave., at W. 13th St., Meatpacking District* ☎ *212/660–6766* ⊕ *www. hotelgansevoort.com* Ⓜ *A, C, E to 14th St.; L to 8th Ave.*

Spice Market. The posh come here to gorge on Asian street fare served with upscale twists and the equally exotic cocktails. Ginger margaritas, anyone? Or a kumquat *mojito* (when in season)? And if you're looking for tranquillity, the multilevel open space has slowly rotating fans, intricately carved woodwork, and flowing curtains that create a palpable aura of calm. ✉ *403 W. 13th St., at 9th Ave., Meatpacking District* ☎ *212/675–2322* ⊕ *spicemarketnewyork.com* Ⓜ *A, C, E to 14th St.; L to 8th Ave.*

★ **The Standard Hotel Beer Garden, Grill, and Living Room.** Practically the official bar of the High Line park, the Standard is a lush diversion. The media was quick to pick up on the riotous behavior of hotel guests here who displayed themselves to High Line visitors, leaving their shades wide open during salacious activities. But the real story is in the sprawling and already riotous beer garden, grill bar, and very cool indoor Living Room lounge. As for the chic hot spot on the top floor, unofficially called the Boom Boom Room, it's currently the hardest "door" in town ("hardest," that is, to get through), but given the quality of the accessible fun down below, we'll forgive their snobbery. ✉ *848 Washington*

St., at W. 13th St., Meatpacking District ☎ *212/645–4646* ⊕ *www. standardhotels.com* Ⓜ *A, C, E, L to 14th St.*

COMEDY CLUBS

Comix. With big-name comics in its main room and up-and-comers in the smaller Ochi's Lounge, Comix brings comedy to the Meatpacking District (whose pretensions can be pretty comical in themselves). Another plus: it looks a whole lot better than most local lairs of laughter. ⊠ *353 W. 14th St., between 8th and 9th Aves., Meatpacking District* ☎ *212/524–2500* ⊕ *www.comixny.com* Ⓜ *A, C, E to 14th St.*

DANCE CLUBS AND DJ VENUES

Cielo. Relatively mature dance club goers (if the word mature can ever be applied to such a crowd) gravitate to this small but sturdy Meatpacking District "music-head" mecca to toss back cocktails, dig the high-quality sound system, groove to top-flight DJs spinning soulful Latin beats and techno, boogie on the sunken dance floor, and smoke in the no-frills garden outside. On Monday nights are the award-winning Deep Space parties, where resident DJ François K. (as well as guest spinmeisters like Dmitri from Paris) rev up the faithful with everything from dubstep to Stravinsky. ⊠ *18 Little W. 12th St., between 9th Ave. and Washington St., Meatpacking District* ☎ *212/645–5700* ⊕ *www.cieloclub.com* Ⓜ *A, C, E to 14th St.; L to 8th Ave.*

Kiss And Fly. One of New York's most discerning nightlife experts, the dance-music artist Sir Ivan, swears by Kiss And Fly, and it's obvious why: this modest-size dance club has sensational music (pumped as loud as can be, of course), a beautiful interior design (dig all the butterfly motifs), and creative lighting that actually lets you see who you're dancing/speaking/kissing/sipping with. It's pricey, tough to get into, and a bit snooty, but now that you've been duly warned, have a ball. ⊠ *409 W. 13th St., between 9th Ave. and Washington St., Meatpacking District* ☎ *212/255–1933* ⊕ *www.kissandflyclub.com* Ⓜ *A, C, E to 14th St.; L to 8th Ave.*

CHELSEA

BARS

Half King. Writer Sebastian Junger (*The Perfect Storm*) is one of the owners of this would-be literary mecca. We say "would-be" because the ambience can be more pub-like than writerly—but that's fine, since the King draws such a friendly crowd (media types, mostly). We like it best for its frequent readings, gallery exhibits, and Irish-American menu. ⊠ *505 W. 23rd St., between 10th and 11th Aves., Chelsea* ☎ *212/ 462–4300* ⊕ *www.thehalfking.com* Ⓜ *C, E to 23rd St.*

Tillman's. Nothing in Chelsea is quite like this glorious "Old Harlem" lounge, resplendent as it is with fireplace, banquettes, good eats, even better cocktails, inventive decor, jazz and blues sounds on the soundtrack, and tastefully uniformed servers complete with a cigarette girl. ⊠ *165 W. 26th St., between 6th and 7th Aves., Chelsea* ☎ *212/627– 8320* ⊕ *www.tillmansnyc.com* Ⓜ *F, M, 1 to 28th St.*

16

COMEDY CLUBS

★ **Upright Citizens Brigade Theatre**. Raucous sketch comedy, audience-initiated improv, and classic stand-up take turns onstage here at the city's absolute capital for alternative comedy. There are even classes available; the Upright Citizens bill their program as the world's largest improv school, where you can catch indie comic darlings like *SNL*'s Amy Poehler or *Human Giant*'s Rob Huebel. ⊠ *307 W. 26th St., between 8th and 9th Aves., Chelsea* ☎ *212/366–9176* ⊕ *www.uprightcitizens.org* Ⓜ *C, E to 23rd St.*

GAY NIGHTLIFE

Big Apple Ranch. Taking *Brokeback Mountain* style to the dance floor, the Ranch lets you unleash your inner "cowboy dancer" every Saturday night, with half-hour two-step lessons at 8 pm, line dancing at 8:30 pm, and then a down-home country-and-western dance party. Make sure the DJ plays some Hank Williams, just to keep things honest (and remember these immortal words from Hank: "I don't need nobody standing by me in a barfight 'cept for my mama with a broken bottle in her hand"). ⊠ *Dance Manhattan, 39 W. 19th St., 5th fl., between 5th and 6th Aves., Chelsea* ☎ *212/358–5752* ⊕ *www.bigappleranch.com* Ⓜ *F, R, M to 23rd St.; 1 to 18th St.*

Gym Sports Bar. At New York's first gay sports bar, the plentiful flat-screen TVs and cheap Budweisers draw athletic enthusiasts of every stripe, from athlete to armchair. Nobly enough, the bar sponsors—and frequently hosts parties for—a number of local gay sports teams. The only problem: couldn't they have thought up a more savory name for the place? ⊠ *167 8th Ave., at W. 18th St., Chelsea* ☎ *212/337–2439* ⊕ *www.gymsportsbar.com* Ⓜ *A, C, E to 14th St.; L to 8th Ave.*

Splash Bar New York. At this large, perennially crowded Chelsea bar-club, beefy go-go boys vie for attention with equally buff bartenders who, for some reason (can't the management afford uniforms?) don't have on much more than underwear. The daily happy hour, with campy music videos on three huge screens, is a hit. Our only caveat: late-night covers can be high. ⊠ *50 W. 17th St., between 5th and 6th Aves., Chelsea* ☎ *212/691–0073* ⊕ *www.splashbar.com* Ⓜ *6 to Astor Pl.*

UNION SQUARE, GRAMERCY, THE FLATIRON DISTRICT, AND MURRAY HILL

GRAMERCY

BARS

★ **The Ace Hotel**. A hot spot for the digital set, the lobby and adjoining restaurant spaces—the Breslin and the John Dory—have been packed since they've opened at this Pacific Northwest import. If your bearded hipster friend came into some cash, it would look like the lobby here, with reclaimed wood tables, beer signs, and beautiful folks in oversize eyeglasses. ⊠ *20 W. 29th St., between Broadway and 5th Ave. Gramercy* ☎ *212/679–2222* ⊕ *www.acehotel.com* Ⓜ *R to 28th St.*

Flatiron Lounge. Here resident mixologists rely on the freshest (and sometimes most exotic) ingredients available. The cocktail menu changes often, but if you're stumped, tell the bartenders what you like and they'll happily invent a new concoction on the spot. ⊠ *37 W. 19th St., between 5th and 6th Aves., Flatiron* ☎ *212/727–7741.*

★ **Old Town Bar & Restaurant.** The proudly unpretentious bi-level Old Town is redolent of old New York, and why not—it's been around since 1892. Tavern-style grub, mahogany everywhere, and atmosphere, atmosphere, atmosphere make this a fun stop on any pub crawl. Men, don't miss the giant, person-size urinals. ⊠ *45 E. 18th St., between Broadway and Park Ave. S, Gramercy* ☎ *212/529–6732* ⊕ *www.oldtownbar.com* Ⓜ *4, 5, 6, L, N, Q, R to 14th St./Union Sq.*

Rye House. A welcoming bar with slick cocktails and clever takes on comfort food, the Rye House beckons just steps from the chain-store overload of Union Square. From boiled peanuts and fried pickles to their own take on a Sazerac, the space is a welcome respite from the hustle and bustle outside. ⊠ *11 W. 17th St., between Broadway and 5th Ave., Union Square* ☎ *212/255–7260* ⊕ *www.ryehousenyc.com* Ⓜ *4, 5, 6, L, N, Q, R to 14th St./Union Sq.*

ROCK CLUBS

Irving Plaza. This two-story venue is known for its solid rock performances, both indie (DJ Shadow and Sleater-Kinney) and more mainstream (Lenny Kravitz, Blues Traveller)—even if they can get a little pricey. Red walls and chandeliers add a Gothic touch. And if the main floor gets too cramped, seek sanctuary in the form of the chill upstairs bar. ⊠ *17 Irving Pl., at E. 15th St., Gramercy* ☎ *212/777–6800* ⊕ *www. irvingplaza.com* Ⓜ *4, 5, 6, L, N, Q, R to 14th St./Union Sq.*

UNION SQUARE

Pete's Tavern. Allegedly the place where that great transplanted New Yorker O. Henry wrote his sweet tale *The Gift of the Magi* (in the booth up front), Pete's has charm to spare even today, when it's crowded with locals enjoying a beer or a (fantastic) burger. ⊠ *129 E. 18th St., at Irving Pl., Gramercy* ☎ *212/473–7676* ⊕ *www.petestavern.com* Ⓜ *4, 5, 6, L, N, Q, R to 14th St./Union Sq.*

MURRAY HILL

JAZZ VENUES

Jazz Standard. The Standard's sizable underground room draws the top names in the business. As a part of Danny Meyer's southern-food restaurant Blue Smoke, it's one of the few spots where you can get dry-rubbed ribs to go with your bebop. Bring the kids for the Jazz Standard Youth Orchestra concerts every Sunday afternoon. ⊠ *116 E. 27th St., between Park and Lexington Aves., Murray Hill* ☎ *212/576–2232* ⊕ *www.jazzstandard.net* Ⓜ *6 to 28th St.*

ROCK CLUBS

Fodor's Choice ★ **Rodeo Bar.** If the honky-tonk tunes, the bison over the front bar, and the peanut shells littering the floor at this neighborhood institution don't clue you in, the rockin' vibe and friendly service will: this is the go-to spot for good times and free live music every night of the week. The Tex Mex food is good (try the Cowboy kisses: shrimp and jalapeños wrapped in bacon) but the real draw is the music: local bands and touring pros play blues, bluegrass, country, alt-country, rockabilly, and sometimes rock 'n' roll. There's never a cover charge but always a reason

16

to hang out with a margarita or a beer from the quality selection. ⊠ *375 Third Ave. Murray Hill* ☎ *212/683–6500* ⊕ *www.rodeobar.com* Ⓜ *6 to 28th St.*

MIDTOWN

MIDTOWN EAST
BARS

Bar in the Cellar. The bar without a name in the basement of the newly opened Andaz Fifth Avenue may lack a moniker, but it certainly has a pedigree. Alchemy Consulting, a joint venture from Chicago's Violet Hour and New York's Death and Co., designed the cocktails here; look for spins on the Negroni and Manhattan in the sleek subterranean space. The food menu is similarly up-market, with a variety of nebulously Spanish small plates on offer. ⊠ *485 5th Ave., at 41st St., Midtown East* ☎ *212/601–1234* Ⓜ *6 to 42nd St.*

The Cabin Club at the Pine Tree Lodge Bar. Who says that the zaniest places are all below 14th Street? This insane theme bar offers serious competition. Think "summer camp on psychedelics"—we're talking mounted wildlife, rafts, and other outdoorsy-kitsch decor. Don't overlook the very spacious backyard or the racy raccoon picture in the comfy side room—you'll never view those critters the same way again. ⊠ *326 E. 35th St., between 1st and 2nd Aves., Midtown East* ☎ *212/481–5490* Ⓜ *6 to 34th St.*

★ **Campbell Apartment.** Commuting professionals pack into this Grand Central Terminal bar on their way to catch trains home during the evening rush, but don't let the crush of humanity scare you away—you can have a deeply romantic time here in one of Manhattan's more beautiful rooms. The restored space dates to the 1920s, when it was the private office of an executive named John W. Campbell, and as the exquisite decor suggests, old JWC knew how to live. Sample the good life as you knock back a well-built cocktail from an overstuffed chair. Just try to avoid that evening rush. ⊠ *15 Vanderbilt Ave. entrance, Grand Central Station, Midtown East* ☎ *212/953–0409* ⊕ *www.hospitalityholdings. com* Ⓜ *4, 5, 6, 7, S to 42nd St./Grand Central.*

Four Seasons. Maybe it's true that, as some wag once said, "History is made at night." But New York City (and American) history are made at lunchtime, too, here in Philip Johnson's landmark temple of modern design. Come nightfall, watch for politicos and media moguls at The Bar. ⊠ *99 E. 52nd St., between Park and Lexington Aves., Midtown East* ☎ *212/754–9494* ⊕ *www.fourseasonsrestaurant.com* Ⓜ *E, M to Lexington Ave./53rd St.; 6 to 51st St.*

Galway Hooker. The name actually refers to a kind of Irish fishing boat (but then, you knew that already, right?). It's sought out as one of Midtown's most authentic, and best, Irish pubs. Even on a block with a high number of fine drinking establishments, the Hooker stands out thanks to its gorgeous circular bar, intriguing orange lighting, spirited after-work crowd, and bartenders, some of whom might just actually hail from the Emerald Isle. Snag one of their business cards, too—on the back are words of wisdom from the best Irish writers. ⊠ *7 E. 36th*

St., between 5th and Madison Aves., Midtown East ☎ *212/725–2353* ⊕ *www.galwayhookernyc.com* Ⓜ *6 to 34th St.*

King Cole Bar. A justly beloved Maxfield Parrish mural of "Old King Cole" himself, as well as his psychedelic court, adds to the already considerable elegance at this romantic and essential Midtown meeting place. Try a Bloody Mary—this is where the drink was introduced to Americans. ✉ *St. Regis Hotel, 2 E. 55th St., between 5th and Madison Aves., Midtown East* ☎ *212/753–4500* ⊕ *www.starwoodhotels.com* Ⓜ *E, M to 5th Ave./53rd St.*

P. J. Clarke's. Mirrors and polished wood and other old-time flair adorn New York's most famous Irish bar, a redbrick brawler of a joint. Steeped in Hollywood lore—Steve McQueen was once a regular, and scenes from the 1945 movie *Lost Weekend* were shot here—Clarke's draws in the after-work crowd that appreciates drinking beer and eating exceptionally juicy burgers around a sense of history. ✉ *915 3rd Ave., at E. 55th St., Midtown East* ☎ *212/317–1616* ⊕ *www.pjclarkes.com* Ⓜ *4, 5, 6, N, R to 59th St.–Lexington Ave.*

Top of the Tower. There are lounges at higher altitudes, but this one on the 26th floor wins wide acclaim for its atmosphere of subdued elegance and East Side location, within spitting distance of the United Nations. (But no spitting on the diplomats, please—it's not diplomatic.) There's live piano music Wednesday–Sunday nights. ✉ *Beekman Tower Hotel, 3 Mitchell Pl., near 1st Ave. at E. 49th St., Midtown East* ☎ *212/980– 4796* ⊕ *www.thebeekmanhotel.com* Ⓜ *6 to 51st St./Lexington Ave.; E, M to Lexington Ave./53rd St.*

The Volstead. Named for the Volstead Act, which instituted Prohibition back in the '20s, this new subterranean bastion of cool is simply indispensable. In a gorgeous though tasteful setting that features just the right mix of mirrors, chandeliers, polished wood, and velvet wallpaper, a friendly staff and an ace barkeep serve up specialties like jalapeño margaritas and strawberry caipiroskas. ✉ *125 E. 54th St., between Park and Lexington Aves., Midtown East* ☎ *212/583–0411* ⊕ *www. thevolstead.com* Ⓜ *E, M to 53rd St.*

GAY NIGHTLIFE

Evolve Bar and Lounge. Rising from the ashes of a popular gay club on the same site, this glossy, raucous Chelsea-style bar–club gets the Upper East Side rocking, with its sexy-yet-genial staff and its theme nights like Pop-off Thursday, Bulge Friday, and Disco Balls Sunday. ✉ *234 E. 58th St., between 2nd and 3rd Aves., Midtown East* ☎ *212/355–3395* ⊕ *www. evolvebarandloungenyc.com* Ⓜ *4, 5, 6, N, R to 59th St./Lexington Ave.*

The Townhouse. It's the elegant yin to the rowdy yang of **Evolve**, which is just across the block at East 58th Street. Distinguished mature men from the Upper East Side meet younger would-be versions of themselves at this "gentlemen's club," which looks like the home of a blueblood with superb taste. As always the attire is "uptown casual," if not fancier. ✉ *236 E. 58th St., between 2nd and 3rd Aves., Midtown East* ☎ *212/754–4649* ⊕ *www.townhouseny.com* Ⓜ *4, 5, 6, N, R to 59th St.–Lexington Ave.*

16

MIDTOWN WEST
ACOUSTIC AND BLUES VENUES

B. B. King Blues Club & Grill. This lavish Times Square club is vast and shiny and host to a range of musicians, from the Harlem Gospel Choir to George Clinton and the P-Funk All-Stars. It's also where surviving rock legends like Little Richard, Chuck Berry, and, yes, the still-relentlessly-touring owner play as well. (If you happen to meet Mr. King here, give our regards to Lucille, his guitar.) ✉ *237 W. 42nd St., between 7th and 8th Aves., Midtown West* ☏ *212/997–4144* ⊕ *www. bbkingblues.com* Ⓜ *1, 2, 3, 7, A, C, E, N, Q, R, S to 42nd St./Port Authority.*

BARS

Cellar Bar. Underneath the Bryant Park Hotel—and a tiled, arched ceiling—is one of the more spectacular spaces in Midtown. As a DJ with a taste for classic R&B spins the night away, a fashion-industry crowd gets up to dance—and spills its collective drink. ✉ *40 W. 40th St., between 5th and 6th Aves., Midtown West* ☏ *212/642–2260* ⊕ *www. bryantparkhotel.com* Ⓜ *B, D, F, M to 42nd St.; 7 to 5th Ave.*

Hudson Bar. Not quite as popular as it once was, though its rotating DJs can still hold their own, the Hudson Hotel's signature bar features a hand-painted ceiling as well as lights shining up from the glass floor. ✉ *356 W. 58th St., between 8th and 9th Aves., Midtown West* ☏ *212/554–6303* ⊕ *www.hudsonhotel.com* Ⓜ *1, A, B, C, D to 59th St.*

Joe Allen. Everybody's en route either to or from a show at this "old reliable" on the boisterous Restaurant Row, celebrated in the musical version of *All About Eve*. Chances are you'll even spot a Broadway star at the bar or in the dining room. Still, our favorite thing about Joe's is not the fun show crowd but the hilarious "flop wall," adorned with posters from musicals that bombed, sometimes spectacularly. (Check out the ones for *Paradox Lust, Got To Go Disco,* and *Dude,* which was the unfortunate sequel to *Hair.*) ✉ *326 W. 46th St., between 8th and 9th Aves., Midtown West* ☏ *212/581–6464* ⊕ *www.joeallenrestaurant. com* Ⓜ *A, C, E to 42nd St.*

Oak Room. One of the great classic cabaret venues, the Algonquin's Oak Room is formal (jackets are mandatory; ties are the norm) and decorated sumptuously. You might find the hopelessly romantic singer Andrea Marcovicci, among other top-notch performers, crooning here. ✉ *Algonquin Hotel, 59 W. 44th St., between 5th and 6th Aves., Midtown West* ☏ *212/840–6800* Ⓜ *B, D, F, M to 42nd St.; 7 to 5th Ave.*

Russian Vodka Room. Forget **Russian Samovar** across the block—here's where the serious vodka drinking goes down, along with (almost) everything that goes along with serious vodka drinking. The Vodka Room features a glowing, sophisticated front room with nightly piano player (and the superlative Dmitri Kolesnik Jazz Trio on Monday, free of charge), a more sumptuous back room, a generous Attitude Adjustment Hour (that's Russki for "Happy Hour"), and more exotically infused vodkas (horseradish! ginger! pepper!) than you can shake a babushka at. For those who crave variety, a vodka tasting menu is available, as are culinary standards like borscht. ✉ *265 W. 52nd St., between*

Broadway and 8th Ave., Midtown West ☎*212/307–5835* ⊕*www. russianvodkaroom.com* Ⓜ *C, E, 1 to 50th St.*

Salon de Ning. Take a break from 5th Avenue shopping at this glass-lined penthouse bar on the 23rd floor of the über-ritzy Peninsula Hotel. Drinks are pricey, of course, but what isn't in this neighborhood? Plus, the views are inarguably worth it, especially from the rooftop terraces. ✉*Peninsula Hotel, 700 5th Ave., at W. 55th St., Midtown West* ☎*212/956–2888* Ⓜ *E, M to 5th Ave./53rd St.*

'21' Club. A row of lawn jockeys welcomes you to this former speakeasy, celebrated for having pulled in famous writers and movie stars through most of the past century. Privilege and whimsy are mixed together here: the well dressed can enjoy well-prepared American cuisine in the well-appointed Bar Room as well as enjoy well-made drinks next to a roaring fire in the cozy front lounge. ✉*21 W. 52nd St., between 5th and 6th Aves., Midtown West* ☎*212/582–7200* ⊕*www.21club.com* Ⓜ *B, D, F, M to 47–50th Sts./Rockefeller Center.*

COMEDY CLUBS

Caroline's on Broadway. This high-gloss club presents established names as well as comedians on the edge of stardom. Janeane Garofalo, David Alan Grier, Colin Quinn, and Gilbert Gottfried have headlined. ✉*1626 Broadway, between W. 49th and W. 50th Sts., Midtown West* ☎*212/757–4100* ⊕*www.carolines.com* Ⓜ *N, R to 49th St.; 1 to 50th St.*

Chicago City Limits. This crew touts itself as performing in the longest-running improv show in the city. The shows, heavy on audience participation, take place Wednesday through Saturday and seldom fail to whip visitors into what the comics might call a "phun phrenzy." ✉*318 W. 53rd St., between 8th and 9th Aves., Midtown West* ☎*212/888–5233* ⊕*www.chicagocitylimits.com* Ⓜ *C, E to 50th St.*

DANCE CLUBS AND DJ VENUES

Pacha. Maybe you've been to the exclusive Pacha clubs in Buenos Aires, Ibiza, and London. Congratulations. But the jewel in the crown of the Pacha empire may well be here. Assuming you pass muster to enter, you'll find four stories' worth of high-tech fittings (blinding lights, go-go girls, humungous sound), plus celeb DJs, celeb customers, even celeb bathroom attendants. (OK, maybe not that last part.) ✉*618 W. 46th St., between 11th and 12th Aves., Midtown West* ☎*212/209–7500* ⊕*www.pachanyc.com* Ⓜ *C, E to 50th St.*

GAY NIGHTLIFE

Posh. Lest you think that Hell's Kitchen has no fine gay lounges, Posh has walls covered in fine canvases by local artists, trophies over the bar, ample room for kibitzing and dancing, plenty of neon decor, and hours that are "4 pm to 4 am GUARANTEED." Who says nothing is certain anymore in these confusing times? ✉*405 W. 51st St., at 9th Ave., Midtown West* ☎*212/957–2222* ⊕*www.poshbarnyc.com* Ⓜ *C, E to 50th St.*

JAZZ VENUES

Birdland. This place gets its name from bebop saxophone great Charlie "Yardbird" (or just "Bird") Parker, so expect serious musicians such as John Pizzarelli, the Dave Holland Sextet, and Chico O'Farrill's

16

Afro-Cuban Jazz Orchestra (on Sunday night). The dining room serves moderately priced American fare with a Cajun accent. If you sit at the bar, your cover charge includes a drink. ⊠ *315 W. 44th St., between 8th and 9th Aves., Midtown West* ☎ *212/581–3080* ⊕ *www.birdlandjazz. com* Ⓜ *A, C, E to 42nd St./Port Authority.*

Iridium. This cozy, top-drawer club is a sure bet for big-name talent like the David Murray Black Saint Quartet and Michael Wolff. The sight lines are good, and the sound system was designed with the help of Les Paul, the inventor of the solid-body electric guitar, who used to play here every Monday night. The rest of the week sees a mix of artists like Chuck Mangione and the Eddie Daniels Band. ⊠ *1650 Broadway, at W. 51st St., Midtown West* ☎ *212/582–2121* ⊕ *www.iridiumjazzclub. com* Ⓜ *1 to 50th St.; N, R to 49th St.*

UPPER EAST SIDE

BARS

American Trash. You might tell from the name that this isn't exactly your granddad's UES drinking establishment. Bicycle tires, golf clubs, and other castoffs cover the walls and ceiling, ensuring that the 20-year-old Trash, a sanctum of sleaze, merits its descriptive name. Eight plasma TVs, three video games, a defiantly rock-and-roll jukebox, and a pool table keep the neighborhood crowd (as well as stray bikers who hate them) busy. Some nights local bands play classic rock. ⊠ *1471 1st Ave., between E. 76th and E. 77th Sts., Upper East Side* ☎ *212/988–9008* ⊕ *www.americantrashnyc.com* Ⓜ *6 to 77th St.*

Auction House. This Victorian lounge brings a touch of downtown chic to the sometimes suburban-feeling Upper East Side with its candle-lighted tables, high tin ceilings, and velvet couches. Rap and hip-hop fans should look elsewhere (the only tunes coming out of this joint are alternative and rock), and baseball caps and sneakers are strictly forbidden here, as are—at the other end of the spectrum—fur coats. ⊠ *300 E. 89th St., between 1st and 2nd Aves., Upper East Side* ☎ *212/427–4458* Ⓜ *4, 5, 6 to 86th St.*

Bar Pleiades. The cocktail bar companion to Café Boulud, also in the Surrey Hotel, Bar Pleiades is a livelier alternative to the more staid atmosphere at the Carlyle's Bemelmans. The decor is classic to a fault, employing a black-and-white theme that's positively Audrey Hepburn-esque. Drinks rotate seasonally, and there are nibbles from the café kitchen to create a base layer. Though it doesn't have the same drink menu, the rooftop bar is a cozy aerie good for people- (and skyscraper-) watching. ⊠ *20 E. 76th St. , between 5th and Madison Aves., Upper East Side* ☎ *212/905–1477* Ⓜ *4, 5, 6 to 77th St.*

Opia. The motto for this upscale-yet-unpretentious bar–restaurant—"If you like us, tell your friends, and if you don't, tell your enemies!"— isn't necessary, given its manifold charms: a drop-dead-gorgeous design, plenty of space for canoodling and cavorting, a romantic balcony (though 57th Street isn't exactly a scenic beach), plus no cover or minimum for the live jazz on Monday night. Opia is ideal for couples in full-on infatuation or spouses hoping to remember the wine-and-roses days before the kids. ✉ *130 E. 57th St., between Lexington and 3rd Aves., Upper East Side* ☎ *212/688–3939* ⊕ *www.opiarestaurant.com* Ⓜ *N, R, 6, to 59th St.*

CABARET AND PIANO BARS

The Carlyle. The hotel's discreetly sophisticated Café Carlyle hosts such top cabaret and jazz performers as Christine Ebersole, John Pizzarelli, and Steve Tyrell. Stop by on a Monday night and take in Woody Allen, who swings on the clarinet with the Eddy Davis New Orleans Jazz Band. The less fancy-schmancy (though still pricey) **Bemelmans Bar**, with a mural by the author of the *Madeline* books, features a rotating cast of pianist-singers. ✉ *35 E. 76th St., between Madison and Park Aves., Upper East Side* ☎ *212/744–1600* ⊕ *www.thecarlyle.com* Ⓜ *6 to 77th St.*

Feinstein's at the Regency. That the world-touring Michael Feinstein performs a residency here only once a year (usually in winter) and still gets the venue named after him speaks volumes about the charismatic cabaret star. This tastefully appointed space in Loews Regency Hotel presents Broadway babe and *30 Rock* regular Jane Krakowski and other top names in the business—plus, when we're lucky, Tony Danza. ✉ *540 Park Ave., at E. 61st St., Upper East Side* ☎ *212/339–4095* ⊕ *feinsteinsattheregency.com* Ⓜ *4, 5, 6, N, R to 59th St.–Lexington Ave.*

GAY NIGHTLIFE

Brandy's Piano Bar. A singing waitstaff warms up the mixed crowd at this delightful and intimate Upper East Side lounge, getting everyone in the mood to belt out their favorite tunes. In fact, the Brandy's scene is so cheerful that some patrons have used this as a musical Prozac, keeping depression at bay. ✉ *235 E. 84th St., between 2nd and 3rd Aves., Upper East Side* ☎ *212/744–4949* ⊕ *www.brandysnyc.com* Ⓜ *4, 5, 6 to 86th St.*

UPPER WEST SIDE

BARS

Ding Dong Lounge. "Gabba gabba hey," kids—the CBGB's punk ethos is most alive and well not downtown but way up near Columbia University, at this out-and-out rock-and-roll bar. All manner of music posters (along with punk chanteuse Patti Smith's actual birth certificate) adorn the walls; the bathrooms are wallpapered entirely with do-it-yourself concert fliers. An exuberant young student crowd swills the many beers on tap, and candles at every table do little to dispel the near-total darkness. Just wear night-vision goggles—and maybe a crash helmet, given how often the DJs really shake up the joint. ✉ *929 Columbus Ave., between W. 105th and W. 106th Sts., Upper West Side* ☎ *212/663–2600* ⊕ *www.dingdonglounge.com* Ⓜ *B, C to 103rd St.*

The Empire Hotel Rooftop Bar. The only thing better than hanging out in Lincoln Center on a lovely night is hanging out a dozen stories above Lincoln Center. Thanks to the radically refurbished Empire Hotel's sprawling new rooftop bar, you can enjoy that pleasure even on nights that are less than lovely. We're talking thousands of square feet here, most of it outdoor and heated, with three terraces' worth

16

of elegant furnishings, lighting, cabanas, and chaise longues. We're talking an attractive crowd, the single-friendliest hostess in New York City, plus fabulous Friday night parties overseen by the great promoter Adam Sands. And we're talking cameras, because you'll want to bring yours and snap the great vistas and the towering red-neon "EMPIRE HOTEL" right above your head. ⊠ *44 W. 63rd St., between Broadway and Columbus Ave., Upper West Side* ☎ *212/956–3313* Ⓜ *1 to 66th St./Lincoln Center.*

Shark Bar. The fantastic bar at this soul-food (and soul-music) restaurant fills with eye candy every night. As if that's not enough to bite you, rapper LL Cool J ("Ladies Love Cool James" to his mother) has been known to mingle among the usual young black executives, music-industry bigwigs, and professional athletes. ⊠ *307 Amsterdam Ave., between W. 74th and W. 75th Sts., Upper West Side* ☎ *212/874–8500* Ⓜ *1, 2, 3 to 72nd St.*

JAZZ VENUES

Smoke. If you can't wait until sunset to get your riffs on, head uptown to this lounge near Columbia University, where the music starts as early as 6 pm. Performers include some of the top names in the business, including turban-wearing organist Dr. Lonnie Smith and the drummer Jimmy Cobb (who laid down the beat on Miles Davis's seminal album *Kind of Blue*). ⊠ *2751 Broadway, between W. 105th and W. 106th Sts., Upper West Side* ☎ *212/864–6662* ⊕ *www.smokejazz.com* Ⓜ *1 to 103rd St.*

HARLEM

JAZZ VENUES

Lenox Lounge. This impeccably detailed Art Deco lounge opened in the 1930s, and hosts jazz ensembles, blues acts, and jam sessions in the Zebra Room. The restaurant in back serves great food to go with the soulful music. ⊠ *288 Lenox Ave., between W. 124th and W. 125th Sts., Harlem* ☎ *212/427–0253* ⊕ *www.lenoxlounge.com* Ⓜ *2, 3 to 125th St.*

Shopping

WORD OF MOUTH

"At Century 21, I've purchased beautiful ties for $16; a first quality Polo Ralph Lauren wool suit for $200 and all cotton Queen size sheet sets for $30.

— Anthony

Updated
by Christina
Valhouli

New Yorkers love to say that everything here is bigger and better, and the same rule applies to shopping. The Big Apple is one of the best shopping destinations in the world, rivaled perhaps only by London, Paris, and Tokyo.

Its compact size, convenient subway system, and the fact that there's rarely a shortage of cabs (unless it's raining) make it easy to navigate with plenty of bags in tow. But what it really comes down to is the staggering number and variety of stores. If you can't find it in New York, it probably doesn't exist.

But where to start? Nearly every neighborhood in New York offers some kind of shopping experience—but it all depends on what you're looking for and how you like to shop. If you like coolly elegant flagships and money is no object, then head to Midtown, where you'll find international megabrands like Louis Vuitton, Yves Saint Laurent, and Gucci. It's also a short stroll to famed department stores Bergdorf Goodman and Barneys. Nearby Madison Avenue offers couture from Carolina Herrera and Vera Wang, and 5th Avenue is lined with some of the most famous jewelry stores in the world, including Tiffany, Van Cleef & Arpels, and Harry Winston. This is also the neighborhood to indulge in bespoke goods, such as ordering handmade shoes from John Lobb or designing a custom yacht at OC Concept Store. But if you like designer pieces but can't afford them, don't despair—there are plenty of upscale consignment shops dotted around the city where you can find last season's Chanel suit or a vintage YSL jacket.

If your tastes run more toward the funky, then head downtown. The small, independent shops that once lined SoHo have largely been swallowed up by big chains like J.Crew and Uniqlo, but if you want to hit the chains, this is a great place to do it and combine it with high-quality people-watching and superb lunches. If you're craving some of SoHo's artistic spirit, don't discount the street vendors' stalls, which sell handmade jewelry and simple cotton dresses. You never know—you might buy something from a soon-to-be-famous designer.

The East Village and Lower East Side are hotbeds of creativity and quirky coolness, with little boutiques selling everything from retro furniture to industrial-inspired jewelry tucked among bars and tenement apartments. The nearby Meatpacking District is another great shopping destination, where you'll find chic stores like Diane Von Furstenberg and Catherine Malandrino alongside old-school-style meat companies.

And of course there are plenty of only-in–New York stores, such as the cheerfully off-kilter Patricia Field or Trash and Vaudeville. Whether you're looking to buy a case of fine wine, a yacht, or the latest Apple tech toys, you can find it all in New York—and have plenty of fun people-watching while you're hunting. Happy shopping.

LOWER MANHATTAN AND TRIBECA

LOWER MANHATTAN

CAMERAS AND ELECTRONICS

J&R Music World. Just south of City Hall, J&R has emerged as the city's most competitively priced one-stop electronics outlet, with an enormous selection of video equipment, cameras, computers, and stereos. The hands-on staff is super-knowledgeable; many of them are A/V wizards who've worked here since the early 1990s. Home-office supplies are at No. 1, computers at No. 15, small appliances at No. 27. ⊠ *23 Park Row, between Beekman and Ann Sts., Lower Manhattan* ☎ *212/238–9000* Ⓜ *4, 5, 6 to Brooklyn Bridge/City Hall.*

DISCOUNT SHOPPING

Fodor'sChoice ★ **Century 21.** For many New Yorkers this downtown fixture—right across the street from the former World Trade Center site—remains the mother lode of discount shopping. Four floors are crammed with everything from Marc Jacobs shoes and half-price cashmere sweaters to Donna Karan sheets, though you'll have to sift through racks and fight the crowds to find the gems. Best bets for men are shoes and designer briefs; the full floor of designer women's wear can yield some dazzling finds, such as a Calvin Klein leather trench coat for less than $600. Don't miss the children's section, either, for brands like Lucky Jeans and Ed Hardy. ■TIP➜ Since lines for the communal dressing rooms can be prohibitively long, do what the locals do: wear leggings and change discreetly in the aisles. ⊠ *22 Cortlandt St., between Broadway and Church St., Lower Manhattan* ☎ *212/227–9092* Ⓜ *R to Cortlandt St.*

TRIBECA

CHILDREN'S CLOTHING

Aminah et Les Amis. Trendy downtown moms flock to this shop for stylish American and European fashion for newborns up to age 12. Brands stocked include Petite Bateau, Lola et Moi, and Glug Baby. ⊠ *2 World Financial Center, between Vesey and Liberty St., Battery Park* ☎ *212/227–0117* Ⓜ *R to Cortlandt St.*

Tips for Finding Sample Sales

CLOSE UP

Everyone loves a bargain—including a temporary New Yorker. Scoring a good deal is a rite of passage, and the city offers everything from low-cost department stores like Century 21 to hawkers of pseudo-Rolex watches and Kate Spade bags stationed at street corners and in Canal Street stalls. And then there are the sample sales.

If a seasonal sale makes New Yorkers' eyes gleam, a sample sale throws shoppers into a frenzy. With so many designer flagships and corporate headquarters in town, merchandise fallout periodically leads to tremendous deals. Although technically, the term sample sale refers to stock that's a sample design, a show model, a leftover, or is already discounted, the term is now also used for sales of current-season goods. Location adds a bit of an illicit thrill to the event: sales are held in hotels, warehouses, offices, or loft spaces, where items both incredible and unfortunate jam a motley assortment of racks, tables, and bins. Generally, there is a

makeshift communal dressing room, but mirrors are scarce, so veteran sample-sale shoppers come prepared for wriggling in the aisles; some wear tank tops with tights or leggings for modest quick changes. Two rules of thumb: grab first and inspect later, and call in advance to find out what methods of payment are accepted. One of the ultimate experiences is the Barneys Warehouse Sale, held in February and August in Chelsea. Other luscious sales range from the Vera Wang bridal-gown sale (early winter) to Dwell Studio (spring and late fall).

How to find out about these events? The level of publicity and regularity of sales vary. The print and online versions of *New York* magazine are always worth checking for sample sale tip-offs, as are regular bulletins on Racked (⊕ *racked.com*) and Daily Candy (⊕ *www.dailycandy.com*). If you're interested in specific designers, call their shops and inquire—you may get lucky.

17

Bu and the Duck. Vintage-inspired children's clothing, shoes, and toys distinguish this shop. The Italian-made spectator boots might make you wish your own feet were tiny again. ✉ *106 Franklin St., between West Broadway and Church St., TriBeCa* ☎ *212/431–9226* Ⓜ *1 to Franklin St.*

Shoofly. Children's shoes and accessories imported from all over the world are the name of the game here. Choose from Mary Janes, trendy sneakers, and motorcycle boots along with pom-pom hats, brightly patterned socks, eclectic toys, and jewelry. ✉ *42 Hudson St., between Thomas and Duane Sts., TriBeCa* ☎ *212/406–3270* Ⓜ *1 to Franklin St.*

CLOTHING

Issey Miyake. This flagship, designed by Frank Gehry, attracts a nonfashion crowd who come just to gawp at his undulating titanium sculpture, *The Tornado*. Miyake's signature style offers clothes that are sleek and slim-fitting, and made from polyester or ultra-high-tech textiles. This flagship carries the entire runway collection, as well as Pleats Please and Issey Miyake Fete. ✉ *119 Hudson St., at N. Moore St., TriBeCa* ☎ *212/226–0100* Ⓜ *1 to Franklin St.*

Tips for Street Vendor Shopping

If you're looking for original or reproduced artwork, the two areas to visit for street vendors are the stretch of 5th Avenue in front of the Metropolitan Museum of Art (roughly between 81st and 82nd streets) and the SoHo area of West Broadway, between Houston and Broome streets. In both areas you'll find dozens of artists selling original paintings, drawings, and photographs (some lovely, some lurid), as well as photo reproductions of famous New York scenes (the Chrysler building, South Street Seaport). Prices can start as low as $10, but be sure to haggle.

The east–west streets in SoHo are an excellent place to look for handmade crafts: Spring and Prince streets, especially, are jammed with tables full of beaded jewelry, tooled leather belts, cotton sundresses, and homemade hats and purses. These streets are also great places to find deals on art books; several vendors have titles featuring the work of artists from Diego Rivera to Annie Leibovitz, all for about 20% less than you'd pay at a chain.

It's best to know which books you want ahead of time, though; street vendors wrap theirs in clear plastic, and can get testy if you unwrap them but don't wind up buying.

Faux-designer handbags, sunglasses, wallets, and watches are some of the most popular street buys in town—but crackdowns on knockoffs have made them harder to find. The hub used to be Canal Street, roughly between Greene and Lafayette streets, but many vendors there have swept their booths clean of fake Vuitton, Prada, Gucci, and Fendi merchandise. You might have better luck finding a Faux-lex near Herald Square or Madison Square Garden, and good old-fashioned fake handbags are still sold by isolated vendors around such shopping areas as Rockefeller Center and the stretch of lower 5th near Union Square. If you're looking for cheap luggage, skip Canal Street, as the bags there might not last beyond the flight home, and instead pick up a bargain at Marshalls, TJ Maxx, or Loehmann's.

J. Crew Men's Shop at the Liquor Store. It would be easy to walk right past this place and think it's a bar rather than an outpost of J.Crew for men, because it's filled with manly knickknacks like old Jack Kerouac books and vintage photographs. Some of the best finds are accessories: Borsalino hats and Selima Optique sunglasses (both in exclusive designs), and vintage tie bars in addition to limited-edition suits and cashmere sweaters. ⊠ *235 West Broadway, at White St., TriBeCa* ☎ *212/226–5476* Ⓜ *1 to Franklin St.*

SOHO, NOLITA, AND LITTLE ITALY

SOHO

ANTIQUES AND COLLECTIBLES

Jacques Carcanagues, Inc. Crammed with goods from Japan to India, this SoHo gallery offers an eclectic array of objects, from pillboxes to 18th-century Burmese Buddhas and teak tables. ⊠ *21 Greene St., between Grand and Canal Sts., SoHo* ☎ *212/925–8110* Ⓜ *4, 5, 6, R to Canal St.*

BEANTY

★ **Lafco NY/Santa Maria Novella.** A heavy, iron-barred door leads to a hushed, scented inner sanctum of beauty products. This location is the official retailer of the 600-year-old Santa Maria Novella products from Italy, which include intriguingly archaic colognes, creams, and soaps such as Tooth Cleansing Water and pomegranate soap. Everything is packaged in bottles and jars with antique-style apothecary labels. ⊠ *285 Lafayette St., between E. Houston and Prince Sts., SoHo* ☎ *212/925–0001* Ⓜ *N, R to Prince St.*

Korres. This all-natural, Greece-based company has a cult following for its line of all-natural herb- and flower-based skin treatments. Best sellers include quince body butter, wild rose moisturizer, and pomegranate cleansing wipes. ⊠ *110 Wooster St., between Prince and Spring Sts., SoHo* ☎ *212/219–0683* Ⓜ *N, R to Prince St.*

BOOKS AND STATIONERY

Kate's Paperie. If you're a fan of good old-fashioned paper and ink, it's impossible not to feel inspired here, among the stacks of brightly colored stationery and note cards. Kate's also rustles with fabulous wrapping papers, ribbons, blank books, writing implements of all kinds, and gift items. ⊠ *72 Spring St., between Crosby and Lafayette Sts., SoHo* ☎ *212/941–9816* Ⓜ *6 to Spring St.*

★ **McNally Jackson.** This cozy, independent bookstore manages to be comprehensive without overwhelming visitors. Check the tables up front for hot-off-the-press novels, nonfiction, and manifestos. There is a newly expanded literature and architecture section, along with foreign-language books. The staff is clearly literary minded, so ask for recommendations if you're browsing. Literature extends beyond the packed shelves here—just grab a coffee from what owner Sarah McNally calls the "booksiest bookstore café" to see for yourself—even the light fixtures are made from books. ⊠ *52 Prince St., between Lafayette and Mulberry Sts., SoHo* ☎ *212/274–1160* Ⓜ *R to Prince St.*

Scholastic Store. Kids and the young at heart will be delighted by the whimsical design here, including an 11-foot orange dinosaur, a life-size Magic School Bus, and a massive Harry Potter. In addition to the thousands of books, kids can amuse themselves with games, toys, DVDs, computers, and arts-and-crafts workshops. It is so kid-friendly that parents will find a separate entrance just for strollers (at 130 Mercer St.). ⊠ *557 Broadway, at Prince St., SoHo* ☎ *212/343–6166* Ⓜ *R to Prince St.*

CAMERAS AND ELECTRONICS

Apple Store. Located in a former SoHo post office, this sleek space sells everything Apple related. The Genius Bar can help with any tech problems, and there's also a small area for those doing business as well as a space dedicated just for iPods. Climb the glass staircase for the children's section and accessories like printers. ■TIP➔ In-store events

17

SOHO

Somehow, everything looks a bit more beautiful here. Maybe it's because of the way sunlight filters down the cast-iron façades, glinting off the shop windows. Maybe it's because the uneven cobblestone streets prompt you to slow down, giving you time to notice details.

Jaded locals call this neighborhood a touristy outdoor mall. True, you'll see plenty of familiar company names, and several common, less expensive chains, like Banana Republic and Sephora, have made land grabs on Broadway. There's also a certain amount of luxury one-upmanship, as stores like Prada, Chanel, and Louis Vuitton have planted themselves here for downtown cred. But you can still hit a few clothing and housewares boutiques you won't find elsewhere in this country. The hottest shopping area runs west from Broadway over to 6th Avenue, between West Houston and Grand streets. Don't overlook a couple of streets east of Broadway: Crosby and Lafayette each have a handful of intriguing shops.
—by Jennifer Paull

BEST TIME TO GO

Wednesday through Friday afternoons, when all the stores are open and the people-watching is prime but the streets aren't hideously crowded. On weekends, Broadway and Prince Street can feel like a cattle drive.

BEST SOUVENIR FOR YOUR IN-LAWS

If they're caffeine fiends, consider the house-blend coffees and teas at **Dean & Deluca** (⊠ *560 Broadway, at Prince St.*), which you can pair with sophisticated snacks in a D&D tote or metal lunch box.

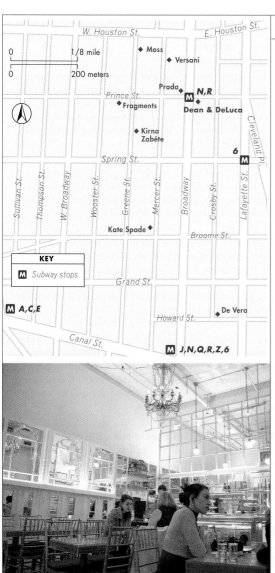

0   1/8 mile
0   200 meters

KEY

M   Subway stops

M   A,C,E

M   J,N,Q,R,Z,6

BEST FOR

WHAT TO WEAR

Prada: the high-concept, Rem Koolhaas–designed store steals the spotlight from the clothes.

Kirna Zabête: uncommon, sought-after women's clothing in a cheerful, unpretentious space.

Kate Spade: the mother lode for clever handbags, plus retro-ish shoes and a few baubles.

HOUSEWARES

Moss: exquisite, innovative design for everything from wineglasses to bathtubs.

De Vera: eclectic selection of antiques and new objets d'art, from Murano glass to Japanese lacquer.

ACCESSORIES

Fragments: scoop up innovative jewelry from emerging or established designers.

Versani: if you believe that bigger and bolder is better, you'll love the jewelry here.

17

REFUELING

For something on the fly, drop by **Balthazar Bakery** (✉ 80 Spring St., between Broadway and Crosby St. ☎ 212/965–1785) for a scone, canelé, or sticky bun with a potent cup of coffee. If you'd rather have a seat, make your way to the tearoom hidden in the back of MarieBelle for a cup of their excellent hot chocolate.

include hour-long tutorials on topics like getting to know your iPhone and navigating new Mac software. ⊠ *103 Prince St., at Greene St., SoHo* ☎ *212/226–3126* Ⓜ *R to Prince St.*

CHILDREN'S CLOTHING

Bundle. This SoHo boutique goes above and beyond selling fashionable onesies by offering a concierge service. If you can't make it to the store to choose a gift, just email them and they'll reply with suggestions. Visit and choose adorable clothes from brands including Kissy Kissy, Baby CZ, and Tea. ⊠ *128 Thompson St., between Prince and Houston Sts., SoHo* ☎ *212/982–9465* Ⓜ *C, E to Spring St.*

Crew Cuts. If you don't like to dress your child in clothes that are too cute or painfully trendy, head to Crew Cuts. Offering pint-size versions of the preppy classic clothes that J.Crew is famous for, this shop is stocked with cords, cashmere sweaters, and wool blazers for the junior set. ⊠ *99 Prince St., between Greene and Mercer Sts., SoHo* ☎ *212/966–2739* Ⓜ *C, E to Spring St.*

Giggle. This high-end baby store is often crammed with stroller gridlock, but it stocks nearly everything a stylish parent (and baby) could ever need. The Giggles flagship carries all the gear and accessories to build a chic nursery, including Dwell bedding, plush toys, and funky kids' clothing. Even the basic gear, such like strollers and high chairs, are sold. The staff is often extra helpful and attentive. ⊠ *120 Wooster St., between Spring and Prince Sts., SoHo* ☎ *212/334–5817* Ⓜ *N, R to Prince St.*

Les Petits Chapelais. Designed and made in France, these kids' clothes (from newborn up to age 12) are cute and stylish but also practical. Corduroy outfits have details like embroidered flowers and contrasting cuffs, and soft, fleecy jackets are reversible. There's also a line of sailor-inspired clothes. ⊠ *86 Thompson St., between Spring and Prince Sts., SoHo* ☎ *212/625–1023* Ⓜ *C, E to Spring St.*

CLOTHING

A Bathing Ape. Known simply as BAPE to devotees, this exclusive label has a cult following in its native Tokyo. At first it may be hard to see what the fuss is about. A small selection of camouflage gear and limited-edition T-shirts is placed throughout the minimalist space; the real scene stealers are the flashy retro-style sneakers in neon colors. ⊠ *91 Greene St., between Prince and Spring Sts., SoHo* ☎ *212/925–0222* Ⓜ *R to Prince St.*

Agent Provocateur. If Victoria's Secret is too tame for you, try this British lingerie shop, which has a naughty twist. Showpieces include boned corsets, lace sets with contrast-color trim, bottoms tied with satin ribbons, and a few fetish-type leather ensembles. A great selection of stockings is complemented by the garter belts to secure them. ⊠ *133 Mercer St., between Prince and Spring Sts., SoHo* ☎ *212/965–0229* Ⓜ *R to Prince St.*

Anna Sui. The violet-and-black salon, with its Victorian rock-chick vibe, is the ideal setting for Sui's bohemian and rocker-influenced designs and colorful beauty products. ⊠ *113 Greene St., between Prince and Spring Sts., SoHo* ☎ *212/941–8406* Ⓜ *R to Prince St.*

A.P.C. This hip French boutique sells deceptively simple clothes in an equally understated setting. Watch your step on the uneven wooden floorboards while choosing narrow gabardine and corduroy suits or dark denim jeans and jackets. For women, best bets include striped sweaters and skinny jeans. ✉ *131 Mercer St., between Prince and Spring Sts., SoHo* ☎ *212/966–9685* Ⓜ *6 to Spring St.; R to Prince St.*

Betsey Johnson. The SoHo store departs from the traditional (if such a word can be applied) hot-pink interior; instead, its walls are white-washed with painted roses, and there's a bordello-red lounge area in back. Most of her dresses, coats, and accessories have slightly kooky patterns; the calmest items are the little black dresses. This is not the place for natural fibers—it's ruled by rayon, stretch, and the occasional faux fur. ✉ *138 Wooster St., between Prince and W. Houston Sts., SoHo* ☎ *212/995–5048* Ⓜ *R to Prince St.*

Catherine Malandrino. Celebs like Halle Berry love this French-born designer for her sexy-without-trying-too-hard looks. Shop for silk V-neck gowns or one-shouldered ruched wool dresses. ✉ *468 Broome St., SoHo* ☎ *212/925–6765* Ⓜ *C, E to Spring St.*

Christopher Fischer. Featherweight cashmere sweaters, wraps, and throws in every hue from Easter-egg pastels to rich jewel tones have made Fischer the darling of the preppy set. His shop also carries leather accessories and such home wares as throw pillows and baby clothes. ✉ *80 Wooster St., between Spring and Broome Sts., SoHo* ☎ *212/965–9009* Ⓜ *R, W to Prince St.*

17

Comptoir des Cotonniers. The "cotton counter" angles for multigenerational shopping, lining up stylish, comfortable basics for babies, twentysomethings, ladies of a certain age, and everyone in between. There's a subtle Parisian vibe to the understated tunics, dresses, and separates; colors tend to be earthy. The brand's first U.S. branch has a nature-friendly minimalist look, with pale-wood floors and lots of natural light. ✉ *155 Spring St., at West Broadway, SoHo* ☎ *212/274–0830* Ⓜ *C, E to Spring St.*

Costume National. Everything about this boutique is sexy and minimalist, with an edge. The clothes—and lighting—are dark. Shoppers will find sharply tailored wool pants for men and silky tops for women in muted shades of black, gray, and charcoal, along with motorcycle boots and leather gloves. ✉ *160 Mercer St., between Prince and W. Houston Sts., SoHo* ☎ *212/431–1530* Ⓜ *C, E to Spring St.*

Emporio Armani. At this middle child of the Armani trio, the clothes are dressy without quite being formal, and are frequently offered in cream, muted blues, and ever-cool shades of taupe. ✉ *410 West Broadway, at Spring St., SoHo* ☎ *646/613–8099* Ⓜ *C, E to Spring St.*

Intermix. This boutique is stocked with a healthy mid- to high-range lineup of established and emerging designers—think Chloé, Stella McCartney, and La Rok. You'll find everything from denim to silk frocks, along with stylish outerwear. ✉ *98 Prince St., between Greene and Mercer Sts., SoHo* ☎ *212/966–5303* Ⓜ *R to Prince St.*

Isabel Marant. The cool, slouchy clothes this Parisian designer is known for have made their mark in the U.S. market, as she recently opened her first store here. The tailored jackets, shorts, and flirty dresses are eclectic and sophisticated, with their textured, deeply hued fabrics. ⊠ *469 Broome St., at Greene St., SoHo* 🕾 *212/219–2284* Ⓜ *R to Prince St.*

Kiki de Montparnasse. Named for Man Ray's mistress and muse from the 1940s, this upscale lingerie store serves up decadent styles in a seductive but artistic setting. Shoppers will find exquisitely made corsets and bra and underwear sets, but a large portion of the store is used as a rotating art gallery for erotic art. ⊠ *79 Greene St., at Spring St., SoHo* 🕾 *212/965–8150* Ⓜ *R to Prince St.*

★ **Kirna Zabête.** A heavy-hitting lineup of prestigious designers—Balenciaga, Alexander Wang, Lanvin, Proenza Schouler—is managed with an exceptionally cheerful flair. Step downstairs for dog apparel, coffee-table books, and hip infant gear from Kit and Lili. ⊠ *96 Greene St., between Spring and Prince Sts., SoHo* 🕾 *212/941–9656* Ⓜ *R to Prince St.*

Marc Jacobs. The West Village is steadily being infiltrated with boutiques carrying the more casual lines of the Jacobs juggernaut. The saturation zone teems with tongue-in-cheek tees, downplayed duds in plaids and stripes, and the eternally popular shoes and bags. This location, housed in a former garage, is filled with ladylike designs made with luxurious fabrics: silk, cashmere, wool bouclé, and tweeds ranging from the demure to the flamboyant. The details, though—oversize buttons, circular patch pockets, and military-style grommet belts—add a sartorial wink. ⊠ *163 Mercer St., between W. Houston and Prince Sts., SoHo* 🕾 *212/343–1490* Ⓜ *R to Prince St.*

Marni. If you're a fan of the boho chic look, stock up on Consuelo Castiglioni's bright-colored, happy clothes here. Silk dresses are printed in bold fabrics, and trousers are sharply tailored. Jackets and accessories are also eye-popping. ⊠ *161 Mercer St., between W. Houston and Prince Sts., SoHo* 🕾 *212/343–3912* Ⓜ *R to Prince St.*

Miu Miu. Prada front woman Miuccia Prada established a secondary line (bearing her childhood nickname, Miu Miu) to showcase her more experimental ideas. Look for Prada-esque styles in more daring colors and cuts, such as high-waist skirts with scalloped edges, Peter Pan–collar dresses in trippy patterns, and patent-leather pumps. ⊠ *100 Prince St., between Mercer and Greene Sts., SoHo* 🕾 *212/334–5156* Ⓜ *R to Prince St.*

Moncler. Many New York women swear by Moncler coats to keep them warm but still looking stylish throughout the brutal winters. This store is the Italian brand's first foray into New York, and is the largest Moncler store in the world. The knee-length puffer is a firm favorite, but there are also shorter ski jackets and accessories, along with choices designed by Thom Browne and Pharrel Williams. ⊠ *90 Prince St., between Mercer St. and Broadway, SoHo* 🕾 *646/350–3620* Ⓜ *R to Prince St.*

Opening Ceremony. Just like Colette in Paris, Opening Ceremony bills itself as a concept store, which means you never know what you will find. The owners are constantly globetrotting to soak up the style and designers in a foreign country, and bring back the best clothing, products, and vintage items to showcase in their store. Hong Kong, Japan, Brazil, and the United Kingdom have all been represented. There's also a gallery space here. ⊠ *35 Howard St., between Broadway and Lafayette St., SoHo* ☎ *212/219–2688* Ⓜ *N, R to Canal St.*

Paul Smith. Fans love Paul Smith for his classic-with-a-twist clothes, and his 5,000-square-foot flagship is a temple to his design ethos and inspirations. Victorian mahogany cases complement the dandyish British styles they hold. Embroidered vests; brightly striped socks, scarves, and shirts; and tongue-in-cheek cuff links leaven the classic, double-back-vent suits for men. Women head for the tailored suits and separates, classic outerwear, and dresses. Plus, you'll find furniture and a selection of photography books and ephemera. ⊠ *142 Greene St., between Prince and W. Houston Sts., SoHo* ☎ *646/613–3060* Ⓜ *R to Prince St.*

Philosophy di Alberta Ferretti. The designer's eye for delicate detailing and soft, feminine design is evident in the perforated hemlines, embroidered stitching, and sprinkling of beads across gauzy fabrics and knits. ⊠ *452 West Broadway, between W. Houston and Prince Sts., SoHo* ☎ *212/460–5500* Ⓜ *F, M to Broadway–Lafayette St.*

Prada. This ultramodern space, designed by Rem Koolhaas, incorporates so many technological innovations that it was written up in *Popular Science.* The dressing-room gadgets alone include liquid crystal displays, changeable lighting, and scanners that link you to the store's database. ⊠ *575 Broadway, at Prince St., SoHo* ☎ *212/334–8888* Ⓜ *R to Prince St.*

R by 45rpm. Shopping here is a Zen-like experience, thanks to a stone pathway, limestone dressing rooms, and denim dangling from wooden trees. Although it's pricey, fans love the label for its attention to detail, like hand-dyed denim that has been woven on antique looms. The T-shirts are particularly funky. ⊠ *169 Mercer St., between W. Houston and Prince Sts., SoHo* ☎ *917/237–0045* Ⓜ *R to Prince St.*

Reiss. Think of Reiss as the Banana Republic of Britain—a go-to place for casual-but-tailored clothes at a relatively gentle price. Standouts for women include cowl-neck sweater dresses and A-line skirts. Men's wool combat trousers are complemented by shrunken blazers, military-inspired peacoats, and trim leather jackets. ⊠ *387 West Broadway, between Spring and Broome Sts., SoHo* ☎ *212/925–5707* Ⓜ *R, W to Prince St.*

Sean. Not to be confused with Sean John, this French-owned shop carries low-key, well-priced, and comfortable menswear imported from Europe. Wool and cotton painter's coats are best sellers, along with corduroy pants and a respectable collection of suits and dress shirts. ⊠ *199 Prince St., between Sullivan and MacDougal Sts., SoHo* ☎ *212/598–5980* Ⓜ *R, W to Prince St.*

Seize sur Vingt. In bringing a contemporary sensibility to custom tailoring, this store realized an ideal fusion. Brighten a suit or cotton moleskin flat-front pants with a checked or striped shirt; all can be made to order. Women are also the beneficiaries of the store's crisp button-downs and

17

single-pleat trousers. ⊠ *78 Greene St., between Spring and Broome Sts., SoHo* ☎ *212/625–1620* Ⓜ *R, W to Prince St.*

7 for All Mankind. If Brooks Brothers is the opposite of your clothing personality, head to this hip boutique that specializes in made-to-measure clothing for men and women. Create a button down shirt or a suit from hundreds of fabric options. ⊠ *348 West Broadway, between Grand and Broome Sts., SoHo* ☎ *212/226–8615* Ⓜ *1, 2 to Canal St.*

Seven New York. This massive store is a temple to all things denim and in every wash and cut. Want them straight, skinny, boot cut, or pleated? No problem. Not content with dressing just customers' lower halves, 7 for All Mankind also sells trendy tops, sweaters, and jackets to complete the look. There are also nondenim dresses and trousers. ⊠ *110 Mercer St., between Prince and Spring Sts., SoHo* ☎ *646/654–0156* Ⓜ *N, R to Prince St.*

Topshop. Americans no longer need to cross the pond to scoop up cheap-chic fashions from British cult favorite Topshop, thanks to the opening of its first stateside boutique. It can be a madhouse, and items sell quickly, but it's a great place to purchase on-trend clothes. Slinky dresses are around $130, and jeans and jumpsuits are about $90. Coats and shoes are also standouts. Male stylistas can browse through the ground-level Topman. ⊠ *480 Broadway, at Broome St., SoHo* ☎ *212/966–9555* Ⓜ *6 to Spring St.; R to Prince St.*

★ **UNIQLO.** The SoHo location is the brand's global flagship, and shoppers will find items here they can't find anywhere else. Seasonal staples like cashmere sweaters and tees in a rainbow of colors are stacked up to the ceiling. The tri-level space bursts with affordable, well-tailored basics. Cashmere crew- and V-necks (most under $100), slim-fit denims, and casual coats share space with edgier tees designed by Japanese graphic artists. Most of the clothing has been tweaked or made specifically for the American market. ■TIP➔ Weekday mornings are the best time to avoid long lines for the dressing rooms. ⊠ *546 Broadway, between Prince and Spring Sts., SoHo* ☎ *917/237–8800* Ⓜ *R to Prince St.*

Vera Wang. Not content designing just wedding dresses, Wang is also a star at evening wear and casual-but-chic daywear. Her entire ready-to-wear collection is showcased here in this gleaming, all-white store. Choose from clothes ranging from sexy one-shouldered satin gowns and cashmere sweaters to wool pencil skirts. ⊠ *158 Mercer St., between Prince and W. Houston Sts., SoHo* ☎ *212/382–2184* Ⓜ *N, R to Prince St..*

Vivienne Tam. Tam is known for her playful "China chic" take on familiar Asian images. Cold-weather creations in jewel-color silk are embroidered; the warm-weather clothes are floaty and romantic. ⊠ *40 Mercer St., at Grand St., SoHo* ☎ *212/966–2398* Ⓜ *R to Prince St.*

What Goes Around Comes Around. Professional stylists flock here to dig up vintage items like Levi's, Azzedine Alaia dresses, and one-of-a-kind rock-concert T-shirts. WGACA also sells its own line of vintage-inspired clothing. If the idea of forking over $100 for an Alice Cooper number pains you, just remember: unlike the copies everyone else is wearing, you'll be sporting the real deal. ⊠ *351 West Broadway, between Grand and Broome Sts., SoHo* ☎ *212/343–1225* Ⓜ *J, M, N, Q, R, Z, 6 to Canal St.*

DISCOUNT SHOPPING

★ **Pearl River Mart.** Whether you're looking for a decorative birdcage or a massive bag of jasmine rice, this mega–department store has everything Asian under one roof—at bargain prices. Browse through housewares like bamboo rice steamers and ceramic tea sets, or decorate your apartment with paper lanterns and bamboo plants. On the main floor, under a ceiling festooned with dragon kites and rice-paper parasols, you can buy kimono-style robes, pajamas, and embroidered satin slippers for the whole family. There's also a dry-goods section, where you can load up on packages of ginger candy, jasmine tea, and cellophane noodles. ⊠ *477 Broadway, between Broome and Grand Sts., SoHo* ☎ *212/431–4770* Ⓜ *N, R, Q to Canal St.*

FOOD AND TREATS

Harney & Sons. Fancy a cuppa? Harney & Sons is famous for producing more than 250 varieties of loose tea, and recently opened its first retail location and tea salon in SoHo. The design is sleek and dramatic, with a 24-foot-long tasting bar and floor-to-ceiling shelves stocked with tea. Shoppers will find classic brews like English Breakfast and Oolong, along with the company's own blends. And no cup of tea would be complete without a scone or two, available at the tea salon. ⊠ *433 Broome St., between Broadway and Crosby St., SoHo* ☎ *212/933–4853* Ⓜ *4, 6 to Spring St.*

Jacques Torres Chocolate Haven. Visit the café and shop here and you'll literally be surrounded by chocolate. The glass-walled downtown space is in the heart of Torres's chocolate factory, so you can watch the goodies being made while you sip a richly spiced cocoa. ■TIP➜ Signature taste: the "wicked" chocolate, laced with cinnamon and chili pepper. ⊠ *350 Hudson St., at King St., SoHo* ☎ *212/414–2462* Ⓜ *1 to Houston St.*

Kee's Chocolates. Owner Kee Ling Tong whips up delicious truffles and macaroons with unusual, Asian-inspired flavors. Try the ginger peach and rosewater lychee macaroons, or truffles flavored with lemongrass mint and tamarind. ⊠ *80 Thompson St., between Spring and Broome Sts., SoHo* ☎ *212/334-3284* Ⓜ *A, C to Spring St.*

MarieBelle. The handmade chocolates here are nothing less than works of art. Square truffles and bonbons—which come in such flavors as Earl Grey tea, cappuccino, passion fruit, and saffron—are painted with edible dyes (cocoa butter dyed with natural coloring) so each resembles a miniature painting. Or relax in the Cacao Bar and Tea Salon while sipping an Aztec hot chocolate. ⊠ *484 Broome St., between West Broadway and Wooster St., SoHo* ☎ *212/925–6999* Ⓜ *R, W to Prince St.*

Vosges Haut Chocolat. This chandeliered salon lined with apothecary bookshelves takes a global approach to chocolate. Many of the creations are travel inspired: the Budapest bonbons combine dark chocolate and Hungarian paprika, and the Black Pearls contain wasabi, but the most unexpected treat might be the chocolate bacon bars. ⊠ *132 Spring St., between Greene and Wooster Sts., SoHo* ☎ *212/625–2929* Ⓜ *R, W to Prince St.*

17

HOME DECOR

Armani Casa. In keeping with the Armani aesthetic, the minimalist furniture and home wares have a subdued color scheme (gold, grays, cream, and black). Big-ticket items include luxuriously upholstered sofas and sleek coffee tables. The desk accessories and throw pillows are equally understated. ⊠ *97 Greene St., between Prince and Spring Sts., SoHo* ☎ *212/334–1271* Ⓜ *R to Prince St.*

Design Within Reach. This sprawling SoHo store is the place to buy midcentury modern classics like Arne Jacobsen and Eames molded chairs and round Knoll pedestal tables. Newer pieces designed in-house include a chunky wood harvest table. ⊠ *110 Greene St., between Prince and Spring Sts., SoHo* ☎ *212/475–0001* Ⓜ *F, M to Broadway–Lafayette St.*

de Vera. Owner Federico de Vera crisscrosses the globe searching for unique decorative products, so shoppers will never know what they might find here. Venetian glass vases, Thai Buddhas, and antique rose-cut diamond rings are typical finds. ⊠ *1 Crosby St., at Howard St., SoHo* ☎ *212/625–0838* Ⓜ *N, Q, R, 6 to Canal St.*

Kiosk. Is it a gallery or a boutique? Duck under the neon arrow sign, head up the stairway, and you'll come upon this novelty shop–cum–art installation. The owners travel the globe in search of locally unique, interestingly designed or packaged items, then sell their gleanings at this outpost. A new destination is highlighted every few months. You might find pipe tobacco from Massachusetts or a sled from Sweden. ⊠ *95 Spring St., 2nd fl., at Broadway, SoHo* ☎ *212/226–8601* Ⓜ *R to Prince St.*

Moss. All of the products at this design store are displayed as if they are in a museum—and some of them are. Owner Murray Moss showcases cutting-edge designs from Tord Boontje, Ted Muehling, and Philippe Starck, along with limited-edition studio works from Dutch designers Studio Job and Maarten Baas. ⊠ *150 Greene St., between W. Houston and Prince Sts., SoHo* ☎ *212/204–7100* Ⓜ *R to Prince St.*

☺ **Pylones.** It's hard to beat Pylones for crazily cheerful products. Utilitarian products like toasters and thermoses have been given makeovers of stripes or flowers, hairbrushes have pictures of frogs or ladybugs on their backs, and pepper mills are turned into pirates. ■TIP➜ There are plenty of fun gifts for less than $20, such as old-fashioned robot toys and candy-color boxes. ⊠ *69 Spring St., between Crosby and Lafayette Sts., SoHo* ☎ *212/431–3244* Ⓜ *6 to Spring St.*

Room & Board. Fans of streamlined, midcentury modern furniture will be in heaven here. This location, one of only a handful in the country, is stocked with sleek sofas, beds, and other pieces of furniture that look like they could have been designed by the Eames Brothers. Instead, it is all new and comes with a relatively affordable price tag. Design afficionados can also choose from designer classics like seating cubes from Frank Gehry and Eames molded plywood chairs. ⊠ *105 Wooster St., between Spring and Prince Sts., SoHo* ☎ *212/334–4343* Ⓜ *N, R to Prince St.*

JEWELRY AND ACCESSORIES

Alexis Bittar. Bittar began selling his first jewelry line, made from Depression-era glass, on a corner in SoHo. Now the Brooklyn-born designer counts A-list celebs and fashion editors among his fans. He makes clean-line, big-statement jewelry from vermeil, colored Lucite, pearls, and vintage glass. The stores mirror this aesthetic with a mix of old and new, like antiqued-white Victorian-era lion's-claw tables and Plexiglas walls. ⊠ *465 Broome St., between Mercer and Greene Sts., SoHo* ☎ *212/625–8340* Ⓜ *R to Prince St.*

★ **Fragments.** This spot glitters with pieces by emerging designers, many of them local, as well as established ones. Most use semiprecious stones— you could try on turquoise-bead shoulder-duster earrings, an oversize opal ring, or a tourmaline pendant—but a few bust out the bling. ⊠ *116 Prince St., between Greene and Wooster Sts., SoHo* ☎ *212/334–9588* Ⓜ *R to Prince St.*

Robert Lee Morris. If you buy into the mantra that bigger is better, make a stop here. Morris designs big, chunky jewelry that is anything but understated. Gold and silver cuffs have a serious weight to them, and necklaces and earrings have dangling hammered disks for a "wind chime" effect. Some pieces incorporate diamonds; others have semiprecious stones like turquoise or citrine. ⊠ *400 West Broadway, between Broome and Spring Sts., SoHo* ☎ *212/431–9405* Ⓜ *C, E to Spring St.*

Stuart Moore. Everything about this boutique is minimalist, from the architecture to the jewelry. Most of the designs (from Heinrich + Denzel to Beatrice Mueller) have a streamlined, almost industrial look: diamonds are set in brushed platinum, and gold bangles are impossibly delicate. ⊠ *411 West Broadway, at Spring St., SoHo* ☎ *212/941–1023* Ⓜ *A, C, E to Spring St.*

Swarovski Crystallized. A shrine to all things sparkly, this crystal superstore is a combination boutique and café, and allows shoppers to customize their purchases. Shoppers mix and match pieces from the striking "library of light" to create designs. If you're lacking ideas, there's always ready-made jewelry. Jean Paul Gaultier's Medieval Chic line starts at $250, and shiny iPhone covers are $46. For more inspiration, hit the exhibition space downstairs. ⊠ *499 Broadway, between Spring and Broome Sts., SoHo* ☎ *212/966–3322* Ⓜ *R to Prince St.; 6 to Spring St.*

Versani. Most of the jewelry here is big, bold, and unisex—and more than a little quirky. Silver teams up with all kinds of materials here: leather, denim, and snakeskin, as well as semiprecious stones. There's a good selection of silver rings and pendants under $50. ⊠ *152 Mercer St., between Prince and W. Houston Sts., SoHo* ☎ *212/941–7770* Ⓜ *R, W to Prince St.*

SHOES, HANDBAGS, AND LEATHER GOODS

Camper. These Euro-fave walking shoes, with their sturdy leather uppers and nubby rubber soles, have also proved popular on the cobblestone streets of SoHo. Comfort is a priority; all the slip-ons and lace-ups

17

here have generously rounded toes and a springy feel. ⊠ *125 Prince St., at Wooster St., SoHo* ☎ *212/358-1841* Ⓜ *R to Prince St.*

Kate Spade. Spade's runaway success with classic kicky, retro-style tote bags has blossomed into a full-fledged lifestyle company. The flagship looks—and feels—like an elegant living room. The totes are still for sale, along with leather handbags, kitten heels, and accessories like eyeglasses and paper. Even the diaper bags are ridicu-

lously stylish. Around the corner you'll find **Jack Spade,** filled with bags, dopp kits, and other men's accessories in a nostalgic setting. ⊠ *454 Broome St., between Mercer and Greene Sts., SoHo* ☎ *212/274-1991* Ⓜ *C, E to Spring St.*

Longchamp. Its Le Pliage foldable nylon bags have become an Upper East Side and Hamptons staple, but don't think this label is stuffy. Kate Moss designs a line for Longchamp that includes wallets, satchels, and hobos. The store carries the entire line of luggage, leather handbags, and totes in a rainbow of colors. ⊠ *132 Spring St., at Elizabeth St., SoHo* ☎ *212/343-7444* Ⓜ *N, R to Prince St.*

TOYS

☺ **Kidrobot.** This shop will appeal to kids, nerds, and the young at heart, who all flock here to stock up on the latest toys from Asian designers. This is a far cry from Mattel—the shelves are stocked with Dunny bunnies, Tokidokis, and Devilrobots. There's also a selection of cool silk-screened T-shirts and hoodies. ⊠ *118 Prince St., between Greene and Wooster Sts., SoHo* ☎ *212/966-6688* Ⓜ *N, R to Prince St.*

NOLITA
CLOTHING

Creatures of Comfort. Owner Jade Lai has brought her popular L.A. outpost to New York. The open, airy boutique offers cool clothes from emerging designers alongside products sourced from around the world. Most of the colors are muted, and brands carried include Acne, MM6, and the house label, Creatures of Comfort. There's a small selection of shoes, plus you never know what you might find for sale on a side table, such as candy and lip gloss from Asia. ⊠ *205 Mulberry St., between Spring and Kenmare Sts., NoLIta* ☎ *212/925-1005* Ⓜ *6 to Spring St.*

Duncan Quinn. Shooting for nothing less than sartorial splendor, this designer provides everything from chalk-stripe suits to cuff links and croquet shirts, all in a shop not much bigger than its silk pocket squares. Only a few of each style of shirt are made, so the odds are slim that you will see someone else in your blue, violet, or orange button-down with contrast-color undercuffs. Bespoke customers can choose from thousands of fabrics. ✉ *8 Spring St., between Elizabeth and Bowery Sts., NoLIta* ☎ *212/226–7030* Ⓜ *6 to Spring St.*

Frock. Models and stylists frequent this tiny shop for vintage women's wear from the 1960s, '70s, and '80s. The store carries pieces from Ossie Clark, Karl Lagerfeld, and Missoni, as well as Valentino, Alaia, and Chanel. ✉ *170 Elizabeth St., between Spring and Kenmare Sts., NoLIta* ☎ *212/594–5380* Ⓜ *B, D, F, M to Broadway–Lafayette St.*

INA. Although you may spot something vintage, like a 1960s Yves Saint Laurent velvet bolero, most clothing at this designer consignment store harks back only a few seasons, and in some cases the item has never been worn. Although there are multiple locations around the city, this flagship also carries menswear. ✉ *15 Bleecker St., at Elizabeth St., NoLIta* ☎ *212/228–8511* Ⓜ *6 to Bleecker St.*

Malia Mills. Fit fanatics have met their match here—especially those gals who are different sizes on top and bottom (bikini tops go up to a size D). Bikini tops and bottoms are sold separately: halters, bandeaus, and triangle tops, plus boy-cut, side-tie, and low-ride bottoms. There are a few one-pieces, too. If you've got a warm-weather honeymoon coming up, you may want the bikini with "Just Married" across your bum. ✉ *199 Mulberry St., between Spring and Kenmare Sts., NoLIta* ☎ *212/625–2311* Ⓜ *6 to Spring St.*

Nanette Lepore. "Girly" may well be the description that comes to mind as you browse through this cheerful shop; skirts are pleated and adorned with bows, jackets are enhanced by embroidery and floral appliqués, fur shrugs have tiny sleeves. ✉ *423 Broome St., between Lafayette and Crosby Sts., NoLIta* ☎ *212/219–8265* Ⓜ *6 to Spring St.*

Paul Frank. The store's mascot, the cheeky Julius monkey, is plastered everywhere here—on flannel PJs, skateboards, and, of course, T-shirts. Also look for tees evoking such formative elements of '80s youth as corn dogs and break dancing. A selection of monkey-free accessories, including perfect weekender bags, is more stylish than sassy. ✉ *195 Mulberry St., at Kenmare St., NoLIta* ☎ *212/965–5079* Ⓜ *6 to Spring St.*

Rebecca Taylor. Taylor is known for her soft, feminine designs in subdued hues of taupe, cream, and lavender. Racks are crammed with silky shirtdresses, embroidered tunics, and ruffled overcoats. ✉ *260 Mott St., between Prince and W. Houston Sts., NoLIta* ☎ *212/966–0406* Ⓜ *6 to Spring St.*

★ **Resurrection.** This small but tidy crimson shop is a mother lode of vintage clothing. Stocked with Chanels, Puccis, and Yves Saint Laurent, it's a retro-chic gold mine—but be prepared to pay dearly. Designers like Marc Jacobs and Anna Sui have sought inspiration among the racks, and the store returns the love by presenting occasional in-store designer exhibits, often with pieces from an honoree's personal collection. ✉ *217 Mott St., between Prince and Spring Sts., NoLIta* ☎ *212/625–1374* Ⓜ *6 to Spring St.*

Tory Burch. Bright-orange lacquer zings through this space, which has the same boho-luxe feel as the clothing. Orange joins navy, flamingo

NOLITA

The Nabokovian nickname NoLITa, shorthand for "North of Little Italy," covers a neighborhood that has taken the commercial baton from SoHo and run with it.

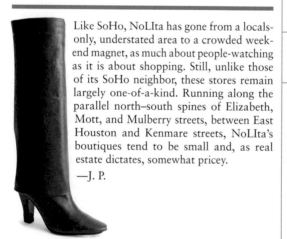

Like SoHo, NoLIta has gone from a locals-only, understated area to a crowded weekend magnet, as much about people-watching as it is about shopping. Still, unlike those of its SoHo neighbor, these stores remain largely one-of-a-kind. Running along the parallel north–south spines of Elizabeth, Mott, and Mulberry streets, between East Houston and Kenmare streets, NoLIta's boutiques tend to be small and, as real estate dictates, somewhat pricey.

—J. P.

BEST TIME TO GO

Wednesday through Friday afternoons if you're keen to shop without too many distractions, weekends for more people to scope out. Shops stay open latest (usually until 8 pm) Thursday through Saturday.

BEST SOUVENIR FOR YOUR BABYSITTER

Beautifully packaged candles exclusive to **Red Flower** (✉ *13 Prince St., at Elizabeth St.* ☎ *212/966-5301*) in dreamy scents like Italian blood orange and Japanese peony. Or perhaps some calming chamomile or lavender bath products from the ancient Italian perfumer-pharmacist **Lafco/Santa Maria Novella**.

0 ____ 1/8 mile
0 ____ 200 meters

E. Houston St.
◆ Calypso
Bowery St.
Chrystie St.

B,D,F,M Ⓜ
6

Lafco, NY ◆
Santa Maria
Novella
Prince St.
Me+Ro ◆
◆ Red Flower

Ⓜ
N,R
Sigerson ◆
Morrison

Resurrection ◆
Duncan
◆ Quinn

Ⓜ
6
Spring St.
Mulberry St.
Mott St.
Elizabeth St.

Kenmare St.

Broadway
Crosby St.
Lafayette St.

J,Z Ⓜ
Calypso Outlet ◆ ◆ Calypso Home
Broome St.
◆
Calypso
Cleveland Pl.
Centre St.

KEY
Ⓜ Subway stops

Grand St.

REFUELING

Hit the takeout window of **Café Gitane** (✉ *242 Mott St., at Prince St.* ☎ *212/334–9552*) for an espresso, or head inside for Moroccan French dishes like avocado toast or couscous. If you don't mind getting your fingers messy, stop by **Café Habana to Go** (✉ *17 Prince St., at Elizabeth St.* ☎ *212/625–2002*) for an addictive grilled ear of corn, topped with chili powder, cheese, and a splash of lime.

BEST FOR

TOO-COOL-FOR-SCHOOL CLOTHES
Creatures of Comfort: the funky separates here are in pale, muted colors.

Duncan Quinn: whether customized or off the rack, these button-downs and suits are perfectly cut.

Resurrection: mint-condition vintage Pucci and Courrèges make this a stylist's gold mine.

Calypso: almost half-a-dozen boutiques in NoLIta alone for softly exotic clothes and housewares.

Tory Burch: score a pair of her signature ballet flats or bohemian chic tunics and skinny cords in eye-popping colors.

FOXY SHOES
Sigerson Morrison: this strappy-sandal success has the biggest footprint in the 'hood.

. . . AND OTHER ACCESSORIES
Me&Ro: Indian-inspired gold and silver jewelry, from shoulder-duster ear-rings to tiny lotus-petal pendants.

17

pink, and mossy green on embellished tunics, printed dresses, and super-skinny cords. The medallion flats are one of Burch's best sellers. ✉ *257 Elizabeth St., between E. Houston and Prince Sts., NoLIta* ☎ *212/334–3000* Ⓜ *R to Prince St.*

JEWELRY AND ACCESSORIES
Dinosaur Designs. Translucent and colorful, this antipodean work uses an untraditional medium: resin. Some resins look like semiprecious stone, such as onyx or jade. The rest delve into stronger colors like aqua or crimson. Cruise the stacks of chunky bangles and cuffs or rows of rings; prices start at $50. There's some striking tableware, too. ✉ *250 Mott St., between Prince and E. Houston Sts., NoLIta* ☎ *212/680–3523* Ⓜ *R to Prince St.*

Me&Ro. Minimalist, Eastern styling has gained these designers a cult following. The Indian-inspired, hand-finished gold bangles, earrings, and necklaces are covered with tiny dangling rubies, sapphires, or brown diamonds. Although the fine jewelry is expensive, sterling-silver pendants start at $85. ✉ *241 Elizabeth St., between Prince and E. Houston Sts., NoLIta* ☎ *917/237–9215* Ⓜ *R to Prince St.*

SHOES, HANDBAGS, AND LEATHER GOODS
Belle by Sigerson Morrison. The company's secondary shoe line will appeal to those with high taste but a low budget. Choose from knee-high boots, gladiator sandals, or chunky wedges. ✉ *242 Mott St., between Prince and E. Houston Sts., NoLIta* ☎ *212/941–5404* Ⓜ *R to Prince St.*

High Way. The bags here marry form and function. Totes and messenger bags come in durable leather and nylon, and some handbags open to disclose a wealth of inner pockets. ✉ *238 Mott St., between Prince and Spring Sts., NoLIta* ☎ *212/966–4388* Ⓜ *6 to Bleecker St.*

John Fluevog Shoes. The inventor of the Angelic sole (protects against water, acid, "and Satan"), Fluevog designs chunky, funky shoes and boots for men and women. ✉ *250 Mulberry St., at Prince St., NoLIta* ☎ *212/431–4484* Ⓜ *R to Prince St.*

Sigerson Morrison. The details—just-right T-straps, small buckles, metallic leathers—make the women's shoes irresistible. Prices rise well above $300, so the sales are big events. ✉ *28 Prince St., between Mott and Elizabeth Sts., NoLIta* ☎ *212/219–3893* Ⓜ *F, M to Broadway–Lafayette St.*

Token. Although messenger bags are now ubiquitous, pay homage to the store that started it all. Super-durable messenger bags come in leather as well as nylon, and the line has expanded to include totes, duffels, and travel bags. ✉ *258 Elizabeth St., between E. Houston and Prince Sts., NoLIta* ☎ *212/226–9655* Ⓜ *R to Prince St.*

EAST VILLAGE AND LOWER EAST SIDE

EAST VILLAGE
ANTIQUES AND COLLECTIBLES
Lost City Arts. This sprawling shop is one of the best places to shop for 20th-century-design furniture, lighting, and accessories. Lost City can help you relive the Machine Age with an in-house, retro-modern line of

Best Bets for Souvenirs

What to get from the city that has everything? Major tourist attractions keep their gift shops well stocked with all the standard souvenirs, and dozens of gift shops dot the Times Square area. If you're looking for grungier souvenirs of downtown (T-shirts with salty messages, tattoos), troll St. Marks Place between 2nd and 3rd avenues in the East Village. *But for more unique mementos of the city, see this chapter's neighborhood spotlights for ideas and try the sources below.*

City Store. The official store of N.Y.C. sells anything and everything having to do with the city, from books and pamphlets to fun gift ideas. Pick up NYPD T-shirts, taxicab medallions, garbage truck toys, and dishtowels silk-screened with the skyline. The store shuts at 4:30 on weekdays and is closed weekends. ⊠ *1 Centre St., at Chambers St., Lower Manhattan* ☎ *212/669–8246* Ⓜ *4, 5, 6 to City Hall/Brooklyn Bridge.*

Eleni's. Take a bite out of the Big Apple—in cookie form—with these perfectly decorated treats. The "New York, New York" tin includes sugar cookies that mimic local icons like yellow cabs, the Wall Street sign, and the Statue of Liberty. ⊠ *Chelsea Market, 75 9th Ave., between W. 15th and W. 16th Sts., Chelsea* ☎ *212/255–6804* Ⓜ *A, C, E to 14th St.; L to 8th Ave.*

H&H Bagels. Looking for a taste of the city? Although a slice of pizza may not travel so well, bagels are another story. H&H can pack its bagels to withstand any plane ride—and in true New York spirit, the store is open 24 hours a day. ⊠ *2239 Broadway, at W. 80th St., Upper West Side* ☎ *212/595–8003* Ⓜ *1 to 79th St.*

New York City Transit Museum Gift Shop. In the symbolic heart of New York City's transit system, all the store's merchandise is somehow linked to the MTA, from straphanger ties to earrings made from old subway tokens. ⊠ *Grand Central Terminal, Vanderbilt Pl. and E. 42nd St., Midtown East* ☎ *212/878–0106* Ⓜ *4, 5, 6, 7 to 42nd St./Grand Central Terminal.*

17

furniture. ⊠ *18 Cooper Sq., at E. 5th St., East Village* ☎ *212/375–0500* Ⓜ *6 to Astor Pl.*

Partners & Spade. Owners Andy Spade and Anthony Perduti have lined this small space with all kinds of carefully curated knickknacks, ranging from the silly to the sublime. You might find a metal helicopter sprinkler or antique globes. The shop's own line of books is wonderfully quirky, covering everything from girls on bikes to the benefits of looking up in Manhattan. The shop is open by appointment only midweek but is open to the public on weekends. ⊠ *40 Great Jones St., between Lafayette and Bowery Sts., East Village* ☎ *646/861–2827* Ⓜ *4, 6 to Bleecker St.*

BEAUTY

Bond No. 9. Created by the same fragrance team as Creed, this line of scents is intended to evoke the New York City experience. Perfumes are named after neighborhoods: Central Park, a men's fragrance, is woodsy and "green," and the new Washington Square pairs purple rose with tarragon and a hint of leather. The shop, with its airy space and wood-panel Tea Library, is a lovely place to linger. ⊠ *9 Bond St., between Lafayette St. and Broadway, East Village* ☎ *212/228–1732* Ⓜ *6 to Bleecker St.*

Kiehl's Since 1851. At this favored haunt of top models and stylists, white-smocked assistants can help you choose between the lotions and potions, all of which are packaged in simple-looking bottles and jars. Some of the products, such as the Ultra Facial Cream, Silk Groom hairstyling aid, and superrich Creme de Corps, have attained near-cult status among beautyphiles. ■TIP→ **Kiehl's is known for being generous with samples, so be sure to ask for your own bag of take-home testers.** ⊠ *109 3rd Ave., at E. 13th St., East Village* ☎ *212/677–3171* Ⓜ *4, 5, 6, L, N, Q, R, W to 14th St./Union Sq.*

BOOKS AND STATIONERY

St. Mark's Bookshop. Downtown residents, NYU students, and intellectuals in general love this store, spending hours poking through popular and oddball fiction and nonfiction. You'll find a truly eclectic, attitudinal collection of books here, not unlike the salespeople. On the main floor, books on critical theory are right up front, across from new fiction titles—this is perhaps the only place where you can find Jacques Derrida facing off against T. C. Boyle. Cultural and art books are up front as well; literature and literary journals fill the back of the store. ■TIP→ **It's open daily until midnight.** ⊠ *31 3rd Ave., between 8th and 9th Sts., East Village* ☎ *212/260–7853* Ⓜ *6 to Astor Pl.*

Fodor's Choice ★ **The Strand Bookstore.** This downtown hangout proudly claims to have "18 miles of books." Craning your neck among the tall-as-trees stacks will likely net you something from the mix of new and old. Take an elevator ride to the third floor for rare-book selections. ⊠ *828 Broadway, at E. 12th St., East Village* ☎ *212/473–1452* Ⓜ *L, N, Q, R, 4, 5, 6 to 14th St./Union Sq.*

CLOTHING

John Varvatos. Over the past few years Varvatos has amplified his rock-and-roll ties, with rock-star photos in his stores and ad campaigns starring Franz Ferdinand and ZZ Top. It's apropos, considering that he's taking over the CBGB club space to use as another boutique for hawking expensive, soft-shouldered suits, cotton crewnecks, and jeans in leather, velvet, or denim. ⊠ *315 Bowery, between E. 1st and E. 2nd Sts., East Village* ☎ *212/358–0315* Ⓜ *F to Lower East Side/2nd Ave.*

Pas de Deux. Fashion editors love this little boutique—which looks like it was imported straight from Paris—thanks to the marble checkerboard floor, chandeliers, and fine woodwork. The well-edited selection includes dresses, trench coats, and denim from Rag & Bone, Philip Lim, and Vena Cava. There are also lots of lovely little accessories, like eyeglasses, cardholders, and delicate necklaces. ⊠ *328 E. 11th St., between 1st and 2nd Aves., East Village* ☎ *212/475–0075* Ⓜ *4, 6 to Astor Pl.*

Patricia Field. If you loved Carrie Bradshaw's wild outfits on *Sex and the City,* this is the place for you. As well as designing costumes for the show, Field has been a longtime purveyor of flamboyant and campy club-kid gear. Her 4,000-square-foot East Village emporium is chockablock with teeny kilts, lamé, marabou, pleather, and vinyl, as well as wigs in every color and stiletto heels in some very large sizes. ⊠ *302 Bowery, between Bleecker and E. Houston Sts., East Village* ☎ *212/966–4066* Ⓜ *6 to Bleecker St.*

Screaming Mimi's. Browse through racks bulging with vintage finds from the 1950s through '80s. Retro wear includes everything from dresses to soccer shirts and prom dresses. Although most of the nondesigner finds are affordable, Screaming Mimi's also carries vintage designer duds from Valentino, Chloe, and Gaultier. ⊠ *382 Lafayette St., between 4th and Great Jones Sts., East Village* ☎ *212/677–6464* Ⓜ *B, D, F, M to Broadway–Lafayette St.*

Tokio 7. Even fashion designers like Alexander Wang have been known to pop into this high-end consignment store to browse. Racks are loaded with goodies from A-list designers such as Gucci, Stella McCartney, DVF, and Philip Lim. ⊠ *83 E. 7th St.,, between 1st and 2nd Aves., East Village* ☎ *212/353–8443* Ⓜ *4, 6 to Astor Pl.–8th St.*

Trash and Vaudeville. This punk mecca is famous for dressing stars like Debbie Harry and the Ramones back in the '70s, and its rock-and-roll vibe lives on. Goths, punks, and pro wrestlers shop here for bondage-inspired pants and skirts, as well as vinyl corsets and mini-kilts. ⊠ *4 St. Marks Pl., between 2nd and 3rd Aves., East Village* ☎ *212/982–3590* Ⓜ *6 to Astor Pl.*

17

FOOD AND TREATS

Max Brenner: Chocolate by the Bald Man. This Aussie arrival is all about a Wonka-ish sense of entertainment. The cafés encourage the messy enjoyment of gooey creations like chocolate fondues and chocolate burgers for kids. Take-away treats include caramelized pralines and tins of hot-chocolate powder. ⊠ *841 Broadway, between E. 13th and E. 14th Sts., East Village* ☎ *212/388–0030* Ⓜ *L, N, Q, R, 4, 5, 6 to 14th St./Union Sq.*

HOME DECOR

White Trash. Looking for a midcentury modern Danish desk? This is your place. Owner Stuart Zamsky crams his store with surprisingly affordable pieces that are mostly from the '40s through '70s, including tables, lamps, and chairs. Some pieces you might find include paper mobiles from the '70s, old fondue sets, and antique medical-office cabinets. ⊠ *304 E. 5th St., between 1st and 2nd Aves., East Village* ☎ *212/598–5956* Ⓜ *4, 6 to Astor Pl./8th St.*

MUSIC STORES

Other Music. DJs and musicians flock to this antidote to music megastores for hard-to-find genres on CD and vinyl, from Japanese electronica and Krautrock to acid folk and Americana. You can buy concert tickets at the in-house box office. ■**TIP**➜ There's also a great selection of used CDs, including seminal punk classics from the Clash and the Stooges. ⊠ *15 E. 4th St., between Lafayette St. and Broadway, East Village* ☎ *212/477–8150* Ⓜ *6 to Astor Pl.*

LOWER EAST SIDE

Once home to multitudes of Jewish immigrants from Russia and Eastern Europe, the Lower East Side has traditionally been New Yorkers' bargain beat. The center of it all is Orchard Street, where vendors still holler, "Lady, have I got a deal for you!"

Here tiny, no-nonsense clothing stores and scrappy stalls hang on to the past while funky local designers gradually claim more turf. A few cool vintage clothing and furniture spots bridge the two camps. Ludlow Street, one block east of Orchard, has become the main drag for twentysomethings with attitude, its boutiques wedged in between bars and low-key restaurants. Anything too polished is looked on with suspicion—and that goes for you, too. For the full scope of this area, prowl from Allen to Essex streets, south of East Houston Street down to Broome Street. A tip: wear closed shoes to stay clear of broken glass and other crud on the sidewalks.

—J. P.

BEST TIME TO GO

Come on a Sunday afternoon, when Orchard Street between East Houston and Delancey streets becomes a vehicle-free pedestrian zone. On Saturday the old-school stores close for the Jewish Sabbath.

BEST SOUVENIR FOR YOUR FAVE KITCHEN AIDE

Raid the **Lower East Side Tenement Museum** gift shop (⊠ *108 Orchard St., between Delancey and Broome Sts.* ☎ *212/982-8420*) for a cheery reproduction 1950 Empire State souvenir kitchen towel or a ceramic version of the Greek key coffee cup.

BEST FOR

VINTAGE

Edith Machinist: big names from the 1970s and '80s, whopping shoulder pads, and often hefty price tags.

Las Venus: Danish modern furniture, princess phones, boomerang ashtrays in punchy colors.

CLOTHES WITH BITE

J.D. Fisk: classic but cool menswear like distressed boots, vintage T-shirts, and denim jackets.

Foley & Corinna: mixes vintage-y new clothes with the truly vintage.

OLD-WORLD FOOD

Russ & Daughters (⊠ 179 E. Houston St., at 1st Ave.): smoked salmon, pickled herring, and babka, oh my.

The Pickle Guys (⊠ 49 Essex St. ☎ 212/656–9739): move beyond the half-sours to the zingy full-sour and horseradish pickle spears.

17

REFUELING

Get your calcium with a stop at **il laboratorio del gelato** (⊠ 188 Ludlow St., between Stanton and E. Houston Sts. ☎ 212/343–9922) for creamy scoops of ice cream and sorbet in unusual flavors like basil, grapefruit hibiscus, and wasabi. Cake with your gelato? Zip to **Sugar Sweet Sunshine** (⊠ 126 Rivington St., between Essex and Norfolk Sts. ☎ 212/995–1960), a homey little bakery where you can nibble on a cupcake with chocolate-almond frosting or a slice of red velvet cake. For something healthy, get a table at the **teany café** (⊠ 90 Rivington St., between Orchard and Ludlow Sts. ☎ 212/475–9190), a vegetarian spot with light meals, sweets, and more than 90 teas to try.

TOYS

Dinosaur Hill. Forget about Elmo. This little shop stocks quirky gifts for kids like hand puppets and marionettes from Asia, mini-bongos, and wooden rattles. A small selection of children's clothing is also for sale. ⊠ *306 E. 9th St., between 1st and 2nd Aves., East Village* ☎ *212/473–5850* Ⓜ *R to 8th St.; 6 to Astor Pl.*

WINE

Astor Wines & Spirits. Stock up on wine, spirits, and sake at this beautiful shop. For unwinding, and learning more about food and wine, there's also a wine library and kitchen for cooking classes. ⊠ *399 Lafayette St., at E. 4th St., East Village* ☎ *212/674–7500* Ⓜ *6 to Astor Pl.*

Union Square Wine & Spirits. Tastings are easy at this well-stocked store, thanks to Enomatic machines. These card-operated contraptions let you sample dozens of wines. If machines don't do it for you, generous tastings are held most Fridays and Saturdays. ⊠ *140 4th Ave., at 13th St., East Village* ☎ *212/675–8100* Ⓜ *L, N, Q, R, 4, 5, 6 to 14th St./Union Sq.*

LOWER EAST SIDE
ANTIQUES AND COLLECTIBLES

Las Venus. Step into this kitsch palace and you may feel as though a time machine has zapped you back to the '50s, '60s, or groovy '70s. Look for bubble lamps, lots of brocade, and Knoll knockoffs. Midcentury modern Danish credenzas are also big here. ⊠ *163 Ludlow St., between E. Houston and Stanton Sts., Lower East Side* ☎ *212/982–0608* Ⓜ *F to 2nd Ave.*

CLOTHING

Foley & Corinna. Images of flowers and butterflies waft along the walls, and the racks divulge both vintage finds, like embroidered leather jackets and Foley's own line of new clothes. Many looks are lingerie inspired, with flounces and lace. ⊠ *114 Stanton St., between Ludlow and Essex Sts., Lower East Side* ☎ *212/529–2338* Ⓜ *F to 2nd Ave. or Delancey St.*

TG-170. Named for owner Terry Gillis, this shop showcases up-and-coming as well as established designers. Cotton dresses from Rachel Mara and jumpsuits from San & Sonni are perfectly on trend. Complete your designer look with fierce heels and a huge cocktail ring from Netti. ⊠ *77 Ludlow St., between Ludlow and Broome Sts., Lower East Side* ☎ *212/995–8660* Ⓜ *F, J, M, Z to Delancey St./Essex St.*

SHOES, HANDBAGS, AND LEATHER GOODS

Altman Luggage. Having trouble bringing all your purchases home? Altman sells top-of-the-line luggage from Samsonite, Delsey, and Tumi at discount prices. A wide selection of pens is also for sale. ⊠ *135 Orchard St., between Delancey and Rivington Sts., Lower East Side* ☎ *212/254–7275* Ⓜ *F, J, M, Z to Delancey St./Essex St.*

J. D. Fisk. Although the shoes are the main attraction, think of J. D. Fisk as a one-stop shop for men. The footwear has a rugged American classic look, although some are punk inspired. There's also a small selection of clothing, such as denim jackets and vintage-inspired T-shirts.

✉ *159½ Ludlow St., between Rivington and Stanton Sts., Lower East Side* ☎ *212/475–0565* Ⓜ *F, J, M, Z to Delancey St./Essex St.*

GREENWICH VILLAGE AND WEST VILLAGE

GREENWICH VILLAGE
ANTIQUES AND COLLECTIBLES

Kaas Glassworks. From the outside, this shop is cuter than cute, with its old-fashioned sign and ivy-covered brick façade. The specialty here is decoupage that has been turned into quirky coasters and trays. Owner Carol Kaas uses vintage postcards, maps, and botanical prints in her works. ✉ *117 Perry St., between Greenwich and Hudson Sts., Greenwich Village* ☎ *212/366–0322* Ⓜ *1 to Christopher St./Sheridan Sq.*

BEAUTY

★ **Aedes De Venustas.** Arguably the best place to buy fragrance in town, the super-knowledgeable staff here will help shoppers find the perfect scent. High-end brands like Anick Goutal and Lubin are stocked here, along with luxurious skin-care products and pricey candles from Diptyque and L'Artisan Parfumeur. Their signature gift wrap is as beautiful as what's inside the box. ✉ *9 Christopher St., between 6th and 7th Aves., Greenwich Village* ☎ *212/206–8674* Ⓜ *1 to Christopher St./Sheridan Sq.*

C. O. Bigelow. If you find shopping at Duane Reade and CVS a little boring and impersonal, try this old-fashioned pharmacy. Founded in 1838, it is the oldest apothecary-pharmacy in the United States; Mark Twain used to fill prescriptions here. They still fill prescriptions, but the real reason to come is for the hard-to-find-brands like Klorane shampoo and Elgydium toothpaste. Bigelow also has its own line of products, including green-tea lip balm and quince hand lotion. ✉ *414 6th Ave., St., between W. 9th and W. 10th, Greenwich Village* ☎ *212/473–7324* Ⓜ *B, D, F, M to W. 4th St.*

BOOKS AND STATIONERY

bookbook. Published diaries, letters, biographies, and autobiographies fill this neighborly store. There's also a thoughtful assortment of general nonfiction, fiction, guidebooks, and children's books. But the real focus here is the carefully selected sale tables that spill out onto the sidewalk—they have deals on everything from Graham Greene to Chuck Palahniuk. ✉ *266 Bleecker St., between 6th and 7th Aves., Greenwich Village* ☎ *212/807–8655* Ⓜ *1 to Christopher St./Sheridan Sq.*

Partners & Crime Mystery Booksellers. Signed first editions, helpful staff, a rental library, and whodunits galore—new and out-of-print—make this a must-browse for fans. Books are organized by fun categories, including "Hardboiled," "Softboiled," and "Espionage—non 007." ✉ *44 Greenwich Ave., between 6th and 7th Aves., Greenwich Village* ☎ *212/243–0440* Ⓜ *F, M, 1, 2, 3 to 14th St.*

Three Lives & Co. Three Lives has one of the city's best book selections. The display tables and counters highlight the latest literary fiction and serious nonfiction, classics, quirky gift books, and gorgeously illustrated tomes. The staff members' literary knowledge is formidable, so

17

don't be afraid to ask them for their own picks. ✉ *154 W. 10th St., at Waverly Pl., Greenwich Village* ☎ *212/741–2069* Ⓜ *1 to Christopher St./Sheridan Sq.*

CLOTHING

Cynthia Rowley. Rowley delivers flirty, whimsical dresses that are perfect for cocktail parties. To complete the look, throw on some of her colorful pumps and sharply tailored coats. The handbags with small inset mirrors are ideal for checking your lipstick. ✉ *376 Bleecker St., between Charles and Perry Sts., Greenwich Village* ☎ *212/242–3803* Ⓜ *1 to Christopher St./Sheridan Sq.*

Írma. This unprepossessing nook with its squeaky plank floors and dressmaker's dummies is home to some of the most elegant designers in the city. Besides carrying a good selection of Vivienne Westwood, the store stockpiles whisper-light cashmere by Kristensen du Nord and gauzy separates from Ilaria Nistri. ✉ *378 Bleecker St., between Charles and Perry Sts., Greenwich Village* ☎ *212/206–7475* Ⓜ *A, C, E, F, M to W. 4th St./Washington Sq.*

La Petite Coquette. Everything at this lingerie store is unabashedly sexy, and the helpful staff can find the perfect fit. The store's own line of silk slips, camisoles, and other underpinnings comes in a range of colors. ✉ *51 University Pl., between E. 9th and E. 10th Sts., Greenwich Village* ☎ *212/473–2478* Ⓜ *R to 8th St.*

Limelight Marketplace. Housed in a former nightclub (which used to be a church), this massive space is now a bustling marketplace for clothing and accessories. Browse through the various boutiques, selling everything from organic oils and Hunter wellies to handcrafted jewelry. Refuel at Baci Gelato and Cupcake Stop on the ground floor, or save your appetite for brick-oven pizza from Grimaldi's. ✉ *47 W. 20th St., at 6th Ave., Greenwich Village* ☎ *212/359–5600* Ⓜ *F, V to 23rd St.*

Ludivine. Ignore the tacky surroundings and make a beeline for this store if you love French designers. Owner Ludivine Grégoire showcases of-the-moment Gallic (and a few Italian) designers like Vanessa Bruno, Jerome Dreyfuss, and Carvin. ✉ *172 W. 4th St., between Jones and Cornelia Sts., Greenwich Village* ☎ *646/336–6576* Ⓜ *1 to Christopher St./Sheridan Sq.*

Nom de Guerre. This basement-level hipster hideaway has an army-meets-preppy vibe. Racks are filled mainly with the house men's line, plus a selection of items by A.P.C., Comme de Garçons, and others. The plaid shirts, belted trench coats, and cargo pants are some of the top picks. ✉ *640 Broadway, at Bleecker St., Greenwich Village* ☎ *212/253–2891* Ⓜ *F, M to Broadway–Lafayette St.*

FOOD AND TREATS

Li-Lac Chocolates. They've been feeding the Village's sweet tooth since 1923. Indulge with almond bark and coconut clusters as well as such specialty items as chocolate-molded Statues of Liberty. ✉ *40 8th Ave., at Jane St., Greenwich Village* ☎ *212/924–2280* Ⓜ *A, C, E to 14th St.*

HOME DECOR

Mxyplyzyk. Named after a character from Superman, this shop is hard to pronounce (*mixy-plit-sick*) and equally hard to resist. The specialty is creative riffs on household standbys such as measuring cups fashioned from Russian dolls and a squirrel-shape nutcracker. More serious items include Lucite chairs and George Nelson clocks. ⊠ *125 Greenwich Ave., at W. 13th St., Greenwich Village* ☎ *212/989–4300* Ⓜ *A, C, E, L to 14th St./8th Ave.*

Olatz. Olatz Schnabel modeled her linen shop on a historic Havana pharmacy after a visit to Cuba. The black-and-white checkerboard floors and mint-green walls breathe a sort of lazy, faded elegance, a spot-on backdrop to her collection of luxurious sheets, blankets, and pajama sets, all of which have sky-high thread counts and are bordered with bold stripes or intricate damask embroidery. ⊠ *43 Clarkson St., between Hudson and Greenwich Sts., Greenwich Village* ☎ *212/255–8627* Ⓜ *1 to Houston St.*

MUSIC STORES

Bleecker Bob's Golden Oldies Record Shop. One of the oldest independent record stores in town, this pleasingly messy place with occasionally surly staff sells punk, jazz, metal, and reggae, plus good old rock on vinyl, until the wee hours. ⊠ *118 W. 3rd St., at MacDougal St., Greenwich Village* ☎ *212/475–9677* Ⓜ *A, C, E, F, M to W. 4th St./Washington Sq.*

SHOES, HANDBAGS, AND LEATHER GOODS

Flight 001. Frequent flyers can one-stop-shop at this travel-theme store that puts a creative spin on everyday accessories. Shop for bright luggage tags, passport holders, satin sleep masks, and even paper soap. ⊠ *96 Greenwich Ave., between W. 12th and Jane Sts., Greenwich Village* ☎ *212/989–0001* Ⓜ *A, C, E to 14th St.*

Lulu Guinness. Hit this black-and-white-stripe salon for cheerfully eccentric accessories such as handbags (some lip-shaped) adorned with appliqué, beads, and bows; polka-dot scarves; and umbrellas patterned with poodles. ⊠ *394 Bleecker St., between W. 11th and Perry Sts., Greenwich Village* ☎ *212/367–2120* Ⓜ *1 to Christopher St./Sheridan Sq.*

WEST VILLAGE

BOOKS AND STATIONERY

Idlewild Books. Named for the pre-1960s JFK Airport, this travel-inspired bookstore groups its goods by destination. It has much more than guidebooks, though; novels, histories, cookbooks, and children's books share each segment, giving you a fascinating look at any given locale. If those chairs look familiar, it may be because you spent a layover in one of them once upon a time in the American Airlines terminal. ⊠ *12 W. 19th St., 2nd fl., at 5th Ave., West Village* ☎ *212/414–8888* Ⓜ *4, 5, 6, L, Q, R to 14th St./Union Sq.*

CLOTHING

Castor & Pollux. The store's interior signals a finely tuned balance of high taste (vintage Bergdorf Goodman display cases) and quirkiness (grass-cloth wall coverings and small horse sculptures). Hard-to-find brands like Hache are mixed with better-known names like Acne and

17

WEST VILLAGE

It's easy to feel like a local, not a tourist, while shopping in the West Village. Unlike 5th Avenue or SoHo, the pace is slower, the streets are relatively quiet, and the scale is small. This is the place to come for unusual finds rather than global-brand goods (well, if you don't count Marc Jacobs).

Bleecker Street is a particularly good place to indulge all sorts of shopping appetites. Foodies love the blocks between 6th and 7th avenues for the specialty purveyors like Murray's Cheese (254 Bleecker St.). Fashion foragers prowl the stretch between West 10th Street and 8th Avenue, and avid readers lose themselves in the book-book bookshop. Hudson Street and Greenwich Avenue are also prime boutique-browsing territory. Christopher Street, true to its connection with the lesbian and gay community, has a handful of rainbow-flag stops. High rents mean there are fewer student-oriented shops around NYU than you might expect.

BEST TIME TO GO

Tuesday through Friday afternoons for a focused shopping stint, Saturday afternoon if you get a buzz from people-watching or the competitive aspect of busier boutiques. (Keep in mind that most stores here are small, so even a half dozen fellow browsers can make a shop feel crowded.) On Sunday the area's a bit bogged down by brunchers, and stores have shorter hours.

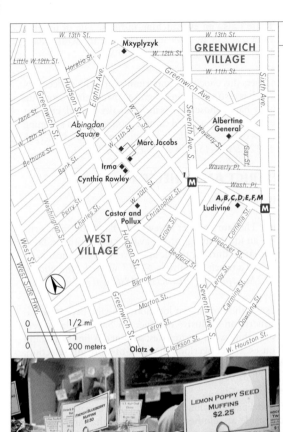

LEMON POPPY SEED
MUFFINS
$2.25

FRENCH BLUEBERRY
MUFFINS
$2.50

BEST FOR

NONCHALANT-CHIC CLOTHES

Marc Jacobs: the casual (but not cheap) line with seemingly unstoppable downtown street cred.

Castor & Pollux: feminine pieces that feel simultaneously vintage and modern.

Írma: the place to pair cult jeans, motorcycle boots, and a revealing top.

Ludivine: a direct feed to the Parisian femme's fashion scene.

Cynthia Rowley: party-friendly outfits for when a girl needs a halter top or a filmy dress.

HOME DECOR

Mxyplyzyk: household necessities and accessories get a jolt of saucy humor.

Olatz: divine bedding and pajamas in a Havana-inspired setting.

17

REFUELING

Skip Magnolia Bakery; there's always a line, and besides, a vast number of other places are great for a pick-me-up in this neighborhood. The house-made sweets at **Amy's Bread** (✉ 250 Bleecker St., at Leroy St. ☎ 212/675–7802), like the layer-cake slices and "kitchen sink" cookies, are both homey and delicious. Try an Irish soda roll or a sandwich on raisin-and-fennel bread. At **Cones** (✉ 272 Bleecker St., between Morton and Jones Sts. ☎ 212/414–1795), you can lap up a rich ginger or pistachio ice cream.

3.1 Philip Lim. There's also an eye-catching in-house line of jewelry, clutches, and sweaters. ⊠ *238 W. 10th St., at Hudson St., West Village* 🕾 *212/645–6572* Ⓜ *1 to Christopher St./Sheridan Sq.*

FOOD AND TREATS

Chocolate Bar. What sets this chocolate emporium apart is its midcentury modern design, which is also evident in the groovy packaging. Scoop up some retro chocolate bars, whose flavors include salty pretzel, coconut cream pie, and key lime. Or try a salted caramel bonbon and a steaming cup of spicy hot chocolate. ⊠ *19 8th Ave., between Jane and W. 12th Sts., West Village* 🕾 *212/366–1541* Ⓜ *A, C, E, to 14th St.*

THE MEATPACKING DISTRICT AND CHELSEA

MEATPACKING DISTRICT

CLOTHING

Alexander McQueen. The late designer's New York flagship is a futuristic, podlike space—an ideal setting for the avant-garde clothing. Now under the helm of Sarah Burton, the designs are still theatrical with exquisite tailoring and a touch of softness. ⊠ *417 W. 14th St., between 9th and 10th Aves., Meatpacking District* 🕾 *212/645–1797* Ⓜ *A, C, E to 14th St.*

Charles Nolan. Despite the downtown location, the vibe here is decidedly uptown. Formerly an exclusive designer for Saks, Nolan offers impeccable craftsmanship: wool shirtdresses, sequined A-line skirts, and billowy white blouses. Don't overlook the front-of-store gift selection, including chunky glass candlesticks and cashmere scrunch scarves. ⊠ *30 Gansevoort St., at Hudson St., Meatpacking District* 🕾 *212/924–4888* Ⓜ *A, C, E to 14th St.*

Destination. The model pigs guarding this store fit right in with the Meatpacking District. Inside are clothes and accessories that are imaginative and quirky. There are dramatic, sculptural coats from Lia Lintern, Jacques le Corre bags, and pieces of statement jewelry from Serge Thoraval. ⊠ *32–36 Little W. 12th St., between Greenwich and Washington Sts., Meatpacking District* 🕾 *212/727–2031* Ⓜ *1 to Christopher St./Sheridan Sq.*

Diane von Furstenberg. Browse for a classic DVF wrap dress or a long, gauzy blouse here. The gleaming white space has just a hint of disco, with mirrored discs sparkling on the ceiling. ⊠ *874 Washington St., at 14th St., Meatpacking District* 🕾 *646/486–4800* Ⓜ *A, C, E to 14th St.*

Iris. As the Italian shoe manufacturers for stylish brands like John Galliano, Marc Jacobs, Veronique Branquinho, and Chloé, Iris's sole U.S. store is able to carry every style from those lines, including pieces not previously available on our shores. ⊠ *827 Washington St., at Little W. 12th St., Meatpacking District* 🕾 *212/645–0950* Ⓜ *A, C, E, L to 14th St.*

Jeffrey. The Meatpacking District really arrived when this Atlanta-based mini-Barneys opened its doors. You can find an incredible array of designer shoes—Valentino, Lanvin, and red-soled Christian Louboutin are some of the best sellers—plus überlabels like Marni, Prada, and

Gucci. ✉ *449 W. 14th St., between 9th and 10th Aves., Meatpacking District* ☎ *212/206–1272* Ⓜ *A, C, E, L to 14th St./8th Ave.*

Stella McCartney. A devout vegetarian setting up shop in the Meatpacking District may seem odd, but it's further proof that chic trumps many other considerations. Her gauzy, muted clothes look best layered or teamed with shredded denim. In keeping with McCartney's vegetarianism, leather is verboten, so shoes and accessories come in satin, canvas, and synthetics. The dressing rooms are so beautiful, you might just want to move in. ✉ *429 W. 14th St., between 9th and 10th Aves., Meatpacking District* ☎ *212/255–1556* Ⓜ *A, C, E to 14th St.*

Tracy Reese. Unabashedly girly but wearable garb is Reese's specialty, as she plays with lush fabrics (silk chiffon is a favorite), quirky color combos, and notice-me embellishments like rhinestones and ruffles. The cuts flatter all sorts of figures, often emphasizing the waist. This flagship carries both the ladylike Tracy Reese line and the funkier, lower-price Plenty label. ✉ *641 Hudson St., between Horatio and Gansevoort Sts., Meatpacking District* ☎ *212/807–0505* Ⓜ *A, C, E to 14th St.*

JEWELRY AND ACCESSORIES

Ten Thousand Things. You might find yourself wishing for 10,000 things from the showcases in this elegant boutique. Designs run from delicate gold and silver chains to long Peruvian opal earrings. Many shapes are abstract reflections of natural forms, like twigs or seedpods. Unusual stones beckon from the glass cases, such as the pendants of purple rubies or labradorite. ✉ *423 W. 14th St., between 9th and 10th Aves., Meatpacking District* ☎ *212/352–1333* Ⓜ *A, C, E to 14th St.*

The Crangi Family Project. It's a family affair at this jewelry shop owned by designer Philip Crangi. On display are Crangi's own line of baubles as well as Giles & Brothers, which Philip designs with his sister (another sibling designed the space's dramatic green upholstered walls). Both collections combine an antique look with an industrial vibe. The thick cuffs are popular, as well as long, thin necklaces with charms like feathers and old shotguns. ✉ *9 9th Ave., between Little W. 12th and W. 13th Sts., Meatpacking District* ☎ *212/929–0858* Ⓜ *L to 8th Ave.*

CHELSEA

★ **Books of Wonder.** Readers young and old will delight in Manhattan's oldest and largest independent children's bookstore. The friendly, knowledgeable staff can help select gifts for all reading levels. Don't miss the extensive Oz section as well as the collection of old, rare, and collectible children's books and original children's book art. An outpost of the Cupcake Café gives little browsers a second wind. ✉ *18 W. 18th St., between 5th and 6th Aves., Chelsea* ☎ *212/989–3270* Ⓜ *F, M to 14th St.*

Skyline Books. An endearingly scruffy, small, old-school space makes this the Woody Allen of used-book stores. Come here for out-of-print books in all categories, a large Beat Generation selection, literary first editions, and books on photography and art. ✉ *13 W. 18th St., between 5th and 6th Aves., Chelsea* ☎ *212/759–5463* Ⓜ *4, 5, 6, N, Q, R to 14th St./Union Sq.*

17

THE MEATPACKING DISTRICT

For nearly a century, this industrial western edge of downtown Manhattan was defined by slaughterhouses and meatpacking plants, blood-splattered cobblestone streets, and men lugging carcasses into warehouses way before dawn.

But in the late 1990s the area between West 14th Street, Gansevoort Street, Hudson Street, and 11th Avenue speedily transformed into another kind of meat market. Many of the old warehouses now house ultrachic shops, nightclubs, and restaurants packed with angular fashionistas. Jeffrey, a pint-size department store, was an early arrival, followed by edgy but established designers like Stella McCartney and a few lofty furniture stores. Despite the influx of a few chains—albeit stylish ones like Scoop—eclectic boutiques keep popping up. The one thing it's hard to find here is a bargain.

—J. P.

BEST TIME TO GO

Wednesday through Friday afternoons. Most stores are open daily, but a few are closed Monday and Tuesday. On weekends some stores stay open until 7 or 8 pm, overlapping with the overeager nightlife crowd.

BEST SOUVENIR FOR YOUR GIRLFRIEND (OR BOHO AUNT)

Jewelry from **Ten Thousand Things** or **The Crangi Family Project**. You can find something sweet, funky, or industrial—or a combination of them all.

BEST FOR

FABULOUS FROCKS

Jeffrey: culls the coolest outfits from high-end labels.

Alexander McQueen: impeccably tailored, take-no-prisoners style.

Catherine Malandrino: romantic chiffon and swingy layers, at more-reasonable prices.

DENIM

Earnest Sewn (✉ *821 Washington St.* ☎ *212/242–3414*): customize the cut, buttons, and pockets of your cult jeans.

KILLER ACCESSORIES

La Perla: the most minxy outpost for this brand's lace lingerie.

Christian Louboutin: vampy heels with telltale crimson soles.

REFUELING

Hit the buzzing bistro **Pastis** (✉ *9 9th Ave., at Little W. 12th St.* ☎ *212/929–4844*) for a croque monsieur, a bracing coffee, or a cocktail with the namesake hooch. For a quick stop, follow the smell of grilled meat to **Pop Burger** (✉ *58–60 9th Ave., between 14th and 15th Sts.* ☎ *212/414–8686*). The miniburgers are tempting, but locals swear by the sides: crispy fries and onion rings, and thick-as-cement milk shakes.

CLOTHING

Balenciaga. Creative director Nicolas Ghesquière continues to wow the fashion world with his avant-garde looks. In this cavelike boutique you might luck onto a reissue from the (Cristobal) Balenciaga archives, made up in modern fabrics. The stash of more accessible handbags and shoes is worth a browse. ⊠ *542 W. 22nd St., between 10th and 11th Aves., Chelsea* ☏ *212/206–0872* Ⓜ *C, E to 23rd St.*

Comme des Garçons. The designs in this stark, white, swoopy space consistently push the fashion envelope with brash patterns, unlikely juxtapositions (tulle and neoprene), and cuts that are meant to be thought-provoking, not flattering. Architecture students come just for the interior design. ⊠ *520 W. 22nd St., between 10th and 11th Aves., Chelsea* ☏ *212/604–9200* Ⓜ *C, E to 23rd St.*

New York Vintage. Stylists to the stars, TV costumers, and the odd princess descend upon this boutique to browse racks of prime vintage clothing. Everything is high-end, so don't expect any bargains. If money is no object, take your pick from Yves Saint Laurent, Madame Grès, and Thierry Mugler pieces. There's a good selection of handbags and pumps, too. ⊠ *117 W. 25th St., between 6th and 7th Aves., Chelsea* ☏ *212/647–1107* Ⓜ *1 to 28th St.*

DISCOUNT SHOPPING

Fisch for the Hip. The racks at this high-end consignment store are evenly split between men's and women's clothes, with a well-edited selection throughout. You may find 7 for All Mankind jeans, Gucci suits, and Marni dresses. Hermès bags are a specialty. ⊠ *153 W. 18th St., between 6th and 7th Aves., Chelsea* ☏ *212/633–9053* Ⓜ *F, M, 1, 2, 3 to 14th St.*

Loehmann's. This discount store doesn't attract the hordes of tourists like Century 21, but you'll still have to dig through crammed racks to unearth bargains. Label searchers can find DVF wrap dresses for $100 and Betsey Johnson coats for around $200, and men can find Juicy Couture T-shirts and Versace ties. The "back room" has the best women's designers. ⊠ *101 7th Ave., at W. 16th St., Chelsea* ☏ *212/352–0856* Ⓜ *1, 2, 3 to 14th St.*

MUSIC STORES AND MEDIA

Jazz Record Center. If you're seeking rare or out-of-print jazz recordings, this is your one-stop shop. Long-lost Ellingtons and other rare pressings come to light here; the jazz-record specialist also stocks collectibles, DVDs, videos, posters, CDs, and LPs. ⊠ *236 W. 26th St., between 7th and 8th Aves., 8th fl., Chelsea* ☏ *212/675–4480* Ⓜ *1 to 28th St.*

Movie Star News. As you flip through images from blockbusters, cult faves, and memorable bombs, it's hard to doubt their claim that they have the world's largest variety of movie photos and posters. Behind the counter are signed photos of many of the stars seen on the posters. ■TIP→ A poster of a New York film such as *Manhattan, The Royal*

Tenenbaums, or *Taxi Driver* makes a good souvenir for less than $20. ⊠ *134 W. 18th St., between 6th and 7th Aves., Chelsea* ☎ *212/620–8160* Ⓜ *1, 2, 3 to 14th St.*

WINE

★ **Bottlerocket Wine & Spirit.** Fun and approachable, this shop puts a new spin on wine shopping. Vintages are organized by quirky factors like their compatibility with Chinese takeout and whom they'd best suit as gifts (ranging from "Someone You Barely Know" to "The Boss"). A reference library, kids' play nook, and doggie area make the space extra welcoming. ⊠ *5 W. 19th St., between 5th and 6th Aves., Chelsea* ☎ *212/929–2323* Ⓜ *N, R, Q, 4, 5, 6 to 14th St.*

UNION SQUARE TO MURRAY HILL

FLATIRON DISTRICT
CHILDREN'S CLOTHING

★ **Space Kiddets.** The funky (Elvis-print rompers, CBGB onesies) mixes with the old-school (retro cowboy-print pants, brightly colored clogs, Bruce Lee T-shirts) and the high-end (Lilli Gaufrette, Kenzo, Boo Foo Woo from Japan) at this casual, trendsetting store that is a favorite of Julianne Moore. ⊠ *26 E. 22nd St., between Broadway and Park Ave., Flatiron District* ☎ *212/420–9878* Ⓜ *6 to 23rd St.*

DISCOUNT SHOPPING
JEWELRY AND ACCESSORIES

Beads of Paradise. Not your ordinary bead store, the baubles here are sourced from around the world. Shoppers can choose silver from Bali and Mexico and ancient glass beads from China, along with semiprecious stones. Sign up for a class to learn how to put it all together. ⊠ *16 E. 17th St., between 5th Ave. and Broadway, Flatiron District* ☎ *212/620–0642* Ⓜ *4, 5, 6, N, Q, R to 14th St./Union Sq.*

HOME DECOR

Fodor'sChoice **ABC Carpet & Home.** If you love eclectic goods from around the world, ★ then this is your place. Spread over 10 floors is a superb selection of rugs, antiques, textiles, furniture, and bedding. Shoppers can find sleek sofas or Balinese daybeds. The ground floor is a wonderland of silk pillows and jewelry. To refuel, there's an in-house restaurant from Jean-Georges Vongerichten. More rugs and carpets are unrolled across the street at 881 Broadway. ⊠ *888 Broadway, at E. 19th St., Flatiron District* ☎ *212/473–3000* Ⓜ *L, N, Q, R, 4, 5, 6 to 14th St./Union Sq.*

The Conran Shop. This British stylemonger sells a sleek, understated lifestyle. Everything from kitchen and garden implements, fabrics, furniture, and glassware is for sale. Even the shower curtains are cool. ⊠ *888 Broadway, at E. 19th St., Flatiron District* ☎ *866/755–9079* Ⓜ *L, N, Q, R, 4, 5, 6 to 14th St./Union Sq.*

Fishs Eddy. The dishes, china, and glassware for resale come from all walks of crockery life, from corporate dining rooms to failed restaurants and ocean liners. Fishs Eddy also sells its own line of dishes, which have a classic look. ⊠ *889 Broadway, at E. 19th St., Flatiron District* ☎ *212/420–9020* Ⓜ *L, N, Q, R, 4, 5, 6 to 14th St./Union Sq.*

17

The Best Holiday Markets

Between Thanksgiving and Christmas, holiday markets—rows of wooden stalls, many with red-and-white-stripe awnings—spring up around town. The gifts and goods vary from year to year, but there are some perennial offerings: colorful handmade knitwear and jewelry; sweet-smelling soaps, candles, and lotions with hand-lettered labels; glittery Christmas ornaments of every stripe; and New York–theme gift items (a group called Gritty City offers T-shirts, coin purses, and undies printed with pictures of taxicabs and manhole covers).

Though the holiday market in **Grand Central Terminal's Vanderbilt Hall** is indoors, most vendors set up outside. There's one every year at **Columbus Circle**, near the southwest entrance to Central Park, and another at **Bryant Park**, behind the New York City Public Library. The largest and most popular, however, is at the south end of **Union Square**, where you can go from the greenmarket to the stalls like the downtowners who meet in the afternoon or after work to look for unique or last-minute gifts.

TOYS

Kidding Around. This independent shop is piled high with old-fashioned wooden toys, sturdy musical instruments, and plenty of arts-and-crafts materials. The costume racks are rich with dress-up potential. ⊠ *60 W. 15th St., between 5th and 6th Aves., Flatiron District* ☎ *212/645–6337* Ⓜ *L, N, Q, R, 4, 5, 6 to 14th St./Union Sq.*

MURRAY HILL

BOOKS AND STATIONERY

The Complete Traveller Antiquarian Bookstore. Founded in the '80s by two former travel writers, this store specializes in rare and antique voyage-related books, and holds the largest selection of out-of-print Baedeker travel guides. They stock surprisingly affordable vintage maps, unusual tomes with New York City themes, and a full spectrum of books—from history and geography to poetry and fiction—that emphasize travel. ⊠ *199 Madison Ave., at 35th St., Murray Hill* ☎ *212/685–9007* Ⓜ *6 to 33rd St.*

MIDTOWN

MIDTOWN EAST

ANTIQUES AND COLLECTIBLES

Chinese Porcelain Company. Though the name of this prestigious shop indicates one of its specialties, its stock covers more ground, ranging from lacquerware to Khmer sculpture as well as European decorative arts. ⊠ *475 Park Ave., at E. 58th St., Midtown East* ☎ *212/838–7744* Ⓜ *N, R to 5th Ave.*

Flying Cranes Antiques. At this world leader in Japanese antiques, shoppers will find a collection of rare, museum-quality pieces from the Meiji period, the time known as Japan's Golden Age. Items include ceramics, cloisonné, metalwork, baskets, and samurai swords and fittings.

✉ *Manhattan Art and Antiques Center, 1050 2nd Ave., between E. 55th and E. 56th Sts., Midtown East ☎ 212/223–4600 Ⓜ N, R, 4, 5, 6 to 59th St./Lexington Ave.*

Newel Art Galleries. Housed in a six-story building, this huge collection spans the Renaissance through the 20th century. The nonfurniture finds, from figureheads to bell jars, make for prime conversation pieces. Newel is also a major supplier of antiques for Broadway shows, television, and film. ✉ *425 E. 53rd St., between 1st Ave. and Sutton Pl., Midtown East ☎ 212/758–1970 Ⓜ 6 to 51st St./Lexington Ave.; E, M to Lexington– 3rd Aves./53rd St.*

BOOKS AND STATIONERY
Argosy Bookstore. Family owned since 1925, Argosy keeps a scholarly stock of rare books and autographs. It's also a great place to look for low-price maps and prints that make ideal gifts. ✉ *116 E. 59th St., between Park and Lexington Aves., Midtown East ☎ 212/753–4455 Ⓜ N, R, 4, 5, 6 to 59th St./Lexington Ave.*

CAMERAS AND ELECTRONICS
Apple Store. Apple's New York flagship is topped by a giant translucent cube and is open 24 hours a day, every day, to satisfy those wee-hours computer cravings. At all stores you'll have to elbow through a crowd, but they're the best places to check out the latest equipment, software, demos, and troubleshooting Genius Bars. ✉ *767 5th Ave., between E. 58th and E. 59th Sts., Midtown East ☎ 212/336–1440 Ⓜ R to 60th St.*

SONY Style. Located on the ground floor of the Sony Building, this sunny space is a wonderland of electronics. You'll find all the latest stereo and entertainment systems, digital cameras, high-def TVs, and MP3 players on the shelves. ✉ *550 Madison Ave., at E. 55th St., Midtown East ☎ 212/833–8800 Ⓜ E, M, 6 to 51st St./Lexington Ave.*

CLOTHING
BCBG/Max Azria. If flirtation's your sport, you'll find your sportswear here: fluttering skirts, beaded camisoles, chiffon dresses, and leather pants fill the racks. ✉ *770 Madison Ave., at E. 66th St., Upper East Side ☎ 212/717–4225 Ⓜ 6 to 68th St./Hunter College.*

Brooks Brothers. The clothes at this classic American haberdasher are, as ever, traditional, comfortable, and fairly priced. Summer seersucker, navy-blue blazers, and the peerless oxford shirts have been staples for generations. The women's and boys' selection have variations thereof. ■ TIP→ Get scanned by a digital tailor for precisely measured custom shirts or suits; appointments are recommended. ✉ *346 Madison Ave., at E. 44th St., Midtown East ☎ 212/682–8800 Ⓜ 4, 5, 6, 7, S to 42nd St./ Grand Central*

Burberry. This six-story glass-and-stone flagship is a temple to all things plaid and British. The iconic trench coat can be made-to-measure here, and the signature plaid can be found on bikinis, scarves, and wallets. For children, there are mini-versions of quilted jackets and cozy sweaters. ✉ *9 E. 57th St., between 5th and Madison Aves., Midtown East ☎ 212/407–7100 Ⓜ N, R, W to 5th Ave./59th St.*

17

FIFTH AVENUE AND 57TH STREET

Fifth Avenue from Rockefeller Center to Central Park South pogos between landmark department stores, glossy international designer boutiques, and casual national chains. What they all have in common: massive flagship spaces.

The intersection of 5th Avenue with 57th Street distills this mix of old and new, exclusive and accessible. From these corners you'll see blue-chip New York classics (jeweler Tiffany & Co., the Bergdorf Goodman department stores), luxury giants (Gucci and the glass box of Louis Vuitton), a high-tech wonderland (another glass box for Apple), and show-off digs for informal brands (NikeTown, Abercrombie & Fitch). Capping this shopping stretch at East 58th Street is the colossal, exceptional toy store FAO Schwarz. If you're keen to shop the high end or to see the impressive flagships, it's worth coming to this neighborhood—but if large-scale doesn't do it for you, you're better off heading downtown.
—J. P.

BEST TIME TO GO

Wednesday through Friday if you're trying to avoid crowds. Weekends before the winter holidays get extremely hectic and can spark "sidewalk rage" in even the most patient shopper—try to come earlier in the week, especially if you want to see the fantastic department-store window displays.

BEST SOUVENIR FOR KIDS

An incredibly lifelike stuffed animal from **FAO Schwarz**. They've got exclusive Steiff "purebred" dogs, for instance, that come with authenticity certificates from the American Kennel Club.

REFUELING

Soothe frazzled nerves with a stop at **Fika** (⊠ *41 W. 58th St., between 5th and 6th Aves.* ☎ *212/832–0022*), a calm, friendly Swedish café. Settle in for a meatball sandwich, a bracing cup of coffee, and a chocolate truffle. If you'd like to stay in the energetic current of 5th Avenue, nab a table, or a seat with a fold-down tray, at the stuck-in-the-'60s **Primeburger** (⊠ *5 E. 51st St., between 5th and Madison Aves.* ☎ *212/759–4729*). Go for a diner classic like an all-day omelet or a burger with a side of curly fries.

BEST FOR

DEPARTMENT STORES

Saks Fifth Avenue: fashion and nothing but.

Bergdorf Goodman: these partner stores (one for women, the other for men; guess which has the housewares) are both genteelly tasteful.

FLAGSHIP STORES

Louis Vuitton: every permutation of the signature handbags and leather goods, plus the jet-set clothing line upstairs.

Chanel: all the hallmarks, from little black dresses to double-C jewelry.

Apple: all sorts of chip-driven devices, 24 hours a day.

Gucci: check out classic designs and goodies exclusive to this store.

SERIOUS JEWELRY

Tiffany & Co.: hum "Moon River," check out the dazzling gems and pearls, then head upstairs for all sorts of silver ornaments.

Cartier: both classic and slinky new designs glitter in a turn-of-the-20th-century mansion.

Harry Winston: the ultimate for diamonds (just ask Marilyn Monroe).

Van Cleef & Arpels: the jewels may be big, but the logos and styles are understated.

17

Chanel. The Midtown flagship has often been compared to a Chanel suit—slim, elegant, and timeless, and decorated in the signature black-and-white colors. Inside wait the famed suits themselves, along with other pillars of Chanel style: chic little black dresses and evening gowns, chain-handled bags, and yards of pearls. There's also a small cosmetics area where you can stock up on the famed scents and nail polish. ⊠ 15 E. 57th St., between 5th and Madison Aves., Midtown East 🕾 212/355–5050 Ⓜ N, R to 5th Ave./59th St.

Christian Dior. John Galliano's over-the-top designs are showcased in this very white, very glossy, serene space. The designs bring elements of everything from raceways to skate punks to haute couture. If you're not in the market for an investment gown or fine jewelry, peruse the glam accessories, like the latest status bag. The Dior menswear boutique is next door; the rocking cigarette-thin suits are often pilfered by women. ⊠ 21 E. 57th St., at Madison Ave., Midtown East 🕾 212/931–2950 Ⓜ E, V to 5th Ave./53rd St.

Dunhill. If you're stumped on what to buy the man in your life, head to Dunhill. The menswear is exquisitely tailored; the accessories like wallets and cuff links are slightly more affordable. The walk-in humidor stores top-quality tobacco and cigars. ⊠ 545 Madison Ave., at E. 55th St., Midtown East 🕾 212/753–9292 Ⓜ F to 57th St.

Gianni Versace. The architecture here, with its marble floor and glittering chandeliers, provides the perfect backdrop for the outrageous designs and colors of Versace clothes. The brand's housewares and bedding collection is also available here. ⊠ 647 5th Ave., near E. 51st St., Midtown East 🕾 212/317–0224 Ⓜ E, M to 5th Ave./53rd St.

Gucci. Located in the Trump Building, this 46,000-square-foot flagship with floor-to-ceiling glass windows is the largest Gucci store in the world. Shoppers will find a special "heritage" department, plus goods exclusive to the store. The clothing is less aggressively sexy than it was in the Tom Ford era, but still edgy. Skintight pants might be paired with a luxe leather jacket; silk tops leave a little more to the imagination. The accessories, like wraparound shades or snakeskin shoes, many with signature horsebit detailing, continue to spark consumer frenzies. ⊠ 725 5th Ave., at 56th St., Midtown East 🕾 212/826–2600 Ⓜ N, R to 5th Ave./59th St.

Tommy Hilfiger. The global flagship oozes old-school Americana, with its dark-wood paneling, shirts displayed on bookshelves, and scattering of antiques. It's filled with tailored suits for men, smart sweater sets and pencil skirts for women, and evening wear along with sportswear, plus a whole floor devoted to denim. ⊠ 681 5th Ave., at 54th St., Midtown East 🕾 212/223–1824 Ⓜ E, M to 53rd St.

Yves Saint Laurent. Tom Ford's successor, Stephano Pilati, is lightening up the fabled French house. Think seduction instead of sexpot, with white trench coats, Grecian column dresses, and ruffled silk blouses. ⊠ 3 E. 57th St., between 5th and Madison Aves., Midtown East 🕾 212/980–2970 Ⓜ N, R to 5th Ave./59th St..

DEPARTMENT STORES

Bloomingdale's. Only a few stores in New York occupy an entire city block; the uptown branch of this New York institution is one of them. The main floor is a crazy, glittery maze of mirrored cosmetic counters and perfume-spraying salespeople. Once you get past this dizzying scene, you can find good buys on designer clothes, bedding, and housewares. ✉ *1000 3rd Ave., main entrance at E. 59th St. and Lexington Ave., Midtown East* ☎ *212/705–2000* Ⓜ *N, R, 4, 5, 6 to 59th St./Lexington Ave.*

Saks Fifth Avenue. A fashion- and beauty-only department store, Saks sells an astonishing array of clothing. The choice of American and European designers is impressive without being esoteric—the women's selection includes Gucci, Narciso Rodriguez, and Marc Jacobs, plus devastating ball gowns galore. The footwear collections are gratifyingly broad, from Ferragamo to Juicy. In the men's department, sportswear stars such as John Varvatos counterbalance formal wear and current trends. The ground-floor beauty department stocks everything from the classic (Sisley, Lancôme, La Prairie) to the fun and edgy (Nars, M.A.C.). ✉ *611 5th Ave., between E. 49th and E. 50th Sts., Midtown East* ☎ *212/753–4000* Ⓜ *E, M to 5th Ave./53rd St.*

HOME DECOR

Muji. If you're into simple, chic, cheap style, Muji will be your trifecta. The name of this Japanese import translates to "no brand," and indeed, you won't find a logo plastered on the housewares or clothes. Instead, their hallmark is streamlined, often monochromatic design. The whole range of goods, from milky porcelain teapots to wooden toys, is invariably user-friendly. At this branch, you can glimpse the lobby of the *New York Times.* ✉ *620 8th Ave., at W. 40th St., Midtown West* ☎ *212/382–2300* Ⓜ *A, C, E to 42nd St./Port Authority.*

JEWELRY AND ACCESSORIES

A La Vieille Russie. Antiques dealers since 1851, this shop specializes in European and Russian decorative arts, jewelry, and paintings. Behold bibelots by Fabergé and others, enameled or encrusted with jewels. If money is no object, there are also antique diamond necklaces and pieces of china once owned by Russian nobility. ✉ *781 5th Ave., at E. 59th St., Midtown East* ☎ *212/752–1727* Ⓜ *N, R to 5th Ave./59th St.*

Cartier. Pierre Cartier allegedly won the 5th Avenue mansion location by trading two strands of perfectly matched natural pearls with Mrs. Morton Plant. The jewelry is still incredibly persuasive, from such established favorites as the Trinity ring and Tank watches to exquisite cuff links for men. ✉ *653 5th Ave., at E. 52nd St., Midtown East* ☎ *212/753–0111* Ⓜ *E, M to 5th Ave./53rd St.*

H. Stern. Sleek designs pose in an equally modern 5th Avenue setting; smooth cabochon-cut stones, most from South America, glow in pale wooden display cases. The designers make notable use of semiprecious stones such as citrine, tourmaline, and topaz. ✉ *645 5th Ave., between E. 51st and E. 52nd Sts., Midtown East* ☎ *212/688–0300* Ⓜ *E, M to 5th Ave./53rd St.*

17

Ivanka Trump. Compared with the style of Trump *père*, this small jewelry boutique is quite discreet. All things being relative, though, The Donald's daughter would like to see you dripping with her diamonds. Drop earrings, tassel lariats, and lots of bold cocktail rings are shown in an unstuffy yet glam salon. ⊠ *685 Madison Ave., between E. 61st and E. 62nd Sts., Midtown East* ☎ *212/756–9912* Ⓜ *N, R, 4, 5, 6 to 59th St./Lexington Ave.*

Tiffany & Co. The display windows can be soigné, funny, or just plain breathtaking. Alongside the $80,000 platinum-and-diamond bracelets, a lot here is affordable on a whim (check out the sterling silver floor)—and everything comes wrapped in that unmistakable Tiffany blue. ⊠ *727 5th Ave., at E. 57th St., Midtown East* ☎ *212/755–8000* Ⓜ *N, R to 5th Ave./59th St.*

Van Cleef & Arpels. This French jewelry company is considerably more low-key than many of its blingy neighbors, in both the designs and marketing ethos (you won't see them opening a store in a suburban mall). Their best-known design is the cloverleaf Alhambra, which can be found on rings, necklaces, and earrings. Other designs are just as understated. ⊠ *744 5th Ave., between E. 57th St. and E. 58th Sts., Midtown East* ☎ *212/644–9500* Ⓜ *N, R to 5th Ave./59th St.*

SHOES, HANDBAGS, AND LEATHER GOODS

Bally. A few curveballs, like olive-green or canary-yellow pumps, liven up the mainly conservative selection. Carryons and clothing, such as deerskin or lamb jackets, join the shoe leather. ⊠ *628 Madison Ave., at E. 59th St., Midtown East* ☎ *212/751–9082* Ⓜ *N, R, 4, 5, 6 to 59th St./Lexington Ave.*

Bottega Veneta. The signature crosshatch weave graces leather handbags, slouchy satchels, and shoes; the especially satisfying brown shades extend from fawn to deep chocolate. The stylish men's and women's ready-to-wear collection is also sold here. ⊠ *697 5th Ave., between E. 54th and E. 55th Sts., Midtown East* ☎ *212/371–5511* Ⓜ *N, R, 4, 5, 6 to 59th St./Lexington Ave.*

Fendi. Once known for its furs, Fendi is now synonymous with decadent handbags. The purses are beaded, embroidered, and fantastically embellished within an inch of their lives, resulting in prices that skyrocket to more than $1,000. Fancy leathers, evening dresses, coats, and other accessories are also available. ⊠ *677 5th Ave., between E. 53rd and E. 54th Sts., Midtown East* ☎ *212/759–4646* Ⓜ *E, F to 5th Ave./53rd St.*

Fratelli Rossetti. Don't come here expecting sexy, skyscraper stilettos. This Italian leather goods company excels at beautiful, classic shoes. Their riding boots are among the most popular items, but there are also pumps, loafers, and slouchy ankle boots. Men can choose from oxfords and boots. There's also a line of leather handbags. ⊠ *625 Madison Ave., between E. 58th and E. 59th Sts., Midtown East* ☎ *212/888–5107* Ⓜ *N, R, 4, 5, 6 to 59th St.*

Furla. Shoulder bags, oblong clutches, and roomy totes can be quite proper or attention-getting, from a cocoa-brown, croc-embossed zippertop to a patent leather, cherry-red purse. ⊠ *598 Madison Ave., at E. 57th St., Midtown East* ☎ *212/980–3208* Ⓜ *N, R, 4, 5, 6 to 59th St.*

Louis Vuitton. In the mammoth 57th Street store vintage examples of Vuitton's famous monogrammed trunks float above the fray on the ground floor, where shoppers angle for the latest accessories. Joining the initials are the Damier check pattern and colorful striated leathers, plus devastatingly chic clothes and shoes designed by Marc Jacobs. ⊠ *1 E. 57th St., at 5th Ave., Midtown East* ☎ *212/758–8877* Ⓜ *E, V to 5th Ave./53rd St.*

Salvatore Ferragamo. Elegance and restraint typify these designs, from black-tie patent to weekender ankle boots. The company reworks some of their women's styles from previous decades, like the girlish Audrey (as in Hepburn) ballet flat, released seasonally for limited runs. Don't miss the silk ties for men. ⊠ *655 5th Ave., at E. 52nd St., Midtown East* ☎ *212/759–3822* Ⓜ *E, M to 53rd St.*

Stuart Weitzman. The broad range of styles, from wing tips to strappy sandals, is enhanced by an even wider range of sizes and widths. Bridal shoes are hugely popular, if pricey. ⊠ *625 Madison Ave., between E. 58th and E. 59th Sts., Midtown East* ☎ *212/750–2555* Ⓜ *N, R, 4, 5, 6 to 59th St./Lexington Ave.*

TOYS

American Girl Place. No pink toy convertibles here; instead, the name-sake dolls are historically themed, from Felicity of colonial Virginia to Kit of Depression-era Cincinnati. Each character has her own affiliated books, furniture, clothes, and accessories. There's a doll hairdressing station, a café, and a Dress Like Your Doll shop. ⊠ *609 5th Ave., at E. 49th St., Midtown East* ☎ *212/371–2220* Ⓜ *B, D, F, M to 47th–50th Sts./Rockefeller Center.*

Fodor's Choice ★ **FAO Schwarz Fifth Avenue.** A New York classic that's better than ever, this children's paradise more than lives up to the hype. The ground floor is a zoo of extraordinary stuffed animals, from cuddly $20 teddies to towering, life-size elephants and giraffes (with larger-than-life prices to match). FAO Schwartz stocks M&Ms in every color of the rainbow. Upstairs, you can dance on the giant musical floor keyboard, browse through Barbies wearing Armani and Juicy Couture, and design your own Muppet puppet. ⊠ *767 5th Ave., at E. 58th St., Midtown East* ☎ *212/644–9400* Ⓜ *4, 5, 6 to E. 59th St.*

MIDTOWN WEST

BEAUTY

The Plaza Beauty. If the sticky samples at Sephora make your skin crawl, try an all-together more civilized experience here. The Plaza Beauty, inside the legendary hotel, is a futuristic, all-white space stocked with elite brands like Tocca, Youngblood, and Aquiesse. For more pampering there's an eyebrow bar and men's area. Best of all, the sales staff is calm and helpful and won't attack you with perfume. ⊠ *1 W. 58th St., Grand Concourse Level, between 5th and 6th Aves., Midtown West* ☎ *212/223–4694* Ⓜ *N, Q, R to 34th St./Herald Sq.*

CAMERAS AND ELECTRONICS

★ **B&H Photo Video and Pro Audio.** As baskets of purchases trundle along on tracks overhead, you can plunge into the excellent selection of imaging, audio, video, and lighting equipment. The staff is generous with

17

advice, and will happily compare merchandise. Low prices, good customer service, and a liberal returns policy make this a favorite with pros and amateurs alike. ■TIP→ Be sure to leave a few extra minutes for the checkout procedure; also, keep in mind that the store is closed Saturday. ✉ 420 9th Ave., between W. 33rd and W. 34th Sts., Midtown West ☎ 212/444–6615 Ⓜ N, Q, R to 5th Ave./59th St.

CLOTHING

Cheap Jack's. Jack's two-floor space may be 12,000 square feet, but it's still jammed with interesting duds—although they are not as cheap as the name would suggest. There's almost everything you could wish for: track suits, bomber jackets, early 1980s madras shirts, old prom dresses, and vintage concert T-shirts with the eau-de-mothball stamp of authenticity. ✉ 303 5th Ave., at 31st St., Midtown West ☎ 212/777–9564 Ⓜ N, Q, R to 34th St./Herald Sq.

Forever 21. The pounding music, plethora of jeggings, and graffiti-covered N.Y.C. taxicab parked inside will appeal to tween shoppers. But even if you are older than 21, you'll still find a reason to shop here. This location, clocking in at a whopping 90,000 square feet, is the biggest Forever 21 on the East Coast. Come for supertrendy clothes that won't break the bank, such as slouchy sweaters, shirtdresses, and pouffy skirts. Menswear and children's clothes are also sold here, and the jewelry is surprisingly well done. ✉ 303 5th Ave., at 31st St., Midtown West ☎ 212/777–9564 Ⓜ B, D, F, M to 47th–50th St./Rockefeller Ctr.

Norma Kamali. A fashion fixture from the 1980s has a newly modern, though still '80s-influenced, line. Her luminously white store carries bold black-and-white-pattern bathing suits, Grecian-style draped dresses, and her signature poofy "sleeping-bag coats." The in-house Wellness Café sells olive oil–based beauty products and healthful snacks like kale chips. ✉ 1540 Broadway, between W. 45th and W. 46th Sts., Midtown West ☎ 212/302–0594 Ⓜ E, M to 5th Ave./53rd St.

DEPARTMENT STORES

Fodor's Choice
★ **Bergdorf Goodman.** Good taste reigns here in an elegant and sophisticated setting. Bergdorf's carries some brilliant lines, such as Marchesa, Narciso Rodriguez, and Balenciaga. In the basement Level of Beauty, find a seat in the manicure–pedicure lounge or go for Bergdorf Blonde highlights at the in-house John Barrett salon. The home department has rooms full of magnificent linens, tableware, and gifts. To fully be a lady who lunches, grab a bite at the seventh-floor BG Salon, with Central Park views. ✉ 754 5th Ave., between W. 57th and W. 58th Sts., Midtown West Ⓜ N, R to 5th Ave.

Henri Bendel. Behind the graceful Lalique windows you'll discover a mecca of niche boutiques stocking beauty products, accessories, and gifts (but no clothing). Bendel's dedication to the unusual begins in the ground-floor cosmetics area and percolates through the floors of women's lingerie and jewelry, scarves, and sunglasses. The in-house lines are displayed throughout. ⊠ *712 5th Ave., between W. 55th and W. 56th Sts., Midtown West* ☎ *212/247–1100* Ⓜ *E, M to 5th Ave./53rd St.*

Lord & Taylor. This is not your mother's Lord & Taylor. The department store has been working hard to attract a younger, hipper crowd. Thanks to a recent makeover, the clothing departments are easier to navigate and shoppers will find classic brands like Coach, Donna Karan, and Ralph Lauren. The ground-floor beauty department also got a face-lift, with store exclusives like Lancôme's first mascara bar. ⊠ *424 5th Ave., between W. 38th and W. 39th Sts., Midtown West* ☎ *212/391–3344* Ⓜ *B, D, F, N, Q, R, M to 34th St./Herald Sq.*

Macy's. Macy's headquarters has more than 1 million square feet of retail space, so expect to lose your bearings at least once. Fashion-wise, there's a concentration on the mainstream rather than on the luxe. One strong suit is denim, with everything from Hilfiger and Calvin Klein to Earl Jeans and Paper Denim & Cloth. There's also a reliably good selection of American designs from Ralph Lauren, DKNY, and Sean John. For cooking gear and housewares, the Cellar nearly outdoes Zabar's. ⊠ *Herald Sq., 151 W. 34th St., between 6th and 7th Aves., Midtown West* ☎ *212/695–4400* Ⓜ *B, D, F, N, Q, R, M to 34th St./Herald Sq.*

JEWELRY AND ACCESSORIES

Bulgari. This Italian company is certainly not shy about its name, which encircles gems, watch faces, and an ever-growing accessories line. There are beautiful, weighty rings, pieces mixing gold with stainless steel or porcelain, and the brand's signature cabochon multicolored sapphires. Wedding and engagement rings are slightly more subdued. ⊠ *730 5th Ave., at W. 57th St., Midtown West* ☎ *212/315–9000* Ⓜ *N, R to 5th Ave.*

Harry Winston. These jewels regularly adorn celebs at the Oscars, and you'll need an A-list bank account to shop here. The ice-clear diamonds are of impeccable quality, and are set in everything from emerald-cut solitaire rings to wreath necklaces resembling strings of flowers. No wonder the jeweler was immortalized in the song "Diamonds Are a Girl's Best Friend." ⊠ *718 5th Ave., at W. 56th St., Midtown West* ☎ *212/245–2000* Ⓜ *F to 57th St.*

Mikimoto. The Japanese originator of the cultured pearl, Mikimoto presents a glowing display of high-luster pearls. Besides the creamy strands from their own pearl farms, check out diamond-and-pearl earrings, bracelets, and rings. ⊠ *730 5th Ave., between W. 56th and W. 57th Sts., Midtown West* ☎ *212/457–4600* Ⓜ *F to 57th St.*

MUSEUM STORES

Museum of Arts and Design. In this museum's new home, the gift shop stocks crafts such as beautiful handmade tableware, unusual jewelry, and rugs, often tied in to ongoing exhibits. ⊠ *2 Columbus Circle, at 8th Ave., Midtown West* ☎ *212/299–7777* Ⓜ *1, A, B, C, D to 59th St./Columbus Circle.*

★ **Museum of Modern Art Design and Book Store.** The redesigned MoMA expanded its in-house shop with a huge selection of art posters and a gorgeous selection of coffee-table books on painting, sculpture, film, and photography. Across the street is the **MoMA Design Store,** where you can find Charles and Ray Eames furniture reproductions, vases designed by Alvar Aalto, and lots of clever trinkets. ⊠ *11 W. 53rd St., between 5th and 6th Aves., Midtown West* ☎ 212/708–9700 Ⓜ *E, M to 5th Ave./53rd St.*

MUSIC STORES

Colony Music. Siphoning energy from Times Square, this place keeps its neon blinking until 1 am Monday through Saturday, and midnight on Sunday. Inspired by the Broadway musical or concert you've just seen? Snap up the sheet music, CD, or karaoke set here. ⊠ *1619 Broadway, at W. 49th St., Midtown West* ☎ 212/265–2050 Ⓜ *R to 49th St.*

PERFORMING ARTS MEMORABILIA

Drama Book Shop. If you're looking for a script, be it a lesser-known Russian translation or a Broadway hit, chances are you can find it here. The range of books spans film, music, dance, TV, and biographies. The shop also hosts Q&As with leading playwrights. ⊠ *250 W. 40th St., between 7th and 8th Aves., Midtown West* ☎ 212/944–0595 Ⓜ *A, C, E to 42nd St./Port Authority.*

One Shubert Alley. This was the first store to sell Broadway merchandise outside of a theater. Today souvenir posters, tees, and other knick-knacks memorializing past and present Broadway hits still reign at this Theater District shop. ⊠ *1 Shubert Alley, between W. 44th and W. 45th Sts., Midtown West* ☎ 212/944–4133 Ⓜ *N, Q, R, S, 1, 2, 3 to 42nd St./Times Sq.*

Triton Gallery. Theatrical posters large and small are available, and the selection is democratic, with everything from Marlene Dietrich's *Blue Angel* to recent Broadway shows represented. ⊠ *630 9th Ave., between W. 44th and W. 45th Sts., Suite 808, Midtown West* ☎ 212/765–2472 Ⓜ *A, E to 42nd St./Port Authority.*

SHOES, HANDBAGS, AND LEATHER GOODS

Christian Louboutin. Lipstick-red soles are the signature of Louboutin's delicately sexy couture slippers and stilettos, and his latest, larger downtown store has carpeting to match. The pointy-toe creations come trimmed with brocade, tassels, buttons, or satin ribbons. ⊠ *965 Madison Ave., between E. 75th and E. 76th Sts., Upper East Side* ☎ 212/396–1884 Ⓜ *6 to 77th St.*

Cole-Haan. This once-conservative brand now shines with shoes made in exotic skins like python and crocodile; for warm weather, check out the orange suede thongs for men and metallic gladiator sandals for women. If comfort is key, many shoes have Nike Air cushioning in the heels. ⊠ *620 5th Ave., at Rockefeller Center, Midtown West* ☎ 212/765–9747 Ⓜ *E, M to 5th Ave./53rd St.*

Manolo Blahnik. These sexy status shoes are some of the most expensive on the market. The signature look is a pointy toe with a high, delicate heel, but there are also ballet flats, gladiator sandals, and over-the-knee dominatrix boots that cost nearly $2,000. Pray for a sale. ⊠ *31 W. 54th St., between 5th and 6th Aves., Midtown West* ☎ 212/582–3007 Ⓜ *E, M to 5th Ave./53rd St.*

Smythson of Bond Street. Although Smythson still sells stationery fit for a queen—check out the royal warrant from England's HRH—its newly expanded line of leather goods includes on-trend handbags and wallets. The hues range from sedate brown and black to eye-popping tangerine. The softbound leather diaries, address books, and travel accessories make ideal gifts. ⊠ *4 W. 57th St., between 5th and 6th Aves., Midtown West* ☎ *212/265–4573* Ⓜ *F to 57th St.*

TOYS

Toys "R" Us. The Times Square megastore is so big that a three-story Ferris wheel—complete with 14 individually themed cars—revolves inside. With all the movie tie-in merchandise, video games, yo-yos, stuffed animals, and what seems to be the entire Mattel oeuvre, good luck extracting your kids from here. ⊠ *1514 Broadway, at W. 44th St., Midtown West* ☎ *646/366–8800* Ⓜ *1, N, Q, R to 42nd St./Times Sq.*

THE UPPER EAST SIDE

ANTIQUES AND COLLECTIBLES

Florian Papp. Established in 1900, this store has an unassailed reputation among knowledgeable collectors. Expect to find American and European antiques and paintings from the 18th to 20th century. Gilt mirrors and mahogany tables abound. ⊠ *962 Madison Ave., between E. 75th and E. 76th Sts., Upper East Side* ☎ *212/288–6770* Ⓜ *6 to 77th St.*

L'Antiquaire & The Connoisseur, Inc. Proprietor Helen Fioratti has written a guide to French antiques, but she's equally knowledgeable about her Italian and Spanish furniture and decorative objects from the 15th through the 18th centuries, as well as about the medieval arts. ⊠ *36 E. 73rd St., between Madison and Park Aves., Upper East Side* ☎ *212/517–9176* Ⓜ *6 to 77th St.*

Keno Auctions. Leigh Keno of *Antique Roadshow* fame presides over this auction house, which specializes in Americana. As expected, he has a good eye and an interesting inventory; he's sold silver sauceboats from Paul Revere, paintings, and Chippendale furniture. ⊠ *127 E. 69th St., between Park and Lexington Aves., Upper East Side* ☎ *212/734–2381* Ⓜ *6 to 68th St./Hunter College.*

Leo Kaplan Ltd. The impeccable items here include Art Nouveau glass and pottery, porcelain from 18th-century England, antique and modern paperweights, and Russian artwork. ⊠ *114 E. 57th St., between Park and Lexington Aves., Upper East Side* ☎ *212/355–7212* Ⓜ *N, R, 4, 5, 6 to 59th St./Lexington Ave.*

BEAUTY

Fresh. All of the products here sound good enough to eat, with ingredients like brown sugar, soy, and black tea. The zingy Sugar fragrance is one of the company's best sellers. This location also has a tiny spa, and treatments are often redeemable against products. ⊠ *1367 3rd Ave., at E. 78th St., Upper East Side* ☎ *212/585–3400* Ⓜ *6 to 77th St.*

Jo Malone. Tangy scents such as lime blossom and mandarin, and pomegranate noir can be worn alone or layered for the Malone style. Since Malone uses colognes, not perfumes, it's not overpowering. You can

17

MADISON AVENUE

GIORGIO ARMANI

If you're craving a couture fix, cab it straight to Madison Avenue between East 57th and East 79th streets. Here the greatest Italian, French, and American fashion houses form a platinum-card corridor for ladies who lunch. (If you're going to be pointedly overlooked by a salesperson, odds are it will happen here.)

Most occupy large, glass-façade spaces, but there are some exceptions, from intimate boutiques in old brownstones to the pair of mansions that are home to Ralph Lauren. Barneys, a full-fledged if very select department store, fits right in with the avenue's recherché roll call. But Madison isn't just a fashion funnel. A couple of marvelous booksellers and several outstanding antiques dealers and art galleries share this address as well.

—J. P.

BEST TIME TO GO

Saturday is the busiest day and thus better for people-watching. Perhaps because of the European influence, the pace is calmer here, especially on weekdays. Avoid coming on a Sunday, since several stores close, especially in summer when they figure their main clientele is out in the Hamptons.

BEST SOUVENIR FOR AN EX-MANHATTANITE

Take a whiff of the Manhattan-inspired perfumes like Chelsea Flowers and Park Avenue at **Bond No. 9**. Can't decide? Snap up the sampler box with travel-size spray scents wrapped like bonbons.

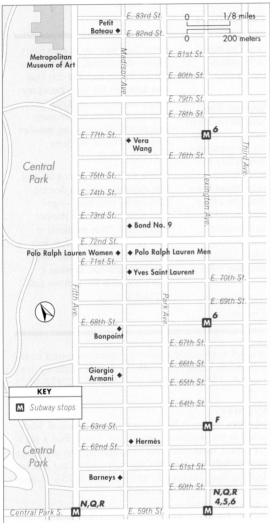

E. 83rd St.

Petit
Bateau ◆   E. 82nd St.

0   1/8 miles
0   200 meters

Metropolitan
Museum of Art

E. 81st St.

E. 80th St.

Madison Ave.

E. 79th St.

E. 78th St.

E. 77th St.   ◆ Vera
              Wang

Ⓜ 6

E. 76th St.

Third Ave.

Central
Park

E. 75th St.

E. 74th St.

E. 73rd St.

Lexington Ave.

◆ Bond No. 9

E. 72nd St.

Polo Ralph Lauren Women ◆   ◆ Polo Ralph Lauren Men
E. 71st St.

◆ Yves Saint Laurent

E. 70th St.

Fifth Ave.

E. 69th St.

Park Ave.

Ⓜ 6

E. 68th St.
◆
Bonpoint

E. 67th St.

E. 66th St.

Giorgio
Armani ◆

E. 65th St.

E. 64th St.

KEY

Ⓜ *Subway stops*

E. 63rd St.

Ⓜ F

E. 62nd St.   ◆ Hermès

Central
Park

E. 61st St.

Barneys ◆

E. 60th St.

N,Q,R
4,5,6

N,Q,R

E. 59th St.

Ⓜ

Central Park S. Ⓜ

17

BEST FOR

INTERNATIONAL MEGA-DESIGNERS

Barneys: dozens of the most cutting-edge names.

Polo Ralph Lauren: haute-WASP style in two beautiful mansions.

Hermès: those divine silk scarves and handbags are waiting. . . .

Giorgio Armani: a sleek setting for perfectly cut suits and dramatic evening wear.

Yves Saint Laurent: Left Bank chic, *fabuleux* accessories.

Vera Wang: the classic bridal gown.

FANCY CHILDREN'S CLOTHES

Bonpoint: precious European designs with hand embroidering, velvet ribbons—you get the picture.

Petit Bateau: all superfine, hypoallergenic, colorful cotton, all the time.

REFUELING

Join the Upper East Side yummy mummies and their trilingual children at the local branch of **Le Pain Quotidien** (✉ *1131 Madison Ave., between E. 84th and E. 85th Sts.* ☎ *212/327–4900*) for a fruit tart, ham-and-Gruyere tartine, or steaming bowl of cocoa. If you're willing to pull yourself away from Madison Avenue, the front room of American-style bakeshop **Two Little Red Hens** (✉ *1652 2nd Ave., between E. 85th and E. 86th Sts.* ☎ *212/452–0476*) has a handful of small tables where you can order a latticed pie or a walnut-pear tart.

The Best Local Chains

New Yorkers in the know hit these fabulous local chains for unique frocks and the best of the city's one-stop-shopping.

Ricky's. Loud and fun, these drugstores sprinkled around the city attract an eclectic, mostly young crowd who come just as often for the crazy-color wigs or false eyelashes as they do for Dove body wash and Neutrogena soap. Every fall the stores turn into Halloween Central, with a huge assortment of feather boas, masks, and trendy costumes referencing everything from Avatar to Jersey Shore. The flagship store is located in TriBeCa. ☒ *375 Broadway, TriBeCa* ☎ *212/925–5490.*

Scoop. These clothes help you fit in with the too-cool-to-dress-up

crowd. They have lots of jeans (Levi's, Citizens of Humanity), slinky tops, vintage-looking tees, and cozy knits from designers like Stella McCartney, Theory, and Halston Heritage. Other locations in the city feature menswear. ☒ *473–475 Broadway, between Broome and Grand Sts., SoHo* ☎ *212/925–3539.*

Searle. Mostly strung along the East Side, these stores have a devoted following for their coats—especially sleek designs from Moncler and Postcard. There are plenty of other designer items to layer, from cowl-neck sweaters to fitted tees. ☒ *635 Madison Ave., between E. 59th and E. 60th Sts., Midtown East* ☎ *212/750–5153.*

also stop by for a quick fragrance-combining consultation or a hand-and-arm massage from one of the store's stylists. ☒ *946 Madison Ave., between E. 74th and E. 75th Sts., Upper East Side* ☎ *212/472–0074* Ⓜ *6 to 77th St.*

BOOKS AND STATIONERY

Crawford Doyle Booksellers. You're as likely to see an old edition of Wodehouse as a best seller in the window of this shop. You'll find a high-quality selection of fiction, nonfiction, and biographies, plus some rare books on the balcony. Salespeople offer their opinions *and* ask for yours. ☒ *1082 Madison Ave., between E. 81st and E. 82nd Sts., Upper East Side* ☎ *212/288–6300* Ⓜ *4, 5, 6 to 86th St.*

Shakespeare & Co. Booksellers. The stock here represents what's happening in just about every field of publishing today: students can grab a last-minute Gertrude Stein for class, then rummage through the homages to cult pop-culture figures. ☒ *939 Lexington Ave., between E. 68th and E. 69th Sts., Upper East Side* ☎ *212/570–0201* Ⓜ *6 to 68th St./Hunter College*

CHILDREN'S CLOTHING

Bonpoint. The sophistication here lies in the beautiful designs and impeccable workmanship—pony-hair baby booties and hand-embroidered jumpers and blouses. Older kids can rock Liberty print dresses and peacoats. ☒ *1269 Madison Ave., at E. 91st St., Upper East Side* ☎ *212/722–7720* Ⓜ *4, 5, 6 to 86th St.*

Flora and Henri. The padded twill coats, slate-blue pleated skirts, and skinny cords here are cute with a vintage vibe. They'll stand up to wear and tear, and many of the boys' and girls' clothes are interchangeable. Witness the sturdy Italian-made shoes. ✉ *1023 Lexington Ave., between E. 73rd and E. 74th Sts., Upper East Side* ☎ *212/249–1695* Ⓜ *6 to 77th St.*

Infinity. Prep-school girls and their mothers giggle and gossip over the preteen slinky clothes (with more than a few moms picking up T-shirts and jeans for themselves) with Les Tout Petits dresses, Juicy Couture jeans, and slogan tees. ✉ *1116 Madison Ave., at E. 83rd St., Upper East Side* ☎ *212/734–0077* Ⓜ *4, 5, 6 to 86th St.*

Petit Bateau. Fine cotton is spun into comfortable clothes for babies and kids. Stock up on white onesies and bodysuits, as well as T-shirts and pants. ✉ *1094 Madison Ave., at E. 82nd St., Upper East Side* ☎ *212/988–8884* Ⓜ *4, 5, 6 to 86th St.*

CLOTHING

Barbour. The signature look here is the company's waxed cotton jacket, available for men and women. The quilted jackets, tweeds, moleskin pants, lamb's-wool sweaters, and tattersall shirts invariably call up images of country rambles. ✉ *1047 Madison Ave., at E. 80th St., Upper East Side* ☎ *212/570–2600* Ⓜ *6 to 77th St.*

Bra Smyth. Chic and sweetly sexy French and Canadian underthings in soft cottons and silks line the shelves of this Uptown staple. In addition to the selection of bridal-ready white bustiers and custom-fit swimsuits (made, cleverly, in bra-cup sizes), the store is best known for its knowledgeable staff, many of whom can offer tips on proper fit and size you up on sight. Cup sizes run from AA to J. ✉ *905 Madison Ave., at 73rd St., Upper East Side* ☎ *212/772–9400* Ⓜ *6 to 68th St./Hunter College.*

Calvin Klein. Though the namesake designer has bowed out, the label keeps channeling his particular style. This stark flagship store emphasizes the luxe end of the clothing line. Men's suits tend to be soft around the edges; women's evening gowns are often a fluid pouring of silk. There are also shoes, accessories, housewares, and makeup. ✉ *654 Madison Ave., at E. 60th St., Upper East Side* ☎ *212/292–9000* Ⓜ *N, R, 4, 5, 6 to 59th St./Lexington Ave.*

Carolina Herrera. A favorite of the society set (and Renee Zellweger), Herrera's designs are ladylike and elegant. On her suits, gowns, and cocktail dresses, expect anything from demure, shimmering bands of decoration to knockout swaths of beaded lace. ✉ *954 Madison Ave., at E. 75th St., Upper East Side* ☎ *212/249–6552* Ⓜ *6 to 77th St.*

DKNY. The signature style here is casual sophistication—in other words, a very New York look. Slinky wrap dresses, chunky-knit sweaters, and dark denim are some of the best bets here. If hunger strikes, head to the second floor for a wrap or a salad at Blanche's Organic Café. ✉ *655 Madison Ave., at E. 60th St., Upper East Side* ☎ *212/223–3569* Ⓜ *N, R, W, 4, 5, 6 to 59th St./Lexington Ave.*

Dolce & Gabbana. It's easy to feel like an Italian movie star amid these exuberant (in every sense) clothes. Pinstripes are a favorite; for women, they could be paired with something sheer, furred, or leopard-print, and for men they elongate the sharp suits. ✉ *825 Madison Ave., between E. 68th and E. 69th Sts., Upper East Side* ☎ 212/249–4100 Ⓜ *6 to 68th St./Hunter College.*

Etro. Trademark paisleys and bold patterns sprawl over richly covered suits, dresses, and lustrous pillows at this Italian designer's boutique, while juicy colors and rich detailing and embroidery keep things modern. ✉ *720 Madison Ave., between E. 63rd and E. 64th Sts., Upper East Side* ☎ 212/317–9096 Ⓜ *6 to 68th St./Hunter College.*

J. Crew. The preppy-chic brand that is a staple in so many people's closets continues to push the envelope. Yes, you can still get cardigans, cords, and tees in every pastel color of the rainbow, but some of the separates are downright sexy. The leather jackets and sequined skirts are also perfect for that casual, thrown-together look. ✉ *1035 Madison Ave., at 79th St., Upper East Side* ☎ 212/249–3869 Ⓜ *6 to 77th St./Lexington Ave.*

J. Crew Bridal Boutique. Brides on a budget—and those seeking a simple frock—sighed with relief when preppy favorite J.Crew started selling bridal gowns. And now, the line is featured in an elegant town house, the first boutique the company opened. One floor is filled with cocktail and occasion dresses, and bridal gowns and bridesmaid dresses are on the ground level. For one-stop shopping, jewelry and undergarments are also sold here. Appointments are required to view the bridal and party collections. ✉ *769 Madison Ave., at 66th St., Upper East Side* ☎ 212/824–2500 Ⓜ *6 to 68th St./Hunter College.*

Lanvin. This French label has been around since 1889, and is the oldest French fashion house still in existence. After a period of hibernation, Lanvin reemerged on the fashion radar in 2001, when designer Alber Elbaz took over the reins. The signature look is fluid and sexy; think one-shouldered cocktail dresses, cigarette pants, and ruffled blouses. This elegant town house is the first U.S. outpost. The interior design itself is a showstopper; the three-story space oozes old money and glamour with its Art Deco chandeliers and soothing gray walls. And the clothes? Just as slinky. ✉ *815 Madison Ave., between E. 68th and E. 69th Sts., Upper East Side* ☎ 646/439–0381 Ⓜ *6 to 68th St./Hunter College.*

La Perla. If money is no object, shop here for some of the sexiest underthings around. Choose from items ranging from sheer lace sets and corsets to bathing suits and racy nightgowns. ✉ *803 Madison Ave., between E. 67th and E. 68th Sts., Upper East Side* ☎ 212/570–0050 Ⓜ *6 to 68th St./Hunter College.*

Lisa Perry. Perry takes an artist's approach to her designs in this white loftlike space. She has created dresses printed with famous Andy Warhol photographs, such as the image of him drowning in a Campbell's Soup can. Pop art aside, her store is filled with a mix of '60s and '70s vintage clothes as well as her own designs. Accessories like vintage cocktail glasses and evening bags are also available. ✉ *976 Madison Ave., between E. 76th and E. 77th Sts., Upper East Side* ☎ 212/334–1956 Ⓜ *4, 6 to 77th St./Lexington.*

Marina Rinaldi. If you are a curvy size 10–22 and want to celebrate your figure rather than hide it, shop here. Marina Rinaldi sells form-flattering knit dresses, wool trousers, and coats that are tasteful and luxurious. ⊠ *13 E. 69th St., between Madison and 5th Aves., Upper East Side* ☎ *212/734–4333* Ⓜ *6 to 68th St./Hunter College.*

Max Mara. Think subtle colors and plush fabrics—straight skirts in cashmere or heathered wool, tuxedo-style evening jackets, and several choices of wool and cashmere camel overcoats. The suits are exquisitely tailored. ⊠ *813 Madison Ave., at E. 68th St., Upper East Side* ☎ *212/879–6100* Ⓜ *6 to 68th St./Hunter College.*

Michael Kors. In his deft reworkings of American classics, *Project Runway* judge Kors gives sportswear the luxury treatment, as with cream-color cashmere pullovers. An industrial element is creeping in, too, with chunky gold-chain detailing on buttery leather bags and jewelry. ⊠ *974 Madison Ave., at E. 76th St., Upper East Side* ☎ *212/452–4685* Ⓜ *6 to 77th St.*

Morgane Le Fay. The clothes here have a dreamy, ethereal quality that is decidedly feminine. Silk gowns are fluid and soft; fitted velvet jackets have covered buttons. Her dresses are also popular with brides who want a minimalist look. ⊠ *980 Madison Ave., between E. 76th and E. 77th Sts., Upper East Side* ☎ *212/879–9700* Ⓜ *6 to 68th St./Hunter College.*

Oscar de la Renta. The ladylike yet lighthearted runway designs of this upper-crust favorite got their first U.S. store here. Skirts swing, ruffles billow, embroidery brightens up tweed, and even a tennis dress looks like something you could go dancing in. ⊠ *772 Madison Ave., at E. 66th St., Upper East Side* ☎ *212/288–5810* Ⓜ *6 to 68th St./Hunter College.*

Polo Ralph Lauren. Even if you can't afford the clothes, come just to soak up the luxe RL lifestyle. This brand-new women's flagship is housed in a 22,000-square-foot building built to look like a historic Beaux-Arts mansion (or small palace), complete with a curving marble staircase and stone floors. In addition to the complete women's collection, the brand's lingerie and home wares, and its first fine-jewelry and watch salon are here. The men's collection is just across the street in the Rhinelander Mansion. ⊠ *888 Madison Ave., at E. 72nd St., Upper East Side* ☎ *212/606–2100* Ⓜ *6 to 68th St./Hunter College.*

Reed Krakoff. Coach's president and creative director has branched out to launch his own luxury lifestyle store. The clothing has an edgy look, with little black dresses in heavy wool, and massive cuff bracelets. The handbags and shoes, however, lean more toward ladylike. ⊠ *831 Madison Ave., between 69th and 70th Sts., Upper East Side* ☎ *212/988–0560* Ⓜ *6 to 68th St./Hunter College.*

Roberto Cavalli. Rock-star style (at rock-star prices) delivers denim decked with fur, feathers, animal prints, and even shredded silk overlays in this temple to the over-the-top. ⊠ *711 Madison Ave., at E. 63rd St., Upper East Side* ☎ *212/755–7722* Ⓜ *N, R to 5th Ave./59th St.*

Tom Ford. Ford is famous for making Gucci supersexy, but the menswear here veers toward the traditional—albeit impeccably made. Shirts come in more than 300 hues, and off-the-rack suits start around $3,000. Glide up the ebony staircase for the made-to-measure services, which will customize anything from suits to pajamas. Don't miss the fragrance chamber either. ⊠ *845 Madison Ave., at E. 70th St., Upper East Side* ☎ *212/359–0300* Ⓜ *6 to 68th St./Hunter College.*

Valentino. The mix here is at once audacious and beautifully cut; the fur or feather trimmings, low necklines, and opulent fabrics are about as close as you can get to celluloid glamour. No one does a better red. ⊠ *747 Madison Ave., at E. 65th St., Upper East Side* ☎ *212/772–6969* Ⓜ *6 to 68th St./Hunter College.*

Vera Wang. This star wedding-dress designer churns out dreamy dresses that are sophisticated without being over-the-top. Choose from A-line and princess styles, and slinky sheaths. If money is no object, bespoke wedding dresses are available. Appointments are essential. ⊠ *991 Madison Ave., at E. 77th St., Upper East Side* ☎ *212/628–3400* Ⓜ *6 to 77th St.*

Vilebrequin. Allow St-Tropez to influence your swimsuit; these striped, floral, and solid-color French-made trunks come in sunny hues. Waterproof pocket inserts keep your essentials safe from beachcombers. Many styles come in boys' sizes, too. ⊠ *1070 Madison Ave., at E. 81st St., Upper East Side* ☎ *212/650–0353* Ⓜ *6 to 77th St.*

DEPARTMENT STORES

★ **Barneys New York.** Barneys continues to provide fashion-conscious and big-budget shoppers with irresistible, must-have items at its uptown flagship store. The extensive menswear selection has a handful of edgier designers, though made-to-measure is always available. The women's department showcases posh designers of all stripes, from the subdued lines of Armani and Nina Ricci to the irrepressible Alaïa and Zac Posen. The shoe selection trots out Prada boots and strappy Blahniks; the cosmetics department will keep you in Kiehl's, Sue Devitt, and Chantecaille; jewelry runs from the whimsical (Mark Davis) to the classic (Ileana Makri). ⊠ *660 Madison Ave., between E. 60th and E. 61st Sts., Upper East Side* ☎ *212/826–8900* Ⓜ *N, R, 4, 5, 6 to 59th St./Lexington Ave.*

FOOD AND TREATS

François Chocolate Bar. On the fourth floor of the ultraglam jewelry store Mauboussin, you'll find a chocolate shop owned by famed patissier François Payard. Here, amid exposed brick and *"chocolat"*-painted walls, pastries are displayed like jewels in glass cases. Choose from pound cakes and parfaits, or *verrines,* boasting layers like dark chocolate and *fleur de sel* (hand-harvested sea salt). Macaroons go for only $2.25 a pop. ⊠ *714 Madison Ave., between E. 63rd and E. 64th Sts., Upper East Side* ☎ *212/759–1600* Ⓜ *F to Lexington Ave./63rd St.*

La Maison du Chocolat. Stop in at this chocolatier's small tea salon to dive into a cup of thick, heavenly hot chocolate. The Paris-based outfit sells handmade truffles, chocolates, and pastries that could lull you into a chocolate stupor. ⊠ *1018 Madison Ave., between E. 78th and 79th Sts., Upper East Side* ☎ *212/744–7117* Ⓜ *6 to 77th St.*

HOUSEHOLD ITEMS/FURNITURE

Jonathan Adler. Everything at this newly expanded flagship is fun, groovy, and happy. Adler funks up midcentury modern designs with his striped, striated, or curvy handmade pottery (ranging from a $30 vase to a chunky $400 lamp) as well as the hand-loomed wool pillow covers, rugs, and throws with blunt graphics (stripes, crosses, circles). There's also a new children's line. ⌧ *1097 Madison Ave., at 83rd St., Upper East Side* ☎ *212/772–2410* Ⓜ *4, 5, 6 to 86th St.*

JEWELRY AND ACCESSORIES

Asprey. Its net spreads to cater to all luxury kinds of tastes, from leather goods and rare books to polo equipment and cashmere sweaters. Asprey's claim to fame, though, is jewelry; its own eponymous diamond cut has A-shape facets. ⌧ *853 Madison Ave., between 70th and 71st Sts., Upper East Side* ☎ *212/688–1811* Ⓜ *6 to 68th St./Hunter College.*

Fred Leighton. If you're in the market for vintage diamonds, this is the place, whether your taste is for tiaras, Art Deco settings, or sparklers once worn by a Vanderbilt. The skinny, stackable diamond eternity bands are hugely popular. ⌧ *773 Madison Ave., at E. 66th St., Upper East Side* ☎ *212/288–1872* Ⓜ *6 to 68th St./Hunter College.*

OC Concept Store. This boutique, founded by jeweler Orianne Collins (ex-wife of singer Phil), sells high-end jewelry from Chopard, Jacob & Co., and Audemars Piguet as well as her own designs. Shoppers can browse for one-of-a-kind art, but many of the gifts are aimed at the person who has everything and might enjoy a Lucite foosball table or crocodile-embossed dumbbells. There are also interactive screens so customers can build their own yacht. To make shopping even more enjoyable, there's also a fully stocked champagne and caviar bar. ⌧ *655 Madison Ave., between E. 60th and E. 61st Sts., Upper East Side* ☎ *212/759–9220* Ⓜ *N, R, 4, 5, 6 to 59th St./Lexington Ave.*

MUSEUM STORES

Cooper-Hewitt, National Design Museum. Prowl the shelves here for intriguing urban oddments and ornaments, like sculptural tableware, rare design books, colorful Band-Aids from Cynthia Rowley, and ceramic versions of iconic New York deli coffee cups. ⌧ *2 E. 91st St., at 5th Ave., Upper East Side* ☎ *212/849–8355* Ⓜ *4, 5, 6 to 86th St.*

Metropolitan Museum of Art Shop. This sprawling shop offers a phenomenal book selection, as well as posters, art videos, and computer programs. Reproductions of statuettes and other *objets* fill the gleaming cases in every branch. Don't miss the jewelry selection, with its Byzantine- and Egyptian-inspired baubles. ⌧ *1000 5th Ave., at E. 82nd St., Upper East Side* ☎ *212/570–3894* Ⓜ *4, 5, 6 to 86th St.*

Museum of the City of New York. Satisfy your curiosity about New York City's past, present, or future with the terrific selection of books, cards, toys, and photography posters. ⌧ *1220 5th Ave., at E. 103rd St., Upper East Side* ☎ *212/534–1672* Ⓜ *6 to 103rd St.*

Neue Galerie. Like the museum, this bookshop focuses on German, Austrian, and Central European art. The solid selection includes catalogs, literature, and decorative items, including lovely wrapping papers. Many designs found in the collection have been reproduced as part of

17

the museum's own Neue Haus line. ✉ *1048 5th Ave., between E. 85th and E. 86th Sts., Upper East Side* ☎ *212/628–6200* Ⓜ *4, 5, 6 to 86th St.*

SHOES, HANDBAGS, AND LEATHER GOODS

Billy Martin's. Urban cowboys flock here for high-quality hand-tooled and custom-made boots that count Neil Young and Billy Bob Thornton among their fans. To complete the look, you can add a suede shirt or a turquoise-and-silver belt. ✉ *1034 3rd Ave., between 61st and 62nd Sts., Upper East Side* ☎ *212/861–3100* Ⓜ *N, R, 4, 5, 6 to 59th St.*

Church's English Shoes. Beloved by bankers and lawyers, these shoes are indisputably of high quality. You could choose something highly polished for an embassy dinner, a loafer or crepe-sole suede ankle boot for a weekend, or even a black-and-white spectator style worthy of Fred Astaire. ✉ *689 Madison Ave., at E. 62nd St., Upper East Side* ☎ *212/758–5200* Ⓜ *N, R, 4, 5, 6 to 59th St.*

Devi Kroell. You may have spotted her snakeskin hobo on celebs such as Halle Berry and Ashley Olsen. This serene space is a perfect backdrop for the designer's luxury handbags and shoes, which are crafted from premium leather. Roomy shoulder bags come in python and calf leather, and evening bags have a touch of sparkle. There's also a selection of jewelry and scarves. ✉ *717 Madison Ave., between E. 63rd and E. 64th Sts., Upper East Side* ☎ *212/644–4499* Ⓜ *N, R, 4, 5, 6 to 59th St.*

Hermès. This legendary French retailer is best known for its iconic handbags, the Kelly and the Birkin, named for Grace Kelly and Jane Birkin, as well as its silk scarves and neckties. True to its roots, Hermès still stocks saddles and other equestrian items in addition to a line of beautifully simple separates. ✉ *691 Madison Ave., at E. 62nd St., Upper East Side* ☎ *212/751–3181* Ⓜ *N, R, 4, 5, 6 to 59th St./Lexington Ave.*

Jimmy Choo. Pointy toes, low vamps, narrow heels, ankle-wrapping straps—these British-made shoes are undeniably vampy, and sometimes more comfortable than they look. ✉ *716 Madison Ave., between E. 63rd and E. 64th Sts., Upper East Side* ☎ *212/759–7078* Ⓜ *M to 68th St./Hunter College.*

John Lobb. If you truly want to be well heeled, pick up a pair of these luxury shoes, whose prices start at around $1,100. Owned by Hermès, John Lobb offers classic styles such as oxfords, loafers, boots, and slippers. ✉ *680 Madison Ave., between E. 61st and E. 62nd Sts., Upper East Side* ☎ *212/888–9797* Ⓜ *N, R, 4, 5, 6 to 59th St.*

Judith Leiber. A door handle twinkling with Swarovski crystals signals the entrance to the Kingdom of Sparkle. Instantly recognizable handbags are completely frosted in crystals, from simple, colorful boxes to minaudières shaped like pigs or stars. Crystals also spangle the heels of satin pumps and the bows of oversize (to cut the glare?) sunglasses. ✉ *680 Madison Ave., at E. 61st St., Upper East Side* ☎ *212/223–2999* Ⓜ *4, 5, 6 to E. 59th St.*

Robert Clergerie. Although best known for its chunky, comfy wedges, this French brand is not without its sense of fun. The sandal selection includes beaded starfish shapes, and for winter the ankle boots have killer heels but the soles are padded. ⊠ *19 E. 62nd St., between 5th and Madison Aves., Upper East Side* ☎ *212/207–8600* Ⓜ *R to 5th Ave.*

Tod's. Diego Della Valle's coveted driving moccasins, casual loafers, and boots are the top choice for jet-setters who prefer low-key, logo-free luxury goods. Though most of the women's selection is made up of low-heel or flat styles, an increasing number of high heels are bent on driving sales, rather than cars. The handbags and satchels have the same fine craftsmanship. ⊠ *650 Madison Ave., near E. 60th St., Upper East Side* ☎ *212/644–5945* Ⓜ *N, R to 5th Ave./59th St.*

HOME DECOR

Sachin and Babi for Ankasa. Owners Sachin and Babi Ahluwalia used to source textiles for luxury designers like Oscar de la Renta. Now they are using that same design sensibility to produce a gorgeous line of housewares and accessories, which are globally inspired. The bedding is done in muted colors such as slate and duck-egg blue. They've also recently launched a ready-to-wear collection for women that has a downtown, edgy look. ⊠ *135 E. 65th, between Park and Lexington Aves., Upper East Side* ☎ *212/861–6800* Ⓜ *4, 6 to E. 68th St./Hunter College.*

WINE

Best Cellars. In a novel move, the wines here are organized by their characteristics (soft, luscious, juicy) rather than by region. Even better, the prices are amazingly low—the majority of the stock is less than $15 per bottle. ⊠ *1291 Lexington Ave., between E. 86th and E. 87th Sts., Upper East Side* ☎ *212/426–4200* Ⓜ *4, 5, 6 to 86th St.*

THE UPPER WEST SIDE

ANTIQUES AND COLLECTIBLES

Maxilla & Mandible. It's hard not to do a double take when you walk past this shop, which may have a human skeleton or a gigantic spider in its window display. Maxilla & Mandible bills itself as the "world's first and only osteological store" and is run by a group of scientists. Goths love it for the ghoulish items (skulls, anyone?), but geeks will also appreciate the butterfly-specimen, shark-teeth, and resin bug bracelets. ⊠ *451 Columbus Ave., between W. 81st and W. 82nd Sts., Upper West Side* ☎ *212/724–6173* Ⓜ *1 to 79th St.*

BOOKS AND STATIONERY

Westsider Rare & Used Books. This wonderfully crammed space is a lifesaver on the otherwise sparse Upper West Side. Squeeze in among the stacks of art books and fiction; clamber up the steep stairway and you'll find all sorts of rare books. ⊠ *2246 Broadway, between W. 80th and W. 81st Sts., Upper West Side* ☎ *212/362–0706* Ⓜ *1 to 79th St.*

CHILDREN'S CLOTHING

A Time for Children. When you shop at this funky boutique, you'll also be doing some good, as 100% of the profits go to the Children's Aid Society. Choose from toys, books, and clothing, which includes classics such as Petit Bateau as well as cool vintage-inspired onesies. ⊠ *416 Amsterdam Ave., between W. 79th and W. 80th Sts., Upper West Side* ☎ *212/724–7445* Ⓜ *1 to 79th St.*

CLOTHING

BOC. Who needs to go downtown for cutting-edge designers? Short for Boutique on Columbus, this store has an industrial chic look, and the labels are just as sleek. Separates from Rebecca Taylor, Vivienne Westwood, and Alexander Wang all line the shelves. There's also a small selection of candles and cosmetics. ⊠ *506 Amsterdam Ave., between W. 84th and W. 85th Sts., Upper West Side* ☎ *212/362–5405* Ⓜ *1, 2 to 86th St.*

Allan & Suzi. This consignment shop is the kind of place where you could score a vintage Pauline Trigere dress, or your next Halloween costume, if you like '70s go-go boots and massive wigs. The goods here veer toward the slightly wacky, but in between the flamboyant pieces, browsers will find real gems like past-season Zac Posen, Prada, and Yves Saint Laurent, as well as vintage David Bowie concert T-shirts and gently worn Jimmy Choos. ⊠ *506 Amsterdam Ave., between W. 84th and W. 85th Sts., Upper West Side* ☎ *212/580–8202* Ⓜ *1 to 79th St.*

Intermix. Whether you're looking for the perfect daytime dress, pair of J Brand jeans, or a puffer coat that won't make you look like the Michelin man, Intermix offers a well-edited mix of emerging and established designers. Expect to see designs from DVF, Chloe, and Missoni. ⊠ *210 Columbus Ave., between W. 69th and W. 70th Sts., Upper West Side* ☎ *212/769–9116* Ⓜ *1, 2, 3 to 72nd St.*

Mint. Trendy dresses that won't break the bank are what Mint is all about. The collection includes BB Dakota, Susana Monaco, and Joe's Jeans. The walls are painted, of course, in mint. ⊠ *448 Columbus Ave., between W. 81st and W. 82nd Sts., Upper West Side* ☎ *212/724–7445* Ⓜ *1 to 79th St.*

SHOES, HANDBAGS, AND LEATHER GOODS

Tani. Fashionable Upper West Side ladies love this shoe store for its huge selection and patient staff. Tani's selection is mostly classic-with-a-twist, and shoppers will find slightly off-the-radar brands such as Bensimon, Mugumi Ochi, and Butter. ⊠ *2020 Broadway, between 69th and 70th Sts., Upper West Side* ☎ *212/787–1700* Ⓜ *1, 2, 3 to 72nd St.*

WINE

Acker Merrall & Condit. Founded in 1820 and billing itself as America's oldest wine shop, Acker Merrall & Condit carries a superb selection of red burgundies. There's also a wide range of rare and fine wines. ⊠ *160 W. 72nd St., between Amsterdam and Columbus Aves., Upper West Side* ☎ *212/873–4361* Ⓜ *1, 2, 3 to 72nd St.*

Where to Eat

WORD OF MOUTH

"On my last trip, a friend asked me to buy her a tin of the amazing chocolate at MarieBelle. I discovered a wonderful shop I'd never heard of, met up with a delightful Fodorite there and we wandered a bit in the area (her neck of the woods) and had a great dinner."

—starrs

Updated
by Adeena
Sussman

Ready to take a bite out of New York? Hope you've come hungry. In a city where creativity is expressed in many ways, the food scene takes center stage, with literally thousands of ways to get an authentic taste of what Gotham is all about. Whether they're lining up at street stands, gobbling down legendary deli and diner grub, or chasing a coveted reservation at the latest celebrity-chef venue, New Yorkers are a demanding yet appreciative audience.

Every neighborhood offers temptations high, low, and in between, meaning there's truly something for every taste, whim, and budget. No matter how you approach dining out here, you can't go wrong. Planning a day of shopping among the glittering boutique flagships along Fifth and Madison? Stop into one of the Upper East Side's storied restaurants for a repast among the ladieswho lunch. Clubbing in the Meatpacking District? Tuck into a meal at eateries as trendy as their patrons. Craving authentic ethnic? From food trucks to hidden joints, there are almost more choices than there are appetites. Recent years have also seen entire food categories, from ramen to meatballs to mac 'n cheese, riffed upon and turned into fetishistic obsessions.

Amid newfound economic realities, there's been a revived appreciation for value, meaning you can tap into wallet-friendly choices at every end of the spectrum. At many restaurants you'll also notice an almost religious reverence for seasonal cuisine. And don't forget—New York is still home to more celebrity chefs than any other city. Your chances of running into your favorite cookbook author, Food Network celeb, or paparazzi-friendly chef are higher, adding even more star wattage to a restaurant scene with an already through-the-roof glamour quotient. Ready, set, eat. Rest assured, this city will do its part to satisfy your appetite.

NEW YORK CITY DINING PLANNER

EATING OUT STRATEGY

Where should we eat? With thousands of Manhattan eateries competing for your attention, it may seem like a daunting question. But fret not—our expert writers and editors have done most of the legwork. The 160-plus selections here represent the best this city has to offer—from hot dogs to haute cuisine. Search "Best Bets" for top recommendations by price, cuisine, and experience. Sample local flavor in the neighborhood features. Or find a review quickly, listed alphabetically by neighborhood. Dive in and enjoy! For restaurants in the Outer Boroughs, see the Brooklyn chapter, and the Queens, Bronx, and Staten Island chapter.

CHILDREN

Though it's unusual to see children in the dining rooms of Manhattan's most elite restaurants, dining with youngsters in New York does not have to mean culinary exile. Many of the restaurants reviewed in this chapter are excellent choices for families, and are marked with a ☾ symbol.

RESERVATIONS

It's still a good idea to plan ahead. Some renowned restaurants are booked weeks or even months in advance. If that's the case, you can get lucky at the last minute if you're flexible—and friendly. Most restaurants keep a few tables open for walk-ins and VIPs. Show up for dinner early (5:30 pm) or late (after 10 pm), and politely inquire about any last-minute vacancies or cancellations. Occasionally, an eatery may take your credit-card number and ask you to call the day before your scheduled meal to reconfirm: don't forget or you could lose out, or possibly be charged for your oversight.

WHAT TO WEAR

When in the nation's style capital, do as the natives do: dress up to eat out. Whatever your style, dial it up a notch. Have some fun while you're at it. Pull out the clothes you've been saving for a special occasion and get glamorous. Unfair as it is, the way you look can influence how you're treated—and where you're seated. Generally speaking, jeans and a button-down shirt will suffice at most table-service restaurants in the $ to $$ range. Moving up from there, some pricier restaurants require jackets, and some insist on ties. In reviews, we note dress only when a jacket or jacket and tie are required. If you have doubts, call the restaurant and ask.

TIPPING AND TAXES

In most restaurants, tip the waiter 15%–20%. (To figure out a 20% tip quickly, just move the decimal point one place to the left on your total and double that amount.) Bills for parties of six or more sometimes include the tip already. Tip at least $1 per drink at the bar, and $1 for each coat checked. Never tip the maître d' unless you're out to impress your guests or expect to pay another visit soon.

SMOKING

Smoking is prohibited in all enclosed public spaces in New York City, including restaurants and bars.

18

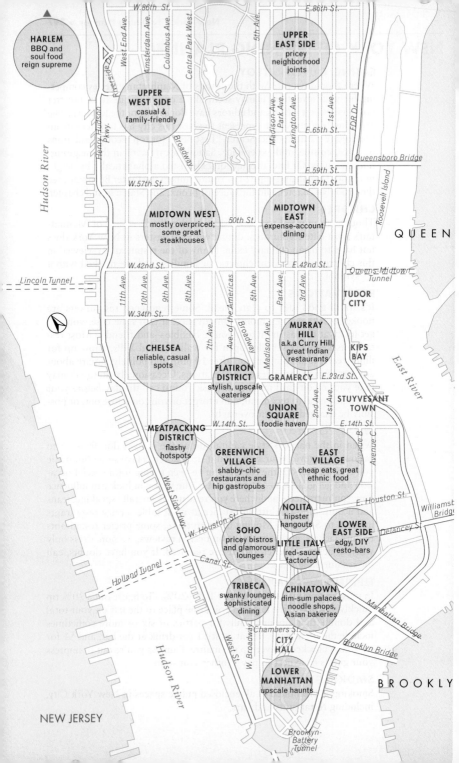

HOURS

New Yorkers seem ready to eat at any hour. Many restaurants stay open between lunch and dinner, some offer late-night seating, and still others serve around the clock. Restaurants that serve breakfast often do so until noon or later. Restaurants in the East Village, the Lower East Side, SoHo, TriBeCa, and Greenwich Village are likely to remain open late, whereas Midtown spots and those in the Theater and Financial districts and uptown generally close earlier. Unless otherwise noted, the restaurants listed in this guide are open daily for lunch and dinner.

PRICES

If you're watching your budget, be sure to ask the price of the daily specials recited by the waiter. The charge for specials at some restaurants is noticeably out of line with the other prices on the menu. Beware of the $10 bottle of water; ask for tap water instead. And always review your bill.

If you eat early or late, you may be able to take advantage of a prix-fixe deal not offered at peak hours. Most upscale restaurants offer great lunch deals, with special menus at cut-rate prices designed to give customers a true taste of the place.

Credit cards are widely accepted, but many restaurants (particularly smaller ones downtown) accept only cash. If you plan to use a credit card, it's a good idea to confirm that it is acceptable when making reservations or before sitting down to eat.

Some restaurants are marked with a price range ($$–$$$, for example). This indicates one of two things: either the average cost straddles two categories, or if you order strategically, you can get out for less than most diners spend.

18

WHAT IT COSTS AT DINNER				
¢	$	$$	$$$	$$$$
RESTAURANTS under $10	$10–$17	$18–$24	$25–$35	over $35

Price per person for a median main course or equivalent combination of smaller dishes. Note: if a restaurant offers only prix-fixe (set-price) meals, it has been given the price category that reflects the full prix-fixe price.

USING THE MAPS

Throughout the chapter, you'll see mapping symbols and coordinates (✢ 3:F2) after property names or reviews. To locate the property on a map, turn to the New York City Dining and Lodging Atlas at the end of this chapter. The first number after the ✢ symbol indicates the map number. After that is the property's coordinate on the map grid.

CHECK BEFORE YOU GO

The nature of the restaurant industry means that places open and close in a New York minute. It's always a good idea to phone ahead and make sure your restaurant is still turning tables.

BEST BETS FOR NEW YORK CITY DINING

With thousands of restaurants to choose from, how will you decide where to eat? Fodor's writers and editors have selected their favorite restaurants by price, cuisine, and experience in the Best Bets lists below. In the first column, Fodor's Choice properties represent the "best of the best" in every price category. You can also search by neighborhood for excellent eats—just peruse the following pages. Or find specific details about a restaurant in the full reviews, listed later in the chapter.

Fodor's Choice ★

A Voce, $$$, p. 442
ABC Kitchen, $$, p. 442
Adour Alain Ducasse, $$$$, p. 450
Aldea, $$$, p. 443
Baoguette, $, p. 427
Bar Boulud, $$, p. 464
Burger Joint, ¢, p. 455
Candle 79, $$, p. 462
Daniel, $$$$, p. 463
DBGB Kitchen & Bar, $$, p. 428
Eleven Madison Park, $$$$, p. 444
Emporio, $$, p. 423
Fatty Crab, $, p. 440
Hundred Acres, $$, p. 424
Katz's Delicatessen, $, p. 431
Marea, $$$$, p. 467
Nha Trang, ¢, p. 418
Northern Spy Food Co., $$, p. 430

Per Se, $$$$, p. 467
Shake Shack, ¢, p. 446
Tía Pol, $$, p. 433

Best by Price

¢

Burger Joint, p. 455
Financier Patisserie, p. 419
Gray's Papaya, p. 436
Nha Trang, p. 418
Shake Shack, p. 446
Veniero's Pasticceria, p. 430

$

Back Forty, p. 427
Baoguette, p. 427
Bubby's, p. 420
Cascabel Taqueria, p. 463
City Bakery, p. 443
Fatty Crab, p. 440

Katz's Delicatessen, p. 431
Mexicana Mama, p. 441
Momofuku Noodle Bar, p. 429

$$

ABC Kitchen, p. 442
Balthazar, p. 423
Bar Boulud, p. 464
Candle 79, p. 462
DBGB Kitchen & Bar, p. 428
Emporio, p. 423
Hundred Acres, p. 424
Northern Spy Food Co., p. 430
Tía Pol, p. 433

$$$

A Voce, p. 442
Aldea, p. 443
Babbo, p. 435
BLT Steak, p. 450
Craft, p. 448

Minetta Tavern, p. 441
Osteria Morini, p. 425
Scarpetta, p. 438
The Standard Grill, p. 439

$$$$

Adour Alain Ducasse, p. 450
Daniel, p. 463
Del Posto, p. 438
Eleven Madison Park, p. 444
Jean Georges, p. 466
L'Atelier de Joël Robuchon, p. 451
Le Bernardin, p. 457
Marea, p. 467
Momofuku Ko, p. 429
Per Se, p. 467

Best by Cuisine

AMERICAN

Back Forty, p. 427
Gramercy Tavern, p. 445
Hundred Acres, p. 424
Marc Forgione, p. 422
Northern Spy Food Co., p. 430
Per Se, p. 467

BARBECUE

Blue Smoke, p. 447
Dinosaur Bar-B-Que, p. 469
Hill Country, p. 445
R.U.B. BBQ, p. 433
Wildwood Barbecue, p. 446

CHINESE

Chinatown Brasserie, p. 427

Grand Sichuan, p. 428

Great New York Noodletown, p. 418

Joe's Shanghai, p. 418

Shun Lee Palace, p. 453

FRENCH

Adour Alain Ducasse, p. 450

Bar Boulud, p. 464

Daniel, p. 463

Jean Georges, p. 466

Le Bernardin, p. 457

The Modern and Bar Room, p. 459

INDIAN

Tamarind, p. 446

ITALIAN

Babbo, p. 435

Del Posto, p. 438

Emporio, p. 423

Marea, p. 467

Osteria Morini, p. 425

Scarpetta, p. 438

JAPANESE

Ippudo, p. 407

Kuruma Zushi, p. 451

Sushi of Gari, p. 464

Sushi Yasuda, p. 453

MEDITERRANEAN

Aldea, p. 443

August, p. 439

Kefi, p. 467

Il Buco, p. 428

Picholine, p. 468

MEXICAN

Cascabel Taqueria, p. 463

Maya, p. 463

Mexicana Mama, p. 441

Toloache, p. 460

NEW AMERICAN

Blue Ribbon, p. 423

Craft, p. 448

Eleven Madison Park, p. 444

Hundred Acres, p. 424

The Lambs Club, p. 457

PIZZA

Arturo's, p. 434

Lombardi's, p. 426

Motorino, p. 430

SEAFOOD

BLT Fish, p. 443

Marea, p. 467

Mary's Fish Camp, p. 437

SPANISH

Boqueria, p. 443

Casa Mono, p. 447

Tía Pol, p. 433

STEAKHOUSE

BLT Prime, p. 447

BLT Steak, p. 450

Porter House, p. 468

VIETNAMESE

Baoguette, p. 427

Nha Trang, p. 418

Best by Experience

BRUNCH

Aquavit, p. 450

Balthazar, p. 423

Bubby's, p. 420

Cookshop, p. 433

Marc Forgione, p. 422

Sarabeth's, p. 468

BUSINESS DINING

DB Bistro Moderne, p. 456

Four Seasons, p. 451

Gotham Bar & Grill, p. 436

Jean Georges, p. 466

The Lambs Club, p. 457

The Modern, p. 459

CELEB-SPOTTING

Balthazar, p. 423

ABC Kitchen, p. 442

DBGB Kitchen & Bar, p. 428

Four Seasons, p. 451

Minetta Tavern, p. 441

The Standard Grill, p. 439

CHILD-FRIENDLY

Bubby's, p. 420

Carmine's, p. 455

City Bakery, p. 443

Fatty Crab Upper West Side, p. 466

Joe's Shanghai, p. 418

Lombardi's, p. 426

Odeon, p. 422

Serafina, p. 460

Veniero's Pasticceria, p. 430

GOOD FOR GROUPS

ABC Kitchen, p. 442

Buddakan, p. 432

Carmine's, p. 455

Churrascaria Plataforma, p. 455

Emporio, p. 423

Hundred Acres, p. 424

GREAT VIEW

Asiate, p. 464

Marea, p. 467

Michael Jordan's The Steakhouse NYC, p. 452

Per Se, p. 467

Porter House, p. 468

LATE-NIGHT DINING

Balthazar, p. 423

Blue Ribbon Brasserie, p. 423

DBGB Kitchen & Bar, p. 428

Emporio, p. 423

Fatty Crab, p. 440

Pastis, p. 438

Minetta Tavern, p. 441

Osteria Morini, p. 425

The Standard Grill, p. 439

WINE LIST

Babbo, p. 435

Corton, p. 421

Del Posto, p. 438

'inoteca, p. 431

Marea, p. 467

18

LOWER MANHATTAN

A wave of development and attractive pricing have meant thousands of new residents in Lower Manhattan, fueling an up-and-coming—yet still slow-moving—neighborhood scene.

The most visible changes? Restaurants in and around the Financial District no longer adhere to banker's hours, and formal dining rooms have been outnumbered by casual cafés and wine bars. On the pedestrian-only Stone Street, throngs of young professionals gather for after-work drinks and dinner at nearby bistros, oyster bars, and steak houses.

To the north, Chinatown beckons adventurous diners with restaurants representing numerous regional cuisines of China, including Cantonese-, Szechuan-, Hunan-, Fujian-, Shanghai-, and Hong Kong–style cooking. Malaysian and Vietnamese restaurants also have taken root here, and the neighborhood continues to grow rapidly, encroaching into what was Little Italy.

To the west, TriBeCa still holds an air of exclusivity, though glamorous dining rooms in converted warehouses have now been joined by more casual spots with later hours.

TRIBECA BRUNCH

Iron Chef winner Marc Forgione serves indulgent brunches in the warm, wood-and-brick dining room of his eponymous restaurant (⊠ *134 Reade St., between West Broadway and Hudson* ✛ *1:C2*). Try the Eggs Benny, lavished in a preserved-lemon Hollandaise; or the over-the-top sliders featuring suckling pig braised in beer, butter, and bacon fat. If you're looking for a more elegant atmosphere, try **Capsouto Frères** (⊠ *451 Washington St., near Watts St.* ☎ *212/966–4900* ✛ *2:C5*), a landmark French bistro that makes the city's best sweet and savory soufflés. We love the praline soufflé with hazelnut crème anglaise.

CHINATOWN CHOWDOWN

With more than 200 restaurants in just under 2 square mi, deciding where to dine may take longer than the actual meal. Here are our favorite places to enjoy Chinatown's diverse bounty.

Cantonese: For Hong Kong–style dim sum, head to **Ping's Seafood** (✉ *22 Mott St., near Worth St.* ☎ *212/602–9988 ✛ 2:F6*) or **HSF** (✉ *46 Bowery, near Canal St.* ☎ *212/374–1319 ✛ 2:F5*). Both spots are crowded but offer addictive fare like turnip cakes, steamed pork buns, and fried sesame-seed balls.

One of the best deals in Chinatown is at **Dumpling House** (✉ *118 Eldridge St., near Broome St.* ☎ *212/625–8008 ✛ 2:G4*), where sizzling pork-and-chive dumplings are four for a buck.

Malaysian: There's something for everyone at **New Malaysia** (✉ *48 Bowery, near Canal St.* ☎ *212/964–0284 ✛ 2:G5*), like roti flatbread with curry and delicious red-bean and coconut-milk drinks.

Shanghainese: The city's best soup dumplings—doughy pouches filled with ground pork and meaty broth—are ripe for the slurping at **Joe's Shanghai** (✉ *9 Pell St., near Bowery* ☎ *212/233–8888 ✛ 2:F5*).

Szechuan: Foodies go ga-ga for the twice-cooked pork in bean sauce and scallion pancakes at **Grand Sichuan** (✉ *125 Canal St., at Chrystie St.* ☎ *212/625–9212 ✛ 2:G5*). At the **Peking Duck House** (✉ *28 Mott St., near Mosco St.* ☎ *212/227–1810 ✛ 2:F5*), don't miss the stunning signature dish. Crispy-skin Peking duck comes with pancakes, scallions, cucumbers, and hoisin sauce.

FINANCIAL DISTRICT'S RESTO ROW

Nestled alongside skyscrapers and the towering New York Stock Exchange, Stone Street is a two-block restaurant oasis that feels more like a village than the center of the financial universe. After the market closes, Wall Streeters head to **Ulysses'** (✉ *95 Pearl St., near Hanover Sq.* ☎ *212/482–0400 ✛ 1:E4*), a popular pub with 19 beers on tap and more than 50 bottled beers.

Clerks might stop in for a broccoli rabe–and–sausage pie (they don't do slices) at **Adrienne's Pizza Bar** (✉ *54 Stone St., near Hanover Sq.* ☎ *212/248–3838 ✛ 1:E4*) while high-rolling brokers continue down the block to **Harry's Steak** (✉ *1 Hanover Sq., at Stone St.* ☎ *212/785–9200 ✛ 1:E4*) for a dry-aged porterhouse and a reserve-collection cabernet from a 2,800-strong cellar. Those with a sweet tooth end up at **Financier Patisserie** (✉ *62 Stone St., between Mill La. and Hanover Sq.* ☎ *212/344–5600 ✛ 1:E4*), pictured below.

DIM SUM DO'S AND DON'TS

Weekends in Chinatown are synonymous with one thing: dim sum. There may be newer, trendier spots, but **Jing Fong** (✉ *20 Elizabeth St., 2nd fl., between Bayard and Canal Sts. ✛ 2:F5*) is a classic spot worth visiting. Take the seats you're given (most likely at a communal table) and simply let your appetite guide your ordering from the jaw-dropping array of dishes that roll by on carts. Point at your choices, then hand over your card to be stamped; the total will be tallied at the end and you'll pay on the way out. Pace yourself—it's easy to get full fast. And don't be afraid to ask questions; the cart attendants often know more English than they let on! Top choices include shrimp folded inside a floppy giant noodle and topped with a squirt of sweet soy; plump spinach dumplings (one of the few choices for vegetarians), and the elusive, spongy barbecue pork buns—pounce if you find them, and you won't be sorry.

18

SOHO, NOLITA, AND LITTLE ITALY

In this high-rent neighborhood dining options are somewhat limited, resulting in crowded restaurants with steep prices. But snacking is a great strategy for experiencing the local flavor without buyer's remorse.

Longtime New Yorkers lament that SoHo has evolved from a red-hot art district into a big-brand outdoor mall. Shoppers engulf the neighborhood on weekends like angry bees, turning Lafayette Street into a buzzing hive of commerce. As a result, popular spots can be tough to get into during prime times.

In NoLita, the trendy next-door neighborhood of indie boutiques and restaurants, the spirit of old SoHo prevails. Modest eateries are squeezed between boutiques featuring products from up-and-coming designers.

If you want authentic Italian food, don't head south to Little Italy: most of the pasta factories along the main strip of Mulberry Street have developed reputations as tourist traps. As with SoHo, it's a better bet to snack your way through this area.

FRESH-BAKED

Follow the beguiling scent of fresh-baked bread to **Balthazar Bakery** (✉ *80 Spring St., near Crosby St.* ☎ *212/965–1785* ✛ *2:E4*), where you'll find baguettes, boules, batards, brioche, and several other different breads. The bakery—an extension of Keith McNally's always-packed Balthazar restaurant—boasts an extensive menu of panini, sandwiches, quiches, and homemade soups, plus newly added fresh breakfast egg dishes. The pastry chefs also turn out custom-made pastries, cakes, and cookies. Try the berry noisette tart or coconut cake, or keep it simple with a few of Balthazar Bakery's buttery lemon or chocolate madeleines.

SOHO SIPS AND SNACKS

3 QUICK BITES

Relax and refuel at one of these neighborhood haunts.

Cuban sandwich at Café Habana (✉ *17 Prince St., at Elizabeth St.* ☎ *212/625–2002* ✛ *2:F3*): This popular pan-Latin dive also boasts excellent Mexican-style grilled corn and café con leche (with milk). The Cuban sandwich features roasted pork, ham, Swiss cheese, pickles, and chipotle mayo.

Tacos at La Esquina (✉ *106 Kenmare St.* ☎ *646/613–7100* ✛ *2:F4*): Order tasty pulled chicken or char-grilled steak tacos and tortas to go from the counter-service taqueria, or squeeze into the small café around the corner for a bigger sit-down meal.

Apertivo at Emporio (✉ *231 Mott St., near Prince St.* ☎ *212/358–1707* ✛ *2:F3*): Visit this cozy Italian restaurant at happy hour, weekdays 5 to 7 pm, when cocktails and wine come with free snacks. The daily selection may include olives, ricotta frittata, cheeses, pizzas, and cubed Italian ham.

ELEVATE YOUR COCKTAIL CONSCIOUSNESS

The American cocktail renaissance is under way at **Pegu Club** (✉ *77 W. Houston St., near West Broadway* ☎ *212/473–7348* ✛ *2:D3*), where renowned mixologist Audrey Saunders developed impeccable modern cocktail recipes steeped in pre-Prohibition tradition.

Inspired by a 19th-century British officers club in Burma, the intimate second-floor lounge has a colonial aura, outfitted with palm trees, dark woods, and low-slung brown-velvet couches.

Since Pegu opened several years ago, many imitators have followed, but Saunders's libations still hold their own, with fresh-squeezed juices and house infusions in every cocktail. Watching the barkeeps in their natty vests and shirtsleeves ply their trade making drinks like an Earl Grey martini with tea-infused gin, or the Jamaican Firefly, featuring fresh ginger beer with rum and lime, makes the bar a prime perch. Ice is hand-chipped, bitters and syrups are brewed on the premises, and the results show in every glass.

"You have to look at well-crafted cocktails as fine cuisine with elements of sweet, sour, bitter, and spicy," Saunders says. "They're not just fruit and booze. You need spices, herbs, and other ingredients to add complexity."

AND FOR DESSERT . . .

Slip into **MarieBelle** (✉ *484 Broome St., between Wooster St. and West Broadway* ☎ *212/925–6999* ✛ *2:D4*) to experience chocolate nirvana in a Parisian-style café setting. At the front of the shop you'll find an assortment of artisanal chocolates filled with velvety ganache. But real chocoholics head to the Cacao Bar at the back of the store for MarieBelle's überrich hot chocolate, crafted from ground cacao beans instead of cocoa powder, then mixed with boiling water (European-style) or steamed milk (American-style). For an unusual treat, try the spicy hot chocolate—it has a real kick to it. Tea lovers will be delighted by MarieBelle's diverse hand-blended selection. Not to worry if you're visiting during the late spring or summer: skip the hot chocolate and cool off with MarieBelle's Aztec iced chocolate—the warm-weather version of her decadent cacao elixir—or the house-made chocolate gelato.

18

EAST VILLAGE AND LOWER EAST SIDE

With luxury condos stretching as far east as Avenue C, the East Village—once Manhattan's edgiest enclave—has become yet another high-rent neighborhood. Nearby, the Lower East Side, home to generations of immigrant newcomers, has nearly completed a similar transformation.

Both neighborhoods still offer some of the best meal deals in the city, and the influx of flush new residents has steadily raised the bar on high-quality eats. Legends like **Katz's**, the late-night Jewish deli, coexist these days with high-end destinations featuring tasting menus and hard-to-score tables. There's something for every budget and craving, from yakitori parlors to midprice trattorias. St. Marks Place is the center of New York's downtown Little Tokyo, and 6th Street is its Indian row. On the Lower East Side, meanwhile, cute little bistros and some restaurant heavy hitters have been inching into new gentrified stretches south of Delancey Street. And the neighborhoods have even given birth to their own homegrown star chefs, wildly creative renegades with cultish followings like **Momofuku**'s David Chang and **wd~50**'s Wylie Dufresne.

TOP BUDGET EATS

Be careful with the incendiary hot sauce at **Mamoun's Falafel** (⊠ 22 St. Marks Pl., between 2nd and 3rd Aves. ☎ 212/674–8685 ✦ 3:G5), where tahini-topped pitas are packed with fresh, green-on-the-inside falafel balls. Gluttony reigns at **Crif Dogs** (⊠ 113 St. Marks Pl., at Ave. A ☎ 212/614–2728 ✦ 3:H5); indulge in a bacon-wrapped, deep-fried hot dog and chili-cheese tater tots. Next door, **Tuck Shop** (⊠ 115 St. Marks Pl., between Ave. A and Ave. B ☎ 212/979–5200 ✦ 3:H5) offers Australian street food. Try a spicy beef meat pie followed by a dense, sweet vanilla slice (vanilla custard surrounded by puff pastry and topped with icing).

RAMEN REVOLUTION

A Japanese ramen noodle revolution has stormed the East Village, starting with **Momofuku Noodle Bar** (✉ *171 1st Ave., between 10th and 11th Sts.* ☎ *212/777–7773* ✛ *3:H5*), David Chang's flagship restaurant. Chang's ramen features fatty slabs of Berkshire pork belly and shredded pork shoulder in savory broth topped with fresh vegetables and a slow-poached egg. At **Ippudo** (✉ *65 4th Ave., between 9th and 10th Sts.* ☎ *212/388–0088* ✛ *3:G5*), the first American branch of the Japanese chain, crowds wait more than two hours for noodles in a thick miso brew and a slick of spicy oil (not to mention the sleeper dish: peppery chicken wings). Japanese expats flock to **Rai Rai Ken** (✉ *214 E. 10th St., between 1st and 2nd Aves.* ☎ *212/477–7030* ✛ *3:H5*) for ramen sunk into one of three signature broths. **Minca** (✉ *536 E. 5th St., between Ave. A and Ave. B* ☎ *212/505–8001* ✛ *2:G2*) has received the least fanfare, but its ramen may very well be the best. Start your meal with light, panfried whole shrimp dumplings and then dive into the shoyu (soy sauce) pork ramen.

LATE-NIGHT EATS

From dirt cheap to stylish, the city's best late-night eats can be found right here. Grab a gargantuan slice at table-less **Artichoke Pizza** (✉ *328 E. 14th St., between 1st and 2nd Aves.* ☎ *212/228–2004* ✛ *3:H4*), where lines snake until 5 am for the artichoke-spinach slice, which tastes like cheesy dip on crackers. For authentic Ukrainian cuisine, 24-hour diner gem **Veselka** (✉ *144 2nd Ave., at 9th St.* ☎ *212/228–9682* ✛ *3:H5*) offers a solid burger and even better potato pierogi. Grab a chewy chocolate chip–M&M cookie for dessert. The swanky tapas restaurant and lounge **Stanton Social** (✉ *99 Stanton St., between Orchard and Ludlow Sts.* ☎ *212/995–0099* ✛ *2:G3*) offers shareable Kobe beef sliders, French onion soup dumplings, and fresh doughnut holes until 2 am nightly (3 on weekends).

AND FOR DESSERT . . .

The standing-only, workbench-like tables at **Momofuku Milk Bar** (✉ *207 2nd Ave., at 13th St.* ☎ *212/254–3500* ✛ *3:H4*) provide clear views of pastry chef Christina Tosi tinkering with her constantly evolving menu of creations such as curiously flavored soft-serve ice cream (cereal-milk, lemon verbena) and Candy Bar Pie, a sweet bomb of caramel, peanut-butter nougat, and pretzels atop a chocolate-cookie crust. If taking a seat is preferred, scoot into the cozy couches and chairs at **Sugar Sweet Sunshine** (✉ *126 Rivington St., between Essex and Norfolk Sts.* ☎ *212/995–1960* ✛ *2:G3*), the brainchild of two former Magnolia Bakery employees. Sugar Sweet's cupcakes are far superior; try the chocolate-almond Gooey Gooey, or the cream cheese frosting–topped pumpkin flavor. The real star showstopper? Swoon-inducing banana pudding incorporating slices of ripe fruit and crumbled Nilla wafers suspended in decadent vanilla pudding.

18

GREENWICH VILLAGE

Dining styles collide on the West Side, with quaint, chef-driven eateries in Greenwich Village facing off against the Meatpacking District's massive, celebrity-fueled hot spots.

Greenwich Village's bohemian days may have faded with the Beatnik era, but the romantic allure of its tiny bistros, bars, and cafés remains. Around New York University, shabby-chic eateries and takeout joints line the streets and are patronized by a student clientele. Avoid heavily trafficked thoroughfares like Bleecker Street (unless you're tapping into the new artisan pizza craze), as most of the Village's culinary gems lie tucked away on side streets and alleyways, especially west of 7th Avenue, in the West Village. The vibe here is low-key and friendly, with patrons squeezed together at tiny tables in matchbox-size eateries.

For a glitzier scene, head to the Meatpacking District, which has been transformed in recent years from a gritty commercial warehouse area to the celebrity-chef–driven epicenter of the city's dining scene. The vibe is flashy, favored by actors, models, and their suitors.

PEANUT BUTTER & CO.

For a childhood classic kicked up a notch, head to **Peanut Butter & Co. Sandwich Shop** (✉ *240 Sullivan St., near W. Third St.* ☎ *212/677–3995* ✛ *2:D2*). Start with a standard PB&J, or go Proustian with any of the menu's 21 options like the Elvis (grilled with peanut butter, bananas, and honey), the Pregnant Lady (peanut butter and pickles), or the sandwich of the week, with expertly paired ingredients such as cherry jam and cream cheese with Crunch Time peanut butter. You can also pick up jars in different flavors as a sticky souvenir.

BEST BAR SEATS: WEST VILLAGE

Belly up to the bar for dinner at these neighborhood institutions:

At **Babbo** (✉ *110 Waverly Pl., between MacDougal St. and 6th Ave.* ☎ *212/777–0303* ⊹ *2:C1*), if reservations are hard to come by, stake your place outside before opening and at 5:30 pm you'll have a decent shot of nabbing a seat or two at the bar, ideal for sampling Mario Batali's iconic dishes like squid-ink spaghetti with sausage.

Gotham Bar and Grill (✉ *12 E. 12th St., between 5th Ave. and University Pl.* ☎ *212/620–4020* ⊹ *3:E4*) is almost better known for its bar seating than its dining room. It's the place solo diners and couples alike sit at the long, deep bar top for a taste of attentive service (and generous pours) from knowledgeable bartenders paired with Chef Alfred Portale's iconic New American cuisine.

And at **Wallsé** (✉ *344 W. 11th St., at Washington St.* ☎ *212/352–2300* ⊹ *3:B6*), chef Kurt Guttenbrunner's modern-Austrian cuisine (think dishes like schnitzel and spaetzle, only with a twist) is best enjoyed at the U-shape bar, as is the impressive art collection with works by the likes of Julian Schnabel and the late Dennis Hopper.

PIZZA THREE WAYS IN THE WEST VILLAGE

SLICE

Flavor reigns at **Bleecker Street Pizza** (✉ *69 7th Ave. S, at Bleecker St.* ☎ *212/924–4466* ⊹ *2:B2*), where the thin-crusted Nonna Maria is topped with garlicky marinara, grated mozzarella, fresh mozzarella, and freshly grated parmigiano-reggiano. You may not find a seat inside tiny **Joe's Pizza** (✉ *7 Carmine St., at 6th Ave.* ☎ *212/366–1182* ⊹ *2:C2*), but you will get one of the best versions of a purist's New York slice.

CLASSIC COAL OVEN

Founded in 1957, **Arturo's** (✉ *106 W. Houston St., at Thompson St.* ☎ *212/677–3820* ⊹ *2:D3*) is a double throwback: it's a jazz bar and friendly neighborhood coal-oven pizza restaurant where crackly-crusted pies are a guarantee. If you can brave the organized chaos and the usual wait, a gooey meatball pie awaits.

AUTHENTIC NEAPOLITAN

At the back of the long, narrow **Keste Pizza & Vino** (✉ *271 Bleecker St., between 6th and 7th Aves.* ☎ *212/243–1500* ⊹ *2:C2*) sits a beautiful, tiled, wood-fired oven that cooks Manhattan's most authentic Neapolitan pies at 1,000 degrees. Blistered and chewy around the edges, each pie gives way to a softer center pooled with San Marzano tomato sauce and imported buffalo mozzarella.

AND FOR DESSERT . . .

Everyone loves beer, wine, and cupcakes, but only Sweet Revenge (✉ *62 Carmine St., between Bedford St. and 7th Ave.* ☎ *212/242–2240* ⊕ *www.sweetrevengenyc.com* ⊹ *2:C2*) brings them all together in a cozy neighborhood spot. Vibrantly flavored and delicately rich, the cupcakes are the real draw. Nut-studded peanut butter–buttercream tops a moist, crumbly peanut-butter cake housing a chocolate ganache center you'll want to measure out in every bite. Pair it with the suggested Argentinean red or German Hefeweizen or combine one of the other 15 wines and beers with a special cupcake of the day, such as the Very Strawberry, with fresh strawberries baked into vanilla cake topped with strawberry cream-cheese frosting. There are also sandwiches and savory cakes, but indulgence is a dish best served sweet. Ten dollars gets you a glass of sangria or wine and a cupcake from 4 to 8 pm Monday through Friday.

18

UNION SQUARE

WITH GRAMERCY, MURRAY HILL, AND FLATIRON DISTRICT

The blocks around Union Square and its open-air Greenmarket are filled with upscale foodie havens featuring market-driven menus. But fancy seasonal fare isn't all the area offers: Curry Hill and Koreatown are just blocks away.

Some of the city's most popular restaurants, including **Craft** and **Union Square Cafe**, are in the area northwest of Union Square, called the Flatiron District. The neighborhood is also a hot shopping destination, with plenty of refueling spots like City Bakery, a gourmet deli and sweets spot that's a standby for many New Yorkers. Heading up from Union Square, Park Avenue South and streets nearby are packed with crowd-pleasers like Blue Smoke and Dos Caminos.

Lexington Avenue between 27th and 29th streets is known as Curry Hill (it borders Murray Hill) for its wall-to-wall Indian restaurants, spice shops, and takeout joints. The area near Koreatown, on West 32nd Street, between 5th and 6th avenues, may look deserted, as eateries often lack visible signage—it's best to go with a specific spot in mind rather than try your luck window shopping.

BURGER BLISS

This area is prime burger turf. The **Stand** (✉ 24 E. 12th St., near University Pl. ☎ 212/488–5900 ✛ 3:F4) offers upscale fast fare in a sleek setting. We recommend the bacon-and-egg cheeseburger, topped with cheddar and hard-boiled-egg mayo. For an Old New York feel, try the classic burgers at the **Old Town Bar** (✉ 45 E. 18th St., near Park Ave. S ☎ 212/529–6732 ✛ 3:F3), where they've been serving 'em up for more than 100 years. Or, if the weather is nice, head up to Madison Square Park, where burger lovers are always queued up at the original **Shake Shack** (✉ 23rd St. near Madison Ave. ☎ 212/889–6600 ✛ 3:F2). Leave room for frozen custard.

THE GREENMARKET CHEF

The popular upscale restaurant Gramercy Tavern is famous the world over for its seasonal, produce-driven menu. Their top purveyor—the Union Square Greenmarket—is a stone's throw away, at the northwest corner of Union Square (⊠ *Broadway at East 17th Street*). Executive chef Michael Anthony is uniquely positioned to take advantage of this beloved New York City culinary treasure. "It's one of the most precious resources this city has," says Anthony, who, along with his staff, visits the market four times a week to pick up the very best raw ingredients for his top-rated eatery. "It's where we get our inspiration."

In addition to waving to fellow chefs who shop the market, he catches up with the many farmers he's befriended over the years. "They're cultivating more than a business," Anthony says. "They're cultivating a community."

Anthony's typically dressed in civilian clothing when he hits the market, but shoppers often sense his passion as he inspects and buys unusual produce. "They'll ask me, 'How do I use that? What does that taste like?'"

At some restaurants greenmarket finds are scrawled on a chalkboard or highlighted on the menu as daily specials. Anthony likes to maintain a bit of drama. "We want people to bite into our food and ask, 'What is this? Where did this come from?'"

The food at Gramercy Tavern is seductively simple, letting the ingredients speak for themselves. "When a dish is shouting with the flavors [of] soft, seductive sweet potatoes, roasted sweet shallots, or the very best organically raised New York State chicken, we know we're doing our job right."

ANTHONY'S TOP GREENMARKET SNACKS

On Friday—Anthony's day off—you'll typically find him back at the Greenmarket, shopping for his personal "VIP customers"— his wife and young child. "If I stay focused, I can get through in half an hour," he says. Still, there are some worthy distractions. He rarely escapes without downing a cup of cider or a drinkable yogurt from Ronnybrook Farms, and a few samples of toasty Martin's pretzels. Then there's the nut-flecked granola from Hawthorne Valley Farms. "I'm lucky if that makes it home."

AND FOR DESSERT . . .

Sure, it's an international chain, but if you're looking for a major chocolate fix, you can count on **Max Brenner: Chocolate by the Bald Man** (⊠ *841 Broadway, near 13th St.* ☎ *212/388-0030* ✛ *3:F4*) to provide your poison. Max Brenner: Chocolate by the Bald Man is a Willy Wonka–esque chocolate emporium filled with college kids, families, and tourists—chocolate lovers, one and all. The extensive chocoholic menu boasts flavored chocolate beverages in custom-made sipping "hug mugs," chocolate fondues, cookies, cakes, brownies, and ice creams, even chocolate pizzas. If the Max Brenner scene isn't for you, check out the more sophisticated City Bakery (⊠ *3 W. 18th St., between 5th and 6th Aves.* ☎ *212/366-1414* ✛ *3:E3*) a few blocks to the north and west, where you can sip gourmet cocoa as thick as mud and nosh on crème brulée tartlets with chocolate crusts or bag some addictively salty pretzel croissants to go.

18

MIDTOWN WEST AND CHELSEA

Big is the buzz in Times Square and neighboring hoods, where neon-lighted billboards, towering skyscrapers, and Broadway theaters play starring roles. But watch out for restaurant rip-offs in this urban-theme-park environment.

It's true that tourist traps abound on the Great White Way, but fortunately you needn't head far from Times Square to score a stellar meal. Just move away from the bright lights and unrelenting foot traffic that clogs the area. On calmer side streets and in adjoining Hell's Kitchen there are excellent dining options for budget travelers and expense-account diners alike. Some of the best steak houses and Italian restaurants are here, and many eateries offer budget pretheater dinners and prix-fixe lunch menus to draw in new business.

But if the constant hustle and bustle unsettles your stomach, head south to Chelsea, a calmer neighborhood filled with art galleries and casual eateries. Chelsea may not be a white-hot dining destination, but you can eat well if you know where to go.

STEAK WITH STYLE

The design at **Quality Meats** (✉ 57 W. 58th St., near 6th Ave. ☎ 212/371-7777 ✛ 4:D1), *pictured above*, is inspired by classic New York City butcher shops in its use of warm wood, stainless steel, and white marble. Sit at the bar to peruse the extensive menu of wines and single-malt scotches. Then retire to the dining room for sophisticated riffs on steak-house classics like beef Wellington. Steak aficionados should know that Midtown has high-quality meats on every block. Here are more sure bets: **Ben Benson's** (✉ 123 W. 52nd St., near 6th Ave. ☎ 212/581-8888 ✛ 4:D2) and **Uncle Jack's** (✉ 440 9th Ave., at 35th St. ☎ 212/244-0005 ✛ 4:B6).

DINING IN TIMES SQUARE

There are plenty of chain eateries here that charge a premium for a substandard, rushed meal. But we've narrowed the field, selecting the best spots for a range of experiences and prices—from fun family dining to pretheater favorites.

For family-style fun, you can't miss the retro, 1950s-style **Ellen's Stardust Diner** (⊠ *1650 Broadway, at 51st St.* ☎ *212/956–5151* ✛ *4:C3*), complete with a singing waitstaff. Enjoy all-American classics such as meat loaf and chicken potpie while your waiters and waitresses serenade you with Broadway tunes.

Unlike the mostly kitschy theme restaurants that occupy Times Square, the sleek **Blue Fin** (⊠ *1567 Broadway, near 47th St.* ☎ *212/918–1400* ✛ *4:C3*) seafood restaurant is a refreshing departure. Watch the crowds go by from the corner glass bar or head upstairs.

Toloache (⊠ *251 W. 50th St., between Broadway and 8th Ave.* ☎ *212/581–1818* ✛ *4:B3*), a festive Mexican cantina, is a top foodie destination for its fresh ceviches, guacamoles, and standout dishes like the Negra Modelo–braised brisket taco or the quesadilla with black truffle and *huitlacoche* (corn fungus).

A mixed crowd of tourists, theatergoers, and thespians frequents **Joe Allen Restaurant** (⊠ *326 W. 46th St., between 8th and 9th Aves.* ☎ *212/581–6464* ✛ *4:B3*), a pretheater favorite. This casual yet classy restaurant serves reliable American cuisine. Don't fret about missing the show—the Broadway-knowledgeable staff will make sure you get to the theater in time for the opening number.

Plates of fresh antipasti are displayed right as you walk into **Bond 45** (⊠ *154 W. 45th St., between 6th and 7th Aves.* ☎ *212/869–4545* ✛ *4:C4*). This Italian eatery, with a dark-wood bar and leather-backed booths, serves a variety of pizzas, pastas, and steaks. With a separate pretheater menu, this Theater District hot spot is an ideal option for dining and then dashing to your show of choice.

Havana Central (⊠ *151 W. 45th St., between 6th and 7th Aves.* ☎ *212/398–7440*) is a great place for reasonably priced group dining and for sampling Cuban-Latino standards like garlicky chicken and well-seasoned skirt steak with a cucumber-and-mango salad. There's also a full menu of tropical-flavored mojitos, including coconut, blueberry, and passion fruit.

Ça Va (⊠ *310 W. 44th St., between 8th and 9th Aves.* ☎ *212/803–4545*) in the new InterContinental Hotel is chef Todd English's paean to French brasserie cuisine. There's a nice-looking bar with good wines by the glass, and hearty dishes like cassoulet, braised pork shank, and halibut with roasted Provençale vegetables.

AND FOR DESSERT . . .

Even if you're not crazy about tofu, the soy-based delights at **Kyotofu** (⊠ *705 9th Ave., near 48th St.* ☎ *212/974–6012* ✛ *4:A3*) will make you reconsider the merits of the soybean. Kyotofu's signature sweet tofu with Kuromitsu black sugar syrup is so creamy and delicious, you'd think it was a traditional panna cotta. The strawberry shortcake with strawberry sake sorbet and the warm miso chocolate cake with chocolate soybean ganache and green-tea cream are two more totally compelling favorites. Kyotofu's menu is full of intriguing options, so your best bet, on your first visit, is to go for the Kaiseki prix-fixe, a three-course tasting menu that enables you to try six different mini-desserts. Their menu changes seasonally, and it also includes savory brunch, lunch, and dinner options as well as an extensive sake and shochu cocktail list.

18

MIDTOWN EAST/UPPER EAST SIDE

Power brokers like to seal their deals over lunch on the East Side, so that means more than a few suits and ties at the restaurants during the day.

At night Midtown's streets are relatively quiet, but the restaurants are filled with expense-account diners celebrating their successes. Some of the most formal dining rooms and most expensive meals in town can be found here, at restaurants like the landmark **Four Seasons** and **L'Atelier de Joël Robuchon** or the **Modern**.

Farther uptown, the Upper East Side is jam-packed with pricey neighborhood eateries that cater to the area's well-heeled residents, but a few more reasonable choices are cropping up. Long viewed as an enclave of the privileged, these neighborhoods have plenty of elegant restaurants that serve the society "ladies who lunch" and bankers looking forward to a steak and single-malt scotch at the end of the day. However, visitors to Museum Mile and 5th Avenue shopping areas need not be put off. Whether you're looking to celebrate a special occasion or just want to grab a quick bite, you're sure to find something here for almost any budget.

URBAN PICNIC

For a uniquely New York experience, take a picnic lunch to one of the outdoor plazas that line Park Avenue from 51st to 53rd streets and seat yourself alongside scores of local office workers. (For architecture buffs, the Mies van der Rohe–designed Seagram Building is at 375 Park Avenue, at 52nd Street.) First, pick up your wares at the **Market at Grand Central Terminal** (Main Concourse, East), a trusted resource for gourmet goods on-the-go. Your menu could include fresh-baked bread from **Corrado Bread & Pastry**, olives or prosciutto from **Ceriello Fine Foods**, and fresh mozzarella from **Murray's Cheese**.

MIDTOWN 2 WAYS

	SAVE	SPLURGE
Museum of Modern Art	The La Bonne Soupe (⌧ 48 W. 55th St., between 5th and 6th Aves. ☎ 212/586–7650 ✛ 4:E2) special includes a bowl of soup with bread, salad, a glass of wine, and dessert for $17.25.	The Modern's Bar Room (⌧ 9 W. 53rd St., near 5th Ave. ☎ 212/333–1220 ✛ 4:D2) offers Alsatian-inspired fare like tarte flambé, a charred flat bread topped with bacon, onion, and crème fraîche.
Neue Galerie	Pintaile's (⌧ 26 E. 91st St., at Madison Ave. ☎ 212/722–1967 ✛ 6:F5) pizza offers delicious slices with a thin whole-wheat crust and gourmet toppings like roasted eggplant, wild mushrooms, and chorizo.	Café Sabarsky (⌧ 1048 5th Ave., near 86th St. ☎ 212/288–0665 ✛ 6:E6) entices museum goers with hearty sandwiches and entrées like sausage and goulash. Rich pastries complete the caloric spree.
Metropolitan Museum of Art	Grab a bite at Belgian chain Le Pain Quotidien (⌧ 1131 Madison Ave., between 84th and 85th Sts. ☎ 212/327–4900 ✛ 5:F1), which offers an array of light fare, like cheese boards and gourmet salads.	E.A.T. (⌧ 1064 Madison Ave., between 80th and 81st Sts. ☎ 212/772–0022 ✛ 5:F2), Eli Zabar's upscale American diner, may have high prices, but devotees return for excellent soups, sandwiches, and salads.

AND FOR DESSERT . . .

The Grand Central Dining Concourse is not your typical food court—it contains outposts for some of the city's most popular edibles, including a pie-lover favorite: the **Little Pie Company** (⌧ *107 E. 42nd St., Grand Central Terminal's Lower Dining Concourse* ☎ *212/983–3538 ✛ 4:F4*). The flaky crusts here are baked from scratch with fresh, all-natural ingredients. And they don't skimp on the fillings either, like fresh fruit, chocolate, or custard. Little Pie Company favorites include the Sour Cream Apple Walnut Pie, which is topped with a brown sugar, cinnamon, and walnut streusel, the Three Berry Pie (strawberry, blueberry, and raspberry), the Key Lime Pie (yep, made with real key lime juice), and the decadent triple-chocolate Mississippi Mud Pie. You'll also find seasonal pies, such as a 100% pure pumpkin pie and their Southern Pecan Pie with Texas pecans.

FORAGING IN CENTRAL PARK

There are plenty of pushcarts offering hot dogs and sodas, but if you're looking to soak up Central Park's magical ambience in an elegant setting, head for the **Central Park Boathouse Restaurant** (⌧ *E. 72nd St. at Park Dr. N* ☎ *212/517–2233 ✛ 5:E3*), which overlooks the gondola lake. There you can relax on the outdoor deck with a glass of wine and a cheese plate, or go for a more formal meal inside the restaurant. In warmer months the restaurant can get crowded: go for a late lunch or early-evening cocktail.

18

UPPER WEST SIDE/HARLEM

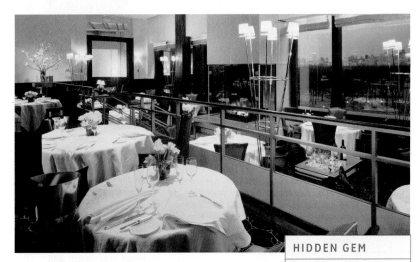

Anchoring the dining experience in this section of town are the high-end restaurants at the Time Warner Center, which some call a "fine-dining food court." Head farther uptown for cheaper eats, but also a burgeoning gourmet dining scene.

With Lincoln Center theatergoers, hungry shoppers, and visitors to Central Park nearby, chefs are finally waking up to the captive built-in audience of tourists and locals alike. The main avenues are indeed lined with restaurants, but until recently many of them have been mediocre. Now the better-known destination-dining spots beyond the Time Warner Center—among them **Jean Georges, Picholine, Telepan, and Dovetail**—have been joined by newcomers like **Salumeria Rossi, Fatty Crab,** and **Ed's Chowder,** all second or third restaurants from well-known chefs. Brunch is still a good bet, too. The flaky scones and fluffy omelets at **Sarabeth's,** not to mention blintzes and bagels at **Barney Greengrass,** are worth seeking out. For more adventurous eating, head up to Harlem for the city's best southern cooking.

HIDDEN GEM

Fairway Supermarket is a neighborhood institution, living up to its reputation for great prices on gourmet products—and shopping-cart jockeying down the narrow aisles. Upstairs, though, is the respite of **Fairway Café** (✉ 2127 Broadway, between 74th and 75th Sts. ☎ 212/944–9555), a large, brick-walled room with windows overlooking Broadway. Up front you can grab a pastry and coffee to go, but there's a full menu of fairly priced entrées as well. The place is run by Mitchell London, who's known for his juicy, well-marbled steaks—try the rib eye and you may never go back to Brooklyn's Peter Luger steak house again.

WHAT'S HOT IN HARLEM

Visitors in decades past may remember Harlem as an area scarred by crime and poverty. But times have changed: the Harlem of today is a vibrant community with excellent restaurants of all stripes. The bottom line? Harlem's ethnic eats are worth the trip.

Here are our top picks for savoring the multicultural flavor of the neighborhood:

Miss Mamie's Spoonbread Too (⊠ *366 W. 110th St., near Manhattan Ave.* ☎ *212/865–6744* ✛ *6:B2*) is a much-loved southern spot that's known for its friendly staff as well as its fried chicken, grits, and cornbread. Local politicians are sometimes seen rubbing elbows with the Columbia University students who gather here.

Native (⊠ *161 Lenox Ave., at 118th St.* ☎ *212/665–2525* ✛ *6:C1*) is a mildly Caribbean restaurant serving flavorful rice bowls and entrées that span a broad range of cuisines. Boasting a curry chicken, smoked salmon linguine, and Moroccan fried chicken with collard greens and mashed potatoes, this eatery manages to be all over the map and still find its way.

Sylvia's (⊠ *328 Lenox Ave., near 127th St.* ☎ *212/996–0660* ✛ *6:D1*): This Harlem mainstay has been serving soul-food favorites like smothered chicken, barbecue ribs, collard greens, and mashed potatoes to a dedicated crowd of locals, tourists, and college students since 1962. The food is so popular that owner Sylvia Woods bottles her signature sauces and spices for the masses, available for purchase at the restaurant and online.

AND FOR DESSERT . . .

A big cookie for the big city. Completely unpretentious and utterly delicious, **Levain Bakery's** (⊠ *167 W. 74th St., near Amsterdam Ave.* ☎ *212/874–6080* ✛ *5:B3*) cookies are rich and hefty. In fact, they clock in at 6 ounces each! Choose from the chocolate-chip walnut, dark-chocolate chocolate chip, dark-chocolate peanut-butter chip, or oatmeal raisin. Batches are baked fresh daily, and they taste best when they're warm and melty right out of the oven, so it's definitely worth seeking out this small basement bakery for a cookie craving. Levain's also bakes artisanal breads, including banana chocolate chip and pumpkin ginger spice, sour cream coffee cake, chocolate-chip and cinnamon brioche, sourdough rolls stuffed with Valrhona chocolate, blueberry muffins, a variety of scones, and bomboloncini—their unique jelly doughnuts.

18

RESTAURANT REVIEWS

Listed Alphabetically Within Neighborhoods

LOWER MANHATTAN

CHINATOWN

¢   ✕ **Great New York Noodletown.** Although the soups and noodles are
CHINESE   unbeatable at this no-frills restaurant, what you should order are the
☺   window decorations—the hanging lacquered ducks and roasted pork,
which are listed on a simple board hung on the wall and superb served
with pungent garlic-and-ginger sauce on the side. Seasonal specialties
like duck with flowering chives and salt-baked soft-shell crabs are excellent. So is the *congee*, or rice porridge, available with any number of
garnishes. Solo diners may end up at a communal table. ⊠ *28 Bowery,
at Bayard St., Chinatown* ☎ *212/349–0923* ▭ *No credit cards* Ⓜ *6, J,
M, Z to Canal St.; B, D to Grand St.* ✛ *2:F5.*

$ ✕ **Jing Fong.** Come to this dim sum palace for a jolting taste of Hong
CHINESE   Kong. On weekend mornings people pour into the escalator to Jing
☺   Fong's carnivalesque third-floor dining room. Servers push carts of
steamed dumplings, barbecue pork buns, and shrimp balls. For adventurous eaters, there's chicken feet, tripe, and snails. Arrive early for the
best selection, and save room for mango pudding. ⊠ *20 Elizabeth St.,
2nd fl., between Bayard and Canal Sts., Chinatown* ☎ *212/964–5256*
▭ *AE, MC, V* Ⓜ *6, J, M, N, Q, R, Z to Canal St.* ✛ *2:F5.*

$ ✕ **Joe's Shanghai.** Joe opened his first Shanghai restaurant in Queens in
CHINESE   1995, but buoyed by the accolades accorded his steamed soup dump-
☺   lings—filled with a rich, fragrant broth and ground pork or pork-crab-
meat mixture—he saw fit to open in Manhattan's Chinatown. There's
always a wait, but the line moves fast. Try the crisp turnip shortcakes
to start, homemade Shanghai noodles, and rich pork meatballs braised
in brown sauce. Other, more familiar Chinese dishes are also excellent.
Another Joe's Shanghai is at 24 W. 56th Street, between 5th and 6th
avenues (credit cards are accepted at this Midtown location). ⊠ *9 Pell
St., between the Bowery and Mott St., Chinatown* ☎ *212/233–8888*
⊕ *www.joeshanghairestaurants.com* ▭ *No credit cards* Ⓜ *6, J, M, N,
Q, R, Z to Canal St.* ✛ *2:F5.*

¢   ✕ **Nha Trang.** You can get a great meal for less than $10 at this low-atmo-
VIETNAMESE   sphere Vietnamese restaurant in Chinatown, a favorite with employees
Fodor'sChoice   and jury-duty candidates from nearby courthouses. Start with crispy
★   spring rolls, sweet-and-sour seafood soup, or shrimp grilled on sugarcane. For a follow-up, don't miss the thin pork chops, which are
marinated in a sweet vinegary sauce and grilled until charred. Another
favorite is deep-fried squid on shredded lettuce with a tangy dipping
sauce. If the line is long, which it usually is, even with a second location around the corner at 148 Centre Street, you may be asked to sit
at a table with strangers. ⊠ *87 Baxter St., between Bayard and Canal
Sts., Chinatown* ☎ *212/233–5948* ▭ *No credit cards* Ⓜ *6, J, M, N, Q,
R, Z to Canal St.* ✛ *2:F5.*

$$$ ✕ **Peking Duck House.** This Chinatown institution is the place to go in
CHINESE   New York for authentic Peking duck. Although the restaurant offers a

full Chinese menu, everyone—and we mean everyone—orders the duck. Begin, as most tables do, with an order of Shanghai soup dumplings, then move on to the bird. It's carved up table-side with plenty of fanfare—crisp burnished skin separated from moist flesh. Roll up the duck, with hoisin and scallions, in tender steamed pancakes. ⊠ *28 Mott St., at Mosco St., Chinatown* ☎ *212/227–1810* ⊕ *www.pekingduckhousenyc.com* ⊟ *AE, MC, V* Ⓜ *6, J, M, N, Q, R, Z to Canal St.* ✛ *2:F5.*

WORD OF MOUTH

"For old school steak, head to the Financial District and enjoy Delmonico's, the original NYC steakhouse."—Bowsprit

$$
CHINESE
Ⓒ
✕ **Ping's Seafood.** Although the original location in Queens still has the most elaborate menu with the most extensive selection of live seafood, the Manhattan location is more accessible both geographically and gastronomically. Helpful menus have pictures of most of the specialties. Among them are Dungeness crab in black-bean sauce, crisp fried tofu, silken braised *e-fu* noodles, and crisp Peking duck. Pricier than some other Chinatown haunts, Ping's is thought by many to be a notch above in setting and service. ⊠ *22 Mott St., near Pell St., Chinatown* ☎ *212/602–9988* ⌂ *Reservations essential* ⊟ *AE, MC, V* Ⓜ *6, J, M, N, Q, R, Z to Canal St.* ✛ *2:F6.*

FINANCIAL DISTRICT

$$$$
STEAKHOUSE
✕ **Delmonico's.** As the oldest continually operating restaurant in New York City, opened in 1837, austere Delmonico's is steeped in cultural, political, and culinary history. Lobster Newburg and Baked Alaska were invented here—and are still served. Inside the stately mahogany-panel dining room, tuck into the classic Delmonico's steak, a 20-ounce boneless rib eye smothered with frizzled onions, and don't forget to order creamed spinach on the side. Also worth trying: cheesy spaetzle with pancetta. The dining room gets busy early with an after-work Wall Street crowd, making reservations an essential component of the meal. ⊠ *56 Beaver St., at William St., Financial District* ☎ *212/509–1144* ⊕ *www.delmonicosny.com* ⌂ *Reservations essential* ⊟ *AE, D, DC, MC, V* ☉ *Closed Sun. No lunch weekends* Ⓜ *2, 3 to Wall St.; R to Whitehall St./South Ferry; 4, 5 to Bowling Green* ✛ *1:D4.*

¢
CAFÉ
✕ **Financier Patisserie.** On the cobblestone pedestrian street that has become the Financial District's restaurant row, this charming patisserie serves excellent pastries and delicious savory foods, like truffle mushroom bisque and panini pressed with prosciutto, fig jam, mascarpone, and arugula. After lunch, relax with a cappuccino and a *financier* (almond tea cake), or an elegant French pastry. In warm weather, perch at an outdoor table and watch Manhattanites buzz by. Another location is nearby at 35 Cedar Street, between Pearl and William streets. ⊠ *62 Stone St., between Mill La. and Hanover Sq., Financial District* ☎ *212/344–5600* ⊕ *www.financierpastries.com* ⌂ *Reservations not accepted* ⊟ *AE, DC, MC, V* ☉ *Closed Sun. No dinner* Ⓜ *2, 3 to Wall St.; 4, 5 to Bowling Green* ✛ *1:E4.*

$$$$
STEAKHOUSE
✕ **Harry's Steak and Harry's Café.** Its noise-dampening acoustics and maze of underground nooks combine to make Harry's Steak—the fine-dining

18

half of the restaurant (Harry's Café is more casual)—the city's most intimate steak house. Request the grotto for a stealthy rendezvous, or the long dozen-seater for a raucous night out with the boys. Begin with savory baked clams buried in smoked bacon and bread crumbs, or the lively tomato trio, starring thick beefsteak slices topped with bacon and blue cheese, mozzarella and basil, and shaved onion with ranch dressing. The star attraction—prime aged porterhouse for two—is nicely encrusted with sea salt and a good match for buttery mashed potatoes infused with sweet roasted shallots and thick steak sauce spooned from Mason jars. ⊠ *1 Hanover Sq., between Stone and Pearl Sts., Financial District* ☏ *212/785–9200* ⊕ *www.harrysnyc.com* ⌲ *Reservations essential* ⊟ *AE, D, MC, V* ⊘ *Closed Sun.* Ⓜ *4, 5 to Bowling Green; 2, 3 to Wall St.* ✛ *1:E4.*

$$
AMERICAN

✕ **P. J. Clarke's.** This East Side institution has been dispensing burgers and beer for more than a century. Despite a physical upgrade under new owners in 2002, the original P. J. Clarke's (there's now another offshoot way downtown) maintains the beveled-glass and scuffed-wood look of an old-time saloon. Many of the bartenders and patrons are as much of a fixture as the decor. More civilized at lunchtime, the bar area heaves with an after-work mob on weekday evenings. Pull up a stool if you can for superlative bar food, like clams casino and the signature burger smothered in creamy béarnaise. A few other P. J. Clarke locations have sprouted up at 915 3rd Avenue (at 55th Street), 44 West 63rd Street, near Columbus Avenue, and 205 East 55th Street, off 2nd Avenue. ⊠ *4 World Financial Center, at Vesey Street, Financial District* ☏ *212/285–1500* ⊟ *AE, DC, MC, V* Ⓜ *A, C, E, 1, 2, 3, 9 to Chambers St.* ✛ *1:B3.*

$$$$
NEW AMERICAN

✕ **SHO Shaun Hergatt.** This restaurant in the Setai Hotel befits the riches of nearby Wall Street. Though it launched at the height of the 2008 recession, the decor screams all-out extravagance in every way. After passing through a dramatic corridor composed of glass-encased wine bottles, you enter a sprawling series of rooms adorned with framed silver rings, striated wood walls, and luxurious Asian-inspired fabrics. Australian chef Shaun Hergatt, visible in the open kitchen, brings a light touch to the luxurious cuisine in dishes like peekytoe crab with galangal gelee and sea urchin, and an ingot of three-day short rib over a rich parsnip puree that looks—and tastes—like a savory candy bar. The $69 three-course prix-fixe is a reasonable antidote to an expensive à la carte menu. ⊠ *40 Broad St., at Exchange Pl., Financial District* ☏ *212/809–3993* ⊕ *www.shoshaunhergatt.com* ⌲ *Reservations essential* ⊟ *AE, MC, V* Ⓜ *R to Rector St., 2, 3, 4, 5 to Wall St., J, M, Z to Broad Street* ✛ *1:D4.*

TRIBECA

$
AMERICAN
☕

✕ **Bubby's.** Crowds clamoring for coffee and freshly squeezed juice line up for brunch at this TriBeCa mainstay, but the restaurant serves fine lunches and dinners as well. The dining room is homey and comfortable, with big windows; in summer, neighbors sit at tables outside with their dogs. For brunch you can order almost anything, including homemade granola, sour-cream pancakes with bananas and strawberries, and *huevos rancheros* with guacamole and grits. Eclectic comfort food— mac 'n cheese, fried chicken—make up the lunch and dinner menus.

✉ *120 Hudson St., at N. Moore St., TriBeCa* ☎ *212/219–0666* ⊕ *www.bubbys.com* 🖃 *D, DC, MC, V* Ⓜ *1 to Franklin St.* ✥ *1:C1.*

$$$$ ✕ **Corton.** Über-restaurateur Drew Neiporent transformed the former
FRENCH Montrachet space into a spare, elegant dining room. It's the perfect
stage for young whiz-kid chef Paul Liebrandt's understated, mildly
experimental cuisine. The walls are decorated with subtle white trompe-
l'oeil designs of cherry blossoms and birds, but the real adornment is
on the plate, where Liebrandt transports diners with dishes like his
"from the garden" composition: an assemblage of nearly 20 vegetable
components that redefines what produce can do. Heirloom eggs are
presented at the table in a basket, then spirited back to the kitchen for
a slow poach before being served with trumpet mushrooms and serrano
gelee. Desserts include chocolate tart with grapefruit and hazelnuts.
The well-curated wine list has a cost-conscious selection of "country
French" bottles. ✉ *239 W. Broadway, between Walker and White Sts.,
TriBeCa* ☎ *212/219–2777* ⊕ *www.cortonnyc.com* 🔖 *Reservations
essential* 🖃 *AE, D, DC, MC, V* 🕲 *Closed Sun. No lunch* Ⓜ *1 to Franklin St., A, C, E to Canal St.* ✥ *2:D5.*

$$$ ✕ **The Harrison.** Jimmy Bradley's back in the kitchen at this perfect
AMERICAN neighborhood eatery, riffing off the formula he mastered at the Red
Cat in Chelsea. The warm, woody room serves as a relaxed backdrop
for the seasonal American food, like English-cut lamb loin with baby
carrots and fennel, and malt-vinegar mayo. Desserts, including an ice
cream–brownie sandwich with Sazerac caramel, are at once accessi-
ble and sophisticated. ✉ *355 Greenwich St., at Harrison St., TriBeCa*
☎ *212/274–9310* ⊕ *www.theharrison.com* 🔖 *Reservations essential*
🖃 *AE, D, DC, MC, V* 🕲 *No lunch* Ⓜ *1 to Franklin St.* ✥ *2:C6.*

$ ✕ **Kitchenette.** This small, comfy restaurant lives up to its name with
AMERICAN tables so close together, you're likely to make new friends. The dining
☺ room feels like a breakfast nook, and the food tastes like your mom
made it—provided she's a great cook. There are no frills, just solid
cooking, friendly service, and a long line at peak times. For brunch
don't miss the blackberry-cherry pancakes or the baked vanilla brûlée
French toast. Lemon-Parmesan chicken with seasonal vegetables is a
heavenly dinner. ✉ *156 Chambers St., near Greenwich St., TriBeCa*
☎ *212/267–6740* ⊕ *www.kitchenetterestaurant.com* 🖃 *AE, MC, V* Ⓜ *1,
2, 3, A, C to Chambers St.* ✥ *1:C2.*

$$ ✕ **Locanda Verde.** The second time's the charm for Robert De Niro, who
ITALIAN along with his partners closed Ago, their first attempt at a restaurant
in the clubby Greenwich Hotel. Chef Andrew Carmellini, an acolyte of
Daniel Boulud, made a smart move from A Voce to cook here, and he's
clearly in his element. The space is warm and welcoming, with accents
of brick and wood and large windows that open to the street, weather
permitting. The menu is full of aspirational comfort food that hits the
mark, especially the *cicchetti* (small plates) such as blue crab crostino
with jalapeños and a mound of sheep's-milk ricotta scattered with
sea salt and herbs. Several draft beers, along with more than a dozen
wines by the glass, make an already hopping bar scene even more of a
draw. ✉ *379 Greenwich St., at N. Moore St., TriBeCa* ☎ *212/925–3797*

18

⊕ *www.locandaverdenyc.com* ᕦ *Reservations essential* ▭ *AE, MC, V* Ⓜ *1 to Franklin St.* ✛ *1:B1.*

$$$
NEW AMERICAN

✕ **Marc Forgione.** Young chef Marc Forgione had big shoes to fill—his father, also named Marc Forgione, was one of the New York food scene megastars with his 1980s restaurant, An American Place. Dad needn't worry. Forgione has an Iron Chef America winner's jacket and numerous awards to endorse his ambitious, creative New American cuisine. The menu changes with the whims of the chef and the seasonal availability of produce, but whatever you order will be bold, flavorful, and inventive without a hint of preciousness. The bar scene hops with a sceney blend of neighborhood locals and Wall Street boys loosening their ties after work, and almost every table feels like a cozy corner regardless of the right angles surrounding it. Though meats—a well-charred Creekstone Farms steak, for one—are well prepared, Forgione has a special way with seafood. His chili lobster, a take on a dish you'll find all over Asia, comes with Texas toast for mopping up the spicy, buttery sauce. Tartare (it could be kingfish, hamachi, or salmon, depending on the day) is accented with avocado in a pool of sweet, soy-lashed sauce, all accompanied by house-made chips. And his famous Maine scallop is topped with "sauce proposal," so called because a customer proposed to Forgione after trying it. ⊠ *134 Reade St., between Hudson and Greenwich Sts., TriBeCa* ☏ *212/941–9401* ⊕ *www.marcforgione. com* ᕦ *Reservations essential* ▭ *AE, D, MC, V* ⊙ *No lunch* Ⓜ *1, 2, 3 to Chambers St.* ✛ *1:C1.*

$$$
JAPANESE

✕ **Nobu.** At this huge, bustling TriBeCa dining room (or its sister location uptown), you might just spot a celeb or two. New York's most famous Japanese restaurant has gained a lot of competition in recent years, but this is still the destination for the innovative Japanese cuisine Nobu Matsuhisa made famous (even if the chef himself is rarely in attendance these days). Dishes like fresh yellowtail sashimi with jalapeño, rock shrimp tempura, or miso-marinated Chilean sea bass continue to draw huge crowds. Put yourself in the hands of the chef by ordering the tasting menu, the *omakase*, specify how much you want to spend, and let the kitchen do the rest. Can't get reservations? Try your luck at the first-come, first-served **Nobu Next Door** (literally next door), with a similar menu plus a sushi bar. ⊠ *105 Hudson St., at Franklin St., TriBeCa* ☏ *212/219–0500* ⊕ *www.myriadrestaurantgroup.com* ᕦ *Reservations essential* ▭ *AE, D, DC, MC, V* ⊙ *No lunch weekends* Ⓜ *1 to Franklin St.* ✛ *1:B1.*

$$$
BISTRO
☺

✕ **Odeon.** New Yorkers change hangouts faster than they can press speed-dial, but this spot has managed to maintain its quality and flair for more than 25 years. The neo–Art Deco room is still packed nightly with revelers. Now children are also welcome. The pleasant service and well-chosen wine list are always in style. The bistro-menu highlights include *frisée aux lardons* (bacon-enhanced frisee salad) with poached farm egg, grilled NY strip steak, and slow-cooked cod with baby leeks and fennel confit. ⊠ *145 West Broadway, between Duane and Thomas Sts., TriBeCa* ☏ *212/233–0507* ⊕ *www.theodeonrestaurant.com* ▭ *AE, D, DC, MC, V* Ⓜ *1, 2, 3, A, C to Chambers St.* ✛ *2:D6.*

SOHO AND LITTLE ITALY (WITH NOLITA)

SOHO

$$$
SEAFOOD

✕ **Aquagrill.** Owned by a husband-and-wife team, Aquagrill is a popular SoHo standard. The decor's a bit tired, but there's lots of room and warm, welcoming service. The lively neighborhood eatery makes its own pastries and baked goods—including the bread for its brunchtime challah French toast with cinnamon apples and pecan butter. Fans rave about the lunchtime $21.50 prix-fixe Shucker Special—a half-dozen oysters with homemade soup or chowder and a salad. Dinner specialties include roasted Dungeness crab cake napoleon with sun-dried tomato oil, and falafel-crusted salmon. Try the the chocolate tasting plate consisting of a dark molten chocolate cake with milk-chocolate ice cream and white-chocolate mousse. ✉ *210 Spring St., at 6th Ave., SoHo* ☎ *212/274–0505* ⊕ *www.aquagrill.com* ⌔ *Reservations essential* ⊟ *AE, D, DC, MC, V* Ⓜ *E to Spring St.* ✛ *2:D4.*

$$
BRASSERIE

✕ **Balthazar.** Even with long waits and excruciating noise levels, most out-of-towners agree that it's worth making reservations to experience restaurateur Keith McNally's flagship, a painstakingly accurate reproduction of a Parisian brasserie. Like the decor, entrées re-create French classics: Gruyère-topped onion soup; steak frites; and icy tiers of crab, oysters, and other pristine shellfish. Brunch is still one of the toughest tables in town. The best strategy is to go at off-hours, or on weekdays for breakfast, to miss the crush of hungry New Yorkers. ✉ *80 Spring St., between Broadway and Crosby St., SoHo* ☎ *212/965–1414* ⊕ *www.balthazarny.com* ⌔ *Reservations essential* ⊟ *AE, MC, V* Ⓜ *6 to Spring St.; N, R to Prince St.; B, D, F, M to Broadway–Lafayette* ✛ *2:E4.*

$$
NEW AMERICAN

✕ **Blue Ribbon.** After 19 years, Blue Ribbon remains *the* late-night foodie hangout. Join the genial hubbub for midnight noshing, namely the beef marrow with oxtail marmalade and the renowned raw-bar platters. Trustafarians, literary types, chefs, designers—a good-looking gang—fill this dark box of a room until 4 am. The menu appears standard at first blush, but it's not. Try the duck club sandwich, or the matzo-ball soup, a heady brew filled with the sacrilegious combo of seafood and traditional Jewish dumplings. ✉ *97 Sullivan St., between Prince and Spring Sts., SoHo* ☎ *212/274–0404* ⊕ *www.blueribbonrestaurants.com* ⌔ *Reservations not accepted* ⊟ *AE, D, DC, MC, V* ⊗ *No lunch* Ⓜ *C, E to Spring St.; R to Prince St.* ✛ *2:D3.*

$$
JAPANESE

✕ **Blue Ribbon Sushi.** Sushi, like pizza, attracts plenty of opinionated fanatics. Stick to the excellent raw fish and specials here if you're a purist. Others might want to try one of the experimental rolls: the Blue Ribbon—lobster, shiso, and black caviar—is popular. The dark, intimate nooks, minimalist design, and servers with downtown attitude attract a stylish crowd that doesn't mind waiting for a table or for chilled sake. ✉ *119 Sullivan St., between Prince and Spring Sts., SoHo* ☎ *212/343–0404* ⊕ *www.blueribbonrestaurants.com* ⌔ *Reservations not accepted* ⊟ *AE, D, DC, MC, V* Ⓜ *C, E to Spring St.; R to Prince St.* ✛ *2:D3.*

$$
ITALIAN
Fodor'sChoice
★

✕ **Emporio.** In a neighborhood whose long, boutique-lined blocks can sometimes feel deserted after dark, Emporio is a chic, welcoming hangout with warmth to spare. The brick-lined front room is a gathering spot for happy hour at the bar, featuring an appetizing selection of

18

free small bites like frittata, white-bean salad, and ham-and-spinach *tramezzini* (finger sandwiches). The centerpiece of the large, sky-lighted back room—great for small and large parties alike—is a wood-fired oven that turns out crisp, thin-crusted pizzas topped with staples like prosciutto, buffalo mozzarella, and arugula. Service is solicitous but not speedy, allowing time to lin-ger into the late hours over a bottle of wine from a copious selection. Try house-made pastas like chewy garganelli with pork sausage and house-made ragu, and entrées like whole roasted fish with grilled lemon, then finish with a piping-hot dessert calzone filled with ricotta, Nutella, and hazelnuts, or a delicate panna cotta with poached plums. ✉ *231 Mott St., between Prince and Spring Sts. NoLIta* ☎ *212/966–1234* ⊟ *AE, D, DC, MC, V* Ⓜ *B, D, F, M, A, C, E to W. 4th St., 6 to Bleecker St.* ✛ *2:F3.*

CULINARY WALKS

Some of the city's most lively foodie walks come courtesy of food-industry insider Liz Young. The former chef leads themed 3- to 4-hour tours through neigh-borhoods around the city. For a food-filled afternoon, try the dim sum tour of Brooklyn's Chinatown or the West Village food and his-tory tour. ⊕ *www.lizyoungtours. com*

$$
NEW AMERICAN
Fodor's Choice
★

✕ **Hundred Acres.** The latest restaurant from the owners of Cookshop and Five Points, Hundred Acres has a rustic, country feel and offers simple yet sophisticated cooking à la Marc Meyer. Don't count on a big menu: the daily choices are limited to seven main dishes and one special entrée. The steamed littleneck clams appetizer served with garlic-oregano butter, pickled corn, cilantro, and garlic toasts is particu-larly delicious. For the mains, try the Montauk bluefish with spinach, chickpeas, and fiery harissa sauce or the Hampshire pork shank with polenta and rhubarb chutney. The classic burger made from pasture-raised beef, topped with Vermont cheddar and served with fries and Vidalia onion mayonnaise, should not be missed. ✉ *38 MacDougal St., between Houston and Prince Sts., SoHo* ☎ *212/475–7500* ⊕ *hundred-acresnyc.com* ⊟ *AE, DC, MC, V* Ⓜ *1 to Houston; C, E to Spring St.; N, R to Prince St.* ✛ *2:D3.*

$
MEXICAN

✕ **La Esquina.** Anchoring a downtown corner under a bright neon sign, La Esquina looks like nothing more than a fast-food taqueria. But beyond the top-notch, dirt-cheap tacos sold to-go until 2 in the morning lurks an entire restaurant complex. Just around the corner you'll find a modestly priced sit-down café featuring those same tacos along with more ambitious fare like fine chiles rellenos (stuffed peppers) and *carne asada* (grilled meat). Meanwhile, the real hipster draw remains com-pletely hidden from sight. La Esquina's basement brasserie, like a Mexi-can speakeasy, is accessible by reservation only, through an unmarked door just inside the ground-floor taqueria. Once inside, you'll discover a buzzy subterranean scene along with potent margaritas and robust upscale fare. Though prices downstairs are high, portions are huge. ✉ *106 Kenmare St., between Cleveland Pl. and Lafayette St., SoHo* ☎ *646/613–7100* ⊟ *AE, MC, V* Ⓜ *6 to Spring St.* ✛ *2:F4.*

$$$ ✕**Lure.** Outfitted like the interior of a sleek luxury liner, Lure offers oce-
SEAFOOD anic fare prepared in multiple culinary styles. From the sushi bar, feast
on Lure House Rolls, shrimp tempura rolls crowned with spicy tuna
and Japanese tartar sauce. From the kitchen, order creative dishes like
steamed branzino with oyster mushrooms, scallions, and ponzu sauce,
or Manila clams over pancetta-studded linguine. For an all-American
treat, you can't go wrong with a classic lobster roll on brioche. ✉ *142
Mercer St., at Prince St., SoHo* ☏ *212/431–7676* ⊕ *www.lurefishbar.
com* ⊟ *AE, MC, V* ⊗ *No lunch weekends* Ⓜ *6 to Bleecker St.; B, D, F,
M to Broadway–Lafayette St.; N, R to Prince St.* ✛ *2:E3.*

$ ✕**MarieBelle.** Practically invisible from the front of the chocolate empo-
CAFÉ   rium, the back entry to the Cacao Bar opens into a sweet, high-ceiling,
↻   12-table hot-chocolate shop. Most people order the Aztec, European-
style (that's 60% Colombian chocolate mixed with hot water—no
cocoa powder here!). The first sip is startlingly rich but not too dense.
American-style, made with milk, is sweeter. Preface it with a salad or
sandwich from the dainty lunch menu, or request one of the expensive
but ravishing flavored chocolates sold out front, like passion fruit, or
dulce de leche. Another location at 762 Madison Avenue, off 65th
Street, gives Upper East Siders their sweet treats. ✉ *484 Broome St.,
between West Broadway and Wooster St., SoHo* ☏ *212/925–6999*
⊕ *www.mariebelle.com* ⊜ *Reservations not accepted* ⊟ *AE, D, MC, V*
⊗ *No dinner* Ⓜ *6 to Spring St.; A, C, E to Canal St.* ✛ *2:D4.*

$$$ ✕**Osteria Morini.** Less formal than his other Italian joints, Osteria
ITALIAN Morini is Michael White's boisterous play on the food of northern
Italy. It's creamy, heavy—and, as usual, delicious. The atmosphere is
lively and raucous, with communal tables at the center and a rock-
and-roll soundtrack at full volume. Knickknacks and black-and-white
photos line the walls, and other items are displayed in glass cases near
the kitchen. Start with a little crock of silky braised cockscomb with
toasty croutons and a plate of tiny croquettes that ooze ham and bécha-
mel when pierced. Oven-baked polenta comes with either sausage or
mushrooms, and the pasta—a lusty ragu Bolognese, a ham- and cream-
lashed garganelli with prosciutto and truffle butter, for example—are
on point. Waits can be long, so try to come early or stay late, or grab
one of the few bar seats for a celery-infused Campari cocktail or a
glass of Italian wine. ✉ *218 Lafayette St., between Spring and Broome
Sts., SoHo* ☏ *212/965–8777* ⊕ *www.osteriamorini.com* ⊜ *Reservations
essential* ⊟ *AE, MC, V* ⊗ *No lunch weekends* Ⓜ *6 to Spring St.* ✛ *2:E3.*

$$$ ✕**Savoy.** Chef-owner Peter Hoffman's two-story restaurant has the
AMERICAN coziness of a country inn, with blazing fireplaces upstairs and down-
stairs, soft wood accents, and windows looking onto the cobblestone
street. Hoffman is one of the city's strongest proponents of using local,
seasonal ingredients, which shows in disarmingly simple dishes like
a confit of pork shoulder with delicata squash, apple, and chorizo,
and salt-crusted baked duck with mashed turnips, poached plums, and
carrots. The wine list emphasizes small producers. ✉ *70 Prince St., at
Crosby St., SoHo* ☏ *212/219–8570* ⊕ *www.savoynyc.com* ⊟ *AE, MC,
V* ⊗ *No lunch Sun.* Ⓜ *R to Prince St.; 6 to Spring St.; F, M to Broad-
way–Lafayette St.* ✛ *2:E3.*

18

$$
KOREAN

✕ **Woo Lae Oak.** Not so much an authentic Korean eatery, Woo Lae Oak uses traditional Korean flavors to create an elevated cuisine in a tony SoHo setting. The food is spicy and flavorful: kimchi burns the lips and prepares the palate for such dishes as *ke sal mari* (Dungeness crab and leek wrapped in spinach crepes), and *o ree mari* (duck slices wrapped in miso blini sweetened with plum sauce). But fans of tabletop grilling will still be able to get their tender sliced beef *bulgo gi*. Since this is SoHo, the tables are dark granite slabs and the lighting is low. ✉ *148 Mercer St., between Prince and W. Houston Sts., SoHo* ☎ *212/925–8200* ⊕ *www. woolaeoaksoho.com* ▭ *AE, DC, MC, V* Ⓜ *R to Prince St.; 6 to Spring St.; B, D, F, M to Broadway–Lafayette St.* ✛ *2:E3.*

NOLITA

$$$
ITALIAN

✕ **Peasant.** The crowd at this rustic restaurant is stylishly urban. Inspired by the proverbial "peasant" cuisine where meals were prepared in the kitchen hearth, chef-owner Frank DeCarlo cooks all of his wonderful food in a bank of wood- or charcoal-burning ovens, from which the heady aroma of garlic perfumes the room. Don't fill up on the crusty bread and fresh ricotta, though, or you'll miss out on other flavorful Italian fare like sizzling sardines that arrive in terra-cotta pots, or spit-roasted leg of lamb with bitter *trevisano* lettuce and polenta. ✉ *194 Elizabeth St., between Spring and Prince Sts., NoLIta* ☎ *212/965– 9511* ⊕ *www.peasantnyc.com* ⌦ *Reservations essential* ▭ *AE, MC, V* ☾ *Closed Mon. No lunch* Ⓜ *6 to Spring St.; R to Prince St.* ✛ *2:F3.*

$$
ECLECTIC

✕ **Public.** Public's space is complex and sophisticated, with soaring ceilings and whitewashed brick walls, skylights, fireplaces, three dining areas, a vast bar, and even the occasional elegant bookcase. The menu flaunts its nonconformity, and brunch at Public is a local favorite, with exotic dishes like coconut pancakes topped with fresh ricotta, mango, and lime syrup, and a juicy venison burger. Australian barramundi fish, served with vanilla-celeriac puree and braised garlic greens, demonstrates a light yet adventurous touch. Standout desserts include a chocolate mousse with tahini ice cream and sesame candy. ✉ *210 Elizabeth St., between Prince and Spring Sts., NoLIta* ☎ *212/343–7011* ⊕ *www. public-nyc.com* ▭ *AE, D, MC, V* ☾ *No lunch weekdays* Ⓜ *6 to Spring St.; N, R to Prince St.; J, M to Bowery* ✛ *2:F3.*

LITTLE ITALY

$
PIZZA
🔥

✕ **Lombardi's.** Brick walls, red-and-white checkered tablecloths, and the aroma of thin-crust pies emerging from the coal oven set the mood for some of the best pizza in Manhattan. Lombardi's has served pizza since 1905 (though not in the same location), and business has not died down a bit. The mozzarella is always fresh, resulting in an almost grease-less slice, and the toppings, such as meatballs, pancetta, or imported anchovies, are also top quality. Lombardi's is perhaps best known for its toothsome clam pizza, which features freshly shucked clams, garlic oil, pecorino-Romano cheese, and parsley. ✉ *32 Spring St., at Mott St., Little Italy* ☎ *212/941–7994* ⊕ *www.firstpizza.com* ▭ *No credit cards* Ⓜ *6 to Spring St.; B, D, F, M to Broadway–Lafayette* ✛ *2:F3.*

EAST VILLAGE AND LOWER EAST SIDE

EAST VILLAGE

$$$
NEW AMERICAN

✗ **Apiary.** Set on a busy strip of the East Village, Apiary is a chic refuge for a mature dinner in a young neighborhood. The restaurant is partly owned by furniture design company Ligne Roset, and the contemporary space holds sleek furnishings by the brand. The à la carte menu, courtesy of talented Veritas alumnus Scott Bryan, isn't huge, but is devoted to seasonal and—whenever possible—local food. Expect dishes like crispy sweetbreads with romesco sauce and chanterelle risotto with peas, lemon, and herbs. A cost-conscious $35 prix-fixe menu, offered Monday through Thursday, offers many menu standouts at a fraction of the price. The extensive wine list features many domestic picks, but also takes drinkers on an international oenological tour. Monday is no-corkage night. ✉ 60 3rd Ave., at 11th St., East Village ☎ 212/254–0888 ⊕ www.apiarynyc.com ⊟ AE, D, DC, MC, V ⊗ No lunch weekdays Ⓜ 6 to Astor Pl.; R to 8th St.; L to 3rd Ave. ✚ 3:G5.

$
AMERICAN

✗ **Back Forty.** Pioneering chef Peter Hoffman, a longtime leader in promoting local, sustainable food, attracts a devoted crowd at this casual restaurant that feels like a neighborhood joint. Despite Hoffman's pedigree, Back Forty displays plenty of humility. Prices on the short, rustic, greenmarket menu are low, and the homey decor features a pastoral mural behind the bar and rusty farm tools on the walls. Begin with bar snacks like chicken-liver mousse on toast washed down with a fine house cocktail like the rum-and-Concord grape Collins. The simple family-style dinner selections (for parties only) include a perfect grilled trout; a moist, shareable pan-roasted chicken; and a wide array of seasonal sides, including the roasted Brussels sprouts with maple-cider vinegar and lemon-thyme butter. A hearty and popular brunch is served on Saturday. ✉ 190 Ave. B, at 12th St., East Village ☎ 212/388–1990 ⊕ www.backfortynyc.com ⊟ AE, MC, V ⊗ No lunch Mon.–Sat. Ⓜ L to 1st Ave. ✚ 3:H4.

$
VIETNAMESE
Fodor's Choice
★

✗ **Baoguette.** Vietnamese *Banh Mi* have taken New York by storm in the past couple of years, and Baoguette, a chainlet from restaurateur Michael Hunh, is a great place to try these spicy, multilayered baguette sandwiches. This is the flagship decorated with raffia walls and large photos of Vietnamese street scenes, and though there a few tables, the majority of customers get take-out sandwiches. Try the namesake sandwich, layered with savory pâté, flavorful pulled pork, and aromatic herbs, or the addictive Sloppy Bao, a sweet and savory sloppy joe with curried beef, mango, and lemongrass. ✉ 37 St. Marks Pl., between 2nd and 3rd Aves., East Village ☎ 212/380–1487 ⊕ www.baoguette.com ⌖ Reservations not accepted ⊟ MC, V Ⓜ R to 8th St./NYU; 6 to Astor Pl./4th Ave. ✚ 2:F1.

$$
CHINESE

✗ **Chinatown Brasserie.** This large, bi-level 175-seat dining room is thrillingly vibrant, featuring dark cherry banquettes and eight stunning crimson pagoda silk lanterns suspended from two central columns. Chicken and pine nuts are wrapped in Bibb lettuce. Crispy Peking duck is roasted in a special barbecuing oven, then sliced and presented on a long platter with the crackling skin still attached to the succulent flesh. Fresh Mandarin pancakes, julienned scallions, and sweet, pungent hoisin sauce

18

are on hand. Dark-chocolate fortune cookies contain salient quotes from Albert Einstein and Ronald Reagan. ✉ *380 Lafayette St., at Great Jones St., East Village* ☎ *212/533–7000* ⊕ *www.chinatownbrasserie. com* 🟰 *AE, MC, M* Ⓜ *6 to Bleecker St.; B, D, F, M to Broadway–Lafayette St.* ✛ *2:E2.*

$$
GASTROPUB
Fodor's Choice
★

✕ **DBGB Kitchen & Bar.** The latest addition to Daniel Boulud's New York City restaurant fleet, DBGB forgoes the white tablecloths, formal service, and steep prices found at the famed chef's fancier digs, and instead pays homage to the grittier, younger feel of its Lower East Side location. (The name is a wink to the legendary rock club CBGB.) Lined with shelves of pots, plates, and pans (not to mention copperware donated by renowned chefs from around the world), the dining room gives way to a partially open kitchen where you can catch the chefs preparing Boulud's take on French- and German-inspired pub fare. The menu features 13 different varieties of sausages (the *tunisienne*, a spicy lamb-and-mint merguez, is a particular standout), decadently sinful burgers (the aptly named "piggy" burger, a juicy beef patty topped with a generous portion of Daisy Mae pulled pork, jalapeño mayonnaise, and mustard vinegar slaw in a cheddar-cornbread bun—not for the weak-willed), and classic entrées like steak frites and lemon-and-rosemary roasted chicken. The $24 three-course, prix-fixe lunch is quite a steal. ✉ *299 Bowery, between Houston and 1st St., East Village* ☎ *212/933–5300* ⊕ *www.danielnyc.com* 🍴 *Reservations essential* 🟰 *AE, D, DC, MC, V* 🕓 *No lunch Mon.* Ⓜ *F to 2nd Ave.* ✛ *2:F2.*

$$
ITALIAN

✕ **Gnocco.** Owners Pierluigi Palazzo and Gianluca Giavonetti named the place not after gnocchi but after a regional specialty—deep-fried dough bites served alongside capicola, salami, and aged prosciutto. Head to the roomy canopied garden out back for savory salads, an endlessly rotating selection of house-made pasta specials, pizza topped with mozzarella, truffles, and mushrooms, and hearty entrées like pork tenderloin in a balsamic emulsion with flakes of Grana Padano cheese. ✉ *337 E. 10th St., between Aves. A and B, East Village* ☎ *212/677–1913* ⊕ *www. gnocco.com* 🟰 *AE* Ⓜ *L to 1st Ave.; 6 to Astor Pl.* ✛ *3:H5.*

$
CHINESE

✕ **Grand Sichuan.** This regional Chinese chainlet may be low on ambience, but it serves delicious Sichuan specialties like fiery *dan dan* noodles or crab soup dumplings. Check the Web site for alternative locations. ✉ *19–23 St. Marks Pl., near 3rd Ave., East Village* ☎ *212/529–4800* ⊕ *www.thegrandsichuan.com* 🟰 *AE, MC, V* Ⓜ *6 to Astor Pl.* ✛ *2:F1, 3:B2, 2:C3.*

$$$
MEDITERRANEAN

✕ **Il Buco.** The unabashed clutter of vintage kitchen gadgets and tableware harks back to Il Buco's past as an antiques store. Each table, two of which are communal, is unique—the effect is a festive, almost romantic country-house atmosphere. The restaurant features meats and produce from local farms for the daily entrées and Mediterranean tapaslike appetizers. Call ahead to book the intimate wine cellar for dinner. ✉ *47 Bond St., between Bowery and Lafayette St., NoHo* ☎ *212/533–1932* ⊕ *www.ilbuco.com* 🟰 *AE, MC, V* 🕓 *No lunch Sun.* Ⓜ *6 to Bleecker St.; B, D, F, M to Broadway–Lafayette St.* ✛ *2:F2.*

$$$$
JAPANESE

✕ **Jewel Bako.** In a minefield of cheap, often inferior sushi houses gleams tiny Jewel Bako. One of the best sushi restaurants in the East Village, the futuristic bamboo tunnel of a dining room is gorgeous, but try to nab a place at the sushi bar and put yourself in the hands of sushi master Yoshi Kousaka. His five-course *omakase,* or chef's menu, starts at $95. (A less expensive sushi or sashimi *omakase* is $50.) You'll be served only what's freshest and best. ✉ *239 E. 5th St., between 2nd and 3rd Aves., East Village* 🕾 *212/979–1012* 🍽 *Reservations essential* 🟰 *AE, MC, V* 🕓 *Closed Sun. No lunch* Ⓜ *6 to Astor Pl.* ✛ *3:G6.*

$$$$ ✕ **Momofuku Ko.** A seasonal tasting menu full of clever combinations
ASIAN and esoteric ingredients explains the deafening buzz for James Beard Award–winning chef David Chang's latest venture. Ko's small, intimate space is sparsely furnished with a counter of blond wood and only a dozen stools. Diners get to see Ko's chefs in action as they prepare all manner of inventive dishes, including a signature preparation of frozen foie-gras torchon grated over lychee fruits and white wine gelee. Reservations can be made only online, no more than 7 days ahead for dinner and 14 days ahead for lunch, and are extremely difficult to get. Log on at 10 am (credit-card number needed just to get in the system), when new reservations are available, and keep hitting reload. ✉ *163 1st Ave., at E. 10th St., East Village* 🕾 *212/777–7773* ⊕ *www.momofuku. com* 🍽 *Reservations essential* 🟰 *AE, MC, V* 🕓 *No lunch Mon.–Thurs.* Ⓜ *L to 1st Ave.; 6 to Astor Pl.* ✛ *3:H5.*

$ ✕ **Momofuku Noodle Bar.** Chef-owner David Chang has created a shrine
ASIAN to ramen with this stylish 70-seat restaurant. His riff on the Japanese classic features *haute* ingredients like Berkshire pork, free-range chicken, and organic produce. His modern take on pork buns with cucumber and scallions is phenomenal—worth the trip alone. Go early or late—the tiny restaurant is packed during regular mealtimes. They also offer a daily prix-fixe menu for lunch ($30 for three courses) and dinner ($40 for four courses). New offerings: a phenomenal fried-chicken meal, featuring triple-fried Korean-style chicken and Old Bay southern-style, with a variety of accoutrements (available by special reservations only on their Web site momofuku.com). ✉ *171 1st Ave., between E. 10th and E. 11 Sts., East Village* 🕾 *212/777–7773* ⊕ *www. momofuku.com/noodle* 🍽 *Reservations not accepted* 🟰 *AE, MC, V* Ⓜ *L to 1st Ave.* ✛ *3:H5.*

$$ ✕ **Momofuku Ssäm Bar.** New York foodies have been salivating over chef
ASIAN David Chang's Asian-influenced fare since he opened his first restaurant, a Japanese noodle shop, in 2004. Momofuku Ssäm Bar, the wunderkind's follow-up, is packed nightly with downtown diners cut from the same cloth as the pierced and tattooed waitstaff and cooks. The no-reservation policy means you'll likely have to wait for a chance to perch at the communal food bar and nibble on Chang's truly original small-plate cuisine. Ssäm Bar is a casual, loud restaurant with an inventive menu that is constantly changing, though country hams and raw-bar items are staples. Chang's not-to-be-missed riff on a classic Chinese pork bun helped build his cult following. On their Web site, momofuku. com, you can special-order a festive Bo Ssäm dinner featuring a slow-roasted pork shoulder, oysters, kimchi, and a variety of sauces—all piled into crispy lettuce leaves. ✉ *207 2nd Ave., at 13th St., East Vil-*

18

lage ☎ *212/777–7773* ⊕ *www.momofuku.com/ssam* ⟨ *Reservations not accepted* ▤ *AE, MC, V* Ⓜ *L to 1st Ave.* ✢ *3:H4.*

$
PIZZA

✕ **Motorino.** The Manhattan branch of the Williamsburg original has brought impossibly high standards—and the long lines to match—to a new borough. This fresh-faced pizzeria serves authentic Neapolitan pies with lightly charred crusts made with glutinous, dough-friendly double-zero flour and San Marzano tomatoes. You can't go wrong with any of chef Matthew Palombino's signature traditional pizzas. Choose from classic marinara made with tomato and oregano; margherita with fresh tomatoes, mozzarella, and basil; or a pie with spicy sopressata sausage and garlic. There are also seasonal selections featuring Brussels sprouts and other vegetables. A value-packed lunchtime prix-fixe offers pizza and salad for $12/person, and antipasti like octopus and fingerling potato salad with celery-chili oil, and cockle-clam crostini round out the menu. ⊠ *349 E. 12th St., at 1st Ave., East Village* ☎ *212/777–2644* ⊕ *www.motorinopizza.com* ⟨ *No reservations* ▤ *AE, MC, V* Ⓜ *L to 1st Ave.* ✢ *3:H4.*

$$
AMERICAN
Fodor's Choice
★

✕ **Northern Spy Food Co.** This gem in the East Village is named for an apple variety, and is run by two San Francisco transplants who have brought with them a fresh perspective on the farm-to-table movement. Start with the freekeh risotto, a traditional dish made with a quirky little-known grain, or a giant mound of shredded kale interspersed with cheddar, pecorino, and toasted almonds. Main courses are winners, too—choose tender meatballs in marinara sauce, roast chicken for two, or baked polenta, eggs, and mushrooms topped with crème fraîche. There is also an interesting, reasonably priced list of wines and beers, and a selection of house-made desserts like chocolate cake with sea salt and caramel. ⊠ *511 E. 12th St., between First Ave. and Ave. A, East Village* ☎ *212/228–5100* ⊕ *www.northernspyfoodco.com* ⟨ *Reservations not accepted* ▤ *AE, D, MC, V.* Ⓜ *L to 1st Ave.* ✢ *3:H4.*

$$
NEW AMERICAN

✕ **Prune.** There's just something very right-on about the food at Prune, a cozy treasure of a restaurant serving eclectic, well-executed American food from cult chef Gabrielle Hamilton. The choices change with the season, but you might find braised rabbit legs in vinegar sauce, whole grilled fish with fennel oil and chunky sea salt, or roasted marrow bones with parsley salad and toast points. There's usually a wait, and the quarters are very cramped, so don't expect to feel comfortable lingering at your rickety wooden table. Desserts, like ricotta ice cream with salted-caramel croutons, are irresistible, and on weekends lines form early for the restaurant's deservedly popular brunch. ⊠ *54 E. 1st St., between 1st and 2nd Aves., East Village* ☎ *212/677–6221* ⊕ *www.prunerestaurant. com* ⟨ *Reservations essential* ▤ *AE, MC, V* Ⓜ *F to 2nd Ave.* ✢ *2:F2.*

¢
CAFÉ
ʘ

✕ **Veniero's Pasticceria.** More than a century old, this bustling bakery-café sells every kind of Italian *dolce* (sweet), from cherry-topped cookies to creamy cannoli and flaky *sfogliatelle* pastry. A wine license means you can top off an evening with a bottle of red. ⊠ *342 E. 11th St., near 1st Ave., East Village* ☎ *212/674–7070* ⊕ *www.venierospastry. com* ⟨ *Reservations not accepted* ▤ *AE, D, DC, MC, V* Ⓜ *6 to Astor Pl.; L to 1st Ave.* ✢ *3:H5.*

LOWER EAST SIDE

$$ ✕ **'inoteca.** The Italian terms on the menu may be a little daunting, but
ITALIAN the food is not. An Italian small-plates concept with an excellent by-the-
glass wine list, this rustic eatery is perpetually packed. (Reservations are
accepted for parties of six or more.) Come for cheese and charcuterie
plates, the famous truffled egg toast, and delicious panini sandwiches
filled with cured meat, runny cheeses, and hot peppers. Menu staples
include fresh salads and creative entrées like lentils, fennel, celery root,
capers, and saffron, and roast lamb cannelloni with white beans, spin-
ach, and pecorino with house-made sausage. ✉ *98 Rivington St., at
Ludlow St., Lower East Side* ☎ *212/614–0473* ⊕ *www.inotecanyc.com*
🖃 *AE, MC, V* Ⓜ *F, J, M, Z to Delancey St.* ✛ *2:G3.*

$ ✕ **Katz's Delicatessen.** Everything and nothing has changed at Katz's since
DELI it first opened in 1888, when the neighborhood was dominated by
Fodor'sChoice Jewish immigrants. The rows of Formica tables, the long self-service
★ counter, and such signs as "Send a salami to your boy in the army" are
all completely authentic. What's different are the area's demographics,
but all types still flock here for succulent hand-carved corned beef and
pastrami sandwiches, soul-warming soups, juicy hot dogs, and crisp
half-sour pickles. ✉ *205 E. Houston St., at Ludlow St., Lower East
Side* ☎ *212/254–2246* ⊕ *www.katzdeli.com* 🖃 *AE, MC, V* Ⓜ *F to 2nd
Ave.* ✛ *2:G2.*

$$$ ✕ **Rayuela.** The young and sexy frequent this vibrant Lower East Side
LATIN restaurant to sample Latin cuisine courtesy of Máximo Tejada, the chef
who built his reputation cooking at the popular (now closed) Lucy's
Latin Kitchen. This bi-level eatery and bar has a dining area, a ceviche
bar, and—growing in the center of the restaurant—an olive tree. The
menu features small plates with more than a dozen ceviches and tapas,
including the must-have lobster with Uruguayan caviar. If you'd like
a predinner drink, arrive early to grab a stool at the bar and enjoy a
standout cocktail, like the pisco made with sour lime juice and foamy
egg white. ✉ *165 Allen St., between Rivington and Stanton Sts., Lower
East Side* ☎ *212/253–8840* ⊕ *www.rayuelanyc.com* 🖃 *AE, D, DC, MC,
V* ⊘ *No lunch* Ⓜ *F to 2nd Ave.; J, M, Z to Essex and Delancey Sts.*
✛ *2:G3.*

$ ✕ **Schiller's Liquor Bar.** It's the kind of hip Lower East Side hangout where
BISTRO you'd be equally comfortable as a celebrity or a parent with a stroller.
⟳ The folks at Schiller's work hard to make it feel as if it's decades old.
Vintage mirrored panels, forever-in-style subway tiles, a tin ceiling,
and a checkered floor lend a Parisian feel. Cuban sandwiches and steak
frites reveal a steady hand in the kitchen. At lunch, dollar doughnuts
with sweet or savory fillings are standouts. At dinner a standard bistro
menu fills out the list. ✉ *131 Rivington St., at Norfolk St., Lower East
Side* ☎ *212/260–4555* ⊕ *www.schillersny.com* 🖃 *AE, MC, V* Ⓜ *F to
Delancey St.; J, M, Z to Essex St.* ✛ *2:G3.*

$ ✕ **Spitzer's Corner.** In warm weather this sprawling Lower East Side
AMERICAN gastropub throws open its windows and doors, and the party inside
seems to consume the whole block. After you see the crowd at the bar
tasting the 40 beers on tap, you'll likely be tempted to pop in for a pint.
Once inside, seated at one of the long wooden communal tables, you

18

may be inclined to stick around for dinner or snacks. The upscale pub grub includes a full raw-bar selection (briny just-shucked oysters) and bar snacks like extra-sinful popcorn cooked in pork fat and topped off with bacon. ⊠ *101 Rivington St., at Ludlow St., Lower East Side* ☎ *212/228–0027* ⊕ *www.spitzerscorner.com* ▭ *MC, V* Ⓜ *F to Delancey St.; J, M, Z to Essex St.* ✛ *2:G3.*

$$ ✕ **The Stanton Social.** A perennial neighborhood favorite, this is the place
ITALIAN to come for an expansive menu of tapas-style dining from talented chef Chris Santos, plus a perfectly calibrated cocktail menu. Come before 7 if you want to be able to hear your fellow diners speak, but the people-watching and shared dishes are good at any hour. Try the gooey, Gruyère-topped onion soup dumplings, juicy Kobe beef sliders, and wasabi-crusted salmon. Downstairs feels like a more traditional dining room, whereas the second level features a buzzy bar. The late-night lounge area, decorated with cherry-blossom wallpaper and red leather upholstery, turns into a quasi-nightclub the later it gets. The Stanton Social is also a great option for brunch—the spicy lobster Benedict is a must. ⊠ *99 Stanton St., between Ludlow and Orchard Sts., Lower East Side* ☎ *212/995–0099* ⊕ *www.thestantonsocial.com* ⌁ *Reservations essential* ▭ *AE, MC, V* ⊗ *No lunch* Ⓜ *F to 2nd Ave.* ✛ *2:G3.*

$$$ ✕ **wd~50.** Chef Wylie Dufresne—the mad genius and early progenitor
NEW AMERICAN of the molecular gastronomy trend—mixes colors, flavors, and textures with a masterful hand here. His staff encourages people to feel at ease trying things like duck breast with apple, cheddar, and kimchi couscous or Iberico pork neck with smoked spaetzle, peach, and marcona almonds. Desserts follow suit: licorice custard with sake sorbet and pears, anyone? ⊠ *50 Clinton St., between Rivington and Stanton Sts., Lower East Side* ☎ *212/477–2900* ⊕ *www.wd-50.com* ▭ *AE, D, DC, MC, V* ⊗ *No lunch Wed.–Sun.* Ⓜ *F to Delancey St.; J, M, Z to Essex St.* ✛ *2:H3.*

GREENWICH VILLAGE, WEST VILLAGE, AND CHELSEA (WITH MEATPACKING DISTRICT)

CHELSEA

$$$ ✕ **Buddakan.** Few—if any—restaurants in Manhattan can rival the
ASIAN 16,000-square-foot Buddakan in terms of sheer magnitude and buoyant theatricality. And in a neighborhood whose eateries often get by on sizzle alone, the food here has real substance as well. Restaurateur Steven Starr created a New York edition of his Philadelphia original. Here the upstairs bar is a great end-of-day meet-up spot for pert cocktails and appetizers, and the vast downstairs is like a dining hall in a medieval castle, complete with a communal table spanning the room. Co-executive chefs Yang Huang and Brian Ray prepare ethereal tuna spring rolls that are narrow flutes of ruby tuna tartare in a crisp contrapuntal fried shell, and edamame dumplings reveal a creamy, light green center. Crisp-tender sizzling short ribs are served with tender, wide noodles and highly comforting results, and there are dozens of other tempting dishes large and small. Considering the droves of patrons, service is surprisingly attentive. ⊠ *75 9th Ave., between 15th and 16th*

Sts., Chelsea ☎ *212/989–6699* ⊕ *www.buddakannyc.com* ⌕ *Reservations essential* ▭ *AE, D, MC, V* ⊗ *No lunch* Ⓜ *A, C, E to 14th St.; L to 8th Ave.* ✛ *3:B4.*

$$
⤬ Cookshop. One of far-west Chelsea's first hot restaurants, Cookshop

AMERICAN (from the same team as Five Points and Hundred Acres) manages a casual elegance while focusing on seasonal, farm-fresh cuisine. Specials and purveyors are scrawled on a large blackboard in the airy, well-lighted space. Outdoor seating is a noisy but great way to survey a cross section of gallery-hoppers and shoppers toting bags from nearby Chelsea Market. Cocktails here are divine, integrating herbs and unique spirits into drinks like the strawberry caipirinha, which infuses fresh berries with cachaca and thyme (snack on salty fried hominy while sipping). Line up early for brunch; it's worth the wait for dishes like baked eggs over duck and Swiss chard, or the fluffiest pancakes in town. Dinner is also a triumph, with a variety of perfectly prepared dishes like whitefish with lemony asparagus and hen-of-the-woods mushroom or a simply roasted chicken. ⊠ *156 10th Ave., at 20th St., Chelsea* ☎ *212/924–4440* ⊕ *www.cookshopny.com* ▭ *AE, D, DC, MC, V* Ⓜ *A, C, E to 23rd St.* ✛ *3:B3.*

$ **⤬ R.U.B. BBQ.** Among the American barbecue capitals, Kansas City's

BARBECUE smoked fare stands out as perhaps the most versatile, characterized by dry rubs with sauces strictly on the side. Executive chef Paul Kirk is from Kansas City and is a legend on the growing New York City barbecue competition circuit. This is not a restaurant for the timid of appetite. Platters are so bountiful that even the side dishes come in overwhelming quantities. The shameless menu promises everything from beef, pork, ham, pastrami, and turkey to chicken, sausage, and, of course, ribs. Burned ends—delicious charred-crisp, rich edges of beef brisket—are legendary, and they sell out every night. For dessert, don't miss the batter-fried Oreos. In fact, many items on the menu sell out by 8 pm, so it's wise to arrive fairly early. ⊠ *208 W. 23rd St., between 7th and 8th Aves., Chelsea* ☎ *212/524–4300* ⊕ *www.rubbbq.net* ⌕ *Reservations not accepted* ▭ *AE, D, MC, V* Ⓜ *1, C, E, F M to 23rd St.* ✛ *3:D2.*

$$ **⤬ Tía Pol.** This tiny, dark, out-of-the-way, but highly popular tapas bar

SPANISH is usually packed, but there are good reasons for that: it's one of the

Fodor's Choice best in town, with a welcoming vibe, a dozen reasonably priced Span-

★ ish wines by the glass, and charm to spare. The tables and stools are small (and high), but the flavors are enormous. One of the most original tapas has become a signature here: bittersweet chocolate smeared on a baguette disc and topped with salty Spanish chorizo. *Patatas bravas* (rough-cut potatoes deep-fried and served with a dollop of spicy aioli) are so addictive, you won't want to share them. The pork loin, piquillo pepper, and mild tetilla cheese sandwich is scrumptious, and so is the Galician octopus terrine. In fact, everything on the menu is transporting and delicious. ⊠ *205 10th Ave., between 22nd and 23rd Sts., Chelsea* ☎ *212/675–8805* ⊕ *www.tiapol.com* ⌕ *Reservations essential* ▭ *AE, MC, V* ⊗ *No lunch Mon.* Ⓜ *C, E to 23rd St.* ✛ *3:A2.*

18

FOOD COURT RENAISSANCE

Everywhere you turn, a new food court is opening. But these are not shopping-mall-style clusters of franchised eateries. Because we're talking New York, you can expect high-quality dining, a boon for hungry pavement-pounders looking for food, fast—not fast food.

At the **Plaza Food Hall** (⊠ *1 W. 59th St., at 5th Ave.* ☎ *212/986–9260* ✛ *4:E1*) in the basement of the Plaza Hotel, celeb chef Todd English oversees a series of mini-restaurants, each with its own counter with seating ideal for a quick snack or a full-fledged meal. Entry is a little confusing; though the place is made up of individual food concepts, you'll be seated by a hostess at any available counter. One you're settled, get up and survey your choices, then sit down and place one order from your waiter. There's a glistening raw bar, a burger joint, and a wood-burning pizza station where you can sample some of English's iconic pies, such as fig and prosciutto. It's one of the most varied and affordable daytime food options in an area of town that can still feel like a lunchtime wasteland.

The cavernous **Eataly** (⊠ *200 5th Ave., at 23rd St.* ☎ *646/398–5100* ✛ *3:E2*), from Mario Batali & Co., is a temple of all things Italian. Ignore the overpriced produce market by the front entrance and make a beeline for La Piazza for sandwiches made with meticulously sourced ingredients (you can eat them at the standup tables nearby); a full-service pizza and pasta restaurant; a raw bar and fish eatery; and a spot for quaffing wines by the glass and beers on tap. There's also a corridor that's a gourmand's dream, with Italian chocolates, coffees, gelati, and pastries.

Adjacent to the new Eventi hotel sits **FoodParc** (⊠ *851 6th Ave., at W. 30th St.* ☎ *646/600–7140* ✛ *3:D1*) a high-design assemblage of food stations perfect for the lunchtime rush and an unhurried, casual dinner. At the 3Bs counter you can craft a custom burger, pair it with addictive snacks like bacon- and cheddar-stuffed hash browns—then top it off with a shake, malted, or egg cream. RedFarm Stand serves dumplings (try the shrimp, bacon, and watercress version) and other fare with a menu devised by Chinatown Brasserie dim sum master Joe Ng, and Fornetti (the weakest link in the bunch) offers Italian standards like subs, sandwiches, and pastas. In a boon to outdoor seating, summertime brings a huge outdoor plaza with room to spread out and watch a giant Jumbotron TV hanging above.

GREENWICH VILLAGE

$$ ✕ **Arturo's.** Few guidebooks list this classic New York pizzeria, but the
PIZZA   jam-packed room and pleasantly smoky scent foreshadow a satisfying
☺   meal. There's a full menu of Italian classics, but don't be fooled: pizza is the main event. The thin-crust beauties are cooked in a coal oven, emerging sizzling with simple toppings like pepperoni, sausage, and eggplant. Monday to Thursday you can call ahead to reserve a table; weekends, be prepared to wait and salivate. ⊠ *106 W. Houston St., near Thompson St., Greenwich Village* ☎ *212/677–3820* ═ *AE, DC, MC,*

V ⊗ *No lunch* Ⓜ *1 to Houston St.; B, D, F, M to Broadway–Lafayette St.* ⊹ *2:D3.*

$$$
ITALIAN
✕ **Babbo.** After one bite of the ethereal homemade pasta or tender bar-becued squab with roast beet farrotto, you'll understand why it's so hard to get reservations at Mario Batali's casually elegant restaurant. The complex and satisfying menu hits numerous high points, such as "mint love letters," ravioli filled with pureed peas, ricotta, and fresh mint, finished with spicy lamb sausage ragout; and rabbit with Brussels sprouts, house-made pancetta, and carrot vinaigrette. Babbo is the per-fect spot for a raucous celebratory dinner with flowing wine and festive banter. But be forewarned: if anyone in your party is hard of hearing, or bothered by loud rock music, choose someplace more sedate. ✉ *110 Waverly Pl., between MacDougal St. and 6th Ave., Greenwich Vil-lage* ☎ *212/777–0303* ⊕ *www.babbonyc.com* ☝ *Reservations essential* ▭ *AE, MC, V* ⊗ *No lunch* Ⓜ *A, B, C, D, E, F, M to W. 4th St.* ⊹ *2:C1.*

$$$
NEW AMERICAN
✕ **Blue Hill.** This tasteful, sophisticated chocolate-brown den of a restau-rant—formerly a speakeasy—on a quiet, quaint side street maintains an impeccable reputation for excellence and consistency under the lead-ership of Dan Barber. The Obamas even stopped by here for dinner, shutting down the street for one of their "date nights." Part of the "slow food," sustainable agriculture movement, Blue Hill mostly uses ingredients grown or raised within 200 mi, including the Four Season Farm at Stone Barns Center for Food and Agriculture, Barber's second culinary project in nearby Westchester County. The chefs produce pre-cisely cooked and elegantly constructed food such as wild striped bass with potato-and-clam chowder and house-cured *guanciale* (pork jowl) and a smoked-tomato soup with tiny knobs of American caviar at the bottom. ✉ *75 Washington Pl., between Washington Sq. W and 6th Ave., Greenwich Village* ☎ *212/539–1776* ⊕ *www.bluehillfarm.com* ☝ *Reservations essential* ▭ *AE, D, DC, MC, V* ⊗ *No lunch* Ⓜ *A, B, C, D, E, F, M to W. 4th St.* ⊹ *2:C1.*

$$
BISTRO
✕ **Blue Ribbon Bakery.** When the owners renovated this space, they uncovered a 160-year-old wood-burning oven. They relined it with volcanic brick and let it dictate the destiny of their restaurant. The bak-ery/restaurant has an eclectic menu featuring substantial sandwiches on homemade bread (from the oven, of course), small plates, a legendary bread pudding, and entrées that span the globe, from hummus to grilled catfish with sautéed collards and sweet potatoes. The basement dining room is dark and intimate; upstairs is a Parisian-style café. ✉ *35 Down-ing St., at Bedford St., Greenwich Village* ☎ *212/337–0404* ⊕ *www.blueribbonrestaurants.com* ▭ *AE, D, DC, MC, V* Ⓜ *1 to Houston St.; A, B, C, D, E, F, M to W. 4th St.* ⊹ *2:C2.*

$$$
ITALIAN
✕ **Centro Vinoteca.** Though *Top Chef* contestant and Eleven Madison Park alum Leah Cohen has left the kitchen, this bi-level Italian spot decked out in gleaming white tiles and a wall of windows looking out onto 7th Avenue remains popular. A recently revamped menu focuses on Italian classics with flair, like a bitter green salad of local mutsu apples, endive, radicchio, frisee, walnuts, and Gorgonzola dressing, and a grilled pizzette with mozzarella, fennel sausage, and arugula. Several dishes use local supplier DiPalo's cheeses, including a ricotta cavatelli

18

with a red wine–braised short rib sauce. Main courses lean toward the substantial, like a grilled Angus rib eye with balsamic braised cipollini mushrooms. And in true Italian form, the kitchen stays open until midnight. ⊠ *74 7th Ave. S, at Barrow St., Greenwich Village* ☎ *212/367–7470* ⊕ *www.centrovinoteca.com* ☰ *AE, MC, V* Ⓜ *1 to Christopher St./ Sheridan Sq.; A, B, C, D, E, F, M to W. 4th St.–Washington Sq.* ✛ *2:B2.*

$$
AMERICAN
✕ **Five Points.** This cheerful restaurant is a refreshing oasis, with a rushing stream of water running through a hollowed-out log for the entire length of the dining room. Chef-owner Marc Meyer's menus are seasonal and market-driven. Expect plump chilled oysters, exemplary Caesar salad, and splendid house-made pasta, followed by the likes of pan-seared day-boat halibut with cucumber gazpacho and chopped tomato salsa; and grilled baby lamb chops with rosemary potatoes, mint-yogurt sauce, and black-olive-stuffed tomato. Weekend brunch is one of the very best in the city, and prices are quite friendly. New to the menu: lunch, meaning Five Points is open all day long. ⊠ *31 Great Jones St., between Lafayette St. and Bowery, Greenwich Village* ☎ *212/253–5700* ⊕ *www.fivepointsrestaurant.com* ⌂ *Reservations essential* ☰ *AE, MC, V* Ⓜ *6 to Bleecker St.; B, D, F, M to Broadway–Lafayette St.* ✛ *3:G6.*

$$$$
AMERICAN
✕ **Gotham Bar & Grill.** A culinary landmark, Gotham Bar & Grill is every bit as thrilling as it was when it opened in 1984. Celebrated chef Alfred Portale, who made the blueprint for "architectural food," that is, towers of stacked ingredients, builds on a foundation of simple, clean flavors. People come for Portale's transcendent preparations: no rack of lamb is tenderer, no seafood salad sweeter. A stellar 20,000-bottle cellar provides the perfect accompaniments—at a price. There's also a fantastic three-course $31 prix-fixe lunch from noon to 2:30 weekdays. ⊠ *12 E. 12th St., between 5th Ave. and University Pl., Greenwich Village* ☎ *212/620–4020* ⊕ *www.gothambarandgrill.com* ☰ *AE, D, DC, MC, V* ☾ *No lunch weekends* Ⓜ *L, N, Q, R, 4, 5, 6 to 14th St./Union Sq.* ✛ *3:E4*

¢
HOT DOG
✕ **Gray's Papaya.** It's a stand-up, takeout dive. And, yes, limos do sometimes stop here for the legendary hot dogs. More often than not, though, it's neighbors or commuters who know how good the slim, traditional, juicy all-beef dogs are. ⊠ *402 6th Ave., at W. 8th St., Greenwich Village* ☎ *212/260–3532* ⌂ *Reservations not accepted* ☰ *No credit cards* Ⓜ *A, B, C, D, E, F, V to W. 4th St.* ✛ *3:D5, 4:B5, 5:B4.*

$$
ITALIAN
✕ **Lupa.** Even the most hard-to-please connoisseurs have a soft spot for Lupa, Mario Batali and Joseph Bastianich's "downscale" Roman trattoria. Rough-hewn wood, great Italian wines, and simple preparations with top-quality ingredients define the restaurant. People come repeatedly for dishes such as ricotta gnocchi with sweet-sausage ragout, house-made salumi, and sardines with golden raisins and pine nuts. The front of the restaurant is seated on a first-come, first-served basis; reservations are taken for the back. ⊠ *170 Thompson St., between Bleecker and W. Houston Sts., Greenwich Village* ☎ *212/982–5089* ⊕ *www.luparestaurant.com* ☰ *AE, MC, V* Ⓜ *A, B, C, D, E, F, M to W. 4th St.* ✛ *2:D3.*

$$
SEAFOOD

✕ **Mary's Fish Camp.** The neighborhood's second New England fish house (the result of a split between Pearl Oyster Bar's partners) proves you can't have too much of a good thing. There's usually a wait here for the excellent fried oysters, chowders, and, of course, the sweet lobster roll with crisp fries. That lobster roll is a citywide favorite—get here early or it may be sold out. ✉ *64 Charles St., at W. 4th St., Greenwich Village* ☎ *646/486–2185* ⌂ *Reservations not accepted* ▭ *AE, MC, V* ⊙ *Closed Sun.* Ⓜ *1 to Christopher St./Sheridan Sq.* ✛ *2:B1.*

$$
SEAFOOD

✕ **Mermaid Oyster Bar.** If you're craving a great raw bar, lobster roll, or soft-shell crab sandwich (in season), this place gives nearby classics Mary's Fish Camp and Pearl Oyster Bar a run for their money. But Chef Lawrence Edelman (who also helms the city's two Mermaid Inn locations) goes beyond the comfort-food classic to offer an alluring menu of sophisticated dinner choice. Almost every dish is a winner here, but try the lobster bisque laced with Manzanilla sherry and toasted pumpkin seeds, blackened striped bass with roasted squash and Swiss chard, and a spicy seafood bucatini fra diavolo. From the bar, try something from the list of perfect-pitch cocktails, like a Dark and Stormy, made with black rum and ginger beer, or a Pimm's cooler with refreshing pieces of fresh cucumber. ✉ *79 MacDougal St., at W. Houston St., Greenwich Village NY* ☎ *212/260–0100* ⊕ *www.themermaidnyc.com* ▭ *AE, D, MC, V* ⊙ *No lunch* Ⓜ *1 to Houston St., A, C, E to Spring St.* ✛ *2:D2*

¢
MIDDLE EASTERN

✕ **Moustache.** There's typically a crowd waiting outside for one of the copper-top tables at this appealing Middle Eastern neighborhood restaurant. The focal point is the perfect pita that accompanies tasty salads like lemony chickpea and spinach, and hearty lentil and bulgur. Also delicious is *lahambajin,* spicy ground lamb on a crispy flat crust. For entrées, try the leg of lamb or merguez sausage sandwiches. Service is slow but friendly. ✉ *90 Bedford St., between Barrow and Grove Sts., Greenwich Village* ☎ *212/229–2220* ⌂ *Reservations not accepted* ▭ *No credit cards* Ⓜ *1 to Christopher St./Sheridan Sq.* ✛ *2:B2.*

$$$
ENGLISH

✕ **The Spotted Pig.** Part cozy English pub, part laid-back neighborhood hangout, part gastronome's lure, the Spotted Pig showcases the impeccable food of Londoner April Bloomfield (Mario Batali and partners consulted). Pair the tang of radishes in a salad with plenty of Parmesan and arugula, or smoked haddock–and-corn chowder with homemade crackers for studies in contrasts in texture and flavor. Shoestring potatoes accompany their Roquefort cheeseburger. Chase it with a glass of foam-dripping Old Speckled Hen. ✉ *314 W. 11th St, at Greenwich St., Greenwich Village* ☎ *212/620–0393* ⊕ *www.thespottedpig.com* ⌂ *Reservations not accepted* ▭ *AE, D, DC, MC, V* Ⓜ *A, C, E to 14th St.; L to 8th Ave.* ✛ *2:A1.*

$$$
AUSTRIAN

✕ **Wallsé.** Kurt Gutenbrunner's modern Austrian menu at this neighborhood restaurant with a quasi–Wiener Werkstätte look is soulful and satisfying, with a strong emphasis on Austrian tradition and urban New York attitude. It's hard to argue with such dishes as Wiener schnitzel with potato-cucumber salad and lingonberries or venison goulash with spaetzle and Brussels sprouts. Desserts do Vienna proud: apple-walnut strudel is served with apple sorbet. ✉ *344 W. 11th St., at Washington St., Greenwich Village* ☎ *212/352–2300* ⊕ *www.wallse.*

18

com ⛳ *Reservations essential* ▱ *AE, DC, MC, V* ☌ *No lunch week-days* ▣ *1 to Christopher St./Sheridan Sq.; A, C, E to 14th St.; L to 8th Ave.* ⊕ *3:B6.*

MEATPACKING DISTRICT

$$$$ ✕ **Del Posto.** Mario Batali's high-profile stab at four-star immortality
ITALIAN helped kick off the big-box restaurant boom in the Meatpacking District. Much more formal than his still hugely popular Babbo, the restaurant initially struck many as too grown-up for a big kid like Batali. The dining room—with its sweeping staircase, formal decor, and live tinkling from a baby grand—has the feel of an opulent hotel lobby. But Del Posto prevailed and is now regarded as one of the most consistently dazzling special-occasion spots in a neighborhood overrun with overpriced eateries—and recently earned the distinction of being the only New York Times four-star-rated Italian restaurant. A partnership with TV chef Lidia Bastianich, the restaurant offers pitch-perfect risotto made fresh to order for two people or more (and served in the oversize pan) and big shareable roast hunks of meat (veal chops), as well as ethereal pastas—all with old-world table-side service. For a little taste of the experience, come for a cocktail and sample the bargain bar menu. ✉ *85 10th Ave., between 15th and 16th Sts., Meatpacking District* ☏ *212/497–8090* ◈ *www.delposto.com* ▱ *AE, MC, V* ☌ *No lunch Tues.–Sat.* ▣ *A, C, E to 14th St.; L to 8th Ave.* ⊕ *3:A4.*

$$$ ✕ **Pastis.** A trendy spin-off of Balthazar in SoHo, Pastis looks like it was
BISTRO shipped in, tile by nicotine-stained tile, from Pigalle. At night, throngs of whippet-thin cell-phone-slinging boys and girls gather at the bar up front to sip martinis and be seen. French favorites are front and center, including toothsome steak frites with béarnaise, mussels steamed in Pernod, and tasty apple tartlet with phyllo crust. ✉ *9 9th Ave., at Little W. 12th St., Meatpacking District* ☏ *212/929–4844* ◈ *www.pastisny. com* ⛳ *Reservations essential* ▱ *AE, MC, V* ▣ *A, C, E to 14th St.; L to 8th Ave.* ⊕ *3:B4.*

$$$ ✕ **Scarpetta.** Chef Scott Conant left L'Impero and Alto to open Scarpetta,
ITALIAN a critical darling since day one, adjacent to the glitz of the Meatpacking District. Walk past the bar into the polished dining room, where orange belts loop around mirrors and a retractable roof ushers in natural light. For a rousing start, try the creamy, rich polenta and mushrooms before enjoying one of the house-made pastas, like the al dente tagliatelle laced with strands of tender lamb ragout or his signature capretto (baby goat). Save room for dessert: the Amadei chcocolate cake with burnt-caramel gelato brings à la mode to a whole new level. ✉ *355 W. 14th St., at 9th Ave., Meatpacking District* ☏ *212/691–0555* ◈ *www.scarpettanyc. com* ▱ *AE, D, DC, MC, V* ☌ *No lunch* ▣ *A, C, E to 14th St.; L to 8th Ave.* ⊕ *3:B4.*

$$$ ✕ **Spice Market.** This playground for New York's elite is set in a cav-
ASIAN ernous space amid embroidered curtains and artifacts from Burma, India, and Malaysia. Chef Jean-Georges Vongerichten's playful takes on Southeast Asian street food will keep you asking the waiters for information: what exactly was in that? Sometimes the playfulness works, sometimes it doesn't, but don't miss the steamed lobster with garlic, ginger, and dried chili, or the squid salad with papaya and cashews.

✉ *403 W. 13th St., at 9th Ave., Meatpacking District* ☎ *212/675–2322* ⊕ *www.jean-georges.com* ✍ *Reservations essential* ▱ *AE, D, DC, MC, V* Ⓜ *A, C, E to 14th St.; L to 8th Ave.* ✛ *3:B4.*

$$$ ✕ **The Standard Grill.** Hotelier Andre Balazs has created an instant scene
AMERICAN for celebs, fashion-industry insiders, and aspirational common folk,
all who cluster at this buzzy restaurant inside his new Standard Hotel.
In warm weather the spacious outdoor seating area is a great place to
watch the new High Line park and sample a strawberry Pimm's cup or
Penny Drop. The indoor bar is low-lighted and sexy, with a raw bar
and charcuterie station that works on overdrive to put out plates of
oysters and Italian cured meats for the two dining rooms—the more
casual one in front, with wainscoted walls and views of Washington
Street, and the larger room in the back, with a floor whimsically made
up of thousands of glittering copper pennies. Chef Dan Silverman's food
is comfort-luxe, with dishes like roast chicken for two in a cast-iron
skillet and delicious moist trout with a currant-and–pine nut relish.
For dessert, there's a nearly obscene chocolate mousse that comes with
four silicone spatulas in lieu of spoons. A late-night menu is offered
until 4 am. ✉ *848 Washington St., between Little W. 12th and 13th
Sts., Meatpacking District* ☎ *212/645–4100* ⊕ *www.thestandardgrill.
com* Ⓜ *A, C, E to 14th St./Broadway, L to 14th St./8th Ave.* ✛ *3:A4.*

WEST VILLAGE

$$ ✕ **August.** Rustic simplicity is the unifying theme at this bustling West
EUROPEAN Village eatery. A wood-burning oven in the dining room turns out
regional European dishes like tarte flambé; an Alsatian flat bread topped
with onion, bacon, and crème fraîche; and Sicilian orata, a meaty white
fish grilled whole and doused with citrus, olive oil, and fresh herbs.
Wood-planed floors and an arched cork ceiling envelop the busy 40-seat
dining room. For a quieter meal, ask for a table in the glass-enclosed
15-seat atrium in back. ✉ *359 Bleecker St., at Charles St., West Village* ☎ *212/929–8727* ⊕ *www.augustny.com* ✍ *Reservations essential*
▱ *AE, MC, V* Ⓜ *1 to Christopher St./Sheridan Sq.; A, B, C, D, E, F, M
to W. 4th St.* ✛ *3:C6.*

$$ ✕ **Barbuto.** In this structural, airy space you'll be facing either the kitchen
ITALIAN or the quiet street outside. The Italian bistro food depends deeply on
fresh seasonal ingredients, so the menu changes daily. Chef Jonathan
Waxman specializes in rustic preparations like house-made duck sau-
sage with creamy polenta, red-wine-braised short ribs, and pasta car-
bonara. Waxman's acclaimed roasted chicken is usually on the menu
in one form or another. ✉ *775 Washington St., between Jane and W.
12th Sts., West Village* ☎ *212/924–9700* ⊕ *www.barbutonyc.com*
▱ *AE, MC, V* Ⓜ *A, C, E, to 14th St.; L to 8th Ave.; 1 to Christopher
St./Sheridan Sq.* ✛ *3:B5.*

$$$ ✕ **Commerce.** This former speakeasy harks back to days gone by with
NEW AMERICAN its Diego Rivera–style murals, vintage sconces, and restored subway
tiles. The young crowd comes not only for the decor, but to taste Chef
Harold Moore's seasonal cuisine. Appetizers range from a red cabbage,
apple, and pecan salad to yuzu-marinated hamachi ceviche. The entrées
are just as vibrant: bright, sweet peas offset pristine halibut, and the
shareable roast chicken, presented table-side, is served with foie-gras

18

bread stuffing. Brunch shows the influence of Israeli-born chef Snir Eng-Sela, who stacks scrambled eggs and hummus atop a pillowy pita, and serves a mean shakshuka—baked eggs nestled in a pepper, onion, and tomato sauce. The smart, nimble waitstaff constantly replenishes your breadbasket with warm baguettes and brioche, and steers you toward the dainty pineapple cheesecake with cilantro sorbet for a sweet ending. For a quieter meal, choose one of the booths near the bar. ☒ *50 Commerce St., West Village* 🕾 *212/524–2301* ⊕ *www.commercerestaurant. com* ▭ *AE, MC, V* ⊘ *No lunch* Ⓜ *1 to Christopher St./Sheridan Sq.; A, B, C, D, E, F, M to W. 4th St.* ✢ *2:B2.*

$$ ✕ **dell'anima.** Lines snake out the door of this neighborhood favorite.
ITALIAN Check out the open kitchen, where the stylish crowd converges to watch chefs prepare authentic Italian dishes like simple arugula salad or a bowl of pasta alla carbonara with speck (smoked and cured pork), egg, and pecorino. The signature *pollo al diavolo* (spicy chicken) with broccoli rabe, garlic, and chili is seared with enough smoke and heat for all seasons. If you can't get a table, head to the 10-seat bar and try one of the restaurant's 400 wines or signature cocktails. Stop in for lunch daily, brunch on weekends, or Anfora, their wine bar next door, for an after-dinner drink. ☒ *38 8th Ave., at Jane St., West Village* 🕾 *212/366–6633* ⊕ *www.dellanima.com* ▭ *AE, MC, V* ⊘ *No lunch weekends* Ⓜ *A, C, E to 14th St.; L to 8th Ave.* ✢ *3:C5.*

$$ ✕ **Do Hwa.** If anyone in New York is responsible for making Korean
KOREAN food cool and user-friendly, it is the mother-daughter team behind this perennially popular restaurant and its East Village sister, Dok Suni's. Jenny Kwak and her mother, Myung Ja, serve home cooking in the form of *kalbi jim* (braised short ribs), *bibimbop* (a spicy, mix-it-yourself vegetable-and-rice dish), and other favorites that may not be as pungent as they are in Little Korea but are satisfying nevertheless. ☒ *55 Carmine St., between Bedford St. and 7th Ave., West Village* 🕾 *212/414–1224* ⊕ *www.dohwanyc.com* ▭ *AE, D, MC, V* ⊘ *No lunch weekends* Ⓜ *1 to Houston St.; A, B, C, D, E, F, M to W. 4th St.* ✢ *2:C2.*

$ ✕ **Fatty Crab.** This rustic Malaysian cantina showcases the exciting cui-
MALAYSIAN sine of chef Zak Pelaccio, who spent years cooking at famous French
Fodor'sChoice restaurants before escaping to Southeast Asia for a year, where he fell
★ in love with the flavors of the region. Start with the addictive pick-led watermelon and crispy pork salad, an improbable combination that's both refreshing and decadent. The can't-miss signature dish is chili crab—cracked Dungeness crab in a pool of rich, spicy chili sauce, served with bread for dipping. It's messy for sure, but worth rolling up your sleeves for. Friday and Saturday the kitchen is open until 2 am. ☒ *643 Hudson St., between Gansevoort and Horatio Sts., West Village* 🕾 *212/352–3590* ⊕ *www.fattycrab.com* ⚞ *Reservations not accepted* ▭ *AE, D, MC, V* Ⓜ *A, C, E to 14th St.; L to 8th Ave.* ✢ *3:C5.*

$ ✕ **'ino.** 'Ino's the kind of place you want in every neighborhood, but the
ITALIAN West Village is the lucky winner here. Every inch of space is economized in this cozy, brick-lined eatery, where the chefs turn out an astonishing variety of fresh bruschetta, tramezzini (soft-bread sandwiches), and panini—not to mention soups and salad—from a tiny, well-organized kitchen. Grab a newspaper from the ledge and sit at one of the bar seats

to sample a great selection of Italian wines by the glass. Everything's delicious, but the truffled egg toast, available for brunch or anytime with an oozing yolk and gooey fontina cheese, is the menu's star attraction. ⊠ *21 Bedford St., between Downing and W. Houston Sts., West Village* 🕿 *212/989–5769* ⊕ *www.inotecanyc.com* ⌕ *Reservations not accepted* ▬ *AE, MC, V* Ⓜ *A, B C, D, E, F, M to W. 4th St.; 1 to Varick St.* ⊹ *2:C2.*

$$
NEW AMERICAN

✕ **The Little Owl.** This tiny neighborhood joint, with seating for 28 people, is exceptionally eager to please. The menu is congruently small, which actually makes it easier to decide what you want. And what you want are the pork-veal-beef-pecorino-cheese meatball "sliders" or miniburgers. The unusually juicy pork loin chop, served with Parmesan butter beans and wild dandelion greens, is gigantic, and hugely satisfying. Raspberry-filled beignets, served with a ramekin of warm Nutella, are otherworldly. ⊠ *90 Bedford St., at Grove St., West Village* 🕿 *212/741–4695* ⊕ *www.thelittleowlnyc.com* ⌕ *Reservations essential* ▬ *AE, MC, V* Ⓜ *1 to Christopher St./Sheridan Sq.; A, B, C, D, E, F, M to W. 4th St.* ⊹ *3:D6.*

$
MEXICAN

✕ **Mexicana Mama.** This colorful—and very popular—space serves vividly flavored fare. The kitchen is serious enough to create four different salsas daily, including a rotating "special salsa" that incorporates an authentic Mexican chili. Several dishes come with your choice of salsa and filling. The tomato-habanero salsa is simply unforgettable; cream tames the habaneros, but only slightly. Three chili-roasted pork tacos are also filled with piquant Chihuahua cheese and black beans, and served over Mexican rice and avocado cubes. Quesadillas are made with fresh corn tortillas (for a change!), filled with that melted Chihuahua cheese and your choice of chicken, barbacoa beef, chicken mole, or a daily special vegetable filling. For dessert, look no further than the eggy flan in flavors like caramel or cinnamon. ⊠ *525 Hudson St., near Charles St., West Village* 🕿 *212/924–4119* ▬ *No credit cards* Ⓜ *1 to Christopher St./Sheridan Sq.; A, B, C, D, E, F, M to W. 4th St.* ⊘ *Closed Mon.* ⊹ *3:C6.*

$$$
NEW AMERICAN

✕ **Minetta Tavern.** By converting a moribund 80-year-old Italian restaurant into a cozy hot spot, restaurateur Keith McNally created another hit. Try early and often to score reservations and sample creations like buttery trout *meunière;* bone marrow on toast; expertly aged steaks; and the celebrated Black Label burger, a pile of meat lashed with clarified butter and topped with caramelized onions and—for the brave—an added layer of cheese. The bar room, with its original details intact, is great for people-watching. A table in the back, with its original mural depicting West Village life and wall-to-wall photos of famous and infamous customers from eras gone by, makes sweet-talking the reservationist worth your while. ⊠ *113 MacDougal St., between Bleecker and West 3rd Sts., West Village* 🕿 *212/475–3850* ⊕ *www.minettatavernny.com* ⌕ *Reservations essential* ▬ *AE, D, DC, MC, V* Ⓜ *A, B, C, D, E, F, M to W. 4th St.* ⊹ *2:C2.*

$$$
NEW AMERICAN

✕ **Perry St.** Pay no mind to the cars whizzing by on the nearby West Side Highway; inside, the clean lines of this austere dining room with its gauze-swaddled wraparound windows and straight-back cream

18

banquettes get you to focus on the main event on your plate. Owner Jean-Georges Vongerichten's son Cedric is manning the stoves, turning out memorable dishes like black-pepper crab dumplings plated with snow peas. Fried chicken is served with mushroom spaetzle and ginger vinaigrette, and a retro char-grilled cheeseburger is lavished with Russian dressing and crispy onions. Vongerichten's restaurants can be pricey, but give the man credit for offering value-oriented prix-fixe specials at lunch and dinner: $26 and $38, respectively. ✉ *176 Perry St., at West St., West Village* ☎ *212/352–1900* ⊕ *www.jean-georges.com* ▭ *AE, D, MC, V* Ⓜ *1 to Christopher St./Sheridan Sq.* ✛ *2:A2.*

UNION SQUARE TO MURRAY HILL (WITH THE FLATIRON DISTRICT AND GRAMERCY)

FLATIRON DISTRICT

$$$
ITALIAN
Fodor's Choice
★

✕ **A Voce.** Executive chef Missy Robbins has a passion for Italian cuisine, and it shows. The American-born Robbins honed her Italian chops in northern Italy at the highly acclaimed Agli Amici restaurant in Friuli. For five years before joining A Voce, she was the executive chef at Chicago's Spiaggia. Her menu is inspired and represents regional dishes from all over Italy. The pasta is prepared fresh every day, and Robbins's fish and meat dishes are exceptional. The *agnello in due modi* entrée is especially well prepared, with tender lamb chops and a flavorful vegetable soffritto. For dessert, try the Tuscan bomboloni doughnuts with dark-chocolate dipping sauce. The attentive staff also help to make the dining experience here a real pleasure. A Voce's atmosphere is warm, and the 90-seat dining room has a retro Italian feel to it—walnut floors, pale green leather-top tables, and Eames chairs. There's additional seating on the patio when weather permits. ✉ *41 Madison Ave., between 25th and 26th Sts., Flatiron District* ☎ *212/545–8555* ⊕ *www.avocerestaurant.com* ▭ *AE, MC, V* Ⓜ *N, R to 23rd St.* ✛ *3:F2.*

$$
AMERICAN
Fodor's Choice
★

✕ **ABC Kitchen.** Jean Georges Vongerichten's latest New York City restaurant is a winning love letter to greenmarket cuisine. Attached to posh housewares emporium ABC Carpet and Home, this eatery makes for a great shopping break and much, much more. In the front bar area, snack on shards of Martin's pretzels from the nearby Union Square Greenmarket and enjoy herb-infused cocktails like the Green Kitchen, made with tarragon syrup and grapefruit juice, on corrugated-cardboard coasters. In the dining room many of the items, from the bread plates to the servers' checked shirts, are vintage or secondhand finds. Underneath the exposed concrete beams a chic crowd devours fresh, flavorful appetizers like the roasted carrot salad with avocado, crème fraiche, and toasted pumpkin seeds or candy-sweet baby Maine shrimp with a sprinkling of sea salt and horseradish. There are pizzas with whole-wheat crust (try the clam or trumpet mushroom versions) and substantial entrées like a well-charred steak served with a lusty red wine–and-carrot puree or a pristine fillet of arctic char served with fractal-looking Romanesco cauliflower. The restaurant is committed to all the right causes—environmentalism, sustainability, supporting local farmers—all of which are announced in a near manifesto-length list on the back of the menu. Thankfully, ABC Kitchen pulls it off without seeming patronizing or preachy. ✉ *35 E. 18th St., between Broadway and Park Ave. S, Flatiron District* ☎ *212/475–5829* ⊕ *www.abckitchennyc.com* ✍ *Reservations essential* ☐ *AE, D, DC, MC, V* Ⓜ *N, R, Q, 4, 5, 6 to 14th St./Union Square* ✛ *3:F3*

$$$
MEDITERRANEAN
Fodor's Choice
★

✕ **Aldea.** Bouley alumnus George Mendes has opened a restaurant that uses his Portuguese heritage as inspiration and takes it to new heights. Although there are no bad seats in the sleekly appointed bi-level space decorated with touches of wood, glass, and blue accents, watching Mendes work in his spotless tiled kitchen from one of the seats at the chef's counter in the back is undeniably exciting. *Petiscos* (small bites) like cubes of crisp pork belly with apple cider and caramelized endive and an earthy pork-and-duck terrine with sweet muscat gelee reveal sophisticated cooking techniques and flavors presented in highly addictive packages. A delicate matsutake mushroom broth floated with a slow-poached egg is edged with a subtle brace of pine. On the $85 five-course chef's tasting menu, the sea urchin on a crispy toast flat is a standout, as is the duck confit with chorizo and shatteringly crunchy duck-skin cracklings. ✉ *31 W. 17th St., between 5th and 6th Aves., Flatiron District* ☎ *212/675–7223* ⊕ *www.aldearestaurant.com* ✍ *Reservations essential* ☐ *AE, MC, V* ⊗ *Closed Sun. No lunch Sat.* Ⓜ *N, R, Q, 4, 5, 6 to 14th St./Union Square; F, M to 14th St. and 6th Ave.* ✛ *3:3E.*

$$$
SEAFOOD

✕ **BLT Fish.** Two stories above the less formal Fish Shack, BLT Fish is an elegantly appointed dining room in a Flatiron town house set under a spectacular skylight. Roasted Alaskan black cod is simply marinated overnight, then roasted. The piping-hot result is among the best seafood dishes in town. Other options include grilled Mediterranean branzino and seared Tasmanian sea trout. Whole fish is sold by the pound, with most fish averaging 1–3 pounds each. At about $32 per pound, that can really add up. ✉ *21 W. 17th St., between 5th and 6th Aves., Flatiron District* ☎ *212/691–8888* ⊕ *www.bltfish.com* ✍ *Reservations essential* ☐ *AE, D, DC, MC, V* ⊗ *Closed Sun. No lunch* Ⓜ *4, 5, 6, L, N, Q, R to Union Sq./14th St.; F, M, L to 6th Ave./14th St.* ✛ *3:E3.*

$$
SPANISH

✕ **Boqueria.** This warm, buzzy restaurant features comfortable wheat-color leather banquettes and, if you want to make friends, a communal table running down the center of the dining room. Fried quail eggs and chorizo on roasted bread are even better than they sound. Salt cod, suckling pig, and mushroom croquettes are perched on dabs of flavored aioli. Traditional churros come with a thick hot chocolate for dipping. ✉ *53 W. 19th St., between 5th and 6th Aves., Flatiron District* ☎ *212/255–4160* ⊕ *www.boquerianyc.com* ✍ *Reservations not accepted* ☐ *AE, D, MC, V* Ⓜ *6, F, R, M, W to 23rd St.* ✛ *3:E3.*

$
CAFÉ
☺

✕ **City Bakery.** This self-service bakery-restaurant has the urban aesthetic to match its name. Chef-owner Maury Rubin's baked goods—giant cookies, addictively flaky, salty-sweet pretzel croissants, elegant caramel tarts—are unfailingly rich. A major draw is the salad bar. It may seem

18

overpriced, but the large selection of impeccably fresh food, including whole sides of baked salmon, roasted vegetables, soups, and several Asian-accented dishes, delivers bang for the buck. Much of the produce comes from the nearby farmers' market. In winter the bakery hosts a hot-chocolate festival; in summer it's lemonade time. Weekend brunch includes limited table-side service, and a happy-hour menu features craft beers, local wines, and a menu with items capped at $10. ⊠ *3 W. 18th St., between 5th and 6th Aves., Flatiron District* ☏ *212/366–1414* ⊕ *www.thecitybakery.com* ⌲ *Reservations not accepted* ⊟ *AE, MC, V* ⊗ *No dinner* Ⓜ *L, N, Q, R, 4, 5, 6 to 14th St./Union Sq.; F, M to 14th St.* ✛ *3:E3.*

$$
NEW AMERICAN

✕ **Craftbar.** The casual sibling to Tom Colicchio's Craft is a spacious and inviting bargain. The menu features assertive seasonal cooking similar to what you can find at the upscale flagship just around the corner. The small-plates category on the menu elevates tiny nibbles like sausage-stuffed fried sage leaves or addictive fluffy salt-cod croquettes to temptations that make you forget the main course entirely. The rest of the menu is eclectic enough to satisfy. ⊠ *900 Broadway, between 19th and 20th Sts., Flatiron District* ☏ *212/461–4300* ⊕ *www.craftbarnyc.com* ⌲ *Reservations essential* ⊟ *AE, D, DC, MC, V* Ⓜ *L, N, Q, R, 4, 5, 6 to 14th St./Union Sq.* ✛ *3:F3.*

$$
MEXICAN
ℭ

✕ **Dos Caminos.** Stephen Hanson, the visionary behind a dozen New York restaurants, has created a hit with the Dos Caminos brand. Start with guacamole, served in a granite mortar called a *molcajete,* and peruse the selection of 150 tequilas. Beef tacos studded with chilies and slow-roasted pork ribs in chipotle barbecue sauce are solid choices. On weekend nights at all three locations, the noise level can get out of control. ⊠ *373 Park Ave. S, between E. 26th and E. 27th Sts., Flatiron District* ☏ *212/294–1000* ⊕ *www.brguestrestaurants.com* ⌲ *Reservations essential* ⊟ *AE, DC, MC, V* Ⓜ *6 to 28th St.* ✛ *3:F2.*

¢
CAFÉ

✕ **Eisenberg's Sandwich Shop.** Since 1929 this narrow coffee shop with its timeworn counter and cramped tables has provided the city with some of the best tuna-, chicken-, and egg-salad sandwiches. On chilly days Eisenberg's classic matzo-ball soup also really hits the spot. The lively and friendly staff use the cryptic language of soda jerks, in which "whiskey down" means rye toast and "Adam and Eve on a raft" means two eggs on toast. Considering the mayhem in the place, it's a pleasant surprise that you always get your meal, quickly and precisely as ordered. ⊠ *174 5th Ave., between E. 22nd and E. 23rd Sts., Flatiron District* ☏ *212/675–5096* ⊕ *www.eisenbergsnyc.com* ⌲ *Reservations not accepted* ⊟ *AE, D, MC, V* ⊗ *No dinner* Ⓜ *R, 6 to 23rd St.* ✛ *3:E2.*

$$$$
NEW AMERICAN
Fodor's Choice
★

✕ **Eleven Madison Park.** Luxury, precision, and creativity are the driving forces at this internationally renowned restaurant overlooking Madison Park. Swiss-born chef Daniel Humm oversees the kitchen, concocting unexpected dishes that change often but may include sea urchin capuccino, duck with lavender honey, and prawn roulade with apple, avocado, and lime, In a new tasting menu-only format, dishes are listed only by their principal ingredients, giving Humm and Co. maximum latitude to work their magic on the plate. Reservations should be made two months in advance. ⊠ *11 Madison Ave., at 24th St., Flatiron*

District ☎ *212/889–0905* ⊕ *www.elevenmadisonpark.com* ⌒ *Reservations essential* ▭ *AE, D, DC, MC, V* ☽ *Closed Sun. No lunch Sat.* Ⓜ *N, R, 6 to 23rd St.* ✛ *3:E2.*

$$$$ ✕ **Gramercy Tavern.** Danny Meyer's intensely popular restaurant tops
AMERICAN many a New Yorker's favorite restaurant list, and chef Michael Anthony
has settled in comfortably in the kitchen of one of New York's classic
settings. In front, the first-come, first-served tavern presents a lighter
menu—including a value-packed three-course prix-fixe—along with
great craft beers and cocktails scrawled on a board at the bar. The
more formal dining room has a prix-fixe American menu; three courses
at dinner is $88. Choose from seasonal dishes such as marinated sea
scallops with pickled peppers and fresh grapes, and rack of lamb with
sunchokes, hazelnuts, and exotic mushrooms. Meyer's restaurants—
he owns several well-regarded eateries in the city—are renowned for
their food and hospitality, and Gramercy Tavern sets the standard.
✉ *42 E. 20th St., between Broadway and Park Ave. S, Flatiron District*
☎ *212/477–0777* ⊕ *www.gramercytavern.com* ⌒ *Reservations essential*
▭ *AE, D, DC, MC, V* Ⓜ *6, R to 23rd St.* ✛ *3:F3.*

$$ ✕ **Hill Country.** This enormous barbecue joint is perfect for big groups
BARBECUE and carnivorous appetites. The menu was devised by 'cue queen Eliza-
beth Karmel, and the current pit master has a championship knack
for real Texas barbecue. The beef-centric menu features meaty ribs
and exceptionally succulent slow-smoked brisket (check your diet at
the door and go for the moist, fatty option). Plump pork sausages, in
regular and jalapeño cheese versions, are flown in directly from Kreuz
Market in Lockhart, Texas. The market-style setup can mean long lines
for meat, sold by the pound, or ribs at cutter-manned stations. Bring
your tray downstairs for a fine bourbon selection and nightly live music.
✉ *30 W. 26th St., between Broadway and 6th Ave., Flatiron District*
☎ *212/255–4544* ⊕ *www.hillcountryny.com* ▭ *AE, MC, V* Ⓜ *N, R to
28th St.; 6 to 28th St.; F, M to 23rd St.* ✛ *3:E2.*

$$ ✕ **Ilili.** Famed Washington, D.C., restaurateur and chef Philippe Mas-
MIDDLE EASTERN soud brings his culinary talents to New York City with this bi-level,
400-seat eatery that showcases cuisine from his native Lebanon. The
menu includes standard Middle Eastern fare, but also unexpected dishes
like bone marrow with sour-cherry tabbouleh and black cod with fragrant rice and tahini. Waiters never fail to refresh the basket of hot,
fluffy, house-baked pita bread. A glass of Lebanese or French wine is a
nice accompaniment to the cuisine. Late-night entertainment includes
belly dancing. ✉ *236 5th Ave., between 27th and 28th Sts., Flatiron
District* ☎ *212/683–2929* ⊕ *www.ililinyc.com* ▭ *AE, D, DC, MC, V*
☽ *No lunch weekends* Ⓜ *N, R to 28th St.* ✛ *3:E2.*

$$$$ ✕ **Primehouse New York.** This sleek steak house comes from the reliable
STEAKHOUSE group that operates Dos Caminos and several other perpetually mobbed
New York restaurants. Here you'll find classic presentations like Caesar
salad and steak tartare prepared table-side, and respectable dry-aged
prime cuts, ranging from hanger steak ($21) to porterhouse for two
($96). For something lighter, try skate sautéed in lemon–brown-butter
sauce, or the Berkshire pork chop with fig glaze and apple compote.
The mod space has a cream-and-black motif that recalls the Jetsons'

18

futuristic 1960s feel, interspersed with geometric M. C. Escher–like patterns. ⊠ *381 Park Ave. S, at 27th St., Flatiron District* ☎ *212/824–2600* ⊕ *www.brguestrestaurants.com/restaurants/primehouse_new_york* ☐ *AE, MC, V* Ⓜ *6, R to 28th St.* ✛ *3:F2.*

$$
ITALIAN

✕ **SD26.** The charming father-daughter restaurant team of Tony and Marisa May closed uptown's San Domenico to open this more casual, yet still impressive, Italian spot. The cavernous main dining room, decorated with a constellation of pinpoint lights and ringed with more intimate tables and banquettes, speaks to a fresher, more modern approach than its predecessor. The food—pappardelle with wild boar ragu, smoked lobster with porcini mushrooms and orange segments—is a refreshing mix of classic and forward-thinking. Expect a personal greeting from either father or daughter before your meal comes to an end. ⊠ *19 E. 26th St., between 5th and Madison Aves., Flatiron District* ☎ *212/265–5959* ⊕ *www.sd26ny.com* ⌧ *Reservations essential* ☐ *AE, DC, MC, V* Ⓜ *R to 23rd St. and 5th Ave.* ✛ *3:2E.*

¢
BURGER
Fodor'sChoice
★

✕ **Shake Shack.** Though the newer, uptown location of Danny Meyer's patties 'n shakes joint is bigger by far, this is where it all began. Here in Madison Square Park there's no indoor seating—just snaking outdoor lines. ■TIP➔ Check the "Shack Cam" from their Web site to gauge your wait. If it's raining, you may be in luck—inclement weather can mean shorter lines. Fresh steer burgers are ground daily, and a single will run you from $3.75 to $4.75, depending on what you want on it. For a burger on-the-go, they're decidedly tasty. For a few more bucks you can also order doubles and stacks or a vegetarian 'Shroom Burger—a super-rich melty Muenster and cheddar cheese–stuffed, fried portobello, topped with lettuce, tomato, and Shack sauce. The Shake Shack also offers beef and bird (chicken) hot dogs, french fries, and a variety of delicious frozen custard desserts, and—of course—shakes! ⊠ *Madison Square Park near Madison Ave. and E. 23rd St., Flatiron District* ☎ *212/889–6600* ⊕ *www.shakeshack.com* ☐ *AE, D, MC, V* Ⓜ *N, R, 6 to 23rd St.* ✛ *3:F2.*

$$$
INDIAN

✕ **Tamarind.** Many consider Tamarind Manhattan's best Indian restaurant. Forsaking the usual brass, beads, sitar, and darkness, you'll find a lustrous skylighted dining room awash in soothing neutral colors and awaft with tantalizing fragrances. Your welcoming hosts, owner Avtar Walia and his nephew, general manager Gary, practically reinvent charm. The busy kitchen offers multiregional dishes, some familiar (tandoori chicken, a searing lamb vindaloo), some unique (succulent venison chops in a vigorously spiced cranberry sauce, she-crab soup with saffron, nutmeg, and ginger juice). The more intriguing a dish sounds, the better it turns out to be. ⊠ *41–43 E. 22nd St., between Broadway and Park Ave. S, Flatiron District* ☎ *212/674–7400* ⊕ *www. tamarinde22.com* ⌧ *Reservations essential* ☐ *AE, DC, MC, V* Ⓜ *N, R, 6 to 23rd St.* ✛ *3:F2.*

$$
BARBECUE

✕ **Wildwood Barbecue.** Prolific restaurateur Steve Hanson's latest venture has been smokin' since day one, appeasing rabid barbecue aficionados. Pit master (and former Queens cop) "Big Lou" Elrose deserves credit for excellent ribs: succulent lamb and saucy baby back. Dine at the bar or at adjacent high tables, where the animated scene is fueled by whiskey and potent mint juleps. Families should settle in the dining room for fiery fried jalapeño slices called "bottle caps," shareable platters of apricot-glazed chicken and pulled pork, and towering carrot and chocolate layer cakes. A crafty combination of reclaimed wood, distressed garage doors, recycled paper, blackboards, and bell jars has made a trendy Manhattan block feel kitschy and comfortable. ⊠ *225 Park Ave. S., at 18th St., Flatiron District* ☏ *212/533–2500* ⊕ *www. brguestrestaurants.com/restaurants/wildwood_bbq* ⊟ *AE, D, DC, MC, V* Ⓜ *4, 5, 6, L, N, Q, R to 14th St./Union Sq.* ✚ *3:F3.*

GRAMERCY PARK

$$$$ ✕ **BLT Prime.** A masculine, vivacious space is the showcase for bold, appealing Franco-American cuisine. Menu specials are scrawled on a blackboard. Everything is served à la carte, and prices are high, but so is the quality of every dish. Former restaurant namesake Laurent Tourondel's signature steaming-hot Gruyère popovers remain on the menu. They're light and buttery with an addictive texture. Although there are poultry, veal, and lamb dishes, from lemon-rosemary chicken to a lamb T-bone, steaks are the main event. The dry-aged USDA prime steaks—pulled from a 30-foot-wide dry-aging room—are broiled at 1,700 degrees, spread lightly with herb butter and offered with a choice of sauce (the béarnaise is perfection). ⊠ *111 E. 22nd St., between Lexington and Park Aves., Gramercy Park* ☏ *212/995–8500* ⊕ *www. bltprime.com* ⚑ *Reservations essential* ⊟ *AE, DC, MC, V* ☾ *No lunch* Ⓜ *6, R to 23rd St.* ✚ *3:F3.*

STEAKHOUSE

$$ ✕ **Blue Smoke.** Ever the pioneer, Danny Meyer led the way for barbecue in Manhattan with a United Nations–like approach representing regional 'cue styles. The menu features Texas salt-and-pepper beef ribs, saucy Kansas City–style ribs, and tangy North Carolina pulled pork on brioche buns. If mac 'n cheese is a weakness, many insist there's none better than Blue Smoke's. Or for something lighter, start with deviled eggs and a blue cheese–topped iceberg wedge. After dinner, waddle downstairs to Jazz Standard, one of the best jazz clubs in New York. ⊠ *116 E. 27th St., between Lexington and Park Aves., Gramercy Park* ☏ *212/447–7733* ⊕ *www.bluesmoke.com* ⊟ *AE, D, DC, MC, V* Ⓜ *6, R to 28th St.* ✚ *3:F2.*

BARBECUE

18

$$ ✕ **Casa Mono.** Andy Nusser put in his time cooking Italian under Mario Batali at Babbo before an obsession with Spain landed him his own acclaimed Iberian niche. The perennially cramped and crowded Casa Mono sends its overflow to Bar Jamón, the annex wine-and-ham bar next door. Pick at plates of *jamon serrano* while awaiting the call for a prime seat at the counter overlooking the chef's open kitchen. Though everything is delectably shareable, of particular note are all things seared *à la plancha*, including blistered peppers and garlic-kissed mushrooms. Like his renowned mentor, Nusser has a weakness for the most neglected cuts of meat. Check your food fears at the door and order up the blood sausage, cockscombs, and tripe. ⊠ *52 Irving Pl., at E. 17th St., Gramercy Park* ☏ *212/253–2773* ⊕ *www.casamononyc.com* ⊟ *AE, DC, MC, V* Ⓜ *4, 5, 6, L, N, Q, R to Union Sq.* ✚ *3:G3.*

SPANISH

MURRAY HILL

$$
BRASSERIE

✕ **Artisanal.** This spacious brasserie is a shrine to cheese, the passion of chef-owner Terrance Brennan. Though service can be spotty, gastronomes and business lunchers still flock here for the more than 150 cheeses—available for on-site sampling or retail sale—then stay to enjoy their selections with one of 160 wines by the glass. Hot *fromage*-imbued fare also is satisfying, with preparations like addictive gougère cheese puffs, onion soup gratiné, and several types of fondue. For curd-adverse customers, steak frites or selections from the raw bar should satisfy. ⊠ *2 Park Ave., at E. 32nd St., Murray Hill* ☎ *212/725–8585* ⊕ *www.artisanalbistro.com* ⌁ *Reservations essential* ⊟ *AE, D, DC, MC, V* Ⓜ *6 to 33rd St.* ✛ *3:F1.*

$
KOREAN

✕ **Gahm Mi Oak.** The deconstructed industrial design, inexpensive 24-hour menu, and late-night hours attract a young and stylish crowd here. Every item on the limited menu goes well with *soju*, a Korean spirit, or beer. There are even photos on the menu to help bleary-eyed revelers order. Korean-style fried mung-bean pancakes with scallions, onions, carrots, and ground pork make for addictive stomach-lining fare. The kimchi is renowned, as is the *sul long tang*, a milky ox-bone soup with thin slices of beef, rice, and noodles that is reputed to be an effective hangover cure. ⊠ *43 W. 32nd St., between 5th Ave. and Broadway, Murray Hill* ☎ *212/695–4113* ⌁ *Reservations not accepted* ⊟ *AE, D, DC, MC, V* Ⓜ *B, D, F, N, Q, R, M to 34th St./Herald Sq.* ✛ *3:E1.*

$$
BRASSERIE
☺

✕ **Les Halles.** This local hangout, owned by Philippe Lajaunie since 1990 and benefiting from the celebrity of former executive chef and writer Anthony Bourdain, is boisterous and unpretentious—just like a true French brasserie. A good bet is steak frites—with fries regarded by some as the best in New York. Other prime choices include crispy duck-leg confit with frisée salad, blood sausage with caramelized apples, and steak tartare, prepared table-side. Another Les Halles is in Lower Manhattan at 15 John St. ⊠ *411 Park Ave. S, between E. 28th and E. 29th Sts., Murray Hill* ☎ *212/679–4111* ⊕ *www.leshalles.net* ⌁ *Reservations essential* ⊟ *AE, DC, MC, V* Ⓜ *6 to 28th St.* ✛ *3:F1.*

$
TURKISH

✕ **Turkish Kitchen.** This striking multilevel room with crimson walls, chairs with red-skirted slipcovers, and colorful kilims is Manhattan's busiest and best Turkish restaurant. For appetizers, choose from the likes of velvety char-grilled eggplant or tender octopus salad, creamy hummus, or poached beef dumplings. The luscious stuffed cabbage is downright irresistible. The restaurant also hosts one of the most alluring Sunday brunch buffets in town, featuring 90 items, Turkish and American—all house-made, including a dozen breads. ⊠ *386 3rd Ave., between E. 27th and E. 28th Sts., Murray Hill* ☎ *212/679–6633* ⊕ *www.turkishkitchen.com* ⊟ *AE, D, DC, MC, V* ☉ *No lunch Sat.* Ⓜ *6 to 28th St.* ✛ *3:G2.*

UNION SQUARE

$$$
NEW AMERICAN

✕ **Craft.** Dining here is like a luscious choose-your-own-adventure game. Every delectable dish comes à la carte, including sides for your roasted guinea hen or braised monkfish. Craft is *Top Chef* head judge Tom Colicchio's flagship in a mini-empire of excellent restaurants around the country, including the upscale Craftbar and Craftsteak brands, as well as grab-and-go sandwich bars called 'wichcraft. Just about everything here is exceptionally prepared with little fuss, from simple yet intriguing starters (grilled French sardines) and sides (the justly famous variety of roasted mushrooms, including oysters, trumpets, chanterelles, and hen-of-the-woods) to desserts (warm chocolate tart with buttermilk ice cream, cinnamon custard, and cashews). The serene dining room features burnished dark wood, custom tables, a curved leather wall, and a succession of dangling radiant bulbs. ☒ *43 E. 19th St., between Broadway and Park Ave. S, Union Square* ☎ *212/780–0880* ⊕ *www. craftrestaurant.com* ☞ *Reservations essential* ▤ *AE, D, DC, MC, V* ☉ *No lunch* Ⓜ *L, N, Q, R, 4, 5, 6 to 14th St./Union Sq.* ✚ *3:F3.*

¢ ✕**Republic.** When Republic first opened, it was one of very few places
ASIAN to get an Asian-style noodle bowl with a stylish edge. Many have followed in its footsteps—and some are better—but for window shoppers, greenmarketers, and anyone else in the Union Square area, this place gets the job done. The look is like a cross between a downtown art gallery and a Japanese school cafeteria, and the young waitstaff dressed in black T-shirts and jeans hold remote-control ordering devices to accelerate the already speedy service. Sit at the long, bluestone bar or at the picnic-style tables and order appetizers such as smoky grilled eggplant and luscious fried wontons. Entrées are all based on noodles or rice. Spicy coconut chicken soup and Vietnamese-style barbecued pork are particularly delicious. ☒ *37 Union Sq. W, between E. 16th and E. 17th Sts., Union Square* ☎ *212/627–7172* ⊕ *www.thinknoodles.com* ☞ *Reservations not accepted* ▤ *AE, DC, MC, V* Ⓜ *L, N, Q, R, 4, 5, 6 to 14th St./Union Sq.* ✚ *3:F4.*

$$$ ✕**Tocqueville.** Hidden just steps from busy Union Square, Tocqueville is
NEW AMERICAN a refined dining oasis that's a secret even to many New York foodies. Guests enter through an austere reception area that gives no indication of the luxury appointments inside. Past heavy curtains and a six-seat bar, the dining area is an intimate, modern room lined with warm gold-and sand-tone fabrics. Chef-owner Marco Moreira's signature starter is the unctuous sea urchin angel-hair carbonara. Main courses are steeped in French tradition, but with international flavors, like honey-glazed Peking duck breast and leg terrine, and curry-dusted Chatham cod. The three-course $24 prix-fixe lunch is a steal. ☒ *1 E. 15th St., between 5th Ave. and Union Sq. W, Union Square* ☎ *212/647–1515* ⊕ *www. tocquevillerestaurant.com* ☞ *Reservations essential* ▤ *AE, MC, V* Ⓜ *L, N, Q, R, 4, 5, 6 to 14th St./Union Sq.* ✚ *3:F4.*

$$$ ✕**Union Square Cafe.** When he opened Union Square Cafe in 1985,
AMERICAN Danny Meyer changed the American restaurant landscape. The combination of upscale food and unpretentious but focused service sparked a revolution. Today chef Carmen Quagliata still draws devotees with his crowd-pleasing menu. Wood paneling and white walls are hung with splashy modern paintings; in addition to the three dining areas, there's a long bar ideal for solo diners. The cuisine is American with a thick Italian accent: for example, the grilled, smoked shell steak can land on the same table as creamy polenta parmigiana. ☒ *21 E. 16th St., between 5th Ave. and Union Sq. W, Union Square* ☎ *212/243–4020* ⊕ *www.*

18

unionsquarecafe.com ⚓ *Reservations essential* ⊟*AE, D, DC, MC, V* Ⓜ*L, N, Q, R, 4, 5, 6 to 14th St./Union Sq.* ✛*3:F4.*

MIDTOWN

MIDTOWN EAST

$$$$
MODERN FRENCH
Fodor'sChoice
★

✕ **Adour Alain Ducasse.** Master chef Alain Ducasse adds to his growing empire with the upscale elegant and wine-focused Adour, in the equally sophisticated St. Regis Hotel. Celebratory couples of all ages gravitate to the Left and Right Bank rooms, and a mix of tourists, shoppers, and businessmen settle on plush burgundy chairs and banquettes in the regal but relaxed main dining room. A chef shuffle brought Ducasse a new aide-de-camp, the talented Didier Elena, who has instituted a vegetarian tasting menu and an increased focus on seasonality. Deep pockets splurge on artfully arranged dishes, such as roasted chicken with mushrooms and herb butter, accompanied by Swiss chard gratin. Sommeliers help decipher an international wine list (displayed on interactive computer screens at the bar) with bottles that range from $35 to $19,000. ⊠*2 E. 55th St., near 5th Ave., Midtown East* ☎*212/710–2277* ⊕*www. adour-stregis.com* ⚓ *Reservations essential* ⊟*AE, D, DC, MC, V* ⊘*No lunch* Ⓜ*E, M to 5th Ave./53rd St.; F to 57th St.* ✛*4:E2.*

$$$$
SCANDINAVIAN

✕ **Aquavit and Aquavit Café.** Celebrity chef and co-owner Marcus Samuelsson may no longer be in the kitchen here, but you'd never know it from the impeccable cuisine and service at this fine-dining restaurant and upscale café, now in the hands of able executive chef Marcus Jenmark. The elegant atmosphere features warm woods and modern decor from a Scandinavian design team. In the café, try a two-course dinner of daily "Swedish home cooking" specials, or order à la carte to try the herring sampler, with boldly flavored selections like curry and apple, and vodka-lime. The main dining room is prix-fixe only, with a three-course dinner for $84 or a chef's tasting at $110. ⊠*65 E. 55th St., between Madison and Park Aves., Midtown East* ☎*212/307–7311* ⊕*www.aquavit.org* ⚓ *Reservations essential* ⊟*AE, DC, MC, V* ⊘*No lunch Sat., except in café* Ⓜ*E, M to 5th Ave./53rd St.* ✛*4:F2.*

$$$
STEAKHOUSE

✕ **BLT Steak.** Chef Laurent Tourondel may no longer be involved with his namesake steak house, but this classy space, decked out in beige with resin-top black tables, still draws crowds. As soon as you're settled, puffy Gruyère popovers arrive still steaming. The no-muss, no-fuss menu is nonetheless large, and so are the portions of supple crab cakes with celery-infused mayonnaise and luscious ruby tuna tartare with avocado, ramped up with soy-lime dressing. A veal chop crusted with rosemary and Parmesan lends new depth to the meat. At lunch, the quintessential BLT includes Kobe beef, foie gras, bacon, and tomato on a split ciabatta bun, with a cute plastic pig toothpick indicating desired doneness. Sides and desserts, like a killer peanut butter–chocolate mousse with banana ice cream, are all superior. ⊠*106 E. 57th St., between Lexington and Park Aves., Midtown East* ☎*212/752–7470* ⊕*www.bltsteak.com* ⚓ *Reservations essential* ⊟*AE, DC, MC, V* ⊘*Closed Sun. No lunch Sat.* Ⓜ*4, 5, 6, N, R to 59th St./Lexington Ave.* ✛*4:F1.*

$$$$ ✕**Four Seasons**. The landmark Seagram Building houses one of America's most famous restaurants, truly an only-in–New York experience.
AMERICAN
Owners Alex Von Bider and Julian Niccolini supervise the seating chart like hawks, placing power players in finance, entertainment, and New York society in prime positions for maximum visibility. The stark Grill Room, birthplace of the power lunch, has one of the best bars in New York. Illuminated trees and a gurgling Carrara marble pool characterize the more romantic Pool Room. The menu changes seasonally; there's a $65 prix-fixe pretheater dinner—a delicious indulgence. You can't go wrong with classic dishes like Dover sole, filet mignon, or crispy duck, but the restaurant moves with the times, so expect roving seasonal specials featuring luxe ingredients and preparations. Finish with pear William, Grand Marnier, or a chocolate soufflé. ⊠ *99 E. 52nd St., between Park and Lexington Aves., Midtown East* ☎ *212/754–9494* ⊕ *www.fourseasonsrestaurant.com* ⌖ *Reservations essential* ⟨Jacket required* ▤ *AE, D, DC, MC, V* ☾ *Closed Sun. No lunch Sat.* Ⓜ *E, M to Lexington Ave./53rd St.; 6 to 51st St.* ✛ *4:F2.*

$$$$ ✕**Kuruma Zushi**. Only a small sign in Japanese indicates the location
JAPANESE
of this extraordinary restaurant that serves only sushi and sashimi. Bypass the tables, sit at the sushi bar, and put yourself in the hands of Toshishiro Uezu, the chef-owner. Among the selections are hard-to-find fish that Uezu imports directly from Japan. The most attentive, pampering service staff in the city completes the wildly expensive experience. The showstopping chef's *omakase* will cost you $250, but it's a multicourse feast you'll never forget. ⊠ *7 E. 47th St., 2nd fl., between 5th and Madison Aves., Midtown East* ☎ *212/317–2802* ⌖ *Reservations essential* ▤ *AE, MC, V* ☾ *Closed Sun.* Ⓜ *4, 5, 6, 7 to 42nd St./Grand Central* ✛ *4:E3.*

$$$$ ✕**L'Atelier de Joël Robuchon**. The New York branch of Joël Robuchon's
FRENCH
superluxurious restaurant, inside the Four Seasons Hotel, features essentially the same food (with a more natural-hue decor) as the Paris original. And that, it turns out, is a very good thing. The perfectionist chef has installed a longtime protégé to uphold the standards that can make a Robuchon meal a life-changing experience. Skip the regular-size appetizers and entrées. Instead, secure a seat at the pear-wood counter and cobble together your own small-plate feast. But be warned: with heady ingredients like Scottish langoustines (tempura fried), Osetra caviar atop crabmeat and coral gelee, and foie gras (paired with caramelized eel), Robuchon's little bites come at a steep price. ⊠ *57 E. 57th St., between Madison and Park Aves., Midtown East* ☎ *212/350–6658* ⊕ *www.fourseasons.com/newyorkfs/dining.html* ⌖ *Reservations essential* ▤ *AE, MC, V* ☾ *No lunch* Ⓜ *4, 5, 6 to 59th St.* ✛ *4:F1.*

$$$$ ✕**Le Cirque**. Impresario-owner Sirio Maccioni still presides over a din-
FRENCH
ing room filled nightly with a who's who of political, business, and society circles—regulars who've table-hopped from Le Cirque's first incarnation to its latest, in a glass-enclosed aerie on the ground floor of the Bloomberg headquarters. Billowing silk, tall gauzy shades, and porcelain monkeys in a display-case pillar create a playful big-top effect. The menu strikes a balance between the creative and classic. Dover sole, filleted table-side, gives way to more avant-garde preparations like a

18

duo of seared foie gras and sushi-grade tuna. Desserts, too, have a split personality, with the menu divided into the "classic" and "new." The foot-tall napoleon that seems to arrive at every second table is an old favorite, but newer creations like the praline tortellini with exotic fruit also satisfy high-society sweet tooths. Though jackets are still required in the dining room, things are more relaxed in the casual wine lounge. ⊠ *151 E. 58th St., at Lexington Ave., Midtown East* ☎ *212/644–0202* ⊕ *www.lecirque.com* ⧌ *Reservations essential* ⊟ *AE, D, DC, MC, V* ⊘ *Closed Sun. No lunch Sat.* Ⓜ *4, 5, 6, N, R to Lexington Ave./59th St.* ✛ *4:F1.*

$$$ ✕ **Michael Jordan's The Steakhouse NYC.** Don't be dissuaded by the fact that
STEAKHOUSE this place is technically part of a chain: there's nowhere remotely like it. The handsomely appointed space in Grand Central Terminal, hung with gracious filigree chandeliers, overlooks one of the most famous interiors in America. Start with the stack of soft, toasted bread soldiers in a pool of hot Gorgonzola fondue. Pristine oysters make a great prelude for a prime dry-aged rib eye or a 2½-pound lobster, grilled, steamed, sautéed, or broiled. Sides, like creamy mac 'n cheese and a crispy rosemary hash-brown cake, are equally tempting. ⊠ *Grand Central Terminal, West Balcony, 23 Vanderbilt Ave., between E. 43rd and E. 44th Sts., Midtown East* ☎ *212/655–2300* ⊕ *www.theglaziergroup.com/restaurants/ michaeljordan* ⧌ *Reservations essential* ⊟ *AE, D, DC, MC, V* Ⓜ *4, 5, 6, 7 to 42nd St./Grand Central* ✛ *4:F4.*

$$ ✕ **Mint.** With a delightful dining room splashed with bright colors and
INDIAN flattering lighting, and executive chef and owner Gary Sikka's brightly seasoned dishes, this newcomer has joined the ranks of the best Indian restaurants in town. The large menu includes rarely encountered specialties from Goa and Sikkim. Freshly grilled, moist ground lamb kebabs deliver a slow burn to the palate. Chili heat punctuates other spices in the lamb vindaloo, resulting in a well-rounded array of savory flavors. Finish with carrot pudding with saffron and coconut flakes. ⊠ *150 E. 50th St., between Lexington and 3rd Aves., Midtown East* ☎ *212/644–8888* ⊟ *AE, D, DC, MC, V* Ⓜ *6, E, M to 51st St./Lexington Ave.* ✛ *4:G3.*

$$$ ✕ **Oyster Bar.** Nestled deep in the belly of Grand Central Station, the
SEAFOOD Oyster Bar has been a worthy seafood destination for more than nine decades. Sit at the counter for the fried oyster po'boy, or slurp an assortment of bracingly fresh oysters before having a steaming bowl of clam chowder washed down with an ice-cold brew. Or experience the forgotten pleasure of fresh, unadorned seafood such as lobster with drawn butter or grilled herring in season. Avoid anything that sounds too complicated, like cream-smothered seafood pan roasts. ⊠ *Grand Central Station, dining concourse, E. 42nd St. at Vanderbilt Ave., Midtown East* ☎ *212/490–6650* ⊕ *www.oysterbarny.com* ⧌ *Reservations essential* ⊟ *AE, D, MC, V* ⊘ *Closed Sun.* Ⓜ *4, 5, 6, 7, S to 42nd St./ Grand Central* ✛ *4:F4.*

$$$ ✕ **Palm.** They may have added tablecloths, but it would take more than
STEAKHOUSE that to hide the brusque, no-nonsense nature of this legendary steak house. The steak is always impeccable, and the Nova Scotia lobsters are so big—3 pounds and up—that there may not be room at the table

for such classic side dishes as rich creamed spinach, served family-style for two or more. The "half-and-half" side combination of cottage-fried potatoes and fried onions is particularly addictive. There may be other locations, but because of its perch near the Theater District and Midtown businesses, this is the one with the most action. ⊠ *837 2nd Ave., between 44th and 45th Sts., Midtown East* ☎ *212/687–2953* ⊕ *www. thepalm.com* ⊟ *AE, D, DC, MC, V* ⊙ *Closed Sun. No lunch Sat.* Ⓜ *4, 5, 6, 7, S to Grand Central* ✚ *4:G4.*

$ ✕**Second Avenue Deli**. It may no longer be on Second Avenue, but the
AMERICAN new incarnation of the East Village institution—one block over and about a mile uptown—is still delivering on its longtime tradition of overstuffed "three-decker" sandwiches filled with house-cured pastrami, matzo-ball soup, and other old-world specialties. Hot open sandwiches, like juicy beef brisket served with gravy and french fries, may be a heart attack on a plate, but hey, you only live once. Even better, you can now get kasha varnishkes, carrot tzimmes, and potato kugel until the wee hours of the night. ⊠ *162 E. 33rd St., between Lexington and 3rd Aves., Midtown East* ☎ *212/689–9000* ⊟ *AE, D, DC, MC, V* Ⓜ *6 to 33rd St./Lexington Ave.* ✚ *4:G6.*

$$$ ✕**Shun Lee Palace**. If you want inexpensive Cantonese food without
CHINESE pretensions, head to Chinatown; but if you prefer to be pampered and don't mind spending a lot of money, this is the place. The cuisine is absolutely classic Chinese. Beijing panfried dumplings make a good starter, and rack of lamb Szechuan-style, grilled with scallions and garlic, is a popular entrée. Beijing duck is sure to please. ⊠ *155 E. 55th St., between Lexington and 3rd Aves., Midtown East* ☎ *212/371–8844* ⊕ *www.shunleepalace.com* ⟁ *Reservations essential* ⊟ *AE, MC, V* Ⓜ *N, R, 4, 5, 6 to 59th St./Lexington Ave.* ✚ *4:G2.*

$$$$ ✕**Sparks Steakhouse**. Magnums of wines that cost more than most
STEAKHOUSE people earn in a week festoon the large dining rooms of this classic New York steak house. Although seafood is given more than fair play on the menu, Sparks is really about dry-aged steak. The extra-thick lamb and veal chops are also noteworthy. Classic sides of hash browns, creamed spinach, sautéed mushrooms, and grilled onions are all you need to complete the experience. ⊠ *210 E. 46th St., between 2nd and 3rd Aves., Midtown East* ☎ *212/687–4855* ⊕ *www.sparkssteakhouse. com* ⟁ *Reservations essential* ⊟ *AE, D, DC, MC, V* ⊙ *Closed Sun. No lunch Sat.* Ⓜ *4, 5, 6, 7, S to 42nd St./Grand Central* ✚ *4:G3.*

$$ ✕**Sushi Yasuda**. Devotees mourned the return of namesake chef
JAPANESE Naomichi Yasuda to Japan, but things are in able hands with his hand-picked successor, Misturu Tamura. Here the sleek bamboo-lined interior is as elegant as the food. Whether using fish flown in daily from Japan or the creamiest sea urchin, the chef makes sushi so fresh and delicate, it melts in your mouth. A number of special appetizers change daily (crispy fried eel backbone is a surprising treat), and a fine selection of sake and beer complements the lovely food. Try to sit at the bar, which was hand-crafted by Yasuda out of imported Japanese materials. ⊠ *204 E. 43rd St., between 2nd and 3rd Aves., Midtown East* ☎ *212/972–1001* ⊕ *www.sushiyasuda.com* ⊟ *AE, D, MC, V* ⊙ *Closed Sun. No lunch Sat.* Ⓜ *4, 5, 6, 7 to 42nd St./Grand Central* ✚ *4:G4.*

18

MIDTOWN WEST

$$$$ ✗ **Aureole.** An island of fine dining in the heart of bustling Times Square,
NEW AMERICAN Aureole is the second act of a New York classic from Charlie Palmer and
his latest executive chef, Christoph Bellanca. From the street, a curved
second-story corridor hosting the restaurant's storied wine collection
beckons. A welcoming front bar room serves a more casual, yet refined,
menu with dishes like a cheddar-bacon burger dolloped with pickled
ramp mayonnaise. The dining room, with its abundance of flowers, is
the place to hobnob with expense-account diners and pretheater revelers alike. For dinner, starters like the sea-scallop "sandwich" topped
with foie gras and passion-fruit coulis is a treat, and the $110 "parallel
tasting" offers the menu's greatest hits, with an optional wine pairing.
✉ *135 W. 42nd St., between Broadway and 6th Ave, Midtown West*
☎ *212/319–1660* ⊕ *www.charliepalmer.com* ⚑ *Reservations essential*
▤ *AE, D, DC, MC, V* Ⓜ *B, D, F, M to 42nd St./Bryant Park; 1, 2, 3,*
9, N, R, Q to 42nd St./Times Sq. ✛ *4:D4.*

$$$ ✗ **Bar Americain.** Celeb chef Bobby Flay's largest Manhattan restaurant
BRASSERIE is the soaring Bar Americain. The 200-seat two-story space looks like
a dining room on a luxury liner (complete with a gift shop: you can
purchase his many cookbooks in the front). This is not food for the
faint-of-heart: Flay piles on the butter, cream, and endless varieties
of bacon. Southern-inflected brasserie fare includes gold corn Johnny-
cakes with barbecued pulled pork and cranberry butter, smoked chicken
with hatch-green-chili spoon bread and black-pepper vinegar sauce, and
roasted duck breast surrounded by dirty wild rice with bourbon-soaked
pecans. Slightly naughtier are the éclairs piped with whiskey-infused
pastry cream and burnished with a burnt-sugar glaze. Brunch, featuring
dishes like biscuits and cream gravy with sausage and scrambled eggs, is
delicious. ✉ *152 W. 52nd St., between 6th and 7th Aves., Midtown West*
☎ *212/265–9700* ⊕ *www.baramericain.com/* ⚑ *Reservations essential*
▤ *AE, D, MC, V* Ⓜ *B, D, E to 7th Ave.; 1, C, E to 50th St.; N, R to*
49th St. ✛ *4:C2.*

$$ ✗ **Becco.** An ingenious concept makes Becco a prime Restaurant Row
ITALIAN choice for time-constrained theatergoers. There are two pricing sce-
narios: one includes an all-you-can-eat selection of antipasti and three
pastas served hot out of pans that waiters circulate around the dining
room; the other adds a generous entrée to the mix. The pasta selection
changes daily, but often includes gnocchi, fresh ravioli, and fettuccine
in a cream sauce. The entrées include braised veal shank, grilled double-
cut pork chop, and rack of lamb, among other selections. ✉ *355 W.*
46th St., between 8th and 9th Aves., Midtown West ☎ *212/397–7597*
⊕ *www.becco-nyc.com* ▤ *AE, D, DC, MC, V* Ⓜ *A, C, E to 42nd St.*
✛ *4:B3.*

$$$$ ✗ **Ben Benson's Steakhouse.** Among the most venerable steak houses
STEAKHOUSE around, Ben Benson's feels like a clubby hunting lodge. The gracefully
choreographed, intensely focused staff will bring you only the finest
dry-aged prime meats and only the freshest seafood, all classically prepared, teeming with familiar and beloved flavors. The trimmings are
ravishing, too: comforting creamed spinach, sizzling onion rings, and
decadent hash browns are essential. Power lunches were practically

invented here; just being in the place makes you feel important. ✉ *123 W. 52nd St., between 6th and 7th Aves., Midtown West* ☎ *212/581– 8888* ⊕ *www.benbensons.com* ⌦ *Reservations essential* ▭ *AE, D, DC, MC, V* ⊘ *No lunch weekends* Ⓜ *B, D, E to 7th Ave.; 1 to 50th St.; N, R to 49th St.* ✛ *4:D2.*

$$$ ✕**Brasserie Ruhlmann.** In a plush 120-seat dining room with just enough
BRASSERIE Art Deco touches to harmonize with its Rockefeller Center setting, the sublime French bistro cookery, courtesy of Laurent Tourondel, is on display. There is a decorous countenance to the room, but the staff is so friendly that the place could never be stuffy. Seventeen excellent wines are available by the glass, as well as 10 half bottles. A pristine raw bar, featuring a selection of pedigreed oysters, is a great way to begin, or opt for a blue crab salad over mache with a honey-lime vinaigrette. If it's on the menu, order braised rabbit nestled in mustard cream on a bed of fresh pappardelle, sprinkled with pitted cherries. Desserts like Floating Island—delicately baked meringue floating on a pond of crème anglaise—are embellished by a tangled flurry of spun sugar. ✉ *45 Rockefeller Plaza, 50th St. between 5th and 6th Aves., Midtown West* ☎ *212/974–2020* ⊕ *www.brasserieruhlmann.com* ⌦ *Reservations essential* ▭ *AE, MC, V* Ⓜ *B, D, F, M to 47th–50th Sts./Rockefeller Center* ✛ *4:D3.*

¢ ✕**Burger Joint.** What's a college burger bar, done up in particleboard
BURGER and rec-room decor straight out of a *Happy Days* episode, doing hid-
Fodor'sChoice den inside a five-star Midtown hotel? This tongue-in-cheek lunch
★ spot, hidden behind a heavy red velvet curtain in the Parker Meridien hotel, does such boisterous midweek business that lines often snake through the lobby. Stepping behind the curtain, you can find baseball cap–wearing, grease-spattered cooks dispensing paper-wrapped cheeseburgers and crisp, thin fries. Forget Kobe beef or foie gras—these burgers are straightforward, cheap, and delicious. ✉ *118 W. 57th St., between 6th and 7th Aves., Midtown West* ☎ *212/245–5000* ⊕ *www. parkermeridien.com* ▭ *No credit cards* Ⓜ *F, N, Q, R to 57th St.* ✛ *4:D1.*

$$ ✕**Carmine's.** Savvy New Yorkers line up early for the affordable fam-
ITALIAN ily-style meals at this large, busy Midtown eatery. Family photos line
☺ the walls, and there's a convivial feeling amid all the Times Square hubbub. Don't be fooled: Carmine's may be huge, but it fills up with families carbo-loading for a day of sightseeing or a night of theater on Broadway. There are no reservations taken for parties of fewer than six people after 7 pm, but those who wait are rewarded with mountains of such popular, toothsome viands as fried calamari, linguine with white clam sauce, chicken parmigiana, and veal saltimbocca. ✉ *200 W. 44th St., between Broadway and 8th Ave., Midtown West* ☎ *212/221–3800* ⊕ *www.carminesnyc.com* ▭ *AE, D, DC, MC, V* Ⓜ *A, C, E, N, Q, R, S, 1, 2, 3, 7 to 42nd St./Times Sq.* ✛ *4:C4.*

$$$$ ✕**Churrascaria Plataforma.** This sprawling, boisterous shrine to meat,
BRAZILIAN with its all-you-can-eat prix-fixe menu, is best experienced with a group of ravenous friends. A *caipirinha,* featuring cachaca sugarcane liquor, sugar, and lime, will kick things off nicely. Follow up with a trip to the salad bar piled with vegetables, meats, and cheeses. But restrain yourself—there's a parade of all manner of grilled meats and poultry, from

18

pork ribs to chicken hearts, delivered to the table on long skewers until you beg for mercy. ✉ *316 W. 49th St., between 8th and 9th Aves., Midtown West* ☎ *212/245–0505* ⊕ *www.plataformaonline.com* ⌦ *Reservations essential* ☰ *AE, D, DC, MC, V* Ⓜ *C, E to 50th St.* ✛ *4:B3.*

$$$ ✕ **DB Bistro Moderne.** Daniel Boulud's "casual bistro" (it's neither, actu-
FRENCH ally) consists of two elegantly appointed dining rooms. The menu features classic dishes like Nantucket Bay scallops or hanger steak exquisitely prepared. Ever the trendsetter, Boulud's $32 db hamburger, available at lunch and dinner, and stuffed with braised short ribs, foie gras, and black truffles, is the patty credited with kick-starting the whole gourmet burger trend. Yes, it's worth every penny. ✉ *55 W. 44th St., between 5th and 6th Aves., Midtown West* ☎ *212/391–2400* ⊕ *www. danielnyc.com/dbbistro.html* ⌦ *Reservations essential* ☰ *AE, DC, MC, V* ⊘ *No lunch Sun.* Ⓜ *B, D, F, M to 42nd St./Bryant Park; 7 to 5th Ave./ Bryant Park* ✛ *4:D4.*

$$$ ✕ **Esca.** The name is Italian for "bait," and this restaurant, courtesy of
SEAFOOD partners Mario Batali, Joe Bastianich, and longtime chef David Paster-
nack, lures diners in with delectable raw preparations called *crudo*—
such as tilefish with orange and Sardinian oil or pink snapper with a sprinkle of crunchy red clay salt—and hooks them with such entrées as whole, salt-crusted branzino, sea bass for two, or *bucatini* pasta with spicy baby octopus. The menu changes daily. Bastianich is in charge of the wine cellar, and you can expect an adventurous list of Italian bottles. ✉ *402 W. 43rd St., at 9th Ave., Midtown West* ☎ *212/564–7272* ⊕ *www.esca-nyc.com* ⌦ *Reservations essential* ☰ *AE, DC, MC, V* ⊘ *No lunch Sun.* Ⓜ *A, C, E to 42nd St.* ✛ *4:A4.*

$ ✕ **Five Napkin Burger.** This perennially packed Hell's Kitchen burger
AMERICAN place/brasserie has been a magnet for burger lovers since day one. Bottles of Maker's Mark line the sleek, alluringly lighted bar in the back, a collection of antique butcher's scales hangs on a tile wall near the kitchen, and meat hooks dangle from the ceiling between the light fixtures. Though there are many menu distractions—deep-fried pick-les, warm artichoke dip, to name a few—the main attractions are the juicy burgers, like the original 10-ounce chuck with a tangle of onions, Gruyère cheese, and rosemary aioli. There's a patty variety for every-one, including a ground lamb *kofta* and an onion ring–topped ahi tuna burger. For dessert, have an über-thick black-and-white malted milk-shake. ✉ *630 9th Ave., between 44th and 45th Sts., Midtown West* ☎ *212/757–2277* ⊕ *www.fivenapkinburger.com* ☰ *AE, D, MC, V* Ⓜ *A, C, E to 42nd St./8th Ave.* ✛ *4:B4.*

$$–$$$$ ✕ **Gordon Ramsay at The London and Maze.** With more than a dozen res-
FRENCH taurants around the world—and an ever-busy TV schedule—you're not likely to find British chef Gordon Ramsay at his eponymous Midtown restaurant. What you will find, however, are Ramsay's trembling aco-lytes producing flawless facsimiles of his classically muted haute cuisine. The flagship fine-dining restaurant is an exorbitant time commitment, with menus that start at $110 for three courses and stretch to $150 for seven. It is hidden behind opaque glass doors just beyond the compara-tively casual, and much more reasonably priced, Maze. The lower-key annex, in a silver-gray dining room, specializes in elegant small-plate

cuisine (often very small). Although dinner is a mix-and-match affair, Maze's $35 prix-fixe three-course lunch is one of the top bargains in Midtown. ✉ *151 W. 54th St., between 6th and 7th Aves., Midtown West* ☎ *212/468–8888* ⊕ *www.thelondonnyc.com* ▭ *AE, D, DC, MC, V* ☉ *No lunch. No dinner Sun. and Mon.* Ⓜ *B, D, E to 7th Ave.; N, Q, R to 57th St.* ⊹ *4:D2.*

$$$
NEW AMERICAN

✕ **The Lambs Club.** Daddy Warbucks would like it here. Restaurateur Geoffrey Zakarian has opened an opulent supper club on the ground floor of the brand-new Chatwal Hotel, complete with Art Deco detailing, red-leather banquettes, and an antique fireplace grill that was discovered and refurbished. Cocktails are from drinks hipster guru Sasha Petraske, but he eschews experimental in the service of classics like the sidecar and the martini, done well. The food is typical Zakarian, meaning New American cuisine with luxe touches in dishes like veal sweetbreads with peppered jus and grilled treviso lettuce, or seared scallops with porcini mushrooms and Indian-spiced sauce. Desserts, like double-chocolate ginger cake with poached pears, are worth the splurge. ✉ *132 W. 44th St., between 6th Ave. and Broadway, Midtown West* ☎ *212/997–5262* ⊕ *www.thelambsclub.com* ▭ *AE, D, DC, MC, V* Ⓜ *1, 2, 3 to 42nd St., B, D, F, M to 47th–50th Sts./Rockefeller Center* ⊹ *4:D4.*

$$$$
FRENCH

✕ **Le Bernardin.** Owner Maguy LeCoze presides over the teak-panel dining room at this trendsetting French seafood restaurant, and chef-partner Eric Ripert works magic with anything that swims—preferring at times not to cook it at all. Deceptively simple dishes such as poached lobster in rich coconut-ginger soup or crispy spiced black bass in a Peking duck bouillon are typical of his style. It is widely agreed that there's no beating Le Bernardin for thrilling cuisine, seafood or otherwise, coupled with some of the finest desserts in town and a wine list as deep as the Atlantic. ✉ *155 W. 51st St., between 6th and 7th Aves., Midtown West* ☎ *212/554–1515* ⊕ *www.le-bernardin.com* 🍴 *Jacket required* ▭ *AE, DC, MC, V* ☉ *Closed Sun. No lunch Sat.* Ⓜ *1 to 50th St.; R to 49th St.; B, D, F, M to 47th–50th Sts./Rockefeller Center* ⊹ *4:C2.*

$
CAFÉ

✕ **Le Pain Quotidien.** This international Belgian chain brings its homeland ingredients with it, treating New Yorkers to crusty organic breads, jams, chocolate, and other specialty products. You can grab a snack to go or stay and eat breakfast, lunch, or dinner at communal or private tables with waiter service. Come for a steaming latte and croissant in the morning or a tartine (open-faced sandwich) at noon. There are more than 20 units in New York City; check the restaurant's Web site for additional locations. ✉ *1271 Avenue of the Americas, at 50th St. Midtown West* ☎ *646/462–4165* ⊕ *www.lepainquotidien.com* Ⓜ *B, D, F, V to 47–50th Sts./Rockefeller Center* ⊹ *3:F3, 3:D3, 5:H4. 2:E4, 5:C5, 4:C1, 5:G2, 5:C4, 2:D1, 5:G5, 3:F4.*

$$
ITALIAN

✕ **Lugo Caffé.** The area around Madison Square Garden is a restaurant wasteland with the rare sparkling exception of Lugo Caffé, founded by an Italian menswear line. Locals rejoiced at the introduction of this spacious Italian "brasserie" offering comfort food with a *Dolce Vita* twist all day long. Stop by for an espresso and pastry in the morning. Later,

18

a single menu presents lunch, *aperitivo*, and dinner options, which include grazing portions of salumi, cheeses, and vegetable dishes like eggplant caponata, Tuscan bean salad, and grilled zucchini with pine nuts. Fuller meals of Neapolitan-style pizzas, house-made pastas, and grilled meats and fish also are commendable. ⊠ *1 Penn Plaza, 33rd St. and 8th Ave., Midtown West* ☎ *212/760–2700* ⊕ *www.lugocaffe.com* ☰ *AE, MC, V* Ⓜ *A, C, E to 34th St.; 1, 2, 3 to 34th St.* ☉ *Closed Sun. (except on some MSG sports game days)* ✛ *4:C6.*

$$$
ASIAN

✕ **Má Pêche.** Any time chef David Chang opens a new property, it merits notice, but this one deserves attention for one extra, very important reason: it's in Midtown. Starkly decorated and set in the basement of the Chambers Hotel on West 56th Street, Má Pêche is blocks from MoMA and is the largest restaurant in Chang's empire, so you've got a better shot of nabbing a seat—either at one of the more conventional perches on the sides, or at the huge X-shape communal table at the center of the room. The menus here are a bit more refined (and expensive) than those at Momofuku Noodle Bar and Ssäm Bar, with elegantly composed plates like lamb shank accompanied by eggplant, raisins, and rice, or seared swordfish with black beans, braised celery, and crisped shallots. In the bar upstairs, try the lettuce-filled summer rolls with pork, shrimp or tofu; the beef tartare with soy, scallion, and mint; or the sticky Niman Ranch pork ribs. At lunchtime, order from the same upscale menu or opt for one of the $10 "Midtown Lunch" specials, like a tasty Banh Mi filled with pork and vegetables, or a beef sausage hero with cucumber and jalapeño. On the way out you can pick up sweets from the uptown offshoot of Momofuku Milk Bar, like the addictive, buttery Crack Pie or a cup of salted pistachio soft-serve. ⊠ *15 W. 56th St., between 5th and 6th Aves., Midtown West* ☎ *212/757–5878* ⊕ *www.momofuku. com/ma-peche* ☰ *AE, D, MC, V* ☉ *No lunch Sun.* ✛ *4:E1.*

$$
MEDITERRANEAN

✕ **Marseille.** With great food and a convenient location near several Broadway theaters, Marseille is perpetually packed. Executive chef and partner Andy d'Amico's Mediterranean creations are continually impressive. His bouillabaisse, the signature dish of the region for which the restaurant is named, is a mélange of mussels, shrimp, rouget, and bass swimming in a fragrant fish broth, topped with a garlicky crouton and served with rouille on the side. Leave room for the spongy beignets with chocolate and raspberry dipping sauces. ⊠ *630 9th Ave., at W. 44th St., Midtown West* ☎ *212/333–2323* ⊕ *www.marseillenyc. com* ⌦ *Reservations essential* ☰ *AE, MC, V* Ⓜ *A, C, E to 42nd St./Port Authority Bus Terminal* ✛ *4:B4.*

$
ETHIOPIAN

✕ **Meskerem.** The tasty Ethiopian delicacies offered in this Hell's Kitchen storefront include *kitfo,* spiced ground steak, which you can order raw, rare, or well done, and *yebeg alecha,* tender pieces of lamb marinated in Ethiopian butter flavored with curry, rosemary, and an herb called *kosart,* and then sautéed with fresh ginger and more curry. The vegetarian combination, served on injera, a fermented and slightly porous flat bread used as a utensil to sop up the food, is a great deal. ⊠ *468 W. 47th St., near 10th Ave., Midtown West* ☎ *212/664–0520* ☰ *AE, D, DC, MC, V* Ⓜ *C, E to 50th St.* ✛ *4:A3.*

$$$–$$$$ ╳**The Modern and Bar Room.** Both spots competing for the title of the
FRENCH country's best museum restaurant sit side by side on the ground floor
of the New York MoMA. The Modern, run by restaurateur Danny
Meyer, is two restaurants in one. Both offer the dazzling food of Alsa-
tian chef Gabriel Kreuther. The formal dining room features a view of
the museum's sculpture garden and an ambitious, pricey, prix-fixe menu
with standouts like chorizo-crusted codfish with white coco-bean puree.
The far more accessible and popular Bar Room lies just beyond a parti-
tion. Here you can find a dizzying collection of shareable plates, like the
refreshing arctic char tartare and oysters with leeks and caviar. Two or
three make a fine if extravagant afternoon snack—double that number
and you have a full meal. ⊠ 9 W. 53rd St., between 5th and 6th Aves.,
Midtown West ☎ 212/333–1220 ⊕ www.themodernnyc.com ▤ AE, D,
DC, MC, V ⊘ Closed Sun. Ⓜ E, M to 5th Ave./53rd St. ✚ 4:D2.

$$$$ ╳**Oceana.** Entering the newly revamped Oceana is like walking into
SEAFOOD the dressy stateroom of a modern luxury ocean liner. Floor-to-ceiling
windows look out both north and west, and the cocktail bar offers
cutting-edge concoctions like a fusion of bourbon, Italian bitters, elder-
flower, and cardamom. The arrestingly designed raw bar backed with
Mediterranean-hue ceramics offers stunningly fresh choices. You would
expect gorgeous oysters at a restaurant called Oceana, and you get
them: they're so full-flavored that they transcend their chilliness. Chef
Ben Pollinger has all the skill and confidence necessary to serve some of
the most vivid and delicious seafood in town. A "contemporary appe-
tizer" section features items like marinated cucumber with cucumber,
apple, and toasted spices. Grilled whole fish like halibut, swordfish,
and crispy wild striped bass are served with a perfect rotating roster of
sauces like classic romesco and grilled pineapple salsa. Thai-style red
snapper comes with tender silk squash, crisp jicama, and a kaffir-saffron
broth. ⊠ 1221 6th Ave., at W. 49th St., Midtown West ☎ 212/759–5941
⊕ www.livanosrestaurantgroup.com ⌖ Reservations essential ▤ AE,
DC, MC, V Ⓜ E, M to 53rd St./5th Ave. ✚ 4:D3.

$$$ ╳**Seäsonal Restaurant and Weinbar.** Partners and executive chefs Wolf-
AUSTRIAN/ gang Ban and Eduard Frauneder have brought something *neu* to Mid-
GERMAN town: a swanky Austrian-German restaurant and Weinbar. With its
sculptural ceiling lighting, elliptical bar, and contemporary Austrian
and German art, Seäsonal feels more "downtown" than you'd expect
from such central Midtown digs. The decor is modern European, with
white walls, wood floors, and leather cubby seating. The cuisine is
sophisticated and contemporary, yet still steeped in regional traditions.
The chefs are committed to using fresh, seasonal ingredients and, when-
ever possible, locally sourced products. Appetizers like the foie-gras
terrine and the cheese ravioli with smoked chanterelle mushrooms will
delight you with their contrasting lightness and intensity of flavor. Main
dishes, such as the pumpkin seed–crusted black sea bass with butternut
squash and black truffles, and the classic Wiener schnitzel served with a
crescent potato-cucumber salad, will pleasure your palate with simple
but striking flavor combinations. Seäsonal's Weinbar features a distinctive selection of wines from emerging Austrian and German winemak-
ers—definitely the right place for your Riesling fix. ⊠ 132 W. 58th St.,

18

Midtown West ☎ *212/957–5550* ⊕ *www.seasonalnyc.com* ▭ *AE, DC, MC, V* Ⓜ *F to 57th St./6th Ave.* ✛ *4:D1.*

$$ ✕ **Serafina.** Each location of Serafina features different design details—
ITALIAN Mediterranean-hue friezes or an outdoor terrace, for instance. Looks
🕙 aside, the real draw here is some authentic Neopolitan pizza—they even
filter the water for the pizza dough to make it more closely resemble the
water in Naples. Beyond the designer pizzas are antipasti, salads, and
pastas. For additional locations, check the restaurant's Web site. ⊠ *210
W. 55th St., at Broadway, Midtown West* ☎ *212/315–1700* ⊕ *www.
serafinarestaurant.com* Ⓜ *N, Q, R, W to 57th St./7th Ave.* ✛ *4:C2,
5:F6, 5:F2, 4:C3.*

$ ✕ **Shake Shack.** Local restaurant legend Danny Meyer has gone a little
BURGER low-brow with his fast-ish food venture, Shake Shack—and New York-
ers are loving it. Area-wise, this Theater District location is the largest
and with the most seating, but be warned: lines still snake out the door,
especially at prime mealtimes. Still, the grub is good and well priced.
Fresh steer burgers are ground daily, and a single will run you from
$3.75 to $4.75, depending on what you want on it. For a few more
bucks you can also order doubles and stacks or a vegetarian 'Shroom
Burger—a melty Muenster and cheddar cheese–stuffed portobello. The
Shake Shack also offers beef and bird (chicken) hot dogs, french fries,
and a variety of delicious frozen custard desserts and—of course—thick
shakes! ⊠ *691 8th Ave. Ave., at W. 44th St., Midtown West* ☎ *646/435–
0135* ⊕ *www.shakeshacknyc.com* ▭ *AE, D, MC, V* Ⓜ *1, 2, 3, A, C, E,
S to 42nd St./Times Sq.* ✛ *4:B4.*

$$ ✕ **Sosa Borella.** This is one of the Theater District's top spots for reliable
ITALIAN food at a reasonable cost. The bi-level, casual Argentinian-Italian eat-
ery is an inviting and friendly space where diners choose from a wide
range of options. The lunch menu features staples like warm sandwiches
and entrée-size salads, whereas the dinner menu is slightly gussied up
with meat, fish, and pasta dishes (the rich agnolotti with lamb Bolognese sauce, topped with a wedge of grilled pecorino cheese, is a must-
try). The freshly baked bread served at the beginning of the meal with
pesto dipping sauce is a nice touch as you wait for your meal. The
service can be slow at times, so leave yourself plenty of time before
the show. ⊠ *832 8th Ave., between 50th and 51st Sts., Midtown West*
☎ *212/262–8282* ⊕ *www.sosaborella.com* ▭ *AE, DC, MC, V* Ⓜ *C, E,
1 to 50th St.* ✛ *4:B3.*

$$ ✕ **Toloache.** Make a quick detour off heavily trafficked Broadway into
MEXICAN this pleasantly bustling Mexican cantina that's one of the best dining
options around Times Square. The bi-level eatery has a festive, cel-
ebratory vibe, with several seating options (bar, balcony, main dining
room, and ceviche bar), oversize bronze chandeliers, and gold and terra-
cotta tones throughout. Foodies flock here for three types of guacamole
(traditional, fruited, and spicy), a trio of well-executed ceviches, and
dishes like the Mexico City–style tacos with Negra Modelo–braised
brisket, and quesadillas studded with black truffle and *huitlacoche* (a
corn fungus). There's an extensive tequila selection—upward of 100
brands. Adventurous palates will be drawn to tacos featuring chili-
studded dried grasshoppers, lobes of seared foie gras, and caramelized

veal sweetbreads. ✉ *251 W. 50th St., near 8th Ave., Midtown West* ☎ *212/581–1818* ⊕ *www.toloachenyc.com* ▭ *AE, D, MC, V* Ⓜ *1, C, E to 50th St.; N, R to 49th St.* ✛ *4:B3.*

$$$$ ✕ **'21' Club.** Tradition's the thing at this town-house landmark, a former
AMERICAN speakeasy that opened in 1929. Toys donated by famous patrons—e.g., John McEnroe's tennis racket or Howard Hughes's model plane—hang from the ceiling. Down below, Chef John Greeley tries to satisfy everyone with standards like the famous '21' burger and Dover sole with brown butter, and more modern dishes, such as smoked Berkshire pork belly with savoy cabbage and green apples, but the food is almost secondary to the restaurant's storied past. Fellas, a jacket is required, but thanks to a more relaxed dress code you can leave your tie at home. ✉ *21 W. 52nd St., between 5th and 6th Aves., Midtown West* ☎ *212/582–7200* ⊕ *www.21club.com* ⌂ *Jacket required* ▭ *AE, D, DC, MC, V* ⊘ *Closed Sun. No lunch Sat.* Ⓜ *E, M to 53rd St./5th Ave.; B, D, F, M to 47th–50th Sts./Rockefeller Center* ✛ *4:D2.*

$$$$ ✕ **Uncle Jack's Steakhouse.** Surpassing even its celebrated flagship res-
STEAKHOUSE taurant in Bayside, Queens, Uncle Jack's soars directly into the pantheon of the best steak houses in Manhattan. As in most great steak houses, you can feel the testosterone throbbing all through the place. The space is vast and gorgeously appointed, and service is swift and focused. USDA prime steaks are dry-aged for 21 days. Australian lobster tails are so enormous, they have to be served carved, yet the flesh is meltingly tender. ✉ *440 9th Ave., between W. 34th and W. 35th Sts., Midtown West* ☎ *212/244–0005* ⊕ *www.unclejacks.com* ⌕ *Reservations essential* ▭ *AE, MC, V* ⊘ *No lunch weekends* Ⓜ *A, C, E to 34th St./Penn Station* ✛ *4:B6.*

$$ ✕ **Virgil's Real BBQ.** Neon, wood, and Formica set the scene at this
BARBECUE massive roadhouse in the Theater District. Start with stuffed jalape-
☺ ños or—especially—unbelievably succulent barbecued chicken wings. Then, what the hell: go for the "Pig Out"—a rack of pork ribs, Texas hot links, pulled pork, rack of lamb, chicken, and, of course, more. It's that kind of place. There are also five domestic microbrews on tap and a good list of top beers from around the world. The place is absolutely mobbed pre-theater, so if that's when you're going, arrive by 6 pm or you'll miss your curtain. ✉ *152 W. 44th St., between 6th Ave. and Broadway, Midtown West* ☎ *212/921–9494* ⊕ *www.virgilsbbq. com* ⌕ *Reservations essential* ▭ *AE, MC, V* Ⓜ *N, Q, R, S, 1, 2, 3, 7 to 42nd St./Times Sq.* ✛ *4:C4.*

18

UPPER EAST SIDE

$$$$ ✕ **Alloro.** Italian chef Salvatore Corea and his wife Gina, a native New
ITALIAN Yorker, are living their dream of opening an old-fashioned family-run restaurant here on the Upper East Side just a block away from the apartment they share with their two young daughters. It's not Corea's first New York restaurant endeavor—he's opened three other successful venues in the city (Cacio e Pepe, Spiga, and Bocca), but Alloro is his first venture with his wife, and judging by the friendly vibe and the delicious dishes coming out of Corea's *cucina*, it's working swimmingly well. Chef Corea's creative take on traditional, regional Italian cuisines leads the

way for delicious dishes, like creamy Parmesan risotto with Lambrusco-wine caramel. Both the sliced rib eye over corn puree and the fillet of sole in pumpkin-Amaretto crust are fantastic. Gluten-free pasta selections are also available. ☒ *307 E. 77th St., near 2nd Ave., Upper East Side* ☎ *212/535–2866* ⊕ *www.alloronyc.com* ═ *AE, MC, V* Ⓜ *6 to 77th St.* ✛ *5:H2.*

WORD OF MOUTH

"Café Boulud is an excellent restaurant if you want a foodie spot on the UES. They have a very good value lunch."—mclaurie

$$$$ ✕ **Café Boulud.** Manhattan's who's who in business, politics, and the art
FRENCH world come to hobnob at this café in name only. The food and service are top-notch at Daniel Boulud's conservative (but not stuffy) restaurant in the Surrey Hotel, which recently underwent a sumptuous renovation. The menu, overseen by Boulud protégé Gavin Kaysen, is divided into four parts: under La Tradition you can find classic French dishes such as roasted duck breast Montmorency with cherry chutney, green Swiss chard, and baby turnips; Le Potager tempts with lemon ricotta ravioli; La Saison follows the rhythms of the season; and Le Voyage reinterprets cuisines of the world. If tables are booked, start out with a drink at the chic Bar Pleiades. ☒ *20 E. 76th St., between 5th and Madison Av es., Upper East Side* ☎ *212/772–2600* ⊕ *www.danielnyc.com* ⌥ *Reservations essential* ═ *AE, DC, MC, V* Ⓜ *6 to 77th St.* ✛ *5:F3.*

$$ ✕ **Café d'Alsace.** Unusually comfortable burgundy banquettes, huge
BRASSERIE antiqued mirrors, and low lighting that makes everyone look fabulous characterize this Alsatian gem. Start with a house cocktail—say, L'Alsacien, in which the aperitif Belle de Brillet meets cognac, pear, and fresh lemon in a happy union. Standouts include the *tarte flambé*, a *fromage-blanc*–topped flat bread scattered with tawny caramelized onions and hunks of bacon. The *choucroute garnie* entrée comes in a cast-iron kettle that keeps it piping hot for the entire meal. Sausages, smoked pork breast, and pork belly are so carefully braised that everything comes out in perfect harmony. Delicious bread pudding is studded with strawberries. ☒ *1695 2nd Ave., at E. 88th St., Upper East Side* ☎ *212/722–5133* ⊕ *www.cafedalsace.com* ═ *AE, MC, V* Ⓜ *4, 5, 6 to 86th St.* ✛ *6:G6.*

$$ ✕ **Candle 79.** The Upper East Side may seem like an unlikely place for
VEGETARIAN gourmet vegan fare, but the people behind Candle 79 have lighted upon
Fodor's Choice a formula that would work in any neighborhood. The elegant, bi-level
★ space, done up in warm, autumnal tones with touches of wood and rich fabric, is far from the health-food stereotype. Try for a second-floor table overlooking the street, and refresh yourself with a house-made elixir made with fresh grated ginger, agave nectar, and lime that will forever convert you from the canned alternative. Appetizers like rice balls with tempeh bacon may sound like hippie throwbacks, but they taste more like well-executed trattoria fare. Signature dishes include the seitan piccata, which replaces the usual protein with a vegetarian substitute and is so well made and well seasoned that you would never miss the meat. Salads, soups, desserts, and entrées are all stunningly fresh and made with local, organic, seasonal produce. There's also an impressive

list of organic wines and sakes. ☒ *154 E. 79th St., at Lexington Ave., Upper East Side* ☎ *212/537–7179* 🌐 *www.candle79.com* ✍ *Reservations essential* ▭ *AE, MC, V* Ⓜ *6 to 77th St./Lexington Ave.* ✣ *5:G2.*

$ MEXICAN ✕ **Cascabel Taqueria.** One of New York's best-rated taqueria's resides in an unexpected neighborhood. At Cascabel, the wrestling-theme decor is a whimsical backdrop for some seriously delicious, reasonably priced Mexican food—something sorely lacking in New York, and especially on the Upper East Side. Tacos, which come two to an order, are inventive without veering too far from the comfort-food norm. The *camaron* scatters plump roasted wild shrimp among fresh oregano, garlic oil, and black beans. The beef tongue is slow braised, then topped with spring onion and serrano chilies, nothing like the stuff you'll find in a deli sandwich containing the same principal ingredient. There's also fresh, creamy guacamole with house-fried chips, pert tortilla soup with *queso fresco* cheese and chicken, and dinner-only platters like adobe-marinated Berkshire pork butt with cucumbers and an alluring onion-tamarind mixture. At lunchtime, one of Cascabel's sandwiches—shredded chicken with mango and smashed avocado, for one—hits the spot with an ice-cold Mexican brew. Inside seating is limited, but in temperate weather the outdoor tables expand your possibilities. ☒ *1538 2nd Ave., between 80th and 81st Sts., Upper East Side* ☎ *212/717–8226* 🌐 *www.nyctacos.com* ▭ *AE, MC, V* ⏲ *No dinner Sun.* ✣ *5:H2.*

$$$$ FRENCH Fodor's Choice ★ ✕ **Daniel.** Celebrity-chef Daniel Boulud has created one of the most elegant dining experiences in Manhattan today, in an expansive space that recently underwent a multimillion-dollar renovation. The prix-fixe–only menu (there are à la carte selections in the elegant lounge and bar) is predominantly French, with such modern classics as turbot on Himalayan salt with an ale-and-gingerbread sauce, and a duo of dry-aged Angus black beef featuring meltingly tender red wine–braised short ribs and seared rib eye with black trumpet mushrooms and Gorgonzola cream. Equally impressive are the serious artwork, professional service, extensive wine list, and masterful cocktails by Xavier, one of the city's most respected mixologists. Don't forget the decadent desserts and overflowing cheese trolley. A three-course vegetarian menu is also available. ☒ *60 E. 65th St., between Madison and Park Aves., Upper East Side* ☎ *212/288–0033* 🌐 *www.danielnyc.com* ✍ *Reservations essential* 🧥 *Jacket required* ▭ *AE, DC, MC, V* ⏲ *Closed Sun. No lunch* Ⓜ *6 to 68th St./Hunter College* ✣ *5:F5.*

$$$ MEXICAN ✕ **Maya.** The upscale-hacienda appearance of this justifiably popular restaurant showcases some of the best Mexican food in the city, courtesy of pioneering Mexican chef Richard Sandoval. Begin with a fresh mango mojito, then tuck into delicious roasted corn soup with huitlacoche dumplings, stuffed poblano peppers, and smoky filet mignon taco with jalapeño escabeche. Finish with caramelized goat's-milk crepes and cinnamon ice cream, and you'll leave wearing a big grin. ☒ *1191 1st Ave., between E. 64th and E. 65th Sts., Upper East Side* ☎ *212/585–1818* 🌐 *www.modernmexican.com/mayany* ✍ *Reservations essential* ▭ *AE, D, DC, MC, V* ⏲ *No lunch* Ⓜ *6 to 68th St./Hunter College* ✣ *5:H5.*

18

$$$ ✕**Park Avenue Summer/Autumn/Winter/Spring.** New York's most self-
AMERICAN consciously seasonal restaurant swaps out much more than its menu
as temperatures change. Four times a year the restaurant—the formerly
staid Park Avenue Café—shuts its doors for a head-to-toe makeover,
switching, for instance, from a summery blond-wood beach-house
motif to dark-wood-and-copper fall-foliage tones. Chef Craig Koketsu's
seasonal food lives up to the striking surroundings. Summer brings a
bounty of fresh-shucked corn, with a big, juicy veal chop and heirloom
tomatoes. Come autumn the kitchen turns its focus to mushrooms, truf-
fles (on a flaky halibut fillet accompanied by a brioche-crusted poached
egg), and game (local quail, big venison chops scattered with pome-
granate and pumpkin seeds). Desserts, by award-winning pastry chef
Richard Leach, include hard-to-resist elegant creations like sweet-corn
ice cream with rhubarb, warm caramel, and popcorn. ⊠ *100 E. 63rd
St., at Park Ave., Upper East Side* ☎ *212/644–1900* ⊕ *www.parkavenyc.
com* ⌂ *Reservations essential* ⊟ *AE, D, DC, MC, V* Ⓜ *F to Lexington
Ave./63rd St.; 4, 5, 6 to 59th St.; N, R to 5th Ave./59th St.* ✛ *5:F6.*

$$$ ✕**Sushi of Gari.** Options at this popular sushi restaurant range from the
JAPANESE ordinary (California roll) to such exotic choices as tuna with creamy
tofu sauce, miso-marinated cod, or Japanese yellowtail with jalapeño.
Japanese noodles (udon or soba) and meat dishes such as teriyaki and
negimaki (scallions rolled in thinly sliced beef) are well prepared. Reservations are recommended. Another location at 370 Columbus Avenue
gives Upper West Siders their udon fix. ⊠ *402 E. 78th St., at 1st Ave.,
Upper East Side* ☎ *212/517–5340* ⊕ *www.sushiofgari.com* ⊟ *AE, MC,
V* ⊙ *No lunch* Ⓜ *6 to 77th St.* ✛ *5:H2.*

UPPER WEST SIDE

$$$$ ✕**Asiate.** The unparalleled view is reason enough to visit Asiate's pris-
ASIAN tine dining room, perched on the 35th floor of the Time Warner Center
in the Mandarin Oriental Hotel. Artfully positioned tables and minimalist decor help direct eyes to the windows, which peer over Central
Park. At night crystalline lights reflect in the glass, creating a magical
effect. Young chef Brandon Kida creates contemporary dishes with an
Asian influence. One of his signature dishes is soba noodles with Osetra
caviar and wasabi cream; another standout is Wagyu beef tenderloin
with smoked potato puree and braised short rib. Professional, attentive service helps foster an atmosphere of dreamlike luxury. The restaurant offers prix-fixe menus only, and an illustrious wine collection
housing 2,000 bottles. ⊠ *Time Warner Center, 80 Columbus Circle,
35th fl., at W. 60th St., Upper West Side* ☎ *212/805–8881* ⊕ *www.
mandarinoriental.com/newyork/dining/asiate* ⊟ *AE, D, DC, MC, V*
Ⓜ *A, B, C, D, 1 to 59th St./Columbus Circle* ✛ *5:C6.*

$$ ✕**Bar Boulud.** Acclaimed French chef Daniel Boulud, known for upscale
FRENCH New York City eateries Daniel and Café Boulud, shows diners his more
Fodor'sChoice casual side with this lively contemporary bistro and wine bar. The long,
★ narrow space accommodates 100 people and has a 14-seat round table
for special wine-theme tastings. An additional level has three rooms for
larger parties. The menu emphasizes charcuterie, including terrines and
pâtés designed by Parisian charcutier Gilles Verot, who relocated just to

work with Boulud, as well as traditional French bistro dishes like steak frîtes and *poulet rôti à l'ail* (roast chicken with garlic mashed potatoes). The 500-bottle wine list is heavy on wines from Burgundy and the Rhône Valley. Wallet watchers won't feel left out: a pretheater three-course menu starts at $42, and weekend brunch has two hearty courses plus coffee and dessert for $42. ✉ *1900 Broadway, between 63rd and 64th Sts., Upper West Side* ☎ *212/595–0303* ⊕ *www.barboulud.com* ⊟ *AE, DC, MC, V* Ⓜ *1 to 66th St./Lincoln Center; 1, A, C, B, D to 59th St./Columbus Circle* ✛ *5:B5.*

$ ✕ **Barney Greengrass.** At this New York Jewish landmark brusque wait-
DELI   ers send out stellar smoked salmon, sturgeon, and whitefish to a happy crowd packed to the gills at small Formica tables. Split a fish plat-ter with bagels, cream cheese, and other fixings, or get your velvety nova scrambled with eggs and buttery caramelized onions. If you're still hungry, go for a plate of cheese blintzes or the to-die-for chopped liver. Beware: the weekend brunch wait can exceed an hour. ✉ *541 Amsterdam Ave., between W. 86th and W. 87th Sts., Upper West Side* ☎ *212/724–4707* ⊕ *www.barneygreengrass.com* ⌂ *Reservations not accepted* ⊟ *No credit cards* ⊙ *Closed Mon. No dinner* Ⓜ *1, B, C to 86th St.* ✛ *6:B6.*

$ ✕ **Big Nick's.** This cramped, 24-hour neighborhood diner is decorated
DINER   with photographs of the celebrities who've visited, but the primary draw is the burgers, which are huge and juicy. The endless menu lists every conceivable burger topping, from avocado and bacon to Greek tzatziki sauce. The classic Bistro Burger has mushrooms, Swiss, and fried onions on toasted challah bread. ✉ *2175 Broadway, between W. 76th and W. 77th Sts., Upper West Side* ☎ *212/362–9238* ⊕ *www.bignicksnyc.com* ⊟ *MC, V* Ⓜ *1 to 79th St.; 1, 2, 3 to 72nd St.* ✛ *5:A3.*

$ ✕ **Bouchon Bakery.** Never mind that you're in the middle of a shopping
CAFÉ   mall under a Samsung sign, soups and sandwiches don't get much more luxurious than this. Acclaimed chef Thomas Keller's low-key lunch spot (one floor down from his extravagant flagship, Per Se) draws long lines for good reason. Share a mason jar of salmon rillettes—an unctuous spread of cooked and smoked salmon folded around crème fraîche and butter—then move on to one of the fork-and-knife open-faced tartines, like the tuna niçoise. When a sandwich has this much pedigree, $13.50 is actually a bargain. Grab dessert to go, a fresh macaroon or éclair, from the nearby bakery window. ✉ *10 Columbus Circle, 3rd fl., at 60th St., Upper West Side* ☎ *212/823–9366* ⊕ *www.bouchonbakery. com* ⊟ *AE, MC, V* Ⓜ *1, A, B, C, D to 59th St./Columbus Circle* ✛ *5:C6.*

$$$ ✕ **Café Luxembourg.** The old soul of the Lincoln Center neighborhood
BRASSERIE   seems to inhabit the tiled and mirrored walls of this lively, cramped restaurant, where West End Avenue regulars—including lots of on-air talent from nearby ABC News—are greeted with kisses, and musicians and audience members pack the room after a concert. The bar's always hopping, and the menu (served until 11 pm Sunday through Tuesday and until midnight from Wednesday through Saturday) includes dishes like steak tartare and lobster roll alongside dishes with a more con-temporary spin like pan-seared trout with haricots verts, hazelnuts, and tomato-caper compote. ✉ *200 W. 70th St., between Amsterdam*

18

and West End Aves., Upper West Side ☎212/873–7411 ⊕*www.cafeluxembourg.com* ⚭ *Reservations essential* ⊟*AE, DC, MC, V* Ⓜ*1, 2, 3, B, C to 72nd St.* ✛*5:A4.*

$$
ITALIAN
☺

✕**Carmine's.** Set on a nondescript block of Broadway, this branch of the Italian family-style mainstay is a favorite for families celebrating special occasions, pre-prom groups of teens, and plain old folks who come for the tried-and-true menu items like fried calamari, linguine with white clam sauce, chicken parmigiana, and veal saltimbocca, all served in mountainous portions. Family photos line the walls, there's a groaning antipasti table filled with savory meats, cheese, and salads, and there's a convivial feeling amid the organized chaos. On weekends, only parties of six or more can make dinner reservations. ⊠*2450 Broadway, between 90th and 91st Sts., Upper West Side* ☎212/362–2200 ⊕*www.carminesnyc.com* ⊟*AE, D, DC, MC, V* Ⓜ*1, 2, 3, to 96th St./Broadway* ✛*6:5A.*

$$$$
AMERICAN

✕**Dovetail.** Inside Dovetail, chef-owner John Fraser's subdued town house and restaurant, cream-color walls and maple panels create a warm, soothing atmosphere, and a recent expansion allows for more dining-room space and a larger bar area. The menu, which changes daily, features refined but hearty dishes. Seek solace from winter temperatures with the earthy gnocchi topped with matsutake mushrooms, poppy seeds, and lemon. Tender lamb is heightened by potatoes, artichokes, and olives. The savory feast continues with pastry chef Michael Shelkowitz's Earl Grey pumpkin cake with lemon curd and cinnamon-toast ice cream. ⊠*103 W. 77th St., at Columbus Ave., Upper West Side* ☎212/362–3800 ⊕*www.dovetailnyc.com* ⊟*AE, DC, MC, V* ☉*No lunch Mon.–Thurs., Sat., or Sun.* Ⓜ*1 to 79th St.; B, C to 81st St./Museum of Natural History* ✛*5:B3.*

$
MALAYSIAN
☺

✕**Fatty Crab.** The uptown branch of Zac Pelaccio's downtown Malaysian street-food joint has two major advantages over its downtown sibling: more seats and a reservations line. Other than that, the menu mimics the Hudson Street locale's laundry list of crowd-pleasing favorites, like coconut-rich short rib Rendang and soft buns filled with Berkshire pork, cilantro, and savory sauce. Perhaps in deference to the child-toting population in the neighborhood, there's spacious outdoor seating perfect for parking strollers. ⊠*2170 Broadway between 76th and 77th Sts., Upper West Side* ☎212/496–2722 ⊕*www.fattycrab.com* ⊟*AE, D, MC, V* Ⓜ*1 to 79th St./Broadway* ✛*5:A3.*

$$$$
FRENCH

✕**Jean Georges.** This culinary temple in the Trump International Hotel and Towers focuses wholly on *chef celebre* Jean-Georges Vongerichten's spectacular creations. Some approach the limits of the taste universe, like foie-gras brûlée with spiced fig jam and ice-wine reduction. Others are models of simplicity, like slow-cooked cod with warm vegetable vinaigrette. Exceedingly personalized service and a well-selected wine list contribute to an unforgettable meal, as do tattooed celeb pastry chef Johnny Iuzzini's rock-and-roll desserts, like a lemon ice cream filled with house-made pop rocks. For Jean Georges on a budget, try the prix-fixe lunch in the front room, Nougatine. ⊠*1 Central Park W, at W. 59th St., Upper West Side* ☎212/299–3900 ⊕*www.jean-georges.com* ⚭*Reser-*

vations essential 🏛 *Jacket required* ▭ *AE, DC, MC, V* ☾ *Closed Sun.*
Ⓜ *A, B, C, D, 1 to 59th St./Columbus Circle* ⊹ *5:C6.*

$ ╳ **Kefi.** Michael Psilakis's homage to his grandmother's Greek cook-
GREEK ing has moved to an expansive space a few blocks north of the now-
closed original location. Among the mezes, the meatballs with roasted
garlic, olives, and tomato is a standout; the flavorful roast chicken,
potatoes, red peppers, garlic, and thyme makes for a winning entrée,
and the béchamel-rich Kefi mac 'n cheese is irresistible. Reasonable
prices—appetizers are no more than $9.95, and main courses max out
at $16.95—make it easy to stick around for a piece of traditional walnut
cake with walnut ice cream. ✉ *505 Columbus Ave., between 84th and
85th Sts., Upper West Side* ☎ *212/873–0200* ▭ *AE, DC, MC, V* ☾ *No
lunch Mon.* Ⓜ *1 to 86th St.; B, C to 86th St.* ⊹ *5:B1.*

$$$$ ╳ **Marea.** Carefully sourced, meticulously prepared fish and seafood
SEAFOOD take center stage at this glossy, well-pedigreed restaurant. Large pic-
Fodor's Choice ture windows in the dining room offer expansive views of Central Park
★ South, and silver-dipped shells on pedestals decorate the dining room.
No expense is spared in importing the very best of the ocean's bounty,
beginning with an entire menu of raw *crudo* dishes—think scallops
with orange, wild fennel, and arugula—that is rapidly becoming the
restaurant's signature and can be enjoyed in the main dining room
or an eight-seat bar at the end of the front room's shimmering onyx
wall. You'd be remiss, though, if you skipped the pastas that made
chef Michael White famous at the now-closed Convivio (and at his
expanding empire, which includes Osteria Morini in NoLIta and Ai
Fiori in the new Setai Hotel). They're served here in lusty iterations
like rich fusilli with octopus and bone marrow and spaghetti with
sea urchin. Whole fish like roasted turbot and salt-baked snapper are
equally showstopping. Service is flawless, and even the dishware—scalloped china embossed with the restaurant's name and tiny shell-shape
espresso cups—is special. ✉ *240 Central Park S, between Broadway
and 7th Ave., Midtown West* ☎ *212/582–5100* ⊕ *www.marea-nyc.com*
⌂ *Reservations essential* ▭ *AE, MC, V* Ⓜ *A, B, C, D, 1 to Columbus
Circle* ⊹ *4:B1.*

$$$$ ╳ **Per Se.** The New York interpretation of what many consider America's
AMERICAN finest restaurant, Napa Valley's French Laundry, Per Se is chef Thomas
Fodor's Choice Keller's Broadway stage. Keller equally embraces French technique, a
★ religious fervor for seasonality, and a witty playfulness that speaks to
his confidence in the kitchen. The large dining room is understated and
elegant, with touches of wood, towering florals, and—the best design
touch of all—sweeping windows with views of Central Park. Keller's
dishes are now world-renowned, such as his tiny cones of tuna tartare topped with crème fraiche, and "oysters and pearls," delicate tiny
mollusks suspended in a creamy custard with tapioca. Dessert service
is a multicourse celebration of all things sweet, including a choice of
27 house-made chocolates and, of course, treats to take home. Waiters, who can, and may, recite the provenance of the tiniest turnip, are
also some of the nicest, most disarming servers in town. There's also a
new à la carte "salon" menu available in the front bar room, but let's
face it: if you manage to snag a reservation, there's nothing else to do

18

but submit to the $275 prix-fixe. ⊠ *Time Warner Center, 10 Columbus Circle, 4th fl., at W. 60th St., Upper West Side* ☎ *212/823–9335* ⊕ *www.perseny.com* ⌁ *Reservations essential* ⌂ *Jacket required* ▭ *AE, MC, V* ⊗ *No lunch Mon.–Thurs.* Ⓜ *A, B, C, D, 1 to 59th St./Columbus Circle* ✛ *5:C6.*

$$$$
MEDITERRANEAN

✕ **Picholine.** Having undergone a spiffy renovation in recent years, Terrence Brennan's classic French restaurant, done up in tones of eggplant and lavender, still has a dignified atmosphere, but it's now caught up with the times. His kitchen maintains a strong emphasis on contemporary Mediterranean cuisine and relies conspicuously on artisanal farmers and food producers. The menu is divided into four relatively small sections: Preludes, Pastas, Day Boats, and the Land, and you are invited to construct your own tasting by selecting three or four sections. The kitchen's spin on chicken Kiev is particularly brilliant: an heirloom chicken breast is pressed into a fat juicy tube and rolled in crushed cornflakes before it is deep-fried. Slice into the soft cylinder and it spills its luscious "liquid foie gras" filling. Don't miss the famous cheese course, which Brennan practically invented here. There's also a more limited three-course pretheater prix-fixe for $58, one of the best deals in the neighborhood. ⊠ *35 W. 64th St., between Broadway and Central Park W, Upper West Side* ☎ *212/724–8585* ⊕ *www.picholinenyc.com* ⌁ *Reservations essential* ▭ *AE, DC, MC, V* ⊗ *No lunch. Closed Sun.* Ⓜ *1 to 66th St./Lincoln Center* ✛ *5:C5.*

$$$$
STEAKHOUSE

✕ **Porter House.** With clubby interiors by Jeffrey Beers and an adjoining lounge area, Porter House marks the splashy return to the scene of former Windows on the World chef Michael Lomonaco. Filling the meat-and-potatoes slot in the Time Warner Center's upscale "Restaurant Collection," the masculine throwback highlights American wines and pedigreed super-size meat. The neighborhood, long underserved on the steak-house front, has quickly warmed to Lomonaco's simple, solid American fare. Begin with his smoky clams casino or rich roasted marrow bones. Steaks are huge and expertly seasoned, and come with the usual battery of à la carte sides—creamed spinach, roasted mushrooms, and truffle mashed potatoes. ⊠ *10 Columbus Circle, 4th fl., at 60th St., Upper West Side* ☎ *212/823–9500* ⊕ *www.porterhousenewyork.com* ▭ *AE, MC, V* Ⓜ *1, A, B, C, D to 59th St./Columbus Circle* ✛ *5:C6.*

$
ITALIAN

✕ **Salumeria Rosi.** Just up the block from Gray's Papaya sits this compact temple to a whole different subset of cured meats. Chef Cesare Casella has created a showcase for dozens of varieties of prosciutto, coppa, mortadella, and more, carved from a professional slicer for consumption on the spot or as indulgent takeout from the immaculate glass-walled display case. There's also a more ambitious menu, including a salad of arugula and lemon with Parmesan, and a lusty osso buco over creamy mashed potatoes. If you're lucky, you may catch a glimpse of the avuncular chef with his signature rosemary sprig peeking out from his breast pocket. ⊠ *283 Amsterdam Ave., between 73rd and 74th Sts., Upper West Side* ☎ *212/877–4700* ⊕ *www.salumeriarosi.com* ▭ *AE, D, MC, V* Ⓜ *1 to 79th St./Broadway* ✛ *5:B3.*

$$
AMERICAN

✕ **Sarabeth's.** Lining up for brunch here is as much an Upper West Side tradition as taking a sunny Sunday afternoon stroll in nearby Riverside

Park. Locals love the bric-a-brac–filled restaurant for sweet morning-time dishes like lemon ricotta pancakes, as well as for the comforting dinners. The afternoon tea includes buttery scones with Sarabeth's signature jams, savory nibbles, and outstanding baked goods. Dinner entrées include chicken potpie and truffle mac 'n cheese. ☒ *423 Amsterdam Ave., at W. 80th St., Upper West Side* ☎ *212/496–6280* ⊕ *www.sarabeth.com* ▭ *AE, D, DC, MC, V* Ⓜ *1 to 79th St.* ✛ *5:B2*

¢ ✗**Shake Shack.** Local restaurant legend Danny Meyer has gone a little low-brow with his fast-ish food venture, Shake Shack—and New Yorkers are loving it. The Upper West Side Shack is an eat-in joint just across Columbus Avenue from the American Museum of Natural History. Although the lines may be long at lunchtime, the grub is good and well priced. Fresh steer burgers are ground daily, and a single will run you from $3.75 to $4.75, depending on what you want on it. For a few more bucks you can also order doubles and stacks or a vegetarian 'Shroom Burger—a melty Muenster and cheddar cheese–stuffed portobello. The Shake Shack also offers beef and bird (chicken) hot dogs, french fries, and a variety of delicious frozen custard desserts and—of course—thick shakes! ☒ *366 Columbus Ave., at W. 77th St., Upper West Side* ☎ *646/747–8770* ⊕ *www.shakeshacknyc.com* ▭ *AE, D, MC, V* Ⓜ *B, C to 81st St.* ✛ *5:B2*.

BURGER
Fodor's Choice
★

$$$ ✗**Telepan.** Chef-owner Bill Telepan is a regular at the neighborhood greenmarket, and it shows in his seasonal, produce-driven menu, which is divided into three courses: appetizers of salads, light fish dishes, and soups; middle courses of eggs, pasta, or vegetables; and main courses of meat and fish. A trio of tiny *amuses-bouches* such as wild mushroom cappuccino arrives to tease your palate, and the servers are refreshingly well versed on the wine list. The menu features brook trout, served on celery-root blini with green-apple sour cream, a well-deserved favorite, as is anything on the menu that contains eggs, like the "egg-in-a-hole" served with spinach and hen-of-the-woods mushrooms. For dessert, a crunchy peanut-butter and milk-chocolate *gianduja* duo with peanut-brittle ice cream is sublime. ☒ *72 W. 69th St., between Columbus Ave. and Central Park W, Upper West Side* ☎ *212/580–4300* ⊕ *www.telepan-ny.com* ▭ *AE, D, DC, MC, V* ☼ *No lunch Mon. and Tues.* Ⓜ *1 to 66th St./Lincoln Center; 1, 2, 3 to 72nd St.; B, C to 72nd St.* ✛ *5:B4*.

AMERICAN

18

HARLEM

$ ✗**Dinosaur Bar-B-Que.** New York's reputation for inferior barbecue improved instantly when John Stage opened the third outpost of his Syracuse-based joint in 2004, installing it in a riverside meatpacking warehouse in Harlem. Now Dinosaur has moved a block away to a larger location with capacious bar seating perfect for downing a plate of knockout wings and a tall beer. Here the city's friendliest waitstaff serves piled-high plates of pulled pork, ribs, chicken, and brisket. A well-stocked bar corrals the Columbia students and worn-out shoppers from the nearby Fairway supermarket. ☒ *646 W. 131st St., at 12th Ave., Harlem* ☎ *212/694–1777* ⊕ *www.dinosaurbarbque.com* ▭ *AE, D, DC, MC, V* Ⓜ *1 to 125th St.* ✛ *6:A2*.

BARBECUE

$$ ✕ **Red Rooster Harlem.** Chef Marcus Samuelsson has fulfilled a longtime
AMERICAN   dream of opening an uptown restaurant—and hopes to spark a foodie's
Harlem Renaissance. Red Rooster is an homage to Samuelsson's poly-
glot history—he's of Ethiopian descent, was raised by Swedish parents,
and earned his culinary stripes in New York City—and a welcome
addition to the Harlem dining scene. Try to get seated in the light-filled
upstairs room, with its distinctive round bar bustling open kitchen in
back, and works from local artists on the wall. The food is a love letter
to Saumelsson's birthplace and adoptive homes—the nut mix on the
bar includes crisped bits of Ethiopian injera bread, fennel-laced, house-
cured gravlax that would make any Swedish mother proud, and a fried
"yardbird" features enough crunch to please regulars at soul-food clas-
sic Sylvia's next door. Expect a wait for Sunday brunch, which features
gospel music and boozy, strong cocktails, and modern takes on dishes
like chicken and waffles. ✉ *310 Lenox Ave., between 125th and 126th
Sts., Harlem* ☎ *212/92-9001* ⊕ *www.redroosterharlem.com* ▭ *AE, MC,
V* Ⓜ *2,3 to 125th St.* ✛ *6:D1.*

New York City
Dining and
Lodging Atlas

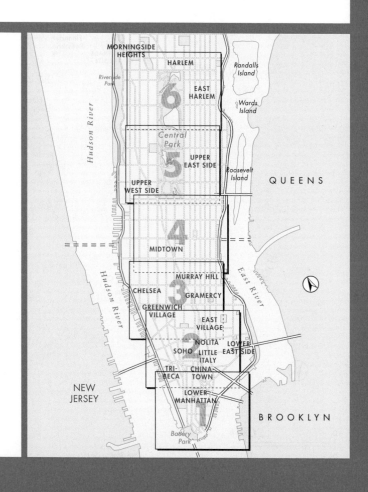

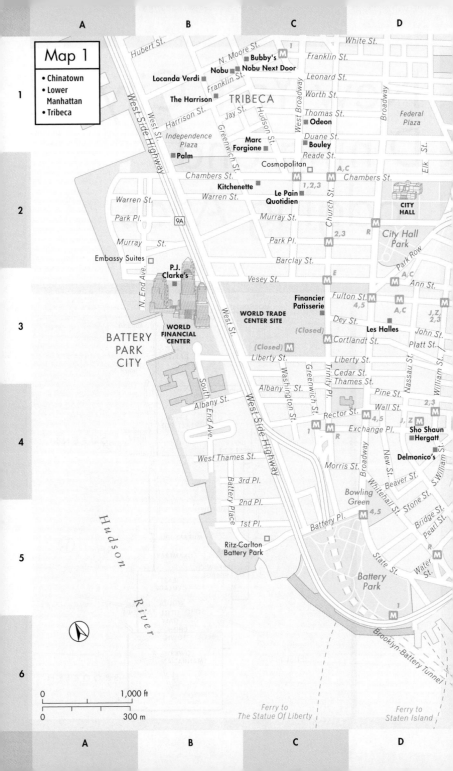

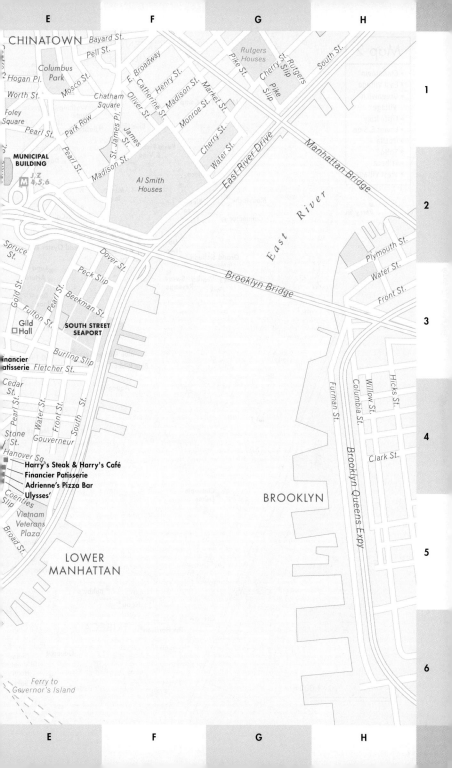

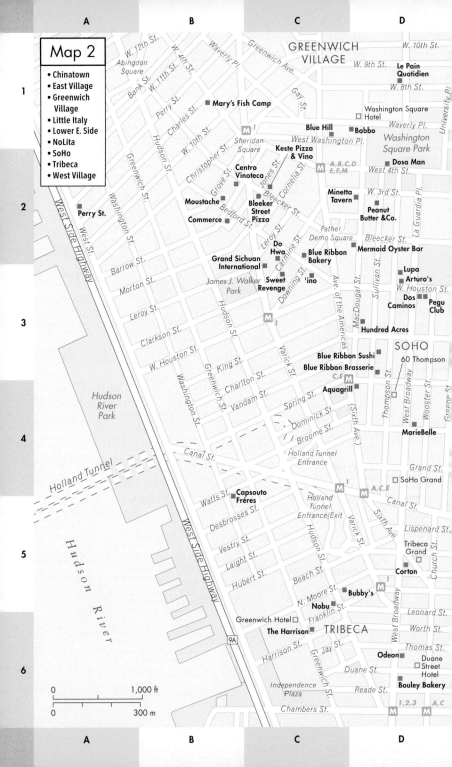

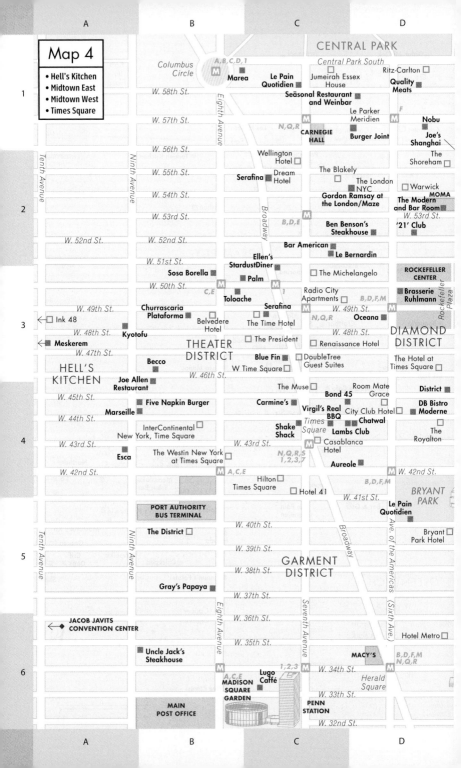

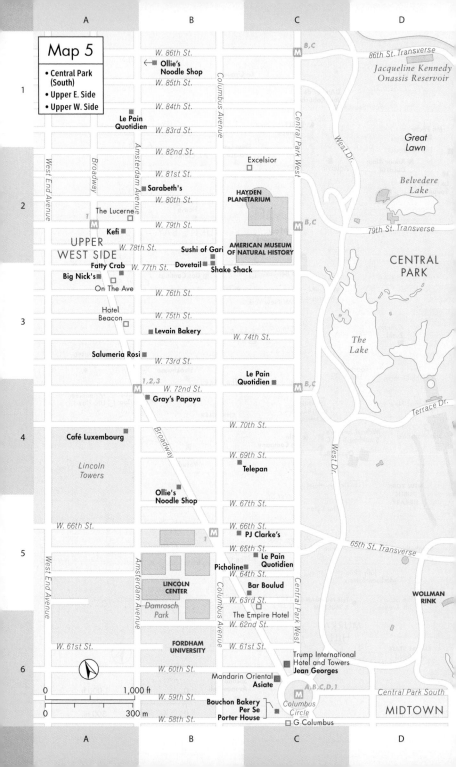

Map 5

- Central Park (South)
- Upper E. Side
- Upper W. Side

A **B** **C** **D**

W. 86th St.

← Ollie's Noodle Shop

W. 85th St.

86th St. Transverse

Jacqueline Kennedy Onassis Reservoir

W. 84th St.

Le Pain Quotidien

W. 83rd St.

Great Lawn

W. 82nd St.

West Dr.

Excelsior

W. 81st St.

Belvedere Lake

Sarabeth's

HAYDEN PLANETARIUM

W. 80th St.

The Lucerne

W. 79th St.

79th St. Transverse

Kefi

UPPER WEST SIDE

W. 78th St.

Sushi of Gari

AMERICAN MUSEUM OF NATURAL HISTORY

CENTRAL PARK

W. 77th St.

Dovetail

Shake Shack

Fatty Crab

Big Nick's

On The Ave

W. 76th St.

Hotel Beacon

W. 75th St.

The Lake

Levain Bakery

W. 74th St.

Salumeria Rosi

W. 73rd St.

Broadway

1, 2, 3

W. 72nd St.

Le Pain Quotidien

Terrace Dr.

Gray's Papaya

W. 70th St.

Café Luxembourg

W. 69th St.

Lincoln Towers

Telepan

West Dr.

W. 67th St.

Ollie's Noodle Shop

W. 66th St.

65th St. Transverse

PJ Clarke's

W. 65th St.

Le Pain Quotidien

Picholine

WOLLMAN RINK

LINCOLN CENTER

W. 64th St.

Bar Boulud

W. 63rd St.

Damrosch Park

The Empire Hotel

W. 62nd St.

FORDHAM UNIVERSITY

W. 61st St.

W. 60th St.

Trump International Hotel and Towers

Jean Georges

Mandarin Oriental

Asiate

A, B, C, D, 1

Central Park South

W. 59th St.

Columbus Circle

MIDTOWN

Bouchon Bakery
Per Se
Porter House

W. 58th St.

G Columbus

0 — 1,000 ft

0 — 300 m

West End Avenue

Amsterdam Avenue

Columbus Avenue

Central Park West

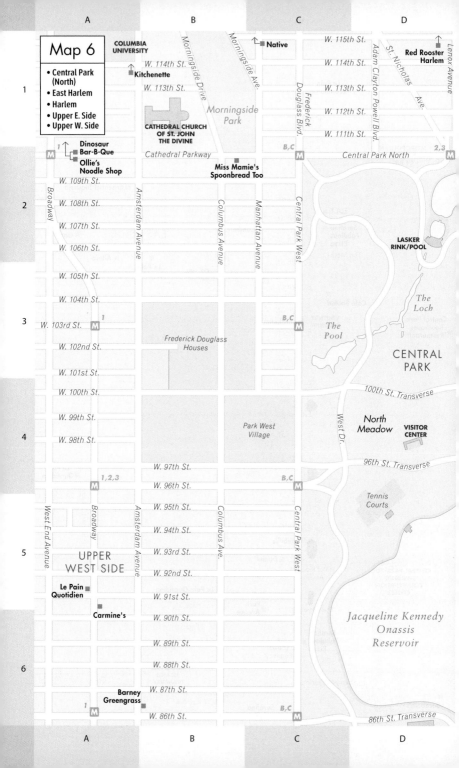

Dining

ABC Kitchen, 3:F3
A Voce, 3:F2
Adour Alan Ducasse, 4:E2
Aldea, 3:E4
Alloro, 5:H2
Apiary, 3:G5
Aquagrill, 2:D4
Aquavit, 4:F2
Artisanal, 3:F1
Arturo's, 2:D3
Asiate, 5:C6
August, 3:C6
Aureole, 3:D4
Babbo, 2:C1
Back Forty, 3:H4
Bagatelle, 3:B4
Baoguette, 2:F1
Balthazar, 2:E4
Bar Americain, 4:C2
Bar Boulud, 5:B5
Barbuto, 3:B5
Barney Greengrass, 6:B6
Becco, 4:B3
Ben Benson's, 4:D2
Big Nick's, 5:A3
BLT Fish, 3:E3
BLT Prime, 3:F3
BLT Steak, 4:F1
Blue Hill, 2:C1
Blue Ribbon Bakery, 2:C2
Blue Ribbon Brasserie, 2:D3
Blue Ribbon Sushi, 2:D3
Blue Smoke, 3:F2
Boqueria, 3:E3
Bouchon Bakery, 5:C6
Brasserie Ruhlmann, 4:D3
Bubby's, 1:C1
Buddakan, 3:B4
Burger Joint, 4:D1
Café Boulud, 5:F3
Café d'Alsace, 6:G6
Café Luxembourg, 5:A4
Candle 79, 5:G2
Carmine's, 6:A5; 4:C4
Casa Mono, 3:G3
Cascabel Taqueria, 5:H2
Centro Vinoteca, 2:B2
Chinatown Brasserie, 2:E2
Churrascaria Plataforma, 4:B3
City Bakery, 3:E3
Commerce, 2:B2
Cookshop, 3:B3
Corton, 2:D5
Craft, 3:F3
Craftbar, 3:F3
Daniel, 5:F5
DB Bistro Moderne, 4:D4
DBGB Kitchen & Bar, 2:F2
dell'anima, 3:C5
Delmonico's, 1:D4
Del Posto, 3:A4
Dinosaur Bar-B-Que, 6:A2
Do Hwa, 2:C2
Dos Caminos, 3:F2;
2:D3; 4;G3

Dovetail, 5:B3
Eisenberg's Sandwich
Shop, 3:E2
Eleven Madison Park, 3:E2
Emporio, TK
Esca, 4:A4
Fatty Crab, 3:C5, 5:A3
Financier Patisserie,
1:E4; 1:C3
Five Napkin Burger, 4:B4
Five Points, 3:G6
Four Seasons, 4:F2
Gahm Mi Oak, 3:E1
Gnocco, 3:H5
Gordon Ramsay at The
London and Maze, 4:D2
Gotham Bar & Grill, 3:E4
Gramercy Tavern, 3:F3
Grand Sichuan, 2:F1
Gray's Papaya, 3LD5
Great New York Noodle-
town, 2:F5
Harrison, The, 2:C6
Harry's Steak and Harry's
Café, 1:E4
Hill Country, 3:E2
Hundred Acres, 2:D3
Il Buco, 2:F2
Ilili, 3:E2
'ino, 2:C3
'inoteca, 2:G3
Irving Mill, 3:F4
Jean Georges, 5:C6
Jewel Bako, 3:G6
Jing Fong, 2:F5
Joe's Shanghai, 2:F5, 4:E2
Katz's Delicatessen, 2:G2
Kefi, 5:B1
Kitchenette, 1:C2; 6:A1
Kuruma Zushi, 4:E3
La Esquina, 2:F4
L'Atelier de Joël Robu-
chon, 4:F1
The Lambs Club, 4:D4
Le Bernardin, 4:C2
Le Cirque, 4:F1
Le Pain Quotidien, 3:F3
Les Halles, 3:F1; 1:D3
Little Owl, The, 3:D6
Locanda Verdi, 2:C5
Lombardi's, 2:F4
Lugo Caffé, 4:C6
Lupa, 2:D2
Lure, 2:E3
Marc Forgione, 1:C1
Marea, 4:B1
MarieBelle, 2:D4; 5:F5
Marseille, 4:B4
Má Peche, 4:E1
Mary's Fish Camp, 2:B1
Maya, 5:H5
Mermaid Oyster Bar, 2:D2
Meskerem, 4:A3
Mexicana Mama, 3:C6
Michael Jordan's The
Steak House NYC, 4:F4
Minetta Tavern, 2:D3
Mint, 4:G3
Modern, The, 4:D2

Momofuko Ko, 3:H5
Momofuko Noodle
Bar, 3:H5
Momofuko Ssäm, 3:H4
Motorino, 3:H4
Moustache, 2:B2
Nha Trang, 2:E5; 2:F5
Nobu, 1:B1, 4:D1
Northern Spy, 3LH4
Oceana, 4:D3
Odeon, 2:D6
Osteria Morini, 2:E3
Oyster Bar, 4:F4
P.J. Clarke's, 1:B3; 4;G2;
5:C5
Palm, 4:G4; 4:B3; 1:B2
Paris Commune, 2:A1
Park Avenue, 5:F6
Pastis, 3:B4
Peasant, 2:F3
Peking Duck House,
2:F5; 4;G2
Per Se, 5:C6
Perry St., 2:A2
Picholine, 5:C5
Ping's Seafood, 2:F6
Porter House, 5:C6
Primehouse New York,
3:F2
Prune, 2:F2
Public, 2:F3
R.U.B. BBQ, 3:D2
Rayuela, 2:G3
Red Rooster Harlem,
6:D1
Republic, 3:F4
Salumeria Rosi, 5:B3
Sarabeth's, 5:B2
Savoy, 2:E4
Scarpetta, 3:B4
Schiller's, 2:G3
SD26, 5:B3
Seäsonal, 4:D1
Second Avenue Deli, 4:G6
Serafina, 4:C2
Shake Shack, 5:B2; 3:F2
SHO Shaun Hergatt, 1:C5
Shun Lee Palace, 4:G2
Sosa Borella, 4:G3
Sparks Steakhouse, 4:G3
Spice Market, 3:B4
Spitzer's Corner, 2:G3
Spotted Pig, 2:A1
Standard Grill, The, 3:B4
Stanton Social, The, 2:G3
Sushi of Gari, 5:H2; 5:B2
Sushi Yasuda, 4:G4
Tabla, 3:F2
Tamarind, 3:F2
Telepan, 5:B4
Tía Pol, 3:A2
Tocqueville, 3:F4
Toloache, 4:B3
Turkish Kitchen, 3:G2
'21' Club, 4:D2
Uncle Jack's, 4:B6
Union Square Cafe, 3:F4
Veniero's Pasticceria, 3:H5
Virgil's Real BBQ, 4:C4

Wallsé, 3:B6
wd~50, 2:H3
Wildwood Barbecue, 3:F3
Woo Lae Oak, 2:E3

Lodging

Ace Hotel, 3:E1
Affinia 50, 4:G3
Alex, The, 4:G4
Algonquin, The, 4:D4
Belvedere Hotel, 4:B3
Benjamin, The, 4:F3
Best Western Seaport
Inn, 1:E3
Blakely, The, 4:C2
Bowery Hotel, The, 2:F2
Bryant Park Hotel, 4:D5
Carlton Arms, 3:G2
Carlton on Madison
Avenue, 3:F1
Carlyle, The, 5:F3
Casablanca Hotel, 4:C4
Chambers, 4:E1
Chelsea Lodge, 3:C3
Chelsea Savoy, 3:C2
City Club Hotel, 4:D4
Cooper Square Hotel,
The, 2:F2
Cosmopolitan, 1:C2
Crosby St. Hotel, 2:E3
DoubleTree Guest Suites
Times Square, 4:C3
Dream Hotel, 4:C2
Duane Street Hotel, 2:D6
Dylan, The, 4:E5
Embassy Suites NY, 1:A2
Empire Hotel, The, 5:C5
Excelsior, 5:C2
Flatotel, 4:C2
Four Seasons, 4:F1
Franklin, The, 6:66
GEM Hotel, The, 3:C3
Gershwin Hotel, 3:E1
Gild Hall, 1:E3
Gramercy Park, 3:G3
Greenwich Hotel, 2:C6
Herald Square Hotel, 3:E1
Hilton New York, 4:D2
Hilton Times Sq, 4:C4
Holiday Inn SoHo, 2:E5
Hotel 41, 4:C4
The Hotel at Times
Square, 4:D3
Hotel Beacon, 5:A3
Hotel Elysée, 4:F2
Hotel Gansevoort, 3:B4
Hotel Giraffe, 3:F2
Hotel Metro, 4:D6
Hotel on Rivington, 2:G3
Hotel Plaza Athénée, 5:F5
Hotel Wales, 6:F5
Ink48, 4:A3
Inn at Irving Place, 3:G3
Inn on 23rd, 3:D2
Iroquois, The, 4:D4
Jane, The, 3:B5
Jolly Hotel Madison, 4:F5
Jumeirah Essex House,
4:C1
Kitano, The, 4:F5

La Quinta Inn, 4:E6
Le Parker Meridien, 4:D1
Library Hotel, 4:E4
Loews Regency, 5:F6
London NYC, The, 4:C2
Lowell, The, 5:F6
Lucerne, The, 5:A2
Mandarin Oriental, 5:C6
Mansfield, The, 4:E4
Marcel at Gramercy, 3:G2
Maritime Hotel, 3:B3
Marriott Marquis, 4:C4
Mercer Hotel, 2:E3
Michelangelo, The, 4:C3
Millennium Hilton, 1:C3
Millennium UN Plaza,
4:H4
Morgans, 4:E5
Muse Hotel, The, 4:C4
New York Palace, 4:E3
Omni Berkshire Place,
4:E2
On the Ave Hotel, 5:A3
Park South Hotel, 3:F2
Peninsula, The, 4:E2
Plaza Hotel, 4:E1
Pod Hotel, 4:G2
Portland Square, 4:C3
President, The, 4:C3
Radio City Apartments,
4C3
Renaissance Hotel, 4:C3
Ritz-Carlton New York,
Battery Park, 1:C5
Ritz-Carlton New York,
Central Park South, 4:D1
Roger Smith, 4:F3
Roger Williams, 3:F1
Room Mate Grace, 4:D4
Roosevelt Hotel, 4:F4
Royalton, The, 4:D4
70 Park Avenue, 4:F5
Sherry-Netherland, 5:E6
Shoreham, The, 4:D2
60 Thompson, 2:D4
Sofitel New York, 4:E4
SoHo Grand, 2:D4
St. Regis, The, 4:E2
Standard, The, 3:B4
Thompson LES, 2:G3
Time Hotel, The, 4:C3
Tribeca Grand, 2:D5
Trump International Hotel
and Towers, 5:C6
W Hotel New York, 4:F3
W New York –The Court,
4:F5
W New York –The Tus-
cany, 4:F5
W New York Union
Square, 3:F3
W Times Square, 4:C3
Waldorf=Astoria, 4:F3
Warwick, 4:D2
Washington Square
Hotel, 2:D1
Wellington Hotel, 4:C2
Westin New York at Times
Square, The, 4:B4
Wolcott Hotel, 3:E1

Where to Stay

WORD OF MOUTH

"Can anyone suggest a decent hotel that would be convenient for the Met, and not cost a fortune?"

—Sue4

"Try the Hotel Wales. My wife stayed there last year for several nights . . . she thought it was a nice boutique hotel."

—Ryan

Updated
by Adeena
Sussman

It's still a buyer's market for hotels here in New York. But does that mean that New York is cheap? Not exactly. Deals are plentiful if you're not set on a specific property. With occupancy down across the city, hotels are slashing rates—especially if you're willing to wait until the last minute. That said, if you want to stay in a specific place and the rate seems reasonable, book it—it's just as likely to go up, especially during peak seasons (spring and fall).

And how to choose? Well, the first thing to consider is location (check out our "Where Should I Stay?" chart on the next page). Many New York City visitors insist on staying in the hectic Midtown area—and options are improving here—but other neighborhoods are often just as convenient. Less touristy areas, such as Gramercy, the Lower East Side, the Upper West Side—even Brooklyn—offer a far more realistic sense of New York life.

Also consider timing: the least expensive months to book rooms in the city are January and February. If you're flexible on dates, ask the reservationist if there's a cheaper time to stay during your preferred traveling month—that way you can avoid peak dates, like Fashion Week and the New York City Marathon. And be sure to ask about possible weekend packages that could include a third night free. (The Financial District in particular can be a discount gold mine on the weekend.)

Another source of bargains? Chain hotels. Many have moved into the city, offering reasonable room rates. In addition to favorites like the Sheraton, Hilton, and Hyatt brands, there are Best Westerns, Days Inns, and Comfort Inns. These rates aren't as low as you'll find outside Manhattan, but they're certainly getting closer.

WHERE SHOULD I STAY?

	NEIGHBORHOOD VIBE	PROS	CONS
Lower Manhattan	Mostly skyscraper hotels in an area that buzzes with activity during weekday hours but can be eerily quiet at night.	Low crime area; easy subway access to uptown sights; great walking paths along the waterfront and in Battery Park.	Construction and congestion near World Trade Center site; limited choice of restaurants and shopping.
SoHo and Little Italy (with NoLIta)	Swanky, high-end hotels with hip restaurants and lounges patronized by New Yorkers and travelers alike.	Scores of upscale clothing boutiques and art galleries nearby; safe area for meandering walks; easy subway access.	Not budget-friendly; streets are crowded on weekends; few major monuments nearby.
Greenwich Village, the West Village and Chelsea (with the Meatpacking District)	More hotels are opening in one of the city's trendiest restaurant and nightlife areas.	Easy subway access to anywhere in town; great shopping, dining, and drinking venues.	Winding streets can be tough to navigate; most hotels are on the pricey side.
Union Square to Murray Hill (with the Flatiron District and Gramercy)	A residential area where you'll get a feel for what it's really like to live in the city.	Patches of calm respite from the hustle-and-bustle of downtown and Midtown; low crime area.	Limited subway access; Gramercy or Murray Hill area may be too quiet for some.
East Village and the Lower East Side	The epicenter of edgy New York, great for travelers looking to party.	Great low-cost options for young adults. Excellent chef-owned restaurants and independent boutiques nearby.	One of the least subway-accessible Manhattan neighborhoods; expect late-night noise.
Midtown	Mostly big-name hotel chains and luxury business suites in the area around Times Square, where out-of-towners tend to congregate.	Near Broadway theaters; easy access to regional trains and most subway lines; budget options are available in chain hotels and indies alike.	Streets are often packed with pedestrians; restaurants are chain-owned and often overpriced; area around Port Authority can feel gritty.
Upper East Side	Well-heeled residential neighborhood with excellent location near many museums.	Removed from Midtown hustle; near tourist attractions like Central Park.	Streets are quiet after 9 pm; few budget dining options; limited subway access (just the 6 line).
Upper West Side	High-priced hotels in a residential neighborhood near Central Park, Lincoln Center, and several museums.	Low crime area; tree-lined streets; great delis and laid-back neighborhood eateries.	Weekend trains can be dreadfully slow; most hotels are on the pricey side.

19

NEW YORK CITY LODGING PLANNER

STRATEGY

Manhattan has hundreds of hotels, so making a choice may seem daunting. But fret not—our expert writers and editors have done most of the legwork. The 120-plus selections here represent the best this city has to offer—from the best budget motels to the sleekest designer hotels. Scan "Best Bets" on the following pages for top recommendations by price and experience. Or find a review quickly in the listings—search by neighborhood, then alphabetically. Happy hunting!

NEED A RESERVATION?

Hotel reservations are an absolute necessity when planning your trip to New York—although rooms are easier to come by these days. Competition for clients also means properties must undergo frequent improvements, especially during July and August, so when booking, ask about any renovations, lest you get a room within earshot of construction. In this ever-changing city travelers can find themselves temporarily, and most inconveniently, without commonplace amenities such as room service or spa access if their hotel is upgrading.

SERVICES

Unless otherwise noted in the individual descriptions, all the hotels listed have private baths, central heating, air-conditioning, and private phones. Almost all hotels have data ports and phones with voice mail, as well as valet service. Many now have wireless Internet (Wi-Fi) available, although it's not always free. Most large hotels have video or high-speed checkout capability, and many can arrange babysitting. Pools are a rarity, but most properties have gyms or health clubs, and sometimes full-scale spas; hotels without facilities usually have arrangements for guests at nearby gyms, sometimes for a fee.

PARKING

Bringing a car to Manhattan can add significantly to your expenses. Many properties in all price ranges do have parking facilities, but they are often at independent garages that charge as much as $20 or more per day, and valet parking can cost up to $60 a day. The city's exorbitant 18.375% parking tax can turn any car you drive into the Big Apple into a lemon.

FAMILY TRAVEL

New York has gone to great lengths to attract family vacationers, and hotels have followed the family-friendly trend. Some properties provide such diversions as Web TV and in-room video games; others have suites with kitchenettes and foldout sofa beds. Most full-service Manhattan hotels provide rollaway beds, babysitting, and stroller rental, but be sure to make arrangements when booking the room, not when you arrive. The hotels that are especially accommodating to those traveling with children are marked with the ☺ symbol.

DOES SIZE MATTER?

If room size is important to you, ask the reservationist how many square feet a room has, not just if it's big. A hotel room in New York is considered quite large if it's 500 square feet. Very large rooms, such as those at the Four Seasons, are 600 square feet. To stay anywhere larger you'll have to get a multiroom suite. Small rooms are a tight 150 to 200 square feet, and sometimes even less. Very small rooms are less than 100 square feet; you'll find these at inns and lodges, and they're sold as a single for only one person. There are studio apartments in the city that are 250 square feet and include a kitchen; 1,000 square feet is considered a huge abode in this very compact and crowded urban playland.

PRICES

There's no denying that New York City hotels are expensive, but rates run the full range. For high-end hotels like the Mandarin Oriental at Central Park, prices start at $895 a night for a standard room in high season, which runs from September through December. At the low end of the spending spectrum, a bunk at the Jane starts at $99 for a single. But don't be put off by the prices printed here—many hotels slash their rates significantly for promotions and Web-only deals.

The price ratings we've printed are based on standard double rooms at high season, excluding holidays. Although we list all the facilities that are available at a property, we don't specify what is included and what costs extra. Those policies are subject to change without notice, so it's always best to ask what's included when you make your reservation.

WHAT IT COSTS				
¢	$	$$	$$$	$$$$
FOR TWO PEOPLE under $150	$150–$299	$300–$449	$450–$600	over $600

Prices are for a standard double room, excluding 14.75% city and state taxes.

USING THE MAPS

Throughout the chapter, you'll see mapping symbols and coordinates (✛ 3:F2) after property names or reviews. To locate the property on a map, turn to the New York City Dining and Lodging Atlas at the end of the Where to Eat chapter. The first number after the ✛ symbol indicates the map number. After that is the property's coordinate on the map grid.

19

HOTEL REVIEWS

Listed alphabetically within neighborhoods. For expanded hotel reviews, visit Fodors.com.

BROOKLYN

$$ 🏨 **New York Marriott at the Brooklyn Bridge.** What Manhattan hotel has room for an Olympic-length lap pool, an 1,100-car garage, and even a dedicated kosher kitchen? Just like many New Yorkers before you, you'll find that one virtue of staying in Brooklyn is all the extra space. **Pros:** near some of New York's hipper neighborhoods; full-service hotel; stylish rooms. **Cons:** on a busy street in downtown Brooklyn. **TripAdvisor:** "wonderful breakfast buffet," "exceptional staff," "first class service." ✉ *333 Adams St., between Johnson and Willoughby*

BEST BETS FOR NEW YORK CITY LODGING

Fodor's offers a selective listing of high-quality lodging experiences in every price range, from the city's best budget motel to its most sophisticated luxury hotel. Here we've compiled our top recommendations by price and experience. The very best properties—in other words, those that provide a particularly remarkable experience in their price range—are designated in the listings with the Fodor's Choice logo.

Fodor'sChoice ★

Ace Hotel, $, p. 499
The Chatwal, $$$$, p. 507
Crosby Street Hotel, $$$, p. 494
Inn at Irving Place, $$, p. 501
Inn on 23rd, $, p. 497
Library Hotel, $$, p. 518
Mandarin Oriental, $$$$, p. 511
The Mark, $$$$, p. 523
The Peninsula, $$$$, p. 519
Plaza Hotel, $$$$, p. 513
Ritz-Carlton New York, Central Park, $$$$, p. 513
The St. Regis, $$$$, p. 520
The Standard, $, p. 499
Thompson LES, $$, p. 496

Best by Price

¢

Best Western President Hotel, p. 505
Carlton Arms, p. 502
La Quinta Inn, p. 510
Pod Hotel, p. 519

$

Ace Hotel, p. 499
Casablanca Hotel, p. 507
Hotel 41, p. 509
Hotel Metro, p. 509
Inn on 23rd, p. 497
Maritime Hotel, p. 497
Room Mate Grace, p. 513
The Standard, p. 499
W Hotel New York, p. 522

$$

Holiday Inn SoHo, p. 494
Inn at Irving Place, p. 501

Library Hotel, p. 518
The Mansfield, p. 511
Thompson LES, p. 496

$$$

Crosby Street Hotel, p. 494
Gramercy Park Hotel, p. 501
The Mercer, p. 494
The Michelangelo, p. 511

$$$$

The Chatwal, p. 507
Mandarin Oriental, p. 511
The Mark, p. 523
Plaza Hotel, p. 513
The Peninsula, p. 519
Ritz-Carlton New York, Central Park, p. 513
The St. Regis, p. 520

Best by Experience

BEST AFTERNOON TEA

The Carlyle, p. 522
The Chatwal, p. 507
Four Seasons, p. 517
Inn at Irving Place, p. 501
London NYC, p. 510
Plaza Hotel, p. 513
The St. Regis, p. 520

BEST BEDS

Four Seasons, p. 517
Ink48, p. 509
Inn at Irving Place, p. 501
The Mark, p. 523
Ritz-Carltons, pp. 492, 513
The Setai, p. 520

BEST FOR BUSINESS

Bryant Park Hotel, p. 507
The Chatwal, p. 507
The Peninsula, p. 519
Ritz-Carlton, Battery Park, p. 492
Trump International Hotel and Towers, p. 526

BEST CELEBRITY RETREAT

Ace Hotel, p. 499
Four Seasons, p. 517
The Mercer, p. 494
The Standard, p. 499

BEST CONCIERGE

Four Seasons, p. 517
Le Parker Meridien, p. 510
The London NYC, p. 510
Mandarin Oriental, p. 511
Ritz-Carlton Battery Park, p. 492

BEST GYM

Le Parker Meridien, p. 510
The London NYC, p. 510
The Mark, p. 523
Trump International Hotel and Towers, p. 526

BEST HIPSTER HOTELS

Ace Hotel, p. 499
Bowery Hotel, p. 495
The Gotham, p. 518
Gramercy Park Hotel, p. 501
The Standard, p. 499
Thompson LES, p. 496

BEST FOR HISTORY BUFFS

The Carlyle, p. 522
The Chatwal, p. 507
Inn at Irving Place, p. 501
Plaza Hotel, p. 513
The St. Regis, p. 520

BEST HOTEL BAR

The Biergarten at the Standard, p. 499
Bemelmans Bar at the Carlyle, p. 522

Breslin Bar at the Ace Hotel, p. 499
King Cole Bar at St. Regis, p. 520
Lobby Bar at the Bowery Hotel, p. 495
Print Lounge at Ink48, p. 509
Rose Bar at the Gramercy Park Hotel, p. 501
Oak Bar at the Plaza Hotel, p. 513

BEST HOTEL RESTAURANT

Asiate at Mandarin Oriental, p. 511
The Breslin and the John Dory at the Ace Hotel, p. 499
Maialino at the Gramercy Park Hotel, p. 501
Jean Georges at Trump International Hotel and Towers, p. 526
L'Atelier de Joël Robuchon at Four Seasons, p. 517
Standard Grill at the Standard, p. 499

BEST FOR KIDS

Ink48, p. 509
Affinia 50, p. 517
Le Parker Meridien, p. 510

BEST LOBBY

Ace Hotel, p. 499
Four Seasons, p. 517
Mandarin Oriental, p. 511
The Peninsula, p. 519
The St. Regis, p. 520

BEST NEIGHBORHOOD EXPERIENCE

The Carlyle, p. 522
The Mark, p. 523
The Franklin, p. 522
Inn at Irving Place, p. 501
The Standard, p. 499

BEST NEW HOTELS

Ace Hotel, p. 499
The Chatwal, p. 507
The Eventi, p. 501
Setai Fifth Avenue, p. 520
The Standard, p. 499
Thompson LES, p. 496

BEST FOR PETS

The Eventi, p. 501
The Carlyle, p. 522
Loews Regency, p. 518
Ritz-Carlton New York, Battery Park, p. 492
Ritz-Carlton New York, Central Park, p. 513
70 Park Avenue, p. 504

BEST POOL

Hotel Gansevoort, p. 499
Mandarin Oriental, p. 511

Millennium UN Plaza, p. 518
The Peninsula, p. 519
Thompson LES, p. 496
Trump International Hotel and Towers, p. 526

BEST-KEPT SECRET

The Franklin, p. 522
Inn at Irving Place, p. 501
Inn on 23rd, p. 497
The Lowell, p. 523

BEST SERVICE

The Carlyle, p. 522
The Chatwal, p. 507
Four Seasons, p. 517
The Peninsula, p. 519
The Mark, p. 523
Plaza Hotel, p. 513
Ritz-Carlton, Battery Park, p. 492

BEST VIEWS

The Carlyle, p. 522
Cooper Square Hotel, p. 495
Ritz Carlton New York, Central Park, p. 513
The Standard, p. 499

MOST ROMANTIC

Inn at Irving Place, p. 501
Library Hotel, p. 518
Ritz-Carlton, Battery Park, p. 492
The Standard, p. 499

19

Sts., Downtown Brooklyn ☎ *718/246–7000 or 888/436–3759* ⊕ *www. marriott.com/nycbk* ⤶ *666 rooms, 25 suites* ⌂ *In-room: a/c, safe, Internet. In-hotel: restaurant, room service, bar, pool, gym, laundry service, Wi-Fi hotspot, parking (paid)* ☰ *AE, D, DC, MC, V* Ⓜ *2, 3, 4, 5 to Borough Hall.*

$–$$ ⊡ **Nu Hotel—Brooklyn.** Sitting atop Smith Street, one of Brooklyn's main drags for nightlife and shopping, the hip-yet-affordable Nu is perfect for visitors seeking a manageable taste of outer-borough New York—and the staff is eager to highlight the neighborhood's charms. **Pros:** great Brooklyn launching pad; knowledgeable staff; fitness center open 24 hours. **Cons:** it's a subway or cab ride to anything in Manhattan; bar area can be a little too quiet; limited in-room amenities. **TripAdvisor:** "clean, spacious, minimalistic rooms," "complimentary continental breakfast," "short to subway." ✉ *85 Smith St., Brooklyn* ☎ *718/852–8585* ⊕ *www.nuhotelbrooklyn.com* ⤶ *3 rooms, 16 suites* ⌂ *In-room: a/c, safe, Wi-Fi. In-hotel: bar, gym, Internet terminal, parking (paid)* ☰ *AE, MC, V* Ⓜ *F to Bergen St.; A, C, G to Hoyt-Schermerhorn.*

LOWER MANHATTAN

FINANCIAL DISTRICT

$$ ⊡ **Gild Hall.** Captains of Industry, here's a boutique hotel for you. Operated by the owners of the successful, chic 60 Thompson Hotel in SoHo, Gild Hall aggressively courts clientele with a Y chromosome: beds have padded leather headboards and tartan throw blankets. **Pros:** central Financial District location; eye-popping lobby; stylish room design. **Cons:** small rooms for the price; untraditional location. **TripAdvisor:** "recommended for business travel," "very nice hotel restaurant," "great sense of customer service." ✉ *15 Gold St., at Platt St., Financial District* ☎ *212/232–7700 or 800/268–0700* ⊕ *www.thompsonhotels.com* ⤶ *126 rooms* ⌂ *In-room: a/c, safe, Wi-Fi. In-hotel: restaurant, room service, bar, laundry service, Internet terminal, Wi-Fi hotspot* ☰ *AE, D, DC, MC, V* ⦿ *CP* Ⓜ *2, 3, 4, 5, 6, A, C to Fulton St./Broadway-Nassau* ✛ *1:E3.*

$$$ ⊡ **The Ritz-Carlton New York, Battery Park.** If you're staying this far downtown, the Ritz is your top choice. The hotel provides the classic Ritz-Carlton experience—you'll be greeted by at least one staffer each time you walk into the lobby—and the big rooms boast sweeping views of the Statue of Liberty and Ellis Island. **Pros:** excellent service; best base for downtown exploring; pet- and kid-friendly; Liberty views. **Cons:** removed from Midtown tourist sights; limited nighttime activities; few neighborhood options for dining and entertainment. **TripAdvisor:** "five star bargain," "beautiful views," "luxurious." ✉ *2 West St., at Battery Park, Financial District* ☎ *212/344–0800 or 800/241–3333* ⊕ *www. ritzcarlton.com/batterypark* ⤶ *298 rooms, 39 suites* ⌂ *In-room: a/c, refrigerator (some), DVD (some), Internet, Wi-Fi. In-hotel: 2 restaurants, room service, bars, laundry service, Internet terminal, Wi-Fi hotspot, parking (paid), some pets allowed* ☰ *AE, D, DC, MC, V* Ⓜ *1, R, J to Rector St.* ✛ *1:C5.*

$$ ▫ **The W New York Downtown.** Located in the heart of the Financial District, this hotel juxtaposes the gritty, unfinished feel of the surrounding area with sleek surfaces and a Lamella LED installation that boasts thousands of color-choreographed hanging lights. **Pros:** near popular tourist attractions; restaurant offers some surprisingly affordable fare; modern workout room. **Cons:** scaffolding-dense neighborhood; WTC construction directly across the street; partially obstructed views; not family-friendly. **TripAdvisor:** "clean and comfortable," "SUPER comfortable beds," "there is construction noice." ⊠ *123 Washington St.at Albany St., Financial District* ☎ *646/826–8600* ⊕ *www.starwoodhotels. com* ⌂ *85 rooms* ♿ *In-room: a/c, safe, DVD. In-hotel: restaurant, bar, Wi-Fi hotspot on 5th fl., gym* ▭ *AE, D, DC, MC, V* Ⓜ *1, N, R to Rector St.* ✢ *1:C2.*

TRIBECA

$ ▫ **Cosmopolitan.** Surprisingly, there's no *Sex and the City* affiliation at the Cosmo, but for those saving for Jimmy Choos (or just on a budget) it's a steal. **Pros:** friendly staff; great location for power shoppers. **Cons:** noisy location; spartan rooms; in mid-2011 the hotel started construction on a new wing. **TripAdvisor:** "window unit A/C was loud," "easy walk to Ground Zero," "porters were polite and helpful." ⊠ *95 West Broadway, at Chambers Sts., TriBeCa* ☎ *212/566–1900 or 888/895–9400* ⊕ *www.cosmohotel.com* ⌂ *125 rooms* ♿ *In-room: a/c, Wi-Fi. In-hotel: Wi-Fi hotspot* ▭ *AE, DC, MC, V* Ⓜ *1, 2, 3, A, C to Chambers St.* ✢ *1:C2.*

$–$$ ▫ **Duane Street Hotel.** Amid TriBeCa's historic warehouses and trendy art galleries sits the Duane Street Hotel, a fashionable addition to the neighborhood. **Pros:** great location; in-room spa treatments available through Euphoria Spa TriBeCa. **Cons:** noisy; small restaurant. **TripAdvisor:** "upscale hotel with outstanding staff," "small rooms," "ideally located." ⊠ *130 Duane St., TriBeCa* ☎ *212/964–6400* ⊕ *www. duanestreethotel.com* ⌂ *45 rooms* ♿ *In-room: a/c, safe, Wi-Fi. In-hotel: restaurant, room service, bar, Wi-Fi hotspot* ▭ *AE, DC, MC, V* Ⓜ *1, 2, 3 to Chambers St.; A, C to Chambers St.* ✢ *2:D6.*

$$$ ▫ **Greenwich Hotel.** You talkin' to me? Yes, Robert De Niro is an owner of the Greenwich Hotel in TriBeCa, De Niro's backyard and a neighborhood he's helped put on the map as a culinary and cultural benchmark. **Pros:** varied yet clever room decoration; great restaurant. **Cons:** odd lobby; price out of sync with quality; can be costly in high season. **TripAdvisor:** "superb dinner at Locanda Verde," "quiet, intimate..and hip," "amazing spa." ⊠ *377 Greenwich St., TriBeCa* ☎ *212/941–8900* ⊕ *www.thegreenwichhotel.com* ⌂ *88 rooms, 16 suites* ♿ *In-room: a/c, safe, DVD, Wi-Fi. In-hotel: restaurant, room service, pool, gym, spa, Internet terminal, parking (paid)* ▭ *AE, MC, V* Ⓜ *1 to Franklin St.* ✢ *2:C6.*

$$ ▫ **Tribeca Grand.** Still popular with the glitterati lo these many years later, the scene at the Tribeca Grand centers on the eight-story atrium's Church Lounge bar and café; now that things have cooled sufficiently, it's a nice place to hang even if you're not an A-lister, though it can get noisy for guests upstairs. **Pros:** great dining and bar scene; iPods in each room; fun social atrium; pet-friendly. **Cons:** rooms get noise

19

from restaurant below; bathroom has slightly cold design. **TripAdvisor:** "very stylish," "great location," "lavish Sunday brunch." ⊠ *2 Ave. of the Americas (6th Ave.), between Walker and White Sts., TriBeCa* ☎ *212/519–6600 or 800/965–3000* ⊕ *www.tribecagrand.com* ⬩ *197 rooms, 6 suites* ⬩ *In-room: a/c, safe, refrigerator, Wi-Fi. In-hotel: restaurant, room service, bar, gym, laundry service, Internet terminal, Wi-Fi hotspot, parking (paid), some pets allowed* ⊟ *AE, D, DC, MC, V* Ⓜ *A, C, E to Canal St.* ✛ *2:D5.*

SOHO AND LITTLE ITALY (WITH NOLITA)

SOHO

$$$ 🖼 **Crosby Street Hotel.** Here in SoHo's heart sits the Crosby Street Hotel,
Fodor's Choice which is the first branch of the U.K.'s Firmdale Hotels to open in the
★ United States. Hotel design in New York is often a man's world of leather and dark colors; here the pieces, all handpicked by co-owner Kit Kemp, are so colorful, light, and whimsical that it's jarring. **Pros:** unique design; big, bright rooms; great bar. **Cons:** breakfast not included; small gym. **TripAdvisor:** "buzzy atmosphere without being intrusive," "deluxe bathrooms," "great décor, service and food." ⊠ *79 Crosby St., between Prince and Spring Sts., SoHo* ☎ *212/226–6400* ⊕ *www.firmdale.com* ⬩ *86 rooms* ⬩ *In-room: a/c, safe (some), DVD, Wi-Fi. In-hotel: restaurant, room service, bar, gym, laundry service, in-room safe, some pets allowed* ⊟ *AE, D, MC, V* Ⓜ *6 to Spring St., R to Prince St.* ✛ *2:E3.*

$$ 🖼 **Holiday Inn SoHo.** "SoHo" and "Holiday Inn" sure don't sound right together, but here they are; once endangered by developers, SoHo's odd man out is more entrenched than ever thanks to rates dwarfed by other hotels in the vicinity. **Pros:** well-priced SoHo solution; well-trained staff. **Cons:** nothing stylish; closer to Chinatown than to SoHo. **TripAdvisor:** "great Internet connection," "very convenient location," "small rooms." ⊠ *138 Lafayette St., near Canal St., SoHo* ☎ *212/966–8898 or 800/465–4329* ⊕ *www.hidowntown-nyc.com* ⬩ *215 rooms, 12 suites* ⬩ *In-room: a/c, safe, Wi-Fi. In-hotel: restaurant, room service, bar, gym, laundry service, Internet terminal, Wi-Fi hotspot, parking (paid)* ⊟ *AE, D, DC, MC, V* Ⓜ *6, M, N, Q, R to Canal St.* ✛ *2:E5.*

$$$ 🖼 **The Mercer Hotel.** Owner André Balazs, known for his Chateau Marmont in Hollywood, has a knack for dating Hollywood starlets and channeling a neighborhood sensibility. Here it's SoHo loft all the way, though it's also a favorite crash pad for Tinseltown names. **Pros:** great location; sophisticated design touches; celebrity sightings in lobby. **Cons:** service inconsistent; tiny rooms. **TripAdvisor:** "scent of candles fill the lobby," "really spacious rooms," "unmatched commitment to service." ⊠ *147 Mercer St., at Prince St., SoHo* ☎ *212/966–6060 or 888/918–6060* ⊕ *www.mercerhotel.com* ⬩ *67 rooms, 8 suites* ⬩ *In-room: a/c, safe, DVD, Wi-Fi. In-hotel: restaurant, room service, bars, Internet terminal, Wi-Fi hotspot, some pets allowed* ⊟ *AE, D, DC, MC, V* Ⓜ *R to Prince St.* ✛ *2:E3.*

$$ 🖼 **60 Thompson.** This successful hotel has served as the blueprint for the mini-chain's four other hotels in Manhattan, and its setup has aged well; it's no longer the center of the universe, scene-wise, and that's been a blessing, improving the service and toning down the attitude of hotel staffers. **Pros:** nightlife central; access to private rooftop club; good gym; some rooms have balconies. **Cons:** not family oriented; no pets allowed. **TripAdvisor:** "staff was very friendly and helpful," "the bar was a great place for a pre-dinner drink," "design of the room is beautiful." ⊠ *60 Thompson St., between Broome and Spring Sts., SoHo* ☎ *212/431–0400 or 877/431–0400* ⊕ *www.thompsonhotels.com* 🛏 *82 rooms, 8 suites* ♿ *In-room: a/c, safe, DVD, Internet, Wi-Fi. In-hotel: restaurant, room service, bars, Internet terminal, Wi-Fi hotspot, parking (paid)* ⊟ *AE, D, DC, MC, V* Ⓜ *C, E to Spring St.* ✛ *2:D4.*

$$$ 🔲 **SoHo Grand.** The SoHo Grand defines what SoHo is today—once pioneering, now expensive, and with a vaguely creative vibe. **Pros:** fashionable, laid-back sophistication; great service; surprisingly discreet setting; diverse eating and drinking options. **Cons:** closer to Canal Street than prime SoHo; rooms on small side. **TripAdvisor:** "great ambience and design," "excellent room service," "great hotel in great location." ⊠ *310 West Broadway, at Grand St., SoHo* ☎ *212/965–3000 or 800/965–3000* ⊕ *www.sohogrand.com* 🛏 *353 rooms, 10 private-access suites, 2 penthouse loft suites* ♿ *In-room: a/c, safe, refrigerator, Internet, Wi-Fi. In-hotel: restaurant, room service, bars, gym, laundry service, parking (paid), some pets allowed* ⊟ *AE, D, DC, MC, V* Ⓜ *6, J, M, N, Q, R to Canal St.* ✛ *2:D4.*

EAST VILLAGE AND THE LOWER EAST SIDE

EAST VILLAGE

$$ 🔲 **The Cooper Square Hotel.** A jarring, 21-story glass-and-steel finger rising up in the low-rise East Village, the Cooper Square Hotel was never going to pass under the radar; the addition of the even more futuristic Cooper Union building next door has alleviated the hotel's out-of-character look somewhat, but it's still a focal point. **Pros:** stylish rooms; excellent amenities; creative guests. **Cons:** out of character with the area; ugly carpeting. **TripAdvisor:** "superior service," "small rooms," "steam shower built into bathrooms." ⊠ *25 Cooper Square, between E. 5th and E. 6th Sts., East Village* ☎ *212/475–5700* ⊕ *www. thecoopersquarehotel.com* 🛏 *145 rooms* ♿ *In-room: a/c, safe, Wi-Fi. In-hotel: restaurant, room service, bars, Wi-Fi hotspot, some pets allowed* ⊟ *AE, D, DC, MC, V* Ⓜ *6 to Astor Pl.; R to 8th. St./NYU* ✛ *2:F2.*

LOWER EAST SIDE

$$ 🔲 **The Bowery Hotel.** A stay at the Bowery centers on the lobby, stocked with newspapers for guests, old-world dark wood, and leather chairs; it's an English hunting lodge in Manhattan, warmed by rich floor-to-ceiling tapestries, fireplaces, and chandeliers—the only thing missing is a trusty hound, and there's certainly no shortage of British, who flock to the property. **Pros:** quirky, fun location; ravishing bar and lobby-lounge area; celebrity sightings; interesting views. **Cons:** gritty neighbors; rooms aren't luxurious; restaurant is crowded but underwhelming. **TripAdvisor:** "very large rooms," "great showers," "very relaxed bar area." ⊠ *335 Bowery, at 3rd St., Lower East Side* ☎ *212/505–9100*

19

⊕ *www.theboweryhotel.com* ⤴ *135 rooms, 25 suites* ⌂ *In-room: a/c, safe, Wi-Fi. In-hotel: restaurant, room service, bar, laundry service, Internet terminal, Wi-Fi hotspot, parking (paid), some pets allowed* ⊟ *AE, D, DC, MC, V* ⍍ *CP* Ⓜ *6 to Bleecker; B, D, F, M to Broadway/ Lafayette* ✛ *2:F2.*

$$ 🏨 **Hotel on Rivington.** A pioneer when it opened in 2004, THOR is no longer the only glass-walled hotel on the Lower East Side, and the years are starting to show, as some fixtures in the room are starting to get tatty. Still, the views of downtown remain breathtaking. **Pros:** superhip location and vibe; huge windows with wonderful New York views; happening bar and restaurant. **Cons:** feels like a club on weekends; spotty service; small rooms and suites. **TripAdvisor:** "very helpful and friendly staff," "basic breakfast," "modern and clean rooms." ⊠ *107 Rivington St., between Ludlow and Essex Sts., Lower East Side* ☎ *212/475–2600 or 800/915–1537* ⊕ *www.hotelonrivington.com* ⤴ *110 rooms* ⌂ *In-room: a/c, safe, refrigerator, Internet, Wi-Fi. In-hotel: restaurant, room service, bar, laundry service, parking (paid), some pets allowed* ⊟ *AE, D, DC, MC, V* Ⓜ *F, J, M, Z to Delancey/Essex Sts.* ✛ *2:G3.*

$$ 🏨 **Thompson LES.** The best expression of the Thompson Hotels philosophy, the Thompson LES is a stylish addition to the neighborhood, the smoked-glass tower contrasting with the Hotel on Rivington's wide-open views. **Pros:** great amenities; in the heart of downtown; great views from suites. **Cons:** snobby staff; rooms stylish but dark. **TripAdvisor:** "vibrant atmosphere," "extremely comfortable bed," "absolutely amazing room." ⊠ *190 Allen St., between Houston and Stanton Sts., Lower East Side* ☎ *212/460–5300* ⊕ *www.thompsonhotels.com* ⤴ *131 rooms* ⌂ *In-room: a/c, safe, refrigerator, Wi-Fi. In-hotel: restaurant, room service, bars, pool, laundry service, Wi-Fi hotspot* ⊟ *AE, MC, V* Ⓜ *F, J, M, Z to Delancey/Essex Sts.* ✛ *2:G3.*

Fodor's Choice
★

GREENWICH VILLAGE, THE WEST VILLAGE, AND CHELSEA (WITH THE MEATPACKING DISTRICT)

CHELSEA

¢   🏨 **Chelsea Lodge.** Popular with Europeans and budget-conscious visitors, the Chelsea Lodge is a great location for guests who don't insist on a lot of amenities. **Pros:** on a gorgeous Chelsea block; great bang for the buck; close to subway. **Cons:** not romantic; shared bathrooms not right for everyone. **TripAdvisor:** "the rooms were a little small," "really quiet gorgeous brownstone street," "safe area, close to subway." ⊠ *318 W. 20th St., between 8th and 9th Aves., Chelsea* ☎ *212/243–4499* ⊕ *www. chelsealodge.com* ⤴ *22 rooms, 2 with bath; 4 suites* ⌂ *In-room: a/c, no phone, kitchen (some), Wi-Fi. In-hotel: Wi-Fi hotspot* ⊟ *AE, D, MC, V* Ⓜ *C, E to 23rd St.; 1 to 18th St.* ✛ *3:C3.*

$ 🏨 **The GEM Hotel Chelsea.** At this stylish, well-priced boutique hotel the modern rooms are small but designed to make the most of the limited space—they come with black-and-white photos on the wall, flat-screen TVs, white linens, iPod docking stations, Gilchrist & Soames toiletries in the bathrooms, full-length mirrors, and free Wi-Fi. **Pros:** great Chelsea location; close to several subway lines. **Cons:** gym and business center, both on the lower level, feel like a work in progress; rooms may be too small for some. **TripAdvisor:** "extremely friendly and helpful staff," "small rooms," "charming hotel in great location." ✉ *300 W. 22nd St., Chelsea* ☎ *212/675–1911* ⊕ *www.thegemhotel.com* ⌑ *81 rooms* ⌂ *In-room: a/c, Wi-Fi. In-hotel: gym, laundry service, Internet terminal* ▭ *AE, D, DC, MC, V* Ⓜ *C, E to 23rd St.; 1 to 23rd St.* ✛ *3:C3.*

$ Ⓣ **Hilton New York Fashion District.** Open since April 2010, the Hilton is part of a neighborhood hotel boomlet that shows no signs of slowing down. Located on the upper edge of Chelsea in a zone that's stretching the limits of what New Yorkers refer to as "downtown," the hotel is designed with the neighborhood's garment district past as its beacon. **Pros:** reasonable prices for a great location; year-round rooftop bar. **Cons:** tiny closets; no on-site gym. **TripAdvisor:** "staff was particularly friendly and helpful," "location was fantastic," "subways are close." ✉ *W. 26th St. between 6th and 7th Aves., Chelsea* ☎ *212/858–5888* ⊕ *www.f26nyc.com* ⌑ *280 rooms* ⌂ *In-room: a/c, safe, Internet, Wi-Fi. In-hotel: restaurant, room service, bar, laundry service, Internet terminal, Wi-Fi hotspot, parking (paid)* ▭ *AE, D, DC, MC, V* Ⓜ *1, 2, 3, A, C, E, B, D, F V, N, Q, R, W to 34th St./Penn Station* ✛ *3:D2.*

$ Ⓣ **Inn on 23rd.** Friendly innkeepers Annette and Barry Fisherman welcome guests to this five-floor, 19th-century building, which also comes with its own cat/mascot. **Pros:** charming innkeepers; comfy and relaxed library; affordable, given location. **Cons:** few business services; some older amenities; beware if you have cat allergies. **TripAdvisor:** "so many thoughtful touches," "staff was very helpful," "excellent breakfasts." ✉ *131 W. 23rd St., between 6th and 7th Aves., Chelsea* ☎ *212/835-5533* ⊕ *www.innon23rd.com* ⌑ *13 rooms, 1 suite* ⌂ *In-room: a/c, DVD (some), Internet, Wi-Fi. In-hotel: laundry service, Internet terminal, Wi-Fi hotspot* ▭ *AE, D, DC, MC, V* ⦿ *CP* Ⓜ *F, M to 23rd St.* ✛ *3:D2.*

Fodor's Choice
★

$ Ⓣ **Maritime Hotel.** In just about any other city, the Maritime would be a major entertainment and cultural center; inside is the Hiro Ballroom nightclub, with room for 800; Matsuri, the cavernous Japanese restaurant below the hotel; and La Bottega, a delightful, expansive plaza-level restaurant and bar. **Pros:** nightlife options galore; great restaurants; fun rooms with big porthole windows. **Cons:** all nightlife all the time; street noise. **TripAdvisor:** "rooms are small," "really inventive design," "staff is incredible." ✉ *363 W. 16th St., at 9th Ave., Chelsea* ☎ *212/242–4300* ⊕ *www.themaritimehotel.com* ⌑ *120 rooms, 4 suites* ⌂ *In-room: a/c, safe, DVD, Internet, Wi-Fi. In-hotel: 2 restaurants, room service, bars, gym, laundry service, Internet terminal, Wi-Fi hotspot, some pets allowed* ▭ *AE, MC, V* Ⓜ *A, C, E to 14th St.* ✛ *3:B3.*

19

GREENWICH VILLAGE

$ Ⓣ **Washington Square Hotel.** This low-key European-style hotel in Greenwich Village is popular with visiting New York University parents—the location near the renovated Washington Square Park and its magnificent arch (and just down the street from Mario Batali's Babbo restaurant) is just a bonus. **Pros:** park-front location; deluxe rooms are charming; great hotel bar. **Cons:** NYU students everywhere; rooms are small. **TripAdvisor:** "well-situated hotel," "price is great," "delicious breakfast." ✉ *103 Waverly Pl., at MacDougal St., Greenwich Village*

Crosby Street Hotel

Thompson LES

The Standard

☎ *212/777–9515 or 800/222–0418* ⊕ *www.wshotel.com* ⤳ *160 rooms* △ *In-room: a/c, safe, Internet (some). In-hotel: restaurant, bar, gym, Wi-Fi hotspot* ⊟ *AE, MC, V* ⓘ◎ⓘ *CP* Ⓜ *A, B, C, D, E, F, M to W. 4th St./Washington Sq.* ⊹ *2:D1.*

MEATPACKING DISTRICT

$$ ⛨ **Hotel Gansevoort.** Don't you hate it when a younger sibling shows you up? Unfortunately, that's the case at the Gansevoort, which is looking a bit frumpy since the Standard opened a few blocks to the west. **Pros:** rooftop pool; wonderful art collection; nice amenities. **Cons:** too-trendy location at times; worn rooms; slipshod service. **TripAdvisor:** "efficient staff," "trendy neighborhood," "rooftop bar/club." ⊠ *18 9th Ave., at 13th St., Meatpacking District* ☎ *212/206–6700 or 877/426–7386* ⊕ *www.hotelgansevoort.com* ⤳ *166 rooms, 21 suites* △ *In-room: a/c, safe, Wi-Fi. In-hotel: restaurant, room service, bars, pool, gym, spa, laundry service, Internet terminal, parking (paid), some pets allowed* ⊟ *AE, MC, V* ⓘ◎ⓘ *CP* Ⓜ *A, C, E, L to 14th St. and 8th Ave.* ⊹ *3:B4.*

¢–$ ⛨ **The Jane.** To some, it's impossibly chic; to others, the rooms are reminiscent of Sing Sing; and to its far West Village neighbors it's just a nuisance. Welcome to the Jane hotel. **Pros:** cheap; hot bar scene; amazing decor in lounge; great branch of weekend brunch favorite Café Gitane; convenient neighborhood for downtown sightseeing. **Cons:** impossibly tiny standard rooms; shared bathrooms; hot bar scene. **TripAdvisor:** "recommended for solo travelers," "very clean cabins," "fun, quirky place to stay." ⊠ *113 Jane St., at West St., West Village* ☎ *212/924–6700* ⊕ *www.thejanenyc.com* ⤳ *150 rooms, 40 suites* △ *In-room: a/c, Wi-Fi. In-hotel: bar, restaurant, Wi-Fi hotspot* ⊟ *AE, D, DC, MC, V* Ⓜ *A, C, E, L to 14th St. and 8th Ave.* ⊹ *3:B5.*

$
Fodor'sChoice
★
⛨ **The Standard.** André Balazs's architectural statement on the West Side, the Standard is one of New York's hottest hotels. It helps to have the High Line, a reclaimed elevated railway–turned-park, running underneath it, but the Standard earned much of the buzz itself, with a lobby full of glamorous types, an authentic beer garden (open year-round; dig the Ping-Pong tables), and, guarding the 18th-floor nightclub, one of the toughest doors in town. **Pros:** beautiful building; beautiful people; impressive restaurant space. **Cons:** noisy at night; tight rooms; sceney. **TripAdvisor:** "impressed with concierge," "cool neighborhood," "beautiful rooms." ⊠ *848 Washington St., between W. 13th and Little W. 12th Sts., Meatpacking District* ☎ *212/645–4646* ⊕ *www.standardhotels.com* ⤳ *337 rooms* △ *In-room: a/c, Internet, Wi-Fi. In-hotel: 2 restaurants, room service, bars, gym, spa, Wi-Fi hotspot* ⊟ *AE, MC, V* Ⓜ *A, C, E, L to 14th St. and 8th Ave.* ⊹ *3:B4.*

19

UNION SQUARE TO MURRAY HILL (WITH THE FLATIRON DISTRICT AND GRAMERCY)

FLATIRON DISTRICT

$
Fodor'sChoice
★
⛨ **Ace Hotel.** Step inside the Ace Hotel, and any notion of what a hotel could and should be is left at the door; the eastern outpost of a West Coast hotel chain (locations are already in Seattle, Portland, and Palm Springs) provides the style and luxury you'd expect to find at a five-star

CLOSE UP

Hotel Hot Spots

Some of the city's most stylish bars and lounges are in hotels. These boîtes occasionally require crossing a velvet-roped entrance, but most extend automatic entry to guests of the hotel.

Downtown in the Financial District, the Library Bar on the second floor of Gild Hall looks like the ultimate luxe club room, with tufted leather banquettes, a dartboard, and a surprisingly friendly staff.

Mega-hotelier Ian Schrager's properties are design temples, with chic lounges favored by jet-setters and locals alike. The new "haute Bohemian" **Gramercy Park Hotel** (⇨ Union Square/Gramercy) is Schrager's latest offering, with its popular—and pricey—Rose Bar and Jade Bar. The hotel also features a private members- and guests-only Roof Club. **The Ace Hotel** (⇨ Union Square/Flatiron) is the sweet spot du jour, with one bar in the eclectic lobby and another at the trendy Breslin restaurant, and also an outpost of Stumptown coffee if you need to sober up.

The Standard (⇨ Greenwich Village/ Meatpacking District) has a happening bar scene at the Standard Grill. The 18th-floor lounge is a tough row to hoe unless you're a friend of the owner, but downstairs you can also sip suds in the outdoor beer garden, which is more egalitarian, and frankly, a lot more fun—they've even got Ping-Pong tables. It's also open year-round now.

On the Lower East Side, the Lobby Bar in the **Bowery Hotel** (⇨ Lower East Side) is a Wes Anderson movie come to life, with worn velvet furniture, Persian rugs, an assortment of taxidermy,

and a back patio that harbors some of the most coveted summertime tables in the neighborhood. Nearby at the **Cooper Square** (⇨ Lower East Side), the Second Floor Bar has a hammered metal bar top and tall glass windows that let the sunlight stream in. It's one of the nicer spots for daytime libation—take it outside to one of the cushioned, low-slung settees if weather permits. In Midtown, the new, Art Deco–designed **Chatwal** (⇨ Midtown West) has a hopping lobby scene with drinks by cocktail guru Sasha Petraske and an elegant second-floor bar decorated with whimsical touches that are a paean to classic New York (look for the shimmering light fixtures shaped like the Chrysler Building).

The **Room Mate Grace** (⇨ Midtown West and Chelsea) in Times Square has a bar that's adjacent to its lobby-level pool; you can see all the underwater action through voyeur windows above the bar. Just make sure to pay attention at the end of the evening, or you might be the hotel's next swimming sensation. At the **Mandarin Oriental** on Columbus Circle (⇨ Midtown West), the 35th-floor lounge is a clutch location for soaking in views of Central Park; grab a perch on a cozy leather couch (and ask the concierge to make you a reservation if you're planning ahead—it gets busy on evenings and weekends).

hotel, minus the pretension and price. **Pros:** in-house restaurants, the Breslin and the John Dory oyster bar, both from star chef April Bloomfield, mean you won't have to travel far for trendy dining or celeb-spotting; lobby java shop is by the excellent Stumptown Coffee Roasters, and the No. 7 Sub shop

offers some of the best sandwiches in the city. **Cons:** dark lobby; caters to a young crowd; may be too sceney for some. **TripAdvisor:** "complimentary breakfast was great," "friendly and unpretentious staff," "the bathroom, while small, was great." ✉ *20 W. 29th St., at Broadway, Flatiron District* ☎ *212/679–2222* ⊕ *www.acehotel.com* ⌗ *251 rooms, 11 suites* ♿ *In-room: a/c, safe, refrigerator (some), Wi-Fi. In-hotel: restaurant, room service, bars, gym, laundry service, Wi-Fi hotspot, parking (paid), some pets allowed* 🖃 *AE, MC, V* Ⓜ *N, R to 28th St.; 1 to 28th St.* ✛ *3:E1.*

$$ 🖵 **The Eventi.** The newest Kimpton property to grace New York City, the Eventi adds a touch of hotel style just below Penn Station in an area desperately in need of new hotel options. **Pros:** great location; fun dining options; nice gym. **Cons:** crowded lobby; dark rooms. **TripAdvisor:** "nice lobby area," "large fitness center," "daily wine hour in lobby." ✉ *851 Avenue of the Americas, at 30th St., Flatiron District* ☎ *866/996–8396* ⊕ *www.eventihotel.com* ⌗ *239 rooms, 53 suites* ♿ *In-room: a/c, safe, refrigerator on request, Internet, Wi-Fi. In-hotel: 2 restaurants, room service, bar, laundry service, Wi-Fi hotspot, parking (paid), some pets allowed* 🖃 *AE, D, DC, MC, V.* Ⓜ *N, R to 28th St.* ✛ *3:D1*

GRAMERCY PARK

$$$ 🖵 **Gramercy Park Hotel.** Ian Schrager, the man who invented the "boutique hotel" concept almost two decades ago, is back, and the property reflects some of his hard-won wisdom. **Pros:** intensely trendy bar scene; opulent rooms; great restaurant; park-side location. **Cons:** inconsistent service; form-over-function rooms; expensive bar. **TripAdvisor:** "beautiful rooftop garden," "huge, comfortable beds," "great location." ✉ *2 Lexington Ave., at Gramercy Park, Gramercy Park* ☎ *212/920–3300* ⊕ *www.gramercyparkhotel.com* ⌗ *140 rooms, 40 suites* ♿ *In-room: a/c, safe, refrigerator, DVD, Internet. In-hotel: restaurant, room service, bars, gym, laundry service, parking (paid)* 🖃 *AE, D, DC, MC, V* Ⓜ *6 to 23rd St.* ✛ *3:F3.*

$$ 🖵 **Inn at Irving Place.** Fantasies of Old New York—Manhattan straight

Fodor's Choice ★ from the pages of Edith Wharton and Henry James, an era of genteel brick town houses and Tiffany lamps—spring to life at this discreet 20-room inn, the city's most romantic. **Pros:** romantic; charming property; big rooms; excellent breakfast and tea service; Mario Batali's Casa Mono is downstairs. **Cons:** twee; rooms aren't flawless, with imperfections like older grouting; street noise. **TripAdvisor:** "lovely hotel," "loved the locale," "quiet oasis of calm in Manhattan." ✉ *56 Irving Pl., between E. 17th and E. 18th Sts., Gramercy Park* ☎ *212/533–4600 or 800/685–1447* ⊕ *www.innatirving.com* ⌗ *5 rooms, 6 suites* ♿ *In-room:*

19

a/c, refrigerator. In-hotel: restaurant, room service, bar, laundry service, no kids under 8 ▭ *AE, D, DC, MC, V* ⦿ *CP* Ⓜ *4, 5, 6, L, N, Q, R to 14th St./Union Sq.* ✛ *3:G3.*

$ 🏨 **Marcel at Gramercy.** A fall 2008 redesign has transformed the Marcel into a chic yet affordable stay that gives guests both style and substance in a prime location. **Pros:** outdoor patio offers great space and spectacular views of the city; good value. **Cons:** elevators are slow; a/c struggles in summer; the wine-and-cheese reception is free but could run longer. **TripAdvisor:** "quirky hotel," "fantastic value for money," "beautiful roof terrace." ✉ *201 E. 24th St., Gramercy Park* ☎ *212/696–3800* ⊕ *www.themarcelatgramercy.com* ⤴ *133 rooms, 2 suites* ♿ *In-room: a/c, safe. In-hotel: restaurant, room service, laundry service, Internet terminal, Wi-Fi hotspot* ▭ *AE, D, MC, V* Ⓜ *6 to 23rd St.* ✛ *3:G2.*

MURRAY HILL

¢ 🏨 **Carlton Arms.** Europeans and students know about the chipper, winning attitude of this friendly, no-frills hotel. **Pros:** rock-bottom prices; chipper attitude; quieter residential Murray Hill location. **Cons:** no elevator; few furnishings; many shared baths. **TripAdvisor:** "inexpensive, funky, artsy hotel," "could have been a little cleaner," "good location." ✉ *160 E. 25th St., at 3rd Ave., Murray Hill* ☎ *212/684–8337, 212/679–0680 for reservations* ⊕ *www.carltonarms.com* ⤴ *54 rooms, 20 with bath* ♿ *In-room: a/c, no phone, no TV. In-hotel: Internet terminal, some pets allowed* ▭ *MC, V* Ⓜ *R to 28th St.* ✛ *3:G2.*

$$ 🏨 **Carlton on Madison Avenue.** A few years ago a five-year, $60 million renovation turned a nearly invisible old dowager into a modern scenestealer. **Pros:** spectacular lobby; stylish rooms; nice amenities. **Cons:** expensive bar; small rooms; lackluster restaurant. **TripAdvisor:** "service was top notch," "room service was prompt," "bathroom was spacious and well-stocked." ✉ *88 Madison Ave., between 28th and 29th Sts., Murray Hill* ☎ *212/532–4100 or 800/601–8500* ⊕ *www.carltonhotelny. com* ⤴ *294 rooms, 22 suites* ♿ *In-room: a/c, safe, Wi-Fi. In-hotel: 2 restaurants, room service, bar, laundry service, Internet terminal, Wi-Fi hotspot, parking (paid), some pets allowed* ▭ *AE, D, MC, V* Ⓜ *6 to 28th St.* ✛ *3:F1.*

$–$$ 🏨 **Herald Square Hotel.** The sculpted cherubs on the facade and vintage magazine covers adorning the common areas hint at the Herald's previous incarnation as *Life* magazine's headquarters. **Pros:** cheap; centrally located. **Cons:** unattractive lobby; readers report inconsistent service. **TripAdvisor:** "very clean and quiet," "hidden gem," "comfortable beds." ✉ *19 W. 31st St., between 5th Ave. and Broadway, Murray Hill* ☎ *212/279–4017 or 800/727–1888* ⊕ *www.heraldsquarehotel.com* ⤴ *120 rooms* ♿ *In-room: a/c, safe, Wi-Fi. In-hotel: Internet terminal, Wi-Fi hotspot, some pets allowed* ▭ *AE, D, MC, V* Ⓜ *B, D, F, N, Q, R, M to 34th St./Herald Sq.* ✛ *3:E1.*

$$ 🏨 **Hotel Giraffe.** Ensconced just off Park Avenue South for more than a decade now, the Giraffe remains a consistent property with friendly service, big rooms, and lots of repeat customers, particularly business travelers. **Pros:** high-quality linens: rooftop terrace for guests; quiet hotel. **Cons:** street noise near lower levels; pricey for the quality you get. **TripAdvisor:** "breakfast buffet," "large rooms," "very comfortable

Ace Hotel

19

Library Hotel,

Inn on 23rd

lobby." ✉ *365 Park Ave. S, at E. 26th St., Murray Hill* ☎ *212/685–7700 or 877/296–0009* ⊕ *www.hotelgiraffe.com* ⇆ *52 rooms, 21 suites* ♿ *In-room: a/c, safe, DVD, Wi-Fi. In-hotel: restaurant, room service, bars, laundry service, Internet terminal, Wi-Fi hotspot, parking (paid)* ▭ *AE, DC, MC, V* ⦿ *CP* Ⓜ *6 to 28th St.* ✛ *3:F2.*

$$ ☷ **Hotel Roger Williams.** A colorful choice in a rather plain neighborhood, the Roger Williams continues to have a following among repeat visitors to New York. **Pros:** colorful room decor; friendly service; good value. **Cons:** no room service; tiny bathrooms. **TripAdvisor:** "wonderfully attentive staff," "lovely amenities," "small rooms." ✉ *131 Madison Ave., at E. 31st St., Murray Hill* ☎ *212/448–7000 or 877/847–4444* ⊕ *www.rogerwilliamshotel.com* ⇆ *193 rooms, 2 suites* ♿ *In-room: a/c, Wi-Fi. In-hotel: restaurant, room service, bar, gym, Internet terminal, Wi-Fi hotspot, parking (paid)* ▭ *AE, D, MC, V* ⦿ *CP* Ⓜ *6 to 33rd St.* ✛ *3:F1.*

$–$$ ☷ **Jolly Hotel Madison Towers.** Italians flock to this hotel operated by Jolly Hotels, the largest hotel chain in Italy. **Pros:** friendly, Italian-style service; good location; attractive bar. **Cons:** no restaurant; no gym; not contemporary in feel; small rooms. **TripAdvisor:** "small rooms," "clean bathrooms," "superb location." ✉ *22 E. 38th St., between Madison and Park Aves., Murray Hill* ☎ *212/802–0600 or 800/225–4340* ⊕ *www.jollymadison.com* ⇆ *238 rooms, 6 suites* ♿ *In-room: a/c, safe, Wi-Fi. In-hotel: bar, laundry service, Internet terminal, Wi-Fi hotspot, parking (paid), some pets allowed* ▭ *AE, DC, MC, V* Ⓜ *6 to 33rd St.* ✛ *4:F5.*

$$ ☷ **The Kitano.** As you might guess from the name, the Kitano imports much of its sensibility from Japan, and such touches include a bilingual concierge and a high-concept Japanese restaurant. **Pros:** extra soundproofing in guest rooms; cute mezzanine bar area; guest pass to great local gym; good value. **Cons:** lower-floor views are limited; very expensive restaurant. **TripAdvisor:** "courteous and professional front desk," "spacious, clean rooms," "sound proofed for location." ✉ *66 Park Ave., at E. 38th St., Murray Hill* ☎ *212/885–7000 or 800/548–2666* ⊕ *www.kitano.com* ⇆ *149 rooms, 18 suites* ♿ *In-room: a/c, safe, refrigerator, Internet. In-hotel: 2 restaurants, room service, bar, laundry service, parking (paid)* ▭ *AE, D, DC, MC, V* Ⓜ *6 to 33rd St.* ✛ *4:F5.*

$ ☷ **Park South Hotel.** In this beautifully transformed 1906 office building, restful rooms feel smartly contemporary, though they've retained some period details. **Pros:** free breakfast and Internet; turndown service; good value. **Cons:** small elevators; tame location; spotty service. **TripAdvisor:** "staff recognizes and cares," "nicely decorated," "comfortable but small rooms." ✉ *122 E. 28th St., between Lexington and Park Aves., Murray Hill* ☎ *212/448–0888 or 800/315–4642* ⊕ *www.parksouthhotel.com* ⇆ *139 rooms, 2 suites* ♿ *In-room: a/c, safe, Internet. In-hotel: restaurant, bar, gym, laundry service, Internet terminal, Wi-Fi hotspot* ▭ *AE, D, DC, MC, V* ⦿ *CP* Ⓜ *6 to 28th St.* ✛ *3:F2.*

$ ☷ **70 Park Avenue.** Branches in the Kimpton hotel chain have something of a cult following with design enthusiasts, but 70 Park is a low-key, slightly disappointing offering that's more for road-warrior business types than style hounds. **Pros:** weekday wine reception; polite service; simple, unobtrusive rooms and hotel layout. **Cons:** bland design; no gym. **TripAdvisor:** "bathroom was also a good size," "comfortable, clean, and customer friendly," "street noise was minimal." ⊠ *70 Park Ave., at 38th St., Murray Hill* ☎ *212/973–2400 or 800/707–2752* ⊕ *www.70parkave.com* ⇱ *201 rooms, 4 suites* ⌂ *In-room: a/c, safe, DVD, Internet, Wi-Fi. In-hotel: restaurant, room service, bar, laundry service, some pets allowed* ⊟ *AE, D, DC, MC, V* Ⓜ *6 to 33rd St.* ✛ *4:F5.*

UNION SQUARE

$ ⚏ **W New York Union Square.** The W chain's iconic New York City property continues to attract a mix of trendsetters and tourists, thanks to the downtown location—and the noticeable lack of other hotel options in the neighborhood. **Pros:** fashionable location; great restaurant. **Cons:** trendy decor; noisy lobby; expensive Wi-Fi. **TripAdvisor:** "extremely friendly staff," "spacious and quiet rooms," "impeccable service." ⊠ *201 Park Ave. S, at E. 17th St., Union Square* ☎ *212/253–9119 or 877/946–8357* ⊕ *www.whotels.com* ⇱ *254 rooms, 16 suites* ⌂ *In-room: a/c, safe, refrigerator, DVD, Wi-Fi. In-hotel: restaurant, room service, bars, gym, spa, laundry service, parking (paid), some pets allowed* ⊟ *AE, D, DC, MC, V* Ⓜ *4, 5, 6, L, N, Q, R to 14th St./ Union Sq.* ✛ *3:F3.*

MIDTOWN

MIDTOWN WEST

$$ ⚏ **The Algonquin.** Even Matilda, the resident cat who holds court in the parlorlike lobby, seems to know that the draw here is the ghosts of its literary past; hordes of literary enthusiasts fill the clubby lobby; signed works of former Round Table raconteurs can be checked out of the library, and their witticisms grace guest-room doors. **Pros:** free Internet; friendly, knowledgable staff; central location. **Cons:** small rooms. **TripAdvisor:** "very well-designed rooms," "location could not be beat," "amazing beds." ⊠ *59 W. 44th St., between 5th and 6th Aves., Midtown West* ☎ *212/840–6800 or 800/555–8000* ⊕ *www.algonquinhotel.com* ⇱ *150 rooms, 24 suites* ⌂ *In-room: a/c, safe, Wi-Fi. In-hotel: 2 restaurants, room service, bar, gym, laundry service, Internet terminal, Wi-Fi hotspot, parking (paid), some pets allowed* ⊟ *AE, D, DC, MC, V* Ⓜ *B, D, F, M to 42nd St.* ✛ *4:D4.*

$ ⚏ **Belvedere Hotel.** Guests choose the Belvedere more for the central location, adjacent to Times Square, and less for the rooms, which lack life (and light). **Pros:** good rates available; renovated rooms are good value. **Cons:** can be loud with street noise; slow elevators. **TripAdvisor:** "bath is small but adequate," "updated, spacious rooms," "not far from Times Square and sightseeing." ⊠ *319 W. 48th St., between 8th and 9th Aves., Midtown West* ☎ *212/245–7000 or 888/468–3558* ⊕ *www.belvederehotelnyc.com* ⇱ *328 rooms, 1 suite* ⌂ *In-room: a/c, safe, kitchen, Wi-Fi. In-hotel: restaurant, laundry facilities, laundry service, Internet terminal, Wi-Fi hotspot, parking (paid)* ⊟ *AE, D, DC, MC, V* Ⓜ *C, E to 50th St.* ✛ *4:B3.*

¢ ⚏ **Best Western President Hotel.** After a $15 million renovation that transformed it from a ho-hum Best Western, the President is the only politically themed hotel in the city. **Pros:** sleek rooms for the price;

19

Romantic Retreats

As the English explorer Sir Walter Raleigh once wrote, "Romance is a love affair in other than domestic surroundings." Indeed, many high-end hotels seem custom-built for romance, with plush feather beds, silky linens, and ultrasoft robes. But some properties go above and beyond in catering to couples, offering services like bath butlers and in-room massage services. Here's our pick of the city's best spots for an intimate getaway.

At the **Ritz-Carlton New York, Battery Park** (⇨ Lower Manhattan) your wish is their command. Take advantage of lower-than-normal weekend rates to book a Liberty Suite, with sweeping views of the Statue of Liberty. With a quick call to the concierge you can arrange to have champagne and strawberries waiting in your room when you arrive. A bath butler can then fill your marble tub with a potion of bath oils and flower petals. If you're here in February, don't miss a trip to the penthouse Chocolate Bar, with its aphrodisiac chocolate-and-champagne buffet.

The **Inn at Irving Place** (⇨ Union Square/Gramercy) does romance the old-fashioned way, with four-poster beds, fireplaces, fur throws, and plenty of privacy in an elegant 1800s brownstone. The complimentary breakfast is served on fine bone china either in the cozy sitting room or in bed.

The 23,000-square-foot Bliss Spa at **W New York** (⇨ Midtown East and Upper East Side), on Lexington Avenue, is an urban oasis, with men's and women's lounges, a gym, and a full menu of facial and body treatments, massage, waxing, and nail services. Couples can spend a full day being pampered and pedicured in the spa or unwind in their rooms with an in-room massage, offered 24 hours a day.

All the rooms at the **Library Hotel** (⇨ Midtown East and Upper East Side) have an inviting charm that makes them a good choice for a romantic weekend away, but if you're looking for a little mood reading, ask for the Erotic Literature room or the Love Room, curated by Dr. Ruth.

---

convenient location; unique theme. **Cons:** cramped lobby; dark bathrooms; poor views. **TripAdvisor:** "wonderful staff," "small but clean rooms," "nice fitness center." ⊠ *234 W. 48th St., between 8th Ave. and Broadway, Times Square* ☎ *212/246–8800 or 800/828–4667* ⊕ *www. presidenthotelny.com* ↘ *334 rooms* ⚲ *In-room: a/c, safe, Wi-Fi. In-hotel: 2 restaurants, room service, bar, gym, laundry service, Internet terminal, Wi-Fi hotspot* ▭ *AE, MC, V* Ⓜ *C, E to 50th St.* ✛ *4:C3.*

$$ 🖼 **The Blakely.** It may be a tried-and-true design motif, but it's hard to resist the English gentlemen's club when it's done right. **Pros:** all rooms have kitchenettes; central location; good-size rooms; acclaimed restaurant. **Cons:** rooms facing 54th Street can be noisy; some rooms have little natural light. **TripAdvisor:** "friendly and attentive staff," "spacious, clean accommodations," "very nice location." ⊠ *136 W. 55th St., between 6th and 7th Aves., Midtown West* ☎ *212/245–1800 or 800/735–0710* ⊕ *www.blakelynewyork.com* ↘ *57 rooms, 54 suites* ⚲ *In-room: a/c, safe, kitchen, refrigerator, DVD, Wi-Fi. In-hotel: restaurant, room service, bar, gym, laundry service, Internet terminal,*

Wi-Fi hotspot, parking (paid) 🖃 *AE, DC, MC, V* Ⓜ *N, Q, R to 57th St.* ✛ *4:C2.*

$$ 🏨 **Bryant Park Hotel.** A New York landmark in brown brick towering over the New York Public Library and Bryant Park, this sleekly modern hotel is still a Midtown hot spot. **Pros:** gorgeous building; fashionable crowd and setting; across from Bryant Park. **Cons:** expensive; Cellar Bar frequently booked for events. **TripAdvisor:** "simple, clean, modern furnishings," "park across the street is lovely," "cellar Bar is superb." ✉ *40 W. 40th St., between 5th and 6th Aves., Midtown West* ☎ *212/869–0100 or 877/640–9300* ⊕ *www.bryantparkhotel.com* ↩ *112 rooms, 17 suites* ♿ *In-room: a/c, safe, Internet, Wi-Fi. In-hotel: restaurant, room service, bars, gym, laundry service, Wi-Fi hotspot, parking (paid)* 🖃 *AE, DC, MC, V* Ⓜ *B, D, F, M to 42nd St.; 7 to 5th Ave.* ✛ *4:D5.*

$ 🏨 **Casablanca Hotel.** Evoking a sultry Mediterranean locale, the Casablanca is outfitted with mirrors and mosaics, ceiling fans, wooden blinds, and dainty little bistro tables in the public spaces. **Pros:** great access to the Theater District; all rooms are smoke-free. **Cons:** exercise facilities at nearby New York Sports Club, not on premises; heavy tourist foot traffic. **TripAdvisor:** "personality and character with great service," "this hotel is very good value," "a brilliant hotel in a great location." ✉ *147 W. 43rd St., Midtown West* ☎ *212/869–1212* ⊕ *www. casablancahotel.com* ↩ *48 rooms* ♿ *In-room: a/c, safe, DVD, Wi-Fi. In-hotel: restaurant, room service, bar, laundry facilities, Wi-Fi hotspot* 🖃 *AE, D, MC, V* Ⓜ *1, 2, 3, 7, N, Q, R, S to Times Sq./42nd St.* ✛ *4:C4.*

$$$–$$$$ 🏨 **Chambers Hotel.** This hotel casts itself as a center for art lovers, with more than 500 contemporary works in public spaces throughout the property. **Pros:** artsy, fun, lighthearted style; great art abounds; buzzing restaurant; wonderful central location. **Cons:** no gym; rooms slightly worn. **TripAdvisor:** "multiple subway stops nearby," "staff is friendly," "fantastic shower." ✉ *15 W. 56th St., off 5th Ave., Midtown West* ☎ *212/974–5656 or 866/204–5656* ⊕ *www.chambershotel.com* ↩ *72 rooms, 5 suites* ♿ *In-room: a/c, safe, DVD, Internet, Wi-Fi. In-hotel: restaurant, room service, bar, laundry service, Internet terminal, Wi-Fi hotspot, parking (paid), some pets allowed* 🖃 *AE, D, DC, MC, V* Ⓜ *F, M to 57th St.* ✛ *4:E1.*

$$$$ 🏨 **The Chatwal.** A place for the Daddy Warbucks in all of us, the Chatwal
Fodor's Choice is the lavishly refurbished reincarnation of a classic Manhattan theater
★ club that lay fallow for decades. **Pros:** gorgeous lobby; state-of-the-art room controls and amenities; excellent service. **Cons:** expensive—some visitors may find justifying such high prices for a Times Square locale difficult. **TripAdvisor:** "service was simply outstanding," " rooms are elegant and beautifully appointed," "setting oozes glamour." ✉ *130 W. 44th St., between 5th and 6th Aves, Midtown West* ☎ *212/264–6200* ⊕ *www.thechatwalny.com* ↩ *83 rooms* ♿ *In-room: a/c, safe, kitchen (some), refrigerator (some), DVD, Internet, Wi-Fi. In-hotel: restaurant, room service, bars, laundry service, Wi-Fi hotspot, parking (paid), some pets allowed* 🖃 *AE, D, DC, MC, V* Ⓜ *B, D, F, M, 7 to 42nd St./Bryant Park* ✛ *4:C4.*

$$ 🏨 **City Club Hotel.** The City Club's ocean-liner-inspired rooms are brisk, bright, and masculine; they're also about the same size as a room on

19

a cruise ship—that means tight quarters, matey, no matter how much you enjoy sharing space with Jonathan Adler ceramics. **Pros:** free Wi-Fi; great restaurant; personal service. **Cons:** no gym; some guests find lighting substandard; no real lobby. **TripAdvisor:** "rates very reasonable for NY," "the rooms are light and airy," "very well designed and kept up." ⊠ *55 W. 44th St., between 5th and 6th Aves., Midtown West* ☎ *212/921–5500* ⊕ *www.cityclubhotel.com* ↪ *62 rooms, 3 suites* ⛄ *In-room: a/c, safe, DVD, Wi-Fi. In-hotel: restaurant, room service, bar, Internet terminal, Wi-Fi hotspot, parking (paid), some pets allowed* ☰ *AE, D, DC, MC, V* Ⓜ *B, D, F, N, R, M, 1, 2, 3, 9 to 42nd St.; 7 to 5th Ave.* ✦ *4:D4.*

$ ⛱ **The Distrikt.** Rising high above Port Authority, the Distrikt, which opened for business in February 2010, tries to approximate the boutique hotel experience in an area of town better known for bus depots. **Pros:** great central location for accessing public transportation; friendly staff; good Midtown views from higher floors. **Cons:** on a gritty block right across from Port Authority; noisy on lower floors. **TripAdvisor:** "immaculate rooms," "huge and comfortable beds," "not scenic location." ⊠ *W. 40th St., between 8th and 9th Aves., Midtown West* ☎ *212/706–6100* ⊕ *www.distrikthotel.com* ↪ *155 rooms* ⛄ *In-room: a/c, safe, laundry service, Internet terminal, Wi-Fi hotspot, parking (paid)* ☰ *AE, D, DC, MC, V* Ⓜ *A, C, W to 42nd St./8th Ave.* ✦ *4:C4.*

$$ ⛱ **DoubleTree Guest Suites Times Square.** A June 2009 renovation of the
⟳   public spaces in this Fodorite favorite has transformed it into a sleek, modern contender for Times Square top dog. **Pros:** free 24-hour gym and Wi-Fi in public areas; extremely helpful, informed concierge; convenient to the Theater District. **Cons:** paid Wi-Fi in guest rooms; pricey for a DoubleTree. **TripAdvisor:** "convenient location," "very clean and safe," "amazing view of Times Square." ⊠ *1568 Broadway, at 47th St., Midtown West* ☎ *212/719–1600* ⊕ *doubletree1.hilton.com* ↪ *460 rooms* ⛄ *In-room: a/c, safe, refrigerator, DVD, Wi-Fi. In-hotel: restaurant, room service, bar, laundry service, Internet terminal, Wi-Fi hotspot, parking (paid), some pets allowed* ☰ *AE, D, DC, MC, V* Ⓜ *B, D, F, M to 42nd St.* ✦ *4:C3.*

$ ⛱ **Dream New York.** Part hotel, part Kafkaesque dream, this Midtown experience is brought to you by hotelier Vikram Chatwal, and it specializes in style over comfort. **Pros:** Ava Lounge penthouse bar; big spa; up-to-the-minute electronics. **Cons:** small rooms; spotty service; trendier-than-thou atmosphere. **TripAdvisor:** "friendly and helpful concierge," "turndown service nice touch," "noisy." ⊠ *210 W. 55th St., at Broadway, Midtown West* ☎ *212/247–2000 or 866/437–3266* ⊕ *www. dreamny.com* ↪ *208 rooms, 20 suites* ⛄ *In-room: a/c, safe, refrigerator, Internet, Wi-Fi. In-hotel: restaurant, room service, bars, spa, laundry service, Wi-Fi hotspot, parking (paid), some pets allowed* ☰ *AE, D, DC, MC, V* Ⓜ *N, Q, R to 57th St.* ✦ *4:C2.*

$$$ ⛱ **Hilton Times Square.** A glass-and-steel skyscraper atop a 335,000-square-foot retail complex that includes a movie theater and Madame Tussaud's Wax Museum, the Hilton reflects Times Square perfectly. **Pros:** immediate access to entertainment; convenient to public transportation; big rooms. **Cons:** impersonal feel; nickel-and-dime charges and

overpriced food and drink, including a $26 buffet breakfast. **TripAdvisor:** "spotless rooms," "not cheap," "recommended for kids." ✉ *234 W. 42nd St., between 7th and 8th Aves., Midtown West* ☎ *212/642–2500 or 800/445–8667* ⊕ *www.hilton.com* ⤵ *444 rooms, 15 suites* ⚭ *In-room: a/c, safe, refrigerator, Internet, Wi-Fi. In-hotel: restaurant, room service, bar, gym, laundry service, parking (paid), some pets allowed* ▭ *AE, D, DC, MC, V* Ⓜ *1, 2, 3, 7, N, Q, R, S to 42nd St./Times Sq.* ✛ *4:C4.*

$ 🖾 **Hotel 41.** Bamboo in the window beckons guests to the warmly lighted lobby of the Hotel 41. This stylish hotel is not meant for family visits; rooms are tiny, even for two people. **Pros:** DVD player in rooms and DVDs to borrow in the lobby; some rooms have refrigerators; Aveda bath amenities. **Cons:** lack of queen-size beds; small rooms; no view. **TripAdvisor:** "friendly and helpful staff," "good air conditioning," "Aveda products in bathroom." ✉ *206 W. 41st St., Midtown West* ☎ *212/703–8600* ⊕ *www.hotel41nyc.com* ⤵ *47 rooms* ⚭ *In-room: a/c, safe, refrigerator (some), DVD, Internet, Wi-Fi. In-hotel: restaurant, room service, bar, laundry facilities, parking (paid)* ▭ *AE, MC, V* Ⓜ *1, 2, 3, 7, N, Q, R, S to Times Sq./42nd St.; A, C, E to 42nd St./Port Authority Bus Terminal* ✛ *4:C4.*

$–$$ 🖾 **Hotel Metro.** With mirrored columns and elegant black-and-white photos in the lobby, the Hotel Metro feels distinctively retro. **Pros:** renovated exercise room has flat-screen TVs; iPod dock and free Wi-Fi in rooms. **Cons:** noise seeps from outside; rooms are tasteful but spartan. **TripAdvisor:** "well-equipped gym," "avoid hotel car service," "excellent Midtown location." ✉ *45 W. 35th St., between 5th and 6th Aves., Midtown West* ☎ *212/279–1310* ⊕ *www.hotelmetronyc.com* ⤵ *179 rooms* ⚭ *In-room: a/c, safe, Wi-Fi. In-hotel: restaurant, room service, bar, Wi-Fi hotspot* ▭ *AE, DC, MC, V* Ⓜ *B, D, F, N, Q, R, M to 34th St./Herald Sq.* ✛ *4:D6.*

$$$ 🖾 **The Hudson.** Budget fashionistas flocked to the Hudson when it first opened, but now it is starting to show its age. **Pros:** fabulous, elegant bar; gorgeous Francesco Clemente fresco in lobby; breathtaking Sky Terrace. **Cons:** staff can be condescending; tiny rooms; worn furnishings. **TripAdvisor:** "serene and comfortable rooms," "sky terrace," "location is a plus." ✉ *356 W. 58th St., between 8th and 9th Aves., Midtown West* ☎ *212/554–6000* ⊕ *www.hudsonhotel.com* ⤵ *1,000 rooms, 2 suites* ⚭ *In-room: a/c, safe, Wi-Fi. In-hotel: restaurant, room service, bar, gym, laundry service, Internet terminal, Wi-Fi hotspot, parking (paid)* ▭ *AE, D, DC, MC, V* Ⓜ *1, A, B, C, D to 59th St./Columbus Circle* ✛ *4:B1.*

19

$$ 🖾 **Ink48.** The Kimpton chain's first foray onto Manhattan's West Side, ☾ the Ink48 (formerly known as the Vu) is all the way west, on 11th Avenue, and a long walk from the nearest subway, three long avenues away. **Pros:** friendly staff; great views; large rooms. **Cons:** strange location; lobby can feel overly quiet at times; street noise. **TripAdvisor:** "pet friendly," "large rooms," "rooftop lounge." ✉ *653 11th Ave., at W. 48th St., Midtown West* ☎ *212/757–0088* ⊕ *www.ink48.com* ⤵ *195 rooms, 27 suites* ⚭ *In-room: a/c, safe, Wi-Fi. In-hotel: restaurant, room*

service, bar, gym, spa, laundry service, Wi-Fi hotspot, parking (paid), some pets allowed ▭ *AE, D, DC, MC, V* Ⓜ *C, E to 50th St.* ✛ *4:A3.*

$$ 🔝 **InterContinental New York Times Square.** The new InterContinental stands to be a top contender among places to stay in Midtown, with a central location (mere blocks from the heart of Broadway, Times Square and Hell's Kitchen) and reasonable room rates. **Pros:** close to many different subway lines and a bus terminal; in-house restaurant helmed by celebrity chef; attentive staff. **Cons:** no pool; fee for Internet. **TripAdvisor:** "room was lovely," "centrally located," "staff was courteous, professional, and gracious." ⊠ *300 W. 44th Street, Midtown West* 🕾 *212/803–4500* ⊕ *www.intercontinental.com* ⤿ *518 rooms, 29 suites* ⌂ *In-room: a/c, Internet, Wi-Fi. In-hotel: 1 restaurant, room service, bar, gym, laundry service, Internet terminal, Wi-Fi hotspot, parking (paid).* ▭ *AE, D, DC, MC, V* Ⓜ *A, C, E to 42nd St./Port Authority Bust Terminal* ✛ *4:B4.*

$$$–$$$$ 🔝 **Jumeirah Essex House.** New managers Jumeirah Hotel Group aimed high with a $90 million refurbishment program for this famed property in 2007, and it still looks fresh several years on. **Pros:** great service; amazing views; impressive restaurant. **Cons:** overly complex room gadgetry; very expensive bar. **TripAdvisor:** "elegant," "pricey minibar," "no traffic noise." ⊠ *160 Central Park S, between 6th and 7th Aves., Midtown West* 🕾 *212/247–0300 or 800/937–8461* ⊕ *www.jumeirahessexhouse.com* ⤿ *515 rooms, 70 suites* ⌂ *In-room: a/c, safe, Internet, Wi-Fi. In-hotel: 2 restaurants, room service, bar, gym, spa, laundry service, Internet terminal, Wi-Fi hotspot, parking (paid), some pets allowed* ▭ *AE, D, DC, MC, V* Ⓜ *F, N, R, Q to 57th St.* ✛ *4:C1.*

¢   🔝 **La Quinta Inn.** The name may conjure a cheapie siesta spot, but don't dismiss it: smack in the middle of Koreatown and close to Penn Station, this budget-friendly hotel in a cheerful old Beaux-Arts building may be one of the best deals in town. **Pros:** self-check-in machines; gift shop on the premises for necessities. **Cons:** no room service; no frills. **TripAdvisor:** "efficient and friendly staff," "clean," "good value." ⊠ *17 W. 32nd St., between 5th Ave. and Broadway, Midtown West* 🕾 *212/736–1600* ⊕ *www.lq.com* ⤿ *182 rooms* ⌂ *In-room: a/c, safe, Wi-Fi. In-hotel: bar, gym, laundry facilities, Wi-Fi hotspot, parking (paid)* ▭ *AE, D, DC, MC, V* Ⓜ *B, D, F, N, Q, R, M to 34th St./Herald Sq.* ✛ *4:E6.*

$$ 🔝 **Le Parker Meridien.** A splash of kookiness in otherwise staid Midtown, ⟳   the Parker is a whimsical place to visit, and the little touches shine through. **Pros:** lively, animated spirit; best hotel gym in the city; fun eating options; tech-friendly rooms. **Cons:** lobby is a public space; small bathrooms. **TripAdvisor:** "stellar views of Central Park," "excellent air conditioning," "rooftop pool." ⊠ *118 W. 57th St., between 6th and 7th Aves., Midtown West* 🕾 *212/245–5000 or 800/543–4300* ⊕ *www.parkermeridien.com* ⤿ *484 rooms, 249 suites* ⌂ *In-room: a/c, safe, refrigerator, DVD, Internet. In-hotel: 3 restaurants, room service, bar, pool, gym, spa, laundry service, parking (paid)* ▭ *AE, D, DC, MC, V* Ⓜ *B, D, E, N, Q, R to 57th St.* ✛ *4:D1.*

$$$ 🔝 **The London NYC.** Boasting the design expertise of David Collins and the cuisine of Gordon Ramsay in his first stateside restaurant, the London NYC merges the style and flair of both of its namesake cities. **Pros:**

posh atmosphere without prissiness; Gordon Ramsay restaurant; great fitness club. **Cons:** inconsistent service; no bathtubs in most rooms; expensive dining options. **TripAdvisor:** "excellent service and amenities," "large rooms," "friendly and helpful staff." ✉ *151 W. 54th St., between 6th and 7th Aves., Midtown West* ☎ *212/307–*

5000 or 866/690–2029 ⊕ *www.thelondonnyc.com* ⤤ *561 suites* ⚐ *In-room: a/c, safe, Internet, Wi-Fi. In-hotel: restaurant, room service, bar, gym, laundry service, parking (paid), some pets allowed* ⊟ *AE, D, DC, MC, V* Ⓜ *B, D, E to 7th Ave.; N, Q, R to 57th St.* ✛ *4:C2.*

$$$$ 🏨 **Mandarin Oriental.** The Mandarin brings some Asian style to a rather
Fodor's Choice   staid corner of New York. **Pros:** fantastic pool views; all the resources
★   of the Time Warner Center; expansive suites. **Cons:** Trump hotel blocks portion of park views; expensive; mall-like surroundings. **TripAdvisor:** "incredible views," "immaculate rooms," "top notch spa facilities." ✉ *80 Columbus Circle, at 60th St., Midtown West* ☎ *212/805–8800* ⊕ *www.mandarinoriental.com/newyork* ⤤ *202 rooms, 46 suites* ⚐ *In-room: a/c, refrigerator, DVD, Internet, Wi-Fi. In-hotel: restaurant, room service, bar, pool, gym, spa, laundry service* ⊟ *AE, D, DC, MC, V* Ⓜ *A, B, C, D, 1 to 59th St./Columbus Circle* ✛ *5:C6.*

$$ 🏨 **The Mansfield.** They sweat the small stuff at the Mansfield; Wi-Fi is free, bathroom products are from Aveda, and even the key cards are snazzily embossed with scenes of old-timey New York. **Pros:** complimentary Wi-Fi; business center; 24-hour gym; great bar. **Cons:** tiny bathrooms; air conditioners are window units. **TripAdvisor:** "spotlessly clean rooms," "very close to Bryant Park," "loved M bar." ✉ *12 W. 44th St., between 5th and 6th Aves., Midtown West* ☎ *212/944–6050 or 800/255–5167* ⊕ *www.mansfieldhotel.com* ⤤ *124 rooms, 25 suites* ⚐ *In-room: a/c, safe, Wi-Fi. In-hotel: restaurant, room service, bar, laundry service, Internet terminal, gym, Wi-Fi hotspot, parking (paid), some pets allowed* ⊟ *AE, D, DC, MC, V* Ⓜ *B, D, F, M to 42nd St.* ✛ *4:E4.*

$$$–$$$$ 🏨 **The Michelangelo.** Italophiles will feel that they've been transported to the good life in the boot at this deluxe hotel, where the long, wide lobby lounge is clad with multihue marble and Veronese-style oil paintings. **Pros:** good location; fantastic restaurant; spacious rooms. **Cons:** noisy air-conditioning units; some rooms have limited views; small closets. **TripAdvisor:** "can't beat the location," "extremely helpful concierge," "top notch service." ✉ *152 W. 51st St., at 7th Ave., Midtown West* ☎ *212/765–1900 or 800/237–0990* ⊕ *www.michelangelohotel.com* ⤤ *123 rooms, 56 suites* ⚐ *In-room: a/c, Internet. In-hotel: restaurant, room service, bar, gym, laundry service, Internet terminal, parking (paid)* ⊟ *AE, D, DC, MC, V* ❧|CP Ⓜ *B, D, E to 7th Ave.; 1 to 50th St.; B, D, F, M to 47th–50th Sts./Rockefeller Center* ✛ *4:C3.*

$ 🏨 **Muse Hotel.** Fresh off a 2009 renovation, the Muse is a bit more staid than it once was. Yes, the Surrealist prints and busts of Thalia, the muse

19

Mandarin Oriental

Plaza Hotel

Ritz-Carlton New York, Central Park South

of comedy, remain, and so do the cheeky robes—now they're zebra print; rooms, however, are slightly toned down, in black and cream. **Pros:** contemporary interiors; good Midtown location; pet-friendly. **Cons:** street noise; small gym. **TripAdvisor:** "friendly and accomodating staff," "wine hour," "amazing room service." ☒ *130 W. 46th St., between 6th and 7th Aves., Midtown West* ☎ *212/485–2400 or 877/692–6873* ⊕ *www.themusehotel.com* ↝ *200 rooms, 19 suites* ♿ *In-room: a/c, safe, Wi-Fi. In-hotel: restaurant, room service, bar, gym, laundry service, Internet terminal, Wi-Fi hotspot, parking (paid), some pets allowed* ▭ *AE, D, DC, MC, V* Ⓜ *B, D, F, M to 47th–50th Sts./ Rockefeller Center* ✛ *4:C4.*

$$$$ 🏨 **Plaza Hotel.** Eloise's adopted home on the corner of Central Park, the
Fodor'sChoice Plaza is back in the hotel game after a $450 million renovation. **Pros:**
★ historic property; great hotel bar; lavish rooms. **Cons:** rooms aren't that big for the money; Oak Room restaurant is pricey. **TripAdvisor:** "staff well-trained in hospitality," "excellent shopping outside door," "extremely comfortable beds." ☒ *768 5th Ave., at Central Park S, Midtown West* ☎ *212/759–3000* ⊕ *www.theplaza.com* ↝ *282 rooms, 102 suites* ♿ *In-room: a/c, safe, DVD, Wi-Fi. In-hotel: 2 restaurants, room service, bar, gym, spa, laundry service, Wi-Fi hotspot* ▭ *AE, D, DC, MC, V* Ⓜ *N, R to 59th St.* ✛ *4:E1.*

$ 🏨 **Renaissance Hotel.** After a $26 million refresh headed by designer Jordan Mozer, the Renaissance shifted in fall 2009 from all business to wacky and whimsical, and it's a rather enjoyable move. **Pros:** contemporary design; latest in-room technology. **Cons:** in the heart of the Square: pandemonium isn't for everyone; over-the-top design not for everyone. **TripAdvisor:** "real boutique vibe," "spacious and clean rooms," "conveniently located." ☒ *714 7th Ave., between W. 47th and W. 48th Sts., Midtown West* ☎ *212/765–7676 or 800/628–5222* ⊕ *www.renaissancehotels.com* ↝ *300 rooms, 5 suites* ♿ *In-room: a/c, safe, Internet, Wi-Fi. In-hotel: restaurant, room service, bars, gym, laundry service, Internet terminal, Wi-Fi hotspot, parking (paid), some pets allowed* ▭ *AE, D, DC, MC, V* Ⓜ *R to 49th St.; 1 to 50th St.* ✛ *4:C3.*

$$$$ 🏨 **The Ritz-Carlton New York, Central Park.** It's all about the park views
☾ here. Service aside, the competition among properties near the park's
Fodor'sChoice south side is fierce, and although the Ritz isn't the foremost of the
★ bunch, it does offer some nice perks. **Pros:** great concierge; personalized service; stellar location; views. **Cons:** pricey; limited common areas. **TripAdvisor:** "supremely comfortable bed," "very large room," "exceptional service." ☒ *50 Central Park S, at 6th Ave., Midtown West* ☎ *212/308–9100 or 866/671–6008* ⊕ *www.ritzcarlton.com/centralpark* ↝ *259 rooms, 47 suites* ♿ *In-room: a/c, safe, DVD, Internet, Wi-Fi. In-hotel: restaurant, room service, bar, gym, spa, laundry service, parking (paid), some pets allowed* ▭ *AE, D, DC, MC, V* Ⓜ *F, M to 57th St.* ✛ *4:D1.*

$ 🏨 **Room Mate Grace.** A favorite of European visitors and business travel-
☾ ers in fashion and entertainment, Grace delivers high-design lodgings on a budget. **Pros:** free, ample continental breakfast; friendly, helpful staff. **Cons:** tiny rooms; little in-room privacy (no door separating shower from main room). **TripAdvisor:** "excellent value for money," "great

19

Kids in Tow

Many New York hotels go out of their way to accommodate families, with special amenities and family-size rooms. However, a hotel claiming that it's child-friendly doesn't always translate to true kid-welcoming style. Ask if cribs come with linens, whether there are high chairs and children's menus in the dining room, and if there are in-house babysitters. Some hotels will even clear out the minibar (for bottle or baby-food storage), baby-proof a room, or provide baby-proofing materials. Here are some of the top picks for traveling with kids.

SUITE LIFE. Space is at a premium in New York hotels, and if you have more than two people in a standard room, you'll really start to feel the squeeze. The answer? A suite, where you can spread out in style. With renovated, spacious suites, **Affinia 50** (⇨ Midtown East and Upper East Side) is the family hotel of choice on the residential East Side.

PURE PAMPERING. Just because you have children in tow doesn't mean your dream of a pampering vacation needs to go down the drain. Several top New York hotels go out of their way to accommodate families. The **Ritz-Carlton's** two hotels (⇨ Lower Manhattan and Midtown West) offer special healthful children's menus,

rubber-duck-filled baths, and toy menus from FAO Schwarz. The **Mandarin-Oriental** (⇨ Midtown West) offers complimentary kids' DVDs and video games, and free coloring books, and crayons for kids.

FUN FLAVOR. Room Mate Grace (⇨ Midtown West and Chelsea) might make the perfect respite if you have teens in tow. There's a funky lobby pool, a kiosk that stocks sweets with which to fill the in-room refrigerators, and rooms with bunk beds that levitate out of the walls and have their own plasma TVs. At the hip **Hotel on Rivington** (⇨ East Village and Lower East Side) a special family suite has two full bedrooms, one with two sets of bunk beds and a big bin of toys. Bonus points: the hotel is across from Economy Candy.

KID KARMA. Family-friendly **Le Parker Meridien** (⇨ Midtown West and Chelsea) has a large pool, a restaurant that serves decadent breakfast foods such as chocolate French toast, and a casual dining spot that serves nothing but burgers and shakes.

KID-SIZE. At the 70 Park, kids get their own mini-size animal-print robes (also available for purchase) so they can feel just like their grown-up travel companions.

---

location," "excessive street noise." ⊠ *125 W. 45th St., Midtown West* ☎ *212/354–2323* ⊕ *www.room-matehotels.com* ⌨ *139 rooms* ⌂ *In-room: a/c, safe, refrigerator, DVD, Wi-Fi. In-hotel: bar, pool, gym, laundry service, parking (paid)* ⊟ *AE, D, DC, MC, V* ⊚*CP* Ⓜ *B, D, F, M to 42nd St.* ✣ *4:D4.*

$$$–$$$$ ⛨ **The Royalton.** During the 1990s the Royalton's dramatic lobby started the craze of local A-listers meeting and greeting in hotel bars; the space, after being completely redesigned by Roman and Williams, now attracts a new generation of movers and shakers to congregate around its sumptuous sofas and the warm glow of its massive cast-bronze fireplace. **Pros:** hip lobby scene; luxe beds and bathrooms; helpful service. **Cons:**

dark hallways; lighting verges on eye-strainingly dim. **TripAdvisor:** "spacious shower," "stylished decorated room," "great Midtown location." ⊠ *44 W. 44th St., between 5th and 6th Aves., Midtown West* ☎ *212/869–4400 or 800/635–9013* ⊕ *www.royaltonhotel.com* ⬎ *141 rooms, 27 suites* ⚹ *In-room: a/c, safe, Internet, Wi-Fi. In-hotel: restaurant, room service, bar, gym, laundry service, Internet terminal, Wi-Fi hotspot, parking (paid)* ▭ *AE, D, DC, MC, V* Ⓜ *B, D, F, M to 42nd St.* ✛ *4:D4.*

$$ ▭ **The Shoreham.** The Shoreham hopes to attract glamorous types, but the result is that all the guests feel like they're stars. **Pros:** stylish decor; tech-friendly. **Cons:** not designed for families. **TripAdvisor:** "very nice staff," "simple clean rooms," "near great restaurants." ⊠ *33 W. 55th St., between 5th and 6th Aves., Midtown West* ☎ *212/247–6700 or 877/847–4444* ⊕ *www.shorehamhotel.com* ⬎ *174 rooms, 37 suites* ⚹ *In-room: a/c, safe, DVD, Wi-Fi. In-hotel: restaurant, room service, bar, laundry service, Internet terminal, Wi-Fi hotspot, parking (paid), some pets allowed* ▭ *AE, D, DC, MC, V* ⦶ *CP* Ⓜ *E, M to 5th Ave.* ✛ *4:D2.*

$$ ▭ **6 Columbus.** A boutique-style hotel nestled in the shadow of the towering Time Warner center, 6 Columbus—part of the ever-proliferating Thompson Hotel Group—offers the vibe and amenities of downtown lodging with the convenience of a more centralized Midtown location. **Pros:** convenient location; fun in-hotel restaurant; reasonably priced for neighborhood; family-friendly. **Cons:** rooms on lower floors facing 58th Street can be noisy. **TripAdvisor:** "pleasant and helpful staff," "good hotel in a great location," "rooms are small." ⊠ *Columbus Circle, Midtown West* ☎ *212/204–3002* ⊕ *www.thompsonhotels.com* ⬎ *72 rooms, 16 suites* ⚹ *In-room: a/c, safe, kitchen (some), refrigerator (some), Internet, Wi-Fi. In-hotel: restaurant, room service, bar, Wi-Fi hotspot, parking (paid), some pets allowed* ▭ *AE, D, DC, MC, V* Ⓜ *1, A, B, C, D to 59th St./Columbus Circle* ✛ *5:C6.*

$$ ▭ **Sofitel New York.** This property brings Gallic flair to the neighborhood. In addition to bilingual signage throughout the hotel, there's plenty of velvet in the lobby, along with leather couches and vases of flowers. **Pros:** central location; great beds. **Cons:** pricey; room views vary. **TripAdvisor:** "blissfully quiet rooms," "luxurious linens and towels," "ideal location." ⊠ *45 W. 44th St., between 5th and 6th Aves., Midtown West* ☎ *212/354–8844* ⊕ *www.sofitel.com* ⬎ *348 rooms, 52 suites* ⚹ *In-room: a/c, safe, Wi-Fi. In-hotel: restaurant, room service, bar, gym, laundry service, Internet terminal, Wi-Fi hotspot, parking (paid)* ▭ *AE, D, DC, MC, V* Ⓜ *B, D, F, M to 42nd St.* ✛ *4:E4.*

$$–$$$ ▭ **The Time Hotel.** One of the neighborhood's first boutique hotels, this spot half a block from the din of Times Square tempers trendiness with a touch of humor. **Pros:** acclaimed and popular Serafina restaurant downstairs; surprisingly quiet for Times Square location; good turndown service. **Cons:** decor makes the rooms a little dated; service is inconsistent; water pressure is lacking. **TripAdvisor:** "prime location," "very small bathroom," "clean and safe." ⊠ *224 W. 49th St., between Broadway and 8th Ave., Midtown West* ☎ *212/320–2900 or 877/846–3692* ⊕ *www.thetimeny.com* ⬎ *164 rooms, 29 suites* ⚹ *In-room: a/c,*

19

safe, Internet. In-hotel: restaurant, room service, bar, gym, laundry service, Internet terminal, parking (paid) ⊟ *AE, D, DC, MC, V* Ⓜ *1, C, E to 50th St.* ✛ *4:C3.*

$ ⊞ **W Times Square.** First opened at the end of 2001, the W Times Square is looking sleek once again thanks to a recent renovation. **Pros:** bustling nightlife and happy-hour scene; sleek rooms. **Cons:** if you want quiet, head elsewhere; no bathtubs in the smaller rooms. **TripAdvisor:** "pleasant front desk staff," "always comfortable rooms," "street noise." ✉ *1567 Broadway, at W. 47th St., Midtown West* ☎ *212/930–7400 or 877/946–8357* ⊕ *www.whotels.com* ↜ *464 rooms, 43 suites* ⚭ *In-room: a/c, safe, DVD, Internet. In-hotel: restaurant, room service, bar, gym, spa, laundry service, Internet terminal, Wi-Fi hotspot, some pets allowed* ⊟ *AE, D, DC, MC, V* Ⓜ *1, 2, 3, 7, N, Q, R, S to 42nd St./Times Sq.* ✛ *4:C3.*

$$–$$$ ⊞ **Warwick.** This grande dame was built by William Randolph Hearst for his mistress, Hollywood actress Marion Davies, and it has hosted many from Tinseltown since then, including Cary Grant in the Presidential Suite for 12 years. **Pros:** excellent restaurant and bar; historic property; spacious suites. **Cons:** not all rooms have been redone; no a/c in the hallways. **TripAdvisor:** "fabulous personnel," "always clean room," "lovely view of Central Park." ✉ *65 W. 54th St., at 6th Ave., Midtown West* ☎ *212/247–2700 or 800/223–4099* ⊕ *www.warwickhotelny.com* ↜ *359 rooms, 66 suites* ⚭ *In-room: a/c, safe, refrigerator, Wi-Fi. In-hotel: 2 restaurants, room service, bar, gym, laundry service, parking (paid)* ⊟ *AE, DC, MC, V* Ⓜ *E, M to 57th St.; N, Q, R, W to 57th St.* ✛ *4:D2.*

$ ⊞ **Wellington Hotel.** A few blocks south of Central Park and Columbus
☾   Circle, the Wellington is a fine jumping-off point for visitors who want to see the sights in Midtown and the Upper West Side. **Pros:** central location; chipper staff; good for big families. **Cons:** dark bathrooms; limited breakfast. **TripAdvisor:** "helpful bell boys," "good sized room," "close to Central Park." ✉ *871 7th Ave., at W. 55th St., Midtown West* ☎ *212/247–3900 or 800/652–1212* ⊕ *www.wellingtonhotel.com* ↜ *600 rooms, 100 suites* ⚭ *In-room: a/c, Wi-Fi. In-hotel: restaurant, bar, laundry facilities, laundry service, Internet terminal, Wi-Fi hotspot, parking (paid)* ⊟ *AE, D, DC, MC, V* Ⓜ *N, Q, R to 57th St.* ✛ *4:C2.*

$ ⊞ **Westin New York at Times Square.** A $24 million renovation is complete at this giant Midtown hotel; all rooms come with the Heavenly Bed, flat-screen televisions, and Wi-Fi. For even more comfort, spa-floor rooms come with massage chairs, aromatherapy candles, and other pampering pleasures. **Pros:** busy Times Square location; big rooms; great gym. **Cons:** busy Times Square location; small bathroom sinks; some rooms need to be refreshed. **TripAdvisor:** "very friendly receptionists," "lovely bed," "smooth check-in." ✉ *270 W. 43rd St., at 8th Ave., Midtown West* ☎ *212/201–2700 or 866/837–4183* ⊕ *www.westinny.com* ↜ *863 rooms, 126 suites* ⚭ *In-room: a/c, safe, refrigerator, Internet, Wi-Fi. In-hotel: restaurant, room service, bars, gym, spa, laundry service, Internet terminal, Wi-Fi hotspot, parking (paid), some pets allowed* ⊟ *AE, D, DC, MC, V* Ⓜ *A, C, E to 42nd St./Times Sq.* ✛ *4:B4.*

MIDTOWN EAST

$$ ⊞ **Affinia 50.** This extremely popular hotel has a businesslike mood, but ☾ it's also supremely comfortable for families or leisure travelers. **Pros:** apartment-style living; good value; kid- and pet-friendly. **Cons:** ugly lobby; old televisions; pricey Wi-Fi. **TripAdvisor:** "rooms were clean and stylish," "real New York experience at a good value," "great location to midtown attractions." ⊠ *155 E. 50th St., at 3rd Ave., Midtown East* ☎ *212/751–5710 or 800/637–8483* ⊕ *www.affinia.com* ⇆ *56 rooms, 151 suites* ⚷ *In-room: a/c, safe, kitchen (some), refrigerator, Internet. In-hotel: room service, gym, laundry facilities, laundry service, Internet terminal, Wi-Fi hotspot, parking (paid), some pets allowed* ▭ *AE, D, DC, MC, V* Ⓜ *6 to 51st St./Lexington Ave.; E, M to Lexington–3rd Aves./53rd St.* ✛ *4:G3.*

$$$ ⊞ **The Alex.** Often overlooked in a part of the city that's heavy with office buildings, the Alex is a sleek little oasis of style on Manhattan's East Side. **Pros:** all suites have kitchens; good service; on-site fitness facilities. **Cons:** cramped lobby; small bathrooms; expensive Wi-Fi. **TripAdvisor:** "comfortable beds," "very good gym," "Frederic Fekkai toiletries." ⊠ *205 E. 45th St., between 2nd and 3rd Aves., Midtown East* ☎ *212/867–5100* ⊕ *www.thealexhotel.com* ⇆ *73 rooms, 130 suites* ⚷ *In-room: a/c, kitchen (some), DVD, Internet. In-hotel: restaurant, room service, bar, gym, laundry service, Internet terminal, Wi-Fi hotspot, parking (paid), some pets allowed* ▭ *AE, MC, V* Ⓜ *4, 5, 6, 7, S to 42nd St./Grand Central* ✛ *4:G4.*

$$$ ⊞ **The Benjamin.** New York bills itself as the City That Never Sleeps, but of course a good night's rest is essential for visitors who plan to tackle a lot during the day. **Pros:** sleep-friendly; gracious staff; kitchenettes in big rooms. **Cons:** paid Internet and Wi-Fi; boring views; dull neighborhood after dark. **TripAdvisor:** "top notch service," "nicely furnished rooms," "excellent Midtown location." ⊠ *125 E. 50th St., at Lexington Ave., Midtown East* ☎ *212/715–2500* ⊕ *www.thebenjamin. com* ⇆ *200 rooms* ⚷ *In-room: a/c, safe, kitchen (some), refrigerator, Internet, Wi-Fi. In-hotel: restaurant, room service, bar, gym, spa, laundry service, Internet terminal, parking (paid), some pets allowed* ▭ *AE, D, DC, MC, V* Ⓜ *6 to 51st St./Lexington Ave.; E, M to Lexington–3rd Aves./53rd St.* ✛ *4:F3.*

$$$ ⊞ **The Dylan.** This hotel made a big splash when it opened at the start of the decade, but there haven't been many changes since then, and it's starting to show. **Pros:** central location; free Internet; new room furnishings. **Cons:** inattentive service; small fitness center; pricey for limited amenities. **TripAdvisor:** "nice amenities," "fantastic location," "excellent choice." ⊠ *52 E. 41st St., between Park and Madison Aves., Midtown East* ☎ *212/338–0500* ⊕ *www.dylanhotel.com* ⇆ *107 rooms, 5 suites* ⚷ *In-room: a/c, safe, Internet, Wi-Fi. In-hotel: restaurant, room service, bar, gym, Wi-Fi hotspot* ▭ *AE, D, DC, MC, V* Ⓜ *4, 5, 6, 7, S to 42nd St./Grand Central* ✛ *4:E5.*

$$$$ ⊞ **Four Seasons Hotel.** It's the Four Seasons, and for better or worse, it remains the blueprint for what a Manhattan luxury hotel should be. **Pros:** spacious and comfortable rooms; perfect concierge and staff service; afternoon tea in the lobby lounge. **Cons:** pricey; confusing room

19

controls; furniture could use updating. **TripAdvisor:** "service is impeccable," "understated and modern," "love it each time." ✉ *57 E. 57th St., between Park and Madison Aves., Midtown East* ☎ *212/758–5700 or 800/487–3769* ⊕ *www.fourseasons.com* ⤳ *300 rooms, 68 suites* ⚲ *In-room: a/c, safe, DVD, Internet, Wi-Fi. In-hotel: restaurant, room service, bar, gym, spa, laundry service, Internet terminal, Wi-Fi hotspot, parking (paid), some pets allowed* ⊟ *AE, D, DC, MC, V* Ⓜ *4, 5, 6, N, Q, R to 59th St./Lexington Ave.* ✛ *4:F1.*

$ ⊡ **The Gotham Hotel.** On the site of the Gotham Book Mart, this sleek, skinny hotel has lots of things going for it, but one clincher for anyone seeking fresh air while in Manhattan: every last room boasts outdoor space. **Pros:** welcoming staff; central location; every room has a balcony. **Cons:** no on-site gym. **TripAdvisor:** "no common areas," "lack of amenities," "good value." ✉ *16 E. 46th St., between 5th and 6th Aves., Midtown East* ☎ *212/490–8500* ⊕ *www.thegothamhotelny.com* ⤳ *66 rooms* ⚲ *In-room: a/c, safe, refrigerator (some), Internet, Wi-Fi. In-hotel: restaurant, room service, bar, laundry service, Wi-Fi hotspot, some pets allowed* ⊟ *AE, D, DC, MC, V* ⦿| *CP* Ⓜ *B, D, F, M to 47th– 50th Sts./Rockefeller Center* ✛ *4:D3.*

$$ ⊡ **Library Hotel.** Bookishly handsome, this stately landmark brownstone,
Fodor's Choice built in 1900, is inspired by the New York Public Library, a block
★ away. **Pros:** fun rooftop bar; playful book themes; stylish rooms. **Cons:** rooftop often reserved for events; more books in rooms themselves would be nice. **TripAdvisor:** "professional and efficient staff," "small rooms," "friendly welcome." ✉ *299 Madison Ave., at E. 41st St., Midtown East* ☎ *212/983–4500 or 877/793–7323* ⊕ *www.libraryhotel.com* ⤳ *60 rooms* ⚲ *In-room: a/c, safe, refrigerator, DVD, Internet, Wi-Fi. In-hotel: restaurant, room service, bar, laundry service, parking (paid)* ⊟ *AE, DC, MC, V* ⦿| *CP* Ⓜ *4, 5, 6, 7, S to 42nd St./Grand Central* ✛ *4:E4.*

$$$ ⊡ **Loews Regency Hotel.** The snazzy lobby sums up the focus of this Park Avenue hotel: service and space. **Pros:** friendly and helpful staff; relatively quiet; good for pets; updated fitness center. **Cons:** rooms are pretty but not a great value; overpriced room service. **TripAdvisor:** "excellent room service," "delightfully quiet rooms," "great location." ✉ *540 Park Ave., at E. 61st St., Midtown East* ☎ *212/759–4100 or 800/233–2356* ⊕ *www.loewshotels.com* ⤳ *266 rooms, 87 suites* ⚲ *In-room: a/c, safe, kitchen (some), refrigerator, Internet. In-hotel: restaurant, room service, bar, gym, laundry service, parking (paid), some pets allowed* ⊟ *AE, D, DC, MC, V* Ⓜ *4, 5, 6, N, Q, R to 59th St./Lexington Ave.* ✛ *5:F6.*

$$ ⊡ **Millennium UN Plaza.** This sky-high tower near the United Nations begins on the 28th floor; the rooms, which make generous use of warm woods and neutral tones, have breathtaking views—get one facing west, toward Manhattan. **Pros:** unbeatable East River and city views; good value; great front-door and bell staff. **Cons:** a walk to the subway; pricey Internet access. **TripAdvisor:** "large rooms," "eclectic decoration," "quiet location." ✉ *1 United Nations Plaza, at E. 44th St. and 1st Ave., Midtown East* ☎ *212/758–1234 or 866/866–8086* ⊕ *www. millenniumhotels.com* ⤳ *382 rooms, 45 suites* ⚲ *In-room: a/c, safe,*

Internet. In-hotel: restaurant, room service, bar, tennis court, pool, gym, laundry service, Internet terminal, Wi-Fi hotspot, parking (paid) ▭ *AE, D, DC, MC, V* Ⓜ *4, 5, 6, 7, S to 42nd St./Grand Central* ✛ *4:H4.*

$$$ 🏨 **New York Palace Hotel.** Want the privileged *Gossip Girl* experience? Stay at these connected mansions, built in the 1880s by railroad baron Henry Villard and supposedly populated by Serena van der Woodsen, circa 2009. **Pros:** gorgeous courtyard with 15th-century Italian-style motifs; great service; unmatched views of St. Patrick's Cathedral. **Cons:** overpriced; harried service from staff. **TripAdvisor:** "top class staff," "spacious and bright rooms," "superbly located." ✉ *455 Madison Ave., at E. 50th St., Midtown East* ☎ *212/888–7000 or 800/697–2522* ⊕ *www.newyorkpalace.com* ↪ *804 rooms, 88 suites* ⌂ *In-room: a/c, safe, refrigerator (some), Internet. In-hotel: 2 restaurants, room service, bars, gym, spa, laundry service, Internet terminal, Wi-Fi hotspot, parking (paid), some pets allowed* ▭ *AE, D, DC, MC, V* Ⓜ *6 to 51st St./Lexington Ave.; E, M to Lexington–3rd Aves./53rd St.* ✛ *4:E3.*

$$$ 🏨 **Omni Berkshire Place.** A recent renovation has reenergized this prop-
🐾 erty, giving it a luxe, modern vibe. **Pros:** location in the heart of a see-it-all New York; 17th-floor fitness center overlooks St. Patrick's Cathedral. **Cons:** no free morning coffee; paid Internet. **TripAdvisor:** "roomy for New York standards," "top notch," "lovely rooms, great service." ✉ *21 E. 52nd St., between 5th and Madison Aves., Midtown East* ☎ *212/753–5800 or 800/843–6664* ⊕ *www.omnihotels.com* ↪ *396 rooms* ⌂ *In-room: a/c, safe, Internet, Wi-Fi. In-hotel: restaurant, room service, bar, gym, laundry facilities, laundry service, Wi-Fi hotspot, parking (paid), some pets allowed* ▭ *AE, D, DC, MC, V* Ⓜ *E, M to 5th Ave.* ✛ *4:E2.*

$$$$ 🏨 **The Peninsula.** Stepping through the Peninsula's Beaux-Arts facade
Fodor'sChoice onto the grand staircase overhung with a monumental chandelier,
★ you know you're in for a glitzy treat. **Pros:** brilliant service; fabulous rooms, with the best lighting of all city hotels (good angles, easy to use); unforgettable rooftop bar. **Cons:** expensive. **TripAdvisor:** "impeccable service," "spacious rooms," "excellent location." ✉ *700 5th Ave., at 55th St., Midtown East* ☎ *212/956–2888 or 800/262–9467* ⊕ *www. peninsula.com* ↪ *185 rooms, 54 suites* ⌂ *In-room: a/c, safe, refrigerator, Internet, Wi-Fi. In-hotel: restaurant, room service, bars, pool, gym, spa, laundry service, parking (paid), some pets allowed* ▭ *AE, D, DC, MC, V* Ⓜ *E, M to 5th Ave.* ✛ *4:E2.*

¢ 🏨 **Pod Hotel.** This is the hotel that made bunk beds cool again—and now they're everywhere; by offering spotless stainless-steel bunks with pullout flat-screen TVs, the Pod makes tiny, tiny rooms tolerable. **Pros:** an inexpensive and fun way to save money. **Cons:** many will hate the small rooms; some shared bathrooms. **TripAdvisor:** "friendly and helpful staff," "small rooms," "roof terrace." ✉ *230 E. 51st St., between 2nd and 3rd Aves., Midtown East* ☎ *212/355–0300 or 800/874–0074* ⊕ *www.thepodhotel.com* ↪ *347 rooms, 195 with bath* ⌂ *In-room: a/c, Wi-Fi* ▭ *AE, DC, MC, V* Ⓜ *6 to 51st St./Lexington Ave.; E, M to Lexington–3rd Aves./53rd St.* ✛ *4:G2.*

$ 🏨 **Roger Smith.** This quirky choice is one of the better budget buys in the city. **Pros:** good location near Grand Central; intimate atmosphere;

19

free Wi-Fi. **Cons:** street noise; small bathrooms. **TripAdvisor:** "pleasant and helpful staff," "warmly recommended," "not far from Grand Central." ⊠ *501 Lexington Ave., between E. 47th and E. 48th Sts., Midtown East* ☎ *212/755–1400 or 800/445–0277* ⊕ *www.rogersmith. com* ↘ *102 rooms, 28 suites* ⑂ *In-room: a/c, kitchen (some), refrigerator, Internet, Wi-Fi. In-hotel: restaurant, room service, bar, laundry service, parking (paid), some pets allowed* ⊟ *AE, D, DC, MC, V* Ⓜ *6 to 51st St./Lexington Ave.; E, M to Lexington–3rd Aves./53rd St.* ✛ *4:F3.*

$ 🏨 **Roosevelt Hotel.** Named after Teddy, not Franklin, this Midtown icon steps from Grand Central has plenty of elbow room for stretching out. **Pros:** great public areas; big bathrooms. **Cons:** dated decor; limited in-room amenities. **TripAdvisor:** "amazing location," "well-maintained and clean rooms," "good value." ⊠ *45 E. 45th St., at Madison Ave., Midtown East* ☎ *888/833–3969* ⊕ *www.theroosevelthotel. com* ↘ *1,015 rooms, 24 suites* ⑂ *In-room: a/c, Wi-Fi. In-hotel: restaurant, room service, gym, parking (paid)* ⊟ *AE, MC, V* Ⓜ *4, 5, 6 to Grand Central/42nd St.* ✛ *4:F4.*

$$$ 🏨 **The Setai Fifth Avenue.** Setting new standards of luxury on lower 5th, the towering, limestone-clad Setai has been conceived as an opulent crash pad for wealthy overseas tourists, captains of industry on long-term stays, and anyone in need of some serious pampering. **Pros:** attentive service; gorgeous spa; great location. **Cons:** street noise reported by guests on lower floors. **TripAdvisor:** "top notch," "treated us like royalty," "very satisfied." ⊠ *400 5th Ave. between 36th and 37th Sts., Midtown East* ☎ *212/695–4005* ⊕ *www.setaififthavenue.com* ↘ *157 rooms, 57 suites* ⑂ *In-room: a/c, safe, kitchen, refrigerator (some), Internet, Wi-Fi. In-hotel: restaurant, room service, bar, gym, spa, laundry service, Wi-Fi hotspot, parking (paid), some pets allowed* ⊟ *AE, D, DC, MC, V* Ⓜ *B, D, F, V to 34th St./Penn Station* ✛ *4:E5.*

$$$$ 🏨 **The St. Regis.** World-class from head to toe, the St. Regis comes as
Fodor's Choice close to flawless as any hotel in New York. **ros:** rooms combine true lux-
★ ury with helpful technology; easy-access butler service; superb in-house dining; prestigious location. **Cons:** expensive; too serious for families seeking fun. **TripAdvisor:** "delicious room service," "lovely afternoon tea," "turndown service." ⊠ *2 E. 55th St., at 5th Ave., Midtown East* ☎ *212/753–4500 or 877/787–3447* ⊕ *www.stregis.com* ↘ *164 rooms, 65 suites* ⑂ *In-room: a/c, safe, refrigerator, DVD, Internet. In-hotel: restaurant, room service, gym, laundry service, parking (paid)* ⊟ *AE, D, DC, MC, V* Ⓜ *E, M to 5th Ave.* ✛ *4:E2.*

$$$ 🏨 **Sherry-Netherland.** With an iconic sidewalk clock on the southeast corner of Central Park and a captivating finial spire atop its slender form, the Sherry is a stately part of the New York landscape. **Pros:** gorgeous lobby; commanding, impeccable location; Cipriani access. **Cons:** small check-in area; rooms vary in taste and decor; nonsuites are on the small side; interior rooms lack views. **TripAdvisor:** "elegant and personal," "amazing views," "gorgeous rooms." ⊠ *781 5th Ave., at E. 59th St., Midtown East* ☎ *212/355–2800 or 800/247–4377* ⊕ *www.sherrynetherland.com* ↘ *30 rooms, 20 suites* ⑂ *In-room: a/c, safe, refrigerator, Internet. In-hotel: restaurant, room service, bar, gym,*

Inn at Irving Place

19

The Peninsula

The St. Regis

laundry service, parking (paid) ▤ *AE, D, DC, MC, V* ▯◯▮ *CP* Ⓜ *N, R, Q to 5th Ave.* ✛ *5:E6.*

$$$ ▦ **Waldorf=Astoria.** The lobby of this landmark 1931 Art Deco masterpiece, full of murals, mosaics, and elaborate plaster ornamentation, features a grand piano once owned by Cole Porter and still played daily. **ripAdvisor:** "high price for Internet access," "gorgeous lobby," "centrally located." ⊠ *301 Park Ave., between E. 49th and E. 50th Sts., Midtown East* ☎ *212/355–3000 or 800/925–3673* ⊕ *www. waldorfastoria.com* ⇖ *1,176 rooms, 276 suites* ⌂ *In-room: a/c, safe, Internet. In-hotel: 3 restaurants, room service, bars, gym, laundry service, Internet terminal, Wi-Fi hotspot, parking (paid), some pets allowed* ▤ *AE, D, DC, MC, V* Ⓜ *6 to 51st St./Lexington Ave.; E, M to Lexington–3rd Aves./53rd St.* ✛ *4:F3.*

$ ▦ **W Hotel New York.** This was the first of the W hotels to open in New York, and after a decade rooms got a much-needed overhaul in 2008. **Pros:** central location; great-looking rooms. **Cons:** thin walls; inconsistent service. **TripAdvisor:** "lovely and stylish," "small bathroom," "superb bar." ⊠ *541 Lexington Ave., between E. 49th and E. 50th Sts., Midtown East* ☎ *212/755–1200 or 877/946–8357* ⊕ *www.whotels.com* ⇖ *629 rooms, 62 suites* ⌂ *In-room: a/c, safe, DVD, Internet. In-hotel: restaurant, room service, bar, gym, spa, laundry service, Internet terminal, Wi-Fi hotspot, some pets allowed* ▤ *AE, D, DC, MC, V* Ⓜ *6 to 51st St./Lexington Ave.; E, M to Lexington–3rd Aves./53rd St.* ✛ *4:F3.*

UPPER EAST SIDE

$$$$ ▦ **The Carlyle, A Rosewood Hotel.** On the well-heeled corner of Madison Avenue and 75th Street, this hotel's fusion of venerable elegance and Manhattan swank is like entering a Chanel boutique: walk in chin high, wallet out, and ready to be impressed. **Pros:** perhaps N.Y.C.'s best Central Park views; refined service; delightful array of dining and bar options. **Cons:** removed from tourist Manhattan; stuffy vibe may not work for families. **TripAdvisor:** "classic style," "rooms are spacious," "expensive but worth it." ⊠ *35 E. 76th St., between Madison and Park Aves., Upper East Side* ☎ *212/744–1600* ⊕ *www.thecarlyle.com* ⇖ *122 rooms, 57 suites* ⌂ *In-room: a/c, safe, refrigerator, DVD, Internet. In-hotel: restaurant, room service, bar, gym, spa, laundry service, parking (paid), some pets allowed* ▤ *AE, DC, MC, V* Ⓜ *6 to 77th St.* ✛ *5:F3.*

$–$$ ▦ **The Franklin.** The Franklin is the best luxury boutique hotel north of 57th Street. **Pros:** neighborhood-y location; free Wi-Fi. **Cons:** far from many N.Y.C. tourist sights except Museum Mile; small rooms. **TripAdvisor:** "great beds," "lovely boutique hotel," "wonderful breakfast." ⊠ *164 E. 87th St., between Lexington and 3rd Aves., Upper East Side* ☎ *212/369–1000 or 877/847–4444* ⊕ *www.franklinhotel.com* ⇖ *50 rooms* ⌂ *In-room: a/c, safe, Wi-Fi. In-hotel: room service, bar, laundry service, Internet terminal, Wi-Fi hotspot, some pets allowed* ▤ *AE, D, DC, MC, V* ▯◯▮ *CP* Ⓜ *4, 5, 6 to 86th St.* ✛ *6:G6.*

$$$$ ▦ **Hôtel Plaza Athénée.** It's easy to be seduced by this luxurious hotel, positioned unobtrusively by Central Park on the Upper East Side, and it's even more of a draw now that the rooms have undergone a renovation that includes refined decor in muted tones and enlarged

bathrooms—some tricked out in marble with soaking tubs. **Pros:** discerning service; exotic bar. **Cons:** nonstandarized rooms hit-or-miss. **TripAdvisor:** "cozy, intimate," "terrific people-watching," "fantastic choice." ⊠ *37 E. 64th St., at Madison Ave., Upper East Side* ☎ *212/734–9100 or 800/447–8800* ⊕ *www.plaza-athenee.com* ↩ *115 rooms, 35 suites* ♨ *In-room: a/c, safe, kitchen (some), refrigerator, Internet. In-hotel: restaurant, room service, bar, gym, laundry service, parking (paid), some pets allowed* ▭ *AE, D, DC, MC, V* Ⓜ *6 to 68th St./Hunter College* ✛ *5:F5.*

$$ ▦ **Hotel Wales.** The hotel underwent a spiffy renovation of its public spas and standard rooms at the end of 2009. **Pros:** on-site fitness facilities; great neighborhood feel, roof garden. Cons: the best rooms, with views of Central Park, haven't been renovated. **TripAdvisor:** "wonderful rooftop terrace," "tastefully decorated rooms," "noisy air conditioning unit." ⊠ *1295 Madison Ave., between E. 92nd and E. 93rd Sts., Upper East Side* ☎ *212/876–6000 or 877/847–4444* ⊕ *www.waleshotel.com* ↩ *46 rooms, 42 suites* ♨ *In-room: a/c, safe, kitchen (some), refrigerator (some), DVD (some), Wi-Fi. In-hotel: restaurant, room service, bar, gym, laundry service, parking (paid), some pets allowed* ▭ *AE, D, DC, MC, V* ⍦ *CP* Ⓜ *4, 5, 6 to 86th St.* ✛ *6:F5.*

$$$ ▦ **The Lowell.** This old-money refuge was built as an upscale apartment hotel in the 1920s, and still delivers genteel sophistication and pampering service in an unbeatable location. **Pros:** great location; service with a personal touch; charming decor. **Cons:** unimpressive, cramped lobby; some rooms need updating. **TripAdvisor:** "service is wonderful," "understated luxury," "class and service." ⊠ *28 E. 63rd St., between Madison and Park Aves., Upper East Side* ☎ *212/838–1400 or 800/221–4444* ⊕ *www.lowellhotel.com* ↩ *23 rooms, 47 suites* ♨ *In-room: a/c, safe, kitchen, refrigerator, DVD, Internet. In-hotel: 2 restaurants, room service, bar, gym, laundry service, parking (paid), some pets allowed* ▭ *AE, D, DC, MC, V* Ⓜ *4, 5, 6, N, R to 59th St./Lexington Ave.; F to 63rd St./Lexington Ave.* ✛ *5:F6.*

$$$$ ▦ **The Mark.** If you took every Upper East Side fantasy and condensed **Fodor's Choice** it into a modern hotel, you'd come up with The Mark, the perfect rep-★ resentation of uptown panache infused with a healthy dose of downtown chic. **Pros:** hip design; scene-making restaurant and bar; cavernous closet space; great service. **Cons:** expensive; surprisingly generic grooming products in the bathrooms. **TripAdvisor:** "room was beautiful," "top-notch hotel," "bar is very chic." ⊠ *25 E. 77th St. at Madison Ave., Upper East Side* ☎ *212/744–4300* ⊕ *www.themarkhotel.com* ↩ *100 rooms* ♨ *In-room: a/c, safe, refrigerator, DVD, Internet, Wi-Fi. In-hotel: restaurant, room service, bar, gym, spa, laundry service, Wi-Fi hotspot, parking (paid), some pets allowed* ▭ *AE, D, DC, MC, V* Ⓜ *6 to 77th St./Lexington Ave.* ✛ *F3.*

19

UPPER WEST SIDE

$ ▦ **The Empire Hotel.** This historic Upper West Side spot, which reopened in 2008 after an extensive redesign, offers a dizzying number of amenities. **Pros:** prime location next to Lincoln Center and just blocks from Central Park; beautiful rooftop pool and bar; complimentary issues of

Lodging Alternatives

APARTMENT RENTALS VS. SUITE HOTELS

For your trip to New York you may want a little more space than the city's typically tiny hotel rooms provide. Some travelers consider apartment rentals, but we tend to recommend hotel suites instead. Why? Unfortunately, apartment-rental scams are prevalent. In some published reports, potential guests have arrived to find that the apartment they rented does not exist, or that they are paying for an illegal sublet. In some cases travelers have lost their deposit money, or their prepaid rent (note: never wire money to an individual's account).

There are a few reputable providers of short-term rentals, noted below. But many Fodorites have turned to suite hotels and bed-and-breakfasts with apartmentlike accommodations to guard themselves from possible scams. We've noted some of their most enthusiastic recommendations.

Local rental agencies that arrange rentals of furnished apartments: **Abode Limited** (⌂ *Box 20022, New York, NY 10028 ☎ 800/835–8880 or 212/472–2000 ⊕ www.abodenyc.com*). **Manhattan Getaways** (⌂ *Box 1994, New York, NY 10022 ☎ 212/956–2010 ⊕ www.manhattangetaways.com*).

Suite suggestions from **Fodor's Forums** (⊕ *www.fodors.com/forums*):

"For a week or less, there's no need to risk being scammed or renting something illegal by renting a private apt. There are LOADS of suite hotels and B&Bs at all price levels that will provide the space and convenience of an apartment, many with the amenities of a hotel including the ability to be able to read reviews of them

before you book and know what you're getting. **Affinia** (⊕ *www.Affinia. com*) is a group of seven suite hotels at various prices that's well regarded. **Milburn Hotel** (⊕ *www.milburnhotel. com*) and **The Salisbury Hotel** (⊕ *www.nycsalisbury.com*) are some of the more popular independent budget options." —mclaurie

BED-AND-BREAKFASTS

B&Bs booked through a service may be either hosted (you're the guest in someone's quarters) or unhosted (you have full use of someone's vacated apartment, including kitchen privileges). Reservation services: **All Around the Town** (⌂ *270 Lafayette St., Suite 804, New York, NY ☎ 212/675–5600 or 800/443–3800 ⊕ www.newyorkcitybestbb.com*). **Bed-and-Breakfast Network of New York** (⌂ *134 W. 32nd St., Suite 602, between 6th and 7th Aves., New York, NY ☎ 212/645–8134 or 800/900–8134 ⊕ www.bedandbreakfastnetny. com*). **City Lights Bed-and-Breakfast** (⌂ *Box 20355, Cherokee Station, New York, NY 10075 ☎ 212/737–7049 ⊕ www.citylightsbedandbreakfast.com*).

"**West Eleventh** (⊕ *www.west-eleventh.com*) and **Abingdon Guest House** (⊕ *www.abingdonguesthouse. com*) are two of many B&Bs in the village with some charm, but are only good for two people." —mclaurie

"Also try **B&B Manhattan** (⊕ *www. bandbmanhattan.com*) which has very nice studio and 1-bed apartments in Chelsea and GV. A friend stayed with them last year and liked it a lot." —tomassocroccante

Time Out New York magazine; fresh apples left at your bedside at turn-down. **Cons:** rooftop bar brings lots of foot traffic through hotel lobby; elevators are beautifully redecorated but still feel rickety; bathrooms are nicely designed but tiny; pool is quite small. **TripAdvisor:** "gorgeous hotel décor," "brilliant service," "nicely priced boutique hotel." ⊠ 44 W. 63rd St., at Columbus Ave., Upper West Side ☎ 212/265–7400 ⊕ www.empirehotelnyc.com ⤵ 50 suites, 370 rooms ⚐ In-room: a/c, safe, refrigerator, Wi-Fi. In-hotel: pool, bar, restaurant ▤ AE, MC, V Ⓜ 1, A, B, C to 59th St./Columbus Circle ✛ 5:C5.

$–$$ 🏨 **Excelsior.** Directly across the street from the American Museum of Natural History, this well-kept spot rubs shoulders with fine prewar apartment buildings (make sure to spring for a room with museum views). **Pros:** unique Upper West Side location near Central Park and foodie mecca Zabar's; tranquil environment. **Cons:** guests report unfriendly front-desk staff; rooms could use updating; Wi-Fi is not free. **TripAdvisor:** "safe neighborhood," "old world charm," "great location." ⊠ 45 W. 81st St., between Central Park W and Columbus Ave., Upper West Side ☎ 212/362–9200 or 800/368–4575 ⊕ www.excelsiorhotelny.com ⤵ 118 rooms, 80 suites ⚐ In-room: a/c, safe, Wi-Fi. In-hotel: gym, laundry service, Internet terminal, Wi-Fi hotspot, some pets allowed ▤ AE, D, DC, MC, V Ⓜ B, C to 81st St. ✛ 5:C2.

$–$$ 🏨 **Hotel Beacon.** The Upper West Side's best buy for the price is 3 blocks from Central Park, 10 from Lincoln Center, and footsteps from the neighborhood's gourmet grocery store gulch—Zabar's, Fairway, and Citarella. **Pros:** kitchenettes in all rooms; heart of UWS location; affordable. **Cons:** rooms emphasize comfort over style. **TripAdvisor:** "no hotel restaurant," "excellent rooms," "small kitchenette available." ⊠ 2130 Broadway, at W. 75th St., Upper West Side ☎ 212/787–1100 or 800/572–4969 ⊕ www.beaconhotel.com ⤵ 120 rooms, 110 suites ⚐ In-room: a/c, safe, kitchen, refrigerator. In-hotel: laundry facilities, parking (paid) ▤ AE, D, DC, MC, V Ⓜ 1, 2, 3 to 72nd St. ✛ 5:A3.

$ 🏨 **The Lucerne.** The landmark façade of this exquisite building has more pizzazz than the predictable guest rooms, with their dark-wood reproduction furniture and chintz bedspreads. **Pros:** free Wi-Fi; clean; close to Central Park. **Cons:** inconsistent room size; some guests report uncomfortable pillows. **TripAdvisor:** "clean and surprisingly large rooms," "great views of Upper West Side," "really good location." ⊠ 201 W. 79th St., at Amsterdam Ave., Upper West Side ☎ 212/875–1000 or 800/492–8122 ⊕ www.thelucernehotel.com ⤵ 142 rooms, 42 suites ⚐ In-room: a/c, kitchen (some), refrigerator (some), Wi-Fi. In-hotel: restaurant, room service, bar, gym, laundry service, Internet terminal, Wi-Fi hotspot, parking (paid) ▤ AE, D, DC, MC, V Ⓜ 1 to 79th St. ✛ 5:A2.

$ 🏨 **On the Ave Hotel.** This tranquil Upper West Side property is also home to the Upper West Side branch of the beloved Fatty Crab; inside, the hotel is tasteful and modern, with the occasional swath of color from a red chair or green drapes. **Pros:** great dining options; excellent value. **Cons:** small charges add up; location not ideal for all N.Y.C. visitors. **TripAdvisor:** "wonderful location," "good value," "very clean." ⊠ 2178 Broadway, at W. 77th St., Upper West Side ☎ 800/509–7598

19

⊕ *www.ontheave-nyc.com* ⤴ *250 rooms, 32 suites* ☼ *In-room: a/c, safe, Internet, Wi-Fi. In-hotel: 2 restaurants, room service, parking (paid)* ▭ *AE, MC, V* Ⓜ *1 to 79th St.* ✢ *5:A3.*

$$$$ ⛨ **Trump International Hotel and Towers.** This iconic New York's property recently underwent a massive renovation, bringing the room's interior design and decor—much conceived with the help of The Donald's equally famous daughter, Ivanka, in line with the rest of the property's stellar standards for personalized service and attention to detail. **Pros:** fine service; stellar views; discerning treatment. **Cons:** expensive; lobby could use a renovation. **TripAdvisor:** "prompt room service," "wonderful hotel," "great fitness center." ⊠ *1 Central Park W, between W. 59th and W. 60th Sts., Upper West Side* ☎ *212/299–1000 or 888/448–7867* ⊕ *www.trumpintl.com* ⤴ *37 rooms, 130 suites* ☼ *In-room: a/c, safe, kitchen, refrigerator, DVD, Internet. In-hotel: restaurant, room service, bar, pool, gym, spa, laundry service, parking (paid)* ▭ *AE, D, DC, MC, V* Ⓜ *1, A, B, C, D to 59th St./Columbus Circle* ✢ *5:C6.*

Travel Smart
New York City

WORD OF MOUTH

"If you are traveling with kids just make sure a parent goes through the [subway] turnstile first and last in case one of the metro cards doesn't work and one of you is stuck on the wrong side from the others."

—richbutnot

GETTING HERE AND AROUND

New York City packs a staggering range of sights and activities into the 322 square mi of its five boroughs. You'll probably want to focus most of your visit in Manhattan, but with more time, taking a trip to the "outer" boroughs (meaning Brooklyn, Queens, the Bronx, and Staten Island) is worthwhile. To experience the most from the city, you need to think like a New Yorker: explore with your eyes open to everything around you; every city block offers new and unexpected sights.

If you're flying into one of the three major airports that service New York—John F. Kennedy (JFK), LaGuardia, or Newark, which is in New Jersey—pick your mode of transportation for getting to Manhattan before your plane lands. The route tourists typically take is to hire a car or wait in the taxi line, but those aren't necessarily the best choices, especially if arriving during rush hour. Public transportation is easy and inexpensive, and should be considered.

Once you're in Manhattan, getting around can be a breeze when you get the hang of the subway system. When not in a rush, just walk—it's the best way to discover the true New York. Not quite sure where you are or how to get where you're headed? Ask a local. You may be surprised at how friendly the city's inhabitants are, debunking their reputation for rudeness. In the same getting-there-is-half-the-fun spirit, find water, land, and air journeys to see the city from a whole new perspective.

■ AIR TRAVEL

Generally, more international flights go in and out of John F. Kennedy Airport, more domestic flights go in and out of LaGuardia Airport, and Newark Airport serves both domestic and international travelers.

Airlines and Airports Airline and Airport Links.com (⊕ www.airlineandairportlinks.com) has links to many of the world's airlines and airports.

Airline Security Issues The Transportation Security Administration (⊕ www.tsa.gov) has answers for almost every question that might come up.

AIRPORTS

The major air gateways to New York City are LaGuardia Airport (LGA) and JFK International Airport (JFK) in the borough of Queens, and Newark Liberty International Airport (EWR) in New Jersey.

■ **TIP→** Long layovers don't have to be only about sitting around or shopping. These days they can be about burning off vacation calories. Check out www.airportgyms.com for lists of health clubs that are in or near many U.S. and Canadian airports.

Airport Information JFK International Airport (☎ 718/244–4444 ⊕ www.jfkairport. com). **LaGuardia Airport** (☎ 718/533–3400 ⊕ www.laguardiaairport.com). **Newark Liberty International Airport** (☎ 973/961–6000 or 888/397–4636 ⊕ www.newarkairport.com).

TRANSFERS—CAR SERVICES

Car services can be a great deal because the driver will often meet you on the concourse or in the baggage-claim area and help you with your luggage. The flat rates and tolls are often comparable to taxi fares, but some car services will charge for parking and waiting time at the airport. To eliminate these expenses, other car services require that you telephone their dispatcher when you land so they can send the next available car to pick you up. New York City Taxi and Limousine Commission rules require that all car services be licensed and pick up riders only by prior arrangement; if possible, call 24 hours in advance for reservations, or at least a half day before your flight's departure. Drivers of nonlicensed vehicles (gypsy cabs) often solicit fares outside the terminal in baggage-claim areas. Don't take them: you run the risk of an unsafe ride, and you'll definitely pay more than the going rate.

⇨ *For phone numbers, see Taxi Travel.*

TRANSFERS—TAXIS AND SHUTTLES

Outside the baggage-claim area at each of New York's major airports are taxi stands where a uniformed dispatcher helps passengers find taxis (⇨ *By Taxi*). Cabs are not permitted to pick up fares anywhere else in the arrivals area, so if you want a taxi, take your place in line. Shuttle services generally pick up passengers from a designated spot along the curb.

New York Airport Service runs buses between JFK and LaGuardia airports, and buses from those airports to Grand Central Terminal, Port Authority Bus Terminal, Penn Station, Bryant Park, and hotels between 23rd and 63rd streets in Manhattan. Fares cost between $12 and $15 one way and $21 to $27 round-trip. Buses operate from 6:05 am to 11 pm from the airport; between 5 am and 10 pm going to the airport.

SuperShuttle vans travel to and from Manhattan to JFK, LaGuardia, and Newark. These blue vans will stop at your home, office, or hotel. There are courtesy phones at the airports. For travel to the airport, the company recommends that you make your request 24 hours in advance. Fares range from $15 to $23 per person.

Shuttle Service New York Airport Service (☎ 718/875–8200 ⊕ www.nyairportservice. com). **SuperShuttle** (☎ 800/258–3826 ⊕ www.supershuttle.com).

TRANSFERS FROM JFK INTERNATIONAL AIRPORT

Taxis charge a flat fee of $45 plus tolls (which may be as much as $6) to Manhattan only, and take 35–60 minutes. Prices are roughly $20–$55 for trips to most other locations in New York City. You should also tip the driver.

The AirTrain links to the A subway line's Howard Beach station, and to Long Island Railroad's (LIRR) Jamaica Station, which is adjacent to the Sutphin

Boulevard/Archer Avenue E/J/Z subway station, with connections to Manhattan. The monorail system runs 24 hours, leaving from Howard Beach and Jamaica stations every 4 to 8 minutes during peak times and every 12 minutes during off-peak times. From Midtown Manhattan, the longest trip to JFK is via the A train, a trip of less than an hour that costs $2.25 in subway fare in addition to $5 for the AirTrain. The quickest trip is with the Long Island Railroad (about 30 minutes), for a total cost of about $13. When traveling to the Howard Beach station, be sure to take the A train marked "Far Rockaway" or "Rockaway Park," not "Lefferts Boulevard."

JFK Transfer Information AirTrain JFK (⊕ www.airtrainjfk.com). **Long Island Railroad** (*Jamaica Station* ⊠ *146 Archer Ave., at Sutphin Ave. Queens* ☎ 718/217–5477 ⊕ www.mta. info/lirr).

TRANSFERS FROM LAGUARDIA AIRPORT

Taxis cost $21–$30 plus tip and tolls (which may be as high as $6) to most destinations in New York City, and take at least 20–40 minutes.

For $2.25 you can ride the M-60 public bus (there are limited luggage facilities on some buses) to 106th Street and Broadway on Manhattan's Upper West Side. From there, you can transfer to the subway to head to your destination. Alternatively, you can take the Q-48 bus to the Main Street subway station in Flushing, where you can transfer to the 7 train. Allow at least 90 minutes for the entire trip to Midtown.

TRANSFERS FROM NEWARK AIRPORT

Taxis to Manhattan cost $50–$70 plus tolls ($8) and take 20 to 45 minutes. "Share and Save" group rates are available for up to four passengers between 8 am and midnight—make arrangements with the airport's taxi dispatcher. If you're heading to the airport from Manhattan, a $15 surcharge applies to the normal taxi rates and the $5 toll.

AirTrain Newark is an elevated light rail system that connects to New Jersey Transit and Amtrak trains at the Newark Liberty International Airport Station. Total travel time to Penn Station in Manhattan is approximately 20 minutes and costs $15. AirTrain runs every 3 minutes from 5 am to midnight and every 15 minutes from midnight to 5 am.

The AirTrain to Newark's Penn Station takes five minutes. From Newark Penn Station you can catch PATH trains, which run to Manhattan 24 hours a day. PATH trains run every 10 minutes on weekdays, every 15 to 30 minutes on weeknights and weekends. After stopping at Christopher Street, one line travels along 6th Avenue, making stops at West 9th Street, West 14th Street, West 23rd Street, and West 33rd Street. Other PATH trains connect Newark Penn Station with the World Trade Center site. PATH train fare is $1.75.

Coach USA with Olympia Trails buses leave for Grand Central Terminal and Penn Station in Manhattan about every 15 to 30 minutes until midnight. The trip takes roughly 45 minutes, and the fare is $15. Between the Port Authority or Grand Central Terminal and Newark, buses run every 20 to 30 minutes. The trip takes 55 to 65 minutes

Newark Airport Information AirTrain Newark (☎ 888/397-4636 ⊕ www.airtrainnewark. com). **Coach USA** (☎ 877/894-9155 ⊕ www. coachusa.com). **PATH Trains** (☎ 800/234-7284 ⊕ www.pathrail.com).

TRANSFERS BETWEEN AIRPORTS

AirTrain provides detailed, up-to-the-minute recorded information on how to reach your destination from any of New York's airports. Note that if you arrive after midnight at any airport, you may wait a long time for a taxi. Consider calling a car service, as there is no shuttle service at that time.

Contacts AirTrain (☎ 800/247-7433 ⊕ www. airtrainnewark.com).

▌ BOAT TRAVEL

The Staten Island Ferry runs across New York Harbor between Whitehall Street next to Battery Park in Lower Manhattan and St. George terminal in Staten Island. The free 25-minute ride gives you a view of the Financial District skyscrapers, the Statue of Liberty, and Ellis Island.

New York Water Taxi, in addition to serving commuters, shuttles tourists to the city's many waterfront attractions between the West and East sides and Lower Manhattan, the South Street Seaport, and Brooklyn's waterfront parks. The hop-on, hop-off one-day pass ticket is $20; the two-day pass is $25.

Information New York Water Taxi (*NYWT* ☎ 212/742-1969 ⊕ www.nywatertaxi.com). **Staten Island Ferry** (⊕ www.siferry.com).

▌ BUS TRAVEL

Most long-haul and commuter bus lines feed into the Port Authority Bus Terminal, on 8th Avenue between West 40th and 42nd streets. You must purchase your ticket at a ticket counter, not from the bus driver, so give yourself enough time to wait in a line. Several bus lines serving northern New Jersey and Rockland County, New York, make daily stops at the George Washington Bridge Bus Station from 5 am to 1 am. The station is connected to the 175th Street Station on the A line of the subway, which travels down the West Side of Manhattan.

A variety of discount bus services, including BoltBus and Vamoose Bus, offer direct routes from cities such as Philadelphia, Boston, and Washington, D.C., with the majority of destinations lying along the East Coast. These budget options, priced from about $20 one way, depart from locations throughout the city.

Most city buses follow easy-to-understand routes along the Manhattan street grid. Routes go up or down the north–south avenues, or east and west on the major two-way crosstown streets: 96th, 86th,

79th, 72nd, 57th, 42nd, 34th, 23rd, and 14th. Usually bus routes operate 24 hours, but service is infrequent late at night. Traffic jams can make rides maddeningly slow, especially along 5th Avenue in Midtown and the Upper East Side. Certain bus routes provide "limited-stop service" during weekday rush hours, which saves travel time by stopping only at major cross streets and transfer points. A sign posted at the front of the bus indicates that it has limited service; ask the driver whether the bus stops near where you want to go before boarding.

To find a bus stop, look for a light-blue sign (green for a limited bus) on a green pole; bus numbers and routes are listed, with the stop's name underneath.

Bus fare is the same as subway fare: $2.25. MetroCards *(⊳ Public Transportation Travel)* allow you one free transfer between buses or from bus to subway; when using coins on the bus, you can ask the driver for a free transfer coupon, good for one change to an intersecting route. Legal transfer points are listed on the back of the slip. Transfers generally have time limits of two hours.

Route maps and schedules are posted at many bus stops in Manhattan and at major stops throughout the other boroughs. Each of the five boroughs of New York has a separate bus map; they're available from some station booths, but rarely on buses. The best places to obtain them are the MTA booth in the Times Square Information Center, or the information kiosks in Grand Central Terminal and Penn Station.

Pay your bus fare when you board, with exact change in coins (no pennies, and no change is given) or with a MetroCard.

Buses in New York Metropolitan Transit Authority (MTA) Travel Information Line (☎ *718/330-1234, 718/330-4847 for non-English speakers* ⊕ *www.mta.info)*. MTA Status information hotline (☎ *718/243-7777 or 718/330-1234),* updated hourly.

Buses to New York Adirondack, Pine Hill & New York Trailways (☎ *800/225-6815* ⊕ *www.trailways.com)*. BoltBus (☎ *877/265-8287* ⊕ *www.boltbus.com).* Coach (☎ *800/631-8405* ⊕ *www.coachusa.com)*. **Greyhound Lines Inc.** (☎ *800/231-2222* ⊕ *www.greyhound.com)*. **New Jersey Transit** (☎ *973/275-5555* ⊕ *www.njtransit.com)*. **Vamoose Bus** (☎ *877/393-2828* ⊕ *www. vamoosebus.com)*.

Bus Stations George Washington Bridge Bus Station (✉ *4211 Broadway, between 178th and 179th Sts., Washington Heights* ☎ *800/221-9903* ⊕ *www.panynj.gov)*. **Port Authority Bus Terminal** (✉ *625 8th Ave., at 42nd St., Midtown West* ☎ *212/564-8484* ⊕ *www.panynj.gov)*.

■ CAR TRAVEL

If you plan to drive into Manhattan, try to avoid the morning and evening rush hours and lunch hour. The deterioration of the bridges to Manhattan, especially those spanning the East River, means that repairs will be ongoing for the next few years. Listen to traffic reports on the radio before you set off, and don't be surprised if a bridge is partially closed or entirely blocked with traffic.

Driving within Manhattan can be a nightmare of gridlocked streets, obnoxious drivers and bicyclists, and seemingly suicidal jaywalkers. Narrow and one-way streets are common, particularly downtown, and can make driving even more difficult. The most congested streets of the city lie between 14th and 59th streets and 3rd and 8th avenues.

GASOLINE

Gas stations are few and far between in Manhattan. If you can, fill up at stations outside the city, where prices are anywhere from 10¢ to 50¢ cheaper per gallon. In Manhattan, you can refuel at stations along the West Side Highway and 11th Avenue south of West 57th Street and along East Houston Street. Some gas stations in New York require you to pump your own gas; others provide attendants.

PARKING

Free parking is difficult to find in Midtown and on weekday evenings and weekends in other neighborhoods. ■TIP➜ Violators may be towed away or ticketed literally within minutes. And you will not be able to talk your way out of a ticket—especially after it's been printed— unless you've mastered the Jedi Mind Trick. Trust us on this one. On the other hand, parking lots charge exorbitant rates—as much as $23 for two hours (this includes an impressive sales tax of 18.375%). If you do drive, use your car sparingly in Manhattan. Instead, park it in a guarded parking garage for at least several hours; hourly rates decrease somewhat if a car is left for a significant amount of time. If you find a spot on the street, check parking signs carefully. Before leaving your car, scour the curb for that bane of every motorist's existence, the painted yellow line that's so faded you had better look twice to ascertain both its existence and its range.

CAR RENTALS

When you reserve a car, ask about cancellation penalties, taxes, drop-off charges (if you're planning to pick up the car in one city and leave it in another), and surcharges (for being under or over a certain age, for additional drivers, or for driving across state or country borders or beyond a specific distance from your point of rental). All these things can add substantially to your costs. Request car seats and extras such as GPS when you book.

Rates are sometimes—but not always— better if you book in advance or reserve through a rental agency's Web site. There are other reasons to book ahead, though: for popular destinations, during busy times of the year, or to ensure that you get certain types of cars (vans, SUVs, exotic sports cars).

■TIP➜ Make sure that a confirmed reservation guarantees you a car. Agencies sometimes overbook, particularly for busy weekends and holiday periods.

Rates in New York City are around $50– $125 a day and $250–$425 a week for an economy car with air-conditioning, automatic transmission, and unlimited mileage. This includes the state tax on car rentals, which is 19.87%. Rental costs are lower just outside New York City, specifically in such places as Hoboken, New Jersey, and Yonkers, New York. The Yellow Pages are also filled with a profusion of local car-rental agencies, some renting secondhand vehicles. If you're traveling during a holiday period, make sure that a confirmed reservation guarantees you a car.

CAR-RENTAL INSURANCE

If you own a car and carry comprehensive car insurance for both collision and liability, your personal auto insurance will probably cover a rental, but read your policy's fine print to be sure. If you don't have auto insurance, then you should probably buy the collision- or loss-damage waiver (CDW or LDW) from the rental company. This eliminates your liability for damage to the car. Some credit cards offer CDW coverage, but it's usually supplemental to your own insurance and rarely covers SUVs, minivans, luxury models, and the like. If your coverage is secondary, you may still be liable for loss-of-use costs from the car-rental company (again, read the fine print). But no credit-card insurance is valid unless you use that card for *all* transactions, from reserving to paying the final bill.

■TIP➜ Diners Club offers primary CDW coverage on all rentals reserved and paid for with the card. This means that Diners Club's company—not your own car insurance—pays in case of an accident. It *doesn't* mean that your car-insurance company won't raise your rates once it discovers you had an accident.

You may also be offered supplemental liability coverage. The car-rental company is required to carry a minimal level of liability coverage insuring all renters, but it's rarely enough to cover claims in a really serious accident if you're at fault.

Your own auto-insurance policy will protect you if you own a car; if you don't, you have to decide whether you are willing to take the risk.

U.S. rental companies sell CDWs and LDWs for about $20 to $40 a day; supplemental liability is usually more than $10 a day. The car-rental company may offer you all sorts of other policies, but they're rarely worth the cost. Personal accident insurance, which is basic hospitalization coverage, is an especially egregious rip-off if you already have health insurance.

■TIP➜ You can decline the insurance from the rental company and purchase it through a third-party provider such as Travel Guard (⊕ www.travelguard.com)—$9 per day for $35,000 of coverage. That's sometimes just under half the price of the CDW offered by some car-rental companies.

■ PUBLIC TRANSPORTATION

When it comes to getting around New York, you have your pick of transportation in almost every neighborhood. The subway and bus networks are extensive, especially in Manhattan, although getting across town can take some extra maneuvering. If you're not pressed for time, take a public bus (⇨ Bus Travel); they generally are slower than subways, but you can also see the city as you travel. Yellow cabs (⇨ Taxi Travel) are abundant, except during the evening rush hour, when many drivers' shifts change. Like a taxi ride, the subway (⇨ Subway Travel) is a true New York City experience; it's also often the quickest way to get around. But New York is really a walking town, and depending on the time of day and your destination, hoofing it could be the easiest and most enjoyable option.

During weekday rush hours (from 7:30 am to 9:30 am and 5 pm to 7 pm) avoid the jammed Midtown area, both in the subways and on the streets—travel time on buses and taxis can easily double.

Subway and bus fares are $2.50 for a single ride ticket, although reduced fares are available for senior citizens and people with disabilities during nonrush hours.

Note that if using a MetroCard, a plastic card with a magnetic strip the cost per ride is reduced. As you swipe the card through a subway turnstile or insert it in a bus's card reader, the cost of the fare is automatically deducted. With the Metro-Card, you can transfer free from bus to subway, subway to bus, or bus to bus. You must start with the MetroCard and use it again within two hours to complete your trip.

MetroCards are sold at all subway stations and at some stores—look for an "Authorized Sales Agent" sign. The MTA sells two kinds of MetroCards: unlimited-ride and pay-per-ride. Seven-day unlimited-ride MetroCards ($29) allow bus and subway travel for a week. If you will ride more than 13 times, this is the card to get.

Unlike unlimited-ride cards, pay-per-ride MetroCards can be shared between riders. (Unlimited-ride MetroCards can be used only once at the same station or bus route in an 18-minute period.)

You can buy or add money to an existing MetroCard at a MetroCard vending machine, available at most subway station entrances (usually near the station booth). The machines accept major credit cards and ATM or debit cards. Many also accept cash, but note that the maximum amount of change they will return is $6.

Schedule and Route Information Metropolitan Transit Authority (MTA) Travel Information Line (☎ 718/330 1234, 718/596–8585 for travelers with disabilities ⊕ www.mta.info)

■ SUBWAY TRAVEL

The subway system operates on more than 840 mi of track 24 hours a day and serves nearly all the places you're likely to visit. It's cheaper than a cab, and during the workweek it's often faster than either taxis or buses. The trains are well lighted and air-conditioned. Still, the New York subway is hardly problem-free. Many trains are crowded, the older ones are noisy, the air-conditioning can break, and platforms can be dingy and damp. Homeless people sometimes take refuge from the elements by riding the trains, and panhandlers head there for a captive audience. Although trains usually run frequently, especially during rush hours, you never know when some incident somewhere on the line may stall traffic. In addition, subway construction sometimes causes delays or limitation of service, especially on weekends.

Most subway entrances are at street corners and are marked by lampposts with an illuminated Metropolitan Transit Authority (MTA) logo or globe-shape green or red lights—green means the station is open 24 hours and red means the station closes at night (though colors don't always correspond to reality). Subway lines are designated by numbers and letters, such as the 3 line or the A line. Some lines run "express" and skip stops, and others are "locals" and make all stops. Each station entrance has a sign indicating the lines that run through the station. Some entrances are also marked "uptown only" or "downtown only." Before entering subway stations, read the signs carefully. One of the most frequent mistakes visitors make is taking the train in the wrong direction. Maps of the full subway system are posted in every train car and usually on the subway platform (though these are sometimes out of date). You can usually pick up free maps at station booths.

For the most up-to-date information on subway lines, call the MTA's Travel Information Center or visit its Web site. The Web site Hopstop is a good source for figuring out the best line to take to reach your destination. (You can also call or text Hopstop for directions.) Alternatively, ask a station agent.

Subway fare is the same as bus fare: $2.50 for a single ride ticket. You can transfer between subway lines an unlimited number of times at any of the numerous stations where lines intersect. If you use a MetroCard ($\Rightarrow$ *Public Transportation*) to pay your fare, you can also transfer to intersecting MTA bus routes for free. Such transfers generally have time limits of two hours.

Pay your subway fare at the turnstile, using a MetroCard bought at the station booth or from a vending machine.

Subway Information Hopstop (☎ *888/246–7867* ⊕ *www.hopstop.com*). **Metropolitan Transportation Authority (MTA) Travel Information Line** (☎ *718/330–1234, 718/330–4847 for non–English speakers* ⊕ *www.mta.info*). **MTA Lost Property Office** (☎ *212/712–4500*). **MTA Status information hotline** (☎ *718/243–7777*), updated hourly.

▌ TAXI TRAVEL

Yellow cabs are in abundance almost everywhere in Manhattan, cruising the streets looking for fares. They are usually easy to hail on the street or from a cabstand in front of major hotels, though finding one at rush hour or in the rain can take some time. Even if you're stuck in a downpour or at the airport, do not accept a ride from a gypsy cab. If a cab is not yellow and does not have a numbered aqua-color plastic medallion riveted to the hood, you could be putting yourself in danger by getting into the car.

You can see whether a taxi is available by checking its rooftop light. If the center panel is lighted and the side panels are dark, the driver is ready to take passengers. Once the meter is engaged (and if it isn't, alert your driver; you'll seldom benefit from negotiating an off-the-record ride), the fare is $3 just for entering the vehicle and 40¢ for each unit thereafter. A unit is defined as either 0.20 mi when the cab's cruising at 6 mph or faster or as 60 seconds when the cab is either not moving or moving at less than 12 mph. A 50¢ night surcharge is added between 8 pm and 6 am, and a much-maligned $1 weekday surcharge is tacked on to rides after 4 pm and before 8 pm.

One taxi can hold a maximum of four passengers (an additional passenger under the age of seven is allowed if the child sits on someone's lap). There is no charge for extra passengers. You must pay any bridge or tunnel tolls incurred during your trip (a driver will usually pay the toll himself to keep moving quickly, but that amount will be added to the fare when the ride is over). Taxi drivers expect a 15% to 20% tip.

To avoid unhappy taxi experiences, try to know where you want to go and how to get there before you hail a cab. ■TIP→ If after naming your destination your driver asks you "the best way to go," suggest that navigation's also part of his job (unless you know the best way and you're in the mood to direct the driver). If he disagrees, abandon the cab. You should assist your driver, however, by directing him to the specific cross streets of your destination (for instance, "5th Avenue and 42nd Street"), rather than the numerical address, which means nothing to drivers. Also, speak simply and clearly to make sure the driver has heard you correctly. A quick call to your destination will give you cross-street information, as will a glance at a map marked with address numbers. When you leave the cab, remember to take your receipt. It includes the cab's medallion number, which can help you track the cabbie down in the event that you lose your possessions in the cab or if, after the fact, you want to report an unpleasant ride.

Taxis can be extremely difficult (if not impossible) to find in many parts of Brooklyn, Queens, the Bronx, and Staten Island. As a result, you may have no choice but to call a car service. Always determine the fee beforehand when using a car service sedan; a 10%–15% tip is customary above that.

Taxi Companies **Carmel Car Service** (☎ *212/666-6666 or 866/666-6666* ⊕ *www. carmelcarservice.com*). **Dial 7 Car Service**

(☎ *212/777-7777* ⊕ *www.dial7.com*). **London Towncars** (☎ *212/988-9700 or 800/221-4009* ⊕ *www.londontowncars.com*).

■ TRAIN TRAVEL

⇨ *For information about traveling by subway within New York City, see Subway Travel.*

Metro-North Railroad trains take passengers from Grand Central Terminal to points north of New York City, both in New York State and Connecticut. Amtrak trains from across the United States arrive at Penn Station. For trains from New York City to Long Island and New Jersey, take the Long Island Railroad and New Jersey Transit, respectively; both operate from Penn Station. The PATH trains offer service to Newark, Jersey City, and Hoboken. All of these trains generally run on schedule, although occasional delays occur.

Information **Amtrak** (☎ *800/872-7245* ⊕ *www.amtrak.com*). **Long Island Rail Road** (☎ *718/217-5477* ⊕ *www.mta.info/lirr*). **Metro-North Railroad** (☎ *212/532-4900* ⊕ *www.mta.info/mnr*). **New Jersey Transit** (☎ *973/275-5555* ⊕ *www.njtransit.com*). **PATH** (☎ *800/234-7284* ⊕ *www.pathrail.com*).

Train Stations **Grand Central Terminal** (✉ *Park Ave. at E. 42nd St., Midtown East* ☎ *212/340-2583* ⊕ *www.grandcentralterminal. com*). **Penn Station** (✉ *W. 31st to W. 33rd Sts., between 7th and 8th Aves., Midtown West* ☎ *212/630-6401*).

ESSENTIALS

■ COMMUNICATIONS

INTERNET

You can check your email or surf the Internet at cafés, copy centers, libraries, and most hotels. By far the best equipped and probably most convenient is Cyber Café in Times Square, which has dozens of computers plus scanners, color printers, and camera chip readers; it's open from 8 am to 11 pm on weekdays and 11 am to 11 pm on weekends. The organization NYCwireless keeps track of free Wi-Fi hot spots in the New York area. The Web site JiWire allows you to find Wi-Fi hot spots in hotels, libraries, parks, and other locations throughout the city.

Contacts JiWire (⊕ www.jiwire.com). NYCwireless (⊕ www.nycwireless.net).

Internet Cafés Cyber Café (⊠ 250 W. 49th St., between 8th Ave. and Broadway, Midtown West ☎ 212/333–4109 ⊕ www.cyber-cafe.com).

Other Internet Locations New York Public Library–Mid-Manhattan Library (⊠ 455 5th Ave., at E. 40th St., Midtown East ☎ 212/340–0863 ⊕ www.nypl.org).

■ DISABILITIES AND ACCESSIBILITY

New York has come a long way in making life easier for people with disabilities. At most street corners curb cuts allow wheelchairs to roll along unimpeded. Many restaurants, shops, and movie theaters with step-up entrances have wheelchair ramps. And though some New Yorkers may rush past those in need of assistance, you'll find plenty of people who are more than happy to help you get around.

Hospital Audiences maintains a Web site with information on the accessibility of many landmarks and attractions. A similar list, "Tourist and Cultural Information for the Disabled," is available from New York City's Web site. Big Apple Greeter

has tours of New York City tailored to visitors' personal preferences. The Andrew Heiskell Braille and Talking Book Library houses an impressive collection of Braille, large-print, and recorded books in a layout designed for people with vision impairments.

Local Resources Andrew Heiskell Library (⊠ 40 W. 20th St., between 5th and 6th Aves., Flatiron District Ⓜ F, V to 23rd St. ☎ 212/206–5400 ⊕ www.talkingbooks.nypl. org). Big Apple Greeter (⊠ 1 Centre St., Lower Manhattan Ⓜ 4, 5, 6, to Brooklyn Bridge-City Hall ☎ 212/669–8159 ⊕ www.bigapplegreeter. org). Hospital Audiences (☎ 212/575–7676 ⊕ www.hospaud.org). New York City (☎ 311 in New York City, 212/639–9675 [212/NEW–YORK] outside New York ⊕ www.nyc.gov).

LODGING

Despite the Americans with Disabilities Act, the definition of accessibility seems to differ from hotel to hotel. Some properties may be accessible by ADA standards for people with mobility problems but not for people with hearing or vision impairments, for example.

If you have mobility problems, ask for the lowest floor on which accessible services are offered. If you have a hearing impairment, check whether the hotel has devices to alert you visually to the ring of the telephone, a knock at the door, and a fire/emergency alarm. Some hotels provide these devices without charge. Discuss your needs with hotel personnel if this equipment isn't available, so that a staff member can personally alert you in the event of an emergency.

If you're bringing a guide dog, get authorization ahead of time and write down the name of the person with whom you spoke.

RESERVATIONS

When discussing accessibility with an operator or reservations agent, ask hard questions. Are there any stairs, inside *or* out? Are there grab bars next to the toilet *and* in the shower/tub? How wide is the doorway to the room? To the bathroom? For the most extensive facilities meeting the latest legal specifications, opt for newer accommodations. If you reserve through a toll-free number, consider also calling the hotel's local number to confirm the information from the central reservations office. Get confirmation in writing when you can.

SIGHTS AND ATTRACTIONS

Most public facilities in New York City, whether museums, parks, or theaters, are wheelchair-accessible. Some attractions have tours or programs for people with mobility, sight, or hearing impairments.

TRANSPORTATION

Other than at major subway exchanges, most stations are still all but impossible to navigate; people in wheelchairs should stick to public buses, most of which have wheelchair lifts and "kneelers" at the front to facilitate getting on and off. Bus drivers will provide assistance.

Reduced fares are available to all disabled passengers displaying a Medicare card. Visitors to the city are also eligible for the same Access-a-Ride program benefits as New York City residents. Drivers with disabilities may use windshield cards from their own state or Canadian province to park in designated handicapped spaces.

The U.S. Department of Transportation Aviation Consumer Protection Division's online publication *New Horizons: Information for the Air Traveler with a Disability* offers advice for travelers with a disability, and outlines basic rights. Visit Disability.gov for general information.

Information and Complaints U.S. Department of Transportation Aviation Consumer Protection Division (⊕ *airconsumer.dot.gov/publications/horizons.htm*.

▌ GAY AND LESBIAN TRAVEL

Attitudes toward same-sex couples are very tolerant in Manhattan and many parts of Brooklyn. Chelsea, Greenwich Village, and Hell's Kitchen are the most prominently gay neighborhoods, but gay men and lesbians feel right at home almost everywhere. The world's oldest gay-pride parade takes place on 5th Avenue the last Sunday in June.

PUBLICATIONS

For listings of gay events and places, check out *Next* and the *Gay City News*, both distributed free on the street and in many bars and shops throughout Manhattan. Magazines *Paper* and *Time Out New York* have a gay-friendly take on what's happening in the city.

Local Information Gay & Lesbian Switchboard of NY (☎ *212/989-0999 or 888/843-4564* ⊕ *www.glnh.org*). **Lesbian, Gay, Bisexual & Transgender Community Center** (✉ *208 W. 13th St., between 7th and 8th Aves., Greenwich Village* ☎ *212/620-7310* ⊕ *www.gaycenter.org*).

Gay Publications Gay City News (⊕ *www.gaycitynews.com*). **Next** (⊕ *www.nextmagazine.net*).

Gay- and Lesbian-Friendly Travel Agencies Different Roads Travel (☎ *760/325-6964 or 800/429-8747 Ext. 14* ✍ *lgernert@tzell.com*). **Skylink Travel and Tour/Flying Dutchmen Travel** (☎ *707/546-9888 or 800/225-5759*), serving lesbian travelers.

▌ KIDS IN NEW YORK

For listings of children's events, consult *New York* magazine. The Friday *New York Times* Arts section also includes children's activities. Other good sources on happenings for youngsters are the monthly magazines *New York Family* and *NY Metro Parents,* both available free at toy stores, children's museums, and other places where parents and children are found. The Web site Parents Connect includes listings of what's going on. If you have access to cable television, check the local all-news channel New York 1, where you'll find a spot aired several times daily that covers current and noteworthy children's events. *Fodor's New York City with Kids* (available in bookstores everywhere) can help you plan your days together.

Publications and Web Sites *NY Metro Parents* (⊕ www.nymetroparents.com). **Parents Connect** (⊕ www.parentsconnect.com).

LODGING

Before you consider using a cot or foldout couch for your child, ask just how large your hotel room is—New York City rooms tend to be small. Most hotels in New York allow children under a certain age to stay in their parents' room at no extra charge, but others charge for them as extra adults; be sure to find out the cutoff age for children's discounts.

PUBLIC TRANSPORTATION

Children shorter than 44 inches ride for free on MTA buses and subways. If you're pushing a stroller, don't struggle through a subway turnstile; ask the station agent to buzz you through the gate (the attendant will ask you to swipe your MetroCard through the turnstile nearest the gate). Keep a sharp eye on your young ones while on the subway. At some stations there is a gap between the train doors and the platform. Unfortunately, New York riders are not known to give up their seats for children, for someone carrying a child, or for anyone else.

▮ MONEY

In New York it's easy to get swept up in a debt-inducing cyclone of $60-per-person dinners, $100 theater tickets, $20 nightclub covers, and $300 hotel rooms. But one of the good things about the city is that because there's such a wide variety of options, you can spend in some areas and save in others. Within Manhattan a cup of coffee can cost from 75¢ to $4, a pint of beer from $5 to $8, and a sandwich from $6 to $10. Generally, prices in

the outer boroughs are lower than those in Manhattan.

The most generously bequeathed treasure of the city is the arts. The stated admission fee at the Metropolitan Museum of Art is a suggestion; those who can't afford it can donate a lesser amount and not be snubbed. Many other museums in town have special times during which admission is free. The Museum of Modern Art, for instance, is free on Friday 4–8. In summer a handful of free music, theater, and dance performances, as well as films (usually screened outdoors) fill the calendar each day.

Prices throughout this guide are given for adults. Substantially reduced fees are almost always available for children, students, and senior citizens.

CREDIT CARDS

The following abbreviations are used: **AE**, American Express; **D**, Discover; **DC**, Diners Club; **MC**, MasterCard; and **V**, Visa.

Record all your credit-card numbers—as well as the phone numbers to call if your cards are lost or stolen—in a safe place, so you're prepared should something go wrong. Both MasterCard and Visa have general numbers you can call if your card is lost, but you're better off calling the number of your issuing bank, since MasterCard and Visa usually just transfer you to your bank; your bank's number is usually printed on your card.

Reporting Lost Cards American Express (☎ 800/992–3404 in U.S., 336/393–1111 collect from abroad ⊕ www.americanexpress. com). **Diners Club** (☎ 800/234–6377 in U.S., 303/799–1504 collect from abroad ⊕ www. dinersclub.com). **Discover** (☎ 800/347–2683 in U.S., 801/902–3100 collect from abroad ⊕ www.discovercard.com). **MasterCard** (☎ 800/627–8372 in U.S., 636/722–7111 collect from abroad ⊕ www.mastercard.com). **Visa** (☎ 800/847–2911 in U.S, 410/581–9994 collect from abroad ⊕ www.visa.com).

TRAVELER'S CHECKS AND CARDS

Both Citibank (under the Visa brand) and American Express issue traveler's checks in the United States, but Amex is better known and more widely accepted; you can also avoid hefty surcharges by cashing Amex checks at Amex offices. Whatever you do, keep track of all the serial numbers in case the checks are lost or stolen.

Contacts American Express (☎ 888/412–6945 in U.S., 801/945–9450 collect outside of U.S. to add value or speak to customer service ⊕ www.americanexpress.com).

▍RESTROOMS

Seinfeld fans might recall George Costanza's claim that if you named any given coordinates in New York City, he could instantly name the closest and most worthy public restroom in the vicinity. Regrettably, unless you're traveling with your own George or a potty-training toddler who can drive even the most hardened retailers to share their private bathrooms, public restrooms in New York are few and far between. Plans are in the works to add coin-operated street toilets at several locations. (At press time, the first toilet was operating in Madison Square Park, with 20 more on the way.)

In the meantime, head for Midtown department stores, museums, or the lobbies of large hotels to find the cleanest bathrooms. Public atriums, such as those at the Citicorp Center and Trump Tower, also provide good public facilities, as do Bryant Park and the many Barnes & Noble bookstores and Starbucks coffee shops in the city. If you're in the area, the Times Square Information Center, on Broadway between 46th and 47th streets, can be a godsend.

Restaurants usually allow only their patrons to use their restrooms, but if you're dressed well and look as if you belong, you can often just sail right in. And if you're too self-conscious for this brand of nonchalance, just ask the host or hostess nicely. Be aware that cinemas, Broadway theaters, and concert halls have limited amenities, and there are often long lines before performances and during intermissions.

Find a Loo The Bathroom Diaries (⊕ www.thebathroomdiaries.com) is flush with unsanitized info on restrooms the world over—each one located, reviewed, and rated.

▍SAFETY

New York City is one of the safest large cities in the country. However, do not let yourself be lulled into a false sense of security. As in any large city, travelers in New York remain particularly easy marks for pickpockets and hustlers.

After the September 11, 2001, terrorist attacks security was heightened throughout the city. Never leave any bags unattended, and expect to have yourself and your possessions inspected thoroughly in such places as airports, sports stadiums, museums, and city buildings.

Ignore the panhandlers on the streets and subways, people who offer to hail you a cab (they often appear at Penn Station, the Port Authority, and Grand Central), and limousine and gypsy-cab drivers who (illegally) offer you a ride.

Keep jewelry out of sight on the street; better yet, leave valuables at home. Men should carry their wallets in their front pants pocket rather than in their back pockets. When in bars or restaurants, never hang your purse or bag on the back of a chair or put it underneath the table.

Avoid deserted blocks in unfamiliar neighborhoods. A brisk, purposeful pace helps deter trouble wherever you go.

The subway runs around the clock and is generally well trafficked until midnight (and until at least 2 am on Friday and Saturday nights), and overall it is very safe. If you do take the subway late at night, ride in the center car, with the conductor, and wait on the center of the platform. Watch out for unsavory characters lurking around the inside or outside of stations.

When waiting for a train, stand far away from the edge of the subway platform, especially when trains are entering or leaving the station. Once the train pulls into the station, avoid empty cars. While on the train don't engage in verbal exchanges with aggressive riders, who may accuse others of anything from pushing to taking up too much space. If a fellow passenger makes you nervous while on the train, trust your instincts and change cars. When disembarking, stick with the crowd until you reach the street.

Travelers Aid International helps crime victims, stranded travelers, and wayward children, and works closely with the police.

■**TIP**➜ Distribute your cash, credit cards, IDs, and other valuables between a deep front pocket, an inside jacket or vest pocket, and a hidden money pouch. Don't reach for the money pouch once you're in public.

Information Travelers Aid (✉ *JFK International Airport, Terminal 4, Queens* ☎ *718/656–4870* ✉ *Newark International Airport, Terminal B, Newark, NJ* ☎ *973/623–5052* ⊕ *www. travelersaid.org).*

■ SENIOR-CITIZEN TRAVEL

The Metropolitan Transit Authority (MTA) offers lower fares for passengers 65 and over.

To qualify for age-related discounts, mention your senior-citizen status up front when booking hotel reservations (not when checking out). Be sure to have identification on hand. When renting a car, ask about promotional car-rental discounts, which can be cheaper than senior-citizen rates.

Educational Programs Road Scholar (☎ *800/454–5768, 978/323–4141 international callers, 877/426–2467 TTY* ⊕ *www.roadscholar. org).*

Information MTA Reduced Fare hotline (☎ *718/243–4999* ⊕ *www.mta.info).*

■ SPORTS AND THE OUTDOORS

The City of New York's Parks & Recreation division lists all of the recreational facilities and activities available through New York's Parks Department. The sports section of *Time Out New York*, sold at most newsstands, lists upcoming events, times, dates, and ticket information.

Contact Information Department of Parks & Recreation (☎ *311 in New York City, 212/639–9675,* ⊕ *www.nycgovparks.org).*

BASEBALL

The subway will get you directly to stadiums of both New York–area major-league teams. A fun alternative, the *Yankee Clipper* cruises from Manhattan's East Side and from New Jersey to Yankee Stadium on game nights. The round-trip cost is $25. The regular baseball season runs from April through September.

In 2009 the New York Mets moved from Shea Stadium to the neighboring, newly constructed CitiField, at the next-to-last stop on the 7 train, in Queens; the New York Yankees also got a new home at the new Yankee Stadium. Affiliated with the Mets since 2001, the minor-league Brooklyn Cyclones are named for Coney Island's famous wooden roller coaster. They play 38 home games at KeySpan Park, next to the boardwalk, with views of the Atlantic over the right-field wall and views of historic Astroland over the left-field wall. Most people make a day of it, with time at the beach and amusement rides before an evening game. Take the D, F, or Q subway to the end of the line, and walk one block to the right of the original Nathan's Famous hot dog stand.

For another fun, family-oriented experience, check out the Staten Island Yankees, one of New York's minor-league teams, which warms up many future New York Yankees players. The stadium, a five-minute walk from the Staten Island Ferry terminal, has magnificent panoramic views of Lower Manhattan and the Statue of Liberty.

Contact Information Brooklyn Cyclones (⊠ *1904 Surf Ave., at 19th St., Coney Island, Brooklyn* ☎ *718/449-8497* ⊕ *www. brooklyncyclones.com* Ⓜ *D, F, Q to Stillwell Ave.*). **CitiField** (⊠ *Roosevelt Ave. off Grand Central Pkwy., Flushing, Queens* ☎ *718/507-8499* ⊕ *www.mets.com* Ⓜ *7 to Willets Pt./Shea Stadium*). **Staten Island Yankees** (⊠ *Richmond County Bank Ballpark at St. George, Staten Island* ☎ *718/720-9265* ⊕ *www. siyanks.com*). **Yankee Clipper** (☎ *800/533-3779* ⊕ *www.nywaterway.com*). **Yankee Stadium** (⊠ *161st St. at River Ave., Bronx* ☎ *718/293-6000* ⊕ *www.yankees.com* Ⓜ *B, D, 4 to 161st St.-Yankee Stadium*).

BASKETBALL

The New York Knicks arouse intense hometown passions, which means tickets for home games at Madison Square Garden are hard to come by. The New Jersey Nets play at the Meadowlands in the Izod Center, but have plans to relocate and possibly become the Brooklyn Nets. Tickets are generally easy to obtain. The men's basketball season runs from late October through April. The New York Liberty, a member of the Women's NBA, had its first season in 1997; some of the team's more high-profile players are already legendary. The season runs from mid-May through August, with home games played at Madison Square Garden.

If the professional games are sold out, try to attend a college game where New York stalwarts Fordham, Hofstra, and St. John's compete against national top 25 teams during invitational tournaments.

Contact Information Madison Square Garden (⊕ *www.thegarden.com*). **New Jersey Nets** (☎ *201/935-3900 box office, 800/765-6387* ⊕ *www.nba.com/nets*). **New York Knicks** (☎ *212/465-5867* ⊕ *www.nba.com/knicks*). **New York Liberty** (☎ *877/962-2849 tickets, 212/564-9622 fan hotline* ⊕ *www.wnba.com/ liberty*).

BICYCLING

Central Park has a 6-mi circular drive with a couple of decent climbs. It's closed to automobile traffic from 10 am to 3 pm (except the southeast portion between 6th Avenue and East 72nd Street) and 7 pm to 7 am on weekdays, and from 7 pm Friday to 7 am Monday. On holidays it's closed to automobile traffic from 7 pm the night before until 7 am the day after.

The bike lane along the Hudson River Park's esplanade parallels the waterfront from West 59th Street south to the esplanade of Battery Park City. The lane also heads north, connecting with the bike path in Riverside Park and the promenade between West 72nd and West 110th streets, and continuing all the way to the George Washington Bridge. From Battery Park it's a quick ride to the Wall Street area, which is deserted on weekends, and over to South Street and a bike lane along the East River.

The 3.3-mi circular drive in Brooklyn's Prospect Park is closed to cars year-round except from 7 am to 9 am and 5 pm to 7 pm on weekdays except holidays. It has a long, gradual uphill that tops off near the Grand Army Plaza entrance. (Biking around Manhattan streets next to the dense traffic is best left to messengers and seasoned cyclists.)

Bike Rentals Bicycle Rentals at Loeb Boathouse (⊠ *Midpark near E. 74th St., Central Park* ☎ *212/517-2233*) Ⓜ *6 to 68th St./Hunter College*). **Bicycles NYC** (⊠ *1400 3rd Ave., between E. 79th and E. 80th Sts., Upper East Side* ☎ *212/794-2929* Ⓜ *4, 5, 6 to 86th St.* ⊕ *www.bicyclesnyc.com*). **Pedal Pusher** (⊠ *1306 2nd Ave., at E. 69th St., Upper East Side* ☎ *212/288-5592* ⊕ *www. pedalpusherbikeshop.com* Ⓜ *6 to 68th St./ Hunter College*). **Toga Bike Shop** (⊠ *110 West End Ave., at W. 64th St., Upper West Side* ☎ *212/799-9625* ⊕ *www.togabikes.com* Ⓜ *1 to 66th St.*).

GROUP BIKE RIDES

For organized rides with other cyclists, call or email before you come to New York. Bike New York runs a five-borough bike ride in May. The Five Borough Bicycle Club organizes day and weekend rides. The New York Cycle Club sponsors weekend rides for every level of ability. Time's Up!, a nonprofit environmental group, leads free recreational rides at least twice a month for cyclists as well as skaters; the Central Park Moonlight Ride, departing from Columbus Circle at 10 pm the first Friday of every month, is a favorite.

Contact Information Bike New York (✉ 891 Amsterdam Ave., at W. 103rd St., Upper West Side ☎ 212/932-2453 ⊕ www.bikenewyork. org). **Five Borough Bicycle Club** (✉ 891 Amsterdam Ave., at W. 103rd St., Upper West Side ☎ 347/688-2925 ⊕ www.5bbc.org). **New York Cycle Club** (✑ Box 4474, Grand Central Station, 10163 ☎ 212/828-5711 ⊕ www.nycc. org).

BOATING AND KAYAKING

Central Park has rowboats (plus one Venetian gondola for glides in the moonlight) on the 22-acre Central Park Lake. Rent your rowboat at Loeb Boathouse, near East 74th Street, from March through October; gondola rides are available only in summer. In summer at the Pier 96 Boathouse in Midtown West, you can take a sturdy kayak out for a paddle for free on weekends and weekday evenings from mid-May through mid-October. Beginners learn to paddle in the calmer embayment area closest to shore until they feel ready to venture farther out into open water. More experienced kayakers can partake in the three-hour trips conducted every weekend and on holiday mornings. Sign-ups for these popular tours end at 8 am. Because of high demand, names are entered into a lottery to see who gets to go out each morning. No reservations are taken in advance. Manhattan Kayak Company runs trips (these are not free) and gives lessons for all levels.

Contact Information Loeb Boathouse (✉ Midpark near E. 74th St., Central Park ☎ 212/517-2233 ⊕ www. thecentralparkboathouse.com) Ⓜ 6 to 68th St./ Hunter College). **Manhattan Kayak Company** (✉ The Boathouse, Pier 66, W. 26th St. at 12th Ave., Chelsea ☎ 212/924-1788 ⊕ www. manhattankayak.com Ⓜ C, E to 23rd St.). **Pier 96 Boathouse** (✉ 56th St. at the Hudson River, Midtown West ⊕ www.downtownboathouse.org Ⓜ 1, A, C, E to 59th St.).

FOOTBALL

The football season runs from September through December. The enormously popular New York Giants play at the New Meadowlands Stadium. Most seats for Giants games are sold on a season-ticket basis—and there's a long waiting list for those. However, single tickets are occasionally available at the stadium box office. The New York Jets also play at New Meadowlands Stadium. Although Jets tickets are not as scarce as those for the Giants, most are snapped up by fans before the season opener.

Contact Information New York Giants (☎ 201/935-8222 for tickets ⊕ www.giants. com). **New York Jets** (☎ 800/469-5387 for tickets ⊕ www.newyorkjets.com).

ICE SKATING

The outdoor rink in Rockefeller Center, open from October through early April, is much smaller in real life than it appears on TV and in movies. It's also busy, so be prepared to wait—there are no advance ticket sales. Although it's also beautiful, especially when Rock Center's enormous Christmas tree towers above it, you pay for the privilege: rates are $15.50–$19 and skate rentals are $12.

The city's outdoor rinks, open from roughly November through March, all have their own character. Central Park's beautifully situated Wollman Rink offers skating until long after dark beneath the lights of the city. Be prepared for daytime crowds on weekends. The Lasker Rink, at the north end of Central Park, is smaller and usually less crowded than

Wollman. Chelsea Piers' Sky Rink has two year-round indoor rinks overlooking the Hudson. Rentals are available at all rinks. The Pond at Bryant Park offers free skating, not including the cost of skate rental, from late October through February, from 8 am to 10 pm from Sunday through Thursday and from 8 am to midnight Friday and Saturday.

Contact Information Bryant Park (✉ 6th Ave. between 40th and 42nd Sts., Midtown West ☎ 212/768–4242 ⊕ www. thepondatbryantpark.com Ⓜ B, D, F to 42nd St.). **Lasker Rink** (✉ Midpark near E. 106th St., Central Park ☎ 917/492–3857 ⊕ www. wollmanskatingrink.com Ⓜ B, C to 103rd St.). **Rockefeller Center** (✉ 50th St. at 5th Ave., lower plaza, Midtown West ☎ 212/332–7654 ⊕ www.therinkatrockcenter.com Ⓜ B, D, F to 47th–50th Sts./Rockefeller Center; E, V to 5th Ave.–53rd St.). **Sky Rink** (✉ Pier 61, W. 23rd St. at the Hudson River, Chelsea ☎ 212/336–6100 ⊕ www.chelseapiers.com Ⓜ C, E to 23rd St.). **Wollman Rink** (✉ North of 6th Ave. entrance, between 62nd and 63rd Sts., north of park entrance ☎ 212/439–6900 ⊕ www. wollmanskatingrink.com) Ⓜ A, B, C, D, 1 to 59th St./Columbus Circle).

JOGGING

All kinds of New Yorkers jog, some with dogs or babies in tow, so you'll always have company on the regular jogging routes. What's not recommended is to set out on a lonely park path at dusk. Jog when and where everybody else does. On Manhattan streets, roughly 20 north–south blocks make a mile.

In Manhattan, Central Park is the busiest spot, specifically along the 1.6-mi path circling the Jacqueline Kennedy Onassis Reservoir, where you jog in a counterclockwise direction. A runners' lane has been designated along the park roads. A good 1.75-mi route starts at the former Tavern on the Green (now closed) along the West Drive, heads south around the bottom of the park to the East Drive, and circles back west on the 72nd Street park road to your starting point; the entire loop

road is a hilly 6 mi. Riverside Park, along the Hudson River bank in Manhattan, is glorious at sunset. You can cover 4.5 mi by running from West 72nd to 116th Street and back, and the Greenbelt trail extends 4 more mi north to the George Washington Bridge at 181st Street. Other favorite Manhattan circuits are the Battery Park City esplanade (about 2 mi), which connects to the Hudson River Park (about 1.5 mi), and the East River Esplanade (just over 3 mi from East 63rd to East 125th streets).

▌ STUDENTS IN NEW YORK

New York is home to such major schools as Columbia University, New York University, Fordham University, and the City College of New York. With other colleges scattered throughout the five boroughs, as well as a huge population of public and private high-schoolers, it's no wonder the city is rife with student discounts. Wherever you go, especially museums, sightseeing attractions, and performances, identify yourself as a student up front and ask if a discount is available. However, be prepared to show your ID as proof of enrollment and/or age.

A great program made available to children between the ages of 13 and 18 (or anyone in middle or high school) is High 5 for the Arts. Tickets to a wide variety of performances are sold for $5 online or by phone. Write or call to receive a free catalog of events, check it out online, or pick up a catalog at any New York public library or at High 5's offices.

IDs and Services High 5 for the Arts (✉ 520 8th Ave., at 36th St., Midtown ☎ 212/750–0555 ⊕ www.highfivetix.org). **STA Travel** (☎ 212/627–3111, 800/781–4040 24-hr service center ⊕ www.sta.com).

▌ TAXES

A sales tax of 8.875% applies to almost everything you can buy retail, including restaurant meals. However, prescription drugs and nonprepared food bought in grocery stores are exempt. Clothing and footwear costing less than $110 does not incur a city sales tax, although there is a 4.375% state sales tax.

▌ TIPPING

The customary tipping rate for taxi drivers is 15%–20%, with a minimum of $2; bellhops are usually given $2 per bag in luxury hotels, $1 per bag elsewhere. Hotel maids should be tipped $2 per day of your stay. A doorman who hails or helps you into a cab can be tipped $1–$2. You should also tip your hotel concierge for services rendered; the size of the tip depends on the difficulty of your request, as well as the quality of the concierge's work. Waiters should be tipped 15%–20%, though at higher-end restaurants, a solid 20% is more the norm. Tip $1 per drink you order at the bar.

▌ VISITOR INFORMATION

The Grand Central Partnership (a sort of civic Good Samaritans' group) has installed a number of information booths in and around Grand Central Terminal (there's one near Vanderbilt Avenue and East 43rd Street). They're loaded with maps and helpful brochures on attractions throughout the city and staffed by friendly, knowledgeable, multilingual New Yorkers.

NYC & Company's Times Square Visitors Center is decked out with lots of fun and helpful tools like multilingual kiosks. The bureau also has a Midtown visitor center on 7th Avenue and runs kiosks in Lower Manhattan at City Hall Park and at Federal Hall National Memorial at 26 Wall St; in Chinatown at the triangle where Canal, Walker, and Baxter streets meet; and in Harlem at the Apollo Theater at 253 West 125th St.

The Downtown Alliance has information on the area encompassing City Hall south to Battery Park, and from the East River to West Street. For a free booklet listing New York City attractions and tour packages, contact the New York State Division of Tourism.

CONTACTS
City Information Downtown Alliance (✉ 120 Broadway, Suite 3340, between Pine and Thames Sts., Lower Manhattan ☎ 212/566–6700 ⊕ www.downtownny.com). **Grand Central Partnership** (☎ 212/883–2420 ⊕ www.grandcentralpartnership.org). **NYC & Company Convention & Visitors Bureau** (✉ 810 7th Ave., between W. 52nd and W. 53rd Sts., 3rd fl., Midtown West ☎ 212/484–1200 ⊕ www.nycgo.com). **Times Square Information Center** (✉ 1560 Broadway, between 46th and 47th Sts., Midtown West ☎ 212/768–1560 ⊕ www.timessquarenyc.org) Ⓜ N, Q, R, S, 1, 2, 3, 7 to 42nd St./Times Square).

Statewide Information New York State Division of Tourism (☎ 518/474–4116 or 800/225–5697 ⊕ www.iloveny.com).

INDEX

A

A & G Merch (shop), 208
A Voce ×, 442
ABC Carpet & Home (shop), 371
ABC Kitchen ×, 442–443
Abyssinian Baptist Church, 185–186, 188
Ace Hotel, 324, 499, 501
Acquavella (gallery), 154
Acoustic and blues venues, 316–317, 328
Adour Alain Ducasse ×, 450
Aedes De Venustas (shop), 361
Affinia 50, 514, 517
African Burial Ground, 57
Air travel, 528–530
Ajna Bar, 101
Al di la ×, 217
Alamo (sculpture), 81
Alan Klotz Gallery, 105
Aldea ×, 443
Alex, The, 517
Alexander McQueen (shop), 101
Algonquin, The, 505
Alice in Wonderland statue, 164
Alice's Teacup ×, 175
Alloro ×, 461–462
Alphabet City, 82
American Folk Art Museum, 253
American Museum of Natural History, 19–20, 21, 174, 175, 269–275
Amy Ruth's ×, 184–185
Andrea Rosen (gallery), 105
Angel of the Waters statue, 162–163
Angel Orensanz Center for the Arts, 86
Angelika Film Center, 283–284
Antonio's Trattoria ×, 238
Apartment rentals, 524
Apiary ×, 427
Apollo Theater, 185, 299
Appellate Division, New York State Supreme Court, 116, 124–125
Applewood ×, 217
APT (dance club), 306
Aquagrill ×, 423
Aquariums, 21, 218–220
Aquavit and Aquavit Café ×, 450
Architecture, 28–29, 69, 72, 100–101, 116
Arlene's Grocery (rock club), 311
Arsenal, 160
Art galleries
Brooklyn, 203, 207
Chelsea, 92–93, 100, 105–110
Lower East Side, 88
Midtown, 145–146
SoHo, 75–76
Upper East Side, 154
Arthur Avenue (The Bronx), 234, 237–238, 240
Arthur Avenue Retail Market, 228, 240
Arthur's Tavern, 305
Artisanal ×, 448
Arts
and children, 283, 288, 290–291, 293, 294, 300
cabaret, 316, 320, 331
dance, 288, 290
festivals and seasonal events, 99, 159, 203, 289
film and television, 229, 283–284, 286–287, 289, 290–291, 295, 300
galleries, 75–76, 88, 92–93, 100, 105–110, 145–146, 203, 207
music, 280, 283, 287, 291, 294, 295–296, 299
opera, 286, 294
performing arts centers, 291–292, 294, 296–300
readings and lectures, 283, 284, 285–286, 287–288, 292, 295
theater, 282, 284–285, 288, 290, 292–294, 295, 300
tickets for, 278–280
Asia Society and Museum, 255, 263
Asiate ×, 464
Astor Place, 81
Astor Place Subway Station, 81, 84
Astoria (Queens), 225–229
Atlantic Avenue, 209
ATM Gallery, 105
August ×, 439
Aureole ×, 454

B

B. Altman Building/New York Public Library–Science, Industry, and Business Library (SIBL), 116, 125
B & H Photo Video and Pro Audio (shop), 379–380
Ba Xuyen ×, 196
Babbo ×, 435
Babeland (shop), 86
Back Forty ×, 427
Bailey Fountain, 215
Balthazar ×, 423
Balto statue, 161
BAMcafé ×, 212
Baoguette ×, 427
Bar Americain ×, 454
Bar Boulud ×, 464–465
Barbè (bar), 217–218
Barbuto ×, 439
Barcade, 207
Barnard College, 175
Barney Greengrass ×, 465
Barney's New York (department store), 390
Bars. ⇨ *See also under specific areas*
gay and lesbian, 316, 320, 324, 331, 327
hotel, 500
Baseball, 219, 232, 237, 540–541
Basketball, 541
Battery Park, 42, 43, 45–46
Battery Park City, 31
Beacon's Closet (shop), 208
Becco ×, 454
Bed-and-breakfasts, 524
Bedford, The ×, 204
Bedford Cheese Shop, 208
Belmont (The Bronx), 237–238, 240
Belvedere Castle, 165–166
Belvedere Hotel, 505
Bemelmans Bar ×, 308
Ben Benson's Steak House ×, 454–455
Benjamin, The, 517
Bergdorf Goodman (department store), 380
Best Western President Hotel, 505–506
Bethesda Fountain, 162–163
Bialystoker Synagogue, 86
Bicycling, 541–542
Bierkraft (shop), 218
Big Nick's ×, 465
Bird (shop), 195, 218
Birdland (jazz club), 131
Blakely, The ×, 506–507

Bleeker Street, *96*
Blockhouse #1, *169*
Bloomingdale's (department store), *131*
BLT Fish ✕, *443*
BLT Prime ✕, *447*
BLT Steak ✕, *450*
Blue Hill ✕, *435*
Blue Note (jazz club), *94–95, 304*
Blue Ribbon ✕, *423*
Blue Ribbon Bakery ✕, *435*
Blue Ribbon Sushi ✕, *423*
Blue Smoke ✕, *447*
Blues clubs, *316–317, 328*
Blueberi (shop), *204*
Boat and ferry travel, *38, 56–57, 240, 241, 530*
Boat tours, *32, 104*
Boating, *542*
Boerum Hill (Brooklyn), *194, 208–210*
Bohemian Hall & Beer Garden ✕, *228*
Books of Wonder (shop), *367*
Booth Theater, *131*
Boqueria ✕, *443*
Borgatti's Ravioli & Egg Noodles (shop), *240*
Bouchon Bakery ✕, *465*
Bow Bridge, *164*
Bowery, *61–62*
Bowery Ballroom (rock club), *310–311, 317–318*
Bowery Hotel ☉, *495–496*
Bowling Green, *44*
Brandy Library (bar), *303*
Brasserie Ruhlmann ✕, *455*
Brighton Beach, *196, 218–220*
Broadhurst Theater, *131*
Broadway, *174, 282*
Broadway theater, *282*
Bronx, The, *16, 223–225, 234–240*
children's activities, 235–236
price categories, 225
restaurants, 238
shopping, 238, 240
Bronx Zoo, *20, 21, 234, 235–236*
Brooklyn, *16, 193–220*
children's activities, 198, 199, 202, 218
galleries, 203, 207
hotels, 489, 492
nightlife, 203, 207–208, 210, 217–218
performing arts, 299–300
price categories, 196

restaurants, 195–196, 199, 202–203, 204–207, 209–210, 212–213, 217, 220
shopping, 203–204, 208, 218
Brooklyn Academy of Music (BAM), *210–212, 299–300*
Brooklyn Art Guide, *207*
Brooklyn Borough Hall, *197*
Brooklyn Botanic Garden, *195, 213–214*
Brooklyn Brewery, *207*
Brooklyn Bridge, *19, 46, 197–198*
Brooklyn Bridge Park, *289*
Brooklyn Children's Museum, *216–217*
Brooklyn Fare ✕, *209*
Brooklyn Flea Market, *211*
Brooklyn Heights, *194, 196–199*
Brooklyn Heights Promenade, *196, 198*
Brooklyn Historical Society, *198*
Brooklyn Ice Cream Factory ✕, *202*
Brooklyn Museum, *213, 214–215*
Brooklyn Social (bar), *210*
Brooklyn Superhero Supply Co. (shop), *218*
Brooklyn Tourism & Visitors Center, *197*
Bryant Park, *131, 289*
Bryant Park Hotel ☉, *507*
Bubby's ✕, *420–421*
Buddakan ✕, *101, 432–433*
Burger Joint ✕, *455*
Bus tours, *32*
Bus travel, *530–531*
Business hours, *13, 399*
Butler Library, *179*
Buttermilk Channel ✕, *210*

C

Cabaret, *316, 320, 331*
Café Boulud ✕, *462*
Café Carlyle, *308*
Café d'Alsace ✕, *462*
Café Kashkar ✕, *196*
Café Luxembourg ✕, *465–466*
Caffè Reggio ✕, *94*
Cake Shop (rock club), *311*
Calabria Pork Store, *240*
Calandra Cheese (shop), *240*
Campbell Apartment (bar), *133, 308, 326*
Canaan Baptist Church of Christ, *184, 186, 188*

Candle 79 ✕, *462–463*
Car rental, *532–533*
Car travel, *531–533*
Carl Schurz Park, *150, 151*
Carlton Arms ☉, *502*
Carlton on Madison Avenue ☉, *502*
Carlyle, A Rosewood Hotel, The ☉, *150, 522*
Carmine's (Midtown) ✕, *455*
Carmine's (Upper West Side) ✕, *466*
Carnegie Hall, *131, 291*
Carroll Gardens (Brooklyn), *194, 208–210*
Casa Mono ✕, *447*
Casabel Taqueria ✕, *463*
Casablanca Hotel ☉, *507*
Casey Kaplan (gallery), *105–106*
Castle Clinton National Monument, *43–44, 46*
Catbird (shop), *195, 208*
Cathedral Church of St. John the Divine, *174, 175, 176–177*
CBGB, *310*
Central Library, *215*
Central Park, *16, 20, 156–170, 174, 295*
Central Park Conservancy tours, *158*
Central Park Zoo, *21, 160*
Centro Vinoteca ✕, *435–436*
Century Building, *124*
Century 21 (discount department store), *335*
Chambers Hotel ☉, *507*
Char No. 4 ✕, *195, 210*
Charging Bull statue, *44*
Charles A. Dana Discovery Center, *169*
Charlton Street, *72*
Chatwal, The ☉, *507*
Cheim & Read (gallery), *106*
Chelsea, *14, 91–93, 100–110*
architecture, 100–101
bars, 323
children's activities, 104
galleries, 92–93, 100, 105–110
hotels, 496–497
museums, 100, 252
nightlife, 306–307, 323–324
performing arts, 288, 290
restaurants, 101, 412–413, 432–433
shopping, 367, 370–371
Chelsea Art Museum, *100, 252*

Chelsea Hotel 🏠 , *100–101, 104*
Chelsea Lodge 🏠 , *496*
Chelsea Market, *101, 104*
Chelsea Piers (sports facility), *104*
Cherry Lane Theater, *95*
Children
aquariums, 21, 218–220
arts, 283, 288, 290–291, 293, 294, 300
dining, 397, 418, 419, 420–421, 422, 425, 426, 430, 431, 434–435, 443–444, 448, 455, 460, 461, 466
hotels, 488, 497, 508, 509–510, 513–514, 516, 517, 519, 523, 538
ice-skating, 160, 542–543
museums, 21, 143, 199, 216–217, 242, 249, 250–251, 253, 255
parks, playgrounds, and gardens, 21, 45–47, 83–84, 98, 132–133, 152, 180, 189, 202, 213–214, 215–216, 232–234
shopping, 104, 218, 335, 342, 348, 350, 360, 371, 379, 383, 386–387, 393
sightseeing attractions, 21, 56, 104, 116, 118, 120, 140–141, 143, 198
travel with, 537–538
zoos, 21, 160–161, 195, 216, 233–234, 235–236
Children's Museum (Staten Island), *242*
Children's Museum of Manhattan, *21*
Children's Museum of the Arts, *250*
Chinatown, *43, 61–64*
museums, 61, 246, 249–250
restaurants, 61, 403, 418–419
Chinatown Brasserie ✕ , *427–428*
Chocolate Room, The ✕ , *196*
Christofle (shop), *151*
Christopher Park, *93–94, 98*
Chrysler Building, *131, 133*
Churrascaria Plataforma ✕ , *455–456*
Cielo (dance club), *307*
Citi Field, *232*
City Bakery ✕ , *443–444*
City Center, *291–292*
City Club Hotel 🏠 , *507–508*
City College, *186*

City Hall, *57*
City Hall Park, *57*
Cleopatra's Needle, *167*
Cleopatra's Needle (jazz club), *176*
Climate, *12*
Cloisters Museum and Gardens, The, *276*
Cobble Hill (Brooklyn), *194, 208–210*
Colonnade Row, *81, 84*
Columbia Heights (Brooklyn), *196*
Columbia University, *175, 178–179*
Columbus Avenue, *174*
Columbus Circle, *177*
Columbus Park, *63–64*
Comedy clubs, *323, 324, 329*
Commerce ✕ , *439–440*
Communications, *536*
Coney Island (Brooklyn), *195, 218–220*
Coney Island Museum, *219, 220*
Conservatory Garden, *169*
Conservatory Water, *164*
Convent Avenue Baptist Church, *188*
Cookshop ✕ , *433*
Cooper-Hewitt, National Design Museum, *263*
Cooper Square Hotel 🏠 , *495*
Cooper Union's Science and Art Building, *81*
Corona (Queens), *232–234*
Corton ✕ , *421*
Cosmopolitan 🏠 , *493*
Craft ✕ , *448–449*
Craftbar ✕ , *444*
Crawford Doyle Booksellers, *151*
Credit cards, *7, 538*
Crosby Street Hotel 🏠 , *494*
Culinary tours, *424*
Cushman Row, *101, 105*
Cyclone, The (roller coaster), *219*

D

Daily News Building, *139*
Dakota, The (apartments), *163, 179*
Dance, *288, 290*
Dance clubs, *306–307, 312, 323, 329*
Daniel ✕ , *463*
David Findlay Jr. Fine Art (gallery), *145–146*

David Zwirner Gallery, *100, 106*
DB Bistro Moderne ✕ , *456*
DBGB Kitchen & Bar ✕ , *428*
Decker Building, *124*
Deitch Projects (gallery), *75*
Del Posto ✕ , *101, 438*
Delacorte Theater, *167*
Delhi Palace ✕ , *230*
dell'amina ✕ , *440*
Delmonico's ✕ , *419*
Deno's Wonderwheel Amusement Park, *219*
Diner ✕ , *205*
Dining, *7, 23.* ⇨ *See also* Restaurants
Dinosaur Bar-B-Que ✕ , *469*
Disabilities and accessibility, *536–537*
Discounts and deals, *13*
shopping, 335, 347, 370, 371
theater tickets, 279–280
Distrikt, The 🏠 , *508*
DJ venues, *312, 323, 329*
Do Hwa ✕ , *440*
Dos Caminos ✕ , *444*
DoubleTree Guest Suites Times Square 🏠 , *508*
Dovetail ✕ , *466*
Doyers Street, *61*
Drawing Center (gallery), *75–76*
Dream New York 🏠 , *508*
Dressler ✕ , *205*
Duane Street Hotel 🏠 , *493*
DUMBO (Brooklyn), *202–204*
DUMBO Arts Center, *203*
DUMBO Arts Festival, *203*
Dumont ✕ , *205*
Duplex (bar), *93*
Dylan, The 🏠 , *517*

E

East Village, *14, 78–85*
bars, 314–316
children's activities, 83–84
hotels, 495
museums, 81, 250–252
nightlife, 314–319
performing arts, 284–286
restaurants, 406–407, 427–430
shopping, 354–360
Economy Candy (shop), *86*
Edward Mooney House, *62*
18 West 11th Street, *93*
Eisenberg's Sandwich Shop ✕ , *444*
El Museo del Barrio, *263*

Eldridge Street Synagogue, *85–86*

Eleanor Proske Visitor Center, *242*

Eleven Madison Park ✕ , *444–445*

Ellis Island, *36–38, 42–43*

Empire-Fulton Ferry Park, *202*

Empire Hotel, The ☎ , *523, 525*

Empire State Building, *18, 115, 116, 118, 120*

Employees Only (bar), *321*

Emporio ✕ , *423–424*

Enid A. Haupt Conservatory, *236–237*

Esca ✕ , *456*

Essex Street Market, *87–88*

Eventi, The ☎ , *501*

Excelsior ☎ , *525*

F

Fairway (gourmet shop), *174*

Family Festival, *289*

Fanelli's (bar), *313*

FAO Schwarz (shop), *379*

Fatty Crab ✕ , *440, 466*

Fatty Cue ✕ , *205–206*

Federal Hall National Memorial, *45, 46*

Federal Reserve Bank of New York, *57, 60*

Feinstein's (bar), *308*

Ferry service, *56–57, 240, 241, 530*

Festivals and seasonal events, *99, 159, 203, 289*

Fette Sau ✕ , *206*

5th Avenue and 57th Street, *374–375*

51-53 Christopher Street, *93*

Film and television, *283–284, 286–287, 289, 290–291, 295, 300*

festivals, 289

series and revivals, 295

studios, 229

tickets, 24–25

Film Forum, *286–287*

Financial District, *42, 43–61*

children's activities, 45–47

hotels, 492–493

museums, 56, 60

restaurants, 403, 419–420

shopping, 354–360

Financier Patisserie ✕ , *419*

First Corinthian Baptist Church, *184, 188, 189*

Five Napkin Burger ✕ , *456*

555 Edgecombe, *190*

Five Points, *63*

Five Points ✕ , *436*

Flatiron Building, *116, 120–121*

Flatiron District, *14, 113–126*

hotels, 499, 501

museums, 115, 252–253

restaurants, 442–447

shopping, 371–372

Flushing (Queens), *232–234*

Flushing Meadows-Corona Park, *232–234*

Food courts, *434*

Football, *542*

Fort Greene (Brooklyn), *210–213*

409 Edgecombe Avenue, *190*

Four Seasons ✕ , *451*

Four Seasons Hotel ☎ , *517–518*

Fragments (shop), *349*

Franklin, The ☎ , *522*

Franny's ✕ , *217*

Fraunces Tavern Museum, *44, 60*

Free events, *26–27*

Frick Collection, *263–264*

Friedsam Memorial Carousel, *160*

Fulton Ferry Landing, *202*

Future Perfect (shop), *195, 208*

G

Gagosian (gallery), *106*

Gahm Mi Oak ✕ , *448*

Galapagos Art Space, *203*

Galarie Lelong, *107*

Gallery Onetwentyeight, *88*

Garage Restaurant & Cafe, *305*

Gardens, *21*

Bronx, The, 234, 236–237, 238

Brooklyn, 195, 213–214

Central Park, 166, 169

Staten Island, 242

Upper East Side, 151, 152

Upper West Side, 276

Gay and lesbian nightlife, *316, 320, 324, 327, 329, 331*

Gay and lesbian travel, *537*

Gay Street, *95–96*

GE Building, *137*

GEM Hotel Chelsea ☎ , *496–497*

General Greene, The ✕ , *212*

Gild Hall ☎ , *492*

Gladstone Gallery, *107*

Gnocco ✕ , *428*

Gordon Ramsay at The London and Maze ✕ , *456–457*

Governor's Island, *30, 43, 46–47*

Gospel tours, *188*

Gotham Bar & Grill ✕ , *436*

Gotham Hotel, The ☎ , *518*

Gracie Mansion, *150, 151–152*

Gramercy Park, *14, 113–126*

hotels, 501–502

nightlife, 324–325

restaurants, 447

Gramercy Park Hotel ☎ , *115, 501*

Gramercy Tavern ✕ , *445*

Grand Army Plaza (Brooklyn), *215*

Grand Central Terminal, *131, 133–135*

Grand Sichuan ✕ , *428*

Grant's Tomb, *179–180*

Gray's Papaya ✕ , *436*

Great Lawn, *166–168*

Great New York Noodletown ✕ , *418*

Greater Refuge Temple, *188*

Green-Wood Cemetery, *195*

Greenwich Hotel ☎ , *493*

Greenwich Village, *14, 90–99*

bars, 319

hotels, 497, 499

nightlife, 304–305, 319–321

performing arts, 286–288

restaurants, 96, 408–409

shopping, 96, 361–366

Grimaldi's Pizzeria ✕ , *202*

Ground Zero, *42, 48–55*

Grove Court, *93*

Guggenheim Museum, *150, 265*

Guided tours, *32, 104, 158, 188, 424*

H

Halloween Parade, *99*

Hamilton Heights, *185, 186*

Hamilton Terrace, *186*

Hans Christian Andersen statue, *164*

Harlem, *16, 183–190*

children's activities, 189

museums, 185, 276

nightlife, 332

performing arts, 299

restaurants, 416–417, 469–470

Harlem Meer, *169*

Harrison, The ✕ , *421*

Harrison Street, *62, 63*

Harry's Steak and Harry's Café ✕, 419–420
Harvey Theater, 211–212
Haughwout Building, 72
Hawks, 170
Helen Hayes Theater, 131
Helmsley Building, 139
Henry's End ✕, 199
Herald Square Hotel ⬚, 502
High Line, 31, 101, 105
Hill Country ✕, 445
Hilton New York Fashion District ⬚, 497
Hilton Times Square ⬚, 508–509
Hirschl & Adler (gallery), 146
Hispanic Society of America, 276
Historic Richmond Town (Staten Island), 240–241
Hogs and Heifers (bar), 101
Holiday Inn SoHo ⬚, 494
Holiday Shops, 132–133
Hotel Beacon ⬚, 525
Hotel 41 ⬚, 509
Hotel Gansevoort ⬚, 101, 499
Hotel Giraffe ⬚, 502, 504
Hotel Metro ⬚, 509
Hotel on Rivington ✕, 496
Hôtel Plaza Athénée ⬚, 522–523
Hotel Roger Williams ⬚, 504
Hotel Wales ⬚, 523
Hotels, 7, 486–526
 atlas, 472–484
 bars in, 500
 best bets, 490–491
 children, 488, 497, 508, 509–510, 513–514, 516, 517, 519, 523, 538
 disabilities and accessibility, 536–537
 Fodor's choice, 490
 lodging alternatives, 524
 neighborhoods, 487
 parking, 488
 price categories, 12, 489
 reservations, 488, 536–537
 romantic retreats, 506
 room size, 488–487
 services, 488
 tipping, 544
Housing Works Used Book Café, 284
Hudson, the ⬚, 509
Hudson River Park, 30, 63, 94, 289
Hundred Acres ✕, 424

I

Ice-skating, 160, 542–543
Il Buco ✕, 428
Ilili ✕, 445
Imperial Theater, 131
Ink48 ⬚, 509–510
Inn at Irving Place ⬚, 114–115, 501–502, 506
Inn on 23rd ⬚, 497
'ino ✕, 440–441
'inoteca ✕, 431
Insurance, 532–533
InterContinental New York Times Square ⬚, 510
International Center of Photography, 253
Internet service, 536
Intrepid Sea, Air & Space Museum, 253, 255
Iridium (nightclub), 131
Irondale Center, 210
Irving Place, 114–115, 122

J

Jack Shainman (gallery), 107
Jackson Heights (Queens), 229–232
Jacobs Theater, 131
Jacqueline Kennedy Onassis Reservoir, 168
Jacques Marchais Museum of Tibetan Art, 240, 241
Jacques Torres Chocolate (shop), 203–204
James ✕, 217
Jane, The ⬚, 499
Jane Kahan (gallery), 154
Japan Society, 255
Jazz at Lincoln Center, 177
Jazz clubs, 304–305, 320–321, 325, 329–330, 332
Jean Georges ✕, 466–467
Jefferson Market Library, 93
Jeffrey (shop), 101
Jewel Bako ✕, 428–429
Jewish Museum, 264
Jing Fong ✕, 418
Joe's Shanghai ✕, 418
Jogging, 543
Jolly Hotel Madison Towers ⬚, 504
Joyce Theater, 100, 288, 290
Jumeirah Essex House ⬚, 510

K

Kabab Café ✕, 228–229
Karaoke bars, 312
Katz's Delicatessen ✕, 431

Kaufmann Concert Hall, 294
Kayaking, 542
Kefi ✕, 467
Kehila Kedosha Janina, 86
Keszler Gallery, 154
Kim Lau Arch, 64
Kim Lau Square, 64
King Cole Bar, 309
King of Greene Street (building), 72
Kirna Zabête (shop), 344
Kiss and Fly (dance club), 307
Kitano, The ⬚, 504
Kitchenette ✕, 421
Knickerbocker Bar & Grill, 305
Knoedler & Company (gallery), 154
Koreatown, 125
Kuruma Zushi ✕, 451

L

La Esquina ✕, 424
La Maison du Chocolat (shop), 151
La Quinta Inn ⬚, 510
La Superior ✕, 206
Lafco NY/Santa Maria Novella (shop), 339
Lambs Club, The ✕, 457
Lani Kai (bar), 313
L'Atelier de Joël Robuchon ✕, 451
Le Bernardin ✕, 457
Le Cirque ✕, 451–452
Le Pain Quotidien ✕, 457
Le Parker Meridien ⬚, 510, 514
Le Poisson Rouge (rock club), 287, 321–322
Lefferts Historic House, 216
Lemon Ice King of Corona ✕, 234
Lenox Lounge, 185
Leo Castelli (gallery), 154
Les Halles ✕, 448
Lexington Bar and Books, 308
Libraries
 Brooklyn, 215
 Greenwich Village, 93
 Midtown, 131, 140
 Union Square, 115, 116, 125, 252–253
 Upper West Side, 179
Library Hotel ⬚, 506, 518
Lincoln Center, 174, 175, 177–178, 296
Litchfield Villa, 215
Literary Walk, 161
Little India, 115

Little Italy, 14, 66–68, 73–76
hotels, 494–495
restaurants, 73, 404–405, 426
shopping, 73
Little Owl, The ✕, 441
Little Singer Building, 72–73
Lobby Lounge, 309
Local 138 (bar), 311
Locanda Verdi ✕, 421–422
Lodging. ⇨ See Hotels
Loeb Boathouse, 164
Loews Regency Hotel 🏨, 518
Lombardi's ✕, 426
London Terrace (building), 101
London NYC, The 🏨, 510–511
Long Island City (Queens),
 225–229
Lord and Taylor (department
 store), 131
Louis Armstrong House
 Museum, 234
Love Brigade (shop), 195
Low Memorial Library, 179
Lowell, The 🏨, 523
Lower East Side, 14, 79–80,
 85–88
bars, 314–316
galleries, 88
hotels, 495–496
museums, 80, 85, 250–252
nightlife, 310–311, 314–319
restaurants, 406–407, 431–432
shopping, 86, 360–361
Lower East Side Tenement
 Museum, 80, 85, 250–251
Lower Manhattan, 14, 40–64
children's activities, 45–47,
 56, 249
hotels, 492–494
museums, 44, 45, 46, 52, 56,
 60, 61, 246, 249–250
nightlife, 303, 312
performing arts, 280, 283
restaurants, 402–403, 418–422
shopping, 335
Lucerne, The 🏨, 525
Lucille Lortel (theater), 93
Lugo Caffé ✕, 457–458
Luhring Augustine (gallery),
 107
Lupa ✕, 436
Lure ✕, 425

M

Má Pêche ✕, 458
MacDougal Alley, 93
Macy's (department store), 122
Madame Tussaud's New York,
 139–140

Madiba ✕, 212
Madison Avenue shopping,
 384–385
Madison Square Park, 114,
 116, 122–123
Madonia Brothers Bakery, 240
Mahayana Buddhist Temple, 64
Majestic Theater, 131
Malcolm Shabazz Harlem Mar-
 ket, 185
Mall, The, 161
Mandarin Oriental 🏨, 511
Mandate of Heaven (shop), 208
Mansfield, The 🏨, 511
Marc Forgione ✕, 422
Marcel at Grammercy 🏨, 502
Marcus Garvey Park, 189
Marea ✕, 467
MarieBelle ✕, 425
Maritime Hotel 🏨, 497
Mark, The 🏨, 523
Mark Morris Dance Center, 210
Marlborough (galleries), 107,
 146
Marquee (dance club), 307
Marseille ✕, 458
Mary Boone (gallery), 107
Mary's Fish Camp ✕, 437
Masa ✕, 175
Masjid Malcolm Shabazz, 185,
 189–190
Matsuri ✕, 101
Matthew Marks (gallery), 100,
 107
Maya ✕, 463
Mayahuel (bar), 315
McNally Jackson (bookstore),
 339
McSorley's Old Ale House, 81,
 82–83
MCU Park, 219
Meal plans, 7
Meatpacking District, 14,
 91–93, 100–105
bars, 322–323
nightlife, 306–307, 322–323
restaurants, 438–439
shopping, 101, 366–367,
 368–369
Memorial Baptist Church, 188
Mercer Hotel 🏨, 494
Merchant's House Museum,
 81, 251
Mercury Lounge, 311, 318
Mermaid Oyster Bar ✕, 437
Meskerem ✕, 458
Metro Pictures (gallery), 108
Metropolitan Life Insurance
 Tower, 116, 125–126

Metropolitan Museum of Art,
 18, 150, 257–262
Mexicana Mama ✕, 441
Michael Jordan's The Steak
 House NYC ✕, 452
Michelangelo, The 🏨, 511
Midtown, 16, 128–146
bars, 326–327, 328–329
children's activities, 132–133,
 140–141, 143, 253, 255,
 290–291
galleries, 145–146
hotels, 505–522
museums, 139–140, 143, 151,
 253, 255
nightlife, 308–309, 326–330
performing arts, 290–294
restaurants, 412–415, 450–461
shopping, 372–383
Millennium UN Plaza 🏨,
 518–519
Milligan Place, 93, 96
Minetta Lane Theatre, 95
Minetta Tavern✕, 95, 441
Mint ✕, 452
Minton's Playhouse, 185
Mitchell-Innes & Nash (gal-
 lery), 154
Modern and Bar Room, The
 ✕, 459
MoMA PS 1, 225
Momofuku Ko ✕, 429
Momofuku Noodle Bar ✕, 429
Momofuku Ssäm Bar ✕,
 429–430
Money matters, 538–539
Money saving tips, 13
Morgan Library and Museum,
 115, 252–253
Morimoto ✕, 101, 430
Morningside Heights, 174
Morris-Jumel Mansion,
 186–187
Mott Street, 61
Mount Morris Park Historic
 District, 189
Mount Vernon Hotel Museum
 and Garden, 151, 152
Moustache ✕, 437
Municipal Art Society, 135
Murray Hill, 14, 113–126
hotels, 502, 504–505
museums, 252–253
nightlife, 325–326
restaurants, 448
shopping, 372
Muse Hotel 🏨, 511, 513
Museum of American Finance,
 246

Museum of American Illustration, *264*

Museum of Arts and Design, *174, 175, 177, 267*

Museum of Chinese in the Americas (MOCA), *61, 246*

Museum of Comic and Cartoon Art, *250*

Museum of Jewish Heritage–A Living Memorial to the Holocaust, *246, 249*

Museum of Modern Art (MoMA), *18–19, 254, 290*

Museum of Modern Art Design and Book Store, *381–382*

Museum of Sex, *253*

Museum of the City of New York, *264*

Museum of the Moving Image, *225, 226–227*

Museum stores, *381–382, 391–392*

Museums, *243–276*
  Brooklyn, *198, 199, 213, 214–215, 216–217, 219, 220*
  Chelsea, *100, 252*
  Chinatown, *61, 246, 249–250*
  East Village, *81, 250–252*
  Harlem, *185, 276*
  Lower East Side, *80, 85, 250–252*
  Lower Manhattan, *44, 45, 46, 52, 56, 60, 61, 246, 249–250*
  Midtown, *139–140, 143, 151, 253, 255*
  Murray Hill and the Flatiron District, *252–253*
  museum stores, *381–382, 391–392*
  planner, *244*
  Queens, *225, 226–227, 233, 234*
  SoHo, *250*
  Staten Island, *240–242*
  Union Square, *115*
  Upper East Side, *150, 152, 255–267*
  Upper West Side, *174, 175, 177, 267–276*

Music. ⇨ *See* Arts

Music Box Theater, *131*

N

Nancy Hoffman (gallery), *108*

Nathan's Famous×, *220*

National Arts Club, *115*

National Museum of the American Indian (Smithsonian Institution), *249*

National September 11 Memorial and Museum at The World Trade Center, *52*

National Shrine of San Gennaro, *74*

Naturalists' Walk, *167–168*

Neighborhoodies (shop), *204*

Neue Galerie New York, *264, 267*

New Museum, The, *251–252*

New York Aquarium, *21, 218–220*

New York Botanical Garden, *21, 234, 236–237*

New York City Fire Museum, *250*

New York City Police Headquarters, *75*

New York City Police Museum, *249*

New York Earth Room (soil sculpture), *76*

New York Film Festival, *289*

New York Hall of Science, *233*

New-York Historical Society, *174, 175, 267, 276*

New York Knicks, *541*

New York Life Insurance Building, *116, 126*

New York Marriott at the Brooklyn Bridge ⬚, *489, 492*

New York Mets, *232*

New York Palace Hotel ⬚, *519*

New York Public Library (NYPL) Humanities and Social Sciences Library, *131, 140*

New York Stock Exchange, *45, 47*

New York Times Building, *131, 140–141*

New York University, *92*

New York Yankees, *237*

Newhouse Center for Contemporary Art, *242*

Nha Trang ×, *418*

Nightlife. ⇨ *See under specific areas*

92nd Street Y, *294*

No. 7 ×, *212*

Noble Maritime Collection, *242*

Nobu ×, *422*

Noguchi Museum, *225, 227*

NoLita, *14, 66–68, 73–76*
  hotels, *494–495*
  restaurants, *404–405, 426*
  shopping, *350–354*

Nom Wah Tea Parlor, *61*

Noodle Pudding ×, *199*

North Garden, *169*

Northern Dispensary building, *93*

Northern Spy Food Co. ×, *430*

Nu Hotel ⬚, *492*

Nuyorican Poets Café, *82*

NY Skyride, *120*

O

Oceana ×, *459*

Odeon ×, *422*

OK Harris Works of Art (gallery), *76*

Old Town Bar & Restaurant ×, *325*

Omni Berkshire Place ⬚, *519*

On the Ave. Hotel ⬚, *525–526*

One World Trade Center, *53*

Opera, *286, 294*

Orchard Street, *85*

Osteria Morini ×, *425*

Our Lady of Pompeii Church, *94*

Outdoor activities and sports, *540–543*

Oyster Bar ×, *452*

P

P.J. Clarke's ×, *420*

Pace Wildenstein (galleries), *108, 146*

Pale Male, *170*

Paley Center for Media, *255*

Palm ×, *452–453*

Paris (movie theater), *290*

Park Avenue Summer/Autumn/Winter/Spring ×, *464*

Park Slope (Brooklyn), *213–218*

Park South Hotel ⬚, *504*

Parks, *30–31*
  Brooklyn, *195, 202, 213, 215–216*
  Central Park, *16, 20, 156–170, 174, 295*
  Chelsea, *101*
  East Village, *82, 83–84*
  film festivals in, *289*
  Greenwich Village, *93–94, 98, 105*
  Harlem, *189*
  Lower Manhattan, *42, 43, 44, 45–47, 57, 63–64*
  Midtown, *131, 132–133*
  Queens, *232–234*
  Union Square, *114, 115, 116, 121–123*

Upper East Side, 150, 151, 152
Upper West Side, 174, 175, 180
Pastis ✕ , *101, 306, 438*
Patel Brothers (shop), *232*
Patchin Place, *93, 96*
Paula Cooper (gallery), *109*
Pearl River Mart (department store), *347*
Peasant ✕ , *426*
Peking Duck House ✕ , *418–419*
Peninsula, The 🏨 , *519*
Per Se ✕ , *175, 467–468*
Performing arts, *278–300*
Performing arts centers, *291– 292, 294, 296–300, 316*
Perry Street ✕ , *441–442*
Peter Luger Steak House ✕ , *206*
Pete's Candy Store (bar), *207*
Pete's Tavern ✕ , *115*
Piano bars, *320, 331*
Pianos (rock club), *311*
Picholine ✕ , *468*
Pier 16, *56*
Pier 17, *56*
Pier 62, *104*
Pierogi (gallery), *207*
Ping's Seafood ✕ , *61, 419*
Pink Pony, The (bar), *311*
Players Club, *115*
Plaza Hotel, The 🏨 , *141, 513*
Plymouth Church of the Pilgrims, *198–199*
Pod Hotel 🏨 , *519*
Porter House New York ✕ , *175, 468*
Postmasters (gallery), *109*
PowerHouse Arena (shop), *204*
Price categories
dining, 12, 196, 225, 399
lodging, 12, 489
Primehouse New York ✕ , *445–446*
Primorski ✕ , *196*
Prometheus statue, *137*
Prospect Heights, *213–218*
Prospect Park, *195, 213–218*
Prospect Park Audubon Center and Visitor Center at the Boathouse, *216*
Prospect Park Band Shell, *215–216*
Prospect Park Carousel, *216*
Prospect Park Zoo, *195, 216*
Prune ✕ , *430*
Public ✕ , *426*
Public Theater, The, *285*

Public transportation, *533, 538*
Puck Building, *72*

Q

Queen of Greene Street (building), *72*
Queens, *16, 223–234*
addresses, 228
children's activities, 232–234
performing arts, 300
price categories, 225
restaurants, 228–229, 230, 234
shopping, 232
Queens Museum of Art, *234*
Queens Zoo, *233–234*

R

R.U.B. BBQ ✕ , *433*
Radegast Hall and Biergarten, *207–208*
Rainbow Room, *137, 308*
Radio City Music Hall, *135– 136, 292*
Ramble, The, *165*
Rayuela ✕ , *431*
Readings and lectures. ⇨ *See Arts*
Realform Girdle Building, *208*
ReBar, *203*
Red Rooster Harlem ✕ , *470*
Renaissance Hotel 🏨 , *513*
Renwick Triangle, *85*
Republic ✕ , *449*
Restaurants, *7, 23*
atlas, 472–484
best bets, 400–401
Bronx, The, 238
Brooklyn, 195–196, 199, 202–203, 204–207, 209–210, 212–213, 217
Chelsea, 101, 412–413, 432–433
children, 397, 418, 419, 420– 421, 422, 425, 426, 430, 431, 434–435, 443–444, 448, 455, 460, 461, 466
Chinatown, 61, 403, 418–419
dress codes, 397
East Village, 406–407, 427–430
Financial District, 403, 419–420
Flatiron District, 442–447
Fodor's choice, 400
food courts, 434
Gramercy Park, 447
Greenwich Village, 96, 408–409
Harlem, 416–417, 469–470

hours, 399
Little Italy, 73, 404–405, 426
Lower East Side, 406–407, 431–432
Lower Manhattan, 402–403, 418–422
Meatpacking District, 438–439
Midtown East, 414–415, 450–453
Midtown West, 412–413, 454–461
Murray Hill, 448
NoLita, 404–405, 426
price categories, 12, 196, 225, 399
Queens, 228–229, 230, 234
reservations, 397
7 Train, 231
smoking, 397
SoHo, 404–405, 423–426
taxes, 397
tipping, 397
TriBeCa, 402, 420–422
Union Square, 410–411, 448–449
Upper East Side, 414–415, 461–464
Upper West Side, 273, 416– 417, 464–469
West Village, 96, 409, 439–442
Restrooms, *539*
Resurrection (shop), *351*
Ritz-Carlton New York, Central Park 🏨 , *513, 514*
Ritz-Carlton New York, Battery Park, The 🏨 , *492, 506, 514*
River Café ✕ , *202*
Rivera, Diego, *142*
Riverside Church, *180*
Riverside Park, *174, 175, 180, 289*
Robert F. Wagner Jr. Park, *46*
Robert Miller Gallery, *100, 109*
Rock clubs, *310–311, 316, 317–318, 321–322, 325–326*
Rockefeller, John D., *142*
Rockefeller Center, *130, 136–137*
Rodeo Bar, *325–326*
Roger Smith 🏨 , *519–520*
Ronald Feldman Fine Arts (gallery), *76*
Rooftop Films, *289*
Room Mate Grace 🏨 , *513–514*
Roosevelt Hotel 🏨 , *520*
Roosevelt Island, *152–153*
Roosevelt Island Tramway, *153*
Rose Center for Earth and Space, *21, 269, 273*

Row, The (town houses), 98
Royalton, The ⚅, 514–515
Rubin Museum of Art, 252
Rum House (bar), 60
Russian and Turkish Baths, 84
Rye✕, 206–207

S

S.O.B.'s (world music club), 314
Safety, 13, 183, 539–540
Sahil Sari Palace (shop), 232
St. Bartholomew's Church, 130, 141
St. George's Ukrainian Catholic Church, 81
St. James Theater, 131
St. Luke's Place, 98–99
St. Mark's Church in-the-Bowery, 84–85
St. Marks Place, 80, 81–82, 83
St. Nick's Jazz Pub, 190
St. Patrick's Cathedral, 137–138
St. Patrick's Old Cathedral, 73, 74
St. Paul's Chapel (Columbia University), 179
St. Paul's Chapel (Lower Manhattan), 60
St. Regis, The ⚅, 520
Saks Fifth Avenue (department store), 131
Salumeria Rosi ✕ , 468
San Remo (apartments), 180
Sant Ambroeus ✕, 151
Santos Party House (dance club), 312
Sarabeth's ✕, 468–469
Sardi's ✕, 131
Saul ✕, 195, 210
Savoy ✕, 425
Scarpetta ✕, 438
Schaller & Weber (shop), 151
Schermerhorn Row, 56
Schiller's Liquor Bar ✕, 431
Schoenfeld Theater, 131
Sculpture for Living (building), 81, 85
SculptureCenter, 227
SD26 ✕, 446
Seagram Building, 141, 143
Sean Kelly (gallery), 109
Seäsonal Restaurant and Weinbar ✕, 459–460
Second Avenue Deli ✕, 453
Senior citizen travel, 540
September 11, 2001, 49–51
Serafina ✕, 460

Serene Rose (shop), 195
Setai Fifth Avenue, The ⚅, 520
Setai Spa, 45
7 Train, 231
75 1/2 Bedford Street, 95
70 Park Avenue ⚅, 504–505, 514
Shake Shack ✕, 115, 446, 460, 469
Shakespeare Garden, 166
Sheep Meadow, 162
Sherry-Netherland ⚅, 520, 522
SHO Shaun Hergatt ✕, 420
Shopping, 334–394. ⇨ See also under specific areas
antiques, 338, 354–355, 360, 361, 372–373, 383, 393
beauty products, 339, 355–356, 361, 379, 383, 386
books, 339, 356, 361–362, 363, 367, 372, 373, 386, 393
cameras and electronics, 335, 339, 342, 373, 379–380
chain stores, 386
children, 104, 218, 335, 342, 348, 350, 360, 371, 379, 383, 386–387, 393
clothing, 335, 337–338, 342–346, 350–351, 354, 356–357, 360, 362, 366–367, 370, 371, 373, 376, 380, 386–390, 393–394
department stores, 377, 380–381, 390
discounts, 335, 347, 370, 371
flea markets, 211
food and treats, 347, 357, 362, 366, 390
greenmarkets, 124
holiday markets, 372
home decor, 348, 357, 363, 371, 377, 393
household items and furniture, 391
jewelry, 349, 354, 367, 371, 377–378, 381, 391
music, 357, 363, 370–371, 382
museum stores, 381–382, 391–392
performing arts memorabilia, 382
sample sales, 337
shoes, handbags, and leather goods, 349–350, 360–361, 363, 378–379, 382–383, 392–393, 394
souvenirs, 340, 352, 355, 358, 368, 374, 384

stationery, 339, 361–362, 363, 372, 386, 393
street vendors, 338
toys, 350, 360, 372, 379, 383
wine, 360, 371, 393, 384
Shoreham, The ⚅, 515
Shubert Alley, 131
Shubert Theatre, 131
Shun Lee Palace ✕, 453
Sideshow Gallery, 207
Sideshows by the Seashore, and the Coney Island Museum, 219, 220
Sightseeing tours, 32, 104, 158, 188, 424
6 Columbus ⚅, 515
651 Arts, 210
60 Thompson ⚅, 494–465
Skyscraper Museum, 249–250
Smack Mellon Studios, 203
Smallpox Hospital, 153
Smalls (jazz club), 95
Smith Street, 195, 209
Smoke Joint ✕, 212
Smoking, 397
Sniffen Court, 126
Snug Harbor Cultural Center, 240, 242
Socrates Sculpture Park, 225, 227–228
Sofitel New York ⚅, 515
SoHo, 14, 20, 66–73
architecture, 69, 72
bars, 313–314
children's activities, 250
galleries, 75–76
hotels, 494–495
museums, 250
performing arts, 283–284
restaurants, 404–405, 423–426
shopping, 69, 338–350
SoHo Grand ⚅, 495
Soldiers' and Sailors' Monument, 180
Solomon R. Guggenheim Museum, 150, 265
Sonnabend (gallery), 110
Sony Building, 143
Sony Wonder Technology Lab, 21, 143, 290–291
Sosa Borella ✕, 460
Sotheby's (auction house), 154
South Garden, 169
South Street Seaport Historic District, 42, 43–61
South Street Seaport Museum, 21, 56
Southpaw (nightclub), 218
Space Kiddets (shop), 371

Spanierman (gallery), *146*
Sparks Steakhouse ✕, *453*
Spas and bathhouses, *45, 84*
Spice Market ✕, *101, 306, 438–439*
Spicy Mina ✕, *230*
Spitzer's Corner ✕, *431–432*
Sports and the outdoors, *540–543*
Spotted Pig, The ✕, *437*
Spring (gallery), *203*
Standard, The ⊤, *101, 499*
Standard Grill, The ✕, *439*
Standard Hotel Beer Garden, Grill, and Living Room, *322–323*
Stanton Social, The ✕, *432*
Staten Island, *16, 223–225, 240–242*
children's activities, 240, 242
price categories, 225
Staten Island Botanical Gardens, *242*
Staten Island Ferry, *56–57, 240, 241*
Staten Island Historical Society Museum, *240–241*
Statue of Liberty, *19, 33–35, 38, 42–43*
Stella McCartney (shop), *101*
Stonehome Wine Bar & Restaurant ✕, *212–213*
Strand Bookstore, The, *123, 286, 356*
Strawberry Fields, *163*
Street layout, *13*
Strivers' Row, *185, 187–188*
Students, *543*
Studio Museum in Harlem, *185, 276*
Stuyvesant Street, *85*
Stuyvesant-Fish House, *85*
Subway travel, *533–534*
Sugar Hill, *185, 190*
Superfine (bar), *203*
Surfside 3 Marinemax Marina, *104*
Sushi of Gari ✕, *464*
Sushi Yasuda ✕, *453*
Sweet Melissa ✕, *195–196*
Sweet Rhythm (jazz club), *305*
Symbols, *7*
Symphony Space, *176*

T

Tacos Matamoros ✕, *196*
Tamarind ✕, *446*
Tammany Hall, *124*
Tanuki Tavern✕, *101*

Tanya Bonakdar (gallery), *110*
Taverna Kyclades ✕, *229*
Taxes, *397, 543–544*
Taxis and car services, *528– 529, 534–535*
Teany (bar), *311*
Teitel Bros (shop), *240*
Telepan ✕, *469*
Television tapings, *24–25*
Temple Emanu-El, *151, 153*
Teresa's ✕, *199*
Theater, *131, 282, 284–285, 288, 290, 292–294, 295, 300*
Broadway, 282
cabaret and performance spaces, 316, 320, 331
children's, 293, 300
Thompson LES ⊤, *496*
303 (gallery), *110*
Tia Pol ✕, *433*
Tibor de Nagy (gallery), *146*
Tickets, *24–25, 278–280*
Time Hotel, The ⊤, *515–516*
Time Warner Center, *175, 177*
Times Square, *18, 130, 131, 413*
Times Square Visitor Center, *138*
Timing the visit, *12*
Tipping, *397, 544*
Tisch Children's Zoo, *160–161*
Titanic, *104*
Titanic Memorial, *56*
TKTS booth (discounted theater tickets), *130*
Tocqueville ✕, *449*
Toloache ✕, *460–461*
Tompkins Square Park, *82*
Tom's Restaurant ✕, *217*
Top of the Rock (observation deck), *130, 138–139*
Tours and packages, *32, 104, 158, 188, 424*
Train travel, *535*
Transit Museum, *199*
Transportation, *12, 22, 38, 41, 67, 79, 91, 113, 129, 149, 153, 173, 183, 193, 223, 237, 528–535, 537*
Transportation Hub, *53*
Traveler's checks and cards, *539*
TriBeCa, *43, 61–64*
bars, 303
hotels, 493–494
nightlife, 303, 312
performing arts, 283–284

restaurants, 402, 420–422
shopping, 335, 337–338
TriBeCa Film Festival, *289*
Tribeca Grand ⊤, *493–494*
Trinity Church, *45, 60–61*
Trump International Hotel and Towers ⊤, *177, 526*
Trump Tower, *143–144*
Tudor City, *131, 144*
Turkish Kitchen ✕, *448*
"21" Club ✕, *131, 308, 309, 461*

U

Uncle Jack's Steakhouse ✕, *461*
Union Hall (nightclub), *218*
Union Square, *14, 113–126*
architecture, 116
children's activities, 116, 118, 120
hotels, 505
restaurants, 410–411, 448–449
shopping, 371–372
Union Square Cafe ✕, *449–450*
Union Square Park and Greenmarket, *124*
UNIQLO (shop), *346*
United Nations Headquarters, *144–145*
University Club, *145*
Upper East Side, *16, 149–154*
bars, 330–331
children's activities, 152
galleries, 154
hotels, 522–523
museums, 150, 152, 255–267
nightlife, 308–309, 330–331
performing arts, 294–295
restaurants, 414–415, 461–464
shopping, 383–393
Upper West Side, *16, 173–180*
children's activities, 180, 294
hotels, 523, 525–526
museums, 174, 175, 177, 267–276
nightlife, 308–309, 331–332
performing arts, 295–299
restaurants, 273, 416–417, 464–469
shopping, 393–394
Upright Citizens Brigade Theatre (comedy club), *324*
USTA Billie Jean King National Tennis Center, *234*

V

Veniero's Pasticceria ✕ , *430*
Village Vanguard (jazz club),
  94–95, 304, 321
Vinegar Hill House ✕ ,
  202–203
Virgil's Real BBQ ✕ , *461*
Visitor information, *544*
  Brooklyn, 197
  Central Park, 169
  Columbia University, 179
  Ellis Island, 37
  Ground Zero, 55
  Prospect Park, 216
  Rockefeller Center, 137
  Staten Island, 242
  Times Square, 138
Voorlezer's House, *240–241*

W

W Hotel New York ☎ , *522*
W New York ☎ , *506*
W New York Downtown, The
  ☎ , *493*
W New York Union Square
  ☎ , *505*
W Times Square ☎ , *516*
Waldorf-Astoria ☎ , *522*
Walking tours, *32, 158, 424*
Wall Street, *44–45*
Wall Street Bath & Spa, *45*
Wallsé ✕ , *437–438*
Warwick ☎ , *516*
Washington Market Park, *64*
Washington Memorial Arch,
  93, 98
Washington Mews, *93, 99*
Washington Square Hotel ☎ ,
  497, 499
Washington Square Park,
  93, 98

Wave Hill (The Bronx), *238*
Wd-50 ✕ , *432*
Weather, *12*
Wellington Hotel ☎ , *516*
West Village, *14, 90–99*
  nightlife, 321–322
  performing arts, 288
  restaurants, 96, 409, 439–442
  shopping, 96, 361–366
Westin New York at Times
  Square ☎ , *516*
White Horse Tavern, *319*
Whitney Museum of American
  Art, *150, 266*
Wildwood Barbecue ✕ ,
  446–447
Williamsburg (Brooklyn), *194,*
  204–208
Willow Street, *196*
Wollman Memorial Rink, *160*
Woo Lae Oak ✕ , *426*
Woolworth Building, *61*
World music venues, *314*
World Trade Center site, *42,*
  48–55

Y

Yankee Stadium, *237*
Yorkville, *150, 151*

Z

Zabars (gourmet shop), *174,*
  175
Zero Otto Nove ✕ , *238*
Ziegfeld (movie theater), *291*
Zoos
  Bronx, The, 20, 21, 234,
  235–236
  Brooklyn, 195, 216
  Central Park, 160–161
  Queens, 233–234

PHOTO CREDITS

1, Bo Zaunders/viestiphoto.com. 2, Kord.com/age fotostock. 5, Liberty Helicopters, Inc. Chapter 1: Experience New York City: 8-9, Rudy Sulgan/age fotostock. 10, Luc Novovitch/age fotostock. 11 (left), LHB Photo/Alamy. 11 (right), Oote Boe Photography/Alamy. 14, ACE Stock Limited/Alamy. 16, Martha Cooper/viestiphoto.com. 18 (left), Ken Ross/viestiphoto.com. 18 (top center), Kord.com/age fotostock. 18 (top right), Doug Scott/age fotostock. 18 (bottom), Ken Ross/viestiphoto.com. 19 (top left), SuperStock/age fotostock. 19 (bottom left), Craig Chesek/AMNH. 19 (right), PictureQuest. 20 (top left), Walter Bibikow/viestiphoto.com. 20 (bottom left), Frances Roberts/Alamy. 20 (right), Diane Hall/viestiphoto.com. 21, Jeff Greenberg/Alamy. 22, Black Star/Alamy. 23 (left), David H. Wells/age fotostock. 23 (right), Richard Levine/Alamy. 25, Everett Collection. 26, Joe Viesti/viestiphoto.com. 27 (left), Frances M. Roberts/Alamy. 27 (right), adactio/Flickr. 31 (left), David Berkowitz/Flickr. 31 (right), emilydickinsonridesabmx/Flickr.32, Corbis. 33, Photodisc. 35 (top), Liberty Helicopters, Inc. 35 (bottom), Ken Ross/viestiphoto.com. 37 (top), Corbis. 37 (bottom), Library of Congress Prints and Photographs Division. Chapter 2: Lower Manhattan: 39, Ambient Images/Alamy. 41, Kord.com/age fotostock. 42, Chuck Pefley/Alamy. 47, Heeb Christian/age fotostock. 48, Silverstein Properties. 49 (top), SpecialKRB/Flickr. 49 (bottom), Sondra Paulson/iStockphoto. 50 (top left), AP Photo/Marty Lederhandler. 50 (top right), AP Photo/Amy Sancetta. 50 (bottom), RodneyRamsey/Flickr. 51 (left), AP Photo/Mark Lennihan. 51 (center), Peter Comitini/Flickr. 51 (right), Bo Zaunders/viestiphoto.com. 52-53 (top) and 52 (bottom), Silverstein Properties. 53 (bottom left and bottom right), Joe Woolhead/Silverstein Properties. 54 (top left), Keith Reicher/iStockphoto. 54 (bottom left), FaceMePLS/Flickr. 54 (center), jorbasa/Flickr. 54 (top right), p_c_w/Flickr. 54 (bottom right), cytech/Flickr. 58-59, Kropic1/Shutterstock 62, SuperStock. Chapter 3: SoHo & Little Italy: 65, Art Kowalsky/Alamy. 67, Ambient Images/Alamy. 68, Yadid Levy/Alamy. 70-71, SIME s.a.s/eStock Photo. 75, CW Harris Works of Art. Chapter 4: East Village & the Lower East Side: 77, Jeff Greenberg/Alamy. 79, peyri/Flickr. 80, Ken Ross/viestiphoto.com. 83, Giovanni Simeone/SIME/eStock Photo. 87, Deutsches Dispensary & Library by Paul Lowry http://www.flickr.com/photos/paul_lowry/4912819725/ Attribution License. Chapter 5: Greenwich Village & Chelsea: 89, Kokyat Choong/Alamy. 91, Black Star/Alamy. 92, Frances Roberts/Alamy. 97, Ambient Images Inc./Alamy. 100, PCL/Alamy. 102-103, Kord.com/SuperStock. 109, Frances M. Roberts/Alamy. Chapter 6: Union Square: 111, David Shankbone/Wikimedia Commons. 113, Kord.com/age fotostock. 114, Yadid Levy/Alamy. 117, Russell Kord/Alamy. 119, Joe Shlabotnik/Flickr. 121, naphtalina/iStockphoto. Chapter 7: Midtown: 127, Kord.com/age fotostock. 129, Bruno Perousse/age fotostock. 130, Michel Friang/Alamy. 135-36, Joe Viesti/viestiphoto. 143, Corbis. 145, Ken Ross/viestiphoto.com. Chapter 8: The Upper East Side: 147, Nicholas Pitt/Alamy. 149, Ken Ross/viestiphoto.com. 150, Janine Wiedel Photolibrary/Alamy. Chapter 9: Central Park: 155, Piero Ribelli. 156 (top), Piero Ribelli. 156 (center), Rudy Sulgan/age fotostock. 157 (left), Bo Zaunders/viestiphoto.com. 157 (right), Sandra Baker/Alamy. 158, Worldscapes/age fotostock. 159 (top), Michal Daniel. 159 (bottom), Chris Lee. 160, Peter Arnold. Inc./Alamy. 161 (left), Ken Ross/viestiphoto.com. 161 (right), Agency Jon Arnold Images/age fotostock. 162 (top left), Bo Zaunders/viestiphoto.com. 162 (top right), Sandra Baker/Alamy. 162 (bottom), Walter Bibikow/age fotostock. 163 (top left), Chuck Pefley/Alamy. 163 (top right), Bo Zaunders/viestiphoto.com. 163 (bottom), Darren Green Photography/Alamy. 164, Piero Ribelli. 165 (left), Sandra Baker/Alamy. 165 (right), Piero Ribelli. 166 (top left), Peter Arnold, Inc./Alamy. 166 (top right), TNT Magazine/Alamy. 166-67 (bottom), Bo Zaunders/viestiphoto.com. 167 (top left), Chuck Pefley/Alamy. 167 (top right), LMR Group/Alamy. 168 (top left), Piero Ribelli. 168 (top right), Ken Ross/viestiphoto.com. 169, Jon Arnold/Agency Jon Arnold Images/age fotostock. 170 (top), Lincoln Karim/palemale.com. 170 (center), Piero Ribelli. 170 (bottom images), Lincoln Karim/palemale.com. Chapter 10: The Upper West Side: 171, Kord.com/age fotostock. 173, Jeff Greenberg/age fotostock. 174, Kord.com/age fotostock. Chapter 11: Harlem: 181, Joe Viesti/viestiphoto.com. 183, Joe Malone/Agency Jon Arnold Images/age fotostock. 184, SuperStock/age fotostock. 189, RIEGER Bertrand/age fotostock. Chapter 12: Brooklyn: 191, Jeff Greenberg/age fotostock. 193, SuperStock/age fotostock. 194, ACE Stock Limited/Alamy. 200-201, Rudy Sulgan/SuperStock. Chapter 13: Queens, The Bronx, and Staten Island: 221, Sylvain Grandadam/age fotostock. 223, Michel Friang/Alamy. 224, Siobhan O'Hare. 233, Paul Hakimata Photography/Shutterstock. 235, Doug Milner. 239, Johnny Stockshooter/age fotostock. Chapter 14: Museums: 243, Bartomeu Amengual/age fotostock. 245, Ken Ross/viestiphoto. com. 254, Ken Ross/viestiphoto.com. 256, Brooks Walker. 257 and 258 (top), Renaud Visage/age fotostock. 258 (center), Metropolitan Museum of Art. 258 (bottom), Ken Ross/viestiphoto.com. 260 (top), Renaud Visage/age fotostock. 260 (bottom), Metropolitan Museum of Art. 261, Wild Bill Studio/Metropolitan Museum of Art. 262 (top and bottom), Metropolitan Museum of Art. 265, Doug Scott/age fotostock. 266, Geoffrey Clements. 268-69 and 270 (top left and right), Ken Ross/viestiphoto.com. 270 (bottom), Dennis Finnin/AMNH. 272, Ken Ross/viestiphoto.com. 273 and 274, Dennis Finnin/AMNH.

275 (top), C. Chesek/AMNH. 275 (bottom), Dennis Finnin and C. Chesek/AMNH. Chapter 15: The Performing Arts: 277, Joan Marcus. 278, Joe Viesti/viestiphoto.com. 281, Ted Pink/Alamy. Chapter 16: Nightlife: 301, Pictorial Press/Alamy. 302, kriskat£afterglowpix.com. 304, Lebrecht Music and Arts Photo Library/Alamy. 305 (top), Michael Belardo/Alamy. 305 (bottom), JAZZ: Joe Wilder, Lewis Nash and John Webber at the Village Vanguard. by Professor Bop - aka Dr. Jazz http://www.flickr.com/photos/professorbop/403537049/ Attribution License. 306 (top), kriskat£afterglowpix.com. 306 (bottom), Gustavo Andrade/age fotostock. 307 (top), Carlos Davila/age fotostock. 307 (bottom), Happy Valley. 308 (top), Grant Winston. 308 (bottom), foodfolio/Alamy. 309, Mark Molloy. 310, Mike Faivre/Arlene's Grocery. 311 (top), Mike Faivre/Arlene's Grocery. 311 (bottom left), Nicole Fournier. 311 (bottom right), Ted Pink/Alamy. 318, Beirut @ Bowery Ballroom by Tammy Lo http://www.flickr.com/photos/tammylo/489390788/ Attribution License. Chapter 17: Shopping: 333, Bruno Perousse/age fotostock. 334, Richard Levine/Alamy. 340 and 341 (left), Piero Ribelli. 341 (right), Jonathan Adler. 352 (top), Yadid Levy/Alamy. 352 (bottom), Sigerson Morrison. 353, Yadid Levy/Alamy. 358 (top), Las Venus. 358 (bottom), Sugar Sweet Sunshine Bakery. 359 (top), Frock. 359 (bottom), lowereastsideny.com. 364, Frances Roberts/Alamy. 365 (top), Amy's Bread. 365 (bottom), Cynthia Rowley. 368, Piero Ribelli. 369, Piero Ribelli. 374 (top), Piero Ribelli. 374 (bottom), Louis Vuitton. 375, Piero Ribelli. 384-85, Piero Ribelli. Chapter 18: Where to Eat: 395, Bo Zaunders/viestiphoto.com. 396, ACE Stock Limited/Alamy. 402, Dina Litovsky/Stregoica Photography. 403, Thomas Schauer. 404, Dina Litovsky/Stregoica Photography. 405, pravin.premkumar/Flickr. 406, Dina Litovsky/Stregoica Photography. 407 (top), Noah Kalina. 407 (bottom), Chickpea. 408, Dina Litovsky/Stregoica Photography. 409, Visual Mercenary Group. 410, Frances M. Roberts/Alamy. 411, nicasaurusrex/Flickr. 412, Quality Meats. 413, Kyotofu. 414, The Modern. 415, Rachel from Cupcakes Take the Cake/Flickr. 416, Per Se. 417 (top), Pamela Weekes. 417 (bottom), Frances Roberts/Alamy. Chapter 19: Where to Stay: 485, Arcaid/Alamy. 486, On the Ave Hotel. 491, Roy Wright. 498 (top), Simon Brown/Firmdale Hotels. 498 (bottom left), Michael Weber. 498 (bottom right), The Standard. 503 (top), Ace Hotel/Eric Laignel. 503 (bottom left), Library Hotel. 503 (bottom right), Claudia Hehr Photography. 512 (top), Mandarin Oriental. 512 (bottom left), The Plaza. 512 (bottom right), The Ritz-Carlton New York, Central Park. 521 (top), Roy Wright. 521 (bottom left), The Peninsula. 521 (bottom right), St. Regis Hotel, New York.

NOTES